FROMMER'S E

CRUISING

By Aaron Saunders

FROMMER'S STAR RATINGS SYSTEM

Every hotel, restaurant, and attraction listed in this guide has been ranked for quality and value. Here's what the stars mean:

★★ Recommended
★★★ Highly Recommended
★★★ A must! Don't miss!

AN IMPORTANT NOTE

The world is a dynamic place. Hotels change ownership, restaurants hike their prices, museums alter their opening hours, and busses and trains change their routings. And all of this can occur in the several months after our authors have visited, inspected, and written about, these hotels, restaurants, museums and transportation services. Though we have made valiant efforts to keep all our information fresh and up-to-date, some few changes can inevitably occur in the periods before a revised edition of this guidebook is published. So please bear with us if a tiny number of the details in this book have changed. Please also note that we have no responsibility or liability for any inaccuracy or errors or omissions, or for inconvenience, loss, damage, or expenses suffered by anyone as a result of assertions in this guide.

The Queen Mary 2.

CONTENTS

The village of Flatts in Harrington's Lagooon, Bermuda (p. 50).

A LOOK AT CRUISING

O ceans cover 71% of the earth's surface. They were, until very recently, the barrier that walled off cultures from one another. To trade, to meet, to emigrate meant undertaking often risky sea voyages. Nobody went to sea just for the fun of it.

That all changed in the 1970s when ocean liner executives, stuck with massive empty ships as passengers switched to air travel for ocean crossings, very creatively created an industry of shipboard vacations. That brash young business is the subject of this guide.

Cruising is a superb way to relax, to see the world, and to bond with the people you bring with you. Because the ship is such a hugely important element of the vacation, we decided that a book was needed to help find not just the right itinerary, but also the right boat.

— Pauline Frommer

The Terrace Pool on the *Emerald Princess* (see p. 195).

DESTINATIONS

Native culture and eye-popping scenery are two of the hallmarks of an Alaskan (p. 71) cruise.

Archeologists believe Xunantunich (pictured) was built around 600 A.D. An easy day trip from Belize City (p. 55), cruisers can climb to its peak and survey the surrounding jungle, dotted with other ruins.

A "Junkanoo" dancer in the Bahamas (p. 51).

Antoni Gaudi's Casa Batilo in Barcelona (p. 90).

Luquillo Beach, Puerto Rico (p. 63).

Gondoliers ply Venice's Grand Canal (p. 90).

St. John is just a quick ferry ride from the port stop of St. Thomas (p. 67). Much of the island is a protected nature preserve.

A regiment parades daily at Halifax's historic, star-shaped Citadel (p. 87).

As ships pass through the Panama Canal (p. 69), they are lifted (or lowered) around 85 feet at each lock. It's awe-inspiring to see this marvel of engineering up close.

A scuba diver explores the undersea world around Cozumel (p. 55).

The slippery climb at Dunn's River Falls in Jamaica (p. 60).

Curaçao's capital Willemstad (p. 57), a UNESCO World Heritage Site, was founded in 1707.

MAINSTREAM LINES

An LED sculpture (pictured) is the focal point of the *Carnival Vista*'s atrium (p. 130).

Aboard the *Disney Fantasy* (p. 154), two girls dance with Minnie.

The *Oasis of the Seas* (p. 208) has vast interior "neighborhoods."

The *Norwegian Gem* (p. 185) sails from the port of Mykonos.

Old-fashioned song and dance aboard the *Star Princess* (p. 195).

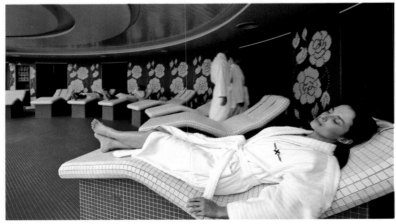

The Persian Garden Spa aboard Celebrity's *Oasis of the Seas* (p. 208).

Guests pedaling recumbent bikes high over the deck of the *Carnival Vista*.

RCL's "North Star" capsule gently lifts to give guests 360-degree views 300 feet above the deck.

The *Disney Dream*'s "AquaDuck" was the first watercoaster at sea.

Carnival's "80's Rock and Glow" deck party.

"Serenity" is an adults-only quiet area, now featured on a number of Carnival ships.

A special occasion meal on the *Celebrity Solstice* (p. 135).

NICHE & LUXURY LINES

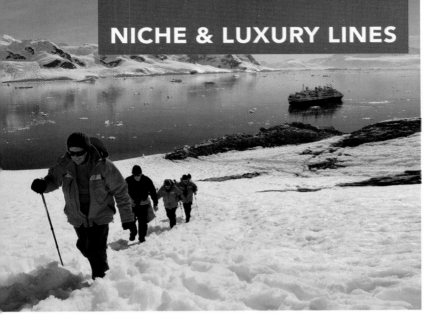

Silversea (see p. 266) passengers hiking in Antarctica.

From the ocean to the ocean—caviar in the surf is a perk on some *Seabourn* (p. 258) cruises.

An Alaska Marine Highway ferry (p. 326) is an affordable way to see lesser-known parts of the "Last Frontier."

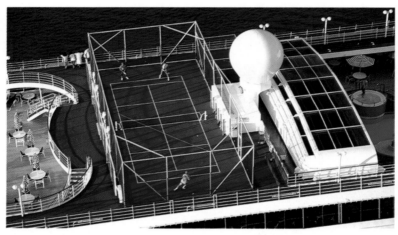

Who says you can play tennis only on land? Not Crystal Cruises (see p. 227).

Hands-on cooking classes are a popular activity aboard Oceania's *Marina* (see p. 248).

The deck of the *Marina*, an Oceania Cruises vessel.

An expedition of Lindblad's *National Geographic Islander* (p. 347) to the Galapagos Islands.

Cunard's *Queen Mary* (see p. 240) plying the majestic fjords of Norway.

The Dirk Weyer suite aboard Lindblad's yacht, the *Sea Cloud*.

Crystal Cruises is known for its polished service.

The Sea Dream Yacht Club (see p. 262).

CHOOSING THE RIGHT SHIP

Choosing a cruise is a complicated decision. You have to decide where in the world you want to go. Then, you have to figure out which line suits your taste as well as your budget, and then which of the ships within the line is the right fit for you (since they can vary greatly, even within the same cruise line).

So why is it such a hard decision? While you may think that the moment you decide to take a cruise is when you define your vacation, it's really the moment when you pick your ship that determines the fate of your holiday. People tend to lump cruising together as one type of vacation, but cruise lines are as different from one another as hotel chains—usually even more so. Some lines are young and fun and loud and even a little messy; some are older and sophisticated with intellectual leanings or a posh and refined atmosphere; others are full of energy and designed for families with children of multiple ages. Choose the wrong ship and you've chosen the wrong vacation.

Get it right and you'll find that cruising is a more varied an activity today than ever, with superb choices for people of all income levels, interests and ages. The problem is, as we said at the start, choosing the perfect ship for you. Fortunately, we're here to help! We hope to make the planning not only enjoyable, but fun as well. So here goes.

THE best OF THE MAINSTREAM SHIPS

Gold Award: Disney Cruise Line
Silver Award: Celebrity Cruises
Bronze Award: Holland America Line

It's hard to beat **Disney Cruise Line,** which has been consistently wowing cruisers young and old since *Disney Magic* first set sail in 1998. Disney's attention to detail is legendary: Staterooms have special "split" bathrooms with separate toilet and vanity areas; kids have their very own deck with age-specific activities and public rooms; and waiters follow families from one dining room to another as they rotate throughout the several options over the course of the week. You don't have to love Mickey Mouse to love a Disney cruise—but you can count them: Designers have hidden the visage of the famous cartoon mouse all over the fleet.

Celebrity Cruises, on the other hand, wows adults with its handsome Solstice-class ships that feature a half-acre of real grass on their top decks; expansive spas bordered by floor-to-ceiling glass windows, and dramatic main dining rooms that span two decks in height. Best of all, Celebrity pays close attention to refitting their existing fleet with new dining and entertainment choices.

Holland America Line sometimes gets a bad rap for their supposedly older clientele, but that's a stereotype that is quickly winding its way into cruising's dust bin. Expect a relaxed, traditional cruise experience aboard these elegant "dam" ships.

THE best SHIPS FOR LUXURY

Gold Award: Silversea Cruises
Silver Award: Viking Ocean Cruises
Bronze Award: Crystal Cruises

Silversea Cruises gets our pick for top luxury cruise line thanks to their diverse fleet and worldwide itineraries. Butler service, pillow menus, and small, intimate ships with superb cuisine set the tone for onboard offerings. Amenities like Wi-Fi, shore excursions and nearly all beverages and gratuities are included in the cruise fare. The line earns bonus points for pioneering the concept of the luxury expedition cruise; in addition to five classic luxury ships, Silversea has three luxury expedition cruise ships that sail from the Arctic to the Galapagos and Antarctica.

Viking Ocean Cruises is hot on their heels, however. This classic river cruise line's first foray into ocean cruising took the form of the 932-guest *Viking Star* in 2015, and she's been wowing guests and media ever since. Rarely do brand-new, first-off-the-line ships get it right on the first try, but *Viking Star* ticks off all the boxes, from the stunning (and complimentary) Thermal Suite in the Nordic Spa to the myriad of dining options. Sumptuous but subtle décor features windows that can fully open in both the main restaurant and the casual buffet eatery. Viking took everything that annoys most guests about ocean cruising (photographers, extra charges, kitschy entertainment) and removed it, and the results are superb.

Crystal Cruises gets the bronze for its new luxury liners, a dedicated expedition yacht with its own submarine and even its own air service. It's playing do-si-do with Viking and is now plying rivers as well as oceans.

THE best OF THE NICHE SHIPS

Gold Award: Lindblad-National Geographic Expeditions
Silver Award: Un-Cruise Adventures
Bronze Award: Windstar

Lindblad-National Geographic Expeditions shines with its onboard naturalists, *National Geographic* tie-in, and overall soft-adventure expertise.

Sailing to some of the world's most remote places—like Antarctica and the Galapagos Islands—Lindblad's onshore experiences are unparalleled.

Seattle-based **Un-Cruise Adventures** shines in Alaska and along the Pacific Coast, where its fleet of small ships offers guests the ability to see the places the big ships can't go—with some of the friendliest, most personable crews and expedition teams at sea.

Windstar Cruises, on the other hand, has undergone a resurgence since emerging from near-bankruptcy in 2011. Since then, the line has heavily refitted its three sailing cruise ships and purchased three ex-Seabourn luxury yachts. Refitted to Windstar's exacting standards, the company managed a massive expansion while actually improving the quality of their onboard cuisine and service.

THE best SHIPS FOR FAMILIES WITH KIDS

Gold Award: Disney Cruise Line
Silver Award: Carnival Cruise Line
Bronze Award: Norwegian Cruise Line and Royal Caribbean

If you have kids, it's hard to beat **Disney Cruise Line,** a line that brings its park prowess to the high seas and manages to teach the competition a thing or two about how to deliver service to families with young children while still catering to the needs of the adults who are, after all, footing the bill. How good is Disney with kids? It starts when you embark and a crew member welcomes families on board by name over the ship's public address system. Even adults aren't immune to Disney's unique brand of cruising whimsy.

Carnival Cruise Lines runs a close second thanks to their much-improved kids' programs and upgraded facilities. Of particular note is the line's new *Seuss at Sea* partnership that includes a special *Cat in the Hat* parade from the ship's atrium to the main theatre; Dr. Seuss story time; and a focus on encouraging kids to read that we absolutely love.

Norwegian Cruise Line and **Royal Caribbean** earn honorary mentions thanks to their diverse kids' programs that are tailored to children and teenagers of all ages and whiz-bang onboard toys, like twisty waterslides, bumper cars and sky diving simulators.

THE best LINES FOR ROMANCE

Gold Award: Oceania Cruises
Silver Award: Celebrity Cruises
Bronze Award: Paul Gauguin Cruises

Finding the right cruise for a romantic vacation can be a challenge. A lot of the more mainstream megaship lines have excellent restaurants and bars, but can carry hundreds of children. For that honeymoon feeling, **Oceania Cruises** gears its offerings to adults, from swank spas run by Canyon Ranch to luxurious digs and a multitude of culinary options. Itineraries tend feature longer port calls than many competitors, meaning you can have a special night out on shore, too (a nice change).

The big, classy ships of **Celebrity Cruises** allow children, but the line tends to cater more to adults with its elaborate onboard spas, chic interior decor and plenty of classy bars and lounges.

Paul Gauguin Cruises' eponymous vessel specializes in year-round sailings throughout French Polynesia. The intimate size of the ship (just 332 guests sail aboard the *Paul Gauguin*), her decidedly French styling, and excursions allowing guests to snorkel lagoons and explore *motu*—deserted isles— are romance-enhancers *par excellence.*

THE best LINES TO SAIL SOLO

Gold Award: Norwegian Cruise Line
Silver Award: Holland America Line
Bronze Award: Cunard Line

Norwegian Cruise Line made a splash when it launched its Studio Staterooms—small, inside Cabins designed exclusively for solo cruisers and loaded with cool features like colored mood lighting and funky design. Introduced aboard *Norwegian Epic* in 2010, Norwegian has since expanded their solo accommodations across the fleet. A key element: These solo areas have a shared lounge that allow people traveling alone to meet likeminded travelers to pal around, and dine, with while on board.

Holland America Line earns brownie points for having some of the most single-friendly amenities in the industry, from cocktail parties for solos to Gentlemen Hosts on longer voyages. The line even has a Single Partners Program that will match travelers of the same sex to a stateroom, supplement-free. If the line can't find another traveler to share the cabin, you're not out any extra money.

Cunard recently refitted their flagship, *Queen Mary 2,* with single-occupancy staterooms, allowing guests to cross the Atlantic in style without having to worry about the dreaded "single supplement."

THE best SHIPBOARD CUISINE, LUXURY

Gold Award: Crystal Cruises
Silver Award: Seabourn Cruises
Bronze Award: Oceania Cruises

Crystal Cruises With Silk Road sushi bar created by Iron Chef Nobuyuki "Nobu" Matsuhisa himself, Crystal has the finest Asian food at sea. But sushi is just one of several onboard culinary offerings, each of which excels. Guests can even elect to dine privately with the ship's Head Sommelier by booking a private dinner at The Vintage Room. How good is it? The first Ultimate

Vintage Room Dinner Crystal offered was an eight-course meal paired with a nearly impossible-to-get 1959 Château Lafite–Rothschild from Bordeaux and a Screaming Eagle 1996 from Napa Valley, considered to be a pinnacle year for the region.

Sometimes who you know matters when it comes to food, and **Seabourn** has partnered with Thomas Keller, creator of what many consider to be the finest restaurant on earth, the Napa Valley's **French Laundry.** Starting in 2016, Keller rolled out special menus, and in some cases, special restaurants, for ships across the Seabourn fleet. The first reviews have been rapturous.

Aboard **Oceania Cruises'** two newest vessels, *Marina* and *Riviera,* the culinary options are memorable, especially the French bistro designed by famed chef and restauranteur Jacques Pépin. Even the Asian restaurant, a sore spot on most ships, impresses with authentic Thai and Malaysian dishes.

THE best SHIPBOARD CUISINE, MAINSTREAM

Gold Award: Carnival Cruise Lines
Silver Award: Royal Caribbean
Bronze Award: Azamara Cruises

You read that right: **Carnival Cruise Lines** beats the competitors in their price point when it comes to their onboard food offerings. We'll take the complimentary poolside burgers from Guy's Burger Joint (where the buns are baked in house and the cheese always oozes over the side) and the made-to-order burritos from BlueIguana Cantina over any others at sea. Carnival can also be classy, too: Their onboard steak houses are better than the competition's, and the Wasabi-infused mashed potatoes are to-die for.

Royal Caribbean gets credit for substantially upping the game, particularly aboard their newer ships like *Allure of the Seas* and *Quantum of the Seas,* where a variety of cuisines are presented in specialty restaurants of all sorts.

Azamara has long offered very fine food on board, and we give it a hat tip for its healthy cuisine, which is not only blessedly low-cal, but also tasty.

THE best SHIPS FOR NIGHTTIME ENTERTAINMENT

Gold Award: Norwegian Cruise Line
Silver Award: Disney Cruise Line
Bronze Award: Carnival Cruise Lines

You've got to hand it to **Norwegian Cruise Line** for making shipboard entertainment cool again. In 2010, they recruited the Blue Man Group to perform aboard *Norwegian Epic,* and quickly expanded that partnership to include Broadway productions like *Legally Blonde* and the New York–based spectacle the Rockettes.

Disney Cruise Line puts on shows with massive production values—and they don't have to worry about copyright issues, either. Expect to see shows based on the Disney catalogue like *Toy Story, Frozen,* and even *Star Wars.*

Carnival has upped its act with both stellar comedians and a concert series of visiting superstar singers and bands (everyone from Gladys Knight to Journey).

THE best SHIPS FOR DAYTIME ONBOARD ACTIVITIES

Gold Award: Royal Caribbean International
Silver Award: Disney Cruise Line
Bronze Award: Carnival Cruises

Royal Caribbean International wins this one with ships that offer unheard-of-at-sea diversions like zip lines, Flowrider surfing simulators, and even a full-sized bumper car arena aboard *Quantum of the Seas.* Much as we hate to admit it, the bumper cars are pretty fun.

Disney Cruise Line is a close second. The line offers up first-run Disney movies, character breakfasts, trivia, animation classes, and even a Disney version of the Oscars, complete with red carpet rollout.

The Fun Ships of **Carnival Cruises** shines when it comes to activities, which can range from morning yoga to belly-flop contests. On sea days, we've counted nearly 100 individual activities from dawn until dusk. On its longer Carnival Journeys voyages, the line even offers a "Throwback Sea Day" designed to replicate the cruising experience way back in 1987. Fish out your Heart cassette tapes and get ready for some Baked Alaska.

THE best SHIPS FOR ENRICHMENT

Gold Award: Cunard Line
Silver Award: Viking Ocean Cruises
Bronze Award: Princess Cruises and Oceania Cruises

Cunard's lectures are some of the best we've seen, particularly on the line's transatlantic crossings aboard *Queen Mary 2.* Guest speakers from all walks of life routinely fill the 493-seat Illuminations Theatre to standing-room only.

Viking Ocean Cruises doesn't skimp on the guest lecturers either, offering up destination-specific speakers who are engaging and knowledgeable. Plus, Viking extends that enrichment ashore, offering complimentary in-depth walking tours in many ports of call.

Princess's onboard ScholarShip@Sea program is a real winner, with hands-on classes in such diverse subjects as photography, computers, cooking, and even ceramics (you can make take-home souvenirs).

DIFFERENT TYPES OF CRUISERS

Choosing the ship that's right for you has as much to do with whom you're cruising with than anything else (and that includes traveling alone). This chapter covers the best options for families, romance-seekers, solos, groups, and travelers with disabilities. Read on.

FAMILY TRAVEL

Many parents take their kids with them on cruise vacations. The big ship lines have responded with youth counselors and supervised programs, fancy playrooms, teen centers, and even video-game rooms to keep kids entertained while their parents relax. Some lines even go so far as to offer special shore excursions and spa treatments for children and teens, and most ships provide additional evening activities and in-cabin babysitting (for an extra charge). You may even find reduced cruise fares for kids; MSC Cruises is famous for offering "kids-sail-free" promotions at certain times of the year.

And children certainly enjoy cruising. The largest ships have splash parks, water slides, game show-style activities, and character meet and greets as well as sea day brunches with costumed favorites. On land, there are often family-friendly activities (sometimes at ships' private islands) such as beachcombing, trampoline parks, splash parks, water slides, zip-lines, and kid-friendly barbecues. Cruise vacations can be a hybrid of a resort, an amusement park, and a shopping mall, meaning plenty of entertainment for kids of all ages.

Infants, Babies & Toddlers

While many lines are kid-friendly, far fewer welcome babies, so if you expect to travel with a baby you'll want to make baby-friendliness a priority in your line selection.

- **Requirements:** Most lines require babies to be at least 6 months old on their cruises, and some require them to be 12 months old. There are outliers: MSC Cruises has no age requirement at all and—on the other end of the spectrum—many luxury and expedition lines have a minimum age requirement of 14 and up.

o **Gear:** The most baby-friendly lines will have cribs or playpens and high chairs at your disposal. Disney Cruise Line, for example, also offers loaner diaper genies and strollers. Many have programs that allow you to order formula, wipes, and diapers in advance and have them waiting on arrival so that you don't have to schlep these products from home. Some luxury lines, including Crystal Cruises, offer handmade baby food in the dining room.

o **Swimming:** Pool access is restricted on all cruises to potty trained children, and in play pools and splash parks lines will expect babies and toddlers to wear swim diapers.

o **Babysitting:** Policies on babysitting vary widely. Cunard, Disney, and Royal Caribbean have nurseries for babies that are full-service. Other lines, including Celebrity Cruises and Regent Seven Seas, offer in-cabin babysitting programs for babies. Plenty of other lines require kids to be potty trained before you can leave them alone with a staff member, so be diligent in your research so that you're not surprised on arrival. Costs can vary wildly, but expect to pay about $19 per hour for this service.

Kids' Clubs

This is one place where what the lines offer ranges widely from full-service for children of most ages at most times, to very limited—or even no—offerings at all. It's also important to ask your travel agent or cruise line whether a supervised program will be available on your specific cruise, because sometimes lines that allow children but don't cater as specifically to them only provide programs if a certain number of children are on board.

For lines that have kids' clubs in a dedicated space with dedicated staffers, you will find the process usually follows this plan: On the first day of the cruise, you need to register your child, filling out paperwork. You'll get a chance to explore the space with your child—which is important because later, once the voyage begins, no adults are allowed in the kids' areas. These kids' clubs are divided by age group. On some lines, they share a large room with dedicated areas; other lines, like Carnival, Disney, and Royal Caribbean feature separate clubs for toddlers, kids, tweens, and teenagers.

Television & In-Room Movies

On the mainstream lines every cabin will have a TV, though some smaller and expedition-style ships will not. Channel selection ranges from a limited number of stations to a full On Demand set-up. Watch out—most lines will charge for movies on-demand, so make sure the kids don't go wild with the remote. If you think what the ship offers may not meet the needs of your family, consider bringing along a laptop or iPad with movies and television shows pre-loaded. This is also a good idea if you're going to find yourself in your stateroom during nap times and once you've put the children to bed.

character PARTNERSHIPS

Think these programs are just frosting on top of the cake of children's programs? The second you see a group of small children squeal as their favorite character walks into the room—like they're seeing a rock star in the flesh for the first time—you'll understand how far these programs go in entertaining the littlest cruisers.

Without a doubt, **Disney Cruise Line** has the most extensive character program. Mickey greets cruisers at embarkation and at the end of the gangway, and the sail-away party on the first evening includes Donald Duck's band. Throughout the cruise there are meet-and-greets with Mickey, Minnie, and their friends, but also the princesses (who line up to sign autographs for a long, long line of little girls, many of whom have dressed up for the photo op). One special option: You can sign your children up to get a phone call from one of their favorite characters telling them how excited they are to meet them on the cruise, a treat that toddlers compared notes on during one of my sailings.

The Dreamworks partnership with **Royal Caribbean Line** includes screenings of Dreamworks films, some of which are 3D movies, as well as an evening parade of *Shrek, Fiona, How to Train Your Dragon, Kung Fu Panda,* and the *Madagascar* animals. Cruisers can also sign up for character breakfast and luck into photo ops throughout the cruise. On *Allure of the Seas* there's a Madagascar-themed aquatic show. **One important note:** Characters are not on all ships, and the line's newest builds, *Quantum of the Seas* and *Anthem of the Seas,* do not feature the Dreamworks experience.

The "Seuss-a-Palooza" program on **Carnival Cruises** is a winner, the highlight of which is the Green Eggs and Ham brunch. Kids can also take part in a parade of characters (think Thing 1 and Thing 2 as well as the Cat in the Hat) which ends in the ship's main show lounge where cruise director's entertain kids with a special story time, read from an oversized copy of *The Cat in the Hat.* The line has also begun rolling out Dr. Seuss' Bookville, a children's reading room.

In recent years, **MSC Cruises** has ramped up its Lego partnership: You'll find plenty of brightly colored classic and Duplo bricks in play rooms and, on some ships, in special Lego-themed play areas with Lego walls. On each sailing, a sea day is designated as the official Lego day, and passengers play games and compete in building contests. Guests can also have their picture taken with the Lego-based character on board.

When you bring your child back and drop him or her off, you will typically pay per hour for the service. You can drop your child off during the day for an hour so you can hit the spa, or for several hours so you can lie in the sun; at night, many lines offer dinnertime and evening kids' club services as well.

If you're worried about safety, you may feel better to learn about the precautions the cruise lines take. Some cruise lines (including Disney and Norwegian) place wristbands on children so that if they're in the club the staff can bring them to the right lifeboat to meet you in the case of an emergency. A few lines—including Disney—offer pagers to parents so they can keep in touch.

Activities vary widely among age groups, but you may find arts and crafts, character-related meet and greets, open playtime with toys, and story hours. Some lines also offer pajama parties, movies under the stars, and other events geared toward kids and teens. On one sailing aboard Norwegian Cruise Line's *Norwegian Sun,* kids were encouraged to make paper airplanes that were then "launched" into the air from the top of the atrium. Carnival throws a kids parade through the main dining rooms, during which the young 'uns, dressed as pirates, chanting, "We want dessert! We want dessert!"

One of the better offerings for parents looking to combine a mix of family time and adult time: Some lines (most consistently Disney, Royal Caribbean, and Carnival) will have members of the kids' club staff pick up children during dinner, so that you can finish your meal as a couple and even catch a show or have some cocktails before picking the children up later.

Discounts for Families & Other Groups

Most cruise lines that cater to families offer discounted fares for the third or fourth passenger in a cabin with two full-paying guests, whether they're adults, teenagers or young children. Some have special children-sail-free programs for kids who share a cabin with two adults paying the full fare. Those discounts are sometimes seasonal, so you will have to do some research but MSC is a line with consistently good deals for families.

SOLO TRAVEL

One of the nice thing about travelling solo on cruises is that you can always ask to be seated with other guests, so you never have to dine alone. (If you don't want to be seated with other guests, seek a ship with alternative-dining options—although a steady diet of "Table for one, please" is likely to raise a few eyebrows among your shipmates.) You also needn't worry much about finding people to talk to because the general atmosphere on nearly all ships is very congenial and allows most to find conversation easily, especially during group activities. Some ships host a party or lunches on sea days to give singles a chance to get to know one another, and some ships provide social hosts as dance partners for women traveling alone.

The downside is that you may have to pay for the privilege of traveling solo. Cruise ship cabins are traditionally designed for two people and so pricing is offered per person based on double occupancy. Historically the cruise lines have charged a single supplement for cruisers who take a whole cabin for themselves, in order to compensate the line for the fact that it is designed for double occupancy revenue. Today the "single supplement" fee ranges from

Roommate Pairing Programs

Some lines, like Holland America and a number of the river cruise lines, have a stateroom-share program. By selecting this, solo travelers can sign up to be paired with another single traveler of the same sex and thus dodge the dreaded singles supplement. If the cruise line can't find you a same-sex roommate, they'll book you in a cabin alone but still honor the shared rate.

HOW TO GET freebies ON BOARD

No need to lug **toiletries** on board with you: Nearly every cruise line offers soap, shampoo, body wash, and conditioner free of charge. On some lines, the amenities can be quite upscale, with Viking and Windstar featuring L'Occitane toiletries and Silversea trotting out the Bulgari and Ferragamo. Stateroom bathrooms often have little extras like cotton balls, nail files and shower caps. If you're trying to minimize packing, ask the line or your travel agent in advance what will be in your loo.

If it's **free drinks** you're looking for, many lines serve them at sail-away parties and others offer them at ship-sponsored cocktail hours. Past guest of the line are usually plied with free drinks (and canapes are typically doled out in liberal quantities) at special parties just for these loyal customers.

Other freebies vary from line to line. Some have **lanyards** for your cabin card, others have **playing cards, postcards, combs,** and **wine keys.** Many will offer **seasickness** or **pain-relief medicine** gratis if you ask. After all, it's in their best interest to see that you enjoy your cruise. In addition, many lines give out **logo-covered items**—such as T-shirts—for people who win onboard competitions. Holland America, Princess and Windstar provide guests with handy little **tote bags** before setting out on shore excursions, while Viking ships out leather **luggage tags** and destination guides with guests' tickets that can be very valuable.

If you're taking an expedition cruise to colder climates, you may not have to pack that hefty **parka:** Hurtigruten, Seabourn, and Silversea each equip guests with jackets and parkas that are theirs to keep on cruises to the Arctic and Antarctic. Many expedition lines also provide guests with complimentary backpacks.

Sadly, the days of leather document holders and printed tickets have gone the way of the 8-track: Most cruise lines nowadays issue electronic tickets and luggage tags in PDF form that guests print off themselves.

10% to 100% of the double-occupancy fare, with a few exceptions (see below). If you must pay one, find a line with a reasonable single supplement rate—Holland America, Regent Seven Seas, and Silversea frequently offer lower-than-average solo supplements on entry-level staterooms; top-of-the-line suites will always carry a hefty surcharge for single occupancy.

Studio Cabins

Your best choice as a cruiser who wants to travel alone, but hates the idea of a single supplement: Book a cruise with a line that offers cabins specifically for solo travelers. In 2010, **Norwegian Cruise Line** launched *Norwegian Epic* with a block of 128 single-occupancy cabins known as "Studio Staterooms". Created to be smaller, but efficiently and even playfully designed, these cabins are all insides but they have access to a shared lounge that serves as a coffee shop, bar, and meeting place. The line has rolled additional studio staterooms on its new builds, with *Norwegian Breakaway* and *Norwegian Getaway* each blessed with 59 single occupancy cabins and *Norwegian Escape* with 82.

Other cruise lines are following suit. **Royal Caribbean** has 28 studio cabins on board the new *Quantum of the Seas* and *Anthem of the Seas*. **Cunard Line** added nine single staterooms on *Queen Elizabeth* and *Queen Victoria*, along with the first solo staterooms on board *Queen Mary 2*. **Holland America**'s *Koningsdam* has 12 solo cabins, its *Prisendam* has 3. **Costa Cruises** has singles cabins on about half of its fleet.

Gentleman Hosts & Social Hostesses

A few decades ago, most cruise lines had gentleman hosts. These single male travelers would get free passage, and in exchange they would commit to dining and dancing with the single women on board. All but a few lines have eliminated the program. Today, Cunard, Crystal, and Silversea still offer gentleman hosts, and they often do more than just dancing and dining—some lines have them accompany single travelers on shore excursions, as well.

Most cruise ships have what are known as a Social Hostess. These crew members do a lot to make single travelers feel included: They organize morning coffee chats on sea days and group lunches, and make an effort to introduce people who travel alone to others. On luxury lines like Silversea, the Social Hostess may also be the International Hostess, able to assist guests who need information in languages other than English.

LARGER GROUP TRAVEL

Traveling with 10 other people or more? You may be surprised to learn how much the line will do to bring you and your group on board.

o **Discounts:** Crystal Cruises' offers free passage to the 11th person in a group; Carnival Cruises and Costa Cruises' offer free fare to the 15th passenger. Some lines offer a free upgrade for the "leader" of a group instead, and many provide onboard credits for everyone in the group.

o **Freebies:** When it comes to free stuff for everyone in the group, many lines—including Holland America and Norwegian Cruise Line—start offering per-person handouts when you get up to eight cabins. It's also worth asking if your line will host a private cocktail party as a value-add.

o **Coordinated Booking:** Booking as a group has another benefit: It allows your travel agent and cruise line to "link" your reservations together, ensuring you are all given the same dining times and seating arrangements and, if requested, staterooms that are in a block next to each other.

CRUISERS WITH DISABILITIES

It's important to let the cruise line know about any special needs when you make your booking. If you use a wheelchair, you'll need to know if wheelchair-accessible cabins are available (and how they're equipped), as well as whether public rooms are accessible and can be reached by elevator, and whether the cruise line has any special policy regarding travelers with

holiday CRUISES

The way cruise lines celebrate holidays tends to vary from line to line and holiday to holiday, so it's important to ask in advance what programs and activities will be offered if the celebration is important to you.

That said, most mark Thanksgiving with a proper turkey dinner with all the fixings—from stuffing to cranberry sauce and pumpkin pie—regardless of where the ship is sailing in the world on that day. In fact, if you don't like to cook, a Thanksgiving cruise is a wonderful way to toast the holiday with your family over a proper and traditional meal without having to turn on the oven or wash a single dish.

New Year's may actually be one of the best times of year to be on a ship, as the cruise lines tend to throw a great party. The tone—from formal to mild or wild—depends on the line, but you can expect plenty of music, noise makers and toasts regardless of the ships you choose.

Christmas, too, is festive on many cruise ships, with twinkling lights, trees, and both traditional Christmas Eve and Christmas Day meals. A variety of lines celebrate the Jewish holidays as well, with Passover Seders and Hanukkah candles (usually of the electric variety for safety reasons). That said, if a certain type of religious service is important to you, you should always inquire about it in advance.

Of course, holiday cruising comes with a significant downside: Prices rise into the stratosphere and voyages sell out early. It's not uncommon for Christmas and New Year's voyages to double in cost, particularly for the top-of-the-line suites. Airlines and hotels know the score, too, and raise prices accordingly. Cruise ships *always* operate at full capacity during this time, with many lines filling nearly all third and fourth berths as well—and that means more battles on the pool deck for your favorite lounge chair.

As an alternative, you might want to sail during the first week of January, when prices fall into the bargain-basement. You won't get the holiday festivities, but your savings account will be in better shape.

disabilities—for instance, whether it's required that a fully mobile companion accompany you. Based on various court cases, it's clear that when operating in U.S. waters, ships are expected to comply with the Americans with Disabilities Act (ADA). Newer ships tend to be better equipped, however, offering a larger number of cabins at various price points for passengers in wheelchairs as well as those who are sight- or hearing-impaired. But even older ships undergoing renovations are being retrofitted to provide more access.

Travelers with disabilities should inquire when booking whether the ship docks at ports or uses "tenders" (small boats) to go ashore. Tenders cannot always accommodate passengers with wheelchairs; in most cases, wheelchair-bound passengers require crew assistance to board tenders—though Holland America, for one, uses a special lift system to get passengers into the tenders without requiring them to leave their wheelchairs. Once aboard the ship, travelers with disabilities will want to seek the advice of tour staff before choosing shore excursions that are wheelchair-friendly.

theme CRUISES

Theme cruises have exploded in popularity in recent years, giving cruisers an opportunity to dive into their favorite hobbies or see performances by their favorite artists while at sea. No matter what you're into, chances are that there's a sailing that focuses on your interests.

Carnival kicked the concept of the theme cruise up a notch a few years ago when it introduced its Carnival LIVE sailings. Initially focused on musical artists like Journey and Martina McBride, the line has expanded its entertainment offerings to include comedians and actors like Chris Tucker and Kathy Griffin.

Sometimes, outside companies charter out an entire ship for music-related cruises. Norwegian Cruise Line has partnered with a company called Sixthman to operate full-ship music charters that feature bands like KISS, Train, and events like the first Ubersoca cruise at sea aboard *Norwegian Pearl*. The line maintains a webpage at www.ncl.com/theme-cruises with all the details.

Food and wine-themed cruises have become popular in recent years, too. The focus can be on regional cuisines, local wineries and breweries, or cuisine in general. Many sailings feature headlining chefs; Jacques Pépin and his daughter occasionally host sailings on Oceania Cruises, home to his eponymous bistro restaurant. On these sailings the chef does cooking demos, signs autographs, and designs special menus. On cruises hosted by winemakers, there are often full degustation dinners on offer.

Hobbyists and crafters also have their own sailings, with knitting, needlepoint, and scrapbooking sailings. Sports fans often sell out their theme sailings early, whether the focus is on a sport or an individual team. Lines like Cunard, Seabourn and Silversea frequently feature guest speakers and lecturers that talk about political and intellectual topics. Usually, these are related to the itinerary that your ship is sailing, but quite often lecturers can present other topics, as well. Expedition lines take things one step further, with full-blown naturalists, botanists, and geologists (not to mention photographers, documentarians, and noted authors) who help add insight to the adventuresome destinations you'll visit.

There are also cruises that cater to nudists, swingers, and gay and lesbian travelers, though these tend to be full-ship charters, meaning there's not much chance of you accidentally winding up on a ship full of nudists if that's not your thing.

A comprehensive list of theme cruises is maintained at **ThemeCruiseFinder.com.**

Just consider yourself warned: Many theme cruises are annual sailings and so you may have to plan your vacation time around their availability. The good news: Itineraries and departure dates are typically released well in advance.

Tip: Because able bodied passengers have discovered that accessible cabins are often roomier, it's become harder of late to get an accessible cabin (since able-bodied passengers have been booking them under false pretenses). So book early to ensure that you get what you need.

If you have a chronic health problem, we advise you to check with your doctor before booking a cruise and, if you have any specific needs, to notify the cruise line in advance. This will ensure that the medical team on the ship is properly prepared to offer assistance.

WEDDINGS

Can you get married on a cruise ship? You sure can: Most big-ship lines offer wedding packages that allow guests to be married either on embarkation day or in a port of call. **Azamara Club Cruises, Celebrity Cruises, Cunard Line,** and **Princess Cruises** even have legally licensed Captains that can perform this ceremony at sea, if you so choose.

Most cruise lines recommend you start planning your oceangoing wedding at least 1 year in advance, though some will let you do the whole thing in 60 whirlwind days. Although each line puts its own twist on the wedding festivities, most packages offered by the cruise lines include the services of a wedding planner, flower bouquets and boutonnieres, decor for the chosen venue (typically, each ship will have one or more venues to choose from), along with officiants and wedding coordinators, sparkling wine, and dinner in one of the ship's formal specialty restaurants.

Some lines, like Cunard, really pull out all the stops for the bride and groom, offering pressing services, priority embarkation and disembarkation, a bottle of Veuve Cliquot champagne, and a white-gloved bellman to escort the bride to the wedding venue.

If you love Mickey Mouse, you can tie the knot aboard the classy ships of Disney Cruise Line, or its private island in the Bahamas, Castaway Cay. And because Disney owns the copyright, Disney's own pianist can play a selection of your Disney favorites as you walk down the aisle, if you so choose.

Have a big wedding party? See our section above about group travel for info on discounts.

HONEYMOONS

A cruise is a great choice for a honeymoon, especially because it is an easy trip to plan for, and couples are generally distracted by wedding planning up until the big day itself. You will want to make sure to request a cabin with a double, queen, or king-size bed, instead of twins.

Rooms with private verandas are particularly romantic; you can take in the sights in privacy and even enjoy a quiet meal, assuming the veranda is big enough for a table and chairs and the weather doesn't turn chilly. If you want to dine alone at dinner, request a table for two in advance; the same goes for couples' spa treatments, which can fill up in advance.

Some ships—among them those of Princess, Royal Caribbean, Carnival, Celebrity, and Holland America—offer special packages and sometimes honeymoon suites. Most lines provide special amenities, such as champagne and chocolates, if you let them know in advance that you'll be honeymooning.

CHOOSING & BOOKING YOUR CRUISE

Cruise lines have detailed websites and brochures, or sometimes many different brochures—including e-brochures—full of beautiful glossy photos of beautiful glossy people enjoying fabulous vacations. They're colorful! They're gorgeous! They're enticing! They're also confusing in that they all blur together very quickly. Sadly, while the lines themselves are very different from one another, their marketing strategies are not.

This chapter is about comparing and contrasting, so you can pick the cruise that's right for you. And about not getting taken, so you can feel good about your vacation costs.

If you dig a little deeper, you'll find that picking the right cruise is a lot like buying a car: Any one will get you where you want to go, but there are some that will make you happier than others.

QUESTIONS TO ASK BEFORE YOU BOOK

When you look at the attributes of the various ships and itineraries to make your choice, some determining factors will be no-brainers. For instance, if you're traveling with kids, you'll want a ship with a good kids' program. If you're a foodie, you'll want a ship with gourmet cuisine. If you usually stay at B&Bs when you travel, you'll probably prefer one of the small ships.

Also ask yourself whether you require resortlike amenities, such as a heated swimming pool, spa, casino, aerobics classes, and state-of-the-art gym. Or do you care more about having an adventure or an educational experience? If you want the former, choose a large cruise ship; if you prefer the latter, a small ship may be more your speed. Here are some more pertinent questions to help you narrow the field:

What Size Is Best for You?

The size of the ship contributes significantly to the atmosphere. Cruise ships range from small, adventure-type vessels or yacht-style options to megaships that carry thousands, and will have multiple dining venues, many types of entertainment, cutting edge gyms and elaborate spas. Size also dictates the social atmosphere aboard the vessel. Do you want, or do you need, to be with people and, if so, in an intimate daily setting or only on an occasional basis?

On a small ship, there's no escape: The people you meet on a 22-passenger or even a 100-passenger vessel are the ones you're going to be seeing every day of the cruise. The truth is that it will impact your vacation if they turn out to be boring, or bombastic, or slow-witted, or in some other way not to your taste. Personal chemistry plays a big part in the success or failure of any cruise experience—especially the small-ship cruise experience.

Some people may think that the megaships are too big, but they do have at least one saving grace: On a 2,000- or 5,000-passenger ship, there's plenty of room to steer clear of people who turn you off. And because all these big, newer ships have lots of alternative restaurants, it's even easier to avoid those types at mealtimes, something that's not so easy on a smaller ship.

The hotel director on a Holland America ship once noted, "If you want to stay out until 4am, gamble wildly, and pass out in a lounge, you don't come on Holland America." And he's right. Picking the ship that's right for you is the key to a successful cruise experience.

How Much Time Does the Ship Spend in Port?

This varies widely, from Mediterranean cruises that are in ports every day to longer sailings in Asia with a handful of sea days required to cover the distance between ports. In the Caribbean, you may have 1 or 2 sea days on an itinerary and, generally, Alaska itineraries spend 3 or 4 days in port with 1 or 2 days of scenic cruising in-between.

Coming into port, ships generally dock right after breakfast, allowing you the morning and afternoon to take a shore excursion or explore on your own. Ships usually depart in the early evening, giving you an hour or two to rest up before dinner (although some ships do stay in specific ports, such as Juneau or Cozumel, as late as 10pm, giving passengers a chance to sample a dinner on shore). Some lines, like Azamara and Oceania, make a point of designing their itineraries with multiple overnight stays in port. And voyages to Bermuda, for example, typically feature 2 or 3 days docked in Hamilton before ships set sail across the Atlantic for the eastern seaboard.

This is where your own personal tastes will come into play: You can easily find a Mediterranean voyage that is packed with port calls, or one that is interspersed with sea days in between. While a week of solid ports sounds like fun, the truth is that it can be very exhausting. A nice mix of sea days can provide that much-needed "down time" to relax and recuperate without having to worry about FOMO: the Fear Of Missing Out.

On days at sea, the emphasis will be on activities (think bingo, pool games, and wine tasting) or, in some parts of the world exploring natural areas and scanning for wildlife. Big ships stick to prearranged schedules on these days, but on small-ship, soft-adventure-type cruises, days at sea can be unstructured, with the captain choosing a destination based on reports of whale sightings, for example. Some small-ship itineraries include almost no ports, sticking instead to isolated natural areas that passengers explore by kayak, Zodiac boat or on foot.

Is the Cruise Formal?

If you don't care to get dressed up, select a less formal cruise, such as those offered by many of the small ships, or larger ships such as those of Norwegian Cruise Line and Oceania Cruises, which do not have official formal nights. If, on the other hand, having the chance to put on your finery appeals to you, select Celebrity, Cunard, or Holland America (and, to a lesser extent, mass-market lines, such as Royal Caribbean and Carnival) or posh lines like Crystal and Silversea. These ships will have casual and formal nights over the course of a week, when women can show off everything from a sundress to an evening gown (though on formal nights, most show up in cocktail dresses), and men will go from shirtsleeves to jacket and tie. You can wear a tuxedo on formal night if you like, but many men are now opting for dark suits. Most lines also now have an option for those who do not want to dress up on formal nights—you can skip the dining room and eat casually at the buffet, or order room service in your cabin, where the dress code is pretty much whatever you feel like wearing.

What Are the Other Passengers Like?

Each ship attracts a fairly predictable type of passenger. On small ships, you'll find a more physically active bunch that's highly interested in nature, but you'll find fewer families and single travelers. Larger ships cater to a more diverse group—singles, newlyweds, families, and couples over 55. A good general rule to follow: the longer the itinerary, the older the crowd.

For nightlife seekers, big ships are the way to go. The nightlife aboard Carnival, MSC, Norwegian, and Royal Caribbean ships is plentiful and varied, and goes on well into the night. Princess cruise ships tend to quiet down around 11pm, while Holland America guests typically turn in even earlier.

What Daytime Activities Does the Ship Offer?

On small ships, activities are limited by the available public space and are usually up to the passengers to organize—maybe a game of Scrabble or Trivial Pursuit. There may be a showing of a video or two, and there will typically also be a lecture series dealing with flora, fauna, history, or religion. These enrichment lectures are also popular on larger cruise ships, along with "edutainment" classes that focus on cooking, art, photography, personal finance, computers and history. Cooking is particularly hot, no pun intended, with certain lines installing purpose-built demonstration kitchens.

Many big and small ships alike will offer beer or wine tastings, often under the supervision of the onboard Sommelier. Bridge, shuffleboard and poolside games are common; on ships with more retired passengers you may find bridge and mahjong, too. And then there are the "behind-the-scenes" tours that take guests into some of the more typically off-limits spaces, including the ship's galley, provisioning areas, laundry rooms, and backstage theatre areas. Some of these tours are complimentary; others can run well over $100 per person and can include some special goodies like T-shirts, hats and complimentary photos. A handful of tours may include a supervised visit to the ship's navigation bridge, though this is far more common on smaller vessels.

What Entertainment Does the Ship Offer at Night?

Forget the old jokes about the so-so quality of cruise ship entertainers: Productions at night are *de rigueur* on all but the smallest vessels, and they've gotten a lot better in the last few years. Now, on large the big ships, you'll find Broadway-caliber productions complete with sets that rise and turn, smoke, lighting effects, and directional sound. Sure, the "Tribute to ABBA!" shows crop up every now and again, but they're gradually fading into the sunset in favor of smarter and more elaborate productions.

Live music is also making a comeback on board many big ships. Carnival's Fun Ships offer a surprising amount of music, with piano bars, pop and rock duos, and on-deck DJ's. Cunard kicks things up a notch for classical music lovers with some of the best instrumental artists on the high seas, and themed voyages featuring the National Symphony Orchestra. Holland America Line has dedicated an entire area of their new *Koningsdam* to music, and even small-ship lines like Windstar Cruises employ at least a pianist to dance the night away to.

Obviously, entertainment varies from line to line—and a few lines have some additional perks. Disney Cruise Line, for example, gets to run the entire Disney library on board its whimsical ships, while Carnival spearheaded some of the best comedy clubs at sea with their Punchliner Comedy Club.

And kudos to Princess Cruises for reinventing the way vacationers watch movies on board. In 2004, they outfitted the then-new *Caribbean Princess* with a gigantic poolside movie screen and sound system, and "Movies Under the Stars" was born. The technology has since been adopted by many other lines.

Will I Get Seasick?

You'll want to choose your ship carefully if you're concerned about seasickness. Keep in mind that big ships tend to be more stable than smaller ships, but that all ships will move around if the winds or the swells are high enough. That being said, ship stability has improved dramatically in recent years. The vast majority of cruise ships built nowadays have stabilizers: finlike surfaces that swing out from the hull underwater, much like the wings of an airplane. These help to reduce the rolling (left-to-right) of the ship, which is what causes people the most discomfort. Stabilizers, however, do not counteract pitch, which is the ship rising at the bow and the stern.

What Do You Do If You Start to Feel Seasick?

There are pill-based medications that can help, including Dramamine, Bonine, and Marezine, which are available over the counter and also stocked by most ships—the purser's office may even give them out for free. The downside is that they can make you tired, and even the non-drowsy formulas can make you feel a bit sleepy.

Another option is the Transderm patch, which is applied behind your ear and has time-released medication. The patch can be worn for up to 3 days, but you should be aware that it comes with a slew of warnings about side effects, including the possibility of blurry vision.

Non-medicinal alternatives are also available. Chewing on candied ginger or taking ginger capsules relieves the onset of seasickness for some; the products are available at most health food stores. Acupressure wristbands, known as SeaBands, are another strategy, available at most pharmacies. These are worn around both wrists like a watch, and feature a small buttonlike appendage that pushes into your skin. Generally, both of these remedies work best if you start them *before* the onset of seasickness. We swear by our candied ginger, Ginger Ale, and Sea Bands when the seas get rough.

If you are generally prone to seasickness, you should ask for recommendations from your doctor before your cruise. However, if you do get sick on board, the ship's doctor may be able to prescribe a cure—for a hefty fee.

You'll also want to pick your itinerary carefully. Unless you're particularly prone to seasickness, you probably don't need to worry much on itineraries that stay close to the shore, such as those in the Mediterranean and Caribbean waters (with some exceptions; see below). At certain points, however, on some sailings—including Alaska—you may end up in open water. You may experience rough water around Sitka and at the entrance to Queen Charlotte Strait, for example, which shouldn't be surprising since there is nothing between you and Japan but a lot of wind, water, and choppy seas. Although ships that ply these routes tend to be very stable, you'll probably notice some rocking and rolling. Other routes, including a variety of ocean crossings and other around-the-world voyages, hit open seas for more substantial amounts of the trip, and those are the times when seasickness is most likely to strike.

Two other notoriously choppy areas are the Bay of Biscay, just off the coast of France and Spain in the Atlantic and the Drake Passage which separates South America from Antarctica. You'll have to cross the Drake if you're sailing from Ushuaia to the Antarctic Peninsula. Good news, though: If you get the "Drake Shake" heading across to Antarctica, you'll likely have the "Drake Lake"—very calm conditions—coming back. And once you're in Antarctica, seas are generally smooth as glass.

In addition, time of year can be a factor. Some routes, particularly those in the Caribbean, offer smooth sailing most of the year, but can be rougher during hurricane season (particularly Sept–Oct), when tropical storms change the sea from calm to stormy. This is true of the Mediterranean as well, which is noted for its fierce winter storms in the colder months.

If you are worried about seasickness, you want to choose your cabin carefully as well. Those in the middle tend to be the most stable while cabins at the stern and bow feel the movement more. Staterooms on lower decks, closer to the water line, tend to move around less. It's somewhat ironic, given that most cruise lines place their largest and most luxurious suites near the top of the ship—where the views are great, but movement can be felt the most.

BOOKING A CRUISE

We won't lie: The cruise itself will be very relaxing. Booking the cruise? Not so much. There are a number of factors, which we'll go through below, that you need to understand so that a) you don't get taken and b) you end up with the cruise you want.

First issue: What are the costs involved in a cruise? As in any venture, it's important that you understand the overall price of what you are buying. The truth is the base price for cruises constantly fluctuate based on a variety of factors, including the number of available staterooms left, the amount of time remaining until sailing day, your past passenger status (if any), and your residence (localized specials can often be found). Some lines give discounts for those with active or past military service. Rates are heavily influenced by the volume of travelers interested in cruising to a particular region, how long the season is, and how many individual departures are on offer.

Generally speaking, though, the various lines fall into three budget categories, though we'll note that sometimes fares at some of the cruise lines marked "moderate" below—like Celebrity and Princess—can fall into the "budget" category and every once in a while, starting fares on Holland America, Norwegian and Royal Caribbean will be in the moderate range:

General Cruise Costs

Budget ($100 per day or less)	Moderate ($100–$400 per day)	Expensive ($400 per day or more)
Alaska Marine Highway System	Azamara Club Cruises	Alaskan Dream Cruises
Carnival Cruise Lines	Celebrity Cruises	American Cruise Lines
Costa Cruises	Cunard Line	Blount Small Ship Adventures
Holland America Line	Disney Cruise Line	Crystal Cruises
MSC Cruises	Princess Cruises	Lindblad Expeditions
Norwegian Cruise Line	Star Clippers	Oceania Cruises
Royal Caribbean International	Viking Ocean Cruises	Paul Gauguin Cruises
	Windstar Cruises	Regent Seven Seas Cruises
		Seabourn Cruises
		SeaDream Yacht Club
		Silversea Cruises
		Un-Cruise Adventures

The price you pay for your cabin represents the bulk of your cruise vacation cost, but there are other fees to consider. Are you getting a price that includes the cruise fare, port charges, taxes, fees, and insurance, or are you getting a cruise-only fare? Are airfare and airport transfers included, or do you have to book them separately (either as an add-on to the cruise fare or on your own)? One agent might break down the charges in a price quote, while another might bundle them all together. Make sure you're comparing apples with apples. Your total price should include an itemized analysis of your total cruise fare, much like the breakdown you'd see on an airline ticket. Read the fine print.

It's important when figuring out what your cruise will cost to remember what extras are *not* included in your cruise fare. While the high-end luxury lines will throw in everything but the kitchen sink, you need to be prepared to reach into your wallet while on board in order to enjoy some fun diversions on most cruise lines. A big misconception about cruises is that they're all-inclusive; with the exception of the top-end lines, that just isn't the case.

Having said that, none of these costs are deal-breakers—if you know about them in advance. Here's a look at what you can expect to have to shell out money for on board if you're booking a mainstream, big-ship cruise:

Shore Excursions

Some of the priciest additions to your overall cruise cost are the shore excursions sold by the cruise lines. Expect to pay about $30 to $99 per person for a comprehensive walking or bus-based sightseeing tour, $30–$50 per person or thereabouts for a beach break in the Caribbean, and between $199 and $699 or more for high-profile tours like flightseeing and dog sledding in Alaska, or going for a swim with the dolphins in Mexico. By and large, Caribbean-based excursions tend to be the cheapest, while Alaska and the Mediterranean duke it out for high-cost supremacy.

Of course, you don't have to take a ship-sponsored shore excursion in order to enjoy your cruise. In many ports of call, passengers can simply step off the ship and explore independently; this form of travel offers a more authentic sense of place than simply seeing the destination through the tinted windows of a motor coach can. In the old days, it wasn't uncommon for cruise lines to try to scare passengers away from solo exploration, saying they'd be left behind if they got back to the port late and weren't on a ship-sponsored tour. Our advice: Check your watch or phone periodically, and take a copy of your ship's printed Daily Program with you: It will have the ship's telephone number and the Port Agent's telephone number on it, along with your scheduled "All Aboard" and "Departure" times listed.

Between going off on your own and taking a cruise ship-sponsored tour, there's a middle road, particularly doable if you're travelling with three or more people: arranging an independent shore excursion. You may be able to save by booking your tours through such private companies as **Viator** (www.viator. com), **ShoreTrips** (www.shoretrips.com), or **Cruising Excursions** (www. cruisingexcursions.com), a UK company. All three act as clearinghouses for

Fancy Dining Choices for a Fee

As if multicourse dining room meals and endless buffets were not enough, cruise lines have added premium restaurant venues where, in most cases, they charge a fee to cover especially attentive service and a menu featuring extra-special cuisine. These alternative restaurants tend to be small venues done up in fancy furnishings—just the kind of place you'd want for a date night or special celebration. In most cases, the spaces are reserved for adults only. Prices vary from line to line and restaurant to restaurant. For example, you can dine for $20 per person at Disney Cruise Line's impressive Northern Italian-themed Palo, a classy (and delicious) venue designed just for adults. Carnival's steakhouses serve extrava-gant prime aged cuts for $35, along with surf-and-turf options. Norwegian Cruise Line charges $75 and Royal Caribbean $95 for a Chef's Table experience where multiple courses are presented by the ship's executive chef and accompanied by specially paired wines. On some of the luxury lines, a meal at one of the specialty restaurants is included in the cruise fare (but does require advance reservations).

Beyond the extra costs, is there a downside to these specialty restaurants? Some cruisers feel that the quality of the food in the main dining rooms, on some ships, has slipped to encourage people to take on the extra fees. We've noted, in our reviews later in the book, when that seems to be the case.

local tour operators. Because the latter two work exclusively with tour passengers, each offers guarantees that if you arrive back at port after the ship has set sail, they'll get you to the next port free of charge. Most of Viator's vendors offer the same guarantee, with the exception of those tours that are offered to both cruise passengers and land tourists.

Tips

Tips comprise a good percentage of what you'll pay overall for a cruise. We've broken down the expectations on p. 104.

Beverages

Most ships charge extra for alcoholic beverages (including wine at dinner) and soda. Non-bubbly soft drinks such as lemonade and iced tea and hot drinks such as coffee and tea are usually included in your cruise fare. On Disney ships, soda from fountains and at meals is free, but you'll pay extra if you want a can from a bar. A can of soda will cost about $2.50, beer $3.50 and up, a glass of wine or mixed drinks $6 and up. Bottled water is extra, too, from $2 per bottle. Bringing your own re-usable bottle of water is a good idea, but some lines may frown on refilling it from the water taps in the buffet, due to the risk of spreading germs. Filling it up with a glass of water from the lido or from your stateroom tap (it's perfectly safe to drink unless otherwise noted) is fine.

If you're a big soda drinker, you'll want to consider buying a soda package that offers unlimited refills. Prices vary by cruise line, but start at around $42 for adults ($28 for kids) for a weeklong cruise. You may be required to book the package in advance of your cruise; check the info sent from the cruise line.

WHAT'S not INCLUDED?

Generally speaking, cruise fares covers your accommodations, meals (except for those in specialty restaurants) shipboard entertainment, and most shipboard activities. There are, however, a number of expenses not covered in the typical cruise package, and you should factor these in when planning your vacation budget. Here's a quick checklist:

Airfare The largest of these costs will undoubtedly be airfare to and from your port of embarkation and debarkation, unless you're within driving distance of the embarkation and debarkation points. See p. 32 for more on this topic.

On-Shore Accommodations If you think you don't need a pre-cruise hotel, think again: Unless you live near the port of embarkation, flying in on the day-of embarkation is not a good idea. If anything goes wrong, from flight delays to cancellations to mechanical issues, you can find yourself at-risk of missing the entire cruise. Arrive the day before; you'll be glad you did. See p. 32 for more on that expense.

Gratuities Tips are typically extra on most lines, with the exception of luxury cruise lines that include them in the cost of your fare. See p. 104.

Shore Excursions These are rarely included in the cruise fare if you're on a standard, mass volume cruise line. River boats, expedition lines and luxury cruise lines are starting to offer at least one in most ports of call. Excursion prices also vary depending on your cruise destination; a beach break in the Caribbean can set you back as little as $30 per person, while a flightseeing tour in Alaska can run into the hundreds of dollars. See p. 101 for more on costs.

Drinks Alcohol is typically extra (though river cruise lines and luxury lines like Regent and Silversea include all or most drinks in the cruise fare), as are sodas (with a few exceptions, including Oceania and Disney).

Incidentals Need to do laundry or require babysitting? Those will be extra, sometimes a LOT extra. And then there are such optional splurges as beauty and spa services, wine tastings, dining in alternative restaurants, select fitness classes, fancy ice cream sundaes, and photos taken by ship photographers.

Internet Internet access has historically been incredibly slow and shockingly expensive, but there have been improvements, at least in speed, in recent years. That being said, Viking Cruises offers complimentary Wi-Fi aboard their *Viking Star*, as do some of the river cruise companies and a few of the luxury lines.

A bottle of wine with dinner will run anywhere from $15 to upwards of $300, though most big-ship lines offer wine packages which can reduce the cost of each bottle (you buy, say, five bottles for a discounted price). There are also packages that offer up inclusive alcoholic drinks—beers, wines, spirits and mixed drinks—typically up to a certain price point (the most premium spirits or mixed drinks in souvenir glasses will always be extra). Celebrity Cruises, Carnival, Holland America Line, MSC Cruises, Norwegian Cruise Line, and Royal Caribbean all offer alcohol and wine packages. You'll have to do the math on how much you typically drink in a week in order to figure out if you can imbibe enough to make it worth it. *Note:* Most lines have made the inclusive alcohol packages mandatory purchases for *both* guests in the stateroom; unless you're a heavy drinker, these can get very expensive, very quickly. *Tip:* Many lines will put a cork in an unfinished bottle of wine at dinner and let you have the rest the next day.

Port Charges, Local Taxes & Fees

Every ship has to pay docking fees at each port. Cruise lines are also required to pay local taxes and per-passenger "head taxes" at many ports of call. Like landing fees airlines have to pay at airports, these can vary from place to place and from one itinerary to another. Transiting the Panama Canal, unsurprisingly, costs cruise lines a lot of money. Port charges, taxes, and other fees are sometimes included in your cruise fare, but not always, and these charges can add on average between $200 and $250 to the price of a 7-day cruise. There can be other fees, too. For example, in Alaska, a $35 per passenger head and berth tax imposed by the State of Alaska and $7 and $8 taxes in Juneau and Ketchikan, respectively, are usually rolled into your cruise fare. Make sure you know whether these fees are included in the cruise fare when you're comparing rates; most websites and advertisements, by law, are required to list whether port taxes and other charges are included.

Booking Through Travel Agencies vs. Online Travel Agencies vs. Cruise Lines

So how do you book your cruise? Traditionally (meaning over the past 30 years or so), people have booked their cruises through travel agents. But you may be wondering: Hasn't the traditional, bricks-and-mortar travel agent gone the way of typewriters and eight-track tapes and been replaced by the Internet? Not exactly. Travel agents are alive and kicking, though the Internet has indeed staked its claim alongside them and even knocked some out of business.

But even in this digital age, the vast majority of cruise passengers still book through travel agents. The cruise lines are happy with this system and—unlike airlines—typically have only a small dedicated reservations staff on-hand to take direct bookings. In some cases, if you try to call a cruise line directly to book your own passage, the line will advise you to contact an agent in your area. The cruise line may even offer a choice of names from its list of preferred agencies (you'll often find links to preferred agencies on cruise-line websites).

This isn't a bad thing: A good travel agent can save you both time and money. Booking a cruise is far more complex than booking a stay at a Marriott, or planning a flight to Rome. A cruise has a number of moving parts and decisions that need to be made. You may be the rare type that doesn't need a travel agent, but most of us—including the most experienced cruisers—are better off working with one, at least in the complex world of cruising.

Good agents can give you expert advice, save you time, and (best of all) usually work for you for free or for a nominal fee—the bulk of their fees are paid by the cruise lines. (Many agents charge a consultation fee—say, $25 or

WATCH OUT FOR scams

The travel business tends to attract more than its share of scam operators trying to lure consumers with incredible come-ons, and cruises are no exception. To keep yourself safe:

Get a Referral A recommendation from a trusted friend or colleague is one of the best ways to hook up with a reputable agent.

Use the Cruise Lines' Agent Lists Many cruise-line websites include agency locator lists, naming agencies around the country with which they do business. These are by no means comprehensive lists of all good or bad agencies, but an agent's presence on these lists is usually a good sign of experience.

Beware of Snap Recommendations If an agent suggests a cruise line without asking you a single question about your tastes, beware. Because agents typically work on commissions from the lines, some may try to coerce you into cruising with a company that pays them the highest rates, even though that line may not be the right fit for you.

Always Use a Credit Card to Pay for Your Cruise A credit card gives you more protection in the event the agency or cruise line fails. (Trust us! It happens occasionally.) When your credit card statement arrives, make sure the payment was made to the cruise line, not the travel agency. If you find that payment was actually made to the agency, it's a big red flag that something's wrong. If you insist on paying by check, you'll be making it out to the agency, so it may be wise to ask if the agency has default protection. Many do.

Follow the Cruise Line's Payment Schedule Never agree to a different schedule that the travel agency comes up with. The lines' terms are always clearly printed in their brochures and usually require an initial deposit, with the balance typically due no later than 45 to 75 days before departure, depending on the cruise line. If you're booking 2 months or less before departure, you'll often be required to pay in full at the time of booking. However, the cruise lines have been making changes in this regard, so read the fine print carefully.

Keep on Top of Your Booking If you ever fail to receive a document or ticket on the date it's been promised, inquire about it immediately. If you're told that your cruise reservation was canceled because of overbooking and that you must pay extra for a confirmed and rescheduled sailing, demand a full refund and/or contact your credit card company to stop payment. Ensure that names are spelled properly and that your receipt reflects the date, ship and itinerary you had booked. Even good, competent travel agents can make mistakes sometimes, so it always pays to be attentive to any documents you receive.

THE MOST COMMON SCAMS

Contests Targeted victims fill out a "Win a Free Cruise!" card at a fair or trade show, or receive an unsolicited card in the mail claiming that they've won a free cruise. The name "Caribbean Cruise Line" is usually printed somewhere on the card. Of course, there is no "Caribbean Cruise Line" as such. Typically, the victim is convinced to hand over increasing sums of money to access a 2-night cruise to the Bahamas....and the sailing is paired with high-pressure timeshare condo sales. And that's if you're ever "lucky" enough to set sail.

"Cold Calls" If you get an unexpected solicitation by phone, fax, mail, or e-mail be wary, especially if the agency in question won't give you a street address. Legit agencies don't tend to "cold call" potential customers; they have enough business without having to resort to such tactics.

$50—which they refund if you eventually give them the booking.) In addition to advising you about the different ships, an agent can help you help you make decisions about the type of cabin you need, your dining room seating choices, and whether you want to extend your cruise vacation with any pre- and post-cruise land offerings—all of which can have a big impact on your cruise experience. We have seen complaints from people who booked a really cheap inside cabin and were angry that it was "a noisy cabin." Had they asked an experienced cruise agent, they might have been advised that the cabin was cheap because it was practically in the engine room—and that simply selecting a different stateroom within that category would have dramatically improved their cruise experience. (Note that the days where cruise ships offered less-desirable staterooms is gradually coming to an end. Most new ships tend to offer staterooms that are more similar than not across a single category, with most differences listed in detail on the vessel's deck plan. It's a far cry from the former *Celebrity Mercury,* which featured a large metal pole smack in the middle of one of its inside staterooms.)

Having a dedicated travel agent—whether online or in-person in standard "brick-and-mortar" offices that you can physically go into—can also be a lifesaver if things go south. Think of the travel agent as your liaison to the cruise lines. Fog, storms, and strikes can all delay ships unexpectedly. Knowing what your options are and having someone in-the-know acting fast on your behalf can make a huge difference.

FINDING A GREAT AGENT

If you don't know a good travel agent, ask your friends for recommendations, preferably those who have cruised before. For the most personal service, look for an agent in your area, and for the most knowledgeable service, look for an agent with cruising experience.

Of course, the easiest way to do this is to find a travel agency that specializes exclusively in cruises or cruisetours. But there are also good cruise specialists who work within full-service travel agencies. If you are calling a full-service travel agency, ask for the cruise desk.

It's also a good idea to ask the agent you are working with if he or she has actually been to the region you want to visit, and on the ships that you are considering booking. Even if they haven't sailed on that particular ship, travel agents are routinely treated to familiarization trips (FAMs) that can consist of a ship tour and lunch on board when the vessel is in port.

An easy rule of thumb to maximize your chances of finding an agent who has cruise experience, and won't rip you off, is to book with an agency that's a member of the **Cruise Lines International Association** (**CLIA;** www. cruising.org; ℂ **754/224-2200**), the main industry association. Members are cruise specialists; agents accredited as Certified Cruise Counselors by CLIA have particularly extensive training. Membership in the **American Society of Travel Agents** (**ASTA;** www.asta.org; ℂ **800/275-2782**) ensures that the agency is monitored for ethical practices, although it does not designate cruise experience. Tap into the websites of these organizations to find reliable agents.

OTHER WAYS TRAVEL AGENTS CAN HELP

Travel agents are frequently in contact with the cruise lines and are continually alerted by the lines about the latest and best deals and special offers. The cruise lines tend to communicate such deals and offers to their top agents first, often throwing in **incentives** like reduced deposits, complimentary stateroom category upgrades, or onboard credits (OBCs) that can be applied toward shipboard costs like beverages, shore excursions or spa treatments.

Experienced agents know how to play the cruise lines' game and get you the best deals. For example, many cruise lines run promotions that allow you to book a specific stateroom category without being assigned an actual stateroom number. This is called a **"guarantee cabin,"** or GTY, and these offers tend to work out to be some of the most economical. Typically, a few weeks before sailing you'll see your stateroom appear on your online Cruise Personalizer or on your documents. You're guaranteed at least the stateroom category you booked—or better. Playing the guarantee game can really pay off (we once went from an inside stateroom to a full-blown balcony stateroom), but you have limited control over your actual stateroom once it's assigned. An informed agent will know about these offers, and may also be able to direct you to a category on a specific ship in which your chances of an upgrade are better. The cruise lines sometimes even upgrade passengers as a favor to their top-producing agents or agencies, though this happens more rarely today than it did 10 years ago.

Depending on the agency you choose, you may run across other incentives for booking through an agent. Some agencies buy big **blocks of space** on a ship in advance and offer it to their clients at a group price available only through that agency. These are called group rates, although "group" in this instance strictly means "savings"; you won't have to hang out with the other people booking through the agency.

One word of advice: Be wary of an agent promising to give you a cash rebate. It's against the rules of most cruise lines, and they have been clamping down on violators—most legit agents follow the rules. The cruise lines themselves post Internet specials on their websites, and the same deals are usually also available through travel agents. The lines don't want to upset their travel-agent partners and generally try not to compete against them.

The Most Important Question to Ask Your Would-Be Agent

The big thing to remember when using a travel agent: Not all agents represent all cruise lines. To be experts on what they sell, and to maximize the commissions the lines pay them (they're often paid more based on volume of sales), some agents may limit their offerings to, say, one luxury line, one mid-price line, one mass-market line, and so on. If you have your sights set on a particular line or have narrowed down your preferences to a couple of lines, you should find an agent who handles those. And whenever approaching a new agent ASK if they specialize in this way, and if so, with which cruise lines.

BOOKING A small-ship CRUISE

The small-ship cruise lines—such as Un-Cruise Adventures, American Cruise Lines, and Lindblad Expeditions—provide cruise experiences that tend to attract passengers who have a very good idea of the kind of experience they want (usually educational or adventurous, and always casual and small-scale). In many cases, a large percentage of passengers on any given cruise will have sailed with the line before. Because of all this, and because the passenger capacity of these ships is so low (22–100 passengers) in general you won't find the kinds of deep discounts often offered by the large ships. For the most part, these lines rely on agents to handle their bookings, taking very few reservations directly. All the lines have a list of agents with whom they do considerable business on their websites.

BOOKING WITH AN ONLINE TRAVEL AGENCY (OTA)

For those who know exactly what they want and don't need the personalized care a smaller travel agency provides, there are deals to be had on the Internet. Popular sites selling cruises include mega travel clearinghouses like **Expedia. com, Orbitz.com,** and **Flightcenter.ca** in Canada; plus big agencies that specialize exclusively in cruises (**icruise.com, Cruise.com, CruisesOnly. com, Cruise411.com, VacationsToGo.com, 7blueseas.com,** and **Cruise ExpertsTravel.com** in Canada). Some online cruise sellers also offer standard brick-and-mortar retail locations, like **Expedia Cruise Ship Centers,** the dedicated cruise arm of Expedia that offers retail locations in the United States, Canada, Mexico and Puerto Rico. All online sites have phone numbers you can call or chat forums where you can ask questions. Also selling cruises on the Web are search engines (**Kayak.com**), and auction sites (**Allcruise auction.com** and **Priceline.com**).

The Internet also has some good sites that specialize in providing cruise information rather than selling cruises. Two popular cruise fan sites are **Cruiseline.com** and **Cruisecritic.com,** which feature reviews by professional writers, ratings and reviews by cruise passengers, plus useful tips and message boards. You can read what past passengers have said about your line, your ship, your itinerary, and the ports included. The online message boards frequently descend into petty bickering and offer more than a bit of misinformation, but taken with a grain of salt these cruise message boards can provide information on a huge range of topics.

MONEY-SAVING STRATEGIES
Early-Bird & Last-Minute Discounts

How you save will depend on where you're going. The best way to save on a cruise to a region with a short season (such as Alaska in summer) is to book in advance. In a typical year, lines offer their lowest published fares—typically with savings of 25% or more—to those who book those cruises by mid-February of the year of the cruise. If the cabins do not fill up by the cutoff date, the early-bird rate, sometimes referred to as an early-booking discount, may be extended, but any discount may also be lowered—meaning fares rise.

In more crowded areas with lots of cruise choices—such as the Caribbean in wintertime, before some of the ships move on to Alaska and Europe—you may do better with a last-minute booking deal, if you have the flexibility to take advantage of slashed rates with little notice. We've occasionally seen prices slashed as much as 75%. But remember: Often, the deepest last-minute discounts are for cruises leaving from ports near airports where the airfares in tend to be quite high. So crunch *all* the numbers before booking.

We also have to bring up a new wrinkle: Recently Royal Caribbean announced it would no longer discount their voyages if they were less than 30 days from sailing. The rationale was that those who booked well in advance were (understandably) angry that those who booked last-minute got a better deal. Whether or not this vow will stick remains to be seen. We're guessing if two many ships go out with too many empty cabins, RCL may have to pedal backwards on that promise.

Beyond pricing, early-bird bookings always offer consumers the best selection of cabins, important if you're traveling with a group that wishes to bunk near to one another; or if you need one of the limited number of accessible cabins that are aboard each vessel. That's especially true of river cruises, which tend to sell out *well* in advance. Many lines try to encourage booking up to a year in advance, a strategy that does have some advantages: Booking so far in advance secures your cruise and stateroom, and gives you plenty of time to research airfare and hotel options.

Keep in mind that the most expensive and cheapest cabins tend to sell out first. This is as much price-driven as supply-driven: Those who want the top-of-the-line suites know there are only a handful on the ship, and will pay the price to secure one. Inside staterooms are desirable because they represent the most economical way to get on the cruise. That leaves "the meaty center," which on most cruise ships would be your standard balcony stateroom, open for booking. As they say in the cruise business, ships sell out from the top and bottom first.

Third- & Fourth-Passenger Discounts

Many cruise lines offer highly discounted rates for third and fourth passengers sharing a cabin with two full-fare passengers, even if those two have booked at a discounted rate. You can add the four rates together and then divide by four to get your per-person rate. This is a good option for families (or very good friends) on a budget, but remember that travelling four to a stateroom—particularly in smaller oceanview and inside categories—will be a tight fit, with at least two guests sleeping either on pull-out couches or Pullman-style berths that fold down from the wall or their housing in the stateroom's ceiling.

Group Discounts

One of the best ways to get a cruise deal is to book as a group, so you may want to gather family together for a reunion or convince your friends or colleagues they need a vacation, too. A "group," as defined by the cruise lines, is generally at least 16 people occupying eight staterooms. By doing so, the potential savings include discounted cruise fares all around, and at least the cruise portion of the 16th ticket will be free. On some upscale ships, you can negotiate a free ticket for groups of 10 or more. The gang can split the proceeds from the free berth or hold a drawing for the ticket, maybe at a cocktail party on the first night. If your group is large enough, you may even be able to get that cocktail party for free, and perhaps some other onboard perks as well (contact Group Services—though cruise lines have wildly varying policies on this point.)

Senior Citizen & Military Discounts

Senior citizens might be able to get extra savings on their cruise. Some lines will take about 5% off the top for those who are 55 and older on select sailings, and the senior rate applies even if the second person in the cabin is younger. Membership in groups such as AARP is not required, but such membership may bring additional savings. Discounts may also be available for active or retired military personnel, so let your travel agent know if you fit into this category.

Localized Specials

Sometimes, discounts are offered on select sailings and destinations depending solely on where you live. Residents living near Vancouver or Seattle, for example, may find special British Columbia or Washington State resident's rates for cruises to Alaska and the Pacific Coast. Likewise, offers targeting the same residents might be designed to encourage them to take a Mexican Riviera cruise, or a trip to the Caribbean. So make sure you ask your travel agent about any region-specific offers, and be sure you've added your State or Province of residence when searching for your next cruise vacation online.

Booking Your Next Cruise On Board

If you like your cruise so much that you decide to take a vacation with the cruise line again, consider booking your next cruise on the spot. Cruise lines cannily recognize the value in having a captive audience to whom to pitch future vacation plans—and no doubt at some point during your journey your Future Cruise Consultant will host a little sparkling wine-infused powwow. You don't have to choose a set itinerary or a set ship; by putting down a deposit (usually $200–$300 USD), you can book any itinerary aboard any cruise ship the line has, as long as you do it within a set amount of time—usually 3 years. Should you not book a cruise during that timeframe, your deposit is refundable.

So why should you consider doing this *during* the cruise that took you so long to plan? The answer is simple: Booking your next cruise on board usually opens up valuable onboard credit offers and other early-booking incentives. Not only do you get first dibs at the sailing and ship you want, but you can always transfer the booking to your existing travel agent—even if you haven't picked a ship or an itinerary yet. Frequent cruisers swear by booking on board, and we recommend it if you're enjoying the line you're sailing with. As always, though, never feel pressured to book on board: The choice remains yours.

AIRFARE & HOTELS

Depending on where you are sailing, the airfare and the pre- and post-cruise hotel stays can add a significant amount of money to the cost of your overall vacation. That doesn't mean, however, that you should tempt fate by flying into town the day of your cruise. It's *critically* important to arrive at your port of embarkation a day early, as storms can delay or even cancel flights throughout the year (statistically speaking, summertime storms cause even more delays than winter storms, but both can sock in airports). Or, like us, you could just have bad luck: Airplanes are complicated machines, and mechanical delays and cancellations aren't uncommon.

When booking flights to and from your cruise, look for either direct flights or flights with generous connection times. Just because an airline says a 45-minute connection at Chicago O'Hare is legal doesn't mean that you can actually *make* that connecting flight. Sure, airports aren't a lot of fun to hang around in, but trust us: Missing your connecting flight—and potentially your cruise—is a whole lot worse.

Air Add-Ons

Unless you live within driving distance of your port of embarkation, you'll probably be flying to join your ship. Most cruises won't include airfare in the purchase price, so you'll have to book your flights separately.

The cruise lines will offer to book your airfare for you, but in practice we've found this isn't a good option: By booking air directly with the cruise line, you're generally waiving your right to choose which airline you travel on, what cities you connect through, and even where you'll sit on the plane. Need to make changes? Expect a hefty fee (around $50 USD) every time you need to have the cruise line alter your air—and that goes for seat assignments, too.

It's not that the cruise line won't do a good job—they will—but why give up control over something most people feel very strongly about? Nearly all of us have a preferred airline we like to fly, an airport we want to connect through, or a route we want to fly because it offers us perks with our frequent flier status. And once the cruise line issues that air ticket, you're stuck with it: Changes are typically not allowed.

A better option is to book airfare yourself. Once upon a time, purchasing air was a complicated exercise but today, booking online—either through an online travel agency (like Expedia, Priceline, and the rest) or directly with the airline itself—is easy and advantageous. Booking your own airfare lets you determine what airline you fly, what cities (if any) you connect through, and even what aircraft you fly on. We highly recommend both **Kayak.com** and **Momondo.com,** sites that do not sell airfares, but simply aggregate that information, allowing you to see prices from a number of different sources quickly and easily.

If you're a **frequent-flier,** you *might* be able to cash in your frequent-flier points in order to fly to your cruise for (nearly) free. Keep in mind, however, that airlines are mindful of cruise schedules: Those prime flights that show up on reward bookings for other days of the week have a funny way of disappearing the day before a major cruise ship is set to depart the city in question. Likewise, you might find yourself routed through four cities you'd rather not pass through on small (often overworked and late) regional jets. We've personally had some great success with reward bookings—and we've also had some real stinkers that made us wish we'd just paid full-fare in the first place. And those were in the "good old days" when it didn't take a gazillion points to nab a ticket (and points could be earned with miles flown rather than by the cost of the ticket).

Pre- & Post-Cruise Hotel Deals

Consider spending a day or two in your port of embarkation or debarkation either before or after your cruise. An advantage to arriving a day or two early is that you don't have to worry if your flight is running late. Plus, many embarkation ports—the cities into which most passengers fly in order to board their cruise ship—happen to be great places to explore.

As with airfare, each cruise line always has a handful of partner hotels in each port of embarkation that they are willing to book on your behalf, should you choose to. Unless your cruise line is throwing it in *gratis,* as many luxury lines do, we'd recommend taking a pass on the cruise line's offer: The properties they sell are usually some of the best in the city, but they're also typically some of the priciest—and the cruise line will display *per person* rates instead of the normal *per room* rate that's typically offered by the hotel. Bottom line: You'll pay more than you need to if you book your hotel through the cruise line.

Instead, the best rates are likely to be through the hotels themselves, as all of the major chains are now undercutting the rates offered by both the cruise lines and the online travel agencies, with special deals given only to members of their loyalty programs. To suss out how much you should be paying, look at such sites as **HotelsCombined.com** or **Kayak.com** both of which search a number of sources. Then, if you find a hotel you like, contact it directly to see if it will undercut what can be found at the online travel agency sites. (*Tip:* These super-discounted rates will *only* be offered to loyalty program members, but that shouldn't be a big issue, as signing up for these programs is free.)

It's also worth checking out **Airbnb.com, Wimdu.com, HomeAway.com,** or **FlipKey.com** to book either a full apartment or a room within an apartment. Not only are there hundreds of options to choose from in most locations, these local residences usually provide more space, and a more authentic experience of these vibrant locales, often at a fraction of the cost of what a hotel might run you for the evening. Airbnb alone has over 1,500,000 listings in 34,000 cities in 190 countries around the world, so chances are good that your port of embarkation has a rental option or two.

CHOOSING YOUR CABIN

Modern cruise ship staterooms are nothing like the small, cramped staterooms found just a few years ago. While cabins typically vary in size according to price, most contemporary cruise ships have staterooms that hover around the 150- to 180-square-foot mark and increase in size from there. Suites, obviously, offer the most personal space, but also come with the highest cost. These can contain marbled bathrooms, private dining areas, and even your very own baby grand piano—not to mention butler service, private elevators, you name it. For most of us, though, a standard stateroom will be our likely home.

Most cabins on cruise ships today have queen-sized beds that can separate into two twins upon request. Some staterooms may have either a queen bed that won't be convertible into two twins, or—in rare instances—two twin beds that cannot convert into a queen bed. Either way, these restrictions will be listed on the deck plan for your cruise ship, as will staterooms that are suitable for third or fourth occupancy.

Although they're becoming increasingly rare, some staterooms—notably Carnival Cruise Line's Category 1A Interior staterooms—have bunk beds, which are typically referred to as "upper and lower berths." While it seems like a downside, these staterooms can be convenient for friends travelling together, or as an add-on stateroom for extended families travelling together.

Speaking of which, many cruise lines have special cabins designed for families, with "regular" twin beds that can be pushed together to create a double bed, plus fold-down bunks. Families may also be able to book connecting cabins (although they'll have to pay for two cabins to do so). Disney Cruise Line takes things one step further, creating segmented bathrooms that feature individual compartments for showering and washing up, allowing up to two guests to utilize bathroom spaces at once while still maintaining privacy. Norwegian Cruise Line also wins brownie points for the separated, family-friendly bathrooms found aboard their Jewel Class ships.

INSIDE & OUT

Larger megaships often have "hybrid" staterooms that can be a smart pick for those who want to stretch their cruising dollar further. For example, on Royal Caribbean's Voyager-class ships, like *Voyager of the Seas*, Promenade Staterooms have bay windows overlooking the ship's massive horizontal atrium. Priced between standard inside staterooms with no view and Oceanview Staterooms with windows looking out on the ocean, these offer a "happy-medium" for travelers who want the affordability of an inside staterooms but don't like the idea of not having a window.

Specially designated staterooms for travelers with disabilities are ideally located near elevators and other public areas, and feature accessible bathrooms and showers.

In the past, solo cruisers would have to contend with paying a massive Single Supplement fare but today, many modern cruise ships—including select Cunard, Holland America and Norwegian Cruise Line ships, to name a few—feature dedicated staterooms designed expressly for the solo cruiser (see p. 4).

The vast majority of cruise ship staterooms have TVs, and increasingly these units are interactive, to allow passengers to book meals and activities, as well as see daily schedules. Some cruise lines employ an on-demand service that allows you to watch movies like you would in a hotel. And just like in a hotel, these movies typically carry a hefty fee. A handful of complimentary broadcast-television channels are available (depending on satellite connectivity), along with channels that display a live view from a camera mounted on the ship's navigation bridge, and a voyage tracker that alternates between the current weather conditions, your ship's heading and speed, and any relevant voyage information, Some staterooms have amenities such as safes, mini-fridges, bathrobes, slippers, and hair dryers. A bathtub is considered a luxury on ships and is usually found only in more expensive suites, though Holland America is noted for having bathtubs in nearly all of its staterooms on most of the fleet.

Cabin Types

What kind of cabin is right for you? Price will likely be a big factor here, but so should the vacation style you prefer. (Please see p. 21 for our take on which cabins are best for those who suffer from seasickness.)

The typical ship has several types of cabins, each of which is listed on the deck plans for each cruise ship. The cabins are usually described by price (highest to lowest), category (suite, deluxe, superior, standard, economy, and other types), and furniture configuration ("sitting area with two lower beds"). The cabins will also be described as being inside or outside, balcony or suite. Simply put, inside cabins do not have windows (or even portholes), and

HOW TO CHOOSE A quiet CABIN

Cruise ships are like little cities and—as such—there are quiet parts of "town" and loud parts of town. When you're looking at the deck plan and trying to pick a quiet cabin, consider these spots you may want to avoid:

Near Elevators Just as this is a problem in hotels, it is also an issue on ships. Elevators may ping, or have a voice that tells you the deck level—something that can keep you from getting a good night's sleep. In addition, these tend to be areas that cruisers congregate in, so there may be conversational noise as well. Newer ships, though, have employed designs that separate out elevator lobbies which works to eliminate this excess noise.

Below the Pool Deck Ironically, the pool deck is at its most loud at times when passengers aren't using it. At the end of each day, the crew stacks up the deck chairs and hoses down the deck for the night. In the morning, they unstack everything and set up the chairs. Neither action is particularly quiet.

Above or Below a Dance Floor or Concert Space Do you see a space that may have speakers and a DJ above or below a cabin space? Then you really don't want that cabin unless you're likely to be the last one dancing on the ship every single night.

Near Service Areas The doors to crew quarters open and slam a hundred times a day, as people go on and off shift,

bring out room service deliveries, and roll out carts to refill mini bars and clean up staterooms. In addition to the sounds of doors slamming and carts rolling and attendants talking, you may also be near an entrance with an ice machine. Service areas are sometimes, but not always, shown on deck plans; a knowledgeable travel agent will be able to help you avoid them.

Above Any Machinery A good rule of thumb is to assume that staterooms that are near the water line at the extreme forward and aft ends of the ship will be within range of the anchors, bow thrusters, stern thrusters, or tender shell doors (mechanical platforms that can open to facilitate tendering operations). The sounds made by these pieces of equipment don't last long, but they can be very loud. We once never set an alarm on a cruise aboard *Grandeur of the Seas* because our extreme-forward stateroom rattled with the sound of the anchor chain each time we docked, waking us up. And if your stateroom is positioned near the ship's lifeboats drills and tendering operations might mean being awoken by the sound of the hydraulics firing up, though this is only likely to happen sporadically throughout the voyage.

Please note that noise issues, in general, are more of a problem on older cruise vessels, thanks to poor insulation and public venues clustered uncomfortably close to the ships' accommodations.

outside cabins do. However, views from some outside cabins may be obstructed—usually by a lifeboat—or look out onto a public area; an experienced travel agent should be able to advise you on which cabin to choose, and most cruise lines will list major obstructions on their deck plans and categorize these staterooms as such.

On the big ships, deluxe outside cabins may also come with verandas (also known as balconies), giving you a private outdoor space to enjoy the sea breezes. But remember that the verandas vary in size, so if you're looking to do more than stand on your balcony, make sure the space is big enough to accommodate deck chairs, a table, or whatever else you require. Also keep in mind that these verandas are not completely isolated—your neighbors may be able to see you and vice versa. With few exceptions, veranda cabins will not have obstructed views. It's also worth reiterating that most cruise lines have completely banned smoking on stateroom balconies, so if you're thinking of booking one with the intention of lighting up, you might end up disappointed—and penalties for doing so against the rules are stiff.

These basic categories—inside, outside, balcony and suite—are then divided even further into sub-categories that each carry a different price. Let's look at the *Carnival Breeze* to get some idea of the many categories of cabins one ship can hold. It has seven different sub-categories of just the basic balcony stateroom: categories 8A, 8B, 8C, 8D, 8E, 8F, and 8G. What differentiates these seven categories is their physical location on the ship. The lower the letter, the less the price—but the location may not be as "desirable"; higher categories are typically placed near the center of the ship, while lower categories like 8G might be positioned at the extreme front or back of a deck (not ideal; see box above). When prices are listed on the cruise line's website or in print advertisements, these are almost always "lead-in" prices for lower-category staterooms. Expect the price to rise, sometimes significantly, if you absolutely have to have that midships, Category 8A balcony stateroom. It's also good to be flexible: That Category 8G stateroom might be near the front of the ship, but it could also save you hundreds of dollars.

Carnival Breeze also has "cove," or sheltered balconies, on her lower deck below the lifeboats. Known as Category 7C, these staterooms are desirable for their location closer to the water, but they tend to be sheltered by the lifeboats above them and feature steel, rather than clear Plexiglas, balcony railings.

To complicate things further, *Carnival Breeze* also offers two categories of Aft Extended Balconies (8M and 8N) that feature abnormally large balconies and are situated overlooking the ship's wake, and a Premium Vista Balcony known as Category 9C. And that's all without even looking at the 10 categories of interior staterooms, five categories of oceanview staterooms, and three

Cabin Size by Square Foot

The size of a cabin is described in terms of square feet. This number may not mean a lot unless you want to mark it out on your floor at home. But to give you an idea: 120-square-feet and under is low end and cramped, 180-square-feet is the typical size of your average big ship stateroom, and suites on luxury ships start around 250-square-feet and go up from there. The current reigning king of the suite is Regent Seven Seas: Their new *Seven Seas Explorer* has the largest seagoing suite in the world, measuring an astonishing 3,875 square feet, the equivalent of 21.5 standard 180-square-foot "big ship" staterooms put together.

different suite categories. Determining what kind of stateroom you want—then consulting a deck plan—is a very important step in choosing your cruise vacation. We've highlighted the *Carnival Breeze* deck plans as an example, but every single cruise line uses this same methodology.

There's no rule of thumb for which stateroom to book: Generally speaking, the one that offers the best mix of price and features is the right way to go. You'll also find you will tend to adjust your style of cruising based on the type of stateroom you've chosen. If, for example, you pick a more economical inside stateroom that lacks a window, you might find you're only in your cabin to change and sleep. Book a more expensive (and spacious) stateroom or suite and you'll want to adjust your cruising style to linger in your own private oasis.

Luxury suites are usually located on the ship's uppermost decks and the swankiest ones can be apartment-sized. They afford some of the best views (and largest balconies) on the entire vessel, along with some of the best amenities. On the downside, the most stable cabins during rough seas are those in the middle and lower parts of the ship. And, not surprisingly, these lavish accommodations come with the highest price tag—and tend to sell out first.

On small ships carrying fewer than 100 guests, cabins range from spartan to lavish; size alone isn't a good predictor of amenities. Generally, the difference lies in the orientation of the cruise line: Those promising a real adventure experience tend to feature somewhat utilitarian cabins, while lines that focus on the private yacht experience will pull out all the stops in terms of luxury. Some cruise lines, like Un-Cruise Adventures, make up for their more basic accommodations by offering complimentary beverages (both alcoholic and nonalcoholic) and other luxury-style amenities on certain vessels.

Aboard both large and small ships, keep in mind that the most expensive and least expensive cabins tend to sell out fast. Also, just as with real estate, it's sometimes better to take a smaller cabin on a nicer ship than a bigger cabin on a less pleasant ship.

DINING OPTIONS

It probably doesn't come as a surprise that small ships offer fewer dining options, while big ships offer a plethora of culinary delights that can range from basic room service to multi-course meals prepared under the direction of Michelin-starred chefs.

What you might not know is that there is also a world of choice when it comes to simply choosing *when* and *how* you'd like to dine. Gone are the inflexible dining times and rigid dress codes of old…unless you prefer a fixed early or late dinner seating for dinner. Most big ships still offer that as a time-tested option. If you like more flexibility, many cruise lines have adopted open-seating options that invite you to dine when you'd like, with whomever you'd like to, during the restaurant's opening hours.

Small ships are the exception here, but even they offer open seating that lets you sit where you want and with whomever you want, though generally at a set time. Which brings us to...

Mealtimes

Traditional dining on most big ships means choosing between one of two predetermined dinner times: early (typically 6pm) and late (usually 8:30pm). There are advantages and disadvantages to both times. Early seating is usually far more crowded and is the preferred time for families with small children and seniors. The dining experience can be a bit more rushed (the staff needs to make way for the next wave of guests coming for the second seating), but you'll still have the rest of your evening to enjoy the ship: You can see a show right after dinner and have first dibs on other nighttime venues as well.

Late seating, on the other hand, allows you time for a good long nap or late spa appointment before dining. Dinner is not rushed at all, and guests tend to linger at the table until well after 10:00 p.m. Folks who like to watch sailaway may find this dining time to be more advantageous, as 5:30 p.m. or 6:00 p.m. departure times from many ports are fairly common. Don't worry about missing your favorite shows: Main production shows are often run twice in an evening, and scheduled entertainment options usually run until midnight.

Most big ships will offer some form of **flexible dining,** though each cruise line gives this a different name. Holland America Line calls it "As You Wish" dining. Princess Cruises dubs it, "Anytime Dining." But whatever you call it, the basic system remains the same: Guests are invited to dine in one of the ship's main dining rooms in an open-seating environment. You can choose who (if anyone) you would like to sit with, and simply waltz in at any time during the room's published opening hours. Like a land-based restaurant, though, you might find yourself in for a wait during peak times; typically, you'll be given an electronic buzzer that will light up when your table is ready.

The vast majority of large ships today also have alternative dining options. Most have a buffet-style restaurant offering an extensive spread of both hot and cold food items at breakfast, lunch, and dinner (as an alternative to the dining room). Some ships also have reservations-only restaurants, seating fewer than 100, where—except on some luxury ships—a fee is charged.

Table Size

Do you mind sitting with strangers? Are you looking to make new friends? Your dinner companions can sometimes make or break your cruise experience. Most ships have tables configured for two to eight people. For singles or couples who want to socialize, a table of eight seats generally provides enough variety that you don't get bored and also allows you to steer clear of any individual you don't particularly care for. Tables are assigned, but seats aren't. Couples may choose to sit on their own, but singles may find it hard to secure a table for one. A family of four may want a table for four, or request to sit with another family at a table for eight.

You need to state your table-size preference in advance, unless you're on a ship with an open-seating policy. If you change your mind once you're on board, don't worry; you'll probably have no trouble moving around. Just inform the dining-room maître d' on the afternoon of embarkation, and he or she will review the seating charts for an opening. Check your onboard Daily Program for times; the maître d' generally holds court for an hour or two on embarkation day for guests with dining queries or special dietary needs.

Open Seating

Put off by all this formality? Want guaranteed casual all the way? Back in 2001, Norwegian Cruise Line started serving all meals with open seating—dine when you want (within the restaurants' open hours, of course) and with whom you want—and now other lines are doing this, as well. The catch, particularly with Norwegian, is that you have to be on-top of your "dining game," choosing and reserving a table at the restaurant of your choice early on in the cruise; simply walking up without a reservation when you decide to eat usually doesn't get you a table. Carnival, Celebrity, Holland America Line, Princess, and Royal Caribbean all have a version of this system, allowing guests to choose traditional early or late seating or open restaurant-style seating, typically selecting one or the other during the booking process. Sailing on a luxury line like Regent, Seabourn or Silversea? Your dining is already Open Seating.

Special Requests

The cruise line should be informed at the time you make reservations about any special dietary requirements you have. Some lines provide kosher menus, and all have vegetarian, vegan, low-fat, low-salt, gluten-free, and sugar-free options. Allergies can usually be catered to if the cruise line is notified in advance. Reconfirm your requests with the maître d' on the afternoon of embarkation so they can ensure their dining staff are all on the same page; mistakes do happen and sometimes your request can get lost in the shuffle (though this is very rare).

DEPOSITS & CANCELLATION POLICIES

You'll be asked by your travel agent to make a deposit, either a fixed amount or some percentage of the total cost of your cruise. You'll then receive a receipt and booking confirmation, either electronically as a PDF file or by snail-mail. You'll typically be asked to pay the remaining fare usually no later than 60 to 90 days before your departure date.

Cruise lines have varying policies regarding cancellations, and it's important to look at the fine print in the line's brochure to make sure you understand the policy. Most lines allow you to cancel for a full refund on your deposit and payment any time up to 75 days before the sailing, after which you have to pay a penalty. When in doubt, always ask your travel agent or do a little independent research online.

Large ships usually have a fully equipped medical facility and staff (a doctor and a nurse or two) on board to handle any emergency. They work in a medical center that typically offers set office hours but is also open on an emergency basis 24 hours a day. A fee (sometimes a steep one) is charged to your onboard account. The staff is equipped to do some surgery, but in cases of major medical emergencies, passengers may be airlifted off the ship by helicopter to the nearest hospital—and that can cost a bundle if you're uninsured.

TRAVEL INSURANCE

Given today's unpredictable geopolitical situation, economic woes, and extreme weather conditions, you just never know what might occur. A cruise could be canceled, for example, because of mechanical breakdowns (such as nonfunctioning air-conditioning or propeller issues), or—more rarely—the cruise line going out of business or an act of war. For all these reasons—worries about travel, worries about cruise lines canceling, sudden illness or other emergencies, missed flights that cause you to miss the ship, or even if you just change your mind—you may want to think about purchasing travel insurance.

If you're worried about medical problems occurring during your trip, travel insurance is vital. Except for small coastal cruisers that lack any sort of facilities or onboard medical physician, most cruise ships have an infirmary staffed by a doctor and a nurse or two, but in the event of a dire illness the ship's medical staff can only do so much. Therefore, you may want a policy that covers emergency medical evacuation and for some remote itineraries, like Antarctica and the Arctic, this is required; having a helicopter pick up a sick person on board a ship can cost tens of thousands of dollars. But even for destinations closer to home, medical and medical evacuation insurance are a good idea; the potential cost of major medical treatment while away from home can be prohibitive (especially vital if you're covered primarily by Medicare, which won't cover you in international destinations—and since most ships are flagged internationally, they don't qualify for coverage).

Canadians will want to supplement their medical insurance with third-party insurance, unless your employer already offers supplemental medical insurance. Check to see what your coverage is, and what regions of the world it applies in.

In addition to medical insurance, you might want to invest in something called "Trip Cancellation and Interruption Insurance." This type of insurance, often separate from medical insurance, typically reimburse you in some way when your trip is affected by unexpected events (such as flight cancellations, dockworkers' strikes, or the illness or death of a loved one, as late as the day before or day of departure) but not by "acts of God," such as hurricanes and earthquakes, the exception being if your home is made uninhabitable, putting you in no mood to continue with your cruise plans. Both also typically (but not always—check!) cover cancellation of the cruise for medical reasons (yours or a family member's, whether he or she was a part of your traveling party or not); medical emergencies during the cruise, including evacuation from the ship; lost or damaged luggage; and a cruise missed due to weather-related airline delays (though some only cover if the delay is greater than 3 hr.).

We recommend that you book insurance directly through an insurance company, rather than through the cruise line or through a travel agency. We make this recommendation because you usually can get more coverage for less money if you buy directly. As importantly, if your travel agency goes belly up, you've not only lost the cost of the cruise, but possibly the insurance, too, if they didn't make the payments in time. Reputable insurers include **Allianz** (www.accessamerica.com; ℂ **800/284-8300**), **Travel Guard International** (www.travelgaurd.com; ℂ **800/826-4919**), **Travel Insured International** (www.travelinsured.com; ℂ **800/243-3174**), and **Blue Cross** for Canadian citizens (www.bluecross.ca; phone number varies between provinces). Two useful websites, **Squaremouth** (www.squaremouth.com; ℂ **800/240-0369**) and **InsureMyTrip.com,** let you easily compare various third-party insurance options. For evacuation coverage in the event of a major medical emergency, **MedJet Assist** (www.medjetassist.com; ℂ **800/527-7478**) has both short-term and annual policies. Be aware that travel insurance does not cover changes in your itinerary, which are at the discretion of the cruise line.

CRUISE DESTINATIONS

I n previous chapters, we've taken a look at the "who" and "what" of your cruise choices. Now it's time to focus on the "when" and "where." The next step in ensuring you'll have a successful cruise vacation is to match your expectations to the right itinerary for you and your own personal travel preferences.

While some regions of the world—for example, equatorial regions where there's less seasonal difference in the weather—offer cruises year-round, many others are traditionally limited to certain months of the year. If that's where you know you want to go, you'll have to plan in advance to clear time in that season. Conversely, if you only have certain time windows free, then we'll help you identify the regions that are active in those time periods.

Once you've decided on the season and the region, we'll clue you into the different travel experiences of various routes in that region. And finally, we'll profile a number of major ports of call, and ports of embarkation, so that you can be sure that the itinerary you choose includes experiences you'll enjoy.

WHAT'S IN SEASON?

You can take a cruise any time of the year but, depending on where you want to go, some times are better than others for a visit.

Caribbean cruises are available year-round but are most crowded when children have off from school. This means that spring break, July, August, and December can see prices hit premium levels, whereas the "shoulder season" months of January, September and October are likely to be more cost-effective. There's another reason fall is slow in this region: hurricane season. Officially that lasts from June through November, but historically most storms have hit in September and October. Usually, if a hurricane is predicted the cruise is re-routed, not cancelled, but it's helpful to know that cruises planned during this time frame might be more prone to last-minute itinerary changes. And while its safe to cruise at this time (the ships are faster than the storms), sometimes the result is passengers having to endure rough seas. Cruises to the west coast of **Mexico** run year-round with much less seasonal fluctuation.

shore excursions: THE WHAT, WHEN & WHY

Shore excursions, or tours offered by the cruise lines, can end up being the largest vacation expense after the cost of the cruise itself. It's no secret that the cruise lines mark up these excursions drastically and sell them relentlessly, both before the cruise and during it. That being said sometimes they provide a way for passengers to efficiently see the sites, without having to worry about transportation or being back at the ship on time. The latter is important: The cruise line always waits if its own excursions are late getting back, but will not wait if individual passengers aren't at the dock on time.

A wide variety of shore excursions are available. Some are of the walking-tour or bus-tour variety, allowing you to see the highlights of a port quickly with a tour guide there to provide context; others are just transfers to popular sites, such as beaches or water parks, or reefs for snorkeling. Still others are activity-oriented: Cruise passengers have the opportunity to go sea kayaking, mountain biking, horseback riding, on ATV tours, and even rock climbing. You can see the sights by seaplane or helicopter. You'll find quirky excursions, especially on the luxury lines, such as visits with local artists in their studios or with vintners at wineries.

But, as we said at the start, these experiences usually don't come cheaply and as we didn't say, they're often crowded. In many ports it's possible to simply walk off the ship and see the sights. In others, there are outside companies that have less-expensive, smaller group tours that are the equal, or better, than what the cruiseline is offering. You can find those outside companies through such sites as CruisingExcursions.com, ShoreTrips.com and Viator.com The key is to make some plan before the boat docks. We hope that the rest of the chapter will help with that a bit. As a rule of thumb, if the ship is docking in the middle of the action, you can likely see the sights on your own. However, if you're going to a port where you'll have to travel over 45-minutes to see the sights, or hang at a beach, it's a better idea to take a tour (either with the cruise line or with an outside company) than trying to rent a car while in port. The only exception are those destinations where you'll stay overnight; and the Hawaiian Islands (since car-rental companies are right at the terminal and are expert at dealing with cruise passengers).

Alaska's cruise season is a short one, from May through September, although a few ships get an early jump, starting up in late April. May and September are considered the shoulder seasons, with lower brochure rates and more aggressive discounts offered during these months. *Tip:* We particularly like cruising to Alaska in May, before the crowds arrive; we've generally found locals to be friendlier than they are later in the season, when they're pretty much ready to see the tourists go home for the winter.

The season for cruises to **New England and Eastern Canada** is similarly geared to warmer weather, beginning in May, with the slight difference than it extends deeper into the autumn, well into October, to take advantage of the region's brilliant fall colors.

Ships based in **Hawaii** cruise the islands year-round, but itineraries that link the Hawaiian isles to North American ports are more likely to be in April,

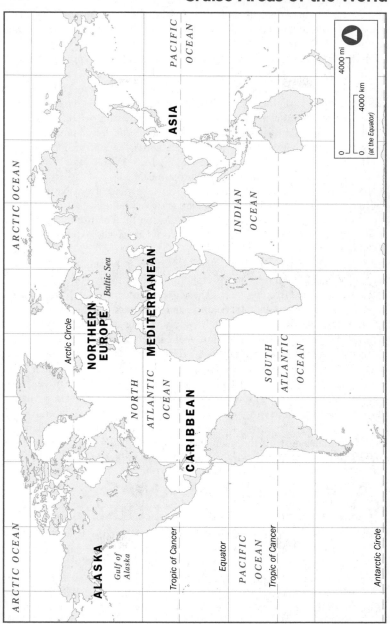

May, September, and October, often as part of a repositioning cruise between Alaska and the Caribbean. There's also cruising year-round in **French Polynesia**—the Pacific Islands that include Tahiti, Bora Bora, Moorea, and many others—with some occasional long cruises that combine the two island chains.

Mediterranean cruises are offered year-round, but the prime season is summertime, when the sea is warm enough to swim in and the beaches fill up with sunbathers from the north. (*Note:* In recent seasons, many cruise companies have been curtailing their Mediterranean operations—see the box on p. 90). As for **Northern Europe** and **The Baltics,** summer offers the best weather and the significant bonus of midnight sun; you'll find the vast majority of departures between May and September. A few cruise lines do offer winter itineraries through Norway, however, which reveal a land blanketed in snow—and possible sightings of the Northern Lights.

Expedition cruises to **Antarctica** tend to take place from November to February, when the Southern Hemisphere is experiencing its summer. At that time of year, days are long, and temperatures on the Peninsula, where most cruises venture, are well above what New York City would experience during the middle of January.

Antarctica's polar counterpart, the **Far Arctic,** is typically visited during July and August. Even then, however, temperatures in much of the High Arctic barely break the freezing mark. These expedition cruises, which generally head for Arctic **Canada, Greenland,** and **Svalbard** (formerly known as **Spitsbergen**), send guests in search (safely) of ice and polar bears, not to mention the stunning array of wildlife that calls these chilly waters home.

Historically, more exotic itineraries—including **Asia, South America,** and **Africa**—tended to be part of longer, around-the-world sailings, which traditionally set sail in January. That's no longer the case: At any time of year now, you can book a weeklong cruise on a mainstream line departing from **Australia,** and 10- and 12-day voyages now visit many parts of Asia and South Africa. Weeklong voyages are common all year around the **Galapagos Islands,** situated just off the mainland coast of Ecuador, and you can even circle **Tahiti** and other parts of the **South Pacific** in just under 2 weeks.

CARIBBEAN, BAHAMAS & PANAMA CANAL CRUISES

The Caribbean is a classic cruise destination, tailored to people who want nice white-sand beaches, tiki bars serving tropical drinks, hot island music, and the chance to perfect their tans. Yet beyond those generalities, the Caribbean islands each provide slightly different versions of fun in the sun. Some—especially St. Thomas and Nassau—are much more touristy and commercial than others, but they'll appeal to shoppers with their large variety of bustling stores. Others—Virgin Gorda, St. John, and Jost Van Dyke, for instance—have more of an eco-tourism appeal. Ports such as St. Barts and Virgin Gorda have a

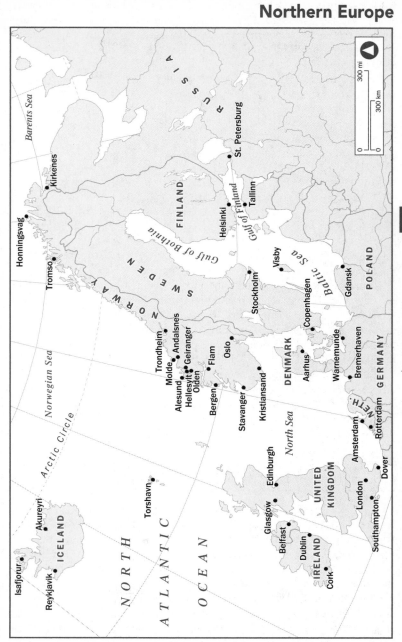

The Caribbean

low-key yachting-port atmosphere, while Key West and Cozumel are all about whooping it up. And if your passion is for coral-reef snorkeling, deep-sea diving, or golf, only certain islands will really fit the bill.

In general, all the Caribbean islands are getting more business by increasingly bigger ships. The more famous and larger the port, the more likely there will be a flotilla of cruise ships lined up in a row and passengers clogging the streets. This is especially true in the busy winter season, before some of the ships that serve Alaska and Europe in the summertime move on to those routes. The crowding may not seem like that big a deal before you arrive; after

all, you're probably going on organized excursions and are only in town for a few hours. But the reality is that these ports can't always handle the masses with elegance: Important attractions might be thronged, and competition for space on popular beaches can be fierce. Also, since many cruise lines use the same shore excursion providers, your excursion could be packed with guests from other ships and lines.

It's harder than ever to find the unspoiled, uncrowded corners of the Caribbean, though they still exist if you have the dough to book a luxury small cruise, one that skips the more mainstream ports of call.

BERMUDA shorts

Cruises to the Atlantic island of Bermuda are distinctly different from Caribbean cruises. Roughly parallel to South Carolina (or Casablanca, if you're measuring from the east), this 21-square-mile oasis is an orderly, beautiful, easy place to visit. A British crown colony since 1620, it's a beguiling mix of British properness and island sun-and-fun. And you'll have a chance to get to know it well, because Bermuda-bound cruises tend to spend several whole days at the island, rather than port-hopping as so many Caribbean cruises do.

The Bermuda cruising season runs from late April through October. Most ships dock at **King's Wharf,** in the West End, although some smaller vessels still visit the piers in **Hamilton,** Bermuda's sophisticated capital, and the charming historic town of **St. George's.** Wherever they dock, visitors tend to fan out across the island, via taxi, motor scooter, or the ferry that runs between King's Wharf and Hamilton; it only takes about an hour to drive from one end of Bermuda to the other.

Whereas Caribbean cruises keep moving from island to island, Bermuda cruises allow passengers plenty of time to enjoy various aspects of the island's considerable charm. Major draws include powdery-soft beaches, with distinctive coral-tinted pink sand. Our favorite beach is **Horseshoe Bay,** in Southampton Parish, with its scenic rocky cliffs at the edges and a vast soft plane of sand in the middle. Other options include **Warwick Long Bay** (Warwick Parish); **Tobacco Bay Beach** (St. George's Parish), where the water is very calm and the beach is tiny; and **Elbow Beach** (in Paget Parish). The more adventurous can rent a scooter and beach-hop among the many unnamed slivers of silky sand tucked into the jagged coastline. Bermuda also has excellent golf courses—in fact, it has more golf courses per square mile than any other place in the world, and the extended stay may allow you to try more than one.

Hamilton's tony shopping district specializes in luxury goods, mostly English (or Irish) in provenance. Meanwhile, history buffs have several old forts and lighthouses to explore, including the excellent **Bermuda Maritime Museum** right by the cruise docks in King's Wharf. The 29km/18-mile **Bermuda Railway Trail** gives joggers and cyclists unique views of the ocean and the island's lush gardens and bird life.

Shore excursions may also include snorkeling and glass-bottom boat tours, which let you peer down at the coral reefs and many shipwrecks (remember the Bermuda Triangle?) in the turquoise waters around Bermuda.

Eastern vs. Western vs. Southern Itineraries

For the purposes of cruising, the Caribbean can be divided into three separate areas, known generically in the industry as the **southern, eastern,** and **western** routes. That said, these delineations really only exist in the cruise world. In addition, there is a lot of overlap on these itineraries.

Most weeklong itineraries will go to the "big three" eastern Caribbean ports of call: St. Thomas, in the U.S. Virgin Islands; Philipsburg, St. Maarten; and Nassau, in the Bahamas. It's worth noting, however, that there's an enormous range of potential ports of call within this one region. And here's a tip: You can add even more time in the Caribbean sun by flying to San Juan, Puerto

Rico, or St. Thomas in the U.S. Virgin Islands, to pick up an Eastern Caribbean sailing that departs directly from there.

Western Caribbean itineraries tend to include visits to some of the more heavily crowded ports: Belize, the Cayman Islands, Jamaica, and Cozumel. Just how busy can they get? Well, multiple ships can visit Grand Cayman in a single day, and Cozumel boasts three separate docking locations for cruise ships. Still, many of these islands offer strong cultural attractions, such as excursions to Mayan ruins.

In fact, if you're wavering between the two, you may be able to have your cake and eat it, too: Many ships operating Western Caribbean cruises alternate their itineraries with Eastern Caribbean sailings, which means you may be able to book two back-to-back voyages without ever repeating ports of call.

Of all the Caribbean itineraries, Southern Caribbean voyages are often the best. Generally lasting from 7 to 15 days, they often depart right from the Caribbean, out of Barbados; Martinique; San Juan, Puerto Rico; or St. Lucia. Since they don't have to traverse long stretches of ocean, they spend fewer days at sea, and frequently call on a mix of the following ports: Aruba, Bonaire, Curacao, St. Lucia, Barbados, Grenada, and the little isles of the Grenadines, a real treat for sun worshippers. Some of these itineraries are so long they also include transit through the Panama Canal—a boon for history buffs, if perhaps a bust for those who are more in search of sand and surf.

Ports of Call in the Bahamas

Although they are often included in Caribbean cruise itineraries, the Bahamas aren't in the Caribbean at all—they're in the Atlantic, north of the Caribbean and less than 161km (100 miles) from Miami. Holdovers from Great Britain's long colonial occupation linger in some architecture and culture here, but the general vibe isn't all that much different from parts of Florida. The temperature is similar, too, meaning you aren't guaranteed beach weather in winter.

FREEPORT/LUCAYA

Freeport, on Grand Bahama Island, is the second-most-popular destination in the Bahamas (after Nassau—see p. 52). Technically, Freeport is the land-locked section of town, while adjacent Lucaya, where cruise ships dock, hugs the waterfront. Though they have none of Nassau's colonial charm, they do have plenty of white-sand beaches, golf, tennis, and watersports.

TOP BEACHES A 20-minute ride east of Lucaya, unspoiled Gold Rock Beach in Lucayan National Park may be the island's best for getting away from it all. Barbary Beach, slightly closer to Lucaya, is great for seashell hunters.

FOR NATURE LOVERS Based at the Lucaya marina, **UNEXSO** (https://unexso.com) organizes dolphin swims in a protected lagoon or diving experiences with dolphins and other marine creatures.

SMELL THE ROSES The well-shaded **Garden of the Groves** (www.thegardenofthegroves.com), once the private meditation garden of Freeport's founder, Wallace Groves, is a peaceful retreat with waterfalls, flowering shrubs, tropical birds, and other wildlife.

SHOPAHOLICS ALERT The village-style mall **Port Lucaya Marketplace,** across the street from Lucaya Beach, offers one-stop shopping and dining right by the cruise ship docks.

NASSAU, THE BAHAMAS

With its beaches, shopping, resorts, casinos, historic landmarks, and active activities (land and water), Nassau is the Bahamas' most visited destination, and one of the world's busiest cruise ship ports. The Nassau/Paradise Island area comprises two separate islands: Nassau is on the northeastern shore of 34km (21-mile) New Providence Island, with tiny Paradise Island linked to New Providence by bridges, protecting the Nassau harbor. Cruise ships dock at Prince George Wharf, in the center of Nassau town at Rawson Square. Downtown Nassau still preserves some vestiges of the Bahamas' British colonial past, including the flamingo-pink government buildings of Parliament Square, surrounding a statue of Queen Victoria.

Shore excursions here tend to center around snorkeling, diving, and boat-tour options. For many visitors, however, duty-free luxury-goods shopping is the town's biggest attraction, with a profusion of shops on and around Bay Street—practically the first thing you see when you step off the ship.

TOP DRAW The fancifully designed **Atlantis Paradise Island** megaresort (www.atlantis.com) keeps its beach and pool off limits to non-guests, but cruise passengers are invited to spend money at its casino and restaurants, and to take a guided tour of the resort's sprawling system of man-made lagoons.

CHEESY BUT FUN Nassau's 18th-century pirate past is mined for yar-har-hars downtown at the interactive **Pirates of Nassau Museum** (www.piratesofnassau.com).

FOR NATURE LOVERS Performing pink flamingos are the star attraction at **Ardastra Gardens** (www.ardastra.com), where you can also see parrots, boa constrictors, honey bears, macaws, and capuchin monkeys in a lush tropical landscape.

TOP BEACH On New Providence Island, sun worshipers flock to beautiful 6.5km (4-mile) **Cable Beach,** which has various watersports and easy access to shops, a casino, bars, and restaurants.

Caribbean Ports of Call
ANTIGUA

Popular with the sailing and yachting crowd, Antigua is the largest of the British Leeward Islands (though it's still only 23km/14 miles long and 18km/11 miles wide), and is much more laid back than some of the glitzier Southern Caribbean islands. Most cruise ships dock at Heritage Quay, Nevis Pier, or the more commercial Deepwater Harbour in **St. John's,** the island's easygoing capital and main town, full of cobblestone sidewalks and weather-beaten

As ships get bigger and cruise line fleets grow, some Caribbean ports are more about traffic jams and crowded shopping malls than frosty margaritas on wind-swept beaches. The antithesis to all of this Caribbean madness, of course, is the cruise line private island, where only one ship or two ships at a time stop for the day. Yes, they still can get crowded but because there's no travel involved to the beach, there's less overall hassle. And, let's be real: These ports are a way for the cruise lines to control more of your travel dollar (*ka-ching, ka-ching*) and you won't be treated to any historic sights. Still, if there's a private island stop on an itinerary you choose, it shouldn't be a deal-breaker: A pure beach day is not such a bad thing.

Norwegian Cruise Line pioneered this concept developing Great Stirrup Cay, a stretch of palm-studded beach-front in the Berry Island chain of The Bahamas. As other cruise lines jumped on the bandwagon, most grabbed islets in the Bahamas—**Holland America**'s Half Moon Cay, known for its ultrasoft sand; **Princess Cruise**'s Princess Cay, which offers tons of water sports; **Royal Caribbean/Celebrity**'s family-oriented CoCo Cay; and **Disney Cruise Line**'s Castaway Cay, which in true Disney style features a barnacle-encrusted ghost ship anchored offshore (a prop from one of the *Pirates of the Caribbean* movies). **MSC Cruises** even went so far as to *make* its own cay in the Bahamas, **Ocean Cay Marine Reserve.**

More off the beaten track are **Costa Cruise**'s palm-fringed Catalina Island, in the eastern Caribbean off the coast of the Dominican Republic, and **Royal Caribbean/Celebrity**'s Labadee, an isolated, sun-flooded peninsula along Haiti's north coast. A completely tourist-oriented and sequestered area, it was untouched by the 2010 Haiti earthquake, and in fact provided locals with some much-needed jobs following that tragedy.

wooden houses. A handful of smaller vessels drop anchor at Falmouth Harbour, on the south side of the island, or the even smaller English Harbour next to it. Shore excursions naturally include diving and sailing, both popular here; there's also decent shopping at restored warehouses near the docks.

TOP DRAW   The restored 18th-century naval base at **Nelson's Dockyard National Park** (www.paradise-islands.org) was once home base for British national hero Admiral Horatio Nelson; it's surrounded by a lovely national park with lots of nature trails and scenic lookouts. It's 18km (11 miles) southeast of St. John's, or within walking distance of English Harbour.

SLICE OF HISTORY   Billed as the only still-working 18th-century sugar mill in the Caribbean, **Betty's Hope** (www.visitantiguabarbuda.com) is near Pares village on the island's east side.

ICONIC SIGHT   On the extreme eastern tip of the island, **Devil's Bridge** is a natural limestone arch carved out over the centuries by powerful Atlantic breakers. Come here at high tide to watch the surf spurt skyward through its blowholes.

4

CRUISE DESTINATIONS

Caribbean, Bahamas & Panama Canal Cruises

TOP BEACH   Antiguans claim that the island has 365 beaches, one for each day of the year. Our top pick is secluded **Half Moon Bay,** at the island's southeast extreme, which has good waves for bodysurfing and a quieter side for snorkeling.

ARUBA

Situated only 32km (20 miles) north of Venezuela, the sunny Dutch island of Aruba has some of the finest beaches in the southern Caribbean, along with scuba diving, snorkeling, windsurfing, and all the other watersports you'd expect. The concentration of stores and malls in Oranjestad, the island's capital, is as impressive as any in the Caribbean, and there are a dozen casinos, two of them just steps from the cruise ship terminals in the Port of Oranjestad.

TOP BEACHES   Just north of crowded Palm Beach, with its high-rise hotels, the sugar-white sands of **Eagle Beach** offer a more relaxed scene. The top beach for families is **Baby Beach,** at the island's easternmost point, a shallow bowl of warm turquoise water protected by an almost complete circle of rock.

UNDER THE SEA   The best snorkeling sites are around **Malmok Beach** (also a great windsurfing spot) and Boca Catalina, where the water is calm and shallow and marine life is plentiful.

OUT AND ABOUT   Aruba's desertlike interior, full of cacti, divi-divi trees, iguanas, and bizarre rock formations, is fun to explore by jeep or ATV. Head for **Arikok National Park** on the northern coast, with its distinctive cave-pocked mesas full of bats and petroglyphs.

SHOPAHOLICS ALERT   Downtown's **Renaissance Mall** and **Renaissance Marketplace** are magnets for high-end shopping. Across from the high-rise hotel area there's fun boutique shopping at Paseo Herencia and the Village.

BARBADOS

No port of call in the southern Caribbean can compete with Barbados when it comes to natural beauty, attractions, and endless stretches of pink and white sandy beaches. Its fertile land once made British colonial plantation owners rich; now it's tourists who pay to see the tropical rainforests and gardens of the island. Cruise ships dock at a modern terminal about 1 mile from the capital, Bridgetown; taxis, tour buses, and shuttles meet the boats to help passengers sample the island's natural beauties.

TOP DRAW   In the island's center, **Harrison's Cave** (www.harrisonscave. com) takes visitors through a massive crystallized limestone cavern aboard an electric tram.

SMELL THE ROSES   Barbados' green center has a wealth of topnotch gardens. Two of our favorites: the preserved rainforest of **Welchman Hall Gully** (www.welchmanhallgullybarbados.com) and the **Flower Forest** (www. barbados.org/flowfrst.htm), a former sugar plantation now overrun with tropical flowers and trees.

SLICE OF HISTORY   Get a sense of Barbados' plantation past at the 300-year-old **Sunbury Plantation House** (www.barbadosgreathouse.com), the only plantation great house on Barbados whose rooms are all open for viewing.

BOTTOMS UP   A variety of tours are offered at Bridgetown's **Mount Gay Rum Distillery** (www.mountgayrum.com), a Barbados institution which claims to be the world's oldest rum.

TOP BEACHES   On Barbados' western coast—a.k.a. the Gold Coast— baby-powder sand and calm waters are ideal conditions for sunning. Bridgetown's Fresh Water Bay has a trio of fine beaches: Brighton Beach, Brandon's Beach, and Paradise Beach.

BELIZE

Situated on the northeastern tip of Central America, the tiny country of Belize combines Central American and Caribbean cultures. It's home to ancient Mayan ruins and a 298km (185-mile) coral reef that runs the entire length of the country—the largest in the Western Hemisphere and the second largest in the world. Belize is serious in its dedication to conservation: One-fifth of its total landmass is dedicated as nature reserves, and 7,770 sq. km (2,973 sq. miles) of its waters are protected as well.

While some cruise ships anchor offshore from the capital, Belize City, smaller boats may moor directly off some of its 1,000-some tiny islands, or cayes, such as Ambergris Caye and Caye Caulker, both of which are also popular short-hop flights from Belize City. Tenders arriving in Belize City pull into the Fort Street Tourism Village, which has four main terminals with shops, restaurants, and tourist information. We'd recommend getting out of the city as quickly as possible—it's a frenetic, none-too-pleasant place. The inland sites and cayes are spectacular though.

TOP DRAW   Numerous operators offer day trips to Belize's major Mayan ruins (they're extraordinary), including **Lamanai,** an immense jungle site with more than 700 structures, most still half-buried; and hilltop **Xunantunich,** where more than 25 temples and palaces include the huge El Castillo ("the castle").

UNDER THE SEA   South of Ambergris Caye, the **Hol Chan Marine Reserve & Shark Ray Alley** (www.holchanbelize.org) are a popular destination for snorkeling and swimming with stingrays and nurse sharks.

FOR NATURE LOVERS   Two major wildlife sanctuaries lie inland from Belize City, off the Northern Highway: the **Community Baboon Sanctuary** (www.howlermonkeys.org), which preserves howler monkey habitat; and **Crooked Tree Wildlife Sanctuary** (www.belizeaudubon.org), which protects a wetland mosaic habitat for more than 360 bird species.

COZUMEL & MEXICO

The island of Cozumel, just off Mexico's Yucatán coast, is one of the busiest cruise ports on the planet, with up to 16 ships visiting every day during high

The largest and most fabled of the Yucatán ruins, **Chichén Itzá** (meaning "Mouth of the Well of the Itza Family") was founded in A.D. 445 by the Mayans and later inhabited by the Toltecs of central Mexico. At its height, the city had about 50,000 residents, but it was relinquished to the surrounding jungle in the early 13th century. The area covers 18 sq. km (7 sq. miles), so you can see only a fraction of it on a day trip. What you will see is the magnificent El Castillo pyramid, intricately built with the Maya calendar in mind; the Sacred Cenote, where sacrificial victims were drowned; the wonderfully preserved Ball Court (Juego de Pelota); the richly carved Temple of the Warriors; the evocative Temple of the Jaguars, and the gruesome Temple of the Skulls (Tzompantli).

Only a 30-minute drive from Playa del Carmen, the small walled city of **Tulum** is the single-most-visited Maya ruin. From its dramatic perch atop seaside cliffs, you can see wonderful panoramic views of the Caribbean. Tulum's ruins include a temple to Kukulkán, the primary Maya/Olmec god; the Temple of the Frescoes, the Temple of the Descending God, the House of Columns, and the House of the Cenote. There's also a sliver of silky beach below the site, so bring your bathing suit for a refreshing dip.

A 35-minute drive northwest of Tulum, **Cobá** was once one of the most important city-states in the Maya empire; its pyramid, Nohoch Mul, is the tallest in the Yucatán. Archaeologists estimate that only a small percentage of this dead city has yet been uncovered; its 81 primitive acres provide excellent opportunities for exploration by hikers.

season, counting those that anchor offshore and ferry in passengers. All that activity can make the port town of San Miguel seem more like Times Square than the sleepy, refreshingly gritty town it once was. Outside town, though, development hasn't destroyed the island's natural beauty, including acres of low-lying scrub forest containing protected plant and animal species.

For us the major allure of Cozumel remains its proximity to the ancient Mayan ruins on the Yucatán Peninsula (see the box above), which are generally offered as day-trip excursions. In recent years, a handful of mainland Yucatán ports have also come onto the scene: Playa del Carmen, which is a 45-miute ferry ride from Cozumel; Calica, just south of Playa, where there's little more than a pier; Progreso, on the Gulf coast of the Yucatán, making it the closest to Chichén Itzá, as well as the city of Mérida; and Costa Maya, about 161km (100 miles) south near the sleepy fishing village of Mahajual.

UNDER THE SEA   Offshore, 32km (20 miles) of coral reefs have been set aside as an underwater national park, including the stunning Palancar Reef, the world's second-largest natural coral formation.

CHEESY BUT FUN   Just south of the cruise terminals, the **Discover Mexico** theme park (www.discovermexicopark.com) offers scale models of Mexico's most famous archaeological sites and colonial buildings.

4

FOR NATURE LOVERS   About a $10 taxi ride from the center of San Miguel, the **Chankanaab Nature Park** (www.cozumelparks.com) is a combination archaeological park, botanical garden, and wildlife sanctuary (crocodiles! sea lions!), with a wide white-sand beach and underwater statues for snorkelers to admire.

TOP BEACH   Cozumel's best powdery white-sand beach, Playa San Francisco, stretches for some 5km (3 miles) along the southwestern shoreline.

CURAÇAO

The largest and most populous of the Netherlands Antilles, just 56km (35 miles) north of the Venezuelan coast, arid Curaçao still retains the storybook look of its 17th-century Dutch trading post heritage. As you sail into the harbor of Willemstad, look for the quaint Queen Emma floating pontoon bridge, which swings aside to open the narrow channel. From the pier, it's a 5- to 10-minute walk to the town center, which is easy to navigate on foot (so don't feel like you have to book an excursion for this port).

TOP DRAW   Willemsted's historic center and the island's natural harbor, Schottegat, have been inscribed on UNESCO's World Heritage list. Fort Amsterdam, site of the Governor's Palace and the 1769 Dutch Reformed church, guards the waterfront.

SLICE OF HISTORY   Jews have lived on Curaçao since the mid–17th century: historic sites include the **Mikve Emmanuel Israel** synagogue (the Western Hemisphere's oldest), **Beth Haim Cemetery** (consecrated in 1659) and **Landhouse Bloemhof,** displaying art and artifacts.

OFF THE BEATEN PATH   In the **Christoffel National Park** (www. christoffelpark.org), on the northwestern tip of Curaçao, you can see ancient Arawak paintings and the Piedra di Monton, a rock heap piled by African slaves who cleared this former plantation.

FOR NATURE LOVERS   The **Curaçao Sea Aquarium** (www.curacao-sea-aquarium.com), displays more than 400 species of fish, crabs, anemones, and other invertebrates, sponges, and coral.

SHOPAHOLICS ALERT   More than 100 stores line Heerenstraat, Breedestraat, and other streets in Willemstadt. Look for good buys on French perfumes, Dutch blue Delft souvenirs, finely woven Italian silks, Japanese and German cameras, jewelry, silver, Swiss watches, linens, leather goods, and liquor, along with island-made rum and liqueurs.

DOMINICA

Distinctly different from the Dominican Republic (for one thing, it's pronounced Dome-i-*nee*-ka, not Doe-*min*-i-ka), the lush and mountainous Commonwealth of Dominica is an independent country in the Eastern Caribbean, where English, not Spanish, is the official language. Dominica claims to have 365 crystal-clear rivers (one for every day of the year), along with dramatic waterfalls, volcanic lakes, and gargantuan foliage, all accessible via river trips or hikes along undemanding jungle trails.

Although the island now has three cruise ship ports (Roseau Harbour, Wood-bridge Bay, and the northwestern town of Portsmouth), the capital Roseau has an authenticity lacking in other, more developed island towns. The island is also notable for its population of some 3,000 Carib Indians, the last remaining descendants of the people who dominated the region when Europeans arrived.

ICONIC SIGHT   Approximately 15 to 20 minutes by car from Roseau, **Trafalgar Falls** is actually two separate falls, with cascading white torrents pummeling the black-lava boulders below.

FOR NATURE LOVERS   Dominica has been hailed by some marine biologists as one of the most reliable spots to see sperm whales. Board a motorized vessel and cruise to a point offshore to search for whales and dolphins.

LOCAL COLOR   Dominica sells handicrafts and art not obtainable any-where else, most notably Carib Indian baskets made of dyed larouma reeds and balizier (heliconia) leaves, their designs handed down from generation to generation.

SLICE OF HISTORY   Near Portsmouth, in Cabrits National Park, the 18th-century **Fort Shirley** is one of the most impressive and historic military complexes in the West Indies and a UNESCO World Heritage Site.

GRAND CAYMAN

Scuba divers love Grand Cayman, the largest of the Cayman Islands. It's actu-ally the top of an underwater mountain; its side—known as the Cayman Wall—plummets straight down for 150m (490 ft.) before becoming a steep slope that falls away for 1,800m (5,900 ft.) to the ocean floor. Scrubby Grand Cayman and its sister islands (Cayman Brac and Little Cayman) boast more than their share of upscale private homes and condos, thanks to the tiny nation's lenient tax and banking laws, meaning that the restaurants are better here than in many other parts of the Caribbean (so splurge on lunch). Grand Cayman, a British Colony, is also popular because of its laid-back civility—so civil that ships aren't allowed to visit on Sunday. You cruise will anchor off of George Town, the colony's capital and commercial hub.

TOP DRAW   In the waters off Grand Cayman's northwest tip, **Stingray City** (www.stingraycitycaymanislands.com) attracts from 30 to 100 relatively tame stingrays to swarm around visiting snorkelers.

FOR NATURE LOVERS   On Grand Cayman's northwest coast, the **Cay-man Turtle Centre** (www.turtle.ky) supports the breeding activities of the endangered green sea turtle. The farm is now part of a marine park called Boatswain's Beach, which has a snorkeling lagoon, a predator tanks, a tank for dolphin swims, and other mostly marine-oriented displays.

TOP BEACH   Though it's lined with condominiums and plush resorts, **Seven-Mile Beach,** which begins north of George Town, has sparkling white sands with a backdrop of casuarina trees, and is known for its array of water-sports and translucent aquamarine waters.

When shopping, be aware that some items sold may not be allowed by U.S. Customs. You might be eyeing that gorgeous piece of **black-coral jewelry,** for instance, but laws prohibiting the trade in endangered species make it illegal to bring many products made from coral and other marine animals back to the United States. (Remember, corals aren't rocks, they're living animals—a single branch of coral contains thousands of tiny marine invertebrates called polyps.) **Sea turtles,** too, are highly endangered, and sea horses and conch (yes, the ones you eat in restaurants), while not yet globally protected by law, are currently threatened with extinction. The shopkeepers selling items made from these creatures probably won't tell you they're questionable from a Customs standpoint, but the Customs agent sure will, and may fine you or, at the very least, confiscate the item if he catches you with it. Better to buy a cheap underwater camera and take pictures of these beauties on a snorkeling expedition—you get the memories, the evidence, a little exercise, and good karma to boot.

Cuban cigars used to be prohibited by U.S. Customs, but that restriction was lifted in late 2016. So feel free to buy, puff, and enjoy—just don't tell your pulmonologist.

GRAND TURK

Grand Turk has long been known as one of the top five diving destinations in the world, with a plunging continental shelf, healthy coral reefs, and great visibility. The whole western shore of the island is a protected underwater park. More recently, it has also opened a deepwater pier, the Grand Turk Cruise Center, to accommodate even the largest megaships. About 5km (3 miles) from the pier, charming Cockburn Town—the administrative capital of the Turks and Caicos Islands—has Bermudan-influenced colonial buildings, guesthouses, and a couple of laid-back bars, near miles of public powder-white beaches.

UNDER THE SEA   Scuba divers will be wowed by the manta rays, whale sharks, and sea turtles, and the beautiful colors of the third-largest coral reef in the world. If you're not a diver, snorkeling cruises depart from the cruise terminal to visit sites such as **Horseshoe Reef** and **Round Cay.**

FOR NATURE LOVERS   From January to April, excursion boats follow the Atlantic humpback whales traveling down Turk's Passage trench on the western side of the island, heading for their breeding grounds south of Grand Turk.

SLICE OF HISTORY   In the plaza of Cockburn Town's historic district, a bronze plaque marks the spot where Christopher Columbus allegedly first set foot in the New World, on October 14, 1492.

TOP BEACH   On Grand Cayman's southwest coast, **Governor's Beach** is one of the few blue-flagged beaches in the Caribbean. It's also reputed to have the best snorkeling on the island.

GRENADA

Once a British crown colony, the now-independent nation of Grenada produces more spices than any other country in the world, including clove, cinnamon, mace, cocoa, tonka beans, ginger, and a fifth of the world's nutmeg—thus its nickname, the Spice Island. St. George's, the country's capital, is one of the most colorful ports in the West Indies, nearly landlocked in the deep crater of a long-dead volcano, full of charming Georgian colonial buildings, and flanked by old forts. Cruise ships dock at the Melville Street Cruise Terminal, or anchor in the picturesque St. George's harbor and send passengers on a short tender ride to the pier.

ICONIC SIGHT At the heart of Grand Etang National Park—with its many hiking trails through rainforest and nutmeg groves—pristine **Grand Etang Lake** is set in an extinct volcanic crater some 530m (1,740 ft.) above sea level.

OUT AND ABOUT Grenada's lush interior has a number of scenic waterfalls, including **Seven Sisters Waterfalls** in the **Grand Etang rainforest** and **Annandale Falls** in the mountains northeast of St. George's.

TOP BEACH South of St. George's, **Grand Anse Beach,** with its 3km (2 miles) of wide sugar-white sands, is one of the best in the Caribbean, boasting calm waters and great views.

JAMAICA

A favorite of North American honeymooners, Jamaica is the third-largest of the Caribbean islands after Cuba and Hispaniola, with dense jungle in its interior, mountains rising as high as 2,220m (7,282 ft.), and many beautiful white-sand beaches along its northern coast, where the cruise ships dock at either **Ocho Rios, Montego Bay,** or **Falmouth.** Montego Bay has better beaches, shopping, and restaurants than Ocho Rios, as well as some of the best golf courses in the Caribbean.

Jamaica's history is rooted in the plantation economy and some of the most impassioned politics in the Western Hemisphere. The island is also the birthplace of Bob Marley (1945–81), whose reggae music has inspired generations of musicians and music lovers.

With its greater land mass, Jamaica offers a wide variety of shore excursion activities, including river tubing, horseback riding, and mountain biking. (Plus golf—did we mention golf?)

TOP DRAW Just west of Ochos Rios, scenic **Dunn's River Falls** (www.dunnsriverfallsja.com) cascade 180m (590 ft.) to the beach. Tourists are allowed to climb the falls, and it's a ball to slip and slide your way up with hundreds of others. The most visited attraction in Jamaica, they can be overcrowded when a lot of cruise ships are in port.

SLICE OF HISTORY Just outside Montego Bay, the 18th-century **Rose Hall Great House** (www.rosehall.com) is the most famous plantation home in Jamaica, with a scandalous history of witchcraft, adultery, and murder. Today it's the centerpiece of the upscale Rose Hill golf resort.

Caribbean, Bahamas & Panama Canal Cruises

CRUISE DESTINATIONS

TOP BEACHES   The tranquil waters of **Aquasol Theme Park** in Montego Bay make it a particular favorite for families. You might also check out the big **James Bond Beach,** in Oracabessa, about 20 minutes from Ochos Rios. Nearby is Goldeneye, home of James Bond author Ian Fleming.

LOCAL COLOR   Adjacent to the Ochos Rios cruise pier, the entertainment-and-shopping complex **Island Village** (www.islandjamaica.com), developed by Island Records' Chris Blackwell, includes such only-in-Jamaica features as the ReggaeXplosion museum and a museum of Jamaican art.

KEY WEST

Located at the end of the Florida Keys, Key West—America's southernmost city—has the vibe of a colorful Caribbean outpost with a dash of New Orleans high life. It's a fun-loving, heavy-drinking town with a lot of history, more than a little touristy goofiness, and a large gay community.

Cruise ships dock on the Gulf side of the island, at Mallory Square (Old Town's tourist central), the nearby Hilton Resort's Pier B, or the U.S. Navy base's Outer Mole pier. Most cruise lines offer guided walking tours and bike tours, but this is really a port to explore on your own, with most attractions in easy proximity to the cruise docks. Wander around touristy Mallory Square and Duval Street, check out some of the theme bars, and then take a walk down some of the quieter side streets. Or, you might want to spend your day playing golf, diving, snorkeling, or—in the spirit of former Key West resident Ernest Hemingway—deep-sea fishing.

ICONIC SIGHT   The **Hemingway Home** on Whitehead Street (www.hemingwayhome.com) is where "Papa" lived in the 1930s, writing *For Whom the Bell Tolls* and *A Farewell to Arms* in his studio out back.

BOTTOMS UP   Bars are an essential part of the Key West experience. Two storied but touristy bars—Sloppy Joe's on Duval Street and Captain Tony's Saloon on Greene Street—compete for bragging rights to the hard-drinking Hemingway legend. Wherever you end up, try some of the favorite local beer, Hog's Breath, or the favorite local rum, Key West Gold.

SLICE OF HISTORY   On Front Street, the **Harry S Truman Little White House** (www.trumanlittlewhitehouse.com) was Truman's vacation home during his presidency and today remains just as he left it, decorated in late-1940s style.

SMELL THE ROSES   Lush tropical gardens surround **The Audubon House** (audubonhouse.com), a restored 19th-century sailor's mansion filled with engravings by famous naturalist and artist John James Audubon.

FOR NATURE LOVERS   On the waterfront at Mallory Square, the **Key West Aquarium** (www.keywestaquarium.com), opened in 1932, displays marine creatures native to the Keys, from sea turtles and jellyfish to alligators and stingrays.

MARTINIQUE

For years, France and England vied to control this lush plantation island in the Southern Caribbean (hint: France won). With its quaint seaside villages,

Across the bay from Fort-de-France, in Trois Ilets, the **Musée de la Pagerie** tells the life of Empress Joséphine, the Martinique-born wife of Napoleon. Set in a humble cottage—the former kitchen of Joséphine's aristocratic family's planation—it's full of artifacts, from her childhood bed to the love letters Napoleon wrote her.

At the eastern end of downtown Fort-de-France, in La Savane park, a statue of Joséphine was erected in 1848. However, today she stands headless—her statue was decapitated in 1995 to protest her role in reinstating slavery on the island in the early 1800s.

colonial ruins, beautiful rainforests, and captivating beaches, it's a popular cruise port of call. Most cruise ships dock in the heart of the capital, Fort-de-France, at the Pointe Simon Cruise Dock, though when things get crowded they may also dock at the Tourelles Passenger Terminal at the main harbor, a 5-minute cab ride from Fort-de-France.

Bustling Fort-de-France is a lovely town to walk around in, full of ochre buildings, wrought-iron balconies, Belle Epoque architecture, cascading flowers, and tall palm trees. The town's narrow streets, cluttered with boutiques and cafes, climb from the bowl of the sea to the surrounding hills, forming a great urban amphitheater. Martinique is known as a great place to eat, with its mixed French and Creole culinary heritage.

Just east of the cruise docks, you can catch a blue ferry to cross the bay to La Pagerie and the resort area of Pointe du Bout.

TOP BEACH   At the island's southern tip, **Grand Anse des Salines** has coconut palms, views of Diamond Rock, and white sand that seems to run for miles. North of Fort-de-France, the silver volcanic sands of Anse Turin are where French painter Paul Gauguin swam when he lived on Martinique.

SLICE OF HISTORY   On the northwest coast, the fishing village of **St. Pierre** was the cultural capital of the island until 1902, when Mount Pelée erupted, killing all but two of St. Pierre's 30,000 inhabitants. Ruins of a church, theater, and other buildings still stand, and there's a small museum.

OUT AND ABOUT   The ruins of a 17th-century sugar plantation are slowly being reclaimed by rainforest at **Habitation Céron** (www.habitation-ceron.com), a haunting reminder of Martinique's colonial past. The on-site French restaurant makes a good lunch stop.

UNDER THE SEA   Across the bay from Fort-de-France, the reef at **Anse Dufour** has excellent snorkeling. The reef is filled with marine animals, including French grunts, blackbar soldierfish, and silversides.

SHOPAHOLICS ALERT   In downtown Fort-de-France, especially on rue Victor Hugo, French luxury items—perfumes, couture fashion, luggage, crystal, and dinnerware—sell for 30% to 40% less than in the U.S. But beware: The island's hefty value-added tax can wipe out much of those savings.

NEVIS

Sonmewhat off the beaten tourist track, Nevis is the junior partner in the combined Federation of St. Kitts and Nevis, which became an independent nation in 1983. Though smaller than neighboring St. Kitts (p. 64), Nevis is nevertheless the more appealing and upbeat of the two islands. Columbus first sighted the island in 1493, naming it Las Nieves, Spanish for "snows," because its mountain reminded him of the Pyrenees. Settled by the British in 1628, Nevis became a prosperous sugar-growing island as well as the most popular spa island of the 18th century, thanks to its hot mineral springs.

The capital city, Charlestown, has a lovely mixture of port-town exuberance and small-town charm. Smaller ships dock at the Charlestown Port, right in the center of town; larger vessels anchor off the coast of Pinney's Beach. Nevis is so small and easy to negotiate on your own that excursions aren't really necessary.

TOP BEACH   North of Charlestown, **Pinney's Beach** is a lovely spot for swimming, snorkeling, beachcombing, or just sitting back and watching the pelicans dive-bomb into the surf.

SLICE OF HISTORY   On Main Street, the **Museum of Nevis History** (www.nevisheritage.org) occupies a rustic little two-level house where Nevis' most famous native son, Alexander Hamilton, may have been born, in either 1755 or 1757.

BONUS   On a hill above downtown, the small but appealing **Nelson Museum** (www.nevisheritage.org) traces the history of Admiral Horatio Nelson's Caribbean career, portrayed in ship models, paintings, and even a scrap from the Union Jack under which the admiral was standing when he was fatally shot in 1805.

SMELL THE ROSES   South of Charlestown, the **Botanical Garden of Nevis** (www.botanicalgardennevis.com) actually has several gardens—a rose and vine garden, a cactus garden, a tropical fruit garden, an orchid garden, and a tropical rainforest conservatory.

PUERTO RICO

San Juan, the capital of Puerto Rico, has the busiest ocean terminal in the West Indies. Caribbean cruises not only stop here, several originate here. While cruise groups, by their sheer size, can overwhelm many ports of call, San Juan absorbs them with ease. Many cruise ships dock at Old San Juan, but some lines use the Pan American Pier in Isla Grande, which is more convenient to the resort area but further from the historic district.

The San Juan metropolitan area, home to about a third of Puerto Rico's 3.8 million people, is one of the largest and most sophisticated urban centers in the Caribbean. Cruise passengers, however, tend to stick to Old San Juan, the handsome historic district, with hilly cobblestone streets lined with brightly painted colonial town houses. However, there are two very good reason to venture beyond Old San Juan: to visit the El Yunque Rainforest, less than an hour's drive east of the city, or to play golf at one of the area's many fine resort courses.

TOP DRAW   Old San Juan has not one but two massive colonial fortresses: the 16th-century **Castillo San Felipe del Morro** (El Morro for short) and the 18th-century **Castillo de San Cristóbal.** Both are managed by the National Park Service (www.nps.gov/saju) and are UNESCO World Heritage sites.

TRY YOUR LUCK   Most large hotels have casinos, which are one of San Juan's biggest draws. Most convenient for cruise ship passengers is The **Sheraton Old San Juan Hotel's casino,** right across from Pier 3, but there are larger and more elegant casinos at **The Hotel InterContinental San Juan** and the **Ritz-Carlton,** both east of Old San Juan in Isla Verde.

TOP BEACH   While Condado Beach, at the western end of Ashford Avenue, is the most famous, we prefer the less rocky beaches of **Isla Verde,** behind the hotels and condominiums along Isla Verde Avenue, with their white sand, palm trees, ocean breezes, and rolling surf.

SHOPAHOLICS ALERT   San Juan has some great bargains, and U.S. citizens pay no duty on items bought in Puerto Rico. The streets of the Old Town, especially Calle San Francisco and Calle del Cristo, are a major shopping area. Local handicrafts can be good buys.

ST. BARTS

Chic, sophisticated St. Barts (or, technically, St. Barthélemy, a name no one ever uses) is one of the ritziest refuges in the Caribbean. Yet despite all the hoopla, St. Barts retains its charm, serenity, natural beauty, and authentically Gallic flavor. In contrast to most Caribbean islands, where descendants of African enslaved peoples form the majority, St. Barts's year-round residents are primarily of French ancestry. Gustavia, the main port, is full of French restaurants and semibohemian nightspots. Many of the small luxe ships that call here stay into the evening so passengers can enjoy a night out. Away from town, the island is full of dramatic hills and pristine white-sand beaches.

TOP BEACH   If you're looking for an active beach strand, with restaurants and watersports, **Grand Cul de Sac** fits the bill, with waters that are shallow, warm, and protected.

LOCAL COLOR   For a taste of the island's celebrity vibe, make a beeline to the laidback dive bar **Le Select** on rue de la France, the epicenter of Gustavia's afternoon social life for more than 60 years.

OFF THE BEATEN TRACK   Visit the quaint fishing village of **Corossol,** about 10 minutes by taxi from the dock, for a glimpse of the old pre-jet-set St. Bart's, when traditional folk still lived off the sea.

SHOPAHOLICS ALERT   Duty-free St. Barts is a good place to buy liquor, perfume, and other French luxury items. Shops are concentrated in Gustavia and St. Jean, where the quality-to-schlock ratio is as high as anywhere in the Caribbean.

ST. KITTS

Separated by only about 3.2km (2 miles) of ocean from its other half, Nevis (p. 63), St. Kitts—or St. Christopher, a name hardly anyone uses—is by far the more populous of the two islands. St. Kitts is almost ridiculously lush and fertile, dotted with rainforests and waterfalls and boasting some lovely beaches; it's also extremely poor, its economy still dependent on sugar cane. Cruise ships put in at modern Port Zante in Basseterre, a pleasant if low-key capital full of colonial architecture.

TOP DRAW   Panoramic views abound at the 17th-century **Brimstone Hill Fortress** (www.brimstonehillfortress.org), up the west coast from Basseterre, one of the largest and best-preserved forts in the Caribbean. Today, it's the centerpiece of a national park crisscrossed by nature trails, with a population of green vervet monkeys to keep things lively.

SMELL THE ROSES   Tropical gardens bedeck the ruins of the **Romney Manor** sugar estate, now home to the popular Caribelle Batik shop and workshop (www.caribellebatikstkitts.com).

TOP BEACH   Like a finger pointing toward Nevis, the narrow southeast peninsula contains the island's finest white-sand beaches. At the far end you'll find laidback **Cockleshell Bay beach,** which has watersports and a couple of fun beach cafes.

UNDER THE WATER   Secluded **Shitten Bay** is a great spot for snorkeling among diverse reef fish and coral formations. You'll need a boat (or a tour operator with a boat) to get here.

ST. LUCIA

St. Lucia (pronounced *Loo*-sha) changed hands often during the colonial period, being British seven times and French seven times. Today, though, it's an independent state that's become one of the most popular destinations in the Caribbean, with top-of-the-line resorts.

The capital, Castries, boasts a lovely hill-ringed harbor that's really an extinct volcanic crater. Most cruise ships arrive at Pointe Seraphine, within walking distance of the center of Castries. Some smaller lines anchor off other sites around the island, such as Rodney Bay to the north or Soufrière to the south.

Because of the difficult terrain, shore excursions are the best means of seeing this beautiful island in a day or less. Snorkeling excursions to St. Lucia's offshore marine reserve are also recommended.

TOP DRAW   Originally a separate island, **Pigeon Island**—now a national park (www.slunatrust.org)—was British admiral Rodney's naval base in 1782, when he defeated the French fleet to win St. Lucia. A few bits of the fort remain—including a mess hall that's now a pub—but mostly it's an ideal spot for picnics and nature walks, with a view that stretches all the way to Martinique.

ICONIC SIGHT   Soufrière, a fishing port and St. Lucia's second-largest settlement, is dominated by the Pitons, two sharply pointed volcanic peaks that rise right from the sea. Cloaked in green vegetation, with waves crashing around their bases, they've become the symbol of St. Lucia.

BONUS   Near the town of Soufrière lies the famous "drive-in" volcano, **La Soufrière,** a rocky lunar landscape of bubbling mud and craters seething with fuming sulfur.

TOP BEACH   St. Lucia is famous for its beaches, and just north of Soufrière is a beach connoisseur's delight, **Anse Chastanet,** a gorgeous expanse of white sand at the foothills of lush mountains. This is a fantastic spot for snorkeling, with coral reefs starting only a little way offshore.

ST. MARTIN/SINT MAARTEN

Who can resist a two-for-one deal? That's what you get on St. Martin, which has been shared by France and the Netherlands for more than 350 years. The French side, with some of the best beaches and restaurants in the Caribbean, emphasizes quiet elegance. The Dutch side, officially known as Sint Maarten, reflects Holland's anything-goes philosophy: Development is much more widespread, flashy casinos pepper the landscape, and strip malls make the larger towns look as much like Anaheim as Amsterdam.

Cruise ships usually dock on the Dutch side, at Dr. A. C. Wathey Pier, about 1.6km (1 mile) southeast of Philipsburg. Smaller vessels sometimes dock on the French side of the island at Marina Port la Royale, adjacent to the heart of Marigot.

Shopping, sunbathing, and gambling are the pastimes that interest most cruise passengers who hit this island, but folks with a taste for culture and history can make a day of those here as well.

UNDER THE WATER   Good snorkeling spots are plentiful. Some of the most rewarding are Maho Bay, Mullet Bay, and Dawn Beach on the Dutch side, and the small offshore island of Ilet Pinel off the French side's northeast coast.

TRY YOUR LUCK   Gamblers will want to stick to the Dutch side, where several casinos are clustered along Front Street in the heart of Philipsburg. All of them open early to snag cruise passengers.

SLICE OF HISTORY   Naturally, each side of the island has its own colonial fort: the Dutch **Fort Amsterdam,** looking out over Great Bay from the hill west of Philipsburg; and the far more intact French **Fort St. Louis,** on the hill flanking Marigot Bay's north end.

TOP BEACH   Far and away the island's most visited strand, **Orient Beach,** on the northeast coast of the French side, fancies itself the St. Tropez of the Caribbean. Hedonism is the name of the game here: plenty of food, drink, music, and flesh. Watersports abound.

SHOPAHOLICS ALERT   St. Martin is a true free port—no duties are paid on any item coming in or going out—and neither side of the island has a sales tax. Shops on the much busier Dutch side are concentrated in Philipsburg, around Front Street; on the French side, Marigot has a calmer ambience, with a wide selection of European merchandise skewed toward an upscale audience.

ST. CROIX, U.S.V.I.

St. Croix, the largest of the USVIs, gets nowhere near as many visitors as St. Thomas, making for a more easygoing port experience. (A few years back, a spate of robberies and muggings against passengers and crew drove most cruise lines out of St. Croix, but a concerted effort by the island recently to improve conditions has brought many lines back.) The island's Dutch heritage is evident throughout its capital, Frederiksted.

TOP DRAW   The offshore **Buck Island Reef National Monument** (www.nps.gov/buis) is full of gorgeous coral reefs.

BOTTOMS UP   Tours of the **Cruzan Rum Distillery** in Frederiksted are refreshingly more about the working factory, the process, and the history than about the tastings at the end (though it has those, too).

ST. JOHN, U.S.V.I.

The most tranquil and unspoiled of the U.S. Virgins, St. John is more than half national park, with miles of serpentine hiking trails, ruins of 18th-century Danish plantations, and panoramic ocean views. A few ships moor directly off St. John, but those that dock in neighboring St. Thomas usually offer excursions here as well, via ferry, to access St. John's pristine white-sand beaches and eco-tourist sensibilities. Surrey-style taxis take visitors around the small island.

TOP DRAW   Founded in 1956 by the wealthy Rockefeller family, **Virgin Islands National Park** (www.nps.gov/viis) includes over two-thirds of St. John's landmass, plus submerged land and water adjacent to the island.

SLICE OF HISTORY   Within the national park, the **Annaberg Ruins,** on Leinster Bay Road, are all that's left of the island's plantations and sugar mill, founded by Danish settlers in 1718.

TOP BEACHES   The great white sweep of **Trunk Bay** is all too often overcrowded, but it's still worth visiting for its underwater snorkeling trail near the shore. Snorkelers also find good reefs at **Cinnamon Bay** and **Maho Bay,** a great place to spot turtles and schools of parrotfish.

LOCAL COLOR   Most cruise passengers enter through Cruz Bay, a cute little West Indian village with intriguing bars, restaurants, boutiques, and pastel-painted houses.

ST. THOMAS, U.S.V.I.

Vacationers discovered St. Thomas right after World War II and have been flocking here ever since. Today the island is one of the busiest and most developed cruise ports in the West Indies, often hosting more than six ships a day during the peak winter season. Its capital town Charlotte Amalie, named in 1691 in honor of the wife of Denmark's King Christian V, has become the Caribbean's major shopping center.

With so much traffic, St. Thomas has several docks for cruise ships: West Indian Dock/Havensight Mall, the Crown Bay Cruise Ship Terminal, and Charlotte Amalie Harbor. Taxis meet all ships and are the best way to get around the island.

The waters off of St. Thomas are rated among the most beautiful in the world, so many shore excursions focus on snorkeling, diving, and kayaking. Many excursions also visit neighboring St. John (p. 67).

TOP DRAW Besides a fascinating array of tanks and touch pools, **Coral World Underwater Observatory and Marine Park** (https://coralworldvi. com) lets visitors plunge to the depths without getting wet, in a 3-story underwater observation tower 100 feet offshore.

SMELL THE ROSES The lush 11-acre hilltop **St. Peter Greathouse Estate and Gardens** (www.greathousevi.com), on the island's northern rim, shows off some 200 varieties of plants and trees, as well as a rainforest, an orchid jungle, waterfalls, and reflecting ponds.

TOP BEACH On the north side of the island, Magens Bay Beach was once hailed as one of the world's most beautiful, but it's often overcrowded. For more serenity, head east of Charlotte Amalie to **Bolongo Bay** for a fine spread of sand and a variety of watersports.

SHOPAHOLICS ALERT Many cruise ship passengers shop at the Havensight Mall, right by the West Indian Dock, but the major shopping is along the harbor of Charlotte Amalie, with Main Street the prime shopping thoroughfare.

TORTOLA, B.V.I.

With small bays and hidden coves that were once havens for pirates, the British Virgin Islands (BVIs) are among the world's loveliest cruising regions. Once-sleepy Tortola, one of the chain's largest islands, has evolved from a yacht-chartering port to a full-bore cruise destination that can handle megaships (many of whose passengers then catch a ferry or take a launch 12 miles farther to Virgin Gorda; see p. 69). Cruise ships dock in the colonial capital, Road Town.

TOP DRAW Dominating Tortola's interior, **Sage Mountain National Park** (www.bvitourism.com), the highest point in the Virgin Islands, offers panoramic views and hiking trails through a native forest of mango, papaya, breadfruit, coconut, birch berry, and guava trees.

SMELL THE ROSES Right in Road Town, the **J.R. O'Neal Botanic Gardens** (on Botanic Road, naturally) packs a lot into 4 acres—a stately palm avenue, a pergola walk, lily pond, waterfall, and mini-rainforests.

UNDER THE SEA Nearby **Norman Island** is one of the BVI's prime snorkel sites, full of coral formations, colorful fish, and a group of caves at Treasure Point, where pirate treasure is reputedly hidden.

TOP BEACH Across the mountains from Road Town, **Cane Garden Bay** on the island's northwest coast is worth the trip. Further down the coast, surfers like **Apple Bay.**

LOCAL COLOR Also on the northwest coast, on Cappoon's Bay beach, **Bomba's Surfside Shack** is the oldest, most memorable bar on Tortola, covered with Day-Glo graffiti and ladies' undergarments and laced with scraps of wire, driftwood, and abandoned rubber tires.

VIRGIN GORDA, B.V.I.

Instead of visiting Tortola (p. 68), some small cruise ships put in at its lovely B.V.I. neighbor Virgin Gorda; megaships that stop at Tortola also usually offer an excursion option to Virgin Gorda. The third-largest island in the colony, it got its name ("Fat Virgin") from Christopher Columbus, who thought the mountain framing it looked like a protruding stomach. Most vessels anchor in Gorda Sound and tender passengers to a pier at the village of Spanish Town, which can accommodate smaller ships.

ICONIC SIGHT   At the island's southwest tip, **The Baths** are truly a spectacular natural attraction—toppled house-sized boulders that form saltwater grottoes, excellent for swimming and snorkeling.

UNDER THE SEA   Just north of the Baths, **Spring Bay** offers white sand, clear water, and good snorkeling. Nearby is the **Crawl,** a natural pool formed by rocks, great for novice snorkelers; a marked path leads here from Spring Bay.

OFF THE BEATEN PATH   **Devil's Bay National Park** can be reached by a trail from the Baths, a 15-minute walk through boulders and dry coastal vegetation to a secluded coral-sand beach.

Panama Canal Ports of Call

The Panama Canal is an awesome feat of engineering and human effort. Construction began in 1880 and wasn't completed until 1914, at the expense of thousands of lives. Transiting the Canal, which links the Atlantic Ocean with the Pacific, is a thrill for anyone even vaguely interested in engineering or history.

Passing through the Canal takes about 8 hours from start to finish. The 80km (50-mile) route includes passage through three main locks, plus artificial lakes. Your ship will line up in the morning, mostly with cargo ships, to await its turn through the Canal. While you're transiting, there will be a running narration of history and facts about the Canal by an expert brought on board for the day.

In June 2016, the Canal opened an expanded channel that allows even bigger ships to pass through, a project that should give cruise lines much greater flexibility in planning itineraries for their largest ships.

Cruises that include a **Canal crossing** are generally 10 to 15 nights long, with popular routes running between Florida and Acapulco; they visit a

Off Panama's Caribbean coast, the **San Blas Islands** are a picture postcard perfect tropical archipelago and home to the Kuna Indians, whose women are well known for their colorful, hand-embroidered stitching. When your ship anchors offshore at the islands, be prepared for throngs of Kunas to emerge from the far-off distance, paddling (or, in a few cases, motoring) dugout canoes up to the ship, where they will spend the entire day calling for money or anything else ship passengers toss overboard.

In **Costa Rica,** many ships call at Puerto Caldera, on the Pacific side, or Puerto Limón, on the Atlantic side.

While there's nothing to see from either cargo port, both are ideal jumping-off points for tours from ships of the country's lush, beautiful rainforests.

In **Guatemala,** most Panama Canal–bound ships call at Puerto Quetzal, on the Pacific coast; a few may call at Santo Tomas, on the Caribbean side. Both are used as gateways to Guatemala's spectacular Mayan ruins at Tikal, the country's most famous attraction, with more than 3,000 temples, pyramids, and other buildings of the ancient civilization—some of them dating as far back as A.D. 300—nestled in a thick, surreal jungle setting.

---

handful of Caribbean and Mexican ports and a few ports in Central America along the way. Many ships also do a **partial crossing** of the Canal, sailing into Gatun Lake from the Caribbean side, docking to let passengers off for excursions, and then sailing back out again.

COLÓN

Since 1999, when Panama took over canal operations from the U.S. government, government agencies and private developers in Panama have worked to expand the Canal Zone's tourism infrastructure. Key to this has been developing new attractions at the Canal's Caribbean entrance in Colon. Opened in 2000, Colón's new glass-and-marble terminal building has a large lounge, an Internet cafe, and a huge duty-free shopping mall (part of the Colón Free Zone, the second-largest tax-free zone in the world). Unfortunately, the town surrounding the splashy new development remains poverty stricken and extremely unsafe, so tourists absolutely should not wander around town.

To keep tourists busy (and to divert their dollars to Panama businesses), local tour operators have developed a number of shore excursions in the area:

NATIVE CULTURE   Visitors paddle dugout canoes to the rainforest village of the Embera Indiana, who perform traditional dances and sell their handmade crafts.

SLICE OF HISTORY   A guided tour visits the ruins of old Panama City—destroyed by pirates in 1671—and its replacement, 17th-century Colonial Panama, with its mix of French, Spanish, and Italian architecture.

FOR NATURE LOVERS   Eco-cruises and kayak tours explore **Gatun Lake,** created when the Chagres River was dammed during Canal construction. Though man-made, the lake is surrounded by rainforest and teems with wildlife.

PANAMA CITY

At the south end of the Canal, the Pacific port of Panama City has (naturally) a large duty-free shopping zone. We'd recommend touring Panama City instead. Its sophisticated, modern downtown area is the heart of Latin America's banking industry, yet it still has Spanish colonial remnants in Casco Antiguo.

TOP DRAW   The new Frank Gehry-designed **Biomuseo** (www.biomuseo panama.org) has exhibits explaining the critical role of the Isthmus of Panama—the link between North and South America—upon the planet's biodiversity.

ICONIC SIGHT   The **Amador Causeway** offers great views of the city skyline and the gleaming Bridge of the Americas that spans the Canal.

FOR NATURE LOVERS   **Metropolitan Nature Park** is the only rainforest within a capital city in the Americas. Observe toucans, woodpeckers and parrots within their natural habitat. Or venture out to **Soberania Rainforest**, just 25km (16 miles) out of Panama City, to view monkeys, sloths, crocodiles, and 500 different bird species.

ALASKA & BRITISH COLUMBIA

There are three basic types of Alaska cruises: **Inside Passage** voyages that begin and end in Vancouver; **Alaska cruises** that depart roundtrip from Seattle; and so-called **Gulf of Alaska** voyages that typically sail one-way, northbound or southbound, between Vancouver and Seward or Whittier, the two turnaround ports for nearby Anchorage.

Gulf cruises offer the most flexibility. You can book them back-to-back to create a 14-day roundtrip journey, or you can use them as the springboard for combination land-and-sea packages, which have grown increasingly popular (and increasingly elaborate) over the decades. (See the box on p. 72.) The downside to this type of cruise—and it can be a major one—are increased airfare costs, as you'll be flying into one gateway and out of another. Sometimes, however, these "one-way" sailings are more reasonably priced than round-trips that embark and debark from the same port. Bottom line: Get out a calculator and factor in all costs before booking.

Timing will also factor into how much you pay. The season typically runs between May and September, but dips into April and October, and deals can abound for the shoulder months (May and Sept are also often cheaper). Which is better? Alaska is famous for its "liquid sunshine" and that can strike at any time during the year, as can cold weather. So bring layers, waterproof clothing and your binoculars—Alaska is spectacular no matter what the weather is doing.

Inside Passage from Vancouver

The Inside Passage runs through the area of Alaska known as Southeast (which the locals also call "the Panhandle"). It's the narrow strip of the state—islands, mainland coastal communities, and mountains—that runs from the

Many cruise companies have developed add-on land tours to complement their cruise packages. The most popular such cruisetour combines a Gulf of Alaska cruise ending in Anchorage with a train excursion to stunning **Denali National Park,** where guests stay in the cruise lines' private lodges, and then on to Fairbanks for a range of activities such as river cruises, jet-boat rides, and excursions to gold mines. A shorter add-on to Anchorage cruises offers fishing, hiking, sightseeing, kayaking, and wildlife-watching on the **Kenai Peninsula,** just across a narrow channel from Anchorage. Tours into Canada's **Yukon Territory** typically follow a Vancouver-to-Juneau/Skagway cruise, taking passengers to historic spots such as Whitehorse, the territorial capital, and Dawson City, a picture-perfect gold-rush town.

Can visitors recreate these journeys on their own? Easily. The Kenai Peninsula is where Anchorage residents go for their own vacations, and it's a wonderful road trip to some of Alaska's most scenic areas (it's also kismet for fishermen). And visitors hoping to see Denali can ride the exact same train cruise passengers do (or rent a car for a speedier trip), and take terrific ranger-led tours of the park. It's up to you whether you want more of a group experience or a solo adventure.

Canadian border in the south to the start of the Gulf in the north, just above the Juneau/Haines/Skagway area. The islands on the western edge of the area give cruise ships a welcome degree of protection from the sea and its attendant rough waters (hence the name "Inside Passage"). Because of that shelter, ships can reach ports such as Ketchikan, Wrangell, Petersburg, and others with less rocking and rolling—and thus less risk of seasickness for their passengers. Sitka is not on the Inside Passage (it's on the Pacific Ocean side of Baranof Island), but is included in a fair number of Inside Passage cruise itineraries because it's a beautiful little port. The "classic" Alaska cruise, these voyages depart roundtrip from Vancouver's Canada Place Cruise Terminal (p. 75). Holland America Line and Princess Cruises offer the most departures from Vancouver to Alaska, but other players, including Disney Cruise Lineand Oceania call Vancouver home, along with luxury lines Crystal, Regent Seven Seas, Silversea and Seabourn Cruises.

Alaska Roundtrip from Seattle

While airfare costs might be cheaper for U.S. travelers flying into SeaTac than Vancouver International Airport, there are some trade-offs to this convenience. Unlike cruises departing from Vancouver, voyages from Seattle typically don't sail the scenic Canadian section of the Inside Passage. Instead, they swing out west of Vancouver Island into the open Pacific Ocean, which carries a threat of rough weather, and seas, during the shoulder months of May and September.

A typical sailing out of Seattle includes similar ports to the Inside Passage cruises from Vancouver, with the addition of the requisite "foreign port"—which in this case is usually the romantically English capital of Victoria,

4

CRUISE DESTINATIONS | Alaska & British Columbia

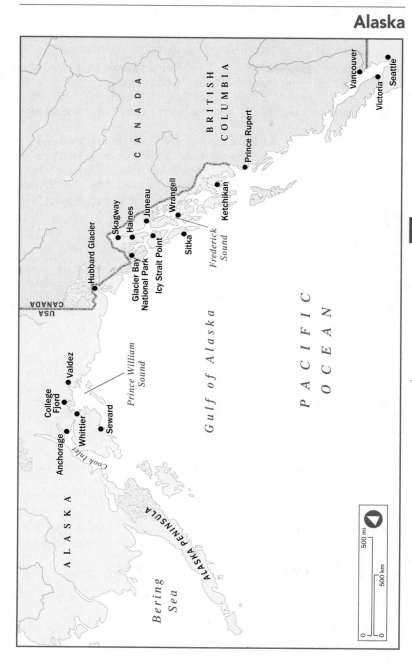

British Columbia (p. 79), though some cruise lines are now calling in Nanaimo, British Columbia, instead (to avoid the summer crowds in Victoria).

The Gulf of Alaska—Vancouver to Anchorage

The other major cruising area is the Southcentral region's Gulf of Alaska, usually referred to by the cruise lines as the "Glacier Discovery Route" or the "Voyage of the Glaciers." "Gulf of Alaska," after all, sounds pretty bland, and on this itinerary you see twice as many glaciers as you do on Inside Passage routes.

Gulf cruises still visit the Inside Passage ports (see above), but then they continue along the coastline of the Gulf, that arc of land from just north of Glacier Bay to the Kenai Peninsula, ending in Anchorage, Alaska's biggest city. Or rather, close to Anchorage: To save a day's travel, most ships choose the turnaround ports of Seward or Whittier instead, carrying passengers from Seward or Whittier on to Anchorage by bus or train.

Alaska Ports of Call

HAINES

Sitting near the northern end of the Lynn Canal, this small, laid-back Alaska town is blessedly free of the tourist gloss of neighboring Skagway. Despite the town's dramatic setting amid the peaks of the Fairweather Mountain Range, few ships come here, partly because it doesn't have a large deepwater dock. Ships that don't stop in Haines regularly provide excursions to the town from Skagway, traveling by boat.

Haines was established in 1879 by Presbyterian missionary S. Hall Young and naturalist John Muir as a place to convert the Chilkoot and Chilkat Tlingit tribes to Christianity. In 1903, the U.S. military built the white clapboard structures of Fort William H. Seward; since decommissioned, it's been turned into private homes, B&Bs, and arts and performances spaces. The town itself has several small, quirky museums; shore excursions here tend to feature nature as wildlife, via rafting, cycling, or hiking.

NATIVE CULTURE   A re-created **Tlingit tribal house** has been built at the center of Fort Seward's former parade ground; in the old fort hospital on the south side of the parade grounds, the **Alaska Indian Arts Gallery** displays native artwork and has a totem carving workshop.

TEE 'EM UP   Just outside town, the 9-hole **Valley of the Eagles Golf Course** (www.hainesgolf.com) allows you the rare opportunity of being able to say you golfed in Alaska.

BOTTOMS UP   On Main Street, the **Haines Brewing Company** (www. hainesbrewing.com), the smallest brewery in Alaska, has a tasting room and beer garden.

FOR NATURE LOVERS   Haines is probably the best place on earth to see bald eagles, especially from October to mid-December. About 20 miles outside town, the **Chilkat Bald Eagle Preserve** is the place to go for a float-trip along the cottonwood-lined Chilkat River, one of their favorite haunts.

Glacier Bay   In little more than 200 years, this area has gone from being a solid wall of ice up to 4,000 feet thick to being a 65-mile bay ecosystem full of wildlife, whales, and slowly returning vegetation. As the ice retreats, it has left behind a series of inlets headed by 11 tidewater glaciers. Among them, the Johns Hopkins, Reid, Lamplugh, Margerie, and Grand Pacific—all in the bay's western arm—are regularly approached by cruise ships. Calving activity (large chunks of ice breaking off) from these glaciers is the big draw (Johns Hopkins has so much that ships can seldom approach closer than 2 miles).

Glacier Bay was named a national park in 1925, and today each ship that enters takes aboard a park ranger to provide information about glaciers and wildlife (which includes mountain goats, brown bears, and minke, orca, and humpback whales) and the history of Native peoples and white men in the bay. A strict rationing of permits to the cruise lines means only two ships a day can sail in the park, preventing the place from getting too busy for its own good.

Tracy Arm & Endicott Arm   Located about 50 miles due south of Juneau, these long, deep fjords reach back from the Inside Passage into the Coastal Mountain Range, their steep-sided waterways ending in active glaciers—the **North Sawyer** and **South Sawyer Glaciers** in Tracy Arm and **Dawes Glacier** in Endicott. All of them calve constantly, filling the waters with miles of brash ice and bergs that ping and thunk off your ship's hull as you approach the ice faces. The passage through either fjord is incredibly dramatic, the sheer mountain walls rising a mile straight from the water, cut by cascading waterfalls and tree-covered, snow-topped mountain valleys. Wildlife here might include Sitka black-tailed deer, bald eagles, mountain goats, and harbor seals.

Misty Fjords National Monument
Covering 2.3 million acres along the Behm Canal, east of Ketchikan, Misty Fjords is actually a flooded cleft between mountains; it's a stunning landscape of volcanic cliffs, rising up to 3,150 feet and plunging hundreds of feet below the waterline. Peace and serenity are the stock in trade of the place, with its namesake mists imparting a *Lord of the Rings* kind of atmosphere, abetted by dense hemlock and spruce forests. Its narrow waterway means that only passengers on small ships will see Misty Fjords close up; bigger ships pass the southern tip of the area, and then veer away northwest to dock at Ketchikan, where shore excursions can take you back into the area.

ICY STRAIT POINT

Situated on Chichagof Island about 50 miles west of Juneau and 22 miles southeast of Glacier Bay, Icy Strait Point isn't actually a town, but a self-contained destination owned and managed by Tlingit Indians from the nearby village of Hoonah. Designed specifically for cruise passengers, the site includes a restored 1930s salmon cannery that now houses a museum, a 1930s cannery display, a restaurant, and shops. Principally, though, Icy Strait Point is a destination for adventure-oriented shore excursions, from fishing to cycling to zip-lining.

NATIVE CULTURE   At the **Native Heritage Center Theater,** near the cannery, a group of Huna Tlingit performs traditional song, dance, and storytelling.

Hubbard Glacier   Lying at the northern end of Yakutat Bay, Hubbard has two claims to fame: It's the largest tidewater glacier on the North American continent (with Alaska's widest ice face, at about 6 miles across), and it's one of the fastest-moving glaciers in Alaska. It's still an active mother, calving off a substantial amount of ice.

Prince William Sound   Located directly south of Anchorage on the bottom side of the Kenai Peninsula, Prince William Sound suffered mightily following the *Exxon Valdez* oil spill in 1989, but after more than 2 decades of cleanup, the area is well on its way to recovery, with whales, harbor seals, eagles, sea lions, sea otters, puffins, and fish all returned to its waters. It's one of Alaska's most appealing wilderness areas, surrounded on three sides by the Chugach Mountains. Scenic **College Fjord,** in the northern sector of Prince William Sound, is visited on many cruises, mostly for Harvard Glacier, which sits at its head. Perhaps the most spectacular of the Sound's ice faces, however, is **Columbia Glacier,** with more than 400 square miles of ice surface and a tidewater frontage of nearly 6 miles.

FOR NATURE LOVERS   Sightseeing boats with onboard naturalists sail through Icy Strait to Point Adolphus, one of Alaska's best whale-watching sites. Sightings include humpbacks and orcas, Steller sea lions, and harbor seals.

OFF THE BEATEN PATH   A bus tour to **Spasski Creek,** about 20 minutes east of Icy Strait, leads to viewing platforms where you may be able to spot bald eagles, land otters, Sitka black-tail deer, and Alaska coastal brown bears—a.k.a. grizzlies.

JUNEAU

Although it's the capital of Alaska, Juneau is unreachable by road, completely surrounded as it is by water, forest, and the massive Juneau Icefield, not to mention two towering mountains, Mount Juneau and Mount Roberts. It is, however, thoroughly accessible by boat—on any given day in season, 4 or 5 cruise ships may be in port, from megaships to microships. Ships dock right in the downtown area, along Marine Way, and downtown can be completely overrun by visitors and tour buses from late May through September.

Tourism woes aside, modern Juneau is a product of Alaska's golden past. It was no more than a fishing outpost for local Tlingit Indians until 1880, when gold was discovered in a creek off the Gastineau Channel. That Gold Rush heritage is kept alive not only in local museums but in several vintage downtown bars with a carefully curated frontier rowdiness.

TOP DRAW   About 13 miles from downtown, the 12-mile-long **Mendenhall Glacier** is the most visited glacier in the world. Visitors go out from Juneau to the glacier by raft, canoe, bicycle, helicopter, or even dog-sled. Nature trails from the visitor center afford good views, but it's well worth the extra effort to book an excursion that allows you to hike on the glacier itself.

LOCAL COLOR Many years ago, a bull terrier named Patsy Ann was Juneau's official town greeter, trotting down to the docks whenever a ship came in. Long dead now, she's memorialized with a bronze statue in Marine Park, where the cruise ships dock.

STRETCH YOUR LEGS From the docks, the **Mount Roberts Tramway** (http://mountrobertstramway.com) will whisk you up the mountain on a 6-minute ride. From the station, a network of paths lead to really incredible views. It's 6 miles round-trip to the summit, though there are also several shorter loops.

SLICE OF HISTORY Just south of town, the **AJ Gold Mine/Gastineau Mill** (http://ajgastineauminetour.com) was once one of the world's richest. Today, you can don a hard hat and venture down a 360-foot mine tunnel, where experienced miners demonstrate hard-rock mining.

BOTTOMS UP East of downtown, there's a tasting room at the popular **Alaskan Brewing Company** (www.alaskanbeer.com).

KETCHIKAN

They call it "Alaska's first city" because it's the first port visited on most northbound cruises, but the way people throng the port area's gift shops, you'd think it was their last chance to use credit cards before Judgment Day. Here's our advice: Walk down the gangway, take three deep breaths, and say to yourself, "I do not need to shop." Instead, walk right past the souvenir stores and head for one of the town's several totem-pole parks or take an excursion to Misty Fjords National Monument (p. 75). Other popular shore excursions here feature salmon fishing, sea kayaking, and wildlife-watching outside of town.

The centerpiece of the historic downtown is Creek Street, a row of quaint wooden houses built on pilings above a busy salmon stream. Once the city's red-light district, today it's filled with boutiques, funky shops and restaurants, and galleries featuring local artists.

TOP DRAW The indoor **Totem Heritage Center** on Deermount Street was built by the city in 1976 to house 33 original 19th-century totem poles, all retrieved from the Tlingit Indian villages of Tongass and Village Islands and the Haida village of Old Kasaan.

Buyer Beware

Shops throughout Alaska are chock-full of knockoff "Native Alaskan" art shipped in from Asia. So, when shopping for the real thing, ask the dealer for details about the artist, and also look for the **Silver Hand sticker,** a state certification that guarantees the item was, in fact, crafted in Alaska by a Native artist. Sky-high prices will also be a tip-off that an item is the real thing. You get what you pay for.

BONUS About 10 miles north of town, at **Totem Bight State Park,** a winding forest trail leads to an old Indian campsite filled with totem poles.

NATIVE CULTURE **Saxman Native Village,** about 2½ miles outside Ketchikan, is home to hundreds of Tlingit, Tsimshian, and Haida, and is a center for the revival of Native arts and culture. Cone here for storytelling sessions, dance performances, and totem-carving demonstrations.

CHEESY BUT FUN Just a few hundred yards from the pier, the **Great Alaskan Lumberjack Show** (alaskanlumberjackshow.com) features logrolling, speed climbing, tree topping, chainsaw carving, and many other skills every lumberjack needs.

SITKA

Geographically speaking, Sitka is not on the Inside Passage at all, but rather on the Pacific coast of Baranof Island. However, it's included in a fair number of Inside Passage cruise itineraries simply because it's such a beautiful little port. Sitka lacks docking facilities for megaships (those that do stop here send passengers ashore in tenders), which means the town has fewer cruise ship visits than Juneau, Ketchikan, and Skagway. Because of this, it retains a more residential feel. History is Sitka's strong suit—for centuries it was the stronghold of the powerful Kiksadi Tlingit clan, until 1799-1804 when, despite armed resistance by the Tlingits, a Russian fur-trading company set up a fort and colony, making it Alaska's earliest white settlement.

Shore excursions here are fairly standard; we recommend skipping them just to walk around this fascinating town.

TOP DRAW Walking tours of Sitka explore the town's Russian heritage at such sites as the onion-domed St. Michael's Russian Orthodox Cathedral, the 1842 Russian Bishop's House, a Russian cemetery, the Russian blockhouse, and—as a corrective to the Russian history—Sitka National Historical Park, where the Tlingit made their last valiant stand against Russia in 1804.

FOR NATURE LOVERS At the nonprofit **Alaska Raptor Center** (www.alaskaraptor.org), located just across Indian River, guests can get close-up views of sick or injured birds of prey (primarily eagles), many of them being treated to be returned to the wild.

NATIVE CULTURE The **Sheetka'Kwaan Naa Kahidi Building** on Katlian Street is a modern version of a traditional Tlingit tribal house; it hosts regular performances of traditional Tlingit dance, often timed to coincide with cruise ship visits.

LOCAL COLOR At **Centennial Hall,** the all-women New Archangel Dancers give 30-minute performances of Russian and Ukrainian traditional dance on most days when cruise ships are in port.

SKAGWAY

Situated at the end of the picturesque Lynn Canal, Skagway is the quintessential Gold Rush Town. When gold fever hit in 1897, it brought total anarchy to Skagway, with a swarm of opportunists arriving with the prospectors to either service or swindle them—usually both. Some things haven't changed: Most of the folks you see in the summer are seasonal workers, brought in essentially as actors to man the set.

It's some set, with the wide main drag, Broadway, lined end to end with gold-rush-era buildings and protected as a National Historic District. A few that look like real businesses turn out to be displays showing how it was back in frontier days, but most house gift shops—lots and lots of gift shops, mostly selling either cheap tourist gimcracks or jewelry. Ships dock at the cruise pier, at the foot of Broadway or off Congress or Terminal Way. Though the docks are in sight of downtown, it's about a 20-minute walk, so free shuttle buses are provided.

TOP DRAW   The famous **White Pass & Yukon Route** narrow-gauge railway (www.frontier-excursions.com) takes you from the town and past waterfalls and still-visible parts of the famous "Trail of '98" to the White Pass Summit, the boundary between Canada and the United States, a 3-hour round trip. *Beware:* On an overcast day, you won't see a damn thing from the train.

OFF THE BEATEN TRACK   The ghost town of **Dyea,** about 9 miles west, was established around the same time as Skagway, but was abandoned completely after the gold rush. Tours head to Dyea by bus, bicycle, or on horseback.

TEE 'EM UP   Over the White Pass, the Yukon town of Carcross has a 9-hole golf course at the **Meadow Lakes Golf & Country Club** (meadowlakesgolfresort.com). Golfing in the Yukon! Now there's something to tell your regular partners.

CHEESY BUT FUN   The *Days of '98 Show* has been playing at the Fraternal Order of Eagles Hall since 1927, which tells you how long Skagway has relied on tourism. A melodrama of the Gay '90s, it features dancing girls, ragtime music, poetry recitations, and actors portraying a legendary shootout.

ALSO CHEESY BUT FUN   On **Skagway Streetcar** tours (www.skagwaystreetcar.com), guides in period costume relate tales of the boomtown days as you tour the sights both in and outside of town in a 1920s limo.

VICTORIA, BRITISH COLUMBIA

Cruises that start in Seattle or San Francisco typically visit Victoria on the way north to Alaska. Located on Vancouver Island, this lovely little city is the capital of British Columbia, and appropriately so, as it's almost more British than Britain. Cruise ships dock at the Ogden Point cruise ship terminal on the Strait of Juan de Fuca, about a mile southwest of the Inner Harbour and the Downtown/Old Town area, where most attractions are located. Cruise lines generally offer a shuttle to the Inner Harbour.

ICONIC SIGHT   The ivy-covered, grandly Edwardian **Fairmont Empress Resort Hotel** (www.fairmont.com/empress-victoria) on Government Street is *the* place to go for British-style high tea. Many shore excursions include tea here; but if you plan to go on your own, call 2 weeks before your cruise for

HAWAIIAN punch

Cruising around the Hawaiian islands allows you to sample several different islands' charms within the space of a few days. In a place where the weather really is perfect all the time, you can learn to surf, go to a luau, snooze on the sand, float in warm water surrounded by rainbow-colored tropical fish, enjoy the local coffee, or check out the native Hawaiian culture, of which the locals are fiercely proud.

By far the most developed of the islands, **Oahu** has some of the best shopping, trendy eateries, and beautiful beaches (including the famous Waikiki Beach). Probably the most important shore excursion here is a visit to Pearl Harbor and USS Missouri (www.nps.gov/vair), site of the 1941 bombing that brought the U.S. into World War II. Honolulu has both America's only royal palace, its oldest Chinatown and the superb Bishop Museum (www.bishopmuseum.org) dedicated to South Pacific culture and history.

The garden isle of **Kauai** is the most spectacular in the chain. There are no opulent shopping malls here, but what Kauai lacks in glitz, it more than makes up for in sheer natural splendor: moody rainforests, majestic cliffs, jagged peaks, emerald valleys, and the breathtaking beaches of the Napali Coast. Shore excursions tend to focus on outdoor adventure, although the historic remnants of sugar cane plantations add a dash of culture.

Maui, also called the Valley Isle, has two ports, industrial Kahului and the far more charming historic town of Lahaina.

Top sights here include the dramatic crater of the Haleakala volcano and the peaceful rainforest of Iao Valley state park; it's the islands' best destination for whale-watch tours, and has a wide range of shopping, from local boutiques to luxury goods.

The island of **Hawaii,** usually called The Big Island, is large enough for more varied terrain, from the waterfalls and rainforests that surround Hilo to the coffee plantations and rugged lava shores of the Kailua-Kona coast. A visit to the Big Island will usually include its volcanoes—snowcapped Mauna Kea, the world's tallest mountain; its neighbor Mauna Loa, is the largest volcano on earth; and still-erupting Kilauea, where you can still see fiery-red lava flow (www.nps.gov/havo). Helicopter tours fly over the crater, or you can hike through the ravaged landscape (often on a free ranger-led tour). Other activities include coffee tastings in the lush Kona plantations, hiking to ancient Hawaiian petroglyphs north of Kailua, horseback riding in the inland plains, or rounds of golf at the island's west coast resorts.

Cruises may also stop at **Lanai** to visit the beautiful beach of Manele Bay, a nature sanctuary, for snorkeling and diving.

The most popular Hawaiian cruises start and end in the islands—which means that travelers fly there and fly home—but it's also possible to sail there from a North American port and fly home. Some longer itineraries even include Hawaii as part of a longer cruise that goes on to French Polynesia.

reservations, and be sure to follow the dress code: no sleeveless shirts, tank tops, short-shorts, or cutoffs.

SMELL THE ROSES Some 13 miles north of downtown Victoria, the world-renowned **Butchart Gardens** (www.butchartgardens.com) features English, Italian, and Japanese gardens, along with water gardens and rose gardens.

FOR NATURE LOVERS Catamaran tours visit the waters off southern Vancouver Island, where passengers can view killer whales, seals, porpoises, and myriad birds.

A SLICE OF HISTORY The stone-turreted **Craigdarroch Castle** (https://thecastle.ca), built in the 1880s, was the home of millionaire Scottish coal magnate Robert Dunsmuir, furnished in opulent Victorian splendor.

SHOPAHOLIC ALERT While handy to the Inner Harbor, the 5-block Government Street promenade is mostly souvenir shops. Worth a stop is Fort Street's Antique Row, renowned for quality British collectibles. In Old Town, the Market Square complex has 35-plus shops, as well as dining and entertainment.

THE MEXICAN RIVIERA & BAJA

The so-called Mexican Riviera—the stretch of port cities and resorts extending from Mazatlán in the north to Acapulco in the south—is one of the classic cruise destinations. Blessed with miles of beaches backed by picturesque mountains, and with a climate that practically guarantees perfect beach weather any day of the year, this is the Caribbean for folks who live on the West Coast.

Spanish conquistadors and missionaries came to this coast in the 16th and 17th centuries to find riches, convert the heathen, and establish ports for sailing to the Far East. But it wasn't until the mid–20th century that other travelers discovered the region. Hollywood stars arrived first, heading south for anonymity and great sport-fishing. Later, the spring-break crowd followed. The region's appeal has broadened since then, offering plenty of family-oriented relaxation and a dash of both history and culture.

Mexican Riviera Ports of Call
ACAPULCO

In Mexico's jet-set days of the 1950s and 1960s, Acapulco was a star destination, with its nearly year-round sunshine, perfectly sculpted bay, and famous cliff divers. The city's glamor has faded since then, as it has been bypassed by newer resort areas, and fewer cruises include it on their itineraries these days. Yet it's still a water-sports playground, with a string of beautiful beaches ringing the bay, all with well-developed facilities. Cruise ships dock west of the Golden Zone hotel strip, a 5-minute walk from Old Acapulco's main plaza, the *zócalo*.

ICONIC SIGHT At the towering cliff of **La Quebrada,** just above downtown, crowds gather daily at 1pm to watch professional high divers plunge from a ledge on the cliff, diving 130 feet into the roaring surf of an inlet that's just 20 feet wide and 12 feet deep. Touristy as it sounds, it's actually low-key and laidback.

LOCAL COLOR Cafes and shops border Acapulco's town square, the *zócalo,* which is shaded by huge mango and rubber trees and cooled by fountains. At its far north end stands the **Nuestra Señora de la Soledad** cathedral with its rounded blue tower domes.

OFF THE BEATEN TRACK From Caleta and Caletilla beaches, south of downtown, brightly painted boats ferry passengers to **Roqueta Island,** a good place to snorkel, sunbathe, hike to a lighthouse, visit a small zoo, or have lunch.

CABO SAN LUCAS

Cabo San Lucas is one big bar-and-beach scene perched at the very tip of the Baja Peninsula, with the Pacific Ocean on one side and the mouth of the Sea of Cortez on the other. (Its quieter twin, San Jose del Cabo, is about 21 miles away, down a resort-lined corridor.) After 1973, when the Transpeninsular Highway finally linked the town to the rest of North America, the Mexican government began pumping in money for new highways, a larger airport, golf courses, and modern marine facilities. There's almost nothing of cultural or historic significance here, beyond the party atmosphere; shore excursions typically include several snorkeling, scuba, sailing, and sport-fishing options (catch-and-release only). A wide walkway wraps most of the way around the harbor, lined with bars, restaurants, and shops.

ICONIC SIGHT At the end of the rugged point that separates the bay from the Pacific, a famous natural arch connects the two seas. At low tide you can walk here from tiny Lovers Beach, accessible only by water taxi from the docks.

FOR NATURE LOVERS Every year from January to March, Cabo San Lucas is visited by humpback, gray, and blue whales. The best, most intimate, and action-packed way to see them is on tours aboard small inflatable craft.

TEE 'EM UP Los Cabos is increasingly gaining a reputation as a golf destination. One of the best is the 18-hole Jack Nicklaus-designed **Ocean Course** west of town at the Cabo del Sol Resort (www.cabodelsol.com).

TOP BEACH **Long Medano Beach** curves west from the harbor, with plentiful shops renting WaveRunners, kayaks, windsurfing boards, and snorkeling gear.

SHOPAHOLICS ALERT Retail opportunities in Cabo range from a large, covered handicrafts market just beyond the tender dock at the harbor to the high-end Puerto Paraíso shops at the west end of the marina.

IXTAPA/ZIHUATANEJO

Located side by side about 158 miles northwest of Acapulco, Ixtapa and Zihuatanejo are the odd couple of twin beach resorts. Ixtapa (Eex-*tah*-pah) is a model of modern infrastructure, services, and luxury resorts, while Zihuatanejo (See-wah-tah-*neh*-hoh, or just "Zihua") is the quintessential rustic Mexican beach village—and, oddly, the place where cruise ships pull in. Only a couple of cruise lines stop here, which is too bad, as it feels much less touristy than some of the other ports of call in this region.

Beaches, scuba diving, deep-sea fishing, and golf are the area's chief draws. The heart of Zihuatanejo is the Paseo del Pescador, a brick waterfront walkway bordering the Municipal Beach with many shops and calm, casual restaurants. A good highway connects Zihua to Ixtapa, where tall hotels line the wide Playa Palmar beach, and resorts offers golf courses and sophisticated restaurants.

TOP BEACH   South of Zihuatanejo, **Playa La Ropa** is a mile-long sweep of sand with calm waters and a great view of the sunset. Palm groves edge the shoreline, and some lovely small hotels and restaurants nestle in the hills.

LOCAL COLOR   Zihuatanejo is a decent place to buy crafts, folk art, and jewelry. The artisans' market on Calle Cinco de Mayo is a good place to start; specialty shops spread inland from the waterfront. Produce and crafts are also sold at the large municipal market sprawling over several blocks off Avenida Benito Juárez (about 5 blocks inland from the waterfront).

OFF THE BEATEN TRACK   Book a ride aboard a trimaran and sail to **Manzanillo Beach,** one of the best snorkeling spots on the bay, where you'll drop anchor for direct access to the water.

MAZATLÁN

Mazatlán—"The Land of the Deer" in the old Nahuatl language—for better or worse made its name as a spring break destination from the 1980s on. Today, however, families and mature vacationers flock here as well, taking advantage of the low prices and 10-plus miles of beaches. Almost straight across the Sea of Cortez from Cabo San Lucas, Mazatlan has Mexico's largest commercial port. Cruise ships dock near the historic downtown area at the south end; the tourist-oriented Zona Dorada (Golden Zone) lies about 4 miles to the north.

ICONIC SIGHT   At the center of Mazatlán's 20-square-block historic district—extensively restored since the early 2000s—pretty little Plazuela Machado is home to the 19th-century Italian-style **Teatro Angela Peralta,** a national historic monument which still hosts concerts. Daytime visitors can tour its sumptuous, jewel-box-like interior.

TOP BEACH   In the Zona Dorado, long **Playa Sábalo** is perhaps the best beach in Mazatlán.

TEE 'EM UP   Mazatlán affords the best golf value in Mexico, with two notable courses open to the public: the 27-hole course at the **El Cid** resorts (http://elcidgolfclub.com), just east of the Zona Dorado; and the 18-hole **Estrella del Mar Golf Club** (www.estrelladelmar.com), across the channel from downtown, designed by Robert Trent Jones, Jr.

OFF THE BEATEN TRACK   Bus tours into the foothills of the Sierra Madre take visitors to 16th-century colonial towns with narrow cobbled streets and old churches.

BOTTOMS UP   Tours of the local **Pacifico Brewery** (www.discoverpacifico. com), which makes one of Mexico's most popular beers, includes tastings and a rooftop bar.

PUERTO VALLARTA

Popularized by Hollywood types in the 1960s, the old silver-mining port of Puerto Vallarta is now a vibrant, bustling resort town with cobblestone streets, red-tiled roofs, and a long art-lined seaside promenade. Cruise ships dock at the Puerto Vallarta Marina, from which you'll probably want a taxi to take you into the historic town, about 3 miles south. Three bridges cross the Rio Cuale river, linking the two sections of downtown. North of the river is the main tourist zone, while south of the river you'll find sidewalk cafes and fine restaurants, plus the town's better beaches. Many shore excursions here will take you up into the nearby foothills of the Sierra Madre, for hiking or jungle adventures.

TOP BEACH   About 6 miles south of town along Highway 200, the public beach **Playa Mismaloya** boasts clear waters and a Hollywood pedigree: This is where the steamy 1964 film *Night of the Iguana,* starring Richard Burton and Ava Gardner, was filmed.

FOR NATURE LOVERS   **Dolphin Discover Vallarta** (www.dolphin discovery.com) offers swims with Pacific bottlenose dolphins or sea lion encounters in a saltwater pool at the Aquaventuras water park in Nueva Vallarta.

LOCAL COLOR   At the corner of Calle Galeana and Calle Morelos, Huichol Collection is the best shop in town for remarkable art by Huichol Indians, descendants of the Aztec who live in the high sierra north and east of Vallarta.

OFF THE BEATEN TRACK   Motor launch tours take visitors out to **Las Caletas,** the palm-lined hideaway cove where director John Huston stayed when he came here in 1964 to film *Night of the Iguana.*

SHOPAHOLICS ALERT   Puerto Vallarta has hundreds of small stores selling everything from fine folk art and modern art to tacky T-shirts, plus tremendous amounts of silver jewelry and sculpture. The municipal market is just north of the Río Cuale; across a plank-and-rope bridge on Río Cuale Island, outdoor stalls sell crafts, gifts, folk art, and clothing. Another popular shopping area is just inland from the *malecón,* around Calle Corona and Calle Morelos.

NEW ENGLAND & EASTERN CANADA

On a cruise in this region, you'll see lots of historical sites, from Newport's Gilded-Age mansions to Québec City's 17th-century Notre-Dame des Victoires Church to the Halifax Maritime Museum's *Titanic* exhibit. But you'll also get a dose of the region's inimitable character: fishing boats piled with

New England & Eastern Canada

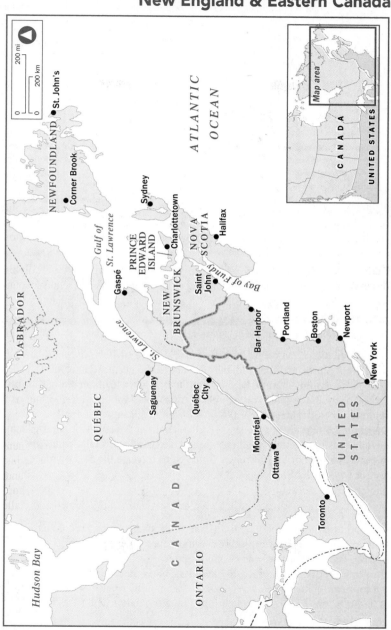

smaller ports: NEW ENGLAND & EASTERN CANADA

A number of smaller ports in New England and eastern Canada host smaller cruise ships. These include:

Block Island, Rhode Island, an 11-square-mile Yankee gem with freshwater ponds, some 17 miles of beach, dramatic seaside bluffs, and a wildlife refuge that covers a full third of the island.

Nantucket, Massachusetts, a classic New England island that was once the world's top whaling hub. Come here for cobblestone streets, old ship captain's mansions, and a yacht-filled harbor.

Martha's Vineyard, Massachusetts, New England's largest island, boasts handsome old towns, lighthouses, white picket fences, and charming ice-cream shops . . . plus lots of summer visitors.

Fall River, Massachusetts, offers some interesting museums, from Battleship Cove's collection of preserved American warships to the quirky Lizzie Borden Museum.

New Bedford, Massachusetts, the 19th century whaling capital of the world, boasts a beautifully restored waterfront area and a great Whaling Museum.

Portland, Maine, draws visitors with its cobblestoned Old Port neighborhood, a revitalized warehouse district stuffed with boutiques and an exciting restaurant scene; there's also fabulous outlet shopping nearby in Freeport.

Sydney, Cape Breton Island, Nova Scotia, wears its Highland Scots heritage proudly, and has a spectacular national park, **Cape Breton Highlands.**

Charlottetown, Prince Edward Island, is prime *Anne of Green Gables* territory, and the island's scenic highways wend past sandstone cliffs, rocky coves, lovely beaches, and fishing villages.

netting, Victorian mansions built by wealthy ship owners, lighthouses atop windswept bluffs, and the cold, hard beauty of the north Atlantic sea.

The classic time to cruise here is in autumn, when a brilliant sea of fall foliage blankets the region. You can also cruise these waters in the spring and summer, aboard either big 3,000-passenger megaships or smaller vessels. Depending on the size of the ship and the length of the cruise, itineraries may include passing through Nantucket Sound, around Cape Cod, or into the Bay of Fundy or Gulf of St. Lawrence. Some ships traverse the St. Lawrence Seaway or the smaller Saguenay River.

Northeast U.S. & Canada Ports of Call
BAR HARBOR, MAINE

Bar Harbor is situated on the mid-Maine coast, overlooking Frenchman's Bay from its perch on the eastern shore of Mount Desert Island. In its 19th-century heyday, Bar Harbor was one of the premier resort areas on the East Coast, attracting Astors, Vanderbilts, Rockefellers, and other wealthy families looking for rustic summer getaways. Today, it's a humbler place, with no shortage of T-shirt shops and ice-cream parlors, but still popular with tourists.

TOP DRAW The lush fir-dotted islands of 35,000-acre **Acadia National Park** (www.acadiainfo.com) are reachable via shore excursion, bicycle, horse-drawn carriage, or kayak.

BONUS   Whale-watching excursions between April and October view the humpbacks, finbacks, minkes, and dolphins that gather in the waters off the island.

TASTE OF THE SEA   Fresh Maine lobster—boiled, baked, broiled, in rolls, in rich bisques and chowders, or any other number of ways—is served at the town's many waterfront restaurants.

HALIFAX, NOVA SCOTIA

Perched midway up the Nova Scotia coast, Halifax is the top port of call for big ships on the New England and Eastern Canada circuit, owing to the city's natural deep-water port, which inevitably led to the town's role as a shipbuilding, naval, and trading center. British settlers in 1621 called the land Nova Scotia ("New Scotland"), and even today bagpipers meet cruise ship when they dock. Pubs and kilt shops continue to trade on the Scottish connection in Halifax's pleasant and easily walkable downtown.

TOP DRAW   On a hill overlooking the town, the star-shaped **Halifax Citadel** is one of Canada's most-visited historic sites, restored to its mid-19th-century appearance, complete with costumed guides, cannon firings, and bagpipers on parade.

BONUS   The **Maritime Museum of the Atlantic** (maritimemuseum. novascotia.ca) and other sites in town commemorate Halifax's leading role in rescuing victims of the *Titanic* shipwreck in 1912.

OFF THE BEATEN TRACK   Just southwest of Halifax, **Lunenburg** is Nova Scotia's main fishing port, with an Old Town that's been restored to its original colonial character.

SMELL THE ROSES   Halifax's famous 17-acre **Public Gardens** (www. halifaxpublicgardens.ca) are the oldest formal Victorian gardens in North America, and look much as they have since the 1870s.

NEWPORT, RHODE ISLAND

In the late 19th century, this Narragansett Bay island became *the* place for America's wealthy aristocrats to spend their summers. From the Vanderbilts to the Astors, all the Gilded Age millionaires had summer mansions (or, as they called them, "cottages") here, each grander than the next. The city is also a major sailing center, hosting more than 40 races each summer and fall. Today, Newport has a beautiful sea, rocky coastline, and a bustling town that's all cobblestone streets, shady trees, cute cafes, and historical buildings, all within a short walk or drive of the downtown area.

TOP DRAW   Ten of Newport's grandest 19th-century mansions are operated by the Preservation Society of Newport County (www.newportmansions. org), which offers several ticket packages that combine admission to different houses. The famed mansions on Bellevue and Ocean avenues are within 1 to 4 miles of the pier; you can take the trolley or a taxi.

BONUS   Newport also boasts a sizeable historic area, with nearly 200 restored 18th- and 19th-century Colonial and Victorian homes and landmarks. Self-guided walking tour maps are available at the tourist office.

The Mediterranean

Bay of Biscay

FRANCE

Genoa

Villefrance-sur-Mer

Nice

Sete

Marseille

Cannes

Toulon

Corsica

Barcelona

Sardinia

SPAIN

Mallorca

Mediterranean Sea

Cartagena

Gibraltar

Malaga

Tangier

MOROCCO

Casablanca

0 — 300 mi
0 — 300 km

STRETCH YOUR LEGS   The 3.5-mile **Cliff Walk** follows Newport's rocky coastline past many of the town's Gilded Age estates, providing a better view of their exteriors than you get from the street.

OFF THE BEATEN TRACK   The **International Tennis Hall of Fame** on Bellevue Avenue (www.tennisfame.com) is one of the few places in North America where you can play on a grass court.

QUÉBEC CITY, QUÉBEC

Perched on a cliff top overlooking the St. Lawrence River, Québec City has a European aura that's rare in North America. Its old city—a tumble of colorful metallic-roof houses clustered around the dominating Château Frontenac—dates back nearly 400 years. The hemisphere's only walled city north of Mexico, it's been named a UNESCO World Heritage Site—one of only three areas so designated in North America.

The **Lower Town** (or **Basse-Ville**) is where the port is; a steep uphill walk or funicular ride will take you to the **Upper Town (Haute-Ville),** the city's historic section.

ICONIC SIGHT The majestic turrets of the **Château Frontenac** hotel (www.fairmont.com/frontenac-quebec) tower over the city from Place d'Armes square in the Haute-Ville. Colonial governors used to live here, and everyone from Winston Churchill to Queen Elizabeth II have visited since. Guided tours are available, or just stop in for a drink or afternoon tea.

STRETCH YOUR LEGS Beginning at the city's star-shaped Citadel fort, the pedestrian promenade la **Terrasse Dufferin** offers magnificent views of the St. Lawrence River, ferries, and the harbor below.

OFF THE BEATEN PATH Bicyclists can ride 8 scenic miles to **Montmorency Falls,** which plummet down a 272-foot cliff into the St. Lawrence River.

SHOPAHOLIC ALERT Québec City has 3 prime shopping areas: the Lower Town's boutique-y Quartier Petit-Champlain and antiques-laden rue St-Paul, and in the old city, avenue Cartier, which has more of a youthful local vibe.

MEDITERRANEAN CRUISES: a slowdown

Due to a number of tragic geopolitical situations, many cruise lines have been suspending, or at least reducing, their presence in the Mediterranean Sea. It's a regrettable state of affairs, because this sun-splashed region, with its world-class cities and spectacular resort towns, has long been one of the world's most rewarding cruise destinations. We sincerely hope the situation will be reversed—and when it has been, we'll restore full coverage of these routes in this book.

Historically, **Western Mediterranean** routes—which often start in Barcelona or Rome—have been more about museums and cultural sites. With ports clustered closer together, they are more likely to offer overnight stays or extended port call—which allow passengers more time on shore to take advantage of the region's spectacular gastronomy.

Meanwhile, ancient civilizations and time in the sun have been the focus of **Eastern Mediterranean** routes. With Istanbul disappearing from cruise itineraries for security reasons, Athens' port, Piraeus, has become the main Eastern Mediterranean gateway, and itineraries spend a lot of time in the Greek islands.

SAINT JOHN, NEW BRUNSWICK

New Brunswick's largest city, Saint John, sits on the Bay of Fundy, at the mouth of the St. John River. Like Halifax, it was an important shipbuilding hub around the turn of the 19th century, and today its deep-water harbor can accommodate the world's largest cruise liners.

Don't expect a picture-postcard harbor town: Saint John is a predominantly industrial city, with large shipping terminals, oil storage facilities, and paper mills. To get past that, take one of the bus-style or horse-trolleys that meet the ships to investigate the restored historic district, known as Trinity Royal.

TOP DRAW Boats head out from the harbor to **Reversing Falls Rapids,** a much-photographed spot where the Bay of Fundy meets the St. John River, creating a massive twice-daily tidal swing of some 2 billion gallons of water, with all the churning rapids and whirlpools you'd expect. It's also reachable via a 3-mile bike and walking trail along the waterfront.

BONUS The bustling centerpiece of the historic district is the still-active **Old City Market,** built in 1876, where you can put together a lunch from various stalls.

BOTTOMS UP Sample Canadian beers like Moosehead at a famous local Irish pub, **O'Leary's** (olearyspub.com), which often has live music.

ocean CROSSINGS

If the romance of open water with nowhere to be appeals to you, then a crossing may just be the cruise for you. There are actually two different kinds of ocean crossings—regular transoceanic voyages by ocean liners and repositioning cruises. Although the Transatlantic Crossing is most famous, a growing number of lines offer Transpacific Crossings from North America to ports in Asia as well.

When it comes to the first type, Cunard is the only line offering regularly scheduled **transatlantic crossings,** the majority of which take place on their enormous flagship, *Queen Mary 2* (p. 240). Typically lasting just 1 week, crossings operate between New York's Brooklyn Cruise Terminal in Red Hook and the Ocean Terminal in Southampton, England; a port city located approximately 90 minutes south of London that served as the embarkation port for the ill-fated RMS *Titanic*. All of the days are "sea days" (there are no ports to visit on this route); the appeal is the luxury of peace and quiet. Days at sea are spent reading—often on deck with a wool blanket and a cup of bouillon, relaxing in the massive Canyon Ranch Spa, or participating in the sophisticated enrichment program built around guest lecturers and visiting academics and notables. Cunard regularly hosts musical guests like the National Symphony Orchestra, James Taylor, and jazz legends as part of their BlueNote Jazz at Sea crossings.

The second type of crossing is a repositioning, when a ship moves from one part of the world where it has spent a season to another—for example, from the Caribbean to the Mediterranean.

Many ships do this twice a year, and while there's still a block of uninterrupted sea days in the middle of the voyage, the sailings tend to offer a few ports on either end of the ocean. For example, westbound repositioning voyages typically stop in Ireland, the Faroe Islands, Iceland, Greenland and Atlantic Canada on their way down to Montreal, Boston or New York.

So just how smooth is the ride? That depends on a great many factors, from the size of the ship, to the stabilizers, to the weather. Spring and summer crossings offer some of the best weather and sea conditions, particularly further south where the weather is warmer, while North Atlantic crossings can get stormy in the winter months. We're huge fans of the transoceanic crossing, and we've had seas ranging from calm-as-glass to hold-onto-your-hat (though the latter is rarer than one might expect).

On the other side of the world, **transpacific** crossings are offered once or twice a year by ships repositioning from Asia to Alaska and the West Coast of North America. One of our favorite itineraries, offered by Holland America and Silversea, departs from Vancouver in the fall bound for Alaska, Unalaska (think Dutch Harbor and *Deadliest Catch*), Russia's Kamchatka Peninsula, and Japan.

If you don't mind being at sea for an extended stretch (indeed, that's the appeal of these voyages), a transoceanic crossing is one of the best cruise values out there, with per diems that are far below typical cruises that span 2 weeks or more. The only exception to this is *Queen Mary 2*, which commands decent fares year-round thanks to her status as the world's only modern ocean liner.

PREPPING FOR THE CRUISE

Packing, budgeting, embarkation…oh my! There are a number of tasks you'll need to accomplish before you can board the boat and start to relax. Here's a quick rundown with our (hopefully) helpful tips, plus some info on shipboard customs, fees and scheduling that you'll want to know well before your trip.

PACKING FOR YOUR CRUISE

The must-haves on any cruise include a raincoat, an umbrella, and comfortable walking shoes that you don't mind getting wet. A swimsuit is also a must if your ship has a pool or hot. You'll also want to pack enough outfits for daytime sightseeing and dinners in the evening.

Packing for Formal, Informal & Casual Events

Some people agonize over what to pack for a cruise, but there's no reason to fret. Except for the addition of a formal night or two, a cruise vacation is really no different from any resort vacation. And in some cases, it's much more casual so don't feel you have to go out and buy "cruise wear." Sweatshirts, jeans, and jogging outfits are the norm during the day. Dinner is dress-up time on most ships, but certainly not on all (and except on smaller vessels, there's always somewhere you can just pick up a quick bite in shorts and a t-shirt). The small adventure-type ships are all casual, all the time.

Generally, ships describe proper dinner attire as **formal, informal,** or **semiformal** (the latter two terms mean the same thing in this case), **smart casual,** or **casual.** There are usually either 2 formal nights and 2 informal (or semiformal) nights during a week-long cruise or 2 formal nights and the rest "smart casual" or all smart casual/country club casual; check with your line for specifics. Although the term has gotten somewhat more relaxed in recent years, **formal** generally means a dark suit with tie for men (some still wear a tuxedo) and a nice cocktail dress, long dress, or dressy

5

Many ships offer dry-cleaning and laundry services—for a fee, of course. Look for deals where they will wash whatever you can squeeze into a laundry bag for a set price, usually around $25. Other lines offer either free or coin-operated laundry facilities (the latter requiring quarters or tokens that you can get at the reception desk). Using these services can save you a lot of packing, especially on long itineraries. Check the line's website for details on what's available on your particular ship before you start filling your suitcase. After all, bringing less clothing will leave more room for any souvenirs you may choose to bring home.

pantsuit for women. **Informal** (or **semiformal**) is a jacket, tie, and dress slacks, or a light suit, for men, and a dress, skirt and blouse, or pants outfit for women (the ubiquitous little black dress is appropriate here).

Smart casual or **country club casual** is pretty much the same as informal without the tie. **Casual** at dinner means a sports shirt or open-collar dress shirt with slacks for men (some will also wear a jacket), and a casual dress, pants outfit, or skirt and blouse for women. In other words, for casual nights, dress as you would to go out to dinner at a midrange restaurant.

Just take the entire thing with a grain of salt: In all dress code situations, don't be surprised if there are some people on board who ignore the suggested dress code altogether.

Preparing for the Weather

Here's a quick rundown of the major cruise areas and what types of weather you'll need to dress for:

- **The Caribbean** tends to be sunny and warm year-round.
- **Europe**'s seasons often mirror the weather on our East Coast, with cooler winters, temperate spring and fall seasons, and hot summers.
- **Alaska**'s weather is sometime extreme and always unpredictable: During a summertime cruise, you may experience temperature variations from the 40s to the 80s or even low 90s Fahrenheit (single digits to low 30s Celsius). The days will be long, with the sun all but refusing to set, especially in the more northern ports, and people will be energized by the extra daylight hours. You'll likely encounter some rain, and you're less likely to encounter snow, but it is still a possibility, especially in the spring. Dressing in layers is smart in this part of the world.
- **Asia**'s weather swings wildly, too. You'll want to know if monsoon season will be a factor before you pick out your clothing (and it's such a large region we can't give seasons here). Light, long sleeved shirts can actually be your friend in Asia, as it protects you from both the sun and potential bug bites.

MONEY MATTERS

While there are plenty of onboard expenses to contend with (at least on main-stream lines), these charges are made easier thanks to the fact that cruises operate on a "cashless" basis; all expenses are charged to your onboard account and settled at the end of the voyage, either by cash or credit card.

When you check in for a large-ship cruise, either at the terminal or online, the cruise line will ask for a major credit card to charge your onboard expenses. They will typically preauthorize your account (through your credit card company) for $50 to $70 per person per day, an amount that is refunded if you don't spend it. This will, however, reduce your available credit on your credit card, so ensure you have sufficient cushion for extra purchases.

On some ships, you must report to the purser's office once on board to establish your **onboard credit account.** On all cruises, you also have the option of paying your account with credit or cash. If you want to establish your onboard account using **cash only,** you'll be asked to put down an initial deposit, usually between $250 to $350 per person for a 1-week sailing. You should let the cruise line know as early as possible if you wish to pay with cash (some lines like to know at the time you make your cruise reservations).

Some lines will now let you establish your onboard account by linking it directly to your **debit card,** but we don't recommend that course of action. Why? The same hold that would be placed on a credit card is placed on a debit card, but this time, it's on your checking account—and numerous preauthorizations can eat that up fast. It's refunded to you if you don't use it all, but that process can take up to 30 days depending on your financial institution.

Your keycard acts as your onboard charge card for the length of your cruise (along with opening your stateroom door). It will work for most everything bought on board, except for any gambling you do in the casino. On most ships, you can even put your crew tips on your credit card, though on some you're expected to use cash (see p. 104 for more on tipping).

On most small ships, things aren't so formal. Because there are so few passengers, and because the only places to spend money aboard are at the bar and the small gift counters, the staff will just mark down your purchases and you'll settle your account at the end of the week.

In all cases, you will need some cash on hand for port stops: to pay for cabs, make small purchases, buy sodas and snacks, tip your tour guides, and so on. Having bills smaller than $20 is useful for these purposes (especially some $1 bills). Some ships have their own ATMs aboard, most often located, not surprisingly, in the casino or adjacent to the Guest Relations desk. These give out U.S. dollars, but typically involve a hefty convenience fee.

Tip: Guests from countries other than the United States should note that many cruise lines provide the option to be billed in U.S. Dollars or in their native currency. It's a good policy to always state you want your onboard account to be charged in USD. Cruise lines use a financial service to do this,

THE COST OF COMMON CRUISE INCIDENTALS	U.S.$
Alternative dining (service charge)	10.00–75.00
Babysitting (per hour)	
Group	6.00–8.00
Private	15.00–19.00
Beverages	
Beer (domestic/imported)	3.50–6.00
Latte	3.25–4.25
Mineral water	2.00–3.95
Mixed drink (more for fine liquors)	5.95–15.00
Soft drink	2.50–4.00
Wine with dinner (per bottle)	15.00–300.00
Cruise-line-logo souvenirs	3.00–60.00
Internet access (per minute)	0.40–0.75
Haircuts	
Men's	29.00–45.00
Women's	52.00–79.00
Laundry/dry cleaning (per item)	2.00–10.00
Massage (50 min.)	119.00–169.00
Phone calls (per minute)	4.95–12.00
Photos	9.95–18.00

which charges you a "conversion fee" on top of the fees your bank will be charging you. It's like paying a tax on a tax, and not generally worth it.

It's recommended that you not leave large amounts of cash in your room. All ships have some sort of safes available, either in-room or at the purser's desk, and passengers are wise to use them. You should also store your plane ticket and passport or ID papers there. Many cruise ships even have safes large enough to hold a small laptop computer, or an iPad.

Budgeting

Cruises, with the exception of a few luxury lines, are not all inclusive. Many pay extra for shore excursions (an average of $600 per person for a weeklong cruise) and tips ($11–$13 per passenger per day). You will also want to budget in the many tempting onboard extras: bar drinks, dry cleaning, phone calls, massage and other spa services, salon services, babysitting, photos taken by the ship's photographer, wine at dinner, souvenirs, and costs for any other special splurges your particular ship might offer (items at the cigar bars, time on the golf simulator, and so on).

WHAT SHOULD YOU DO before you board?

Use this handy checklist for what to do before you leave home to ensure smooth sailing on your cruise.

PLAN YOUR PORT TIME

Regardless of whether you intend to book your sightseeing through the cruise line or do it on your own, you want to figure out what you want to see well in advance and make the necessary arrangements. See p. 102 for a list of outside companies that handle these arrangements, sometimes at a lesser cost. If you do decide to book tours through your cruise line, you will find plenty of details on their website about your options. Many lines allow you to book there as well. The timing varies, though: Some let you book months out, while others are mere weeks. (And the closing dates vary, too.) Just be warned: Your first choice could sell out before you board if you don't plan in advance.

RESERVE TABLES AT SPECIALTY RESTAURANTS

The most popular times to dine in specialty restaurants are in the middle of the dinner service, especially on sea days, as well as the least formal nights on the sailing. On some sailings specialty restaurants book completely before embarkation day, so it's important to think ahead. Most cruise lines will let you make advance reservations for specialty restaurants by using their online cruise personalizers. If that's not available make your reservations for specialty restaurants for the voyage on embarkation day.

BOOK SPA TREATMENTS

Sea days during late morning and early afternoon are the most popular times to get spa treatments, so if you want a treatment during that time you want to book as early as the line permits. Again, you should be able to do this online using the cruise line's voyage personalizer, or by visiting the spa immediately once you're on board. Because sea days are so busy, keep in mind that shipboard spas regularly offer "Port Day Specials" that can be substantially discounted.

BRING EVERYTHING YOU NEED IN YOUR CARRY-ON BAGS

When you pack your carry-on for your flight, make sure that you have everything you need for the first day of the cruise—including medication, a change of clothing and your swimsuit—in case the airline or cruise line delays delivery of your luggage.

If **Internet access** is important to you, you'll certainly need to budget for it. Once horrifyingly slow and expensive, shipboard Internet has improved substantially in the last decade. Though it continues to be slower than land-based connections, it's positively zippy compared with the Internet that first popped up aboard Norwegian Cruise Line's *Norwegian Sky* back in 1999. While some cruise lines still bill Internet on a per-minute basis, with packages averaging anywhere between $40 and $250, that is gradually beginning to change. Carnival is leading the way with reasonably priced packages that are based on your usage habits; a week of connecting to e-mail, Facebook, and Twitter will only run you $5 per day for the Social package. The line's top-end "Premium," at $25 per day, provides Internet fast enough to Skype with family members back home. A few lines—like Viking Cruises—provide free Internet to all guests.

Keep careful track of your onboard expenses to avoid an unpleasant surprise at the end of your cruise. Many ships have interactive television systems that will display a current readout of your bill; on those that don't, a quick trip down to the Guest Relations desk is all it takes to get a current printout of your onboard account. It's a good idea to do this at least midway through your cruise; while it's rare, mistakes do happen (we were once billed for a very expensive bottle of champagne that we never ordered). Sadly, more often than not, all of our onboard expenses are usually just that: ours.

On big ships, a final bill will be slipped under your door on the last night of your cruise. If everything is okay and you're paying by credit card, you don't have to do anything but keep the copy. If there's a problem on the bill, or if you are paying by cash or personal check, you will have to go down to the purser's or guest-relations desk and wait in what will likely be a very long line. On small ships, you usually settle up directly with the purser on the last day of the cruise.

DOCUMENTS

About 1 month (and no later than 1 week) before your cruise, you should receive in the mail, and/or downloadable as online files, your cruise documents, including airline tickets (if you purchased them from the cruise line), a boarding document with your cabin and dining choices on it, boarding forms to fill out, luggage tags, and your prearranged bus-transfer vouchers from the airport to the port (if applicable).

Also included will likely be a description of shore excursions available for purchase either on board or, in some cases, in advance, as well as additional materials detailing things you need to know before you sail. Most lines also now allow you to download this information online.

All this information is important. Read it carefully. Make sure that your cabin category and dining preference are as you requested, and also check your airline tickets to make sure everything checks out in terms of flights and arrival times. Make sure that there is enough time to arrive at the port no later than 2 hours before departure time, and preferably a lot earlier; many ports now require that all guests be on board the vessel no later than 60 minutes prior to departure.

Be sure to carry these documents in your carry-on rather than in your luggage, since you can't board without them.

Check-In

A Department of Homeland Security regulation requires cruise ships to deliver a final passenger manifest at least an hour before sailing. Most cruise lines are now requiring passengers to check in at least 1½ hours before sailing and to complete a check-in form online (with your name, address, and passport or other ID information) at least 3 days prior to sailing. If you do not complete the form, you may be required to show up at least 3 hours before your sailing so that the cruise line has time to prepare and transmit your information. If you don't comply, you may be denied boarding (with no refund).

Passports & Identification

You are required to have a valid passport (whereas a photo ID and birth certificate used to suffice) for all cruises that visit foreign ports. On cruises that begin and end in the same port in the U.S., a government-issued birth certificate and government-issued photo ID (such as a driver's license) will suffice—though cruise lines recommend a passport because if for some reason you need to leave the cruise early from non-U.S. soil you may be in for a big hassle.

If you are not a U.S. citizen but live in the United States, you will have to carry your alien registration card and passport.

U.S. citizens travelling to Canadian ports of embarkation will require a valid passport. They should also be aware that offences like drunk-driving are considered criminal offenses in Canada, and those with a DUI or almost any alcohol-related offence on their record—no matter how old—could be turned away at the border.

EMBARKATION

Before you leave for the airport, attach to each of your bags one of the luggage tags sent by the cruise line, or one of the do-it-yourself ones the cruise line sent for you to print off at home. Make sure that you correctly fill in the tags with your departure date, port, cabin number, and so forth. You can find all this info in your cruise documents. Put a luggage tag on your carry-on as well, but keep your carry-on with you; luggage can take several hours to reach your cabin.

Airport Arrival

If you booked your air travel and/or transfers with the cruise line, you should see a cruise-line representative holding a card with the name of the line either when you get off the plane or at the baggage area. Check in with this person. If you are on a pre-cruise package, the details of what to do at the airport will be described in the cruise line's brochure.

When you arrive at your gateway airport, you will be asked by a cruise line representative to identify your luggage, which will then go straight to the ship for delivery to your cabin. It won't necessarily go in the same bus as you, and it may not (almost certainly will not) be waiting for you when you board, but it will arrive eventually, have no fear.

You'll have to turn over to the bus driver the transportation voucher you received with your cruise documents, so do have it handy.

If you're flying independent of the cruise line, claim your luggage at the baggage area and proceed to the pier by cab, train or whatever other transportation you have arranged. And again, remember to put the luggage tags provided by the cruise line on your bags at this point if you haven't already, because when you get to the pier your bags will be taken from you by a porter for loading onto the ship. The porter who takes your bags may expect a tip of $1 per bag (some will be more aggressive than others in asking for it).

Where's My Luggage?

Don't panic if your bags aren't in your cabin when you arrive: Getting all the bags on board is a rather slow process—on big ships, as many as 6,000 bags need to be loaded and distributed. If it's close to sailing time and you're concerned, call guest relations or the purser's office. If your luggage really is lost rather than just late, the cruise line's customer-relations folks will track it down and arrange for it to be delivered to the ship's first port of call.

WHAT TO DO IF YOUR FLIGHT IS DELAYED

First of all, tell the airline personnel at the airport that you are a cruise passenger and that you're sailing that day. They may be able to put you on a different flight. Second, call the cruise line to advise them of your delay—your cruise documents should include an emergency delay number. Keep in mind that you may not be the only person delayed, and the line just may hold the ship until your arrival. Delays due to weather and unexpected mechanical issues are why we strongly recommend flying in to your port of embarkation at least 1 day prior to your cruise.

WHAT TO DO IF YOU MISS THE BOAT

Don't panic. Go directly to the cruise line's port agent at the pier (the name, phone number, and address of the port agent should be listed in your cruise documents). You may be put up in a hotel for the night—at your expense (unless you booked air through the cruise line)—and provided with other transportation to the next port of call. If you booked your flight on your own, you will likely be charged for this service. Keep in mind that on some itineraries (like transatlantic crossings or cruises to Antarctica), joining the ship late simply isn't possible.

At the Pier

Most ships start embarkation in the early afternoon and depart between 4 and 6pm. You will not be able to board the ship before the scheduled embarkation time, usually about 3 or 4 hours before sailing, and even then it's likely that you'll have to wait in line; unless, that is, you're sailing on a small ship carrying very few passengers.

If you've booked a suite, you may get priority boarding at a special desk. Special-needs passengers may also be processed separately. Ship personnel will check your boarding tickets and ID and collect any documents you've been sent to fill out in advance. You will then be given a boarding card and your cabin key. (On some lines, your key may be waiting in your cabin.)

You have up to 90 minutes before departure to board, but there are some advantages to boarding earlier, like getting first dibs on spa-treatment times. Plus, if you're early enough, you can eat lunch on the ship. Conversely, if you hate lines you might want to hold off until the mad rush has evaporated; we've had decent luck checking in for our cruise about 3 hours before departure.

STAYING IN TOUCH

Using Your Cell Phone at Sea

Before you leave home, check with your cell phone plan provider to see what roaming packages they offer, both to travelers to your region in general and cruisers specifically. Some wireless providers have developed a special cruise ship service plan, with lower rates than regular roaming rates, but you must sign up for the plan before you depart. Your carrier's website should have pricing and phone compatibility information.

If your carrier does not offer a special plan for cruisers, or you don't want to sign up for it, consider ordering a data, messaging, or calling plan for your region. Data plans cost around $25 for 100MB, and text messages cost as much as 50 cents per text. Phone calls, at as much as $2.50 per minute, are still the most expensive way to communicate with friends and family back home—though some mobile providers now offer unlimited calling packages for a small preset fee for cruisers abroad.

If you only plan to use the Internet on your smartphone, turn off the phone's data usage and roaming options so that you will not incur roaming fees, and plan to connect only to the ship's Wi-Fi, or a public Wi-Fi network ashore. Then, purchase a shipboard Wi-Fi package. Rates generally range from 40¢ to 75¢ per minute. It is generally cheaper if you buy a set plan—for instance, paying in advance for 4 hours of usage throughout your cruise (plans vary by line, so check with your ship's Internet cafe to see what plans are available; special discounts may be offered if you sign up the first day of your cruise).

Royal Caribbean now offers fast, inexpensive Wi-Fi on their newer ships, and Viking Ocean Cruises offers complimentary Wi-Fi on their ships. Regent Seven Seas Cruises also offers complimentary Wi-Fi, but only to cruisers in certain suite-level cabins. Other lines, including Holland America, have been offering discount packages toward the end of the cruise as well. Celebrity even offers the ability to pre-purchase an Internet package before you leave home.

On the small ship front, Wi-Fi isn't necessarily guaranteed. However, you can certainly get Wi-Fi at everything from Starbucks to hotel lobbies to major shopping malls when you're in port.

If you don't have a smartphone and you want to get online in port, the port cities you'll be visiting are likely to have Wi-Fi spots you can access, either at a library or in a hotel lobby.

Charge It!

If you are bringing a bunch of electronic gadgets—cellphones, cameras that need recharging, an iPad, a laptop—consider packing a power strip. Most cabins don't have more than two electrical outlets.

Note that cruise lines have begun to check the condition of power strips before allowing their use; bring along a new one *without* a surge protector to ensure it doesn't get confiscated.

Religious services depend, of course, on the ship and the clergy on board. Most ships have a nondenominational service on Sunday and a Friday-night Jewish Sabbath service, usually run by a passenger. On Jewish and Christian holidays, clergy are typically on board large ships to lead services, which are usually held in the library or conference room. If you are looking for a daily Catholic Mass, you may have to visit churches at the ports.

For those who like to stay constantly connected on social media, share a lot of photos in real time, or stream video of TV shows or movies, the slow and often expensive Wi-Fi at sea can be a problem. If you're more tech savvy, you can use short code—short phone numbers that allow you to post your messages to Twitter or Facebook by text.

Sending Mail

If you want to send mail from the ship, the purser's office should have postage stamps and a mailbox. We especially like sending mail from the Cunard's *Queen Mary 2,* which offers an English-style mailbox with outgoing mail stamped, "Posted On Board—*Queen Mary 2*—Transatlantic Crossing."

VISITING PORTS OF CALL

Cruise lines carefully arrange their itineraries to visit places that have a little something for everyone, whether your interest is nature, museum hopping, barhopping, or no hopping at all. You can take in the location's ambience and natural beauty, learn about the local culture and history, eat local foods, and enjoy sports activities. And you'll have the opportunity to shop to your heart's content.

Shore Excursions

When the ship gets into port, you'll have the choice of going on a shore excursion organized by the cruise line or going off on your own. The shore excursions are designed to help you make the most of your limited time at each port of call, to get you to the top natural or historical attractions, and to make sure you get back to the ship on time. They also will keep you in the crowds you've been in on board the ship, which is kismet for some and unpleasant for others. And shore excursions are a big moneymaking area for the cruise line, adding a hefty sum to your vacation costs. Whether you choose to take one of these prearranged sightseeing trips is a matter of both personal preference and budgetary concerns; you should in no way feel that you must do an excursion in every, or any, port.

At most ports, the cruise lines have guided tours to the top sights, usually by bus. The most worthwhile tours take you outside the downtown area or include a dance or music performance, or a crafts demonstration (or

The Essentials: Don't Leave the Ship Without 'Em

You must bring your ship boarding pass (or shipboard ID) with you when you disembark or you will have trouble getting back on board. (You probably have to show it as you leave the ship anyway, so forgetting it will be hard.) You may also be required to show a photo ID (such as your passport or driver's license). The ship will let you know if you have to carry this as well. And don't forget to bring a little cash—although your ship operates on a cashless system, the ports do not. Many passengers get so used to carrying no cash or credit cards while aboard the ship that they forget them when going ashore.

Watch the Clock

If you're going off on your own, whether on foot or on one of the alternate tours or transportation options that we've listed, remember to be very careful about timing. You're generally required to be back at the dock at least a half-hour before the ship's scheduled departure. Passengers running late on one of the line's shore excursions needn't worry: If an excursion runs late, the ship accepts responsibility and won't leave without the late passengers.

If you're on your own, however, and miss the boat, immediately contact the cruise-line representative at the port. (Most lines list phone numbers and addresses for their port agent at each stop in the newsletter delivered to your cabin daily; be sure to take it ashore if you are going any distance from the ship!) You'll probably be able to catch your ship at the next port of call, but you'll have to pay your own way to get there.

---

sometimes all the above). There's a guide on each bus, and the excursion price includes all incidental admission costs. The commentary is sometimes hokey, other times educational, and occasionally barely there at all, especially in parts of the world where language barriers are an issue.

In some ports, it's easy to explore the downtown area on your own. There are advantages to independent exploration: Walking around is often the best way to see the sights, and you can plan your itinerary to steer clear of the crowds. In some ports, however, there's not much within walking distance of the docks. Sometimes the line will offer a shuttle bus, or cruisers can usually share a taxi or take some form of transportation into town. In cases where the sites are extremely far from the port, the cruise line's excursion program may be your best option.

That said, in some cases you can lock in the exact same tour your cruise line is selling you (with the exact same outfitter) at a lower price by cutting out the middleman (the line) and going straight to the source (the outfitter). Sites like **Viator.com, ShoreTrips.com,** and **CruisingExcursions.com** can provide a superb overview of different tour options in selected ports of call, as can a quick Internet search. Want to go cycling to the ghost town of Dyea from Skagway? Type in "Skagway Cycle Tours" and you're set.

If you'd like to track down the operators that cruise lines use, the secret is to examine in great detail the tour you're interested in on your cruise line's website, noting the wording of the description and even the photos you find there, and then comparing that to the descriptions and photos of tour options you'll find on the websites of port towns. In some cases, you'll find an exact match. Keep in mind that some small port towns might have only one operator offering such activities as hiking and biking tours and the like, so no matter where you book you're probably going to end up with the same folks.

A fairly new trend in the world of cruising is **private shore excursions.** Here, the cruise line arranges a guide just for you and others you want to invite along. It's the best of both worlds—you get to see what you want to see with an experienced guide—but, naturally, these tours are pricey, easily running into the hundreds of dollars. Still, some lines charge per vehicle—not per person—so if you're splitting the cost six ways, this can actually be advantageous.

Regular shore excursions usually range in price from about $40 to $99 for a bus tour to $229 and up for elaborate trips. Prices can also vary by destination; Alaska has some of the most expensive shore excursions around, thanks to a proliferation of flightseeing and other grand-scale experiential tours. You may be in port long enough to book more than one option or take an excursion and still have several hours to explore the port on your own. You may well find that you want to do a prearranged shore excursion at one port and be on your own at the next.

The best way to decide which shore excursions you want to take is to do some research in advance of your trip. Your cruise line will send you a booklet listing its shore excursions with your cruise tickets; or a link for an online site with this information. You can compare and contrast. Just remember: The most popular excursions sell out fast. For that reason, if you're planning to travel with the cruise line, you're best off booking your shore excursions online before your cruise or at least by the first or second day of your voyage.

Arriving in Port

You might think that when the ship docks right at the pier, you can walk right off, but you can't. Before the gangway is open to disembarking passengers, lots of papers must be signed and local authorities must give their clearance, a process that can take as long as 2 hours. Don't even bother going to the gangplank until you hear an announcement saying the ship has been cleared.

If your ship anchors rather than docks, you will go ashore in a small boat called a launch or tender, which ties up next to your ship and shuttles passengers back and forth all day. Getting on the tender may require a helping hand from crew members, and the waves may keep the tender swaying, sometimes requiring passengers literally to jump to board. The tenders, by the way, are usually part of the ship's ample complement of lifeboats lowered into the water for the day in port.

To make life easier when tendering, try to not be the first off the ship. Like standard disembarkation pierside, you'll save yourself a lot of pushing, shoving and maddening frustration if you just kick back and have that second cappuccino; most ships will run tender services from ship-to-shore throughout the day. Guests on shore excursions purchased through the ship typically get tendering priority, particularly if they are on a tour that departs soon after the ship drops anchor. *Tip:* If you're going to participate in a ship-sponsored excursion, tender ports are a great time to do so. These ports are typically annotated in some way in the cruise line's brochure (and your own personal schedule), so you shouldn't face any nasty surprises. Plus, tender ports are a great chance to get some photos of your ship at anchor on the deep blue sea.

Whether the ship is docked or anchored, you are in no way required to get off at every port of call. The ship's restaurants will remain open, and there will still be activities on offer throughout the day, though usually on a limited basis. On bigger ships, staying on board in ports you've already been to can have an added advantage: The ship is virtually yours to enjoy, free of the typical crowds.

TIPPING, PACKING & OTHER END-OF-CRUISE CONCERNS

A few hints that should save you time and aggravation at the end of your cruise:

Tips on Tipping

Tipping is a subject that some people find confusing. First, let's establish that you are expected on most ships (with the exception of all-inclusive lines that include gratuities) to tip the crew at the end of the cruise—in particular, your cabin steward, server, and bus person—and *not* to tip is bad form. Recently, lines including Carnival, Holland America, Norwegian Cruise Line, and Princess have made the process easier, adopting a system whereby they automatically add tips of $12 to $16 per passenger, per day to your shipboard account. Daily gratuity amounts are often on the high side of that scale for guests staying in the ship's top-of-the-line suites.

You can visit the purser's office and ask to increase or decrease the amount, depending on your opinion of the service you received. Other lines may suggest that you tip in cash, but some also allow you to tip via your shipboard account.

If there is no automatic tip, the cruise line will give suggested tip amounts in the daily bulletin and in the cruise director's debarkation briefing, but these are just suggestions—you can tip more or less, at your own discretion. Keep in mind, though, that stewards, servers, and bus persons are often extremely underpaid and that their salaries are largely dependent on tips. Many of these crew members support families back home on their earnings.

The minimum tip you should consider is $4 per passenger per day for your room steward and your waiter, and $3 per passenger per day for your bus person. That's a total of up to $77 per passenger for a 7-night cruise (you don't have to include debarkation day). You should also consider leaving about half

Tipping, Packing & More

PREPPING FOR THE CRUISE

of these amounts on behalf of child passengers 12 and under. Of course, you can always tip more for good service. You'll also be encouraged to tip the dining room maître d', the headwaiter, and other better salaried employees. Whether to tip these folks is your decision. If you have a cabin with butler service, tip the butler about $5 per person per day, provided he has been visible throughout your cruise (if he hasn't, reduce that amount). The captain and his officers should not be tipped—it'd be like tipping your doctor.

Regent Seven Seas Cruises and Silversea Cruises include tips in the cruise fare, although some people choose to tip key personnel anyway—it's really up to you. Small-ship lines have their own suggested tipping guidelines.

If you have spa or beauty treatments, you can tip at the time of service (just add it to your ship account; be aware some ships add 15% automatically). Most ships now automatically add a gratuity to bar tabs, but if not, you can hand a bartender a buck if you like. Otherwise, tips are usually given on the last night of your cruise. On some ships (especially small ships), you may be asked to submit your tips in a single sum that the crew will divide among itself after the cruise, but generally, you reward people individually, usually in little preprinted envelopes that the ship distributes.

If a staff member is particularly great, a written letter to a superior is always good form and may earn that person an employee-of-the-month honor, and maybe even a bonus.

Settling Your Shipboard Account

On big ships, your shipboard account will close just before the end of your cruise, but before that time, you will receive a preliminary bill in your cabin. If you are using a credit card, just make sure the charges are correct; your credit card will be charged automatically as part of the end-of-cruise procedures. If there is a problem, you will have to go to the purser's office, where you will likely encounter long lines. If you're paying by cash, you'll be asked to settle your account during the day or night before you leave the ship. This will also require that you go to the purser's office. A final invoice will be delivered to your room before departure.

On small ships, the procedure will be simpler. Often you can just mosey over to the purser's desk on the last evening, check to see that the bill they give you looks right, and sign your name.

Luggage Procedures

With thousands of suitcases to deal with, big ships have established the routine of requiring guests to pack the night before they disembark if they don't want to carry their bags off the ship themselves. You will be asked to leave your bags (except for your carry-ons) in the hallway before you retire for the night—usually by midnight. The bags will be picked up overnight and placed in the cruise terminal before passengers are allowed to disembark. It's important to make sure that your bags are tagged with the luggage tags given you by the cruise line toward the end of your cruise. These are not the same tags you arrived with; rather, they're color-coded to indicate deck number and debarkation order—the order in which they'll likely be arranged on the dock. If you need more tags, alert your cabin steward or the purser's staff. You may also have the option of carrying your own bags off if they aren't too heavy.

If you booked your air travel through the cruise line, you may be able to check your luggage for your flight at the cruise terminal (or even on board the ship for a small fee). Make sure you receive your luggage claim checks. You may even be able to get your flight boarding passes at the cruise terminal, saving you a wait in line at the airport. A bus will then take you to the airport.

Debarkation

You won't be able to get off the ship until it is cleared by Customs and other authorities, a process that usually takes 90 minutes or more. It's important to note that disembarkation *rarely* ever starts at the published arrival time shown in the brochure; if it says you're arriving into port at 7am, it literally means the ship will be tying her lines up at 7am.

If you're planning to fly home on the day of disembarkation, make sure you give yourself plenty of time to get off the ship, go through customs procedures, collect your luggage, and make your way to the airport. In some ports, like Galveston, the nearest airport is a good 70-minute drive away. In general, we don't recommend flying out any earlier than noon on the day of disembarkation; it's just not worth the stress.

In most cases, you'll be asked to vacate your cabin by 8am and wait in one of the ship's lounges. If you have a flight home on the same day, you will disembark based on your flight departure time. Passengers with mobility problems, and those who booked suites are also often treated to early embarkation. Guests who will be staying on at the port and have no pressing arrangements will typically leave last, unless they're on a ship-sponsored tour.

Customs & Immigration

If your cruise visits foreign ports, you'll have to clear Customs and Immigration, which usually means that your name goes on a list that is reviewed by authorities. You must fill out a Customs declaration form, and you may be required to show your passport. After that, you'll collect your luggage and exit the terminal.

Note that not all ports have the same requirements; the state of Texas charges cruisers disembarking in any Texan port levies on cigarettes and alcohol, regardless of nationality or home state. You'll need cash on hand to pay for that.

THE MAINSTREAM LINES

Here's where the rudder hits the road: It's time to choose the ship that will be your home away from home on vacation. We'll start with the cruise lines you know even if you've never set foot on one. They're the ones with the catchy TV spots, glossy magazine spreads, and omnipresent website banner ads that make cruises seem like sheer paradise—and for many people, they really are.

Today's mainstream ships are part theme park, part shopping mall, and part faux downtown entertainment and dining district, all packaged in a sleek hull with an oceanview resort perched on top. The biggest are really big: 14 stories tall, 1,000 feet long, with cabin space for between 2,000 and 5,000-plus passengers and a couple of thousand crewmembers. Most of the mainstream lines have spent the past 15 years pumping billions into ever-newer, bigger, and fancier ships. The newer the ship, the more whoopee you can expect: open-air boardwalk districts, bowling alleys, water parks, ice-skating rinks, outdoor movie theaters, surfing machines, giant spas, rock-climbing walls, full-size basketball courts, and virtual-reality golf, plus classics like hot tubs, theaters, water slides, and bars, bars, bars.

The ships featured in this chapter vary in size, age, and amenities, but they share the common thread of having scads of activities and entertainment. And that includes Azamara (see p. 108) a line that might have just as easily been in our "Luxury" chapter (see p. 227).

HOW TO USE THESE REVIEWS

Each cruise line's review begins with an overview of the line in general and a short summation of the kind of cruise experience you can expect to have aboard that line. The text that follows fleshes out the review, providing all the details you need to get a feel for what kind of vacation the cruise line will provide.

We then divided the ships into "classes" of similar vessels. In a chart at the top, you'll see the average minimum amount a cruise will cost per day, which we've labeled as the "Avg. Starting Per

Diem." We arrived at this number by averaging the prices posted by major cruise travel agencies for the lowest cabin category in high season (Christmas week usually), low season and mid-season. Please note that these numbers are not set in stone: Sometimes you'll pay significantly less, and sometimes the price will be considerably higher than what we've posted here.

Below the price is information about the ships being discussed: how many passengers they tend to carry, what the passenger to staff ration is, and more. In the case of classes with several ships, the first number will represent the smallest ship and the second number the largest (we've been very careful to only group together ships that have very similar amenities and sizes).

People feel very strongly about ships. For centuries mariners have imbued their vessels with human personalities, usually referring to an individual ship as "her." It's a fact that people bond with the ships aboard which they sail. They find themselves in the gift shop loading up on T-shirts with the ship's name emblazoned on the front. We know people who have sailed the same ship a dozen times or more and feel as warmly about it as their summer cottage. That's why, when looking at the reviews, you want to look for a ship that says "you."

AZAMARA CLUB CRUISES

www.azamaraclubcruises.com. ℂ **877/999-9553.**

Pros

o **Overnight Stays:** Azamara takes pride in offering numerous overnight (and, in some cases, multi-night) port calls, an unusual itinerary for a mainstream line. This allows guests time to spend more time on shore without worrying about dashing back to the ship before it leaves port.

o **AzAmazing Evenings:** The line's nighttime excursions are winners, offering unique, exclusive experiences in some of the world's best ports of call from Barcelona to Bangkok.

o **More Inclusive:** Rates include wine, beer and cocktails, and gratuities, as well as self-service laundry and shuttle buses in out-of-the-way docking locations to take you to town.

o **Swell Ships:** These ships, once part of the late, great Renaissance cruise line, offer a slice of classic cruising, with elegant public rooms that have only been enhanced under Azamara's leadership.

Cons

o **Small Pools:** The pools and pool decks should be larger for the number of guests onboard. They get packed to the gills on warm days.

o **No Kids' Programs:** Azamara doesn't cater to kids. At all. You've been warned.

Overview

Launched in mid-2007, Azamara Club Cruises is a high-end and adult-oriented sister brand to Celebrity and Royal Caribbean, offering more out-of-the-way itineraries, better service and cuisine, more enrichment opportunities, and lots of little extras. The line's two ships are midsize gems that were originally built for now-defunct Renaissance Cruises. Essentially, if the thought of sailing with 6,000 people makes you queasy, these vessels will give you that intimate cruise vacation without breaking the bank.

EXPERIENCE

The idea behind Azamara is straightforward: smaller ships sailing longer itineraries, visiting out-of-the-ordinary ports, and offering a casual yet country-clubbish experience, with great service. In an age dominated by bigger and bigger megaships, we welcome the return of midsize vessels with open arms.

Like Oceania (see p. 245), Azamara provides an experience that straddles the mainstream and luxury segments of the cruise biz—somewhere between Celebrity and Crystal or Regent, though its **luxury inclusions** (complimentary house wines at lunch and dinner, free gratuities, free specialty coffees and bottled wines, more overnights in port and high-end excursions) are nudging the line closer to the high end.

Not that it was all that mainstream to begin with. On the Pool Deck, a quiet jazz trio replaces the kind of loud pop/reggae band found on most mainstream ships, and in the cafe you'll often find a harpist plucking out classical tunes. Service is exceptional, from the butlers who attend to all cabins to little touches such as the cold towels offered at the gangway after a hot day in port. Dinner time is flexible—just show up when you like, either at the main restaurant, at two reservations-only alternatives, or at a casual but still waiter-serviced buffet restaurant. Onboard activities run from the usual (bingo, napkin folding, team trivia) to the unusual, including poetry reading/writing get-togethers and seminars on etiquette and art. At night you can take in a floor show at the theater, catch a performance by a guest magician or comedian, do the karaoke thing, watch a late-night movie, or take in music in several of the public rooms.

Azamara has also made longer, overnight port calls one of its key offerings. To complement these overnight stays, the line introduced AzAmazing Evenings: included after-dark experiences exclusive to the line. These can range from a concert in a museum in Split, Croatia, to a private party on a Tuscan hillside with music by three tenors. The line's "Nights and Cool Places" offers evening tours of destinations, focusing on what's special about the port, such as illuminated landmarks or evening-specific nightlife. Another program "Cruise Global, Eat Local" guides passengers off the well-trod tourist paths toward a restaurant beloved by locals—bus tours will even drop you off there after your shore excursion has ended.

ROUTES

The line travels to the Mediterranean, Baltic, Caribbean, and the Panama Canal, but also does more far-flung itineraries in Asia, Australia, and New Zealand, and excels at showing passengers a destination in depth.

PASSENGERS

Azamara draws a primarily English-speaking crowd—mostly North Americans, but also Brits and Australians. These passengers are active, well-traveled, and mostly empty nesters and young retirees.

DINING

Dining service—which is excellent on parent-company Celebrity—is at least as good here, and probably a little better. At mealtimes, passengers have full flexibility in terms of where, when, and with whom they dine. Dinner is available in four restaurants: one traditional, two specialty ($25/person charge at each, except for suite guests who have complimentary access), and one casual. House wines are complimentary with lunch and dinner in all restaurants, and more expensive vintages (including selections from boutique wineries around the world) are available for purchase.

ACTIVITIES

Ships have a small pool, spa, and gym, as well as a small casino, and there are also port lectures onboard and the usual array of trivia contests, wine tasting classes and the like. But the focus on these ships is clearly centered on getting passengers on land, and helping them to explore.

CHILDREN'S PROGRAMS

Azamara allows children, but offers no facilities or programming for them.

ENTERTAINMENT

There are no formal nights onboard, and instead the line policy is "casual elegance" every evening. This creates a relaxed atmosphere for dinner, which is the main event onboard.

SERVICE

In cabins, butlers do the usual cabin steward job but also help with packing/unpacking, making restaurant and spa reservations, serving full breakfasts en suite, delivering daily canapes, shining shoes, and so on. Service is unobtrusive but very personal when it does obtrude: Butlers know your name from day one and will go out of their way to greet you in the corridors. Dining service is good in the main restaurant and excellent in the specialty restaurants.

Gratuities for restaurant, housekeeping, and bar staff are included in the line's base rates, so no additional tipping for these staff members is necessary. Spa services have a gratuity added automatically to your bill.

Regular send-out **laundry and dry cleaning** services are available at cost, and each ship also has a **free self-service laundry** located midship on Deck 7.

Azamara Journey • Azamara Quest

The Verdict

We wish more ships were like *Journey* and *Quest:* large enough to be interesting during long itineraries, but small enough to keep things comfortable and convenient.

Specifications   Avg. Starting Per Diem $200

Size (in tons)	30,277	Crew	390
Passengers (Double Occ.)	710	Passenger/Crew Ratio	1.8 to 1
Passenger/Space Ratio	42.6	Year Launched	2000
Total Cabins/Veranda Cabins	355/241	Last Major Refurbishment	2016

Frommer's Ratings (Scale of 1–5)   ★★★★

Cabin Comfort & Amenities	4	Dining Options	4
Ship Cleanliness & Maintenance	4	Gym, Spa & Sports Facilities	4
Public Comfort/Space	4.5	Children's Facilities	N/A
Decor	4	Enjoyment Factor	4

THE SHIPS IN GENERAL

Like all the vessels that were originally built for Renaissance Cruises, more boutique hotel than Vegas resort, with a decor that hearkens back to the golden age of ocean liners—warm woods, rich fabrics, and clubbily intimate public areas. When Celebrity and Royal Caribbean took over the ships, they put nearly $40 million into refurbishments, moving the walls around on some cabin decks to create 32 new suites on each vessel; designing new specialty restaurants; expanding the spa; adding a cafe; and installing a new art collection, decking, carpets, paint schemes, bedding, cushions, drapes, table linens, and other soft goods. The result is a pair of lovely, practically new-looking ships, with only a few dents in cabin corridors (courtesy of luggage carts) betraying the fact that they've already been in service for over two decades.

CABINS Cabins on *Journey* and *Quest* are divided into just seven configurations, including inside rooms, those with views and those with verandas (the other differentiators are size and included amenities). At the lower tiers, closet space is *only just* adequate for the long itineraries these vessels sail, though an abundance of drawers and storage space under the bed helps matters some. Bathrooms are also on the tight side. Cabin decor is nicely understated, with off-white walls, wood-tone furnishings and upholstery and carpeting done in easy-on-the-eyes blues and golds.

At the highest price level, **Club Ocean Suites** and **Club World Owners' Suites** have separate bedrooms and living rooms, whirlpool tubs and showers, a guest bathroom, and huge balconies.

Four cabins on each ship are wheelchair accessible.

PUBLIC AREAS & ACTIVITIES   In the evening, many guests head to the **Cabaret** for small-scale production shows, late-night movies and (sometimes) bingo. The best seat in the house is a high table at the center of the rear bar area, between and slightly behind the two spotlights. The large **casino** is a draw, as are the ship's two understated retail **shops;** and the **Looking Glass** combo disco/observation deck. Also a two-in-one space: the ship's gentleman's club-like **library/piano lounge.** Gotta love the faux fireplace, racing-dog ceramics, squashy leather chairs and a *trompe l'oeil* conservatory ceiling here.

Come daylight, on sea days, many head to the pool deck which is frankly too small for the numbers of passengers aboard (it has just one not-large pool). You'll find more serenity on the Sun Deck or the Promenade Deck (and lovely, thick cushioned wooden lounge chairs, too). The **gym,** located just forward of the Pool Deck, has all the usual equipment, just-enough space and a large aerobics floor (for pilates, spinning, stretch, abs, and yoga offered at no extra charge). Next door there's a **beauty salon;** a **spa;** and a separate suite for acupuncture, laser hair removal, and microdermabrasion.

A corner of the Pool Deck has Ping-Pong tables, and shuffleboard and a small golf-putting green are found on the Sun Deck.

DINING   The **Windows Cafe** provides snacks and meals 18 hours a day, along with complimentary specialty coffees and teas. Service is buffet-style, though much is cooked-to-order. A harpist and pianist perform here frequently. In the **library** a high tea is served in the afternoons. Dinner is taken, most nights, in the handsome **dining room** (some stop in the wood-paneled bar, with its Sistine Chapel-esque ceiling murals, first). We recommend grabbing a table in the central portion of the room, where they seem to be more widely spaced than those along the periphery. Or guests can head to one of the two specialty restaurants **Aqualina** (Mediterranean fare) or **Prime C** (classic steakhouse). There's also a pool deck grill which supplements the usual burgers and hot dogs with salads, seafood kebabs and gyros.

CARNIVAL CRUISE LINES

www.carnival.com. ✆ **888/CARNIVAL** (227-6482).

Pros

- **Fun, Theme-Park Ambience:** The fanciful, sometimes wacko, decor on these vessels is unmatched.
- **Entertaining Entertainment:** Elaborate production shows, the Punchliner Comedy Club (one of the best comedy venues at sea), and the kids' Seuss-at-Sea program offer distractions for all ages. There's also "make your own fun" type entertainments, like casino tournaments, trivia contests and hairy chest competitions—catnip to some cruisers, too "vulgar" for others.
- **An Insomniac's Delight:** When passengers on most ships are calling it a night, Carnival's guests are just getting busy with diversions such as midnight adult comedy shows, raging discos, and 24-hour pizza parlors.
- **Food:** There was a time when Carnival ranked last in this category, but in the last few years the line has stepped up its game. Just how far has the line improved beyond iceberg lettuce-filled salad bars? The truth is, while some older ships remain stuck in the past—that pizza dough they're tossing in the air? It's for show on some ships; the one they're bringing you was frozen—it's hard not to be impressed with their newer restaurants.

Cons

- **Crowds:** These are big ships with lots of people on board, and you're going to feel it when you're checking in. Disembarking. Waiting in line for lunch at the buffet. Trying to find a deck chair by the pool...
- **Cheesiness:** Line dancing to a DJ by the pool, fueled with bottles of beer, just isn't everyone's taste; nor are hairy back contests.

Overview

The definition of mass market, Carnival is the Big Kahuna of the industry, boasting a modern fleet of loud megaships that cater to a fun-loving crowd. But with the 90's fading into the rearview mirror (and the ships built in that decade and soon thereafter), what you *think* you know about Carnival is probably wrong. The line has toned down the formerly retina-shattering decor found of its earliest ships. Starting with *Carnival Breeze* in 2012, the onboard look became...well, not sedate, bus definitely mellower. Yes, boats still are done up in bold, primary colors, and every once in a while you'll encounter a chandelier in the form of an octopus, but overall the interior of these ships boast sleeker lines, contemporary metallic details and fewer dizzying patterns on the drapes and carpets. In addition, food has improved substantially, as have amenities, with Carnival now featuring the fastest—and cheapest—shipboard Wi-Fi we've ever experienced. These are still Fun Ships—no doubt about it—but Carnival isn't far off when it calls these new vessels Fun Ship 2.0.

EXPERIENCE

Carnival does not pretend to be a luxury experience. It doesn't claim to have gourmet food (although it has recently garnered praise for serving some of the best meals of any mass-market ship), and it doesn't promise around-the-clock pampering. The motto is "fun," with a big focus on entertainment, friendly service, and creative cruise directors (who can be corny sometimes, but at least they're lively). Carnival's *FunTimes* daily program frequently offers more than 100 individual things to do in any given day. That said, the festive atmosphere does vary by region; it's a little more subdued on, say, the line's voyages to Alaska than a similar cruise to the Caribbean might be. Deck parties are, after all, tough to do when it's cold and raining out.

ROUTES

Carnival's bread-and-butter is the Caribbean, with voyages leaving from nearly a dozen U.S. homeports. Many of Carnival's other sailings are to sunny destinations—Bermuda, the Bahamas, Hawaii, and the Mexican Riviera. But the line also travels to Alaska, Canada and New England, and Australia. European cruises are less common: They came back in 2016 with the launch of *Carnival Vista,* but are off the books again for 2017 and beyond.

PASSENGERS

On Carnival, you'll find couples, a few singles, and a good share of families. (In fact, the line carries more than 700,000 kids a year—the most in the cruise industry.) Overall, Carnival has some of the youngest demographics in the industry. But it's far more than age that defines the line's customers. Carnival executives are fond of using the word "spirited" to describe the typical Carnival passenger, and indeed, it's right on target. The line's many fans increasingly come from a wide range of ages as well as occupations, backgrounds, and income levels, but they share an unpretentious and outgoing demeanor.

This is a line for people who don't mind at all that their dinner will be interrupted by the loud music and flashing lights of a dance show starring their waiters. Passengers want to see whales or beaches, but they will also dance the Macarena, stay up all night in the disco, and then order a bucket of beer at the pool bar to drink while they watch friends compete in contests to see how many Ping-Pong balls they can stuff in their bikinis.

DINING

Food in the dining rooms and buffets is bountiful, and the cuisine is traditional American: Red meat is popular on these ships. But preparations of more "nouvelle" dishes are also in evidence today (like broiled Chilean sea bass with truffle butter or smoked turkey tenderloin with asparagus). Spa and vegetarian fare are also always an option. In a nod to more adventurous eaters, Carnival's dining room menus include an item called, "Didja Ever?", a dish that rotates nightly and includes options like frog's legs, alligator fritters (delicious), and escargots bourguignonne.

The alternate eating venues—both those that are complimentary and those that come with a fee—have received a big upgrade in recent years. Even diehard foodies have been surprised by the 180-degree shift. Here are some highlights (which are only on select ships at this time):

o **Guy's Burger Joint:** Carnival teamed up with Food Network star Guy Fieri, host of *Diners, Drive-Ins, and Dives,* and the brain behind a series of restaurants of dubious distinction, to create what are undoubtedly the best burgers at sea. The patties are ground onboard and buns are baked daily. Best of all, the fare at this poolside stand is complimentary.

o **BlueIguana Cantina:** Also located on the pool deck, this Mexican spot (no extra charge) makes its own tortilla chips, offers a salsa bar with plenty of options, and fries up impressive Baja-style fish tacos. Their chili-braised pork tacos are also killer.

o **Fahrenheit 555:** This classic steakhouse is better than many steakhouse specialty restaurants on more expensive ships, with some surprisingly creative dishes, like the wasabi-infused mashed potatoes.

Until recently, meals in the main dining rooms were always served at assigned tables, with two seatings per meal. But the line has also rolled out an alternative, eat-when-you-want dining option for passengers called *Your Time* dining. Passengers must sign up for *Your Time* dining in advance, generally when they first make their cruise booking. It's completely free, and you can use Carnival's online *Cruise Personalizer* to select between *Your Time* dining or traditional Early or Late seating dinner.

The casual lunch buffets include international (Italian, Indian, and so on, with a different cuisine featured daily), deli, rotisserie, and pizza stations; the breakfast buffet has everything from made-to-order egg dishes to cold cereals and pastries. Guests wishing to dine casually often come here for dinner as well. Most Carnival cruise ships also have an onboard steakhouse, similar to Fahrenheit 555 listed above. These all go by different names depending on the ship, but offer the same high-quality dining experience and menu.

ACTIVITIES

If Atlantic City and Las Vegas appeal to you, Carnival will, too. Slot machines begin clanging by 8 or 9am in the casinos when the ships are at sea (tables open at 11am), and servers start tempting passengers with trays of fruity theme cocktails long before the lunch hour. You can learn to country line dance or play bridge, take cooking lessons, compete in a hairy chest contest, hit the comedy club and watch first-run movies. Trivia sessions on nearly every conceivable subject take place from dawn to dusk, particularly onboard the line's newer ships. Overall, though, there's not as much variety of activities as aboard lines such as Norwegian, Holland America, and Celebrity (read: absolutely no enrichment lectures on history or other cerebral topics).

CHILDREN'S PROGRAMS

Recently, the line updated its programming for children ages 2 to 11, with **Camp Ocean** replacing the long-running Camp Carnival program. Camp Ocean features more than 200 marine-themed activities as well as a host of other kid-pleasing activities—everything from arts-and-crafts sessions to lectures by wildlife experts. Carnival also has a separate program for 12- to 14-year-olds, known as **Circle "C,"** and **Club O$_2$** for kids ages 15 to 17, each with dedicated facilities and separate staff. The former offers dedicated lounges for 12- to 14-year-olds where they can play video games, watch late-night movies, sing karaoke, participate in pizza making classes, have dance parties, and more. For the older teens, Club O$_2$ has two big advantages: no kids, and no adults. In their own dedicated public rooms, Club O$_2$ features theme parties, group sports activities, dance parties, video games, and more.

Parents of little kids can request beepers so they can keep in touch.

ENTERTAINMENT

Carnival consistently presents some of the most lavish extravaganzas afloat, spending millions on stage sets, choreography, and acoustical equipment that leave many other floating theaters in their wake. The resulting shows feature flamboyantly costumed dancers and singers who perform production shows that, while sparse on plot, are big on razzle dazzle. The FunShips also feature the Punchliner Comedy Club, which hosts some of the best jokesters on the high seas. But entertainment doesn't end there: On almost all the ships, there will be music most everywhere you wander, with nightly piano bars, jazz clubs, DJ discos, and bands playing contemporary hits. For the ultimate entertainment experience, book one of the Carnival LIVE sailings featuring hit performers like Journey and STYX.

SERVICE

All in all, a Carnival ship is a well-oiled machine, and you'll certainly get what you need—but not much more. Chalk it all up to the size of the line's ships. It's a fact of life that service aboard all megaliners is simply not as attentive as that aboard smaller vessels—with thousands of guests to help, your dining-room waiter and cabin steward have a lot of work ahead of them and little time for chitchat.

On Carnival, gratuities of $12 per passenger per day are automatically charged to your shipboard account, but you can increase or decrease the amount by visiting the guest services desk onboard.

An onboard laundry service (for washing and pressing only) charges by the piece; dry cleaning is available onboard *Carnival Breeze, Carnival Conquest, Carnival Dream, Carnival Freedom, Carnival Glory, Carnival Liberty, Carnival Magic, Carnival Splendor, Carnival Valor, Carnival Victory,* and *Carnival Vista* only. Carnival also offers fleet-wide self-service laundry machines on each accommodations deck. Older ships tend to offer coin-operated machines, while newer vessels will let you use your Sail & Sign card.

FLEET

Carnival has the biggest cruise fleet in the world with ships ranging in size from 2,052 to 4,000 passengers. Regardless of how old the vessel is, each has plenty of activities, pool and hot tub spaces (some covered for use in chillier weather), a big ocean-view gym and spa, and more dining options than you can try in a week.

Carnival Fantasy • Carnival Ecstasy • Carnival Sensation • Carnival Fascination • Carnival Imagination • Carnival Inspiration • Carnival Elation • Carnival Paradise

The Verdict

Known as the Fantasy Class, Carnival has spent a substantial amount of money refreshing these classic ships in recent years. Like a great 90's hit, they're back—and they're better than they were before.

Specifications   Avg. Starting Per Diem $100

Size (in tons)	70,367	Crew	920
Passengers (Double Occ.)	2,052-2,056	Passenger/Crew Ratio	2.2 to 1
Passenger/Space Ratio	34.5	Year Launched	1990-1998
Total Cabins/Veranda Cabins	1,020/54	Last Major Refurbishment	2014-2015

Frommer's Ratings (Scale of 1–5)   ★★★ ½

Cabin Comfort & Amenities	4	Dining Options	3
Ship Cleanliness & Maintenance	4	Gym, Spa & Sports Facilities	3
Public Comfort/Space	4	Children's Facilities	4
Decor	3	Enjoyment Factor	4

THE SHIPS IN GENERAL

Built between 1990 and 1998, Carnival's 855-foot long Fantasy class ships once formed the backbone of the FunShip fleet. Carrying between 2,052 and 2,056 guests, they now mostly operate short 3-and-4-day sailings from U.S. homeports, but Carnival occasionally sends them on the odd weeklong cruise—which always sells out well in advance. These ships have been run hard and still display more than a touch of 1990's cruising nostalgia (what the heck is with that red trim in the staterooms?!). Recognizing that, Carnival has been slowly but surely refreshing each ship, adding features like the Punchliner Comedy Club and the Sanctuary, Carnival's Adults-only oasis. Some ships feature more enhancements than others; *Carnival Inspiration,* for example, is the only member of the Fantasy Class with the popular Alchemy Bar. By and large, though, these are fine ships for short sailings, with a healthy dose of FunShip wackiness.

CABINS   The vast majority of **staterooms** aboard the Fantasy Class ships are either inside cabins with no view, or oceanview staterooms that feature either picture or porthole windows. Balconies weren't a priority when these ships were built, so only the top of the line suites feature them. The exceptions to this rule are *Carnival Ecstasy, Carnival Fascination,* and *Carnival Sensation,* each of which were refitted with exterior balcony staterooms that hang, somewhat unattractively, off the ship's superstructure.

That being said, all are well-sized if a bit plain-Jane in their looks. Curiously staterooms all lack hairdryers, and mini-fridges are only available at the **suite** level. Bathrooms have that clingy shower curtain that is the butt of jokes for every cruise director on the High Seas.

PUBLIC AREAS & ACTIVITIES   Elaborate, sprawling, and a bit garish: That's the best way to describe public areas. Each of is decorated around a different theme, some of which have aged better than others.

Among the rooms that get the most action are the whimsically decorated **show lounge** (nightly production shows along with bingo and Seuss-at-Sea Storytime for the kiddies); the large and loud **casino;** and the many onboard **watering holes** from dance clubs to piano bars. The latter are more intimately sized than most modern megaships, a welcomed throwback to how cruising used to be.

While not nearly as elaborate as their older fleetmates, the Fantasy Class still packs a punch when it comes to onboard pools, with at least one midships pool with two hot tubs, complemented by an aft pool and hot tub combination. All ships except *Carnival Elation* and *Carnival Paradise* include Carnival's new **Waterworks Aqua Park** concept that includes splash parks and waterslides for the kids, plus superfast "racer" slides for the adults. On Sun Deck 14, guests will find a **jogging track** and, in the center of the track, the ship's **Mini-Golf** course. If you get here early on in the cruise, few of your fellow guests will know about it, leaving you to putt around the green in a more relaxed fashion.

Spa Carnival offers the usual treatments and a fitness center overlooking the ship's bow that is well-equipped and maintained. It's nothing fancy, but the forward-facing views are sure nice.

DINING For ships built in the 1990s, the Fantasy Class ships have more dining options than you might expect. Each Fantasy Class ship features two **main dining rooms** that serve multi-course dinners either in an open-seating environment, or as traditional "fixed" early and late-sittings. One dining room is typically open for breakfast and lunch on sea days, which can be a popular alternative to the controlled madness that is the **Lido Restaurant.** While it *is* a buffet, Carnival has made some impressive strides with its cuisine here in recent years; to that end, you can expect to find a Mongolian-style wok station in addition to American "comfort" favorites like burgers, hot dogs, salads, sandwiches, and freshly carved meats. It's open breakfast, lunch and dinner. Hungry in the middle of the night? Head to the 24-hour **Pizza Pirate** station. Room service is also available around the clock, with both free and paid option menu items.

Fans of Carnival's newest eateries will want to take note: **Guy's Burger Joint** (p. 114) and the **BlueIguana Cantina** (p. 114)—with its freshly made burritos— are currently only aboard *Carnival Fantasy* and *Carnival Inspiration.*

Carnival Sunshine

The Verdict

If you're a frequent cruiser, you might know *Carnival Sunshine* better by her former name, *Carnival Destiny*. But a spectacular top-to-bottom reconstruction completely altered her look and feel, which today has more in common with her much-younger fleetmates. If you like your megaships on the smaller scale but want all the new bells and whistles, *Carnival Sunshine* is your pick.

Specifications — Avg. Starting Per Diem $110

Size (in tons)	102,853	Crew	1150
Passengers (Double Occ.)	3,002	Passenger/Crew Ratio	2.6 to 1
Passenger/Space Ratio	38.4	Year Launched	1996/2013
Total Cabins/Veranda Cabins	1,501/563	Last Major Refurbishment	2013

Frommer's Ratings (Scale of 1–5) ★★★★

Cabin Comfort & Amenities	4	Dining Options	4
Ship Cleanliness & Maintenance	4	Gym, Spa & Sports Facilities	4
Public Comfort/Space	4	Children's Facilities	4.5
Decor	4.5	Enjoyment Factor	4

THE SHIP IN GENERAL

When she was launched as *Carnival Destiny* back in 1996, she was the largest ship ever built for Carnival (893 feet in length), and the first passenger ship in the world to exceed 100,000 gross tons. Today, those numbers are no longer a draw, so Carnival announced in 2012 that it would spend $155 million dollars on a refit and it was re-christened 2013 as *Carnival Sunshine.*

The refurbishment was sweeping. Gone are the dark interiors with neon accents that had, in 1996, been trendy but which, nearly two decades later, looked like a mistake from the set of the movie *TRON*. The key words today are muted and sleek when it comes to decor and color choices.

But the changes were structural, too. Among the additions were public rooms, 182 new staterooms (bringing the guest capacity up to 3,002), 8 new dining venues, and every FunShip 2.0 enhancement—like the popular Alchemy Bar, the RedFrog Pub, and Guy's Burger Joint. The adults-only Serenity area is one of the best in the entire fleet, and the refit added a massive waterpark that rivals those aboard *Carnival Dream* and her sisters (see p. 128).

CABINS Like the rest of the Carnival fleet, **staterooms** aboard *Carnival Sunshine* are larger than average. The big plus, however, is the change in decor: Gone are the bizarre sea of pinks and oranges (hallelujah!), replaced with crisp whites and earth tones, accented with nautical blue carpeting (just like what you'll find on the new *Carnival Breeze* or *Carnival Vista*). **Balcony staterooms** feature verandas spacious enough for two chairs and a small table—suitable if you want to kick back with a good book or a couple of margaritas. Carnival also offers a decent assortment of **suites,** with the two, top-of-the-line **Captain's Suites** featuring separate living and sleeping areas, along with a BIG square foot balcony. It's also worth noting that all suites feature an audio/video input plate that allows guests to stream content from their portable DVD players or laptops to the in-suite TV.

PUBLIC AREAS & ACTIVITIES *Carnival Sunshine* features all of the innovations usually only seen on Dream-class ships. That list of new or altered public areas is extraordinary and most extensive when it comes to the ship's hip new nightspots. These include cozy **Piano Bar 88,** the **Alchemy Bar** (inventive cocktails, ordered from equally imaginative, backlit menus), **The RedFrog Pub** (craft beers, adult trivia and bar games like darts and pool), the *Jetsons*-esque **Skybox Sports Bar,** and **Ocean Plaza** (with its huge dance floor; it runs across the centerline of the ship). The Cuban-themed **Havana Bar** may be our favorite: It has a breezy elegance to it, and serves Cuban food all day long, at no extra charge.

On the entertainment front, Carnival completely restyled the ship's main **show lounge,** which now has more of a supper club–style feel than the former massive, three-deck high theatre. But even reduced to two levels the production values of these shows dazzle (and the shows are shorter, which isn't bad for entertaining but plot-free fare). Recently, the ship added a "game show" during which audience members compete on massive versions of classic Hasbro toys (can you say "product placement"?) like Connect Four and Sorry. An alternate lounge, **Limelight,** serves as the setting for Carnival's Punchliner Comedy Club performances.

The **Sunshine Casino** squats right in the main companionway on Deck 5. If you're sensitive to smoke, consider this fair warning: Carnival still allows guests to smoke in the Casino.

Arguably the biggest changes were saved for *Carnival Sunshine*'s pool and sports facilities. The ship now has pools and hot tubs on Deck 9 midships, Deck 14 forward, and Deck 11 forward in the newly added (and much appreciated) adults-only, **Serenity** area. With its plush loungers, faux trees, and din-covering waterfall emptying into a gigantic pool, you'll never want to leave this blessedly tranquil oasis.

Kids (and the young-at-heart) are well taken care of, too with a massive waterworks area that features three humongous waterslides, a selection of smaller waterslides for younger passengers, a splash park, and even a ropes course that was more fun than we'd like to admit.

Up front, *Carnival Sunshine*'s completely remodeled and expanded **Cloud 9 Spa** is a substantial improvement over its previous incarnation. The handsome **gym** is large and overlooks the ship's bow (a nice distraction). A **salon** offers up surprisingly well-priced hair services for men and women plus manicures and pedicures.

DINING *Carnival Sunshine* features two main dining rooms but only the aft-facing Sunrise dining room has traditional fixed-seating dinner. One dining room is typically open on sea days for *a la carte* breakfast and lunch.

Elsewhere, *Sunshine*'s newest eateries, the **BlueIguana Cantina** and **Guy's Burger Joint** (see p. 114 for descriptions); the line's **Steakhouse** (additional charge $35/person); **Cucina del Capitano** (an extra $15/person) in honor of all the Italian captains who have helmed these ships; and, best of all, Pan-Asian **Ji Ji** ($15/person), which presents truly gourmet versions such favorites as spring rolls, slow-braised short ribs and jade shrimp.

Quick, buffet meals are always available at the too-cramped **Lido Marketplace** which has a wide selection of American-style favorites, but also a surprising amount of alternative Asian, Japanese, Indian and Italian-style dishes.

Carnival Sunshine is also one of only two ships in the fleet (the others being *Carnival Vista*) to offer **The Shake Spot,** where you can indulge in a variety of ice cream treats. Adults can even hit the throttle by adding a shot of liqueurs to the mix.

Carnival Triumph • Carnival Victory

The Verdict

The 893-foot long *Carnival Triumph* and *Carnival Victory* are considered "midsize" by today's standards, holding 2,754 guests apiece. They've been around the block a few times, but are just fine for the 3-4 night Caribbean itineraries that are their mainstay.

Specifications   Avg. Starting Per Diem $99

Size (in tons)	101,509	Crew	1090
Passengers (Double Occ.)	2,754	Passenger/Crew Ratio	2.6 to 1
Passenger/Space Ratio	37	Year Launched	1999/2000
Total Cabins/Veranda Cabins	1379/508	Last Major Refurbishment	2016/2015

Frommer's Ratings (Scale of 1–5)

★★★ ½

Cabin Comfort & Amenities	3	Dining Options	4
Ship Cleanliness & Maintenance	4	Gym, Spa & Sports Facilities	3
Public Comfort/Space	4.5	Children's Facilities	4
Decor	3	Enjoyment Factor	4.5

THE SHIPS IN GENERAL

Launched in 1999 and 2000 respectively, *Carnival Triumph* and *Carnival Victory* look identical on the outside, but were given wildly different interior design by Carnival's wildly different designer, Joe Farcus. *Carnival Triumph*'s decor pays homage to the great cities of the world, while *Carnival Victory* is themed after bodies of water. The latter is particularly eye-popping, with every conceivable surface dabbed with shades of green and blue and aqua and royal blue and…well, you get the picture. Coupled with Carnival's 1990's color palette of reds, browns and pinks, it's one loud ship, especially compared to the *Carnival Triumph,* which uses much darker tones throughout. But both offer more than enough fun and new features to woo guests on the primarily shorter runs to the Bahamas and the Caribbean.

CABINS   Some would say the staterooms on these two boats are peachy keen, but we'd say that these pink rooms—that's the overarching color scheme—look dated, with the colors too close to what was used in hospitals in the 1990's. Still, even the cheapest rooms are noticeably larger than those on other lines.

Oceanview staterooms have the same amenities as inside staterooms, but with the addition of a picture window. The **balcony staterooms** add a private balcony with two chairs and a small table to the mix. There's no need to worry about obstructed balcony views; all balconies face the sea, feature transparent plexiglass railings, and look directly down.

Suites are never Carnival's forte. *Carnival Victory* and her sister feature a range, from modestly sized **Junior Suites** to the much larger **Ocean** and **Grand Suites** on Empress Deck 7. Suites feature flat-panel television sets while standard staterooms are stuck with the small, 13" tube TV sets that look positively prehistoric now. Book early; these suites tend to sell out quickly.

PUBLIC AREAS & ACTIVITIES   Fans of understated decor need not apply. These ships lay on the neon with abandon, which, when coupled with the ship's odd decorative objects (like the gigantic backlit fish that's suspended near the entrance to the Pacific Dining Room) and wildly patterned carpeting can either be exciting…or vertigo-inducing, depending on your personal aesthetics.

Still, public rooms offer good passenger flow, with very few bottlenecks (except for that first turn off of the **casino** between the **grand atrium** and the **promenade** on Deck 5, which really plugs up on formal night when everyone wants pictures taken). The main three-story **show lounge** can seat 1,500 passengers in a single go, while the cozier **Club Rio/Adriatic Aft Lounge** provides alternate entertainment, like the Punchliner Comedy Club. Also of note: the **dance club,** the **Alchemy Bar** (impressive mixology), and the usually forgotten, and therefore blessedly serene, **Oxford Bar** (**Ionian Bar** on *Victory*), which is tucked away down on Atlantic Deck 4.

The three **pools** and **spa** aren't anything to write home about, owing to their mid-1990's designs.

And *Carnival Triumph* lacks the **Serenity,** Carnival's adults-only pool oasis, while *Carnival Victory,* thankfully has it (though it doesn't have the onboard **basketball court** its sister ships have).

Both ships have decent, if a bit outdated, **kids' facilities**—still, Carnival's excellent youth coordinators will keep kids busy onboard.

DINING   As an older build, these ships don't have the variety of specialty restaurants that their younger brethren do. But *Carnival Triumph* has been refitted with the popular (and tasty!) **BlueIguana Cantina** and **Guy's Burger Joint** (see p. 114). Alas, *Carnival Victory* lacks these. Other meals are taken in the two main **dining rooms** or the large **buffet.**

Carnival Legend • Carnival Miracle • Carnival Pride • Carnival Spirit

The Verdict

Known collectively as the Spirit Class, these four ships have some of the best passenger to space ratios in the fleet. From their transparent funnels that act as the roof of the specialty steakhouse to their hidden nooks and crannies, they offer the Carnival experience with a fraction of the passengers.

Specifications

Avg. Starting Per Diem $100

Size (in tons)	88,500	Crew	930
Passengers (Double Occ.)	2,124	Passenger/Crew Ratio	2.3 to 1
Passenger/Space Ratio	41.7	Year Launched	2001-2004
Total Cabins/Veranda Cabins	1,062/682	Last Major Refurbishment	2014-2015

Frommer's Ratings (Scale of 1–5)

★★★★ ½

Cabin Comfort & Amenities	4	Dining Options	4.5
Ship Cleanliness & Maintenance	4	Gym, Spa & Sports Facilities	4.5
Public Comfort/Space	4.5	Children's Facilities	4
Decor	4.5	Enjoyment Factor	4.5

THE SHIPS IN GENERAL

Entering service between 2001 and 2004, these ships are big and impressive, but with just 2,124 guests onboard are not nearly as crowded as some of the line's larger ships. They make a great alternative for those who are put off by the idea of sailing on a "city at sea." Carnival's longtime interior designer Joe Farcus worked his quirky madness once again. What does that mean? Well, on *Carnival Pride* interiors have "Icons of Beauty" as their main theme so the ship carries a 12-foot replica of Michelangelo's "David," along with reproductions of works by such masters as Botticelli, Raphael, and Da Vinci. Public rooms that have architectural motifs borrowed from the Victorian era, the Art Deco movement, ancient Greece and the Byzantine empire. Oh, and there's an insect-themed Butterflies Lounge on Deck 1. *Pride* is likely the most elaborate, but each ship features its own creative decor. Unlike her three fleetmates, *Carnival Spirit* makes her home year-round in Australia, and as such is missing from Carnival's U.S.-based website.

CABINS   Nearly 80% of the 1,062 guest cabins onboard feature ocean views and of those, a further 80% have private balconies (substantially more balconies than Carnival's older ships). But alas, they have the pink-on-salmon-on-peach decor that afflicted earlier vessels (a look that hasn't aged well). Still, staterooms (even insides) are generously proportioned. A number of **suites** are also available, offering separate sleeping and living areas.

Sixteen staterooms are wheelchair accessible, and a number of connecting staterooms are also available for families and friends travelling together.

PUBLIC AREAS & ACTIVITIES   These four ships are blessed with more off-the-beaten-path public areas than other ships in the Carnival fleet (like the hard-to-find **piano bar** and the two-story **dance club**). They also carry welcome recent editions like the **Alchemy Bar,** which specialized in hand-crafted cocktails, and the **RedFrog Pub** (it carries the line's ThirstyFrog Ale).

Nightly production shows can be found in the three-story **show lounge.** Unlike other Carnival ships, these four vessels feature a secondary show lounge tucked *underneath* the main show lounge. Carnival's **Punchliner Comedy Club** takes place in these kooky-looking rooms—as we said earlier, decor in the public areas of these ships is out there—the most bizarre of which has to be the *Alice in Wonderland*–patterned Mad Hatter Lounge aboard *Carnival Miracle.*

These ships feature three **swimming pools,** including one that is covered by a retractable magrodome roof. Each ship also has a small kids' splash pool, and a waterslide, though *Carnival Miracle* lacks the **Green Thunder** waterslide that her sisters have been refitted with. The steepest waterslide at sea, Carnival says you can reach speeds of up to 65 miles per hour on this terrifying-looking ride. We'll take the company's word for it.

The **Fitness Center** is positioned at the bow of each ship with spectacular views. It surrounds the **spa's** hydrotherapy pool, when means exercising guests get a view of their fellow guests trying to relax—and vice versa (it's an odd configuration). A **beauty salon** is nearby.

DINING   Thanks to their lower passenger counts, these four ships have just one **main dining room,** a two-story blessed by 180-degree windows. Both fixed-seating and flexible dining are offered and the restaurant is open for breakfast and lunch on sea days. A casual **Lido Buffet** offers all three meals. Right now, only *Carnival Pride* and *Carnival Spirit* offer **Guy's Burger Joint** and the **BlueIguana Cantina** (see p. 114), with the latter also carrying the deliciously unhealthy **Fat Jimmy's C-Side Barbecue.** The most dramatic culinary experience onboard can be found at the **steakhouse** which is topped with bank of transparent red glass; the base of Carnival's iconic funnel (a pretty cool sight). Dining here carries an extra per-person charge.

Carnival Conquest • Carnival Freedom • Carnival Glory • Carnival Liberty • Carnival Valor

The Verdict

You need to be a people person to get the most from these ships, as there will be lots onboard. Sun lovers are also a good fit, thanks to the ships' extensive outdoor facilities, water features, and their beach-driven itineraries.

Specifications

Avg. Starting Per Diem $82

Size (in tons)	110,000	Crew	1,160
Passengers (Double Occ.)	2,974	Passenger/Crew Ratio	2.5 to 1
Passenger/Space Ratio	37	Year Launched	2002-2007
Total Cabins/Veranda Cabins	1,487/556	Last Major Refurbishment	2013-2016

Frommer's Ratings (Scale of 1–5)

★★★★

Cabin Comfort & Amenities	4.5	Dining Options	4
Ship Cleanliness & Maintenance	5	Gym, Spa & Sports Facilities	4
Public Comfort/Space	4	Children's Facilities	4.5
Decor	4	Enjoyment Factor	4

THE SHIPS IN GENERAL

The Conquest-class ships tend to do two-to-nine day sailings of the Caribbean and the Bahamas. These regions are a great match for these Fun Ships, as their main focus is outdoor diversions like pools, hot tubs, waterslides, basketball and volleyball courts, and the relaxing adults-only area known as Serenity. But these are also some of Carnival's most crowded ships, holding nearly 3,000 guests apiece.

CABINS There's a lot to like about the **staterooms** aboard the Conquest Class. At 185 square feet, even the most affordable inside stateroom is larger than the competition. Most guests will stay in either balcony or inside accommodations, although a smattering of oceanview staterooms are available, with glass walls that look out at the sea, a nice touch. Another upgrade from the old Carnival formula: The natural woods and burnt orange color schemes are more attractive than Carnival's old pink-on-pink-on-pink digs. But the best part about Carnival's cabins these days is the beds. Called the Carnival Comfort Bed sleep system, mattresses, duvets, and pillows are superthick and ultracomfy. The towels and bathrobes in each cabin are pretty luxurious, too.

The one downside on many of the vessel's cabins? One measly power outlet per stateroom—a problem in today's wired world.

Suites are more abundant on these vessels than older ships in the fleet, thanks to refittings over the years.

PUBLIC AREAS & ACTIVITIES The Conquest ships are bright and playful—a sort of Mardi Gras feel instead of the dark and glittery Las Vegas look on some of the older ships in the fleet. Architect Joe Farcus was inspired by the great Impressionist and post-Impressionist artists (their color palettes) so ships bursts with sunny yellows and oranges, and vivid blues and greens.

IS THERE smoking ON SHIPS?

The short answer is yes, but on a very restricted basis that changes from line to line. Most major cruise lines have banned smoking in cabins and on cabin balconies. Smoking is generally not allowed in shipboard theaters, show lounges, or dining rooms and may be restricted to certain bars or dedicated Cigar Bars. Expect the casino to allow smoking, though some lines take the extra step of offering at least one "smoke free" evening. Smoking may also be allowed out on designated deck areas (typically all the way aft). Small ships typically allow smoking only in certain outdoor areas. If you are a smoker, check with your line in advance. Note, too, that smoking policies don't just cover traditional cigarettes; many lines have established the same rules for E-cigarettes and vaporizers. Like most hotels, the penalties for disobeying the rules can be stiff, with hundreds of dollars in fines for smoking in your stateroom.

Most used interior spaces include the sprawling **casinos** (almost 300 slot machines and about two dozen gaming tables in each), **EA Sports Bar,** which looks a bit like something from Clockwork Orange, but with red rather than white decor; the **Coffee Bar;** and the onboard **Dance Club** where passengers groove on an enormous floor (each ship themes these areas differently). The mixology-forward **Alchemy Bar,** is also popular, one of some 20-plus bars and lounges aboard, including a dedicated **Piano Bar,** and an aft lounge where alternate shows are performed. *Warning:* Carnival allows smoking in the **casino** and since it's at the heart of Deck 5, with many adjacent lounges, that deck's air ain't the greatest. On one recent *Carnival Freedom* cruise out of Galveston, the cigarette smoke was as thick as San Francisco fog.

While the Conquest Class doesn't have the more elaborate Cloud 9 Spa found on the line's newest ships, they nonetheless have the very-decent **Spa Carnival,** On the pool front, there's nothing groundbreaking here, and the pool decks can get crowded, but most will find the facilities more than adequate for the line dancing that tends to break out on sea days (electric slide anyone?). A Twister waterslide runs from Deck 14 down to Deck 10.

If pools aren't your thing, don't forget about the nine-hole mini-golf course that wraps around Carnival's iconic funnel, or the relaxing (and adults-only!) Serenity area that can be found forward on Deck 14.

The massive **children's facilities** are divided into digs for teens and those for younger children, both with age-appropriate amenities like video games, arts and crafts areas, dipping pools, and more.

DINING Once again, Carnival offers both traditional fixed and come-when-you-want dining in one of **two main two story dining rooms.**

Carnival has vastly upgraded its casual food offerings in recent years, and all of these enhancements have finally worked their way aboard the Conquest Class. In addition to the casual **Lido Deck** buffet (which tends towards heavy, non-dieter friendly fare), guests will also find the **BlueIguana Cantina** and **Guy's Burger Joint** (see p. 114 for reviews). The most unusual venue, **The**

Taste Bar, is opened on select days of the cruise and serves specialty dishes from across the Carnival fleet (even from restaurants that aren't on any of these ships), so we suppose it's a type of advertising, but entertaining nonetheless.

Carnival Splendor

The Verdict

A one-off for Carnival, the 3,006-guest *Carnival Splendor* got everything right, rolling the best features of her predecessors into well-designed (if very colorful) ship. Just be prepared to like the color pink—a lot.

Specifications — Avg. Starting Per Diem $93

Size (in tons)	113,300	Crew	1,150
Passengers (Double Occ.)	3,012	Passenger/Crew Ratio	2.6 to 1
Passenger/Space Ratio	37.1	Year Launched	2008
Total Cabins/Veranda Cabins	1,503/589	Last Major Refurbishment	2016

Frommer's Ratings (Scale of 1–5) — ★★★★ ½

Cabin Comfort & Amenities	5	Dining Options	4
Ship Cleanliness & Maintenance	4.5	Gym, Spa & Sports Facilities	5
Public Comfort/Space	4.5	Children's Facilities	4
Decor	3	Enjoyment Factor	4

THE SHIP IN GENERAL

Launched in 2008, *Carnival Splendor* is an evolution of the Conquest Class but with a few extra bells, whistles, and decks. At 952 feet in length, she features over 20 different bars and lounges, not to mention a plethora of dining options culled from the rest of the fleet. She also introduced Carnival's much-expanded Cloud 9 Spa along with a new two-deck pool design with a retractable glass roof and a giant LED screen for watching movies on-deck. Designed around a "splendid" theme, Carnival's in-house designer Joe Farcus set the color wheel to "pink" on this one; an effect that can be a bit overwhelming. Even still, this is one of the line's best megaships to-date.

CABINS You've got to love Carnival for its **staterooms.** While other lines squish passengers into cramped rooms, even Carnival's inside staterooms measure are bigger than outside cabins (read: higher priced) on other mainstream lines. *Carnival Splendor* was also the first Fun Ship with **Cloud 9 Spa Staterooms,** which feature direct, keycard-access to the spa via a stairway secreted away on the forward end of Deck 10. These spa guests get swank Asian-style decor and complimentary access to the ship's hydrotherapy pool and thermal suite, with its heated ceramic loungers and aromatic steam rooms. Cloud 9 Spa Staterooms are available in interior, obstructed oceanview, balcony, and suite categories (meaning there are some relatively affordable ones in the bunch).

A 2016 refit added six new "**Scenic Oceanview" staterooms** and two **Captain's Suites.** The former feature floor-to-ceiling windows, while the latter are perched above the ship's navigation bridge and have private balconies.

PUBLIC AREAS & ACTIVITIES   On *Splendor,* walls in some public areas are covered with a composite material made of stainless steel and 4-inch circular cut-outs backed by pink-stained wood with black pigment rubbed into the grain, with gold-leaf beams and arches illuminated with hundreds of sparkling lights. It's an amazing look. The vessel sports 22 **bars** and **lounges** (though, sadly, doesn't have the Red Frog Pub or the classy Alchemy Bar). Fans of the one-armed bandits will want to head to the **Royal Flush Casino** on Deck 5. That deck is also home to the **Fun Shops,** the **Coffee Bar,** the **Video Arcade,** and the **Red Carpet Dance Club** which, for better or for worse, brings the 1980's back to life. At the stern on Deck 5 is one of the ship's nicest public rooms: the **El Morocco Lounge.** *Carnival Splendor*'s secondary show lounge holds nightly comedy performances and other events. Sure, the faux-Moroccan theme jumps at you from out of nowhere, but this is one cool lounge to relax in.

Carnival Splendor is one of Carnival's best ships for pool and spa mavens. The ship has three pools, one of which (the midships pool) has a retractable magrodome roof. It also boasts a super-fast Twister-style waterslide, and a delightfully refreshing water-spray park in the area of the massive kid's club.

The ship was the first to feature Carnival's **Cloud 9 Spa,** which spans two decks. In addition to treatment rooms, it features a thalassotherapy pool covered by a glass dome and equipped with jets of water that massage every muscle in your body. Across the hall is the thermal suite, with its heated ceramic loungers, an oriental steam bath and a tepidarium and lanconium (both dry heat saunas). Carnival sells passes to the Thermal Suite and Thalassotherapy Pool; guests in Cloud 9 Spa staterooms have complimentary access.

Despite being relocated to the port side of the ship, *Carnival Splendor*'s **Fitness Center** is still larger-than-average for most ships of this size, and features swell ocean views from banks of windows looking out over the sea.

DINING   *Carnival Splendor* features two, two-story dining rooms. Guests opting for traditional fixed early- and late-seating dinner are seated in the **Gold Pearl Restaurant** (sweeping 180-degree views!). Guests who want "Your Time Dining" get the **Black Pearl Restaurant** which is a kick: Gigantic black "pearls" are affixed to nearly every surface and the swooping ceiling reminds us of the interior of an Airbus A380.

But those are only the start of the options. The buffet at **Lido Restaurant** serves most every cuisine known to man (not kidding). There's also a Manhattan-chic **Steakhouse** (try the Yukon Gold Mash potatoes with Wasabi Horseradish; we crave them incessantly when we're onboard); a make-your-own stir fry joint (The **Mongolian Wok**), the **Taste Bar** (see p. 126) and several other options.

Carnival Breeze • Carnival Dream • Carnival Magic

The Verdict

Not just evolutionary, these three ships were *revolutionary* for Carnival when they burst on the scene. With new bars, lounges, and activities—not to mention a new look for *Carnival Breeze*—these ships are some of the best in the Carnival fleet.

Specifications

Avg. Starting Per Diem $110

Size (in tons)	130,000	Crew	1,386
Passengers (Double Occ.)	3,690	Passenger/Crew Ratio	2.6 to 1
Passenger/Space Ratio	36.1	Year Launched	2009-2012
Total Cabins/Veranda Cabins	1,845/851	Last Major Refurbishment	2016

Frommer's Ratings (Scale of 1–5)

★★★★ ½

Cabin Comfort & Amenities	4.5	Dining Options	4.5
Ship Cleanliness & Maintenance	4	Gym, Spa & Sports Facilities	4.5
Public Comfort/Space	4.5	Children's Facilities	4.5
Decor	4/5 Breeze	Enjoyment Factor	4.5

THE SHIPS IN GENERAL

Launched between 2009 and 2012, these three Dream Class ships represented a brand-new design for Carnival, both inside and out. The most different of the three is *Carnival Breeze,* which introduced a new interior decor scheme designed by Germany's PartnerShip AG firm instead of long-time designer Joe Farcus. What does that mean? More soft, Caribbean sea-like shades of blue and fewer eye-popping patterns. On our first day aboard *Carnival Breeze,* we almost had to remind ourselves we were on a Carnival cruise. (*Carnival Dream* and *Carnival Magic* have the same level of high quality furniture and fittings, but in bolder colors and with busier patterns.)

This class was designed to go toe-to-toe with the latest megaships from Royal Caribbean, but Carnival stays with a much more manageable 3,600 guest count compared to the over 5,000 new RCL ships carry. They certainly are equal (or nearly so) when it comes to fun, with poolside movie screens, the largest Cloud 9 Spa complex in the fleet, massive versions of the adults-only Serenity area, and a wonderful space known as The Lanai, an indoor-outdoor area that runs from one side of the ship to the other, creating a social gathering spot in a space that gets short shrift on most vessels.

Carnival shuttles these three ships around quite a bit, but you can typically find them sailing Eastern and Western Caribbean itineraries, plus the odd jaunt to the Bahamas, from ports like New Orleans, and Port Canaveral.

CABINS Every stateroom aboard these three Dream Class ships is at least 185 square feet, spacious for a ship of this size, and appointed with the fab Carnival Comfort Collection bedding and an overall fit-and-finish that's substantially improved from earlier ships. *Carnival Breeze* introduces a new, lighter stateroom decor.

Maybe it's a bit of nostalgia, but Carnival still offers Category 1A "Interior Upper/Lower" category (i.e., bunk beds) on the ships, a staple of the line for decades. They're a decent value, as they include a porthole window. New to the line are **Dream Class** staterooms which feature "cove balconies." These are inset into the hull of the ship, which keeps them sheltered from the elements and allows for 10 square feet more than average. These cabins are also located close to the waterline, which gives the feeling of being on a much smaller ship. **Aft View Extended Balcony Staterooms** have even deeper balconies and a spectacular view of the ship's wake.

Also worth a look: **Cloud 9 Spa Staterooms,** which are Inside, Oceanview, Balcony and Suite digs that include complimentary access to the Thermal Suite and Hydrotherapy Pool, along with upgraded amenities.

PUBLIC AREAS & ACTIVITIES   The main three-level **show lounge,** is home to large-scale production shows; there's not a bad view in the house, but we appreciate the extra leg room in the center part of the lower level. At the opposite end of the ship is a **lounge** for comedy shows and a variety of other acts plus new features like the **RedFrog Pub,** and **Ocean Plaza** (your go-to place for near-hourly trivia sessions and other fun diversions).

On Deck 5, the **Lanai** straddles the line between indoor entertainment space and outdoor hot-tub mecca, and is one of the best uses of a Promenade Deck we've seen in years. The area has two semicircular, partially covered outdoor seating areas and two large hot tubs that are cantilevered out over the ship's rail, with the sea bubbling below and 180-degree views over the horizon. (Two additional cantilevered hot tubs are located a bit farther forward along the Promenade.) Connecting the two Lanai areas is an indoor entertainment space, with its own bar, dance floor, and cafe.

The **Cloud 9 Spa** aboard these three ships is among largest in the fleet, spanning three decks. In it you'll find an expansive **fitness center,** hydrotherapy pool, a full thermal suite with heated loungers, aromatic steam rooms and saunas; and treatment rooms

The **WaterWorks** facility is one of the most elaborate ever designed for the line, though it's got a lot more "wetting features" on *Carnival Breeze*. *Carnival Breeze* also has a topnotch ropes course, sports square, and mini-golf course situated around the ship's funnel. Each ship has two main **swimming pools.** The main pool deck features a bandstand and outdoor movie screen (along with hundreds of deck chairs). Adults can escape from the kids up at the **Serenity** on Deck 14. Watch out if you're climbing up to Serenity from the starboard side stairs on Deck 12; we inadvertently got soaked by the giant WaterWorks bucket as it dumped water over dozens of excited children.

DINING   The Dream Class is all grown up when it comes to dining, offering far more culinary variety than past ships in the fleet. Each ship has two **main dining rooms.** Guests can choose to dine when they wish, but those who do so are seated in the midships dining room which, regrettably, features no windows on the upper levels, and windows that look out onto the ship's technical lifeboat area on the lower level. It might be worth choosing fixed dining for the great 180-degree views from the stern dining room.

These ships feature some of the largest **Lido Marketplace** casual buffets in the fleet, with food selections that traverse the globe. *Carnival Magic* takes things one step further with **Guy's Pig & Anchor Bar-B-Que Smokehouse** (featuring an authentic, honest-to-gosh Smoker), and both *Carnival Magic* and *Carnival Breeze* serve up tasty burgers at **Guy's Burger Joint,** and excellent Mexican cuisine at the **BlueIguana Cantina.** *Carnival Dream* lacks these for now, but chances are good she'll be refitted with them shortly. All three ships feature Carnival's specialty **steakhouse.**

Carnival Vista

The Verdict

With Cuban-themed staterooms, a dizzying array of activities and more outdoor deck areas, this is Carnival's most radically different ship to-date.

Specifications

Avg. Starting Per Diem $127

Size (in tons)	133,500	Crew	1,450
Passengers (Double Occ.)	3,934	Passenger/Crew Ratio	2.7 to 1
Passenger/Space Ratio	34.1	Year Launched	2016
Total Cabins/Veranda Cabins	1,967/854	Last Major Refurbishment	N/A

Frommer's Ratings (Scale of 1–5)

★★★★

Cabin Comfort & Amenities	4.5	Dining Options	4.5
Ship Cleanliness & Maintenance	5	Gym, Spa & Sports Facilities	5
Public Comfort/Space	5	Children's Facilities	4.5
Decor	5	Enjoyment Factor	5

THE SHIP IN GENERAL

Christened in the spring of 2016, *Carnival Vista* ushered in a completely new era for Carnival when she set sail in the Mediterranean. Although she looks like an enlarged version of the Dream Class from the outside, the similarities end there. On the inside, *Carnival Vista* said goodbye to the "old Carnival" of mirrors, fluorescent lighting and heavily patterned surfaces for good, going instead for a more high-end look that's a love-child somewhere between Carnival, Holland America and Celebrity Cruises…by way of Cuba. And though it's rare to run out of fun activities on a Carnival ship, this may be the first one which has so many attractions—the first IMAX movie at sea, an outdoor Twister board, the SkyRide, dozens of live shows and more—it's near impossible to do them all in just one cruise. *Carnival Vista* is the most significant change the Carnival fleet has seen in decades—and it's a good one.

CABINS What's really unusual about the *Vista* is just how many different kinds of **staterooms** it holds, from traditional inside, outside, balcony and suite categories to Cloud 9 Spa-themed staterooms and brand-new Havana Experience staterooms and staterooms geared towards families. As always with Carnival, all rooms are bigger than the mainstream cruise line norm, but rooms at the lower level (price-wise) on *Vista* have an Italian flair to them, with jaunty royal blue and gold striped banquettes (bed throws in the smaller rooms), and lots of soft edges.

Going up a notch are the **Cloud 9 Spa staterooms,** where guests get special spa amenities, a very Zen fern-green and gold decorating scheme, and complimentary access to the thermal suite and hydrotherapy pool. Guests staying in the swanky **Havana Staterooms or Suites** get boutique hotel-like digs (actual wooden beds, chic throw pillows, and hammock chairs on the balcony) plus private access to the Havana Pool and Lanai aft on Deck 5 until 5:00 p.m. daily. With its umbrellas, faux palm trees and thatched patio huts, it's one of the cutest areas on the ship.

Families travelling together will want to book one of the truly spectacular new **Family Harbor Staterooms and Suites.** Clustered in the new Family Zone, these staterooms have nifty maritime signal flags sewn into bed throws and pillows, and all sorts of nautical photos hung gallery style on the walls— the rooms are cool in a way that both adults and kids will appreciate.

A total of 65 staterooms have been designated for wheelchair users.

PUBLIC AREAS & ACTIVITIES Hold the presses because there's no neon, no brass, no highly patterned surfaces that threaten to blow your retinas apart on this ship. Instead, there's chic contemporary decor throughout and more intimate spaces than usual (like the downright classy **Vista Casino** and the two story show lounge, called **Liquid Lounge**). We're also fans of the groovy **Sports Bar,** and the **Limelight Lounge,** the cozy space that houses Carnival's very funny Punchliner Comedy Club performances.

Not everything is smaller: The always-rollicking **Piano Bar** has been expanded, and the large **Library Bar** "stars" a crowd-pleasing machine for self-serve wine. The latter also offers "reading drinks" (well-balanced cocktails), along with a better-than-you'd-expect selection of actual books. They tempt tipplers alongside the swanky **Alchemy Bar,** the **RedFrog Pub and Brewery** (which brews up batches of Carnival's own ale right onboard) and the brand-new **Havana Bar,** a surprisingly authentic representation of Cuba with its teal faux slatted window, low-slung leather chairs and selection of tropical drinks and food. These are just a few options on a ship that has an unusually rich array of nightspots, even for party-hearty Carnival.

While there are three pools onboard *Carnival Vista,* only the first two ("Beaches" and "Tides") are open to all guests. The **Havana Pool**—the prettiest of all—is reserved exclusively for guests staying in Havana category staterooms until 5pm, when the rest of the ship is allowed to have a go at it. As a result, the main pools and hot tubs can get pretty competitive, especially on sea days.

Carnival Vista also has the largest-ever **Water Works** aquatic park, with a kaleidoscope-themed waterslide, the usual Twister waterslide, a splash park for the kids, and a PowerDrencher bucket that tips gallons of water onto the deck surface at random intervals.

Happily, keeping fit aboard *Carnival Vista,* is no problem at all. It can also be a lot of fun, too. In addition to the usual **Fitness Center** (well stocked!), you might want to go for a spin along the new **SkyRide.** A recumbent bicycle course, guests can pedal their way around the track, which is elevated 150 feet above sea level. (*Note:* High winds and inclement weather can close it, and it's free which can lead to some pretty long lines.) The ship also has a ropes course with two levels of difficulty; a nine-hole mini-golf course, a basketball and volleyball court, and a jogging track.

The **Cloud 9 Spa** is the largest spa the line has constructed to-date. It offers spa treatments designed for both adults and teenagers, and an expansive thermal suite with heated ceramic loungers, aromatic showers and steam rooms, sauna rooms, and a hydrotherapy pool. A **salon** also offers a variety of hair and nail services for men and women.

Of course, you should also be sure to head up to Deck 6 to check out the **Carnival Thrill Teeter** (4-D fun) and the first IMAX theatre at sea.

DINING   There are two main dining rooms aboard the *Carnival Vista,* but it's the aft-facing, two-story **Horizons Restaurant** that really impresses. With its polished woods, aquamarine carpeting and soft lighting sources, it elevates the Carnival dining experience to new heights.

Steaks and surf-and-turf are the name of the game at Carnival's **Fahrenheit 555** steakhouse (extra charge). Across the hall, **Bonsai Sushi** serves up some of the best sushi and sashimi we've had on a ship. Other specialty restaurants include Italian **Cucina del Capitano** and **Ji Ji Asian Kitchen.**

CELEBRITY CRUISES

www.celebritycruises.com. © **800/647-2251** or 305/262-8322.

Pros

o **Stellar Spas:** Beautiful to look at and well stocked, the spas and gyms on this line are among the best at sea, and some have their own spa cafe.

o **Good Food:** Celebrity's cuisine is rated high among mainstream cruise lines, and its menus have long recognized the need for vegetarian, low-sodium, heart-conscious, and other healthy dishes.

o **Impressive Art Collections:** Celebrity's ships were among the first in the industry to display major art collections on board.

o **Contemporary Design:** Their design choices feel more like a boutique hotel than a mainstream cruise ship—reading nooks filled with chic wicker egg chairs, and curtained day beds on the pool deck. In an industry where design tends to lag behind what's on land, Celebrity's newest ships feel current.

Cons

o **Occasional Crowding:** Pack a couple thousand people onto a ship (pretty much any ship), and you'll get crowds at times, such as during buffets and when disembarking.

o **So-So Kids' Programs:** While Celebrity ships offer activities for children, kids' facilities and programs are less elaborate and enticing than those found on more family-focused lines such as Carnival, Royal Caribbean, and Disney.

Overview

With a premium fleet that's among the best designed in the cruise industry, Celebrity Cruises offers a great experience: classy, tasteful, and luxurious. You'll be taken care of at a relatively reasonable price.

EXPERIENCE

The Celebrity ships are spacious and comfortable, mixing contemporary and Art Deco styles and boasting an astounding art collection. The line's polished service is noticeable: Staff members are polite and professional and contribute greatly to the cruise experience. Dining-wise, Celebrity offers innovative cuisine that's a cut above the fare served by some of the other mainstream lines like sister line Royal Caribbean.

Celebrity gets the "best of" nod in a lot of categories: The AquaSpa by Elemis on the line's megaships is tops for mainstream lines, the art collections fleet-wide are the most compelling, and the onboard activities are among the most varied. Like all the big-ship lines, Celebrity has lots for its guests to do, but it focuses on mellower pursuits and innovative programming.

ROUTES

Celebrity sails a lot of Caribbean cruises, as well as the Bahamas, Bermuda, and trans-Panama Canal sailings. The line also has a strong presence in Alaska, but does more exotic routes as well, including the Galapagos, South America, Europe, Asia, and Australia.

PASSENGERS

The typical Celebrity guest is one who prefers to pursue his or her R&R with a minimum of aggressively promoted group activities. Passengers are the type who prefer wine with dinner and maybe a tad more decorum than on some other ships, but they can kick up their heels with the beer-and-pretzels crowd just fine if the occasion warrants. Most give the impression of being prosperous but not obscenely rich, congenial but not obsessively proper, animated but not the type to wear a lampshade for a hat. You'll find everyone from kids to retirees, with a good number of couples in their 40s and 50s.

DINING

Celebrity's cuisine, plentiful and served with style, leans toward American/European. This means that dishes are generally not low-fat, although the line has eliminated trans fats and in 2013 brought in healthy-eating organization SPE Certified to consult on and certify dozens of dishes in Celebrity's main restaurants. The company's dining program is under the leadership of John Suley, a highly talented and experienced chef who was nominated as a "rising star" by the prestigious James Beard Foundation.

Celebrity also has one of the most extensive 24-hour room-service menus in the industry, plus themed lunch buffets and one to two (depending on itinerary length) special brunches. Meals in the alternative dining rooms, generally are worth the extra charges of up to $45 per person.

You can dine formally in the dining room or informally at buffets for breakfast and lunch, with a sushi bar and made-to-order pastas and pizzas served nightly in the Oceanview Cafe. Dinner is served at two seatings in the main dining room. A few years ago, the line also introduced the option of open seating in the dining room; you choose either traditional (i.e., assigned) or open seating Celebrity Select Dining before your cruise. The AquaSpa Cafe, in a corner of the Solarium pool area, serves low-cal treats, including fresh mango with mint, chicken salad made with Greek yogurt instead of mayo, and pretty salads topped with tuna or chicken.

ACTIVITIES

The line offers a laundry list of activities through its all-encompassing enrichment program. A typical day might involve a Rosetta Stone language course, bridge, a culinary demonstration, a chef's cook-off, wine tastings in partnership with the renowned Riedel Crystal company, an art auction, and a volleyball tournament. Celebrity iLounge, the brand's chic version of the Internet cafe, allows e-mail access for 75¢ a minute, with discount packages available. The line was among the first to offer acupuncture at sea.

CHILDREN'S PROGRAMS

For children, Celebrity ships employ a group of counselors who direct and supervise a camp-style children's program with activities geared toward different age groups. Though not as elaborate as the kids' facilities on the ships of some other mainstream lines, Celebrity's ships offer kids' play areas and a separate lounge area for teens that, among other things, now feature Xbox-themed spaces for organized Xbox-related activities and games. Private and group babysitting are both available.

ENTERTAINMENT

Although entertainment is not generally cited as a reason to sail with Celebrity, the line's stage shows are solid. You won't find any big-name entertainers, but you also won't find any obvious has-beens either—there's just a whole lot of singin' and dancin', from an Elton John tribute that's straight out of Las Vegas on one night to a pretty solid comedian the next. Of course, you can always find a cozy lounge or piano bar to curl up in, and the line is home to the Molecular Bar, which was the first at-sea cocktail lounge to use liquid nitrogen in drinks, as well as a serve-yourself wine bar with plenty of taps. If you're up late, the disco and casino are, too.

SERVICE

In the cabins, service is efficient and so unobtrusive that you might never see your steward except at the beginning and end of your cruise. In the dining room, as throughout the ship, service is polite, professional, and cheerful.

Laundry, dry cleaning, and valet services are available on all boats.

If you stay in a suite, you really will be treated like royalty, with a tuxedo-clad butler at your beck and call. The butler will serve you afternoon tea (or complimentary cappuccino or espresso) and bring pre-dinner hors d'oeuvres. The butler will shine your shoes, too, on request. Also available for those who can't quite afford a suite are Concierge Class rooms that come with such perks as fresh flowers and fruit, a choice of pillow types, and oversize towels.

Gratuities of $13.50 per passenger per day are automatically charged to your shipboard account ($14 per person per day for those in Concierge Class and AquaClass cabins and $17 per person, per day for suites), but you can increase or decrease the amount by visiting the guest relations desk on board.

FLEET

Celebrity has 11 ships, which range in size from 2,170 to 2,850 passengers. Five of them are part of the impressive Solstice class, which established the ship as a chic, design-focused line with a boutique hotel style. Celebrity's ships have an elegant combination of artfulness, excitement, and fun, without ever becoming tacky. The fleet includes one expedition-style ship, Celebrity *Xpedition,* which sails nature cruises in the Galapagos Islands all year long.

Celebrity Solstice • Celebrity Equinox • Celebrity Eclipse • Celebrity Silhouette • Celebrity Reflection

The Verdict

The most beautiful megaships at sea today, Celebrity's five Solstice-class sisters manage to simultaneously encapsulate all that was great about Celebrity's older vessels while also moving logically and stylistically into the future.

Specifications

Avg. Starting Per Diem $185

Size (in tons)	122,000	Crew	1,246
Passengers (Double Occ.)	2,850	Passenger/Crew Ratio	2.3 to 1
Passenger/Space Ratio	42.8	Year Launched	2008-2011
Total Cabins/Veranda Cabins	1,426/1,216	Last Major Refurbishment	N/A

Frommer's Ratings (Scale of 1–5)

★★★★

Cabin Comfort & Amenities	5	Dining Options	5
Ship Cleanliness & Maintenance	5	Gym, Spa & Sports Facilities	5
Public Comfort/Space	5	Children's Facilities	4
Decor	5	Enjoyment Factor	5

THE SHIPS IN GENERAL

Since introducing its very first new build in 1990, Celebrity has consistently had the most stylish megaships in the cruise biz. The line's Solstice-class ships are no exception: They're absolute knockouts. On the outside, their massive forms have a sexy sleekness, while inside a unifying aesthetic—neo-Deco lines, top quality art, and rich, quality textures and surface materials—ties the many moods and experiences of their public rooms into a satisfying whole. In the atrium, translucent backlit onyx panels and white drapes recall similar materials used in the Millennium atriums, while the dreamy white interiors of each ship's main restaurant and observation lounge evoke both the past and the future—hinting at elements of the Century class while taking a stylistic swipe at both *2001: A Space Odyssey* and 1930s Hollywood movies.

Balancing all the big "wow" elements are a wealth of subtle details, evident in everything from the ship's art collection—a world-class assemblage of minimalist, and nature-evoking pieces from big names and emerging talents—to its cabins, which could win awards for innovation.

CABINS   When was the last time you got to your cabin, looked around, and thought, "Huh, why haven't other ships done that before?" To break the mold, Celebrity broke the mold, moving away from the rectangular **cabins** you'll find on other lines. On these boats one wall of each cabin bulges slightly, interlocking with the cabin next door in a sort of squared-off yin-yang format. That simple change gives passengers far more sense of space and, as importantly, more maneuvering room around the foot of the bed (Solstice's and Equinox's cabins about 15% larger than those on its older ships).

Standard inside (183–200 sq. ft.) and outside (176–192 sq. ft.) cabins have an open and airy feeling, an ergonomic design, and a modern, modular look. Beds have rounded corners (no more banged ankles!) and are higher than normal to give more storage space underneath. At the wall, the beds are flanked by a tall headboard topped with a narrow, completely unobtrusive storage unit perfect for handbags, shopping bags, and other small items. Some couches offer trundle beds for kids and other additional guests, while closet doors slide shut automatically—which isn't so unusual on land, but is a hard thing to accomplish on a moving ship. All cabins have flatscreen TVs, sitting areas with sofas, minifridges, and hair dryers. Outside, cabin balconies are large and deep, with plenty of room for two reclining deck chairs and a table.

Cabin bathrooms and showers are substantially larger and roomier than aboard most other megaships; and those showers are equipped with an ingenious foot rail that makes it easier for women to shave their legs. Bathrooms also come with a handy dandy collection of small drawers, nooks, and cabinets for storing toiletries and other necessities.

In addition to the usual range of inside, outside, balcony cabins, and suites (300–1,291 sq. ft.), Solstice and Equinox both have 130 adults-only **Aqua-Class** staterooms, where the cabin experience is tied to an overall wellness aesthetic. Grouped together on the Penthouse Deck, each AquaClass cabin has niceties such as large balconies, pillow menus, jetted body-wash showers, and special music/sound and aromatherapy options tied to specific vacation goals (relaxation, invigoration, and so on). AquaClass guests also get special perks around the ship, including unlimited access to the spa's Persian Garden aromatherapy steam room and relaxation room, special wellness classes and invitations to VIP events, and the option of dining at a 130-seat specialty restaurant called Blu (see below).

Each ship has 30 wheelchair-accessible staterooms, spread among the different types of accommodations onboard, from inside cabins to sky suites.

PUBLIC AREAS & ACTIVITIES   The Solstice-class ships have one of the most logical arrangements of public rooms we've seen in a decade and a half of reviewing ships. Most are clustered on the Entertainment and Promenade decks, and rooms were consciously grouped so that different types are in different areas of the ship, cutting down on unnecessary congestion in the corridors. Evening entertainment outlets, for instance (the Equinox Theatre and the several venues of the Entertainment Court), are all located forward and linked directly to the **Sky Observation Lounge** by elevator. Pre- and post-dinner entertainment (the Ensemble Lounge for pre-dinner cocktails and after-dinner jazz; **Michael's Club** (for more intimate piano music and libations) is located immediately adjacent to the ships' specialty restaurants.

The 1,115-guest **main theater** is particularly innovative, its complex ceiling rigging allowing aerialist entertainers to fly right over audience members' heads. Down the corridor, **Celebrity Central** is a 200-seat, multifunction venue that presents late-night comedy shows, films, and other performances and events. Across the hall, the Quasar nightclub has a streamlined, space-age look, with clear plastic "bubble chairs" suspended from the ceiling and huge LED screens curving from the walls into the ceiling, their lights synched with the music's beat. Between these venues, an **Entertainment Court** is the venue for vocal quartets and other small-scale entertainment designed to keep passengers' interest as they move between other nightlife options. Other diversions on these decks include **Cellar Masters,** a Napa-inspired space for formal wine tastings and informal sipping; the **Martini Bar** with its purposefully frosted bar (it's very cool looking, especially with all of the blue decor); and **Crush,** a tasting room where guests sit around an ice-filled table to sample pairings of vodka and caviar.

But the Solstice-class ships' most distinctive and innovative features are out on deck—most visibly way up on the top deck, where the **Lawn Club** has a half-acre of real grass growing 15 decks above the sea. A first for cruise ships, the area has a country-club ambience: refined and calming. On the central lawn, passengers can play croquet or putt some golf balls around, either in individual play or during scheduled tournaments. The two grassy courts along the sides of the ship have space for bocce and other lawn games. Passengers can also picnic on the main lawn, relax at the shaded patio at its aft end (dotted with potted greenery and comfortable lounge chairs and couches), or grab a drink at the aft-facing **Sunset Bar,** with its views of the ship's wake.

At the forward end of the Lawn Club is another of the Solstice-class signature features: the **Hot Glass Show.** Developed by the world-famous Corning Museum of Glass, it provides daily (and surprisingly high-energy) programs in which master artisans explain and demonstrate the art of glass-blowing. Presented in an open-air studio designed specifically for these ships, the shows give the audience a sort of "glassmaking 101" experience, taking them through the process of creating a piece from start to finish—from an undifferentiated blob of glass to bowls, vases, and more complex forms like glass conch shells.

For kids, there's a large, light-filled, multiroom children's center near the very top of the ship, on the same deck as the Lawn Club. A teen center is adjacent, along with a video arcade.

DINING   Celebrity diversified its dining program on the Solstice class ships, a first for the line. On these vessels, you'll find a grand **main restaurant,** a **buffet,** three **casual eateries,** and four specialty restaurants, some with extra charges (the latter are clustered aft on the Entertainment Deck, opening off the Ensemble Lounge). The **Tuscan Grille** ($45 per person; $89 per person with wine pairings) is a high-style spot in the ship's stern, with a menu heavy on steaks and pastas. **Murano** ($50 per person) blends classic and modern Continental cuisine in an elegant, romantic setting inspired by Venice's famous Murano glassmakers. **Blu** (included) is reserved exclusively for passengers booked into the AquaClass staterooms (plus suite guests based on availability). It serves a menu of "clean cuisine" dishes that focus on a few simple ingredients, cutting down on calorie-heavy sauces. Aboard *Solstice* and *Equinox,* **Silk Harvest** ($35 per person) offers a mix of Thai, Vietnamese, Japanese, and Chinese selections, complemented by a variety of sakes, Asian-influenced martinis, and cocktails created with ginger root and acai berries. *Reflection, Silhouette,* and *Eclipse* have the high-style **Qsine** ($45 per person) which presents menus on iPads and feature a variety of international cuisines served on uncommon china (no plates or bowls here). Many dishes are designed to be shared, making this a great venue to come to as a group.

Several other eateries are scattered around each ship. Forward of the Ensemble Lounge, the centrally located **Bistro on Five** is a casual, chic restaurant with a menu of specialty crepes, sandwiches, soups, salads, and entrees including quiche, fish and chips, baked ziti, and chicken pot pie. Right across the corridor, **Café al Bacio & Gelateria** is an upscale coffeehouse for specialty coffees, teas, fresh-baked pastries, traditional gelatos and Italian ices, and other desserts. In the Solarium, the **AquaSpa Café** has, you guessed it, spa cuisine: salads, lean meats, seafood, and fresh fruit smoothies.

POOL, FITNESS, SPA & SPORTS FACILITIES   The Solstice-class Pool Deck is one of the most serene in the cruise biz, owing to the decision to place the ship's buffet restaurant and grill on a separate deck, one level up. That decision automatically changed the pool deck from a busy, multipurpose space into one whose sole purpose is resortlike relaxation. Surrounding two **pools** (one for "sports," one for families) and four hot tubs are 12 white, 25-foot, A-frame canopies supporting cantilevered awnings and providing shade for chaise lounges on both the **Resort Deck** (the ships' pool deck) and the **Lido Deck** above. A dancing fountain occupies a central position at the aft of the pool area, ringed with deck chairs. Forward of the pools, the glass-ceilinged **Solarium** is a peaceful enclave for adults only, with a lap pool, cushioned teak lounge chairs, views all around, and the AquaSpa Café.

The **AquaSpa** itself is done up in a restful white and Aegean blue, its colonnade and domed rotunda reception area designed as a contemporary interpretation of the architecture found on the Greek Isles (think whitewashed buildings topped with brilliant blue domes). Besides massages and facials, the treatment menu includes acupuncture, Botox wrinkle treatments, teeth whitening, and cosmetic dermal fillers to smooth smile lines. The Persian Garden is a steam room in the old style (really old, think Ottoman Empire). It's complimentary for guests booked into AquaSpa staterooms and suites; everybody else has to pay. The ships' gyms are large and extremely well equipped.

Celebrity Millennium • Celebrity Infinity • Celebrity Summit • Celebrity Constellation

The Verdict

Not as big or as elaborate as their Solstice-class siblings, Celebrity has nevertheless done a lot to bring these ships up to a similar standard.

Specifications

Avg. Starting Per Diem $147

Size (in tons)	91,000	Crew	999
Passengers (Double Occ.)	2,158	Passenger/Crew Ratio	2.1 to 1
Passenger/Space Ratio	42.1	Year Launched	2000–2002
Total Cabins/Veranda Cabins	1,079/623	Last Major Refurbishment	2016

Frommer's Ratings (Scale of 1–5)

★★★★ ½

Cabin Comfort & Amenities	5	Dining Options	4.5
Ship Cleanliness & Maintenance	4	Gym, Spa & Sports Facilities	4.5
Public Comfort/Space	4.5	Children's Facilities	4.5
Decor	5	Enjoyment Factor	4.5

THE SHIPS IN GENERAL

Time was, these ships were *it:* bigger than the line's first generation of megaships (the Century class), with larger spas and theaters, more veranda cabins, more dining options, more shopping, more lounges, and more sports and exercise facilities—plus more of the same great service, cuisine, and high-style onboard art. Then *Celebrity Solstice* happened, and the bar got a lot higher—but don't count these ships out yet: Each has received multimillion-dollar refurbishments designed to add some of the most attractive features of the Solstice class. Each ship now has the new Tuscan Grille steakhouse restaurant, a new Bistro on Five casual creperie and comfort food eatery, a new Martini Bar with permafrost bar top, a new vodka-and-caviar tasting bar, and a new Café al Bacio & Gelateria, replacing the Millennium ships' Cova Café. Additionally, staterooms and public areas have been slowly restyled to reflect the Solstice class's more sleek lines and understated color palate.

CABINS   Standard inside (170 sq. ft.) and outside (170–191 sq. ft.) **cabins** are roomy and come with a small sitting area, stocked minifridge, TV, safe, ample storage space, cotton robes, a hair dryer, and shower-mounted shampoo dispensers. Only thing missing? Individual reading lights above the beds, though there are table lamps on the nightstands.

Premium and Deluxe staterooms have slightly larger sitting areas and approximately 40-square-foot verandas. The 12 Family Ocean View staterooms in the stern on Panorama, Sky, and Vista decks measure in at a very large 271 square feet and have two entertainment centers with TVs/VCRs, a partitioned sitting area with two convertible sofa beds, and very, very, very large 242-square-foot verandas facing the ship's wake.

Passengers booking the **Concierge Class** staterooms on Sky Deck get a bunch of cushy extras, from a bottle of champagne on arrival to a choice of pillows, upgraded bedding, oversize towels, double-thick Frette bathrobes, priority for just about everything (dining, shore excursions, luggage delivery, embarkation, and debarkation), and high-powered binoculars on their 41-square-foot balconies. Unfortunately, many of those balconies (as well as those attached to several Deluxe Ocean View cabins at Sky Deck midships) catch shadow from the overhanging deck above. *Tip:* Several Concierge Class cabins on the Sky Deck (9038 and 9043) and Panorama Deck (8045 and 8046) have extra-large verandas at no extra cost; try to book those.

Suites provide 24-hour butler service and come in four levels, from the 251-square-foot Sky Suites with balconies to the eight 467-square-foot Celebrity Suites (with a dining area, separate bedroom, two TV/VCR combos, and a whirlpool bathtub, but no verandas) and the 538-square-foot Royal Suites (also with a separate living/dining room, two TV/VCR combos, a standing shower and whirlpool bathtub, and a huge 195-sq.-ft. veranda with whirlpool tub). At the top of the food chain, the massive Penthouse Suites measure 1,432 square feet and have herringbone wood floors, a marble foyer, a computer station, a Yamaha piano, and a simply amazing bathroom with ocean views and a full-size hot tub. And did we mention a 1,098-square-foot veranda that wraps around the stern of the ship and features a whirlpool tub and full bar?

Passengers requiring use of a wheelchair have a choice of 26 cabins in several categories, from Sky Suites to balcony cabins to inside staterooms.

PUBLIC AREAS & ACTIVITIES   There's simply nothing else at sea like the **Grand Foyer** atrium, the stunning hub of all four ships. Each rectangular, three-deck area features a translucent, inner-illuminated onyx staircase that glows beneath your feet, plus giant silk flower arrangements and topiaries, oceanview elevators, and an attractive Internet center.

In each ship's bow is an elegant three-deck **theater** with a warm glow provided by faux torches spaced all around. Seating on all three levels is unobstructed except in the far reaches of the balconies. You'll also find elegant martini, champagne, and caviar bars, as well as brighter, busier lounges for live music. For the real dancing, head up to the stunning **observation lounge/ disco** on the **Sunrise Deck.** Other rooms include a two-deck **library;** a large **casino;** an oceanview **florist/conservatory** (filled mostly with silk flowers and trees, some of which are for sale); and the huge, high-tech **conference center** and **cinema.** Celebrity's signature **Michael's Club** is a quiet, dignified piano bar replete with a fake fireplace and comfy leather club chairs, which is now an exclusive venue set aside for guests booking top-of-the-line suites. Good for suite guests, but bad news for the rest of us.

The ships' **Emporium Shops** have a nice variety of high-end name brands as well as cheap souvenirs.

For kids, the **Fun Factory** has both indoor and outdoor soft-surface jungle gyms, a wading pool, a ball bin, a computer room, a movie room, an arts-and-crafts area, a video arcade, a teen center, and more. There is no dedicated lounge for teens, though the youth staff does program teen activities at different venues onboard.

DINING   The main dining rooms are beautiful two-level spaces with huge stern-facing windows, oversize round windows to port and starboard, and a dramatic central double staircase. *Summit's* dining room boasts a 7-foot Art Deco bronze of the goddess Athena, which once overlooked the grand staircase on the legendary SS *Normandie* ocean liner. (She resided for years near the pool at Miami's Fontainebleau Hotel before Celebrity bought her and returned her to sea.)

The real *pièce de résistance* on these ships, however, is their alternative, reservations-only restaurants. Revolutionary when they first debuted nearly two decades ago, they still hold their own—though we're disappointed to see the former ocean liner focus start to disappear as Celebrity rebrands them. *Millennium's* is the Edwardian-style **Olympic** restaurant, whose decor features several dozen handcarved French walnut wall panels made by Palestinian craftsmen for the A La Carte restaurant on *Titanic's* sister ship *Olympic,* which sailed from 1911 to 1935. *Constellation's* **Ocean Liners** restaurant has artifacts from a variety of luxury liners, including sets of original red-and-black lacquered panels from the 1920s *Ile de France,* which add a whimsical Parisian air. Dining in either is a 2- to 3-hour commitment, with some 100 guests served by a gracious staff of more than 20, including eight dedicated chefs, six waiters, five maitre d's, and four sommeliers. Waiters remove domed silver dish covers with a flourish revealing continental specialties mixed with original recipes from the ships the restaurants are named after—the original Waldorf Pudding recipe from the White Star Liner *Olympic,* for instance, or the Long Island duckling featured on the original SS *United States.* Exceptional cheeses are offered postmeal, and a pianist or a piano/violin duo performs period music.

Infinity, sadly, has lost her **SS United States** restaurant, with its etched-glass panels from the 1950s liner of the same name. Ditto for *Summit's* **Normandie** restaurant, which has, like *Infinity,* been removed to make way for the **Tuscan Grille** steakhouse. Very high in style, it offers a menu heavy on steaks and pastas (for the curious, each ship still displays the removed nautical memorabilia but sadly, it's now in a forgotten corner near the casino.) For something more casual, **Bistro on Five** serves a menu of specialty crepes, sandwiches, soups, salads, and comfort food entrees.

The huge **buffet restaurant** on each ship is open for breakfast, lunch, and dinner, with regular buffet selections plus pizza, pasta, and ice-cream specialty stations. Depending on how busy the restaurant is, waiters may carry passengers' trays to their tables and fetch coffee. For fancy snacks, visit **Café al Bacio & Gelateria,** which serves specialty coffees, teas, fresh-baked pastries, traditional gelatos and Italian ices, and other desserts.

POOL, FITNESS, SPA & SPORTS FACILITIES The **spas** on the Millennium-class ships are gorgeous and sprawling, their 25,000 square feet taken up with hydrotherapy treatment rooms; New Agey Persian Garden steam suites whose nooks have showers that simulate a tropical rainforest, heated tiled couches, and the aromas of chamomile, eucalyptus, and mint; and large, bubbling thalassotherapy pools with soothing pressure jets in a solarium-like setting under a glass roof. The pool is free to all adult guests, and you can stretch out the experience by grabbing a casual breakfast or lunch at the **AquaSpa Café,** set back by the seaview windows.

Next door to the spa, there's a very large **gym** with dozens of the latest machines and free weights, and a large aerobics floor.

Up top, the **Sports Deck** has facilities for basketball, volleyball, quoits, and paddle tennis. Just below, on the **Sunrise Deck,** is the ship's jogging track. Below that is the well-laid-out **Pool Deck,** where you'll find two pools, four hot tubs, a couple of bars, and a sunning area. Head up to the balcony level above the pool, at both the bow and the stern, for quieter sunbathing spots.

Celebrity Xpedition

The Verdict

Celebrity's year-round vessel in the Galapagos offers up an expedition cruise experience with all the Celebrity touches past guests have come to expect.

Specifications

Avg. Starting Per Diem $740

Size (in tons)	2,842	Crew	66
Passengers (Double Occ.)	100	Passenger/Crew Ratio	1.5 to 1
Passenger/Space Ratio	N/A	Year Launched	2001/2004
Total Cabins/Veranda Cabins	49/13	Last Major Refurbishment	2013

Frommer's Ratings (Scale of 1–5)

★★★★

Cabin Comfort & Amenities	4	Dining Options	3
Ship Cleanliness & Maintenance	4	Gym, Spa & Sports Facilities	3
Public Comfort/Space	4.5	Children's Facilities	N/A
Decor	4	Enjoyment Factor	5

THE SHIP IN GENERAL

Acquired in 2004 and refitted every few years ever since, *Celebrity Xpedition* is Celebrity Cruises only expedition vessel in the Galapagos (though two additional ships have just been purchased as this book went to press, and are tentatively scheduled to enter service in 2017). With capacity for just 100 guests, this often-overlooked gem is a real winner in the Galapagos Islands. Onboard, you'll find Celebrity's stylish decor and excellent service, coupled with all of the little amenities that past guests of the line have come to love. But hard-core expedition and adventure cruisers will find plenty to like here, too, including an onboard expedition team of guides approved by the Galapagos National Park Service and authentic Ecuadorian cuisine and crew members. Celebrity includes all drinks and gratuities aboard *Celebrity Xpedition,* putting her in league with ultra-luxury line Silversea's *Silver Galapagos* (p. 272).

CABINS   **Staterooms** and **suites** aboard *Celebrity Xpedition* are all ocean-view, though private balconies don't make their appearance until you hit the suite level. Standard staterooms come in three category levels (Premium, Deluxe and Standard Oceanview) and vary in size from 145 to 160 square feet. While snug, these staterooms all include flat-panel TV's and DVD players, an mp3 docking station, a decent amount of storage space, a small desk and sitting area, as well as bathrobes, binoculars, and use of snorkel equipment and wetsuits. Most have queen beds that can convert to two twins, with the exception of Stateroom 401, which has a fixed queen.

Suites add both more space and the addition of private balconies, as well as special perks like complimentary sparkling wine, a daily fruit basket, and daily hors d' oeuvres. Junior Suites are 175 square feet, while Expedition and Royal Suites come in at just over 200 square feet with 50 square foot balconies. If you're looking for top-of-the-line luxury, the ship's lone Penthouse Suite (room 601) offers up 460 square feet of living space that includes two balconies, separate living and sleeping areas, two private bathrooms with shower, and a private Jacuzzi on the larger of the two balconies.

PUBLIC AREAS & ACTIVITIES   Like most expedition ships, it's quality not quantity when it comes to the ship's public areas. On Deck 5, the **Discovery Lounge** is the place to be for afternoon cocktails, daily expedition briefings, and nightcaps. The room spans the width of the ship and is lined attractively with windows; our favorite area is the seating tucked away on the starboard side of the lounge, near the entrance to the outdoor Beagle Grill (it's nice and cozy). When the weather's good (and it almost always is), most guests can be found up on the open **Panorama Deck** on Deck 6, which has comfortable padded chairs and couches accented with ocean blue cushions and matching umbrellas to keep the sun's rays at bay. Sun worshippers will want to go one deck up, where unshaded loungers are laid out.

DINING   Surprisingly for a ship of this size, there are two main dining venues onboard. **Darwin's Dining Room** is the ship's main restaurant. Running along the port side of Deck 3, it's a fairly narrow room that nonetheless lets in some pretty decent views from the single wall of picture windows. Breakfast buffets are served here, along with a selection of cooked-to-order specialties. Lunch is a casual affair as well, but dinners are where the line really pulls out the stops, delivering multi-course meals. In keeping with Ecuadorian law, practically all ingredients must be sourced from the Galapagos or the Ecuadorian mainland, so it's not the same quality (or international selection) that's found on the rest of the Celebrity fleet. All the way aft on Deck 4, the **Beagle Grill** serves up casual poolside fare during lunch and dinner (think hamburgers and sandwiches). Impressively for a ship of this size, room service is available as well.

POOL, FITNESS, SPA & SPORTS FACILITIES While most of the adventure happens off of the ship, *Celebrity Xpedition* has a hot tub and a small (very small) Fitness Room on Deck 6.

COSTA CRUISES

www.costacruise.com. *©* **800/462-6782.**

Pros

o **Italian Flavor:** Entertainment, activities, and cuisine are presented with European (mostly Italian) flair. Plus, most of the officers are Italians, too.

o **Very Active, Very Fun:** There are a lot of activities, and Costa passengers love to participate, creating a festive and social environment morning to night (could be all those espressos that keep the adrenaline up!).

o **Budget-Friendly:** These cruises start out at prices that won't break the budget, and there are often discounts available that make them even more reasonable.

o **Family-Friendly:** Much like Carnival, Costa caters to families with kids of all ages with dedicated Kids and Teens programs and plenty of diversions to keep the little ones happy.

Cons

o **Smoking:** While the idea of sailing with lots of people from the Continent sounds romantic, there can be culture clashes on a variety of issues, and the largest issue for many Americans is the smoking. (Smoking is allowed on deck and on balconies, and even bars have special sections for smokers.)

o **Crowding:** These ships are rambunctious, and they're not the right fit for travelers looking for a quiet vacation away from crowds. Expect long lines for, well, pretty much everything.

o **Announcements:** Every day, every announcement on every sailing is made in a variety of languages over the loudspeaker system. A simple, one-minute announcement can stretch to four or five minutes, depending on how many different nationalities are onboard.

Overview

These inexpensive cruises require you to lower a few standards—but with bargain basement deals available, you just might be willing to do that. This Italian line, now sadly most famous for the 2012 *Costa Concordia* disaster, is owned by Carnival Corporation, so some of the "very Italian" things once found onboard (such as fab pasta) are in the past, though you can still get thin crust pizza as well as Italian espresso, charcuterie, and cheeses.

EXPERIENCE

For years, Costa has played up its Italian heritage as the main element that distinguishes it from Carnival, Royal Caribbean, and the rest—even though the line is part of the Carnival Corporation empire, and many members of the service staff are as Italian as Chico Marx. Still, there's an Italianate essence here, with more pasta dishes on the menu than on any other line; more classical Italian music among the entertainment offerings; activities facilitated by a young, usually Italian, and ridiculously attractive "animation staff"; and a huge number of Italian Americans among the passengers. The interiors of the line's newest ships are by Carnival's designer-in-chief Joe Farcus, who took inspiration from Italy's traditions of painting and architecture but still stuck close to his signature "more is more" style—think Florence by way of Vegas.

Costa cruises the Eastern and Western Mediterranean, as well as the Red Sea; Dubai/United Arab Emirates sailings; and as far east as the Indian Ocean and Mauritius and into the Far East. Costa also cruises in the Baltic and the Norwegian fjords. Closer to home, you can find Costa in the Caribbean and into South America as well.

PASSENGERS

You'll find passengers from a variety of countries on most sailings, though with more of a European base than many other lines, and a wide range of ages from groups of 20-something-year-old friends, to families with young children, to retirees. The low rates appeal to many different types of travelers.

On cruises that sail in Europe, that may mean 80% European travelers, about 20% North Americans. In the Caribbean, those ratios are reversed.

DINING

Before it was owned by Carnival, the line used to focus on high-quality Italian ingredients, from mouthwatering imported regional cheeses and cured meats to house-made pasta. Alas, today dining onboard these ships is more comparable to their budget-friendly competitors. That said, some ships have hand-tossed pizzas (for a fee) and Italian gelato (for a fee). They also have Italian-style quirks, such as no tap water at dinner, a move that requires Americans used to having water with their evening meal to buy bottled.

ACTIVITIES

These ships are very port focused, with fewer onboard activities than their American counterparts. Still, they all carry a casino, pools, a kiddie pool, hot tubs, a gym, and a spa as well as a jogging track and volleyball courts. Some of the ships also have a pirate ship and castle feature for kids to play on.

CHILDREN'S PROGRAMS

Costa's kids' programs aren't nearly as extensive as those on Disney or Royal Caribbean (or Carnival's Conquest-class and Spirit-class ships), but then, there are usually far fewer children on board. At least two full-time youth counselors sail aboard, with additional staff whenever more than a dozen or so kids are on the passenger list. **Supervised activities** are offered for kids ages 3 to 18, divided into two age groups unless enough children are aboard to divide them into three (3–6, 7–12, and 13–18 years) or four (3–6, 7–10, 11–14, and 15–18 years). The **Costa Kids Club,** for ages 3 to 12, includes such activities as arts and crafts, scavenger hunts, Italian-language lessons, bingo, board games, face painting, movies, kids' karaoke, and pizza and ice-cream-sundae parties. The ships each have a pleasant children's playroom and a teen disco. If there are enough teens on board, the **Costa Teens Club** for ages 13 to 18 opens and has foosball and darts competitions, karaoke, and other activities.

When ships are at sea in the Caribbean, supervised Kids Club hours are typically from 9am to noon, 3 to 6pm, and 9 to 11:30pm. The program also operates during port days, but on a more limited basis.

On Gala nights, there's a great complimentary **Parents' Night Out program** from 6 to 11:30pm during which kids ages 3 and older (they must be out of diapers) are entertained and given a special buffet or pizza party while Mom and Dad get a night out alone. All other times, **group babysitting** for ages 3 and up is available every night from 9 to 11:30pm at no cost, and from 11:30pm to 1:30am if you make arrangements in advance. No private, in-cabin babysitting is available.

Children must be at least 6 months old to sail with Costa, and kids sail free between ages 6 months and 2 years.

ENTERTAINMENT

Evening entertainment might include acrobats, opera performances (unusual on cruise ships, but it feels right here), and a variety of bars and dance clubs. Don't be surprised if you see small children on the floor late at night with their parents, especially on European sailings.

SERVICE

While Costa used to have a primarily Italian staff, today the line draws from a mix of European and Southeast Asian crew. Service is punctual and efficient, though North American guests may find that it's not quite as friendly as on other mainstream lines.

FLEET

The line now has 15 ships, each more colorful than the last, ranging in size from 2,680 to 3,800 passengers. Picture red ceilings, large chandeliers, oversized statues, and fresco-style wall art; the vast majority of the onboard decor has been designed with the zany whimsy of Carnival's longtime in-house designer, Joe Farcus. The line's newest ship, the *Costa Diadema,* is full of flashing lights and bright colors, and aims to bring back some of the line's original "Italian-ness" with Barilla pasta, house-made gelato and Illy coffee. It also carries a large, two-story German-style beer garden with costumed waitresses and a wide selection of both German and Italian beers.

Costa Deliziosa • Costa Luminosa

The Verdict

These two twins offer all the silly fun Costa is known for, and are quite affordable, to boot.

Specifications		Avg. Starting Per Diem $80	
Size (in tons)	92,600	Crew	1,100
Passengers (Double Occ.)	2,862	Passenger/Crew Ratio	2.6 to 1
Passenger/Space Ratio	32.3	Year Launched	2010/2009
Total Cabins/Veranda Cabins	1,130/768	Last Major Refurbishment	N/A

Cabin Comfort & Amenities	4	Dining Options	3
Ship Cleanliness & Maintenance	4	Gym, Spa & Sports Facilities	4
Public Comfort/Space	4.5	Children's Facilities	3
Decor	3	Enjoyment Factor	4

THE SHIPS IN GENERAL

Based upon the same Vista Class platform that Carnival used for Holland America's Vista class and Cunard's *Queen Elizabeth* and *Queen Victoria,* Costa's *Costa Deliziosa* and *Costa Luminosa* may look familiar on the outside, but don't be fooled: Inside is the line's signature brand of zany Italian froufrou. Carrying just 2,260 guests apiece, these two ships are more spacious and less crowded than many of Costa's other vessels, and they've been a hit in the Caribbean since they arrived.

In many ways, these are some of Costa's best ships, with generous open deck spaces, a wraparound promenade that encircles the ship, a magrodome-covered pool, and plenty of balcony staterooms. With their tall, bright yellow funnel adorned with a blue "C," they're also easily distinguishable in a crowd, plenty of glass windows in the ship's public rooms. Carnival's long-time in-house designer, Joe Farcus, works his "magic" on the ships' public rooms—which may be too loud for some. *Costa Deliziosa*'s theme is "pleasure," while *Costa Luminosa*'s theme is "light." Either way, expect decor that lets you know it's DECOR with plenty of contrasting colors and nary a plain wall panel in sight.

CABINS Staterooms aboard *Costa Deliziosa* and *Costa Luminosa* are a real strong point. Even the lowliest standard inside cabin tends to be larger than Costa's non-Carnival competitors (like MSC). **Inside, Oceanview,** and **Balcony staterooms** all offer the same basic look, a Carnival-esque color scheme of pinks, browns and burnt orange.

Both ships offer a number of **suite** choices positioned throughout the ship. **Mini Suites** bridge the gap between a balcony stateroom and a full-fledged suite, include separate living and sleeping areas and are usually well-priced. The ship's **Grand Suites** are essentially expanded versions of this layout. Those who prize the view from the stern will want to book one of the **Panorama Suites** which have balconies that wrap attractively around the stern of the ship. All suite categories come upgraded amenities, including a pillow menu, complimentary 24-hour room service, and concierge and butler service.

Both ships also boast 52 dedicated **Spa Staterooms** that feature private access to the Samsara Spa and a more Zen decor. Guests in these staterooms are invited to dine in the exclusive Samsara Restaurant on Deck 2.

PUBLIC AREAS & ACTIVITIES What's most noteworthy about the public rooms of these ships is how well they flow into one another. Decks 2 and 3 house the vast majority of the ship's entertainment areas, bars and lounges. At the forward end of the ship is a three-story **theatre** (shows are near-nightly) which spills out onto the large **Grand Bar** a superb space that spans the width of the ship and features an oversized dance floor. **Casinos** on both ships are large, if perhaps not quite the focal point, they are on lines like Carnival and Royal Caribbean. A two-story **disco** doesn't get busy until late.

The **Samsara Spa** is one of the largest in the fleet, with an oversized hydrotherapy pool and a salon. Each ship has two **swimming pools,** one of which is covered by a retractable magrodome roof. When the roof is shut, it can become a bit of a greenhouse: humid and noisy, but in the Caribbean this rarely happens. Other sports and relaxation amenities include a golf driving net, and a combo volleyball, basketball, and tennis court. The oceanview **gym** is a pleasant room overlooking the bow of the ship.

DINING   Aside from an elegant two-story **dining room,** there's an alternative, reservations-only **restaurant,** charging guests $34 per person for the privilege of a meal (suite guests can go free of charge once per cruise). Its atmosphere is its best feature, with dim lights, candlelight, fresh flowers, soft live music, and lots of space between tables. Don't expect haute cuisine or truly Italian dishes; Costa may have Italian heritage, but this is still a mass-market line at heart.

For casual breakfast, lunch, and dinner, head to the sprawling indoor/outdoor **buffet restaurant** on Deck 9.

The **Samsara Restaurant** primarily caters to those guests who have booked Samsara Spa staterooms, though guests in any stateroom category can request to dine here for dinner for a fee of $34. The meals featured are health-conscious, with an emphasis placed on low-sodium and lighter fare.

DISNEY CRUISE LINE

www.disneycruise.com. ✆ **888/325-2500.**

Pros

- o **Superb Children's Programs:** Would you expect anything less from Disney? In both the size of facilities and the range of activities, it's impossible to beat this line.

- o **Disney-Quality Entertainment:** The line's family-oriented musicals are some of the best onboard entertainment today.

- o **Family-Style Cabins:** It's rare in the cruise business to find so many large, cabins that can sleep three, four, or even five people, and have split bathrooms with bath tubs so you can get kids ready for bed even faster.

Cons

- o **Limited Adult Entertainment:** Forget about a night out gambling—this is one of just a few ships at sea without a casino. There's an adult-only night entertainment area on board, but it's often quiet.

- o **Packed Pools:** Though there are multiple pools on each ship, they're packed like sardine cans on sunny days, especially the kids' pools.

- o **Expensive:** Compared to other big ship lines such as Carnival and Norwegian, Disney is pricey, running at least a few hundred dollars more.

Overview

Though a number of big lines including Royal Caribbean, Carnival, and Norwegian Cruise Line have long offered entertaining programs for children, it was Disney that first set out expressly to create a family vacation that would be as relaxing for parents as for their offspring. If you love Disney's resorts on land, you'll love the company's ships.

EXPERIENCE

Both classic and ultra-modern, the line's ships are like no others in the industry, designed to evoke the grand transatlantic liners of old but also boasting truly innovative features, such as extra-large cabins for families and a trio of restaurants through which passengers rotate—along with their waiters. Disney is known for entertainment, of course, and its ships don't disappoint, with inspired stage shows. The vessels also have separate adult pools and lounges and the biggest kids' facilities at sea. In many ways, the experience is more Disney than it is cruise (for instance, there's no casino); on the other hand, the ships are surprisingly elegant, but with little Disney touches everywhere, including subliminal mouse ears in many patterns.

ROUTES

Disney Cruise Line does plenty of Caribbean and Bahamas cruises out of Port Canaveral and Miami, some with visits to Castaway Cay, the line's impressive private island. These ships also sail west, through the Panama Canal, to California, Mexico, Alaska, and Hawaii, and west to Europe.

PASSENGERS

Disney's ships attract a wide mix of passengers, from honeymooners to seniors, but as one might expect, a big percentage is made up of young American families with children. (This isn't a big line for foreign passengers, though you'll see a few.) The bulk of the line's passengers are first-time cruisers, and because the line attracts so many families (sometimes large ones), many of its bookings are for multiple cabins.

DINING

Disney offers a traditional fixed-seating type plan for dinners, but with a twist. Each of its ships has three main restaurants—each with a different theme—among which passengers (and, most importantly, their servers) rotate over the course of a cruise. The result: After the first night, servers have drinks waiting on the table when you arrive, including plastic cups with lids and straws and children's names written on the side. The servers are also able to build a rapport with families over the course of the cruise, and get a sense of which groups need to rush through meals in order to put the kids to bed and which ones want to linger and enjoy their dinner each night.

Rotating through the restaurants keeps things fresh: On one night, passengers dine on dishes such as roasted duck or rack of lamb in a green peppercorn sauce in the nautical-themed **Triton's** restaurant. On another night, they enjoy the likes of creole-crusted grouper, braised jerk seasoned pork chop, or mixed grill in the tropical **Parrot Cay** restaurant. And then it's on to **Animator's Palate,** a bustling eatery with a gimmick: It's a sort of living animation cell, with walls decorated with black-and-white sketches of Disney characters that over the course of the meal gradually become filled in with color. Video screens add to the illusion, and eventually the characters on screen start to interact with the kids in the audience, wowing the little ones. Even the waiters' outfits change during the evening.

Disney also offers a romantic, adults-only Italian specialty restaurant, **Palo,** on board its ships that comes with an extra charge ($25 per person). Breakfast and lunch are served in several restaurants, both sit-down and buffet. **Pluto's Dog House,** on the main pool deck, serves up kid-friendly basics such as chicken fingers, fries, burgers, and nachos; nearby **Goofy's Galley** offers wraps, fresh fruit, and other more healthful fare.

One notable feature of Disney ships that sets them apart from other big, mass-market vessels is that soft drinks are included in the fare, and you can find self-serve soda machines around the pool deck and in the buffet area.

ACTIVITIES

Disney offers an array of activities similar to other big-ship lines, with one big exception: There's no casino. (Disney executives apparently decided a casino just didn't fit with the line's family-friendly image.) Besides lounging at the pool or (for kids) heading to the kids' program, the array of options on board includes basketball, Ping-Pong, and shuffleboard tournaments; sports trivia contests; weight-loss, health, and beauty seminars; bingo, Pictionary, and other games; wine tastings; and singles mixers (though these family-focused cruises aren't the best choice for singles).

Enrichment activities include galley and backstage theater tours; informal lectures on nautical themes and Disney history; animation and drawing classes; and home entertainment and cooking demonstrations (which highlight local cuisine and ingredients, such as wild salmon on Alaska sailings). All these activities come with no extra charge except for wine tastings ($15/person). There also are dance classes and movies, including first-run films shown in a movie theater that's probably nicer than the one in your hometown.

The atmosphere onboard is as celebratory here as it is in the Disney parks: All voyages include a captain's cocktail party with complimentary drinks once per cruise, where the master of the ship and (this being Disney) a gaggle of characters make an appearance and children are given gold streamers to wave in the air as they dance around the pool at sailaway.

CHILDREN'S PROGRAMS

Disney's kids' facilities are, famously, the most extensive at sea, spreading across a good part of an entire deck (what the ship lacks in casino space it makes up for with extra kids' space). The ships carry dozens of children's counselors who look after groups split into five age groups. The children's zone generally is open between 9am and midnight. The **Oceaneer Club,** for ages 3 to 12, is a kiddie-size playroom themed around Captain Hook. Kids can climb and crawl on the bridge, ropes, and rails of a giant pirate ship, as well as on jumbo-size animals, barrels, and a sliding board; play dress-up from trunks full of costumes; dance with Snow White and listen to stories by other Disney characters; or play in the kiddie computer room on PlayStations. The interactive **Oceaneer Lab** offers kids ages 3 to 10 a chance to work on computers, learn fun science with microscopes, do arts and crafts, hear how animation works, and direct their own TV commercial.

There is also an exclusive hangout for tweens (ages 11–13), and dance parties, karaoke, trivia games, improv comedy lessons, and workshops on photography are offered for teens on every voyage.

One thing Disney doesn't do is private babysitting. Instead, there's **Flounder's Reef Nursery** for kids ages 3 months to 3 years ($9 per hour for the first child, $8 per each additional child; hours vary depending on the day's port schedule, and space is limited, so book well in advance). No other lines offer such extensive care for babies; parents are given cell phones so they can check in on their little ones from, say, dinner, if they like, and the phones offer a sense of security since parents know they're reachable should they be needed.

Disney also offers youth activities exclusive to certain regions. In the Caribbean, the line's private island has a variety of kid-friendly activities, including character meet-and-greets and a splash park for toddlers. On Alaska sailings, while the ship sails through Tracy Arm Fjord, kids can participate in "Base Camp" on the upper deck. Games, crafts, and activities in Alaska-themed stations entertain children while immersing them in the splendor of the region. During port days, adventure guides specifically for children and teens introduce them to the unique cultural and natural aspects of each Alaskan port.

ENTERTAINMENT

Family-friendly entertainment is one of the highlights of being on a Disney ship, and as one might expect, Disney characters and movies are front and center. Performances by Broadway-caliber entertainers in the nostalgic Walt Disney Theatre include musical medleys of Disney classics and tributes to Disney films through the years combining song, dance, animated films, and special effects. Family game shows (including a trivia contest called "Mickey Mania") and karaoke take place in the Studio Sea family nightclub. Adults 18 years and older, meanwhile, have their own play zone, an adults-only entertainment area with three themed nightclubs in the forward part of Deck 3. Another nightspot is the Promenade Lounge, where live music is featured daily. The Buena Vista Theatre shows movies day and evening.

SERVICE

Just as at its parks, Disney's cruise ships feature staff from around the globe. Service in the dining rooms is efficient and precise, but leans toward friendly rather than formal. The crew keeps the ship exceptionally clean and well maintained. Overall, things run very smoothly.

Services include laundry and dry cleaning. (The ship also has self-service laundry rooms and 1-hr. photo processing.) Tips can be charged to your onboard account, for which most passengers opt, or you can give them out in the traditional method: cash. Disney suggests a gratuity of $28 per person per week for the dining room server, $21 for the assistant server, and $28 for the cabin steward. Disney also recommends tipping the dining room head server $7.

FLEET

The line has four ships, ranging from 2,700 to 4,000 passengers. Everything from cabin layouts to pool deck flow have been well thought out, just like you would find in the parks. And all have those special touches that make it impossible to ever forget you're on a Disney ship: When the horns blow, you'll hear the iconic first few bars of classic Disney tunes, such as "When You Wish Upon a Star." You'll also find subliminal mouse heads—known as "Hidden Mickey's"—hidden all over the ship.

Disney Magic • Disney Wonder

The Verdict

The grandeur of the golden age of transatlantic ocean liners is channeled into these two beautiful vessels, albeit in a modern, Disney-fied way.

Specifications — Avg. Starting Per Diem $185

Size (in tons)	84,000	Crew	950
Passengers (Double Occ.)	1,754	Passenger/Crew Ratio	1.8 to 1
Passenger/Space Ratio	47.3	Year Launched	1998/1999
Total Cabins/Veranda Cabins	875/374	Last Major Refurbishment	2016

Frommer's Ratings (Scale of 1–5) — ★★★★ ½

Cabin Comfort & Amenities	5	Dining Options	4.5
Ship Cleanliness & Maintenance	5	Gym, Spa & Sports Facilities	3
Public Comfort/Space	4	Children's Facilities	5
Decor	5	Enjoyment Factor	5

THE SHIPS IN GENERAL

Built in 1998 and 1999, these majestic ships carry 1,754 passengers at the rate of two per cabin, but because Disney is a family company and its ships were built expressly to carry three, four, and five people in virtually every cabin, the ship could theoretically carry a whopping 3,325 passengers with all berths full—though that only tends to happen during peak travel times. These high numbers mean certain areas of the ship will feel crowded at times, namely the kids' pool area, the buffet restaurants, and the photo gallery and shops after dinner. Overall, though, the ships are well laid out and have aged gracefully, with frequent updates, refurbishments and new amenities added all the time.

CABINS The Disney ships have the most family-friendly **cabins** at sea, with standard accommodations equivalent to the suites or demisuites on most ships—they're about 25% larger than the industry standard and all have at least a sitting area with a sofa bed to sleep families of three (or four if you put two small children on the sofa bed). Some cabins also have one or two pull-down bunks. Nearly half have private verandas. **One-bedroom suites** have private verandas and sleep four or five comfortably; **two-bedroom suites** sleep seven. ***Note:*** Due to the beds being lower to the ground than on most other ships, you may not be able to stow your suitcases underneath and will have to resort to taking up precious closet space with luggage.

The decor is virtually identical from cabin to cabin, with nostalgic ocean-liner elements such as a steamer-trunk armoire, globe- and telescope-shaped lamps, map designs on the bedspreads, and a framed black-and-white 1930s shot of Mr. and Mrs. Walt Disney aboard the fabled ocean liner *Rex.* Warm wood tones predominate, with Art Deco touches in the metal and glass fittings and light fixtures. The majority of cabins have two bathrooms—a sink and toilet in one and a shower/tub combo and a sink in the other. This is something you won't find in any other standard cabin industrywide, and it's a great boon for families.

Sixteen cabins are fitted for wheelchair users.

PUBLIC AREAS & ACTIVITIES Both ships have several theaters and lounges, including an adults-only area with three separate venues: a **piano/jazz lounge, disco,** and **sports-pub-cum-karaoke bar.** There's also a family-oriented entertainment lounge called **Studio Sea** for game shows, karaoke, and dancing; and a 24-hour Internet cafe. A 270-seat **cinema** shows mostly recent-release Disney movies along with a screen attached to the forward funnel, which shows classic Disney animated films. The **children's facilities** are the largest of any ship at sea (see "Children's Program," above, for details).

Throughout, both ships have some of the best artwork at sea, owing to Disney's vast archive of animation cels, production sketches, costume studies, and inspirational artwork. Canned music pumped into the public areas and corridors tends toward big-band music and crooner tunes or surf-type pop.

The Pool Deck of each ship has three pools: **Mickey's Kids' Pool,** shaped like the mouse's big-eared head, with a great big, white-gloved Mickey hand holding up a snaking yellow slide (this pool can get cr-o-o-o-w-ded!); **Goofy's Family Pool,** where adults and children can mingle; and the **Quiet Cove Adult Pool.** A consolation prize for families with young children is a **splash pool** with circulating water for diaper-wearing babies and toddlers. It's the only one at sea, as usually diaper-wearing children (and that includes pull-ups and swim diapers) are not allowed in any pool, for hygiene reasons. On both ships, there is now a new larger **toddler pool** with interactive fountains and splash zones. *Disney Magic* also has the "AquaDunk," a three-story water-slide with a transparent section of tube that cantilevers out over the side of the ship.

Just beyond the adult pool area is an impressive **spa** and **gym.** Among the many treatments is a selection geared to teens. Both ships' spas have been remodeled and three spa villas were added. Each one is an indoor (and quite pricey) treatment suite that's connected to a private outdoor veranda with a personal hot tub, an open-air shower, and a chaise longue.

Both ships have an outdoor Sports Deck with basketball and paddle tennis. There is also shuffleboard and Ping-Pong.

DINING   Disney's unique rotation dining setup has guests sampling three different restaurants at dinner over the course of their cruise, with an adults-only specialty restaurant also available, by reservation only (see "Dining," earlier in this section). At breakfast and lunch, most go for the buffet-style spread in *Magic*'s **Topsider** and *Wonder*'s **Beach Blanket** restaurants. Though the culinary offerings are fine, the layout and tiny size of these restos are not. Be prepared to head to other options like the poolside **Pinocchio's Pizzeria; Pluto's Dog House** for hot dogs, hamburgers, chicken tenders, fries, and more; and **Goofy's Galley** for wraps, fruit, and ice cream. There's also 24-hour room service from a limited menu.

Disney Dream • Disney Fantasy

The Verdict

Graceful, elegant and fun, these are the most creative ships Disney—or anyone else—has ever built.

Specifications   Avg. Starting Per Diem $240

Size (in tons)	130,000	Crew	1,458
Passengers (Double Occ.)	2,500	Passenger/Crew Ratio	1.7 to 1
Passenger/Space Ratio	50	Year Launched	2011/2012
Total Cabins/Veranda Cabins	1,250/901	Last Major Refurbishment	N/A

Frommer's Ratings (Scale of 1–5)   ★★★★

Cabin Comfort & Amenities	5	Dining Options	4.5
Ship Cleanliness & Maintenance	5	Gym, Spa & Sports Facilities	4.5
Public Comfort/Space	5	Children's Facilities	5
Decor	5	Enjoyment Factor	5

THE SHIPS IN GENERAL

The 4,000-guest *Disney Dream* debuted in 2011, and her sister *Disney Fantasy* followed in 2012. At 1,115 feet in length, they're the largest ships that Disney has ever built, and the first since the launch of *Disney Wonder* back in 1999. Like their siblings, they play up the grand transatlantic ocean liner look to the hilt—and add new and innovative features.

In addition to expanding upon the stellar kids' programs Disney is known for, these two ships have some decidedly cool toys, like the AquaDuck, a 765-foot long "water coaster" that takes guests on a journey through four decks of translucent tubing that cantilevers out over the side of the ship. They also introduced "virtual portholes" in Inside Staterooms: sophisticated LED screens designed to mimic a real window that are linked to position-relative cameras mounted to the outside of the ship. Of course, in true Disney fashion, famous cartoon characters appear in on these windows periodically.

Another neat Disney innovation is the addition of a set of rechargeable "Wave Phones" that can be used to keep tabs on family members around the ship. They're loaned to all guests, regardless of cabin category.

Both ships currently sail the Caribbean, with *Disney Fantasy* offering week-long departures and *Disney Dream* operating shorter three, four and five-night sailings to the Bahamas from Port Canaveral.

CABINS Both ships have 1,250 staterooms and suites onboard, and all of them are among the largest at sea. All feature heavy curtain dividers to section off the bed and pull-out couch sleeping areas, as well as sectional bathrooms with a shower/tub and sink in one room, and a toilet and sink in the other.

The ship's 150 **Inside Staterooms** are designed to sleep three to four guests, and include Disney's "Magic Porthole" window (see above). Although they're not overly huge, these are some of the most handsome inside staterooms we've seen, with real teak accents and plenty of Art Deco touches. **Deluxe Oceanview Staterooms** are the same size, but have a real (and large) porthole though be warned: Categories 9C and 9D have porthole windows with obstructed views. **Deluxe Family Oceanview Staterooms** are larger, can sleep up to five, and feature one or two large porthole windows.

Deluxe Oceanview Stateroom with Verandah categories include a private balcony with a plexiglass railing (an important feature, as kids aren't tempted to climb it), and can sleep up to five.

If you've got cash to burn (we mean it—these rooms are *ex-pen-sive*), you can indulge in one of the top-of-the-line **Concierge Suites** which have upgraded amenities like a pillow menu and access to a Media Library where guests can rent CD's, DVD's, video games and board games to enjoy in the comfort of their suite. The top of the line: the **Royal Suites,** which are as big as a small house and feature a gigantic balcony that has its own dining table and padded lounges, plus two bathrooms, separated living and sleeping areas, a pantry with wet bar, and an open dining salon.

PUBLIC ROOMS & ACTIVITIES Disney does a superb job at keeping kids and adults separate. To that end, nearly all the dedicated kids' facilities, from the onboard nursery to the **Oceaneer Club** and **Oceaneer Lab,** take up the better part of Deck 5. One deck lower, Deck 4 is dedicated to adult pursuits, with a collection of pubs and handsome lounges. Our favorite: the **Skyline Lounge,** which features rotating vistas of famous locales around the world as wall decoration. It sounds chintzy, but it's not: Much like the company's theme parks, it doesn't take long for adults to fall under the Disney spell.

Production shows held in the two-story **Disney Theatre** and are topnotch; first-run Disney movies are shown in the two-story **cinema.** As we said earlier, there's no casino onboard (a rarity on mainstream cruise lines).

In addition to the AquaDuck (see above), each ship has a variety of pools and hot tubs designed for kids and adults alike. Adults can get away from the little ones at the **Quiet Cove Adult Pool** (with its adjacent bar), while kids can enjoy the shallow **Mickey's Pool** and adjacent kid-friendly yellow **Mickey's Slide** waterslide; and the deeper **Donald's Family Pool.** The latter also happens to be located in the shadow of the 24-foot tall LED screen affixed to the funnel. Like Disney's other ships, things can get *very* crowded here on sea days.

Up on Deck 11, the **Senses Spa** is absolutely superb, with an indulgent Thermal Suite, featuring rainforest-themed aromatherapy steam rooms, a dry sauna fashioned after a Roman bath, and private luxury "spa villas" that can be booked as an individual, couples, or as the whole family (for a hefty fee). Disney even offers a special "Chill Spa" for teenagers aged 13 to 17, with customized treatments designed just for them.

Both ships have decently sized Fitness Centers adjacent to the spa. Goofy's Sports Deck includes a mini-golf course, a basketball court, Ping-Pong and foosball tables, shuffleboard, a running track, and virtual sports simulators.

DINING Rotation dining returns to *Disney Dream* and *Disney Fantasy*, with guests moving through the **Animator's Palette, Enchanted Garden,** and the more formal **Royal Palace** along with their tablemates and wait staff. While the change in scenery is a swell touch, it's the waiters that really rise to the occasion, making kids big and small feel welcomed. Guests can choose to dine at either 5:45 p.m. or 8:15 p.m. Food is better-than-average.

Among the many casual dining options aboard are the buffet **Cabanas; Flo's Café** for the usual burgers, pizza by the slice, hot dogs, salads and sandwiches).

The real venues to write home about are reserved for adults. **Paolo** ($30 extra) returns to both ships, with Italian-inspired menus for dinner and a sea day Champagne Bruch that always sells out. The dining venue that will have you exclaiming, however, is **Remy** (ouch: $85 extra). Don't let the fact that it's named for the animated star of the movie *Ratatouille* put you off; this is one of the most elegant specialty restaurants at sea, a cross between a French bistro and a wood-paneled Pullman car on the Orient Express. The food is spectacular, crafted by Chef Arnaud Lallement of l'Assiette Champenoise, a Michelin 3-star restaurant located near Reims, France; and Chef Scott Hunnel from award-winning Victoria & Albert's at Walt Disney World Resort.

HOLLAND AMERICA LINE

www.hollandamerica.com. *(C)* **877/932-4259** or 206/286-3900.

Pros

- **Expertise That Comes with Experience:** Holland America's ships may be young, but the line sure isn't. Formed in 1873 as the Netherlands-America Steamship Company, it's been around more than 141 years, a lot of time to learn a little about operating oceangoing vessels.
- **Warm Interiors:** Holland America ships, especially the more recent ones, tend to be inviting, and easy on the eye. Nothing garish here.
- **Great Service:** HAL's primarily Indonesian and Filipino staff is exceptionally gracious and friendly.
- **Signature of Excellence:** The multi-year, mega-upgrade program has enhanced a lot of the shipboard features and activities to create a more premium experience.

Cons

o **Sleepy Nightlife:** If you're big on late-night dancing and barhopping, you may find yourself partying mostly with the entertainment staff.

Overview

More than any other cruise company except Cunard, Holland America Line (HAL) has managed to hang onto its seafaring history and tradition, with its reasonably priced, classic, ocean-liner-like experience. The line also has somewhat smaller, more intimate vessels than its main competitors, Princess and Celebrity.

EXPERIENCE

Cruising with HAL is less hectic than cruising on most other ships. The line strives for a less intrusive, sometimes almost sedate, presentation, although it has brightened up its entertainment package—with offerings including a "Dancing with the Stars"–inspired dance contest—and its food in recent years. Overall, the ships tend to be evocative of the days of grand liners, with elegant, European styling and displays of nautical artifacts.

About a decade ago, the company embarked on a Signature of Excellence product- and service-enhancements program aimed at elevating the quality of the dining experience, service, and enrichment programs on older ships. HAL's still-ongoing $525-million-plus investment also has meant new amenities in cabins—massage showerheads, lighted magnifying makeup mirrors, hair dryers, extra-fluffy towels, terry-cloth robes, upgraded mattresses, and Egyptian-cotton bed linens. Passengers in all rooms now get a complimentary fruit basket. Suites have plush duvets on every bed and a fully stocked minibar.

Another focus has been on branded partnerships that offer passengers the chance to try new things. The Culinary Arts Center, presented by *Food & Wine* magazine, has free cooking demonstrations several times during each cruise, where video cameras allow guests to watch every move the chefs make. For those who prefer a more hands-on experience, cooking classes cost $29 per person. (The classes are limited to about 12 people and hugely popular, so sign up early in your cruise.) Over 60 guest chefs and culinary experts sail on Holland America ships each year (the line's website lists specific sailings).

The "Digital Workshop Powered by Windows," another branded offering on Holland America vessels, offers free sessions on a variety of topics related to camera basics and photo editing, moviemaking, PC security, and more. "Tech-sperts" trained by Microsoft are on hand. In addition, the recently launched On Location activity program brings local experts on board ships to offer personal insights into each destination through lectures, demonstrations, and cultural entertainment performances.

ROUTES

You can see most of the world on a Holland America ship. That includes such usual suspects as the Caribbean, Europe, Alaska, Bermuda, Mexico, and the Panama Canal; and adds the Pacific Northwest, the Amazon, South America, the South Pacific, Australia, Hawaii, Asia and even Antarctica (no shore landings, though). There are Canada and New England sailings in the fall. For those who really love time at sea, "Grand Voyages" are longer sailings that include World Cruises and "shorter" segments (think voyages up to 60+ days).

PASSENGERS

Holland America's passenger profile used to reflect a much older crowd than on other ships. But the average age is dropping, thanks to both an increased emphasis on the line's Club HAL program for children and updating of the onboard entertainment offerings, the Culinary Arts Center (for cooks), and the Windows workshops (for nerds). The line also seems to be attracting more family reunions than it did in the past.

The more mature among Holland America's passengers are likely to be repeat passengers, often retirees. They are usually not Fortune 500 rich—they are looking for solid value, and they get it from this line.

DINING

Years ago, HAL's meals were as traditional as its architecture—even stodgy. But today the variety of dishes on the menu matches those of other premium lines, and the quality of the food is generally good throughout the fleet. Vegetarian options are available at every meal, and the line has excellent veggie burgers at the on-deck grill. We've also found that Holland America does a particularly good job of catering to special diets, ranging from vegan to kosher to gluten-free. On menus in the main dining room, look for selections from top chefs such as Elizabeth Falkner and David Burke, who advise the line as members of its Culinary Council.

Buffets are offered at the Lido Restaurant and since a large percentage of passengers dine there for breakfast and lunch, there can be serious waiting times for tables and on lines during those meals). Canaletto is a waiter-service casual Italian restaurant open for dinner on the Lido Deck, for a $10 extra charge (reservations are recommended). For a fancier meal, the Pinnacle Grill is the line's excellent steak and seafood venue on all the ships, priced at $29 for dinner and $10 for lunch; reservations are required. One night a cruise, the Pinnacle Grill hosts "An Evening at Le Cirque" dining experience ($49 per person), featuring the cuisine of the famed New York City restaurant.

ACTIVITIES

Young hipsters need not apply. Holland America's ships are heavy on more mature, less frenetic activities and light on boogie-till-the-cows-come-home, party-hearty pursuits. You'll find good cooking classes at the Culinary Arts Center and music to listen to in the bars and lounges, plus health spas and all the other standard activities found on most large ships—photography classes, golf-putting contests (on the carpet in the lobby), art auctions, and the like. Lively piano bars are a real highlight of the line, and guests still enjoy after-dinner dancing and cocktails as a form of evening entertainment. All ships provide Internet access for 75¢ a minute; less if you buy a multi-minute package.

The line does a particularly good job showing off the destination in Alaska, a region this Seattle-based line pioneered. Local travel guides sail on all Alaska-bound ships as part of the new On Location program. The guides bring their knowledge of AK culture, history, art, and flora and fauna, giving lectures and interacting one on one with guests. The program also includes food and beverage events, including an Alaskan Brewing Company beer tasting and Pacific Northwest winetasting. The travel guides also sell souvenirs including artwork by Alaska natives. In addition, a Tlingit cultural interpreter from Hoonah boards each ship at Glacier Bay and Hubbard Glacier to give talks explaining the origins of the Huna people—a tribe that has called Glacier Bay home for centuries. At the glaciers, there is commentary by National Park Service employees.

CHILDREN'S PROGRAMS

Club HAL is more than just one of those half-hearted give-'em-a-video-arcade-and-hot-dogs-at-dinner efforts. This children's program has expert supervisors, a fitness center, and dedicated kids' rooms and teen club rooms (adults, keep out!).

Kids' activities are arranged in three divisions, by age—3 to 7, 8 to 12, and teens. The youngest group might have, say, crafts and games; there's golf putting and disco parties for tweens, and, for the older kids, a chance to try their hand at karaoke and sports tournaments. When there are more than 100 kids on board, a Talent Show is presented. On the *Statendam, Volendam, Zaandam,* and *Amsterdam,* teens get their own outdoor sunning area called The Oasis.

ENTERTAINMENT

The line has been making great strides in entertainment over the past decade, bringing in Broadway veterans to play the main theaters of its ships as well as top-notch illusionists, comedians, and musicians. On the *Eurodam* and *Nieuw Amsterdam,* the line opened a B.B. King's Blues Club, and other vessels began "Dancing with the Stars"–themed programming. Overall, the quality of the professional entertainers has perceptibly improved over the past decade.

And then there are the amateurs! Each week includes a crew talent show in which the international staff members perform their countries' songs and dances. Even if that sounds a bit corny, try it—many of the staff members are fabulous! Your fellow passengers might also be quite the surprise—HAL ships offer live karaoke and an "American Idol"–style competition that sometimes deliver professional-caliber performances.

SERVICE

The line employs primarily Filipino and Indonesian staff members who are gracious and friendly without being cloying.

Onboard services on every ship in the fleet include laundry and dry cleaning. On Holland America ships, a gratuity of $12.50 per person per day is automatically charged to your shipboard account ($13.50 per person per day for suites), but you can increase or decrease the amount by visiting the guest services desk.

CRUISETOURS & ADD-ON PROGRAMS

Over the years, Holland America Line has picked up a lot of "stuff"—Holland America Line Tours (formed by the merger of Westours and Gray Line of Alaska); Westmark Hotels; the *MV Ptarmigan* day boat that visits Portage Glacier outside Anchorage; a fleet of railcars; an almost completely new fleet of motor coaches; and a lot more.

HAL's control of so many of the components of tour packages once gave the cruise company a position of preeminence in the Alaska market, though that's been well and truly challenged in the past decade by Princess, which now has a heavy presence in the accommodations and ground-transportation business as well. (Actually, the similarities don't end there: Both lines have large fleets of primarily late-model ships, both strive for and achieve consistency in the cruise product, and both are pursuing and acquiring younger passengers and families. And both are owned by Carnival Corp.)

As might be expected of a cruise line that owns its own land-tour company in Alaska, HAL offers a variety of land arrangements in combination with its cruises. Dubbed Land + Sea Journeys, HAL's cruisetours range from 10 to 20 days in length, including a 3- to 7-day cruise, a 1- to 3-day visit to Denali National Park, and, in some cases, a few days visiting the Yukon Territory. In a big change that started in 2014, the line's tours that visit the Yukon include a 1-hour flight to the region from Fairbanks that replaces up to 2 days of motor coach travel (in our eyes, a great improvement!). While other lines have focused their land-tour options on the Anchorage-Denali-Fairbanks corridor and the Kenai Peninsula, HAL also has poured resources into the Yukon and is the clear leader there; if you want to see the Yukon as part of your AK trip, Holland America is your line (or do it independently). Prices for Land + Sea Journeys vary widely depending on the type of cabin chosen for the cruise, level of hotel for the land portion, and length of trip.

The Holland America–owned Westmark hotels used on the company's tours in Fairbanks, Anchorage, and Skagway also recently have gotten substantial upgrades.

FLEET

HAL's philosophy is to stick with ships of fewer than 2,650 passengers—many of them significantly smaller—eschewing the 3,000- to 5,000-passenger megaships being built by some other lines. Smallest is the *Prinsendam*, a one-off that operates longer voyages for the company, and rarely sails itineraries less than 14 days in length. She carries just 835 guests. The line flirted with joining the megaship race back in 2002 when *Zuiderdam* debuted. Along with her sisters *Oosterdam, Westerdam,* and *Noordam,* she was designed to appeal to a younger crowd of cruisers—with debatable results. Two near-sister ships, *Eurodam* and *Nieuw Amsterdam,* added more balcony cabins and new dining venues. The line's newest ship, *Koningsdam,* made her debut in 2016.

Holland America has never shown any inclination to plunge into the 100,000-plus-ton megaship market. Keeping the size of its ships down allows HAL to maintain its high service standards and a degree of intimacy while offering all the amenities of its larger brethren.

Eurodam • Nieuw Amsterdam

The Verdict

More modern European and less Holland America—royal in feeling, these sleek ships are for all nations. Their logical evolution integrates HAL's traditionalism with new, sophisticated elements.

Specifications

Avg. Starting Per Diem $102

Size (in tons)	86,000	Crew	929
Passengers (Double Occ.)	2,104	Passenger/Crew Ratio	2.3 to 1
Passenger/Space Ratio	41.2	Year Launched	2008/2010
Total Cabins/Veranda Cabins	1,052/708	Last Major Refurbishment	2016

Frommer's Ratings (Scale of 1–5)

★★★★ ½

Cabin Comfort & Amenities	5	Dining Options	5
Ship Cleanliness & Maintenance	5	Gym, Spa & Sports Facilities	4
Public Comfort/Space	4	Children's Facilities	3
Decor	4	Enjoyment Factor	4.5

THE SHIPS IN GENERAL

Holland America's largest ships to date, *Eurodam* and *Nieuw Amsterdam* offer a stylish, tailored Northern European decor that updates the old HAL aesthetic while keeping many of its signature features in place. Artwork, as throughout the fleet, is typically Dutch. A bit larger than HAL's earlier Vista-class ships, the pair includes a number of in-vogue features, including spa staterooms with special amenities; graceful, tentlike cabanas by the Lido pool and in the Retreat; and three specialty restaurants: Pan-Asian **Tamarind,** Italian **Canaletto,** and the Pacific Northwest-themed **Pinnacle Grill.**

Trivia for ship history buffs: *Nieuw Amsterdam* is the fourth HAL ship to bear that name, going back to 1906 and including the *Nieuw Amsterdam* of 1938, generally regarded as one of the greatest of the great old ocean liners.

CABINS   With these ships, HAL's British country house style moves to sophisticated modern Northern Europe, with a more tailored look and rich, understated olives and golds; woods that run the gamut from blond to cherry; and more nickel and stainless steel than brass. **Standard staterooms** are very much like those on Vista-class ships (read: roomy). All categories have the latest Signature of Excellence features, from pillow-top mattresses to Egyptian cotton towels, to massaging shower heads. Closets are sufficient, but drawer space seems rather scarce until you realize that there are drawers under the beds. *Tip:* The veranda staterooms on Deck 4 have a bit more outside space than others.

Suites come with perks like access to the Neptune Lounge with its personal concierge; **Deluxe** and **Superior Verandah Suites** have sitting and dressing areas, double sinks, whirlpool tubs, and separate showers.

The 56 spa **staterooms** and **suites** have different decor: soothing earth tones accented with fresh green and fernlike tracings on the linens. Oddly there is not a spa package or special spa discount that goes with these accommodations but guests do have a direct connection to the spa, a healthier room service menu and a special concierge at their beck and call. Each room is also equipped with a fitness DVD, a yoga mat, and pedometers, along with a water feature to generate soothing sounds.

Thirty cabins, across the categories, offer wheelchair access.

PUBLIC AREAS & ACTIVITIES On *Eurodam,* the three-deck 890-seat **Mainstage** showroom, with a descending orchestra pit and revolving stage to showcase Vegas-style shows, is flanked by a number of bars and lounges. Heading aft, the **casino** is smaller than most megaships, but as a result feels more action-packed. Adjacent to the casino is a music venue known as **Billboard Onboard** (unfortunately bleed-through noise from the casino kills the classy mood from time to time). The dedicated **movie theater,** complete with popcorn and very cushy leather seats, also sees good use.

One of the nicest features of Holland America ships are their nooks and crannies, little private spaces and tables where peace and privacy are easy to find, and *Eurodam* and *Nieuw Amsterdam* are no exceptions. We're particularly fond of the comfortable corners in the well-stocked **library;** and in the **Explorer's Lounge,** with its excellent after-dinner libations, specialty coffees, and hand-dipped chocolates. Don't mistake that for the **Explorations Café** within the Crow's Nest high up on Observation Deck 11 which offers eye candy views and Internet stations. At night, a live band takes over here.

Shutterbugs and computer aficionados will be pleased by the HAL Digital Workshop powered by Microsoft Windows which offers free workshops. **Club HAL** has an expanded presence on these two and have a computer room, games arcade, craft room, small stage, and the teens-only Loft. The age groups are a little larger than on most family-oriented ships, with three ranges (3–7, 8–12, and 13–17). The cutting edge **Culinary Arts Center** has programs for children as well as adults.

The aptly named **Retreat** sunning and relaxation section, located a deck above the activity of the main pool area, is a new move for HAL, and it's been very well received. The biggest attraction here is the set of 14 cabanas—tented, airy private worlds, very well furnished and loaded with iPods, Evian water, chilled grapes, fruit trays, champagne, and chocolate (rentals: $30–$45 on port days, depending on location, $50–$75 on sea days). The only drawback is space: The cabanas have significantly reduced the amount of sunning space in the Lido area, which could prove to be a problem in the Caribbean.

The Lido pools amidships are covered with a retractable Magrodome. The smaller Sea View pool aft of the Lido has its own bar and the Slice pizzeria.

The ship's **Greenhouse Spa** offers a full menu of treatments and salon services for men, women, and teens, with a particularly attractive central hydrotherapy pool and thermal suite and an aromatherapy steam room. The **fitness center** is well equipped and has a great ocean view. Outdoors on Deck 12 is the net-enclosed **Sports Court** for basketball, volleyball, and the like.

DINING There are eight different dining venues, including three that were introduced on these ships: the Pan-Asian **Tamarind,** the family Italian **Canaletto** (dinner only), and **Slice,** a 24-hour pizzeria. The star is unquestionably Tamarind and its adjacent companion, the very charming and intimate **Silk Den,** decorated in pale purple and yellow and serving signature "saketinis." The $15 fee for evening meals wouldn't even cover the tips for cuisine at this level in a major city; dim sum is served at lunchtime without charge.

The ships' **dining rooms** provide menu choices from steak and lobster to unusually imaginative vegetarian dishes, all served in quietly rich surroundings with a wave effect on the ceiling.

At dinnertime, the **Lido buffet** offers table service, and you can select dishes from the main dining room menu or the Lido's own menu. At breakfast and lunch, you do feel the increased number of passengers on board, with long lines and difficulty finding tables at hours of peak use.

Zuiderdam • Oosterdam • Westerdam • Noordam

The Verdict

These ships were Holland America's first foray into mega-size vessels. They marry traditional HAL style with a partying Caribbean feel—a weird fit that was toned back, somewhat, in each successive sister ship.

Specifications

Avg. Starting Per Diem $90

Size (in tons)	82,000	Crew	800
Passengers (Double Occ.)	1,848	Passenger/Crew Ratio	2.3 to 1
Passenger/Space Ratio	46	Year Launched	2002-2006
Total Cabins/Veranda Cabins	924/623	Last Major Refurbishment	2016

Frommer's Ratings (Scale of 1–5)

Cabin Comfort & Amenities	4.5	Dining Options	4
Ship Cleanliness & Maintenance	4	Gym, Spa & Sports Facilities	4.5
Public Comfort/Space	4	Children's Facilities	3
Decor	3	Enjoyment Factor	4

THE SHIPS IN GENERAL

Built in a design similar to Carnival's Spirit-class ships, *Zuiderdam* (named for the southern point of the Dutch compass, and with a first syllable that rhymes with "eye"), *Oosterdam* (eastern, and with a first syllable like the letter *O*), *Westerdam,* and *Noordam* (northern compass point) were technically Holland America's first megaships, though they're downright cozy compared to the behemoths other lines are churning out these days.

Designed to help HAL shed its image as your grandmother's cruise line, the first of these vessels—2002's *Zuiderdam*—was an unhappy hybrid, mixing ultrabright Carnival-esque colors, stark W Hotel modernism, and the traditional style for which HAL was previously known. That mistake was toned down some for sister ship *Oosterdam*, and by the time *Westerdam* came on the scene in 2004, the new look had been refined. The fourth and final sister, *Noordam* (which replaced the previous *Noordam,* which left the fleet in 2004), seems to do it just right, mixing classic wine reds, dark blues, and earth tones with just a hint of zany, such as the silver-framed benches on the elevator landings and in the Pinnacle Grill and Pinnacle Bar.

In the spirit of learning from their mistakes, HAL has gone back and tweaked parts of the *Zuiderdam,* replacing some of the loudest carpeting and removing some jarring "art" pieces (like the giant-red-lips bench that once graced a corridor). All four sisters are extraordinarily spacious, with large cabins, two-level dining rooms, and distinctive specialty restaurants.

CABINS   Cabins in all categories are comfortable and, as aboard every HAL ship, are among the industry's largest. The simple decor of light woods, clean lines, and subtle floral bedding is very appealing. Overall, more than two-thirds of them have verandas, with the deluxe veranda suites and staterooms in the stern notable for their deep balconies, nearly twice the size of those to port and starboard. You get a romantic view of the ship's wake, too, but because the decks are tiered back here, residents of the cabins above you can see right down.

Standard outside and **veranda cabins** all have a small sitting area and a tub in the bathroom—a relatively rare thing in standard cabins these days. Dataports allow passengers to access the Internet from every cabin via their own laptops.

Guests in every **suite** category have use of a concierge lounge whose staff will take care of shore-excursion reservations and any matters about which you'd normally have to wait in line at the front desk. The suite lounge is stocked with coffee, and juice, and a continental breakfast is served daily.

Twenty-eight cabins are wheelchair accessible.

PUBLIC AREAS & ACTIVITIES   Public rooms on the Vista-class ships run the gamut from the traditional to the modern, and from the lovely to the weird (again, we're talking mostly the *Zuiderdam* and *Oosterdam,* which still have some of their original ill-conceived public rooms). The more traditional spaces, done mostly in blues, teals, burgundies, and deep metallics, include the signature **Explorer's Lounge,** a venue for quiet musical performances and high tea. The top-of-the-ship **Crow's Nest** lounge, an observation lounge during the day and nightclub/disco at night, has wide-open views and even a few rococo thrones, good for "wish you were here" cruise photos.

The Lower Promenade Deck is the hub of indoor activity on these ships as home to the **three-deck Vista Lounge 9** the venue for large-scale production shows), the **Queen's Lounge/Culinary Arts Center** (chef demos by day, comedians and other cabaret-style acts in the evening). Between the two, there's a **piano bar** and a **casino,** the latter really flashy on all but the *Noordam.* You'll also find HAL's first-ever dedicated **discos,** but they're uninspired at best (and, on *Zuiderdam,* just butt-ugly). Our favorite room, the Sports Bar, is as far from the standard rah-rah bar as you can imagine, with comfortable free-form leather seating and table lamps. *Très* chic.

Other public rooms include the wicker-furniture outdoor **Lido Bar** on the Lido Deck (which unfortunately lacks the charm of similar spaces on the line's older ships); and the **KidZone** and **WaveRunner** children/teen centers, which are a bit bare, though roomy and sunny.

Gyms carry a full complement of cardio equipment and weight machines arranged in tiers around the cardio floor; the space is attached to another room where you'll find chaise lounges and a large dipping pool. There's also a basketball/volleyball court on the Sports Deck. The **Greenhouse Spa** is fully 50% larger than any other in the HAL fleet, and has a couple of HAL firsts: a thermal suite (saunas and other heat-therapy rooms) and a hydrotherapy pool, which uses heated seawater and high-pressure jets to alleviate muscle tension.

The main **Pool Deck** doesn't quite work on *Zuiderdam,* where the colors are jarring and the materials cheap-looking. However, as in many other areas aboard, the decor on *Oosterdam, Westerdam,* and *Noordam* are a vast improvement, very pleasant all around. Another pool, in the stern on Lido Deck, is a lovely spot for sunbathing and open views of the sea, and it's also the venue for outdoor movies and videos on a large LED screen.

DINING The main **Vista Dining Room** is a two-deck affair, decorated traditionally but with nice touches of modernism (for instance, in *Zuiderdam's* black, high-backed wooden chairs, which are very sharp). On *Noordam,* the elegant space is a throwback with wine-red fabrics, darkish woods, and a living-room-like feeling. The ship's alternative Pacific Northwest restaurant, the 130-seat **Pinnacle Grill,** wraps partially around the three-deck atrium—ask for a table by the windows. The design is appealing, with marble floors, bright white linens, gorgeous Bulgari place settings, and sculpted chairs by Gilbert Lebirge, who also created the ships' batik-patterned elevator doors.

Diners wanting something more casual can opt for the well-laid-out and attractive Lido buffet restaurant (and its new Italian section called **Canaletto**); the outdoor **Grill** for burgers, dogs, and the like; or, on all but the *Noordam,* the **Windstar Café,** serving specialty coffees (for a price), snacks, and light meals in a tall-ship atmosphere.

Rotterdam • Amsterdam

The Verdict

Modern throwbacks to the glory days of transatlantic travel without the stuffiness or class separation, these attractive, happily midsize sisters have winning features, from classic art to rich mahogany woodwork and elegant yet understated public rooms.

Specifications

Avg. Starting Per Diem $95

Size (in tons)	57,000/61,000	Crew	593/647
Passengers (Double Occ.)	1,316/1,380	Passenger/Crew Ratio	2.2 to 1
Passenger/Space Ratio	43/44.2	Year Launched	1997/2000
Total Cabins/Veranda Cabins	690/172	Last Major Refurbishment	2015

Frommer's Ratings (Scale of 1–5)

★★★★ ½

Cabin Comfort & Amenities	4.5	Dining Options	4
Ship Cleanliness & Maintenance	4	Gym, Spa & Sports Facilities	4.5
Public Comfort/Space	5	Children's Facilities	3
Decor	5	Enjoyment Factor	4.5

THE SHIPS IN GENERAL

With 3 years separating them, near-twins *Rotterdam* and *Amsterdam* combine classic elegance with contemporary amenities and provide a very comfortable cruise, especially on itineraries of 10 nights and longer. Carrying just over 1,300 passengers at double occupancy, they're a breath of fresh air in the sea of supermegaships. *Rotterdam* is the sixth HAL ship to bear that name, following the legendary *Rotterdam V,* which was sold in 1997.

Like the rest of the fleet, the ships were recently upgraded to feature HAL's Signature of Excellence enhancements, including the Explorations Café Internet center and coffee shop, beefed-up kids' facilities, a culinary-arts demonstration kitchen, and upgraded cabin amenities.

CABINS   Unlike the beige color schemes of the older Statendam-class ships, the decor here is livelier, with corals, mangos, blues and whites brightening things up. **Standard cabins** are among the roomiest at sea and have enough hanging and drawer space for 10-night-plus cruises. Bathrooms are generous as well, with bathtubs in all but the standard inside cabins. Beds now have plush, amazingly comfy mattresses. Both ships now also have a handful of **spa staterooms** for convenient access to the spa and health club.

Suites have sitting areas, whirlpool tubs, and are kept stocked with fresh fruit. Guests in these classy digs also have use of a concierge lounge whose staff will take care of all the sorts of reservations those in lower class cabins have to wait at the front desk for. Continental breakfast is served in the suite lounge daily.

Twenty-one cabins are wheelchair accessible.

PUBLIC AREAS & ACTIVITIES   Overall, the ships give you the feeling of an elegant old hotel, with dark red and blue upholstery and leathers, damask fabrics, mahogany tones, and gold accents. Artwork is everywhere, from the stairwells to the walkways. Aboard *Amsterdam,* the theme is Dutch and nautical; aboard *Rotterdam,* it's Continental and Asian.

The **Explorations Café** is a main hub on the ships and the place to surf the Web while enjoying a cappuccino. The **Ocean Bar** serves complimentary hot hors d'oeuvres before dinner nightly, and passengers pack in to listen and dance to a lively trio. More elegant is the **Explorer's Lounge** with its spring ensemble, but many guests prefer the open-sided **piano bar** (featuring a red lacquered baby grand piano on the *Amsterdam*). The **Crow's Nest** observation lounge/disco is a popular spot for after-dinner dancing. Near the room's entrance on *Amsterdam,* you'll see the *Four Seasons* sculptures originally created for the old *Nieuw Amsterdam* in 1938. On *Rotterdam,* a highlight of the Crow's Nest is the life-size terra-cotta human and horse figures, copies of ancient statues discovered in Xian, China.

The *Amsterdam*'s **main showroom** is more a nightclub than a theater. Sit on the banquettes for the best sightlines. Other public rooms include a large **casino, library, card room,** and the **Wajang Theatre**—the spot for movie viewing as well as HAL's Culinary Arts Center demonstration kitchen.

Amsterdam and Rotterdam have spacious, well-equipped **gyms** with very large, separate aerobics areas, floor-to-ceiling ocean views, and nice **spas.** There's a pair of **swimming pools:** one amidships on the Lido Deck, with a retractable glass roof and a pair of hot tubs; and another smaller, less trafficked, and thus more relaxing one in the stern. On Rotterdam, this area was renamed the Retreat because it functions more like a tepid wading pool lined with plastic loungers that allow guests to cool down, but not really bathe. A similar refit was scheduled for Amsterdam, but never performed due to the Retreat's unpopularity amongst HAL guests. Aboard Amsterdam, guests will find a more subdued (and traditional) Seaview Pool overlooking the stern.

Also available: a combo volleyball and tennis court and Ping-Pong tables.

DINING   Aboard both ships, the attractive two-level **formal dining rooms** have floor-to-ceiling windows and a swank, nostalgic feel. Neither ever seems crowded. **The Pinnacle Grill** seats fewer than 100 diners and offers Pacific Northwest cuisine in a romantic setting. The only downside here: no windows. And be careful of those funky chairs; they tip if you lean too far forward. Aboard *Amsterdam,* make a point of looking at the paintings, all of which have a joke hidden on the canvas.

As in the rest of the fleet, buffet-style breakfast, lunch, and dinner are served in the **Lido restaurant,** a cheerful place done in corals and blues. It's a well-laid-out space, with separate salad, drink, deli, dessert, and stir-fry stations. There's a **taco bar** poolside at lunchtime and a new Italian section in the Lido as well as a complimentary, upscale pizzeria called **Slice.**

Volendam • Zaandam

The Verdict

These handsome ships represent a successful marriage of HAL's usual elegance and gentility with a dose of modern pizazz. And they're an ideal size: big enough to offer lots of amenities and small enough to be much more intimate than today's jumbo megaships.

Specifications

Avg. Starting Per Diem $111

Size (in tons)	63,000	Crew	647
Passengers (Double Occ.)	1,440	Passenger/Crew Ratio	2.2 to 1
Passenger/Space Ratio	43.7	Year Launched	1999/2000
Total Cabins/Veranda Cabins	720/197	Last Major Refurbishment	2015

Frommer's Ratings (Scale of 1–5)

★★★★ ½

Cabin Comfort & Amenities	4.5	Dining Options	4
Ship Cleanliness & Maintenance	4	Gym, Spa & Sports Facilities	4.5
Public Comfort/Space	5	Children's Facilities	3
Decor	5	Enjoyment Factor	4.5

THE SHIPS IN GENERAL

Introduced at the turn of this century, *Volendam* and *Zaandam* marked Holland America's first steps into a more diverse future, offering an experience designed to attract the vital 40-somethings while still keeping the line's core older passengers happy. The ships have alternative restaurants, Internet centers, and huge gyms that can't be matched by the lines attracting younger crowds, but their overall vibe is more traditional than Carnival, Princess, and Royal Caribbean—and, for that matter, than HAL's newer and much more glitzy Vista-class vessels. These are classic ships, but with a touch of funk to keep things from seeming too old-fashioned—note the autographed Bill Clinton saxophone and Iggy Pop guitar in *Zaandam*'s elegant Sea View Lounge.

These ships, along with the rest of the HAL fleet, were upgraded over the past few years with the line's Signature of Excellence enhancements, including the Explorations Café Internet center, beefed-up kids' facilities, a Culinary Arts Center demonstration kitchen, and upgraded cabin amenities.

CABINS In a word: roomy. Fabrics are salmon red, burgundy, gold, and bronze, and the walls in a striped pale-gold fabric, hung with gilt-framed prints. All **outside cabins** have shower/tub combos (short tubs, but tubs nonetheless), while **inside cabins** have only showers. There's a storage drawer under each bed. All **suites** and **minisuites** have balconies. The single gorgeous **Penthouse Suite** is massive and adorned with one-of-a-kind pieces such as 19th-century Portuguese porcelain vases and Louis XVI marble table lamps.

Twenty-one cabins are wheelchair accessible.

PUBLIC AREAS & ACTIVITIES *Volendam*'s public areas are floral-themed, which means that each aft staircase landing has a still-life painting of flowers, and a spot outside the library has a collection of elaborate Delft tulip vases, with fake silk tulips. Even the rich, graduated colors in the two-story **show lounge** take their cues from blossoms, going from magenta to marigold to create a virtual garden. Along with all of the flowers is some impressive booty: an authentic Renaissance fountain outside the **casino** (the ship's most pricey piece), an inlaid marble table in the **library,** and a small earthenware mask dating from 1200 B.C. that's kept in a display case near the **Explorer's Lounge** (the popular Internet cafe that's on both vessels).

Zaandam's musical theme is exemplified by one of the more bizarre atrium decorations we know of: a huge, mostly ornamental baroque pipe organ decorated with figures of musicians and dancers. But that's not all: Numerous musical instruments are scattered around the ship in display cases, most notably electric guitars in the atrium stair tower, signed by Queen, Eric Clapton, and the Rolling Stones. They say something about HAL's ambitions to attract younger passengers…even if "younger" means 50-somethings.

The ever-popular **Crow's Nest** nightclub has been redesigned on both vessels and now has banquettes in saturated, bold colors and translucent white floor-to-ceiling curtains that function both as decor and movable enclosures for private events. Mixology classes and other events are held here during the day; after dinner, it becomes the ship's disco. The Culinary Arts Center demo kitchen shares space with **the Wajang Theatre.**

There's welcome elbow at the **gyms** on these ships for the dozens of state-of-the-art machines (and sweaty vacationers). The feeling of spaciousness is enhanced by floor-to-ceiling windows. The ship's **spa** has been upgraded and features a range of treatments.

Three **pools** are on the Lido Deck: a small and quiet aft pool, the main pool and wading pool, located under a retractable glass roof in a sprawling area that includes the pleasant, cafelike **Dolphin Bar**. The **Sports Deck** has a pair of practice tennis courts, as well as shuffleboard.

DINING   The two-story main dining rooms are truly glamorous, framed with floor-to-ceiling windows and punctuated by dramatic staircases. A classical trio serenades guests from a perch on the top level. Both ships also feature HAL's fleetwide Pacific Northwest specialty restaurant, the **Pinnacle Grill** (see "Dining," on p. 165). The **Lido** buffets are attractive and efficiently constructed, with separate stations for salads, desserts, and beverages, cutting down on the chance of monstrously long lines. A sandwich station serves its creations on delicious fresh-baked breads.

Maasdam • Veendam

The Verdict

The perfect midsized antidote to the gigantic, circuslike megaships, public areas on both have just a dash of glitz and lots of classic European and Indonesian art.

Specifications   Avg. Starting Per Diem $135

Size (in tons)	55,451	Crew	602
Passengers (Double Occ.)	1,266	Passenger/Crew Ratio	2.1 to 1
Passenger/Space Ratio	43.8	Year Launched	1993/1996
Total Cabins/Veranda Cabins	633/149	Last Major Refurbishment	2012

Frommer's Ratings (Scale of 1–5)   ★★★★

Cabin Comfort & Amenities	5	Dining Options	5
Ship Cleanliness & Maintenance	5	Gym, Spa & Sports Facilities	4
Public Comfort/Space	4	Children's Facilities	3
Decor	4	Enjoyment Factor	4.5

THE SHIPS IN GENERAL

Holland America's 55,451-ton Statendam-class ships have been in service for two decades but still charm. Touches of marble, teak, polished brass, and multimillion-dollar collections of art and maritime artifacts lend an elegant ambience, and many decorative themes emphasize the Netherlands' seafaring traditions (expect lots of paintings of boats). The onboard mood is low-key (though things get dressy at night), the cabins are large and comfortable, and there are dozens of comfortable nooks all over the ships.

The Statendam-class ships have been upgraded recently and now feature HAL's Signature of Excellence enhancements, most notably an Explorations Café Internet center, improved kids' facilities, a Culinary Arts Center demonstration kitchen, upgraded cabin amenities, a pizzeria and large LED movie screen at the pool area, new bars, and a nightclub.

CABINS Cabins are spacious, unfussy, and comfortable, with light-grained furniture and fabrics in safe shades of blue, beige, and burgundy. All have twin beds that can be converted to a queen and, in some cases, a king, all with HALS's wondrously comfortable new bedding. About 200 cabins can accommodate a third and fourth passenger on a foldaway sofa bed and/or an upper berth. Closets are larger than the norm, and bathrooms have bathtubs in all but the lowest category. There's also a handful of **spa cabins.**

Outside cabins have picture windows and views of the sea, though those on the Lower Promenade Deck have pedestrian walkways (and, occasionally, pedestrians) between you and the ocean. Special reflective glass prevents outsiders from spying in during daylight hours. To guarantee privacy at nighttime, you have to close the curtains. No cabin views are blocked by dangling lifeboats or other equipment.

Minisuites are larger than those aboard some of the most expensive lines; full **suites** are positively palatial. Suite guests have a choice of three pillow types.

Six cabins are outfitted for passengers with disabilities, and public areas are also wheelchair-friendly.

PUBLIC AREAS & ACTIVITIES For the most part, public areas are subdued, consciously tasteful and take advantage of the passing seascapes. For 360-views, but without the roaring winds of the **Sky Deck,** there's the ever-popular **Crow's Nest** nightclub, with its cool, subtly glowing bar and translucent white floor-to-ceiling curtains which cut the room into sexy private areas. Cocktail making classes and other events are held here during the day; after dinner, the music starts to thump and it becomes the ship's disco.

The ships' two-story **showrooms** are contemporary and stylish, but be warned: The balcony has bench seating, with low backs that make it impossible to lean back without slouching.

The trendiest spot is the **Explorations Café,** a well-stocked library and Internet center with a coffee bar and ocean views. If you're a crossword buff, you can tackle the *New York Times* puzzles embedded under glass in the room's cafe tables (wax pencils are provided).

There's a dark and cozy **piano bar,** and a new combo lounge called **Mix,** with three separate bars: one for martinis, another for champagne, and the third for spirits and ales. The **casinos** are spacious, though not as handsomely designed as aboard the line's newer ships. A small **movie theater** shows films a few times a day, and also houses the Culinary Arts Center demo kitchen—the movie screen descends in front of the kitchen during showtimes.

For children, the youngest play in a bright but smallish room decorated like a giant paint box, and preteens have a karaoke machine and video games. Lucky teens, however, get the **Oasis,** a top-deck Sun Deck with a wading pool with a waterfall, teak deck chairs, hammocks, colorful Astroturf, and lamps designed as metal palm trees, all enclosed by a bamboo fence.

Each ship has a sprawling expanse of teak-covered aft deck surrounding a **swimming pool,** and now a pizzeria, bar, and large LED movie screen, too. One deck above and centrally located is a second **swimming pool,** plus a

wading pool, hot tubs, and a **spacious deck**—all under a sliding glass roof to allow use in Alaska, or in inclement weather elsewhere.

The **Sports Deck** on each ship has combo basketball/tennis/volleyball courts. The ships' windowed **Ocean Spa** gyms have a couple dozen exercise machines, a large aerobics area, steam rooms, and saunas. The redesigned **Greenhouse Spas** are an improvement, each including thermal suites with a hydrotherapy whirlpool and heated tile loungers.

The **Forward Observation Deck,** a huge expanse of open teak deck, is accessible only via two stairways hidden away in the forward (covered) portion of the Promenade Deck, and so gets little use. But don't miss going. There's no deck furniture here, but standing in the very bow as the ship plows through the ocean is a wonderful, wonderful experience.

DINING   These ships have refined, two-story main **dining rooms** at the stern, with dual staircases swooping down to the lower level for grand entrances and a music balcony at the top where a duo or trio serenades diners. Ceilings are glamorous with their lotus-flower glass fixtures, and two smaller attached dining rooms are available for groups. HAL's specialty restaurant, the **Pinnacle Grill** (see "Dining," p. 165), has a classy, more modern feel to it.

The casual indoor/outdoor buffet restaurant is smartly laid out, which helps keep lines to a minimum, and features an Italian section called **Canaletto.** An **outdoor grill** on the Lido Deck serves burgers and like; a nearby station allows you to make your own tacos or nachos at lunch.

Prinsendam

The Verdict

Holland America's "Elegant Explorer" offers up a dose of old-world class on its longer voyages. It may be the oldest ship in the fleet, but it's also one of the most well-loved.

Specifications   Avg. Starting Per Diem $115

Size (in tons)	37,848	Crew	428
Passengers (Double Occ.)	793	Passenger/Crew Ratio	1.8 to 1
Passenger/Space Ratio	47.7	Year Launched	1988
Total Cabins/Veranda Cabins	398/82	Last Major Refurbishment	2016

Frommer's Ratings (Scale of 1–5)   ★★★★ ½

Cabin Comfort & Amenities	5	Dining Options	5
Ship Cleanliness & Maintenance	5	Gym, Spa & Sports Facilities	4
Public Comfort/Space	4	Children's Facilities	N/A
Decor	5	Enjoyment Factor	4

THE SHIPS IN GENERAL

Prinsendam is the only ship in the Holland America fleet that wasn't purpose-built for the company. Launched in 1988 as Royal Viking Line's *Royal Viking Sun,* it was acquired by Holland America in 2002 and has been primarily operating longer voyages (think 40 and 60 days in duration) for the line ever since. With just 835 guests onboard, this is one of the most intimate ships in the fleet, if one that's hardly ever talked about.

To step aboard is to discover the way cruising used to be—and that's not a bad thing. Humanly sized with an easy-to-navigate deck plan, *Prinsendam* is a strikingly attractive vessel and one that makes a great long-term home base.

Because of her longer itineraries, *Prinsendam* caters to a much older demographic than the newest ships (it's not a ship to bring kids on).

CABINS   *Prinsendam*'s cabins come in four flavors: **inside, oceanview, verandah,** and **verandah suites.** All include comfy (and we mean comfy!) Sealy beds that can be configured as two twins or one queen; ample storage space and elegant dark wood paneling; and massage showerheads in the bathrooms. They're not as spacious as others in the fleet, however.

Top-of-the-line **Verandah Suites** are the largest onboard and come with a number of exclusive perks for staying from in-suite coffee and espresso machines to Bose docking stations to complimentary mimosas with in-suite breakfasts. Guests booking the **Neptune** or **Pinnacle Suite** category also have access to the exclusive Neptune Lounge, which offers up complimentary refreshments, canapes, a library, sofa, and a big-screen TV.

PUBLIC AREAS & ACTIVITIES   Being a smaller ship, *Prinsendam* doesn't have the variety of public rooms that ships like *Nieuw Amsterdam* or even *Maasdam* have, but the ones that are aboard are united by their graceful elegance: Think plenty of nautical tones, pristine soft furnishings, and soft lighting.

The clubby **Java Bar** and **Café and Oak Room** are tucked away next to the **Casino** on the port side of Promenade Deck 8. This is where the majority of *Prinsendam*'s public rooms lie. Nearby, the **Explorations Café** offers up plenty of books and Internet workstations, while the **Explorer's Lounge**—a Holland America Line staple—features ocean views, leather couches, and comfy chairs. Another Holland America staple is the **Ocean Bar,** with its intimate seating and navy blue decor accented by light walnut woods. Don't forget to head up to Deck 12; all the way forward is the quiet, relaxing **Crow's Nest Lounge.** It has a touch of 1988 about it, with its oddly styled barstools and sectional couches, but it still offers some of the best views on the ship.

The **Greenhouse Spa and Salon** aboard *Prinsendam* is the prettiest in the fleet, even if it lacks the amazing hydrotherapy pool and thermal suites found aboard the line's other ships. It also has a dedicated salon; steam and sauna rooms; and a **Fitness Center** where a stern-mounted **swimming pool** is flanked by two hot tubs. Another **pool** and a single whirlpool are located on Lido Deck 9. Sports facilities on board are somewhat limited, but what self-respecting cruise ship does not include croquet and shuffleboard courts?

DINING   The grand **La Fontaine Dining Room** is the place to be for sit-down meals. Oversized windows grace three sides of this dining room, which curves attractively at the back of the room and features glass chandeliers throughout. All the way forward on the same deck is the **Pinnacle Grill,** Holland America's signature steak-and-seafood specialty restaurant. With its wood-paneled walls, this room takes on a supper-club feel that's swankier than its incarnation on some of the line's other ships (we're looking at you, *Zuiderdam.*) The Pinnacle Grill features "An Evening at Le Cirque" at least once per voyage, recreating the recipes of New York's famous Le Cirque restaurant.

If you just want a quick breakfast or a burger and fries, the **Lido Restaurant** up on Deck 9 aft can help out. Buffet breakfast, lunch and dinner are served here, though at dinner part of the restaurant is annexed off to become the Italian-themed **Canaletto Restaurant.** Thanks to low passenger count, the buffet never becomes quite the zoo it can be on the larger Vista and Signature-class ships.

Complimentary room service is available round-the-clock.

MSC CRUISES

www.msccruisesusa.com. ✆ **877/665-4655.**

Pros

- **Budget-Friendly:** These cruises are affordable to begin with and offer frequent sales.
- **Unusual Entertainment:** While the line's production shows can lapse into the usual song and dance, novelties such as jugglers, magicians, classical pianists, and opera singers add a really nice touch.
- **MSC Yacht Club Is a Different Product:** Splurge on this concierge-class suite level, and you'll feel like you are on an entirely different—and significantly better—ship.

Cons

- **Language Barriers:** Crew and officers have varying command of the English language, creating an environment where miscommunication is rife and service can be impacted.
- **Inconsistent Service:** Staff ranges from superb to surprisingly inattentive, the latter (most evident among the Italian staff) provoking one guest we met to comment, "You get the feeling that everyone has something more important to do than focus on you."

Overview

These cruises tempt budget-minded travelers with their sometimes shockingly low advertised rates. *MSC Divina* sails out of Miami to the Caribbean, year-round, and has been tailored to suit American tastes and habits (like complimentary table water at dinner and earlier dining times).

EXPERIENCE

Like Costa, MSC is a truly international cruise line with plenty of Italian influence. Privately owned, it reflects its Italian heritage in pan-Mediterranean cuisine, grandiose decor, and a very European clientele. Daily programs and shore excursion forms are offered in multiple printed languages, which can create some confusion. On our recent cruise in the Eastern Caribbean, there were some language barriers between us, the crew, and our fellow guests.

Trying to cater to North Americans and Europeans all at once is a balancing act MSC hasn't entirely mastered yet.

ROUTES

While MSC has but one ship in the Caribbean (sailing alternating Eastern and Western Caribbean itineraries), the line maintains a massive presence in the Eastern and Western Mediterranean year-round, and seasonally in the Baltic, South America, the Indian Ocean, and Africa. Since those aren't marketed to a North American audience, we're only covering the *MSC Divina* in this guide.

PASSENGERS

Because your fellow passengers are likely to hail from across Europe, you can expect announcements in a variety of languages every day and European-style behaviors, such as late dinners and keeping children up to spend time as a family in the evening. Although European and North American passengers are pretty evenly split on the company's Caribbean sailings, that doesn't mean that your fellow guests will want to speak English. That can create some awkwardness—or it can be a chance to get to make friends from another country. Your call.

DINING

Food and wait service have been MSC's main problem for years, and still needs to improve if the line ever expects to compete effectively with the American mainstream lines.

Ships boast a variety of venues, from room service to casual poolside fare to complimentary main restaurants and extra-fee specialty dining venues. Main dining rooms on these ships have traditional assigned tables and seating times. There are also buffet restaurants, but the lines can be long and the food subpar. But that doesn't mean spending more will get you more here: Specialty restaurants, including pizzerias, ice cream bars, and Tex-Mex spots, are inconsistent in terms of food quality.

There are also some quirks to be aware of, both in the positive and negative column. MSC is the only line on which we've noticed a kosher category on the wine list—and the only line we've been on where poppy-seed bagels are a staple at the buffet. (On every other line, it's plain bagels, period.) On the annoying side, you may have to specially request coffee in the dining room after meals (only Americans do this, several Italian staff members told us), and you may be asked to order your dessert selection at the same time you make your full meal request (just tell them you haven't decided yet, if you haven't).

ACTIVITIES

Because of the number of languages onboard—there are five officially—you won't find academic-style lectures. Instead, the line offers more physical activities, such as dance classes and water cycling. Onboard, the main action revolves around the spas, casinos, pools, and gyms.

CHILDREN'S PROGRAMS

Children under age 11 sail free and kids from 12 to 18 sail at discounted rates, meaning you'll see lots of kids onboard on summer and holiday sailings.

Along with an ok kids' club, there's miniature golf, volleyball, tennis, and— on the line's newest ships—water parks.

ENTERTAINMENT

The Europeans who cruise this line tend to stay up late and, as a result, the ship has a lively atmosphere into the early hours of the morning. In addition to crowds on the dance floors and in the bars, there are elaborate acrobatic and musical performances at night. Whatever faults MSC may have, entertainment is certainly not one of them.

SERVICE

Service is dramatically inconsistent, and varies wildly, not just from ship to ship, but from sailing to sailing. The line's early Caribbean cruises out of the United States were an unmitigated disaster, with often blatantly indifferent service. While MSC has been making strides to rectify this, service remains an issue. It's worth noting, however, that this uneven service comes primarily from the European crewmembers; the ship's Asian crewmembers generally distinguish themselves with their warmth and attentiveness.

FLEET

The line is currently the fourth largest cruise ship operator in the world, and has 12 ships as well as several new ones under construction, ranging in size from 2,055 passengers to over 4,000 passengers. Only *MSC Divina* homeports in North America. MSC's largest-ever ship to-date, the 4,134-guest *MSC Seaside,* will enter service in December 2017 from Miami.

MSC Divina

The Verdict

A truly beautiful ship (especially inside), the *MSC Divina* would be an unbeatable value if it weren't for her hit-and-miss food and service.

Specifications   Avg. Starting Per Diem $64

Size (in tons)	139,400	Crew	1,388
Passengers (Double Occ.)	3,502	Passenger/Crew Ratio	2.5 to 1
Passenger/Space Ratio	39.8	Year Launched	2012
Total Cabins/Veranda Cabins	1,751/1,206	Last Major Refurbishment	N/A

Frommer's Ratings (Scale of 1–5)   ★★★

Cabin Comfort & Amenities	3	Dining Options	3
Ship Cleanliness & Maintenance	4	Gym, Spa & Sports Facilities	4
Public Comfort/Space	4	Children's Facilities	3
Decor	4	Enjoyment Factor	3

THE SHIP IN GENERAL

Launched in 2012, the 4,345-guest *MSC Divina* was christened by film star Sophia Loren. Since late 2014, the ship has been deployed (somewhat irregularly) out of Miami and into the Caribbean. Word on the street is she's there to stay, offering year-round voyages to the Western, Southern, and Eastern Caribbean.

When it comes to decor, MSC has a certain retro look. We're talking fluorescent orange banquettes and a bowling alley at the 1950s-style Sports Bar, while the '70s are alive and well at the disco-infused Golden Jazz Bar, with its fluorescent back-lit yellow-, orange-, and red-striped columns and bar.

CABINS   Each grade of **cabin** on the ship boasts its own unique color scheme, with vibrant shades of red, blue, and yellow, as well as warm earth tones. The majority are balcony cabins, which have full-sized closets and bathrooms with a unique tub/shower combo in select units.

Inside staterooms are inexpensive but pretty cramped at between 138 and 169 square feet. Some oceanview staterooms are even smaller, at just 130 square feet, while oceanview cabins are larger, with the biggest coming in at 215 square feet. Though suites aren't a priority on the ship, MSC Yacht Club suites do include access to a private dining room, exclusive lounge, concierge service, a dedicated lobby, and even a separate sun deck.

A total of 45 cabins are designated as wheelchair-accessible.

PUBLIC AREAS & ACTIVITIES   The ship centers on a glittering three-story **atrium** with sweeping staircases inlaid with Swarovski crystals. Stop by the **Caffe Italia** on Deck 7 for a good view of the scene as well as a good cappuccino. A seating area with bar service and a grand piano functions as the base of the atrium; it's lovely but tends to get crowded, especially at night.

The ship's pool deck is also attractive, with curving decks, inviting sun loungers, a bandstand, and a place for buying gelato. In addition to hot tubs and **swimming pools,** you'll find an oversized infinity pool stretching toward the horizon. Indoors, the Balinese-themed **Aurea Spa** offers the usual range of massage, wellness, and beauty treatments, as well as two Turkish baths with ornate decorative tiles. The ship's **gym** is small for a vessel this size, but it does offer spectacular views.

On the nightlife front, there's the **Golden Jazz Bar,** a hat tip to the '70s that flows attractively into **La Luna Piano Bar.** A central staircase leads down to the understated **casino** and a re-creation of an Italian piazza under a curved ceiling made to look like a starry sky.

DINING   The ship has two **main dining rooms,** a **buffet restaurant,** an evening **pizzeria,** the **Galaxy Restaurant** up on Deck 16, and an **Eataly Steakhouse** (which looks strangely like an IKEA). Additionally, you can grab pub grub in the **Sports Bar** or try some excellent pizza at **La Cantina di Baccio,** the ship's wine bar.

NORWEGIAN CRUISE LINE

www.ncl.com. (*) **866/234-7350** or 305/436-4000.

Pros

o **Flexible Dining:** Norwegian's dining policy lets you sit where and with whom you want, dress as you want (within reason), and dine when you want, again within reason (dinner is served 5:30–10pm; guests must be seated by 9:30pm) at a wide variety of restaurants, including one that's open 24 hours. Room service is also available.

○ **Above-Average Entertainment:** In addition to quality musical groups and Vegas-style shows that are actually *good* (a rarity in the cruise biz), NCL also has comedy shows by the Second City comedy troupe aboard its newer ships, and performances by the Blue Man Group.

○ **Hawaii-Centricity:** If you want to sail the islands, NCL's U.S.-flagged sub-brand, offers the only big-ship cruises that never leave state waters.

Cons

○ **It's Not All Freestyle:** While Norwegian promotes its pioneering "Free-style Cruising" (see below), shows and activities have specific start and end times; it's not up to the passenger.

○ **Few Quiet Spots:** Other than the library (and even that's not always serene) it's very difficult to escape the non-stop, piped-in pop music on these vessels.

○ **Difficult Dining Reservations:** The most popular of the alternative restaurants can get booked up early; it's best to make reservations as quickly as one can.

Overview

In business since 1966, Norwegian is like the cat of the cruise industry: It's got nine lives, and has continually re-invented itself over the years. Back in 2001, Norwegian was the first line to do away with set dining times and assigned seating; its competitors mocked it mercilessly, then almost immediately followed suit. The intervening years saw the line introduce new features, including a bowling alley aboard *Norwegian Pearl* in 2006 and true Broadway-quality production shows like the Blue Man Group, the Rockettes, and *Legally Blonde.*

Norwegian was also one of the first cruise lines to actively cater to solo travelers, introducing special single-occupancy interior Studio Staterooms aboard the *Norwegian Epic* in 2010 (with their own lounge) to single guests. The concept was so popular that it's appeared (in various forms) on some of the line's newer vessels.

Not everything that Norwegian touches turns to gold (its venture into Hawaii back in 2004, for example, was an unmitigated disaster, though the company has since made it work), but the line is largely responsible for a major shift in *how* we cruise. If it wasn't for Norwegian, well—we'd all still be picking "early" or "late" seating dining with strangers we really didn't like.

EXPERIENCE

Norwegian excels in activities, entertainment, and alternative dining. Recreational and fitness programs are among the best in the industry. The line's youth programs for kids and teens are also top-notch.

The company offers what it calls "Freestyle Cruising" which gives guests freedom in when, where, and with whom passengers dine. Guests can eat in their choice of a variety of restaurants pretty much any time between 5:30 and

10pm (you must be seated by 9:30pm), with no prearranged table assignment or dining time, though you might be sent away with a pager to have a drink and wait during peak times. Other features of Freestyle Cruising are that daily service charges are automatically charged to room accounts, dress codes are more relaxed at all times, and at the end of the voyage, passengers can remain in their cabins until their time comes to disembark, rather than huddling in lounges or squatting on luggage in stairwells until their lucky color comes up. Freestyle Cruising has since been copied, to whatever extent possible, by other lines operating in the U.S.

Each new ship in the line's fleet of late has added some innovative whether it be bowling alleys, ropes courses or an exclusive complex called The Haven which gives the priciest suite guests a dedicated restaurant for breakfast and lunch, a key-card access courtyard, and butler service, among other perks.

ROUTES

The bulk of the line's sailings are in the Caribbean, with Bahamas and Bermuda cruises as well. That said, these ships do head to New England, Europe, and, for those looking for more far-flung destinations, South America (and through the Panama Canal). Norwegian Cruise Line is the only big-ship cruise line to offer sailings to Hawaii that depart roundtrip from Honolulu.

PASSENGERS

Norwegian appeals to a wide range of ages and types. On each sailing you'll find a mix of first-timers and veteran cruisers (many of whom have cruised with this line before). The demographic breakdown does vary by region: In the Caribbean, passengers range from 20-somethings to families with children to retirees; on Alaska cruises the overall demographic tends toward affluent seniors. (Still, even there, you'll find an increasing number of younger couples and families, attracted by the line's flexible dining and relaxed dress code.)

Generally, passengers are not seeking high-voltage activities or around-the-clock action. The disco is seldom the most frequented room on a Norwegian ship, the exception being the Bliss Lounge on *Norwegian Pearl*.

DINING

Norwegian offers an extensive number of alternative restaurants (albeit many at an extra charge). Some ships in the fleet have as many as 28 restaurants, so planning out your meals may take some time and consideration. Depending on the boat, options might include an Italian trattoria, a Japanese restaurant with sushi and sashimi; a Brazilian-style churrascaria steakhouse; an American-style steakhouse; a noodle bar; and a pub. Pricing for the specialty restaurants ranges widely, but it's typical to pay $15 to $30 per person for many of the eateries, and more on some of the finer dining venues on the newest ships. In some specialty restaurants, more expensive items—like high-end steaks and surf and turf—are priced *a la carte*.

In addition, there are always two traditional (and smaller) main dining rooms.

As on all ships, breakfast and lunch are available either in the dining room, on an open-seating basis, or in the buffet up top, which features chefs manning cooking stations.

ACTIVITIES

Activities vary by destination, but you'll always find breakfast with Nickel-odeon characters, including Dora and SpongeBob, much to the little ones' delight, classes that teach Cirque du Soleil–inspired circus tricks, and even (on *Norwegian Breakaway*) dance classes taught by New York's famous Rockettes.

You may also find wine-tasting demonstrations; pub crawls; art auctions; other types of dance classes and a fitness program; daily quizzes; crafts; board games; and bingo, among other activities. Passengers also tend to spend time at sports activities, which include basketball and mini-soccer. In some parts of the world, including Alaska, destination lecturers are aboard to discuss local history, landscape, and culture.

CHILDREN'S PROGRAMS

Norwegian ships tend to be very family-friendly: There's at least one full-time youth coordinator per age group, a kids' activity room, video games, an ice-cream stand, and group babysitting for ages 3 and up, plus a Nickelodeon Pajama Jam Breakfast and sometimes destination-specific activities, such as a visit from a park ranger for the ships that sail to Glacier Bay National Park.

The line is constantly upgrading its kids' program. More family features aboard ships include exclusive Nickelodeon at Sea programming, with char-acter meet-and-greets and special Nickelodeon game shows; a bowling alley and a jungle gym with a ball pit and tunnels on the *Pearl;* and arcades on all Norwegian ships.

ENTERTAINMENT

Entertainment is a Norwegian hallmark, with lavish Vegas-style productions that are surprisingly artistically ambitious (the gymnasts are superb). On some nights, the show rooms also feature magic or juggling acts. These ships boast big, splashy casinos, and all have intimate lounges that present pianists and cabaret acts. On the newer builds entertainment is even more sophisticated, like Blue Man Group (on *Norwegian Epic*) or a Latin-dance extravaganza (on *Norwegian Breakaway*).

While other lines have comedy acts, Second City offers improv in a pur-pose-built lounge on the newer ships, *Norwegian Breakaway*'s Broadway show, "Rock of Ages," may not raise eyebrows in Manhattan, but at sea it's potty-mouth languageand adult themes push boundaries.

Music for dancing—usually by a smallish band and invariably the kind of dancing that mature passengers can engage in (that is, not a lot of rock 'n' roll)—is popular and takes place before or after shows. Each ship also has a late-night disco with contemporary music. Norwegian's hip theme party—"White Hot Night"—really keeps the ships lively into the wee hours.

SERVICE

Generally, room service and bar service fleetwide are speedy and efficient. With the introduction of the line's flexible dining program, additional crew members, mostly waiters and kitchen staff, have been added to each ship and improvement in service resulted quickly.

In order to eliminate any tipping confusion, the line automatically adds a charge of $12 per passenger per day to shipboard accounts, which also can be prepaid at the time of booking (you are free to adjust the amount up or down as you see fit). Full-service laundry and dry cleaning are available.

CRUISETOURS & ADD-ON PROGRAMS

Norwegian offers four cruisetours on Alaska sailings. You can add one on before the 7-day southbound cruise or after the 7-day northbound cruise: the Denali Express, Denali/Alyeska Explorer, the Denali/Fairbanks Explorer, and the Authentic Alaska. All cruisetours are fully escorted by local Alaskan guides, feature two nights in Denali, include a stop at an Iditarod Sled Dog musher's house, and have an airport meet-and-greet by a representative. Please note that it's not difficult to recreate these types of experiences on your own and at a lower cost (you'll even book tickets on the same trains if you decide to do a rail visit to Denali National Park).

FLEET

Norwegian Cruise Line is made up of 14 ships, with plenty of variety among them. They range in size from 2,018 passengers to 3,969 passengers.

Norwegian Breakaway • Norwegian Getaway • Norwegian Escape

The Verdict

Big, bold, and surprisingly classy, these three megaships are everything that *Norwegian Epic* should have been, but wasn't.

Specifications — Avg. Starting Per Diem $127

Size (in tons)	145,645-164,600	Crew	1,663-1,731
Passengers (Double Occ.)	4,000-4,258	Passenger/Crew Ratio	2.4 to 1
Passenger/Space Ratio	36.6	Year Launched	2013-2016
Total Cabins/Veranda Cabins	2,014/1,344	Last Major Refurbishment	N/A

Frommer's Ratings (Scale of 1–5) ★★★★ ½

Cabin Comfort & Amenities	4.5	Dining Options	5
Ship Cleanliness & Maintenance	5	Gym, Spa & Sports Facilities	5
Public Comfort/Space	4	Children's Facilities	4
Decor	5	Enjoyment Factor	4.5

THE SHIPS IN GENERAL

Norwegian Epic debuted to some less-than-stellar reviews in 2010, but *Norwegian Breakaway* and *Norwegian Getaway* have made up for it. These well-designed, thoughtfully laid-out beauties—launched in 2013 and 2014—took the best aspects of *Epic* and combined them with the most loved features of the line's modestly sized Spirit, Star, and Jewel ships. The result: dozens of dining options, hundreds of balcony staterooms, exciting entertainment venues, the largest onboard spas Norwegian has ever created, and a gorgeous wraparound promenade deck known as The Waterfront.

Think of relative newcomer *Norwegian Escape* (2015) as the stretch-limo version, outfitted with the same basic design and amenities, but with additional decks tacked on.

CABINS   Every bad decision that plagued the cabins on *Norwegian Epic* has been scrapped entirely. Gone are the curved walls, translucent bathrooms, and bizarre in-room sinks that got water all over the place. Instead, designers have gone with a crisp, clean look emphasizing bold colors and clean lines and thoughtful touches like bedside reading lights, backlit headboards, and some of the best-designed bathrooms the line has ever come up with.

One feature that did carry over from *Epic,* though, is the **Studio Staterooms** specially designed for solo travelers—a boon for an underserved group. These 100-square-foot rooms are admittedly small, but they're smartly designed to make good use of what space there is, and, as a bonus, Studio guests get access to their own two-deck private lounge where they can meet other solo travelers.

Standard inside staterooms include options for families such as connecting cabins clustered near the kids' facilities. **Oceanview cabins** add a picture window, while the largest cabins have private balconies. Standard balcony staterooms, however, have balconies that are substantially smaller than on past Norwegian ships.

Suites are where things get really interesting. **Spa Suites** come with complimentary access to the spa's massive thermal suite, and **Haven Suites** offer Norwegian's top-of-the-line luxury experience, with priority embarkation and disembarkation, a pillow menu, butler service, and access to private restaurants and lounges.

PUBLIC AREAS & ACTIVITIES   These ships set a new standard for Norwegian, with a refined look that manages to be fun at the same time. Expect lots of dark wood paneling complemented by vibrant teal carpeting, rich reds, and soft accent lighting.

A three-story atrium anchors Decks 6, 7, and 8, where nearly all of the bars, lounges, and entertainment venues are clustered. The arrangement makes it easy to hop around, popping into **Shaker's Cocktail Bar** for a nightcap or settling in at the **Café Atrium** for people watching.

Among the bars and lounges, you'll find tried-and-true Norwegian favorites like **Maltings Beer and Whisky Bar** and the very cool (literally) **SVEDKA Ice Bar.** But *Norwegian Escape* also shakes things up with the first **Five O'Clock Somewhere** and **Tobacco Road** bars at sea, as well as a bar serving up nothing but mojitos and another, **The District Brewhouse,** with 24 beers on tap and over 50 different brews by the bottle.

Entertainment remains Norwegian's strong suit. On Decks 6 and 7, the **main theatre** puts on shows direct from Broadway—as of this writing, *Breakaway* is hosting the musical *Rock of Ages,* while guests aboard *Getaway* enjoy *Million Dollar Quartet,* and *Escape*'s guests are treated to *After Midnight,* a musical featuring Duke Ellington tunes. The massive **casino** on Deck 6, however, won't be to everyone's liking: There's no way to get around it, and cigarette smoke has an annoying tendency to waft up to other decks.

The best public area of all is the wraparound **Waterfront,** which does double duty as a promenade deck and spot for outdoor seating for restaurants and lounges on Deck 8.

Each ship offers a single main **pool** midships. On *Breakaway* and *Getaway,* the pool is flanked by four hot tubs; on *Escape,* there are only two hot tubs— for over 4,000 people. Overall, the pool decks feel disjointed, claustrophobic, and crowded. If you're looking for a quiet corner, you're not going to find it. You'll be lucky to find even a deck chair.

DINING There are so many dining options on board it's almost overwhelming—and some of the restaurants will cost you. If you don't want to spend another dime, each ship features three attractive **main dining rooms,** the best of which, the **Manhattan Dining Room,** boasts a huge dance floor and some pretty spectacular views from two-story windows overlooking the stern. Also in the free category is the sprawling **Garden Café** buffet and **O'Sheehan's Pub.**

As for the restaurants that aren't free, we're fans of the French-themed **Le Bistro** (try the French onion soup) and **Moderno Churrascaria,** a Brazilian steakhouse trotting out a never-ending cavalcade of meats. The latter will run you $24.95 per person; Le Bistro, which used to charge a flat fee, has now gone a la carte across the fleet. Other options include the Japanese **Teppanyaki** experience ($29.95/person), **Cagney's Steakhouse** (a la carte), and, on *Norwegian Escape,* Jimmy Buffet's only **Margaritaville** (a la carte) at sea.

Norwegian Epic

The Verdict

One of the biggest cruise ships at sea, *Norwegian Epic* is busy, bustling, and showy. She's the best ship at sea for entertainment, and she's also a winner for families. But the cabins aren't functional, and the crowds are sometimes oppressive.

Specifications   Avg. Starting Per Diem $121

Size (in tons)	155,873	Crew	1,753
Passengers (Double Occ.)	4,100	Passenger/Crew Ratio	2.3 to 1
Passenger/Space Ratio	38	Year Launched	2010
Total Cabins/Veranda Cabins	2,114/1,351	Last Major Refurbishment	2015

Frommer's Ratings (Scale of 1–5)   ★★★ ½

Cabin Comfort & Amenities	3	Dining Options	5
Ship Cleanliness & Maintenance	4	Gym, Spa & Sports Facilities	4
Public Comfort/Space	3.5	Children's Facilities	4
Decor	4	Enjoyment Factor	3.5

THE SHIP IN GENERAL

Originally designed to be the first of three identical super-megaships, *Epic* almost ended up not being launched at all due to disputes with the shipyard regarding design changes and cost overruns. In the end, a compromise led to her completion, but orders for sister ships were cancelled, leaving *Epic* the sole vessel in her class. That's probably for the best.

Our major complaint is a layout that can feel unintuitive. The main interior public decks often force people to walk through public areas, and the placement of furniture and other impediments leads to bottlenecks. The pool deck is full of odd angles that make it difficult to cross when crowded, and some staterooms are hidden away in corridors behind unmarked doors.

Still, you have to admit the ship is fun—especially at night, when the entertainment venues and numerous bars and lounges come to life. Kids certainly won't be bored either, thanks to the playroom, teen center, water slides, climbing features, and activities with Nickelodeon characters including SpongeBob SquarePants and Dora the Explorer.

CABINS Let's get our major complaint out of the way first: What was NCL thinking with these bathrooms? The shower and toilet have been set in their own separate cubicles, while the sink is out in the cabin. The idea seems to have been that this arrangement would allow two or more people to use the bathroom facilities simultaneously, without having to crowd into a tiny space. The reality, though, is that it all just doesn't work, especially the sink which was designed with a tiny bowl. Since counters are also tiny (and often placed right next to the cabin's sitting area), water often shoots out onto the floor and furniture, major splashing all over the place. It's a mess.

But bathrooms aside, there are some intriguing features—freeform, curving walls in balcony staterooms, concealed contour LED lighting, dark wood trim, and an earth-tone color palette.

Epic's major innovation: 128 **studio cabins** for solo travelers. Years ago, many cruise ships (the old *QE2* comes to mind) were built with a number of small staterooms designed specifically for people traveling on their own. That idea died out over the past 3 decades, but *Epic* brings it back with a vengeance, creating a whole separate wing for solo travelers, who in addition to their staterooms get private keycard access to the Living Room, a modern, double-height space with its own bar, TV screens, and concierge area. You can think of it as a swinging singles hangout, but that all depends on what kind of singles end up on board. The Studios themselves were designed by a different creative team than the rest of the staterooms onboard, and you can tell: They're all neon and bold angles, and pack a lot into their modest 100 square feet of space. Each has a large one-way "porthole" window that looks out into the corridor, and ingenious small storage nooks. Priced for the solo traveler (at about $150 per stateroom more than the per-person price of a double-occupancy inside), they can actually accommodate two hipsters, so long as they like togetherness.

In terms of suites, the big draw on Epic, as aboard NCL's other recent ships, is its **Courtyard Villas,** a separate "ship within a ship" area perched way up on Decks 16 and 17. In addition to knockout suite accommodations, villa guests get access to a private pool, lounge, two restaurants just for folks in this class, and other exclusive features.

A total of 42 staterooms and suites across a range of categories are wheelchair accessible.

PUBLIC AREAS & ACTIVITIES   On Decks 5 and 6, the **Epic Theater** is home to the ship's headlining shows: the edgy Blue Man Group and Legends in Concert, a revue of celebrity impersonators. Getting Blue Man onboard was a huge coup for NCL, and really broke the mold for shipboard shows. Another novelty entertainment, **Spiegel Tent** doesn't work as well; essentially dinner-theater-in-the-round, essentially, it hosts a shrill, disjointed show about out of work circus performers who constantly require audience participation (you've been warned). Other onboard entertainment options: **Headliners Comedy Club** and, for a fun capper to the evening, **Fat Cats Jazz & Blues Club,** where the musicians don't hold back for the tourist crowd and are liable to invite any instrumentalists in the audience onto the stage for an impromptu jam. One of the most intriguing nightlife venues is the **Svedka Ice Bar,** a frozen locker kept at 17 degrees Fahrenheit. All the furniture and artwork are made of ice, and specialty vodka drinks are served to guests wearing parkas.

For kids, *Epic* has an extensive **children's center** with video games, a climbing maze, ball-jump pit, and more. Teens get a hangout called Entourage. Youngsters are also likely to gravitate toward the pool deck's three giant water slides—they're so big, in fact, that the actual pool area seems small in comparison. In fact, we'd say that Epic has one of the busiest, most activity-packed Pool Decks we've ever seen—and whether that's a good thing or not depends on your taste.

Nearby you'll find the ship's 33-foot-high rock-climbing and rappelling wall and a **sports and play area** with a full-size basketball court, bungee trampoline, and 24-foot Spider Web you escape by climbing your way out.

For a more relaxing experience, the enormous **Mandara Spa**—supposedly the largest spa at sea, though we didn't get out our tape measure to check—has 24 treatment rooms and a relaxing thermal suite (extra fee required). The ship's well-stocked **fitness center** has dozens of machines and free weights (including kettlebells, the first we've seen at sea); and four different aerobics studios for classes.

DINING   Of the ship's 21 dining options (!), some are complimentary, some charge extra, and a few are exclusively for guests in the ship's suites or studio cabins. One of the two main restaurants, we prefer the **Manhattan Room,** an art-deco spot with a two-deck window overlooking the ship's wake, and a bandstand and dance floor. While guests sample contemporary fare, musical acts mix it up on the stage, and cocktails are prepared tableside.

Specialty restaurants (all of which charge a per-person cover or price a la carte) include **Cagney's Steakhouse** ($25 per person); **Moderno Churras-caria,** a South American-style steakhouse where servers keep bringing slices of grilled meats to you until you pop or tell them to stop ($18 per person); **La Cucina,** a casual, family-style Italian restaurant ($10 per person); **Shang-hai's,** a classic Chinese restaurant ($15 per person); and **Wasabi,** which serves sushi, sashimi, and a selection of sakes (a la carte pricing).

Norwegian Spirit • Norwegian Star • Norwegian Dawn • Norwegian Jewel • Norwegian Jade • Norwegian Pearl • Norwegian Gem

The Verdict

Has someone finally built megaships for Generations X and Y? With a mix of classy and fun spaces, a lively atmosphere, great facilities for kids, and an amazing number of restaurants, these are some of the most original mainstream megaships to come along in years.

Specifications
Avg. Starting Per Diem $90

Size (in tons)	77,000-93,558	Crew	965-1,150
Passengers (Double Occ.)	1,966-2,394	Passenger/Crew Ratio	2 to 1
Passenger/Space Ratio	39-41	Year Launched	1998-2007
Total Cabins/Veranda Cabins	1,197/538	Last Major Refurbishment	2016

Frommer's Ratings (Scale of 1–5)
★★★★

Cabin Comfort & Amenities	4	Dining Options	5
Ship Cleanliness & Maintenance	5	Gym, Spa & Sports Facilities	4
Public Comfort/Space	5	Children's Facilities	5
Decor	4.5	Enjoyment Factor	4.5

THE SHIPS IN GENERAL

These sexy sisters are some of the most fun megaships at sea today. Each has a supersocial atmosphere, creative decor, and onboard music and pop culture references tailored to a surprisingly young demographic: folks from their 20s to their mid-40s.

Want fun? There are lounges with bowling alleys and bordello-like decor. Want food? Choose from 8 to 10 different restaurants, from fancy steakhouses and teppanyaki restaurants to casual Tex-Mex and burger joints. Want fantasy? The nightclubs and atriums feature furniture right out of *Alice in Wonderland.* Want high style? Check out **Gatsby's Champagne Bar** on the *Dawn* and *Star* ships, and Bar Central on *Jewel, Pearl,* and *Gem.*

Though NCL divides these ships into three classes (*Dawn* and *Star* in the Dawn class; *Jewel, Pearl, Jade,* and *Gem* in the Jewel Class; and *Spirit* all by herself), they share more in common than not, including nearly identical layouts.

CABINS   **Standard inside** and **outside cabins,** though not large compared to some in the industry, are roomier than what's on NCL's older ships. Closets and drawer space are ample, and bathrooms are efficiently designed.

Balconies aren't very spacious, however. As for decor: It's a mix, with stylish elements (such as cherrywood wall paneling and snazzy rounded lights), kitschy elements (bright island-colored carpeting), and cheap touches (spindly chairs and end tables, and wall-mounted soap dispensers in the bathrooms).

Owner's Suites are huge by comparison, with two balconies and 750 square feet of space. But that's nothing when you look at the extravagant **Garden Villas**—the biggest suites at sea today with an incredible 5,350 square feet apiece. Each features private gardens, multiple bedrooms with mind-blowing bathrooms, separate living rooms, full kitchens, and private butler service. The price tag is impressive too: about $13,750 per person, per week.

Four cabins are wheelchair accessible aboard *Spirit,* as are 20 on *Star,* 24 on *Dawn,* and 27 on *Jewel, Pearl,* and *Gem.*

PUBLIC AREAS & ACTIVITIES   Public areas throughout the vessels are fanciful and spacious, adorned with a mix of bright, Caribbean- and Miami-themed decor and high-style art deco, with lots of intimate nooks and some great lounges and bars amid the restaurants. *Spirit* and *Star* have a covered outdoor **Bier Garten** stocked with German pilsner, *hefeweizen,* and wheat beers. *Jewel, Pearl, Jade,* and *Gem,* meanwhile, feature whiskey, wine, and cocktail offerings at **Bar Central** on Deck 6. Aboard *Spirit,* **Maharini's** combines a Bollywood theme with a kind of fashion-world ambience, its mood-lit nooks separated by thick red velvet curtains and outfitted with large, comfortable daybeds strewn with pillows. The similarly decorated **Bliss Ultra Lounges** on *Pearl* and *Gem* add four 10-pin bowling lanes to the bordello vibe, gaining NCL points for retro-chic credibility.

Outside, the pool areas have the feel of a resort, ringed by flower-shaped "streetlamps," deck chairs arrayed around the central pool and hot tubs. On the *Dawn, Star,* and *Spirit* these spaces will be especially alluring for families with kids. On *Dawn,* it's right out of *The Flintstones,* with giant polka-dotted dinosaurs standing around faux rock walls, slides, a paddling pool, and even a kids' Jacuzzi. *Star*'s has a space-age rocket theme. At a huge bar running almost the width of the ship, ice cream is served on one side, drinks on the other.

Of the ships' stylish **spas,** the one aboard *Dawn* takes the prize. At the entrance, a sunlit foyer rises three decks high and is decorated with plants and Maya reliefs, with a juice bar on the side. Further in, you'll find a large lap pool, hot tub, jet-massage pool, and sunny seating areas in front of windows. *Jewel, Pearl, Jade,* and *Gem* have four of the better onboard **gyms** of recent years—large and extremely well appointed, with dozens of fitness machines and a large aerobics/spinning room. Outside there's an extralong **jogging track,** a **sports court** for basketball and volleyball, golf-driving nets, and facilities for shuffleboard and deck chess

DINING   These ships are all about their restaurants, with between 8 and 10 on each ship—two or three formal restaurants plus a buffet, at least one casual establishment, and several alternative specialty eateries serving Italian, steakhouse, French/Continental, and Asian cuisine. The high-end **Le Bistro** serves classic and nouvelle fare amid floral upholstery and original paintings Matisse, Monet, van Gogh, and Renoir. (Specialty restaurants cost between $10 and $20 per person.)

Norwegian Sky • Norwegian Sun

The Verdict

The older (but still not very old) *Sun* and *Sky* have a cozier feel than NCL's bigger, newer ships, yet still feature many restaurants and lots of cabins with balconies.

Specifications

Avg. Starting Per Diem $92

Size (in tons)	77,104/78,309	Crew	1,000/968
Passengers (Double Occ.)	2,002/1,936	Passenger/Crew Ratio	2 to 1
Passenger/Space Ratio	38.5/40.6	Year Launched	1999/2001
Total Cabins/Veranda Cabins	1,001/432	Last Major Refurbishment	2016

Frommer's Ratings (Scale of 1–5)

★★★★

Cabin Comfort & Amenities	4	Dining Options	4.5
Ship Cleanliness & Maintenance	4	Gym, Spa & Sports Facilities	4
Public Comfort/Space	4	Children's Facilities	3.5
Decor	4	Enjoyment Factor	4

THE SHIPS IN GENERAL

Norwegian Sky and *Sun* were the first two megaships built for NCL's modern era, and blazed the trail that all the later ships followed, with multiple restaurants and everything designed with casual cruising in mind. *Sky* spent four years sailing as *Pride of Aloha* for NCL's Hawaii operation, but is now running Bahamas itineraries under her original name.

CABINS The cabins are decorated in bright island colors, but they're quite small and have limited storage space. Bathrooms are also compact, with tube-like shower stalls and slivers of shelving. Oh, and watch out for those reading lamps above the beds: Their protruding shades make sitting up impossible! *Norwegian Sun* is heavy on suites and minisuites, the latter measuring a roomy 264 to 301 square feet and featuring walk-in closets. Twenty large **Penthouse** and **Owner's Suites** include the services of a butler and concierge who will get you on the first tender to port, make dinner reservations, and generally try to please your every whim.

Six cabins on *Sky* and 20 cabins aboard *Sun* are equipped for wheelchairs. It's worth noting that there is no wheelchair access to Oslo Deck 6A, a small forward deck with about two dozen oceanview and inside staterooms.

PUBLIC AREAS & ACTIVITIES Even though *Norwegian Sky* is the older of these two vessels, refurbishments in 2009 left her looking fresher and more fun (another update is scheduled for 2017); while *Sun* is still done up in a pleasing but not too jarring pastiche of mostly cool blues, sages, deep reds, and soft golds blended with marble, burled-wood veneers, and brass and chrome detailing (she was refit in spring of 2016 last). Both ships are bright and sun-filled, thanks to an abundance of floor-to-ceiling windows. Each ship has nearly a dozen bars of several types. With soft music coming from the adjacent piano bar as a soundtrack, the **Windjammer Bar** is the most appealing place on the ship for quiet conversation. A large, attractive **observation lounge** becomes a venue for live entertainment in the evening. *Tip:* Many of the balcony seats in the two-story **show lounge** have obstructed views of the stage so try and sit on the first level. For kids, the ships' huge **children's area** includes a playroom, a teen center with a large movie screen and foosball games, and a video arcade. Each ship also has a wading pool.

The well-stocked oceanview **gyms** on these ships stay open 24 hours a day, and the adjacent aerobics room has floor-to-ceiling windows and a great selection of classes, from spinning to kickboxing. Out on deck, there's a pair of **pools** and four hot tubs.

DINING   Like the rest of the NCL fleet, *Sun* and *Sky* excel in the restaurant department. For breakfast, lunch, and dinner, there are two elegant **dining rooms.** An indoor/outdoor **casual buffet restaurant** also serves all three meals daily, plus snacks like pizza and cookies in between. For dinner, you can opt instead for one of eight specialty restaurants on *Sun* and three on *Sky*. On both ships, the Italian eatery **Il Adagio,** is a fave offering Caesar salads prepared tableside and warm chocolate hazelnut cake that is to die for ($10 cover charge).

Pride of America

The Verdict

Sailing from Honolulu, concentrating solely on the islands, and carrying an American crew, this vessel is literally in a class by herself.

Specifications   Avg. Starting Per Diem $179

Size (in tons)	80,439	Crew	917
Passengers (Double Occ.)	2,186	Passenger/Crew Ratio	2.3 to 1
Passenger/Space Ratio	36.7	Year Launched	2005
Total Cabins/Veranda Cabins	1,073/665	Last Major Refurbishment	2016

Frommer's Ratings (Scale of 1–5)   ★★★★

Cabin Comfort & Amenities	4	Dining Options	5
Ship Cleanliness & Maintenance	4	Gym, Spa & Sports Facilities	4
Public Comfort/Space	4	Children's Facilities	4
Decor	4	Enjoyment Factor	5

THE SHIP IN GENERAL

Pride of America is the only big ship operating cruises entirely within Hawaiian waters, sailing round-trip from Honolulu. Because Hawaii's islands are all relatively close together, the ship can visit a Hawaiian port every single day, and even do overnights in Kauai and Maui, giving you an opportunity to sample nightlife ashore and get a better feel for both of those beautiful islands.

There's a downside, however: Because these cruises put so much emphasis on the port experience, there's not much effort left over for on-board activities. And you can expect lots of extra costs, from expensive drinks to pricey Internet access. You're likely to spend a bundle, too, on shore excursions and car rentals in port. (Because most of the islands' real attractions aren't near port facilities, you have to take an excursion or rent a car to see anything worth seeing.)

CABINS   Cabins on *Pride* are pretty, with their vibrant, tropical hues—but they tend to be small: You get as little as 121 square feet in standard inside cabins and as little as 149 square feet in outside units. (That's 20% smaller than Carnival Cruise Lines cabins, to give some perspective.) Balcony cabins are recommended for the nighttime run between Kona and Hilo, since you can watch lava flowing from Kilauea Volcano without changing out of your pajamas. The captain turns the ship 360 degrees at the optimum viewing point, so cabins on both sides get a view.

There are 23 cabins equipped for wheelchairs. The ship has laundry and dry-cleaning service but no self-serve launderettes.

PUBLIC AREAS & ACTIVITIES   As you might expect from the ship's name, *Pride of America* features patriotic decor including giant photos of the Grand Canyon, the Golden Gate Bridge, the Chicago skyline, and other American icons. The **Gold Rush Saloon** has a prospector motif, **Pink's Champagne and Cigar Bar** salutes with islands with Hawaii-patterned carpeting, while the **Napa Wine Bar** supplies a more elegant, *Mad Men*–esque drinking experience. Because of Hawaiian law, there's no casino on board.

For young ones, the **Rascal's Kids Club** has an elaborate indoor jungle gym, a movie room full of beanbag chairs, and an outdoor splash pool with a tube slide. The main pool deck is underwhelming, but look above and you'll spot a trampoline with a bungee harness, and, next to that, a gyroscope in which passengers can strap themselves in to revolve 360 degrees in any direction, like astronauts in outer space.

America's equipment-packed oceanview **gym** is open 24 hours a day, and the adjacent aerobics room has floor-to-ceiling windows and a great selection of stretching, step, and other traditional classes at no extra charge, plus spinning, kickboxing, and other trendy choices for $10 per class. Nearby, the **spa** and **beauty salon** afford ocean views as well.

DINING   *Pride of America*'s two main restaurants are the **Skyline Restaurant,** with its art-deco skyscraper motif, and the **Liberty Restaurant,** where you're greeted by statues of George Washington and Abe Lincoln, seated beneath a soaring eagle on the ceiling, and surrounded by more stars, stripes, and bunting than you'd see at a political rally. Passengers can also choose from several intimate, extra-cost options: the **Lazy J Texas Steakhouse,** where waiters sport cowboy hats; **Jefferson's Bistro,** an elegant eatery serving French cuisine; and the Pan-Asian **East Meets West.**

Because of the ship's emphasis on port calls, restaurants tend to be busiest in the early evening, with long lines often forming at 5:30pm. The later you dine, the shorter the wait.

PRINCESS CRUISES

www.princess.com. © **800/PRINCESS** (774-6237) or 661/753-0000.

Pros

o **Good Service:** The warm-hearted Italian, British, and Filipino service crew have a gift for making passengers feel welcome.

o **Private Verandas:** Some of these ships have balconies in as many as 75% of the cabins.

Cons

o **Average Food:** The ships' cuisine is perfectly fine if you're not a foodie, but if you are, you'll find that it's pretty banquet hall–esque.

o **Small Gyms:** For such large vessels, the gyms are surprisingly small and can even feel cramped.

Overview

The company strives, successfully, to please a wide variety of passengers. It offers more choices in terms of accommodations, dining, and entertainment than nearly any other line.

EXPERIENCE

If you were to put Carnival, Royal Caribbean, Celebrity, and Holland America in a big bowl and mix them all together, you'd come up with Princess Cruises' megaships. The *Coral Princess, Grand Princess, Crown Princess,* and other big Princess ships are less glitzy and frenzied than the ships of, say, Carnival and Royal Caribbean; not quite as cutting-edge as Celebrity's *Solstice* and *Millennium;* but more exciting, youthful, and entertaining than Holland America's near-megas. The Princess fleet appeals to a wider cross-section of cruisers by offering loads of choices and activities, plus touches of big-ship glamour, along with plenty of the private balconies, quiet nooks, and calm spaces that characterize smaller, more intimate-size vessels. Aboard Princess, you get a lot of bang for your buck, attractively packaged and well executed.

ROUTES

Like other lines that offer a world cruise, you can get to a lot of different destinations on these ships. Most popular for this line are Alaska and the Caribbean, but Princess also does well by Europe (both the Baltic and the Mediterranean), the Panama Canal, California, Hawaii, and Mexico. Other routes are available in Asia; around Australis, New Zealand and the rest of the South Pacific; in South America; and along the coast or Canada.

PASSENGERS

Typical Princess passengers are experienced cruisers between about 50 and 65. They know what they want and are prepared to pay for it. But the line also is popular with families, including multi-generation families, thanks to its solid children's programs and a-little-something-for-everyone vibe. On holidays and summer weeks the number of children on board can really soar.

DINING

In general, Princess serves meals that are good, if hardly gourmet. But you've got to give it points for at least trying to be flexible: About a decade ago, Princess implemented a new fleet-wide dining option known as Anytime Dining. Basically, this plan allows passengers to sign up for the traditional first or second seating for dinner, or for a come-as-you-please restaurant-style dining option. The latter allows you to eat dinner any time between 5:30pm and midnight, though you must be seated by 10pm. Passengers who choose the restaurant-style option may request a cozy table for two or bring along a half-dozen shipmates, depending on their mood that evening. It's also possible to eat all your meals in the Horizon Court cafe on all Princess ships.

If you don't go to the main dining room, though, you may miss one of Princess's best features: its pastas. The newest ships also have several alternative-dining restaurant options, including a steakhouse, and it's our experience that meals at these restaurants are well worth the price of admission.

Specialty restaurants on board include **Sabatinis's,** the line's Italian restaurant, which serves (among other options) creamy burrata, fried calamari, and an artichoke soufflé as appetizers and roasted rack of veal and lobster trio as entrees. There's also the very popular **Crowne Grille,** a steakhouse with quality chops, rib-eyes, and seafood classics.

ACTIVITIES

Princess passengers can expect enough onboard activity to keep them going from morning to night if they've a mind to, and enough hideaways to let them do absolutely nothing if that's their thing. The line doesn't go out of its way to make passengers feel that they're spoilsports if they don't participate in the amateur-night tomfoolery or learn to fold napkins. These activities are usually there, along with the inevitable bingo, shuffleboard, and the rest, but they're low-key. Internet access is provided on all the ships for 75¢ per minute. Various packages that bring the cost down are also available—for instance, $55 for 100 minutes, $75 for 150 minutes, and $100 for 250 minutes.

Specifically in Alaska, the line has naturalists and park rangers on board to offer commentary. It also brings on local entertainers, celebrities, and historians to enhance passengers' Alaska experience; for instance, Iditarod winner Libby Riddles sometimes speaks to passengers on ships.

CHILDREN'S PROGRAMS

Supervised activities are held year-round for ages 3 to 17, clustered in three groups: **Princess Pelicans** for ages 3 to 7, Shockwaves for ages 8 to 12, and **Remix** for ages 13 to 17. For more than a decade now Princess has sought to broaden its appeal and distance itself from its old image as a staid, adults-only line, and all the ships are now well equipped for children and clearly intend to cater to families. Each ship has a spacious children's playroom and a sizable area of fenced-in outside deck for kids only, with a shallow pool and tricycles. Teen centers have computers, video games, and a sound system. Wisely, these areas are placed as far away as possible from the adult passengers.

ENTERTAINMENT

From glittering Vegas-style shows to New York cabaret-singer performances to a rocking disco, this line provides a terrific blend of musical styles, and you'll always find a cozy spot where soft piano or jazz is being performed (there are even strolling musicians on board most ships). You'll also find entertainers such as hypnotists, puppeteers, and comedians, plus karaoke for you audience-participation types. In the afternoons, there are always a couple of sessions of that ubiquitous cruise favorite, the Newlywed and Not-So-Newlywed Game. Each of the ships also has a wine bar selling caviar by the ounce and vintage wine, champagne, and iced vodka by the glass. The Princess casinos are sprawling and exciting places, too, and are bound to lure gamblers with their lights and action.

For years, Princess has had a connection to Hollywood—this is the *Love Boat* line, after all. It's the only line we know of where you can watch yesterday's and today's television shows on your in-room TV. Also shown are A&E, Biography, E! Entertainment TV, Nickelodeon, Discovery Channel, BBC, and National Geographic productions. Like several other lines, Princess also shows recently released movies.

SERVICE

Throughout the fleet, the service in all areas—dining room, lounge, cabin maintenance, and so on—is of consistently high quality. An area in which Princess particularly shines is the efficiency of its shore-excursion staff. Getting 2,600-plus people off a ship and onto motor coaches, trains, and helicopters—all staples of any Alaska cruise program—isn't as easy as this company makes it look. And a real benefit of the Princess shore-excursions program is that passengers are sent the options about 120 days before the sailing and can book their choices on an advanced-reservations basis before the trip (tickets are issued on board), either by mail or on the Internet at www.princess.com. The program improves your chances of getting your first choice of tours before they sell out; it also allows cruisers enough time to compare the cruise line-sponsored options—and their prices—and those of independent operators (sometimes they'll offer a lower rate). All of the Princess Alaskan ships have laundry and dry-cleaning services, plus their own self-service laundromats.

On Princess ships, an $11.50 per-person per-day service charge ($12 for passengers in suites and minisuites) is automatically added to your bill. If you want to raise or lower that amount, you can do so at the passenger services desk.

CRUISETOURS & ADD-ON PROGRAMS

Although its ships serve every corner of the globe, nowhere is the Princess presence more visible than in Alaska. Through its affiliate, Princess Tours, the company owns wilderness lodges, motor coaches, and railcars in the 49th state, making it one of the major players in the Alaska cruise market, alongside Holland America and, increasingly, Royal Caribbean Cruise's two brands, Celebrity and Royal Caribbean International. Princess also operates spectacular wilderness lodges, including the River Princess Wilderness Lodge at Cooper Landing near Wrangell–St. Elias National Park.

In 2004, Princess became the first line to use the rather nondescript Whittier as the northern terminus for its Gulf cruises instead of the more commonly used Seward, and it has done so ever since. Whittier's primary advantage over Seward is that it's about 60 miles closer to Anchorage. Passengers bound for rail tours of Denali National Park are able to board their trains right on the pier instead of taking a bus to Anchorage and then embarking on their rail carriages. The inauguration of the service was yet another effort by a cruise line to gain a competitive edge over its Alaska rivals. Princess Cruises is now a member of the same group that owns Holland America and Carnival, both of them highly visible in the Alaska cruise market. That gives the parent, Miami-based Carnival Corp., control of no fewer than 15 ships in Alaska.

Princess has an array of land packages in Alaska in conjunction with its Gulf of Alaska and Inside Passage voyages. Virtually every part of the state is covered—from the Kenai Peninsula to the Interior to the Far North. The land portions come in 3- to 8-night segments, all combinable with a 7- or 10-night cruise. Four types of land itineraries are offered in conjunction with Princess's five wilderness lodges.

FLEET

Princess's diverse fleet ranges in size from 672 passengers to 3,600 passengers. The ships generally are pretty but not stunning, bright but not gaudy, spacious but not overwhelmingly so, and decorated in a comfortable, restrained style that's a combination of classic and modern. They're a great choice when you want a step up from Carnival and Norwegian but aren't interested in (or can't afford) the luxury of Regent Seven Seas.

Royal Princess • Regal Princess

The Verdict

Princess's newest megaships, these two vessels take everything that made the line's previous ships so popular and roll them into a larger package.

Specifications — Avg. Starting Per Diem $112

Size (in tons)	141,000	Crew	1,346
Passengers (Double Occ.)	3,600	Passenger/Crew Ratio	2.6 to 1
Passenger/Space Ratio	39.1	Year Launched	2013/2014
Total Cabins/Veranda Cabins	1,780/1,438	Last Major Refurbishment	N/A

Frommer's Ratings (Scale of 1–5) ★★★★ ½

Cabin Comfort & Amenities	5	Dining Options	5
Ship Cleanliness & Maintenance	5	Gym, Spa & Sports Facilities	5
Public Comfort/Space	4	Children's Facilities	4
Decor	4	Enjoyment Factor	4.5

THE SHIPS IN GENERAL

When *Royal* and *Regal Princess* were introduced in 2013 and 2014 respectively, they officially became the line's largest ships, with a capacity for 3,600 passengers apiece. They also ushered in a brand-new class of vessels for the line, officially heralding the retirement of the "Grand Class" design that most Princess ships from 1998 to 2010 were based on.

Inside, not much has changed—it's just been made better. Guests will find a larger pool deck, complete with some pretty cool glass catwalks (known as the SeaWalk) that cantilever out over the sea below. There's an expanded version of the Piazza Atrium concept that was first introduced aboard *Crown Princess* back in 2006, and that means more seating and better views. In fact, everything that makes Princess great is here, from the **Movies Under the Stars** poolside screenings to the clubby **Crooner's Bar** to the relaxing, adults-only **Sanctuary.** These ships are *evolutionary* rather than *revolutionary,* and that's okay.

If there is a downside to these ships, it's the lack of a midships staircase, which means you can find yourself walking well out of your way just to get around their 1,083-foot length. Some areas tend to bottleneck with passengers, and overall the ship's layout doesn't feel as free-flowing as the Grand Class or the spectacularly lovely *Coral* and *Island Princess* designs.

CABINS If you've sailed aboard Princess's other megaships, be prepared to keep your expectations in check: While both *Royal* and *Regal Princess* offer some of the same cabin categories, there are changes. **Minisuites**—traditionally located on the Dolphin Deck—are now scattered throughout the ship, and balcony sizes have taken a hit compared with counterparts. Ditto for overall stateroom size: Many categories just feel smaller.

Inside staterooms are roughly the same as always, at 166 square feet. All are done in a style that should be very familiar to past Princess guests: white walls, dark wood trim. **Balconies** come in four sizes; standard ones are smaller than what you'll find on most Grand Class ships, and deluxe balconies aren't much bigger for what can be a hefty. Sadly, bathrooms at these levels still come with showers with that oh-so-clingy shower curtain. Ugh.

Minisuites are also smaller than their Grand-class counterparts, but like those, these are a smart choice if you're looking for more space but don't want to spend the amount of money needed for a full suite. There are 40 **suites**— huge spaces, all with their own private balconies and perks like priority embarkation and disembarkation, priority shore excursion reservations, and use of the exclusive Disembarkation Lounge at the end of the cruise and the Elite Lounge (stocked with hors d'oeuvres and more) during the sailing.

A total of 36 cabins are designated as wheelchair accessible.

PUBLIC AREAS & ACTIVITIES Public rooms are attractive, largely adhering to the style that Princess developed for past vessels while ratcheting up the quality of materials used in certain areas. You can expect lots of recessed lighting accenting a palette of mostly earth tones, with a smattering of polished woods and glittering brass and marble here and there. The Piazza-style **atrium** is the place to be for roving entertainment acts and Princess's famous "Champagne Waterfall" usually set up on the first formal night of the cruise. You can still enjoy coffee and pastries in the **International Café,** wine in **Vines,** and gelato on the lowest level.

On deck 6 you have to walk through the **Princess' Casino** to reach the **Princess Theatre,** a three-story affair hosting evening performances. A secondary venue, the **Vista Lounge** at the stern of the ship, is the go-to spot for dancing, trivia tournaments, and comedy acts. The very British **Wheelhouse Bar** returns to these ships, every bit as clubby as ever. The **Crooner Bar** is a favorite for a pre-dinner cocktail or a nightcap.

The biggest changes were saved for the pools and spas. The pool decks are substantial improvements overall, with better design and layout. The **Fountain Pool** amidships is bordered by the glass-enclosed **Skywalk,** and features an attractive fountain show that changes colors at night. There are only two hot tubs, however, and things can get competitive.

Down on Deck 5, the expanded **Lotus Spa** features a new addition called **The Enclave,** a centrally located area with a hydrotherapy pool, heated tiled ceramic loungers, waterbeds, hot and dry saunas, and aromatic showers infused with relaxing scents. Day and full-cruise passes are available for purchase. Unusually, the **Fitness Center** is separated from the spa on these ships. On its perch on the starboard side of Deck 17, you'll find plenty of exercise equipment of all kinds, and yoga, Pilates and spinning classes.

DINING   Passengers have more options than on Princess predecessors, with 16 different venues onboard, including the main **Symphony** and **Concerto** dining rooms (which are for dine-when-you-like passengers), and **Allegro** (which caters to those who took the traditional, fixed-seating arrangement). The **Horizon Court,** which wraps around the entire aft portion of Lido Deck 16, offers buffet breakfasts, lunches, and dinners (its new outdoor seating is a nice touch). There are also plenty of additional-fee dining venues onboard, ranging from the **Gelateria** to the new Chef's Table **Lumiere,** which focuses on giving small groups a highly personalized culinary experience (it's $95 per person, but that includes wine). The **Ocean Terrace Seafood Bar** is a new addition that serves up raw seafood a la carte—including caviar, which will set you back a pretty penny if you indulge. There are also old favorites onboard, such as **The Crown Grill,** Princess Cruises' signature steakhouse, and **Sabatini's,** which specializes in cooked-to-order Italian fare. We recommend the ravioli.

Grand Princess • Golden Princess • Star Princess • Caribbean Princess • Crown Princess • Emerald Princess • Ruby Princess

The Verdict

These huge, well-equipped vessels are very easy to navigate, never feel as crowded as you'd expect, and are surprisingly intimate for their size.

Specifications

Avg. Starting Per Diem $87

Size (in tons)	109,000-113,000	Crew	1,200
Passengers (Double Occ.)	2,600-3,100	Passenger/Crew Ratio	2.6 to 1
Passenger/Space Ratio	36.8-41.9	Year Launched	1998-2008
Total Cabins/Veranda Cabins	1,538/1,102	Last Major Refurbishment	2015

Frommer's Ratings (Scale of 1–5)

★★★★ ½

Cabin Comfort & Amenities	5	Dining Options	4
Ship Cleanliness & Maintenance	4.5	Gym, Spa & Sports Facilities	4.5
Public Comfort/Space	5	Children's Facilities	4
Decor	4	Enjoyment Factor	4.5

THE SHIPS IN GENERAL

Princess's signature vessels (known as the Grand class) were so ahead of their time when they debuted in 1998 that the design of even newcomers such as *Crown* and *Emerald Princess* isn't significantly changed.

They look like nothing else at sea, with their 18 decks soaring up to space-age discos. Though the vessels give an impression of immensity from the outside, inside they're very easy to navigate and are surprisingly intimate. Public areas never feel as crowded as you'd think they'd be with almost 4,000 people aboard. The dimly lit Explorer's Lounge and traditional Wheelhouse Bar recall a grander era of sea travel, and in the elegant three-story atriums, classical string quartets perform on formal nights and during embarkation.

Caribbean Princess, Crown Princess, Emerald Princess, and *Ruby Princess* are slightly larger versions of the original ships, with a similar layout but one extra deck, plus a cafe serving Caribbean dishes, an international restaurant, a wine and seafood bar, a piazza-style atrium, and a steak and seafood restaurant. *Ruby Princess,* the latest of the series, offers a British pub lunch on sea days (no extra charge) and a range of cheeses to go with the wine and seafood snacks available in Vines.

CABINS   Though staterooms on these vessels are divided into some 35 categories, there are actually fewer than 10 configurations. For the most part, the category differences reflect location, such as midships versus aft. Cabins are pleasing to the eye, decorated in light hues and earth tones, and storage is adequate, with more closet shelves than drawer space. Cabin balconies are tiered so that they get more sunlight, but this also means your neighbors above can look down at you. At 324 square feet, including the balcony, the 180 **minisuites** on each vessel are ultracomfortable, with a roomy sitting area with a full-size pullout couch, a large bathroom with full tub and shower, and generous closet and drawer space. **Grand Suites** feature all the above amenities plus a bathroom with a large whirlpool tub and multidirectional shower.

Be aware that lifeboats partially or completely obstruct views from most cabins on Emerald Deck. Each ship has 28 wheelchair-accessible cabins.

PUBLIC AREAS & ACTIVITIES   Because of the ships' smart layout, passengers are dispersed among six dining venues, expansive outdoor deck space, multiple sports facilities, four pools, and nine hot tubs, rather than concentrated into one or two main areas. Even sailing with a full load of passengers, you might wonder where everyone is. Which is not to say you'll be bored. Three main entertainment venues include a well-equipped two-story theater for big Vegas-style musical revues, a smaller lounge for acts like hypnotists and singers, and the travel-themed **Explorer's Lounge,** where bands, standup comics, and karaoke belters perform amid Middle Eastern tiles and works of African and Asian art. There's also the old-world **Wheelhouse Bar,** offering laid-back pre- and post-dinner dancing and jazz in an elegant setting. Finally, **Skywalkers** is a multilevel disco/observation lounge, sequestered 150 feet above the ship's stern like a high-tech tree house. It's positioned away from any cabins, so the noise won't keep anyone up. Even if you're not a dancer, you'll want to check out the view at sunset.

For kids, the **Fun Zone** has tons of games, toys, computers, and an outdoor, fenced-in play area equipped with a fleet of tricycles and mini basketball setup. A kiddie pool is located nearby. In addition to the teen center on every ship, *Grand* and *Golden* have a teens-only sunbathing area with a hot tub, as well as a truly amazing arcade. If you're inspired by all those youngsters to start your own family, each ship has an attractive chapel where the captain himself performs six or seven legal **weddings** on almost every cruise. Princess is one of the few lines where that's allowed, thanks to the laws of Bermuda, where all Princess cruise ships are registered.

Each ship has 1.75 acres of open deck space, so it's not hard to find a quiet place to soak up the sun. On *Grand, Golden,* and *Star,* our favorite spot on a hot, humid day is portside aft on the deck overlooking the swimming pool, where the tail fin vent blows cool air. In 2006, Princess introduced a space called the **Sanctuary,** which is now installed on all Grand-class ships. Three-quarters canopied and dotted with lounge chairs, trees, and private cabanas, it's a perfect chill-out area, staffed with "serenity stewards" who make sure things stay quiet. Light meals, massages, and beverages are available. Admission carries a $10 fee for half-day use, a measure intended to limit use to those who really want some peace and quiet.

The ships each have four great swimming **pools.** On *Grand, Golden,* and *Star,* one has a retractable roof for inclement weather. A 300-square-foot outdoor LED movie screen is set up for watching films under the stars (and kids' movies during the day). You can reserve deck chairs for evening screenings, and, yes, there's popcorn (for free) and Raisinettes (for a price).

Spa, gym, and **beauty-parlor** facilities are located in a large, almost separate part of each ship, surrounding the lap pool set among tiered, amphitheater-style wooden benches. As is the case fleetwide with Princess, the gym is surprisingly small, although there's an unusually large aerobics floor.

DINING   Three pleasant, one-story main **dining rooms** are laid out on slightly tiered levels. By way of some strategically placed waist-high dividers, they feel private, although the ceilings are on the low side. The 24-hour **Horizon Court** buffet serves breakfast and lunch. With stations serving stir-fry, beef, turkey, pork, and lots of fruit, salads, cheeses, and more, lines are kept to a minimum and you're hardly aware of the space's enormity. This restaurant turns into a sit-down **bistro** from 11pm to 4am, with the same dinner menu each night. If you like the idea of a New York strip sirloin at midnight, this is the place to go.

Alternative restaurants include **Sabatini's** (see p. 191 for more on that) and **Sterling Steakhouse** and on *Caribbean, Crown, Star, Emerald,* and *Ruby,* the **International Café** serves food 24 hours a day, including fresh-baked cookies around the clock (some items are at an extra charge). *Ruby, Crown,* and *Emerald* also serve a no-charge pub-style lunch on sea days with fare like fish and chips, bangers and mash, and cottage pie.

Diamond Princess • Sapphire Princess

The Verdict

Diamond and *Sapphire* are two of the best megaships ever, with beautiful proportions, airy outdoor spaces, and intimate public areas.

Specifications
Avg. Starting Per Diem $128

Size (in tons)	116,000	Crew	1,100
Passengers (Double Occ.)	2,670	Passenger/Crew Ratio	2.4 to 1
Passenger/Space Ratio	42.3	Year Launched	2004
Total Cabins/Veranda Cabins	1,337/748	Last Major Refurbishment	2014

Frommer's Ratings (Scale of 1–5) ★★★★ ½

Cabin Comfort & Amenities	4.5	Dining Options	4
Ship Cleanliness & Maintenance	5	Gym, Spa & Sports Facilities	4.5
Public Comfort/Space	5	Children's Facilities	5
Decor	4.5	Enjoyment Factor	5

THE SHIPS IN GENERAL

Built in Nagasaki, Japan, *Diamond* and *Sapphire* are Princess's best ships ever, with a design that's more graceful than the line's Grand-class ships, while still embodying the ideal of big-ship offerings with a small-ship feel. Inside, the nearly identical vessels have comfortable cabins, woodsy lounges with hints of seagoing history, understated central atrium lobbies, relaxing indoor/outdoor pool areas, and large Asian-inspired spas.

Outside, in the stern, four decks descend in curved, horseshoelike tiers, creating a multilevel resort area with two pools, two hot tubs, two bars, and magnificent views of the ship's wake. One of our favorite things about these ships is that the Promenade Deck wraps around the bow, just below the open top deck, affording a view straight out to where you're going. The only thing that keeps these vessels from a five-star rating is their relative dearth of dining options: Even though there are eight restaurants onboard, five of them have the same basic menu. *Diamond* underwent a massive makeover in 2014 intended to make her appeal more to the Japanese market on her voyages around the Pacific. Additions include an 8,800-square-foot onsen bathing experience and Japanese-style motifs throughout the ship.

CABINS Though cabins on *Diamond* and *Sapphire* are a bit bigger than those on the Grand- and Coral-class ships, they still stick close to the "Princess look," with upholstery and walls done in easy-on-the-eyes earth tones and off-whites, all trimmed in butterscotch wood. **Standard inside** and **outside cabins** are comfortable and stylish, and more than 70% of outside cabins have verandas. **Balconies** are tiered, ensuring direct sunlight for those on Decks 8 and 9 (where most of the popular minisuites are located), but also allowing folks standing on the balconies above to look right down on you. **Minisuites** provide substantially more space without jumping into the cost stratosphere. They're ideal for families with children. The 16 **full suites** have curtained-off sitting and sleeping areas, very large balconies, a walk-in closet, and separate whirlpool tubs and showers in the bathroom. Suite guests are also on the receiving end of numerous perks highlighted in the Service section, above.

Twenty-seven cabins on each ship are wheelchair accessible.

PUBLIC AREAS & ACTIVITIES Most public rooms on these ships are on Decks 6 and 7. Toward the bow, the two-deck **Princess Theater** is the main show space, with tiers of upholstered theater seats (with little cocktail tables that fold out of their armrests, airline-style) and a pair of opera boxes on either side of the stage. Just outside the entrance is **Churchill's,** a *veddy British* cigar bar with TVs for sports. You'll also find a multipurpose entertainment lounge called **Club Fusion,** used principally for games (think bingo and talent shows) and evening music. A spiral staircase in the back of the room leads to one of our favorite spaces: the **Wake View Bar,** a classy nook full of dark wood, leather chairs, and paintings depicting turn-of-the-20th-century tobacconists. Six portholes overlook the namesake wake.

At midships are two of Princess's signature lounge spaces: the English-adventurer-themed **Explorer's Lounge,** a secondary show lounge for comedians, impressionists, and other small-scale entertainment; and the elegant **Wheelhouse Bar,** where a jazz combo plays in the evenings. There's dancing here, but the boogie-happy crowd is more likely to be up in the top-deck disco—the highest point on the ship, where a balcony overlooks the stern. Explorer's jungle theme carries into the **casinos,** with their tree-trunk pillars and leafy ceilings. Next door, the three-story **atrium** is admirably restrained, with lots of creamy marble and wood, and musicians performing throughout the day. Opening off the space is the relaxing library and the charmingly old-fashioned writing room, along with several shops, a coffee bar, and **Crooners,** a Rat Pack–themed bar serving 56 different martini recipes. On Deck 7, the **Internet Café** is notable not only for being large and stylish, but also for being an actual cafe: A bar toward the back dispenses gourmet coffee (for an extra charge), along with free croissants and sweet rolls.

For kids, *Diamond*'s and *Sapphire*'s **Fun Zones** are divided into four sizable rooms, separating young ones by age. Tots get a climbing maze, toys, and a cushiony amphitheater for watching movies. Teens get a sort of Austin Powers–esque room, looking much like a bar for adults, sans the booze.

There are two **pools** at midships: a lively main pool in the sun and a secondary "Conservatory" space with a large pool, two hot tubs, and a retractable roof for bad weather. Another, adults-only resistance pool for swimming laps in place is set in a cleft just outside the large, well-appointed **spa.** That spot has a Zen ambiance with a suite of steam rooms and stone lounging chairs for use before or after treatments. Next door, the **gym** is one of the few sour notes on board—it's way too small for the number of people onboard.

DINING   Passengers opting for traditional dining take their meals in the 518-seat **International Dining Room,** with its simple but elegant wood-panel walls and classical paintings, or in the smaller **Vivaldi Restaurant,** where the decor recalls 18th-century Europe. Passengers on the anytime dining program can eat in any of four smaller themed venues, all with the same menus except for one specialty dish apiece.

Coral Princess • Island Princess

The Verdict

Beautiful, spacious, and yet somehow intimate, *Coral* and *Island* are lovely inside and out, with a nice range of entertainment options and top-drawer onboard learning experiences.

Specifications   Avg. Starting Per Diem $108

Size (in tons)	91,627/92,000	Crew	895
Passengers (Double Occ.)	2,000/2,124	Passenger/Crew Ratio	2.2 to 1
Passenger/Space Ratio	45.8/43.3	Year Launched	2003
Total Cabins/Veranda Cabins	1,000/789	Last Major Refurbishment	2015/2016

Frommer's Ratings (Scale of 1–5)   ★★★★ ½

Cabin Comfort & Amenities	4.5	Dining Options	4
Ship Cleanliness & Maintenance	4	Gym, Spa & Sports Facilities	4
Public Comfort/Space	5	Children's Facilities	4
Decor	4.5	Enjoyment Factor	4.5

THE SHIPS IN GENERAL

Coral Princess and *Island Princess* are two of the loveliest cruise vessels afloat, further refining Princess's vision of big ships with an intimate feel. Outside, there are balconies on some 83% of outside cabins, but their tiered design is a vast improvement over the typical wall-of-balconies look, contributing to a flowing profile. Up top, the ships' futuristic (but purely decorative) jet-engine funnels give the impression that the boats could fly right out of the water and into orbit.

Understated interiors are both classic and modern, with Internet centers and Times Square–style news tickers right around the corner from stately lounges. Our favorite spaces: the clubby **Wheelhouse Bar** before dinner, the New Orleans–themed **Bayou Restaurant** for jazz until around midnight, the peaceful solarium, and the **Universe Lounge** for everything from cooking classes and lectures to full-blown theatrical productions. *Island Princess* was extensively refitted in 2015 to add more balcony cabins—which unfortunately did away with the wraparound promenade deck.

CABINS   **Inside** and standard **outside cabins** are serviceable if smallish at 160 and 168 square feet, respectively. Most private balconies are set up in descending tiers—a positive for soaking up the sun, a negative for total privacy. **Minisuites** provide substantially more space without a big increase in cost, and they have large balconies and sizable sitting areas. Storage space in both cabins and minisuites is more than adequate, with a large shelved closet and open-sided clothes rack facing a small dressing alcove by the bathroom door. Sixteen full **suites** have very large balconies, stocked minibars, whirlpool tubs, and walk-in closets. Suite guests get additional perks highlighted in the Service section (see p. 192).

Twenty cabins on each ship are wheelchair accessible.

PUBLIC AREAS & ACTIVITIES   Layout is one of the areas where these vessels really shine, with decks and public spaces arranged so it's always easy to find your way around. Most of the noteworthy indoor spots are on Decks 6 and 7, starting with the large **Princess Theater** in the bow. Unlike the ornately decorated, two- and three-deck theaters on many new ships, this is a classic, sloping, one-level space, with a good view of the stage from wherever you sit. Farther aft, the **Explorer's Lounge** is a smaller-scale show lounge for comedians, karaoke, game shows, and dancing. In the stern, the **Universe Lounge** is an innovative multipurpose space, hosting cooking demonstrations, lectures, and performances on three interconnected stages that can revolve, rise, and otherwise move around the venue.

Standout bars and lounges include the maritime-themed **Wheelhouse Bar, Churchill's** cigar lounge, and **Crooners,** a piano bar with a Rat Pack vibe. One level down, the ship's **library** and **card room** are both large and comfortable, though the layout—with entrances both from the atrium and from the midships elevators—means that people often use the rooms as a passageway, adding more bustle than you'd prefer in a library. Themed casinos (London on *Coral,* Paris on *Island*) and a wedding chapel round out the offerings for grownups.

At the stern on Deck 12 sits the kids' **Fun Zone, Pelican's Playhouse,** and **Off Limits** teen center. The pottery studio is hidden away nearby. The ships' main **pool** areas are spacious but surprisingly plain, with a pool and three large hot tubs surrounded by sunning areas. A steel-drum duo performs on a tiny stage at one end during the day. Moving toward the stern, the **solarium** is a much more interesting spot, decorated with a tranquil Balinese motif. Both ships also offer Princess's Movies Under the Stars outdoor screenings and adults-only Sanctuary relaxation areas.

Fitness facilities include a disappointingly small (though reasonably equipped) **gym,** plus a separate aerobics room. Up on the top decks, there's a basketball/volleyball court, a computerized golf simulator, and a 9-hole miniature golf course. In the stern on Deck 14, **Lotus Spa** offers massage and beauty services, plus a thermal suite with various heat treatments and a lovely salon overlooking the sea.

DINING   The **Provence** and **Bordeaux** dining rooms are dedicated to traditional fixed-seating and anytime dining, respectively. There are two specialty restaurants aboard: **Sabatini's** ($20 per person, see p. 191) and the **Bayou Cafe and Steakhouse** ($15 per person), for New Orleans favorites like seafood gumbo, fried catfish, grilled jumbo prawns, and jambalaya, while a jazz trio provides accompaniment. The 24-hour **Horizon Court** buffet tends to get chaotic due to the circular layout of the food stations and no clear path for navigating them. Overlooking the main pool, the **Grill** serves burgers, hot dogs, and the like in the afternoon, while some excellent pizza and ice cream are available one deck down at the solarium. At the bottom of the atrium, **La Patisserie** is a good spot to watch the waves roll by while you snack on free cookies and coffee as your ship squeezes through the Panama Canal, with literally only a couple feet to spare.

ROYAL CARIBBEAN INTERNATIONAL

www.royalcaribbean.com. © **866/562-7625.**

Pros

o **Excellent Spas & Recreational Facilities:** Royal Caribbean's ships all have elaborate health club and spa facilities, swimming pools, and large, open sundeck areas.

o **Activity Central:** With rock-climbing walls, surfing machines, zip lines, water parks, basketball courts, miniature golf, ice skating, and bungee trampolines among the many diversions, these ships are tops in the adrenaline department.

o **Quality Entertainment:** Royal Caribbean spends big bucks on entertainment, which includes high-tech show productions.

Cons

o **Gargantuan Ships:** As with some other big ships, you almost need a map to get around, and you'll likely experience the inevitable lines for buffets, debarkation, and boarding of buses during shore excursions. Everything takes longer on these jumbo-megas.

Overview

This bold, brash, innovative company, now in its 45th year, has the largest passenger capacity in the industry on the biggest ships. Royal Caribbean International introduced the concept of the megaship with its *Sovereign of the Seas* in 1988, and the industry hasn't been the same since. The mass-market style of cruising that Royal Caribbean sells aboard its megaships is reasonably priced and has nearly every diversion imaginable.

EXPERIENCE

Royal Caribbean International (RCI) was the first company to launch a fleet specializing exclusively in Caribbean ports of call—hence the company name. In the late 1980s, it expanded its horizons beyond the Caribbean (hence the "International") and now offers cruises in every major cruising region.

The line prides itself on being ultra-innovative and cutting edge, pushing the envelope with each new class of ship it builds. If there's something that's never been done at sea before, Royal Caribbean will figure out how to do it.

The ships are more informal than formal and are well run, with a large team of friendly service employees paying close attention to day-to-day details. Dress is casual during the day and informal most evenings, with two formal nights on a typical seven-night cruise.

The contemporary decor on Royal Caribbean vessels doesn't bang you over the head with glitz like, say, the Carnival line; it's more subdued, classy, and witty, with lots of glass, greenery, and art. All the Royal Caribbean vessels feature the line's trademark **Viking Crown Lounge,** an observation area located in a circular glass structure on the upper deck (in some cases, encircling the smokestack). Another popular trademark feature is the ships' nautically themed Schooner bars.

The range of what's available on different Royal Caribbean ships varies dramatically depending on age, size, and design, so if a certain feature is important to you, it's best to double-check the company's website, brochure, or ask your travel agent first.

ROUTES

You'll find Royal Caribbean vessels across the globe. In the Caribbean, Bahamas and Bermuda yes, but also traversing the Panama Canal, sailing to the Hawaiian isles, the Pacific Northwest and Alaska. And there are other choices as well, including New England, Europe, and, for anyone wanting more exotic itineraries, Dubai in the United Arab Emirates, South America, Asia, Australia and New Zealand, and the South Pacific.

PASSENGERS

The crowd on Royal Caribbean ships represents a wide range of people from all walks of life. You'll find a mix from ages 30 to 60, with a large number of families during school vacation periods. Unlike Carnival (which draws a mostly American audience), don't be surprised to see a handful of European or Asian travelers on Royal Caribbean, thanks to the broad worldwide appeal of the company's newsworthy ships.

DINING

Food on Royal Caribbean has also been improved in recent years, and occasionally a dish will knock your socks off (though not as much as at the "pay-for-play" onboard restaurants; see below). Every menu contains selections designed for low-fat, low-cholesterol, and low-salt dining, as well as vegetarian and children's dishes. A basic menu is available from room service 24 hours a day, and during normal dinner hours, a cabin steward can bring you anything being served in the dining room that night.

The line levies a cover charge of $20 to $30 per person for most specialty restaurants, but in our experience the food soars above what's served in the dining room. You'll find everything from a diner with burgers (the Johnny Rocket's chain restaurant) to Chop's Grille Steakhouse and even a Mystery Dinner Theater on some ships.

ACTIVITIES

On the activity front, Royal Caribbean sets the industry standard. Newer ships have everything from carousels to ice skating rinks and bumper cars, as well as crazy-cool things like sky diving simulators and surfing simulators.

Of course, the line also has plenty of the standard fare across the fleet, from crafts classes to horse racing, bingo, shuffleboard, deck games, line dancing lessons, wine-and-cheese tasting courses, cooking demonstrations, and art auctions. Some of these will carry an extra fee.

But if you want to take it easy and watch the world go by or scan the water-line for dolphins in the Bahamas or sea otters in the Pacific Northwest, nobody will bother you or cajole you into joining an activity. Port lectures are given on topics such as Alaska wildlife, history, and culture. The ships also have an extensive fitness program called **Vitality at Sea,** which includes plenty of different (and sometimes extra-cost) ways for guests to stay in shape at sea, from one-on-one training to organized yoga, spinning and other fitness classes.

CHILDREN'S PROGRAMS

Children's activities are the most extensive afloat and include a teen disco, children's play areas, and the Adventure Ocean and teen programs, which have a full schedule of scavenger hunts, arts-and-crafts sessions, and science presentations—so many activities, in fact, that kids get their own daily activities programs delivered to their cabins. Royal Caribbean also provides teen-only spaces on board every ship in its fleet. On some ships, you'll also find a Royal Babies and Tots nursery, designed by Fisher-Price and Crayola, for youngsters 6 to 36 months of age and up (for a fee of $8 per hour per child). It's a fantastic program; one that sets Royal Caribbean apart from its competitors.

ENTERTAINMENT

Royal Caribbean's entertainment package, which incorporates sprawling, high-tech cabaret stages into each of its ships' show rooms, some with a wall of video monitors to augment live performances, is as good as any other mainstream line. Entertainment begins before dinner and continues late, late into the night. There are musical acts, comedy acts, sock hops, toga parties, talent shows, and that great cruise favorite, karaoke. The Vegas-style shows are filled with all the razzle-dazzle guests have come to expect, and these large-cast revues are among the best you'll find on any ship. Royal Caribbean uses 10-piece bands in its main showroom. Show bands and other lounge acts keep the music playing all over the ships.

SERVICE

Overall, service in the restaurants and cabins is friendly, accommodating, and efficient. You're likely to be greeted with a smile by someone polishing the brass in a stairwell. That said, big, bustling ships like Royal Caribbean's are no strangers to crowds and lines, and harried servers may not be able to get to you exactly when you'd like them to. Considering the vast armies of personnel required to maintain a line as large as Royal Caribbean, it's a miracle that staffers appear as motivated and enthusiastic as they do. Laundry and dry-cleaning services are available on both the ships, but neither has a self-service laundromat.

Royal Caribbean automatically adds daily gratuities in folios of passengers who have not prepaid gratuities prior to boarding, although passengers can modify these payments at any time during the sailing. The line's recommended daily gratuities breakdown is $13.50 per person, per day for guests in standard staterooms; and $16.50 per person, per day for suite guests.

CRUISETOURS & ADD-ON PROGRAMS

Royal Caribbean International offers 10- to 13-night cruisetours in Alaska combining a 7-night cruise with a 3- to 6-night land package in the Denali Corridor, in conjunction with the northbound/southbound Inside Passage sailings on board *Radiance of the Seas*. All tours are escorted and spend at least 1 night in Denali National Park and one leg on the Wilderness Express—plush, glass-domed train cars that offer panoramic views of the grand Alaskan frontier. The 10-night Alaska cruisetour prices start at $1,594 per person, based on double occupancy, with package prices varying depending on cabin category, land package, and departure date. Additionally, Royal Caribbean offers pre- and post-cruise hotel stays in Anchorage (from $233 per person double, including transfers) and Vancouver (from $193 per person double, including transfers).

FLEET

Royal Caribbean owns most of the largest ships in the world, including the recently introduced *Harmony of the Seas* and her sister ships *Oasis of the Seas* and *Allure of the Seas*—the world's largest vessels at 225,282 gross registered tons. But while *Oasis* and *Allure* have room for 5,400 passengers at double occupancy and several other Royal Caribbean ships can hold nearly 4,000, other vessels can only carry around 2,000 passengers.

Quantum of the Seas • Anthem of the Seas • Ovation of the Seas

The Verdict

From robot bartenders to some of the most elaborate performances at sea, this technologically advanced trio supply "wow" experiences.

Specifications   Avg. Starting Per Diem $159

Size (in tons)	168,666	Crew	1,500
Passengers (Double Occ.)	4,180	Passenger/Crew Ratio	2.7 to 1
Passenger/Space Ratio	40	Year Launched	2014-2016
Total Cabins/Veranda Cabins	2,091/1,572	Last Major Refurbishment	N/A

Frommer's Ratings (Scale of 1–5)		★★★★ ½	
Cabin Comfort & Amenities	4	Dining Options	3.5
Ship Cleanliness & Maintenance	4.5	Gym, Spa & Sports Facilities	4
Public Comfort/Space	4	Children's Facilities	4.5
Decor	4	Enjoyment Factor	5

THE SHIPS IN GENERAL

Billed by Royal Caribbean as the most technologically advanced ship ever, the 4,180-guest *Quantum of the Seas* certainly lived up to the hype when she was introduced in late 2014. The boat boasted a high number of firsts, from the robotic bartenders at the **Bionic Bar** to the **RipCord by iFly** skydiving simulator, the **NorthStar** hydraulic observation platform, and the onboard bumper-car arena. Are these things necessary? Well, they're fun for sure—but you probably wouldn't miss them if they weren't there. Instead, the standout quality of *Quantum* and her sisters is how they provide a lot of class at reasonable, mainstream prices. The forward-facing **Solarium,** with its soaring, two-story glass canopy roof, is a beautifully serene space, and the **Windjammer Café** makes even passing through the buffet a pleasant experience.

CABINS   There are 2,091 **staterooms** on these ships, and miles of endless corridors to match. Here's a little trick to navigating the hallways: Cabins with a 1 or a 2 after the deck number are always on the port, or left, side of the ship; cabins on the starboard side always have a 5 or a 6 after the deck number. Royal Caribbean's new take on the traditional inside stateroom is the **Virtual Balcony Stateroom,** inside of which you'll find a real-time view of outside projected onto one of the walls. **Outside Staterooms** deliver ocean views through attractive, oversized portholes. To get real, as opposed to virtual, outside access, guests can opt for **Balcony Staterooms** or **Suites.** The latter are really something to write home about, ranging in size from big to positively gargantuan. There are 15 different types, from **Junior Suites** (276 square feet) with an oversized corner balcony, to the massive 1,640-square foot **Royal Loft Suites** that are spread out over two levels and feature one bedroom, two bathrooms, a media room, a bar, and a balcony with its own whirlpool tub.

Decor across the boards is more modern and upscale than Royal Caribbean's past vessels, with spiral grey-and-navy blue carpeting, cream-colored drapes, slate-grey bed skirts and runners, and cabinetry accented with coffee edges and blonde doors and paneling. Bathrooms feature much-improved lighting, along with stand-up showers that better mimic those found in hotels and move away from the standard, plastic "cylinder" found on older ships.

In 2016, Royal Caribbean rolled out its new **Royal Suite Class** aboard these ships. Offering three levels of service (Star, Sky, and Sea) defined by your suite category, they include meals at a restaurant for suite guests only (**Coastal Kitchen**), unlimited Internet access, priority FlowRider rides, exclusive beach access at **Labadee** (Royal Caribbean's private enclave in Haiti) and other perks.

A total of 34 staterooms are designated as wheelchair accessible.

PUBLIC AREAS & ACTIVITIES   Most of the public spaces aboard these ships are linked by an oversized, three-deck-high corridor running down the center of the ship. Known as the **Royal Esplanade,** it connects many popular spots. Royal Caribbean's past guests will no doubt be happy to see traditional staples like the Latin-themed **Bolero's** lounge, with its live salsa music and locally inspired cocktails. But the emphasis is mostly on cool new stuff here. At the **Bionic Bar,** you can pull up a chair to watch robotic bartenders whip you up an adult beverage. It's gimmicky—and the cocktails aren't always the most balanced concoctions—but it is a compelling show. More to our taste is **Vintages,** one of the most inviting spots onboard, with its dark wood paneling, sepia-toned artwork, and chocolate-and-cream leather-backed chairs.

At the bow, the two-story **Royal Theatre** hosts high-quality productions, but it's often overshadowed by its counterpart at the stern. **Two70** has a two-story wall of windows overlooking the ship's wake and seating areas spread over multiple tiers in a classic dinner-theater layout. But it's the shows that stand out—original and developed expressly for these ships, they make use of that back wall of windows, which transforms into a digital canvas by night. Add in smoke and lighting effects and a dynamic soundtrack, and you've got an often thrilling spectacle.

The **casino** on these ships is positively massive, taking up the better part of Deck 3 (aboard *Quantum,* it's even bigger). *Anthem* and *Ovation* have **Music Hall,** where the menus are made out of pieces of old vinyl records and the cocktails stay in keeping with the same theme. As in some underground club in New York, the place has live performances, two bars, pool tables, and lots of cool velvety furniture.

Pool, spa and fitness facilities on these ships are second-to-none, with a mind-boggling variety. The **SeaPlex** on Deck 14 offers the most unique diversions, from actual bumper cars to a circus school. It also has a full-sized basketball court, roller skating, table tennis, and other games. It's surrounded by an **arcade,** a **jogging track,** and a **rock-climbing wall.** Up one deck the **RipCord by iFly** walks you through a full-blown skydiving simulator in a glass-enclosed tube with high-powered fans. The **Flowrider,** meanwhile, simulates surfing (both simulators tend to draw crowds, so be prepared for an audience if you try them out). Another unique attraction is the **NorthStar,** a glass capsule perched atop a hydraulic arm that can swing out over the ocean, offering views over 300 feet above the water. So far, rides are complimentary, though Royal Caribbean plans to start charging for it on *Ovation* when she heads to China.

For those who'd rather kick back, an outdoor **pool** and two whirlpools are located roughly in the middle of Deck 14, adjacent to the ship's oversized movie screen. Forward of this is an indoor pool and the **Solarium,** a graceful, multi-tiered space overlooking the ship's bow with floor-to-ceiling glass. The views inside are unparalleled. One deck up is the **Vitality Spa at Sea,** offering up the usual salon and spa services, and, above that, the sprawling **fitness center.**

DINING The usual Royal Caribbean staples are here, from the casual buffet to the extra-fee burgers and shakes at **Johnny Rockets.** Specialty restaurants **Chops Grille, Izumi,** and the **Chef's Table,** which have proved popular on other ships, show up here as well. Unfortunately, it's the main dining experience that's disappointing. Rather than have a single grand, multistory dining room as in the past, Royal Caribbean opted to go with a series of smaller complimentary restaurants, which RCL announced (as we went to press would all have the same menu, drawn from favorites across the fleet). So we can't comment on the quality of the fare, but they still won't work numbers-wise with 4,000 guests or so to accommodate in four rooms that seat about 400 each, you could be in for service inconsistencies and long waits.

At the specialty restaurants, on the other hand, you'll find lots to like despite the extra charges. The most creative among these, **Wonderland,** pairs imaginative decor (it's pretty much *Alice in Wonderland* come to life) and inventive cuisine. **Jamie's Italian Kitchen,** created by celebrity chef Jamie Oliver, has tasty dishes like lamb lollipops and aubergine parmigiana; designed with the same cool factor as Oliver's land-based eateries, it's one of the hardest venues to get into each night (the fees: $20/lunch, $30/dinner). The best of the bunch might be **Michael's Genuine Pub,** created in conjunction with James Beard Award-winning chef Michael Schwartz. Mimicking an Irish gastropub, it includes a huge selection of craft beers and a superb selection of a la carte pub favorites like slow-roasted pork sliders and mouth-watering charcuterie boards.

Oasis of the Seas • Allure of the Seas • Harmony of the Seas

The Verdict

Oasis, Allure, and *Harmony of the Seas* are the future—the ultimate extension (so far) of the old "city at sea" chestnut with which big ships have been tagged for decades. They're the biggest cruise ships ever, by far, but they've also got heart, and a design that opens up to the air, sky, and sea.

Specifications — Avg. Starting Per Diem $159

Size (in tons)	225,282	Crew	2,394
Passengers (Double Occ.)	5,400	Passenger/Crew Ratio	2.3 to 1
Passenger/Space Ratio	41.7	Year Launched	2009-2016
Total Cabins/Veranda Cabins	2,076/1,956	Last Major Refurbishment	N/A

Frommer's Ratings (Scale of 1–5) ★★★★

Cabin Comfort & Amenities	4.5	Dining Options	5
Ship Cleanliness & Maintenance	5	Gym, Spa & Sports Facilities	5
Public Comfort/Space	5	Children's Facilities	5
Decor	4.5	Enjoyment Factor	5

THE SHIPS IN GENERAL

Welcome to the future. *Oasis of the Seas* launched in 2009, at a cost of $1.4 billion. This innovative ship is a true game changer—not just because of her size and flashy amenities, but for the way she's laid out: An ingenious split superstructure design and a lot of extra width have somehow given the ship a feeling of light and air that's completely new. To walk around Oasis is to be surrounded by wide-open, all-encompassing views from public and private spaces alike, and they're made even better by architecture that favors curving lines to lead the eye from one stunning visual to the next.

Harmony of the Seas entered service in 2016 and introduced some new features found aboard Royal Caribbean's Quantum-class ships, but for the most part, these vessels are identical.

CABINS One of the more remarkable things about the Oasis ships is that their split-superstructure design allows staterooms to have views inward as well as outward, allowing units that would otherwise have been windowless interior cabins to sport balconies looking out over either the greenery of Central Park or the nighttime excitement of Boardwalk. The 254 **balcony staterooms** and 70 **window-view staterooms** that flank Central Park are by far the most serene, with pleasant greenery below and a shifting skyscape above. The 225 **balcony cabins** and eight window cabins that flank the Boardwalk entertainment space are much more boisterous. There are also 18 window-view cabins facing the interior Royal Promenade, but they seem more of an afterthought, and their bay-window views of the "street" below seem almost claustrophobic by comparison. **Standard interior staterooms,** without windows of any kind, are available, and run 149 square feet. All staterooms have interactive TVs (through which you can book shore excursions).

There are 13 different categories of suites on Oasis-class ships, starting with 287-square-foot **Junior Suites** and reaching to the 27 **Loft Suites** at the very top of the ship near the Viking Crown Lounge. These units are true showstoppers, with two floors, two baths, and balconies with sweeping sea views. At the top of the stairs, the loft bedroom floats like a dream behind transparent glass panels that afford open views through the main floor-to-ceiling windows. All suites, loft or not, offer perks like priority check-in, a dedicated suite attendant, coffee and tea service, bathrobes for onboard use, and additional bathroom amenities.

A total of 46 staterooms aboard each ship are wheelchair accessible.

PUBLIC AREAS & ACTIVITIES Public areas aboard *Oasis, Allure,* and *Harmony* are generally grouped into four themed "neighborhoods." Our favorite is **Central Park,** the 21,000-square-foot, open-air tropical garden that sits in the gap between the ships' split superstructure. Taking up the better part of Deck 8, it has a sophisticated yet bucolic atmosphere, with a wide, tiled pathway undulating through the garden, rising and falling in gentle slopes, flanked by cute red benches and surrounded by garden beds, seating nooks, a sculpture garden, and a number of restaurants and other venues. The parks each contain about 12,000 individual trees, plants, vines, and flowers, all contained within 2,200 individually sized aluminum modules which are in turn housed within 46 large planter beds. Two immense **Living Walls** covered in vines and flowers stand in the center of the park.

Entering from the stern, you first pass the **Rising Tide bar,** which connects to the Royal Promenade below. Paths lead to either side of the glass enclosure that shelters the bar from weather, and restaurants sit to either side. Moving forward, we pass the open-air, glass-topped **Trellis Bar,** which seats just 17 people between planter boxes full of greenery on one side and one of the five-deck-high Living Walls on the other. Continuing our walk forward, we arrive at one of two enormous **Crystal Canopy** skylights that let natural light pass through to the Royal Promenade below. Beyond that is the park's **central square** (which is actually round), a sort of communal meeting spot. At the forward end there are shops. The **Vintages** wine bar sits across from this commercial cluster.

The **Royal Promenade** can be found three levels below Central Park. This all-purpose space houses a number of pleasant drinking spots, shops, cafes, and clubs along its length. Additionally, a parade of costumed characters and stilt-walkers wanders through each night, and there are places for bands to perform. At street level, you'll pass **Bolero's,** a Latin-themed bar that's been a staple aboard Royal Caribbean ships for years, and the **On-Air Club,** another old standby that's been expanded here into a full-service sports bar with a news ticker outside. You'll also stroll past shops and watering holes including the Brit-style **Globe and Atlas Pub,** the **Champagne Bar,** and the quieter **Schooner Bar** on the mezzanine level. There are a number of casual dining spots and the little **Cupcake Cupboard** serving fancy, cream-heavy treats for an extra charge. Toward the stern end of the promenade, the oval **Rising Tide** bar shuttles continually up and down between the promenade and Central Park. *Harmony of the Seas* adds the robot-staffed **Bionic Bar** found aboard RCI's *Quantum* and *Anthem of the Seas.*

Along with Central Park, the other open-air neighborhood is the **Boardwalk.** Stretching for almost a third of the ship's length on Deck 6, this is a family entertainment zone with a carnival mood. Flanked by the **Boardwalk Donut Shop** (free donuts!) and **Ice Cream Parlor** (extra cost) is a **carousel** with intricate, hand-carved wooden animals. The first traditional merry-go-round at sea, it's designed to compensate for a ship's pitch and roll. Throughout the Boardwalk, various permanent and temporary amusements keep things lively. Near the carousel is a classic **photo booth** where you and your closest can mug to your heart's content. The space also hosts a daily **Family Festival** with face-painting and games. Three restaurants offer casual fare, and the **AquaTheater** offers swimming in the largest and deepest freshwater pool at sea during the day and impressive aquatic performances at night.

Traditional entertainment spaces can be found at Deck 4's **Entertainment Place,** which features a jazz club, comedy club, and disco, as well as the ship's huge casino. This is also the location of **Studio B ice rink,** for open skating and elaborate ice shows, and the **main theater.** Note that some shows at various venues require timed—albeit free—tickets, which you can book through your cabin's interactive TV.

The **Youth Zone** for children is one of the best in the business, stretching over an amazing 28,700 square feet, with a central boulevard connecting 10 different areas. They include the **Adventure Ocean Theater,** where kids can put on shows; **Imagination Studio,** an art-oriented space created in collaboration with Crayola; the **Adventure Science Lab,** where kids can make DNA strands out of licorice and learn about dinosaurs; and three play spaces segmented by age group. Lastly, there's the **Royal Babies & Royal Tots** nursery, a real rarity in cruise land. Open daily, the nursery provides child-care drop-off options both day and night, charging $8 per hour and caring for little ones between 6 months and 3 years. Teen spaces are located one deck above, and comprise a disco, arcade, and lounge with computer stations and activities like Scratch DJ classes. On one of the top decks, the **H2O Zone** water park is full of water-spouting sculptures, sprayers, and water cannons.

Unlike any other **pool deck** at sea, the ones here are split into four sections, with the deep canyon that houses Central Park splitting them lengthwise and a large structural bridge quartering them at midships. In addition to the H2O Zone, there's a **main pool, sports pool,** and **beach pool,** where the seating area slopes right into the water, letting guests wade in or just park their lounge chairs in the shallow end and dangle their toes in the water.

Behind the pool zone is where Royal Caribbean keeps some of its best toys—including a **miniature golf course** and **basketball court,** while an elevated platform across the back of the deck holds two **FlowRider Surfing Simulators** and the launch pad for the only **zip lines** at sea, which allow guests to fly across the chasm that houses Boardwalk, a full nine stories below. The ride takes all of about 7 seconds, but it's a rush.

For us, the best part of the ships' enormous **fitness center** is the stairway that leads down one deck, providing direct access to a **nearly 0.5-mile jogging track.** It's by far the longest on any cruise ship and nearly twice as long as a standard Olympic-size track. At the tranquil **Vitality at Sea** spa, guests can unwind in relaxation rooms before partaking in a menu of treatments or visiting the thermal suite with its heated tile loungers, saunas, and steam rooms. There's also a dedicated spa for kids and teens

Each of the ships' valuable top-deck real estate is occupied by the best **Solarium** at sea, a two-deck-high wonder under a curved canopy with open strips to let in the air and a bistro that transforms into a disco at night. A river-like water feature separates seating into various islands on the main level, which also has a small pool and two whirlpools. To both port and starboard, between the Solarium and the main Pool Deck, two **cantilevered whirlpools** sit within domed, semi-open bubbles jutting out over the sides of the ship, 136 feet above the ocean.

DINING Both *Oasis* and *Allure* have a gorgeous three-level **dining room** that can seat more than 3,000 guests at a time. But what distinguishes these ships from their fleetmates is the number of specialty restaurants and casual dining spots on board. Central Park, for instance, has two casual restaurants and two fine-dining establishments. On the casual side, **Giovanni's Table**

($15 per person at dinner, $10 at lunch) is a family-style Italian restaurant serving pizzas, pastas, and various rustic dishes, while the **Park Cafe** (free) is sort of an adjunct to the traditional buffet restaurant upstairs, serving made-to-order salads, panini sandwiches, soups, and the like. On the fancy side, Chicago-style steakhouse **Chops Grill** seats guests both inside and out on its alfresco patio ($25 per person). **150 Central Park** is the fanciest restaurant on board, specializing in six- to eight-course tasting menus with wine pairings ($35 per person)—all overseen by award-winning resident chef Keriann Von Raesfeld. Both Chops and 150 Central Park are open for dinner only.

Boardwalk has three casual eateries: the **Seafood Shack** (lunch $7.95 cover, dinner $9.95), the '50s-style **Johnny Rockets** (breakfast $3.95, lunch and dinner $4.95), and the **Boardwalk Bar.** Down on the Royal Promenade, there's a serviceable **Sorrento's Pizza** and **Cafe Promenade** for light meals. There's also a 24-hour coffee, pastry, and sandwich stand called the **Mondo Cafe.**

Freedom of the Seas • Independence of the Seas • Liberty of the Seas

The Verdict

Supersize versions of the already supersize Voyager-class ships, *Freedom, Liberty,* and *Independence of the Seas* offer everything those ships have and more—though they come close to being too commercial for their own good.

Specifications   Avg. Starting Per Diem $120

Size (in tons)	160,000	Crew	1,360
Passengers (Double Occ.)	3,782	Passenger/Crew Ratio	2.7 to 1
Passenger/Space Ratio	44	Year Launched	2006-2008
Total Cabins/Veranda Cabins	1,891/844	Last Major Refurbishment	2016

Frommer's Ratings (Scale of 1–5)   ★★★★ ½

Cabin Comfort & Amenities	4	Dining Options	4.5
Ship Cleanliness & Maintenance	5	Gym, Spa & Sports Facilities	5
Public Comfort/Space	4.5	Children's Facilities	5
Decor	4	Enjoyment Factor	5

THE SHIPS IN GENERAL

The second-largest class of cruise ships in the world, after Royal's own Oasis boats, these three vessels are, in essence, bigger versions of Royal Caribbean's popular Voyager-class ships, which introduced the line's now-brandwide "active vacation" image, complete with rock-climbing walls, ice-skating rinks, and full-size basketball courts. The Freedom ships also boast some unique features, namely a kids' water park and a surfing simulator. Extremely well designed, the Freedom vessels disperse their large complement of passengers among many public areas—including the four-story, boulevard-like interior **Royal Promenade,** which runs more than a football field's length down the center of each ship and is lined with bars, shops, and entertainment lounges. The promenade, with its urban feel, makes the Freedom vessels a great compromise for couples who can't decide between a cruise and a land-based vacation. They really do feel like cities at sea.

Freedom ships have a nearly identical layout and ambience to Voyager craft, but they carry at least 500 more passengers and things are a bit more stretched out, with a few new eye-catching activities and entertainment features. One drawback to that extra space: the Freedom ships' Royal Promenade has a lot more shops and corporate cobranding arrangements (a Ben & Jerry's ice-cream parlor, a sportswear shop with a dedicated New Balance section, and so on), making it feel like a mall as much as a ship.

A series of refits in 2011 and 2015-16 added a number of new features, including nurseries for babies, big video screens by the main pools, helpful new digital signage to help you get around, and specialty cupcake shops—along with new staterooms. The strange nightclub **The Crypt** disappeared to make way for those, and the jogging track has been done away with, too.

CABINS   Standard outside cabins are a livable if not exactly large 161 square feet, though standard insides seem small at 152 square feet. Bathrooms are on the cramped side, with little storage space, few amenities (soap and shampoo only), and only a thin sliver of counter. The cylindrical shower stalls have RCI's standard sliding doors that keep in the water and warmth. Of 1,815 cabins, more than 1,000 have ocean views and 844 have verandas; all have a pleasant, pastel color scheme. **Suites** range from the affordable junior suites (with sitting area and balcony) to a handful of family suites (with two bedrooms, two bathrooms, and a living area with sofa bed) up to the huge Presidential Suite with its four bedrooms, four bathrooms, and 810-square-foot balcony.

For those who want to spend a lot of time people watching, the 168 atrium cabins on the second, third, and fourth levels of the four-story Royal Promenade have windows facing the action below, with curtains and soundproofing to keep most of the light and noise out when you're ready for some down time.

Thirty-two cabins are wheelchair accessible.

PUBLIC AREAS & ACTIVITIES   These ships have more than 3 miles of public corridors apiece, and it can feel like a real hike if your cabin is on one end of the ship and you have to get to the other. As for what's onboard—where do we start?

Running 445 feet down the center of Deck 5 is the bustling, four-story **Royal Promenade,** designed to resemble an urban entertainment thoroughfare like Beale Street in Memphis or Bourbon Street in New Orleans. It's lined with shops, bars, and cafes, and has evening musical performances by various groups including big bands. Other promenade attractions include a Ben & Jerry's ice cream parlor, an English-style pub with evening entertainment, a champagne bar, a wine bar with tastings, a small bookstore, and—for our money, the best thing on the whole strip—a men's **barbershop** giving old-timey professional shaves spiced with a helping of New Age spa frippery. The half-hour Express Shave includes hot towels, deep-cleansing exfoliation, a superclose shave, and did we mention hot towels? The only inauthentic touch: They use safety razors instead of straight.

There's a huge multistory **theater,** a **casino** with more than 300 slot machines, a Latin-themed bar with live music, a wedding chapel, a "peek-a-boo" bridge where guests can watch the crew steer the ship, and an **ice rink** (for skating and shows held both on the ice and on a sliding floor that covers it). For younger passengers there's a sprawling **kids' area** with an oceanview playroom, and a **teen center.**

In keeping with Royal Caribbean's active image, the line has outfitted the Freedom ships with several features sure to entertain both actual athletes and weekend warriors—as well as their kids. The biggest to-do is each ship's **FlowRider surfing simulator,** which is sort of similar to swim-in-place lap pools with recycling currents, except that this one has a stream that flows up an inclined, wedge-shaped surface 40 feet long and 32 feet wide. At the bottom are powerful jets that pump 30,000 gallons per minute up the slope, creating a wavelike flow on which boarders can ride. At least in theory. The ride is adjoined by bleachers for gawkers and fans who come here expressly to watch people wipe out—and most everyone does.

Also nearby: Royal Caribbean's signature **rock-climbing wall** (the biggest one at sea), a mini-golf course, golf simulator, jogging track, and basketball court. In the ship's **gym,** a 20-by-20-feet boxing ring takes the place of the large hot tub that greets guests on Voyager ships. The ring is part of what the line bills as the largest fitness center at sea, with an enormous number of aerobics and weight machines plus workouts (for a fee) that are rare even in shoreside gyms. Options include Fight Klub training (one-on-one boxing sessions), personal training with Pilates instructors, yoga, and a class on the beach at Labadee, Royal Caribbean's private resort in Haiti. A program of mapped jogging routes is available in the ports of call.

Back outside, the kid-friendly **H2O Zone Water Park** takes up almost half the pool deck, with water cannons, jets, buckets, and sprays hidden among colorful cartoon statues, some controlled by motion sensors, others by the kids themselves. The area also includes two wading pools (one geared to toddlers) and two hot tubs for parental relaxation. Farther forward, the main pool area has two pools and two large hot tubs extending 12 feet over the edge of the ship and some 112 feet above the sea. Extremely popular, they get crowded early. Guests seeking something more peaceful can sometimes find it in the adjacent, adults-only **Solarium,** where a second swimming pool is bisected by a little bridge.

Waterslide aficionados have good reason to choose *Liberty of the Seas* over her sisters: In January 2016, the ship received three brand-new slides, including two racers known as **Typhoon** and **Cyclone,** and **Tidal Wave**—the first boomerang-style waterslide at sea.

DINING The ships' three-level **main dining rooms** are, like those on RCI's Voyager-class ships, among the classiest on any of today's megaships. Each level—linked by a large open area and grand staircase at its center—is considered a separate restaurant, though service and menus are consistent throughout. A pianist or trio entertains from a platform in the aft end of the room and a huge crystal chandelier hangs overhead, setting an elegant mood.

Two alternative restaurants occupy spots immediately to port and starboard at the entrance to the buffet restaurant: **Portofino** ($20 charge) serves Italian meals in a cozy setting, and the handsome **Chops Grille** offers steaks ($39 and up depending on what's ordered). Out in the **buffet,** a section called Jade serves Japanese, Chinese, Indian, and Thai dishes.

Another casual spot for lunch, dinner, and late-night snacks is the popular Johnny Rockets, a 1950s-style diner ($6.95 meals, extra for shakes and sodas).

Voyager of the Seas • Explorer of the Seas • Adventure of the Seas • Navigator of the Seas • Mariner of the Seas

The Verdict

Sports club meets Vegas meets theme park meets cruise ship: These enormous vessels are for those who like their vacations larger than life.

Specifications — Avg. Starting Per Diem $110

Size (in tons)	142,000	Crew	1,176
Passengers (Double Occ.)	3,114	Passenger/Crew Ratio	2.7 to 1
Passenger/Space Ratio	45.6	Year Launched	1999-2003
Total Cabins/Veranda Cabins	1,557/757	Last Major Refurbishment	2016

Frommer's Ratings (Scale of 1–5) ★★★★ ½

Cabin Comfort & Amenities	4	Dining Options	4.5
Ship Cleanliness & Maintenance	4	Gym, Spa & Sports Facilities	5
Public Comfort/Space	5	Children's Facilities	5
Decor	4	Enjoyment Factor	5

THE SHIPS IN GENERAL

Truly groundbreaking when they were first launched, Voyager-class ships are still among the largest and most activity-rich passenger ships at sea. And though each vessel carries 3,114 guests at double occupancy (because many staterooms have third and fourth berths, total capacity can reach as high as 3,838), remarkably, the ships rarely feel as crowded as you'd expect. Kudos go to the crew for efficiency, and also to Royal Caribbean for a design that diffuses crowds comfortably. This design not only keeps traffic moving, but it also means you don't tend to find yourself in the same spots day after day—it's entirely possible to be aboard for 6 days, turn a corner, and find yourself in a room you've never seen before.

One thing that deserves mention about ships this large is that even though ongoing maintenance is standard (replacing stained upholstery or carpeting, for instance), it's tough keeping up with the demands of constant use by thousands of passengers, especially on the ship's soft goods. On one sailing aboard the *Voyager,* for instance, we noticed a torn curtain in the dining room and soiled fabric on some chairs. Royal Caribbean recently committed to a massive refurbishment program on these vessels, which should help and which has already added new features to *Explorer of the Seas* and *Navigator of the Seas,* such as updated stateroom decor and amenities (hello, flat-screen TVs!), along with FlowRider surfing simulators and new dining venues like **Chops Grille** and **Izumi.** Ships are also getting oversized poolside LED movie screens slowly but surely, with *Adventure of the Seas* being the latest scheduled to undergo the refits by the time you read this.

CABINS Though not huge (at 160 sq. ft. for insides and 173 sq. ft. for standard ocean views, including balcony), **cabins** are comfortable, but bathrooms are on the cramped side, with little storage space and thin counters. The cylindrical shower stalls—a tight squeeze for some passengers—have efficient sliding doors that keep in the water and warmth. Of the 1,557 cabins, 939 have ocean views and 757 have verandas. There's a single huge **Penthouse Suite,** 10 **Owner's Suites,** and four **Royal Family Suites** that accommodate a total of eight people with two bedrooms, plus a living room with sofa bed and a pair of bathrooms. Smaller and cheaper family cabins sleep six, some on sofa beds. The 138 atrium cabins on the second, third, and fourth levels of the four-story Royal Promenade have windows facing the action below; curtains and soundproofing keep most of the light and noise out when you want some peace and quiet.

Twenty-six cabins are wheelchair accessible.

PUBLIC AREAS & ACTIVITIES Expect non-stop action on all three ships. Each boasts a full-size ice-skating rink; an outdoor in-line skating track; a 9-hole miniature-golf course and golf simulator; regulation-size basketball, paddleball, and volleyball courts; huge two-level gyms and spas; and the rock-climbing walls that have become one of Royal Caribbean's most distinguishing features. And did we mention they also have monumentally gorgeous, three-story dining rooms, florist shops, and a "peek-a-boo" bridge on Deck 11 that allows guests to watch the crew steering the ship?

There are also huge **kids' areas** with sprawling oceanview playrooms, teen discos, and jumbo arcades.

For those of age, there are some 30 watering holes aboard each ship, including the **Viking Crown complex** on the top deck, with its elegant jazz club and golf-themed **19th Hole** bar; the dark, romantic **Schooner Bar;** and the clubby cigar bar, tucked away behind a dark door and hosting blackjack games on formal evenings. Both tippling and dancing go on in the futuristic, or Gothic-dungeon-themed, **disco** (it varies by vessel) which is entered through a "secret passage." And running down the center of each ship is the bustling, four-story, shop-and-cafe-lined **Royal Promenade,** which has even more kinds of bars—an English/Irish pub, a champagne bar, a raucous sports bar, and **Vintages** wine bar, on *Navigator* and *Mariner* only. Vintages is a collaboration with several notable Napa wineries and showcase more than 60 wines at reasonable prices. Guests can taste any variety before ordering (classes in wine appreciation are also held here).

Of course, the fun isn't all booze-fueled. *Voyager, Explorer,* and *Adventure* carry an arcade stocked with classic 1980s video games. Each ship has a two-story **library and computer room** equipped with webcams that allow you to send your picture as an electronic postcard. Lavish productions entertain each evening in handsome three story **showrooms** with truly lovely stage curtains—the one on *Adventure* decorated with peacock designs, the one on *Explorer* depicts a chorus of women standing under golden boughs amid a rain of leaves.

While crowds tend to disperse around the ships' public areas, on sunny days things can get tight out on the main pool decks, where deck chairs are squeezed into every level of the multistoried, amphitheater-like decks. Guests seeking something more peaceful can usually find it in the adjacent **Solarium,** which has a second swimming pool and two enormous whirlpool tubs under a sliding roof. Behind the Johnny Rockets diner, *Voyager, Adventure,* and *Explorer* have a **kids' pool area** with a water slide, wading pool, hot tub for adults, and dozens of adorable half-size deck chairs for the kids. On *Navigator* and *Mariner,* the area is reserved for teens, with deck chairs for sunbathing and an outdoor dance floor with sound and light systems.

And to get to all of this—whew!—get ready to do some walking. The ship has 3 miles of corridors, so bring comfortable shoes.

DINING The three-level main **dining rooms** on these ships are stunning, with designs that follow a general European theme. Each level—linked by a large open area and grand staircase at its center—is considered a separate restaurant, though service and menus are consistent throughout. To enhance the elegant mood, pianists tickle the ivories from a platform in the aft end of the room and a huge crystal chandelier hangs overhead. Dining alternatives are many, from Italian food at the oceanview **Portofino** restaurant (an additional $20 per person) to diner fare at **Johnny Rockets** ($6.95-per-person service charge; sodas and shakes are a la carte) to **Chops Grill** and Japanese-themed **Izumi** (the last two on *Explorer of the Seas* and *Mariner of the Seas* only).

The spacious **Island Grill** and **Windjammer** casual buffet restaurants are joined into one large space, but have separate lines and stations to keep things moving. On *Navigator* and *Mariner,* this area also incorporates the Asian-themed **Jade** buffet. There's no outdoor seating per se, but the ship's main pool area is on the same deck, just outside the restaurants' entrances.

Radiance of the Seas • Brilliance of the Seas • Serenade of the Seas • Jewel of the Seas

The Verdict

With their classic nautical profiles and interior decor, these are Royal Caribbean's most elegantly traditional ships, though they offer a lot of the fun and games of RCI's larger vessels, including rock climbing and mini golf.

Specifications   Avg. Starting Per Diem $107

Size (in tons)	90,090	Crew	857
Passengers (Double Occ.)	2,100	Passenger/Crew Ratio	2.5 to 1
Passenger/Space Ratio	42.9	Year Launched	2001-2004
Total Cabins/Veranda Cabins	1,050/577	Last Major Refurbishment	2016

Frommer's Ratings (Scale of 1–5)   ★★★★

Cabin Comfort & Amenities	4	Dining Options	4.5
Ship Cleanliness & Maintenance	5	Gym, Spa & Sports Facilities	5
Public Comfort/Space	5	Children's Facilities	4
Decor	5	Enjoyment Factor	5

THE SHIPS IN GENERAL

These ships are just plain handsome, with some of the adventure features of their larger Oasis-, Freedom-, and Voyager-class siblings, but a sleeker seagoing profile outside and a more nautical look and feel inside—and acres of windows to bring the two together. They are of a more manageable size, too. When you first board, you'll see one of Royal Caribbean's typical wiry modern art sculptures filling the bright, nine-story atrium, but venture a little farther and you'll see that the ships have a much more traditional interior, with dark-wood paneling, caramel-brown leather, and deep-sea-blue fabrics and carpeting. Some 110,000 square feet of glass covers about half of their sleek exteriors, affording wide-open views from the many bars, lounges, and eateries. The same goes for the atrium, which is an uninterrupted wall of glass from Decks 5 through 10 portside, and has four banks of glass elevators. All this transparency comes in handy in scenic destinations such as Alaska.

CABINS   Cabins are fairly spacious, with the smallest inside ones measuring 165 square feet and some 75% of outside staterooms measuring at least 180 square feet, some with verandas. The rest have jumbo-size portholes. Decor is appealing, with attractive navy blues and copper tones. All cabins have small sitting areas, lots of drawer space, and roomy closets. Bathrooms are small, with Royal Caribbean's typical hold-your-breath-and-step-in shower stalls—but baths do have lots of storage space.

All but a handful of **suites** are located on Deck 10. The best, the **Royal Suite,** measures 1,001 square feet and has a separate bedroom, living room with baby grand piano, dining table, bar, entertainment center, and 215-square-foot balcony. Six **Owner's Suites** are about half that size, with 57-square-foot balconies, a separate living room, a bar, and a walk-in closet. **Grand Suites** are a step below in size and amenities. Three **Royal Family Suites** have 140 balconies and two bathrooms and can accommodate six people in two separate bedrooms (one with third and fourth berths, and another two on a pullout couch in the living room). Suite guests are treated to complimentary in-cabin butler service in addition to cabin stewards, and there's a Concierge Club on Deck 10, where suite guests can request services and grab a newspaper.

One snag on the balcony front: On each ship, cabin Decks 7 through 10 are narrower than those on the rest of the ship, resulting in cabin balconies on

Deck 10 (many of them suites) being shaded by the overhanging deck above. Meanwhile, cabin balconies on the aft and forward ends of Deck 7, being indented, look out onto the top of Deck 6 instead of directly out onto the sea. Some balconies on Deck 7 aren't completely private because the dividers between them don't go all the way to the edge of the space. Keep your clothes on—your neighbors can look right over at you.

Fifteen cabins on each ship can accommodate wheelchair users.

PUBLIC AREAS & ACTIVITIES   Our favorite place on board is the grouping of five intimate, wood-and-leather lounges on Deck 6, which recall the decor of classic yachts, university clubs, and cigar lounges. Expect low lighting, inlaid wood flooring, comfy couches, and area rugs. The best of these rooms is the romantic **piano bar** and lounge that stretches across each ship's stern and has a bank of floor-to-ceiling windows. Adjacent is a lovely colonial-style **Billiard Club** boasting herringbone wood floors, redwood veneer paneling, and a pair of ultra-high-tech gyroscopic pool tables. No excuse for missing shots: The tables compensate for the ship's movements, staying remarkably level.

The main **theaters** are refreshingly different from most in the cruise biz, with a cool ambience, warm wood tones, and seats in deep-sea blues and greens. Artful handmade curtains, indirect lighting, and fiber optics all come together to create a quiet, ethereal look.

Other public areas include the attractive **Casino Royale,** with more than 200 slot machines and dozens of gaming tables; a baseball-themed sports bar with interactive games on the bar top; a specialty coffee bar with several Internet stations; a small library; and, high up on Deck 13, Royal Caribbean's signature **Viking Crown Lounge,** which is divided between a quiet area and a large disco with a rotating bar. Even the ships' high-style public bathrooms are impressive, with their marble floors and mirrors reminiscent of portholes.

The huge **kids' area** on Deck 12 includes a sprawling playroom divided into several areas, with a video arcade and an outdoor pool with water slide. Teens have their own nightclub, with a DJ booth, music videos, and a soda bar.

At the main pool, passengers pack in like sardines on sunny days at sea, and deck chairs can be scarce during the prime hours before and after lunch. (On *Radiance,* the **Pool Deck** is presided over by a 12-foot-high cedar totem pole carved for the ship by Alaska Native artist Nathan Jackson of Ketchikan.)

Much more relaxing are the ships' large, lush **Solariums.** Tropical foliage and waterfalls impart an Eastern mood, and stone reliefs, regional woodcarvings, and statues drive it home. The area's adjacent (and popular) pizza counter adds a little pandemonium to the otherwise serene scene (as can kids, if they happen to find the place). The adjacent **spa** has 13 treatment rooms and a special steam-room complex with heated tiled lounges and showers that simulate tropical rain and fog.

The **Sports Deck** has a 9-hole miniature-golf course and golf simulators, a jogging track, a rock-climbing wall attached to the funnel, and a combo basketball, volleyball, and paddle-tennis court. The oversized oceanview **gym** has a huge aerobics floor and dozens of exercise machines, including sea-facing treadmills and elliptical stair-steppers.

DINING The two-story main **dining rooms** on all four ships are glamorous and elegant, like something out of a 1930s movie set. Four willowy, silk-covered columns dominate the vaulted main floor, and a wide double staircase connects the two decks dramatically—all that's missing are Cary Grant and Deborah Kerr. On *Serenade,* painter Frank Troia's huge, Impressionist *Gala Suite* amplifies the mood, depicting formally dressed couples dancing amid floating globes of light.

The nautically decorated **Windjammer Café** takes self-serve buffet dining to new levels, with 11 food stations (nine inside and two outside) set up as islands to keep the lines down and the crowds diffused. If you prefer taking your meals while reclining, there's a small strip of cozy tables with oversize rattan chairs and thick cushions between the indoor and outdoor seating areas.

The cozy, 90-seat **Chops Grille** is an oceanview spot with dark woods, rich upholsteries, and high-backed booths that bring home the meat-and-potatoes mood. You can watch your steak being cooked in the open kitchen. Adjacent is the 130-seat Italian eatery **Portofino.** Expect more refined and gracious service than in the main dining room, plus a more leisurely pace (and a cost: Portofino charges a $20 per person cover charge; for Chops, it's $25 per person). Up on the Sport Deck, the **Seaview Café** is a serves quick lunches and dinners of fish and chips, popcorn shrimp, burgers and other comfort foods.

At a counter in the Solarium freshly made pizza is served by the slice, and a coffee shop serves cappuccino and pastries.

Enchantment of the Seas • Grandeur of the Seas • Rhapsody of the Seas • Vision of the Seas

The Verdict

Once the latest and greatest, these four are looking frumpy these days, compared to their newer fleetmates.

Specifications			Avg. Starting Per Diem $92
Size (in tons)	74,140-80,700	Crew	765
Passengers (Double Occ.)	1,920-2,252	Passenger/Crew Ratio	2.5 to 1
Passenger/Space Ratio	35.8-38	Year Launched	1996-1998
Total Cabins/Veranda Cabins	1,000/229	Last Major Refurbishment	2016

Frommer's Ratings (Scale of 1–5)			★★★ ½
Cabin Comfort & Amenities	3	Dining Options	3
Ship Cleanliness & Maintenance	4	Gym, Spa & Sports Facilities	3
Public Comfort/Space	4	Children's Facilities	4
Decor	3.5	Enjoyment Factor	4

THE SHIPS IN GENERAL

These Vision-class ships afford a decent experience, but things have changed so fast in the cruise biz that even the best ships from the late–20th century can seem dated—and these do. Still, they each have an open, light-filled feel and many of the same amenities as aboard the line's newer, larger ships, and to us, their relatively smaller size is a point in their favor. You won't feel overwhelmed or lost here.

All the ships have been retrofitted with crowd pleasers like rock-climbing walls, but *Enchantment of the Seas* is by far the most modernized of the bunch. In mid-2005, RCI revisited a trend common in the mid-'90s, literally sawing the ship in half like a magician's assistant, inserting a new 73-foot midsection, and then welding it all back together. As a result, *Enchantment* offers a lot more than her Vision-class sisters. On the much-enlarged Pool Deck, there's an additional stage and midships bar for adults and an "interactive splash deck" with water jets that kids can control to spray each other or create their own water ballet. Additions to the nearby Sports Deck include four bungee trampolines. New accessibility features for passengers with disabilities include pool and Jacuzzi lifts, access to the Splash Deck, a lift to the bungee trampoline area, and improved thresholds and ramps throughout the vessel. There have been below-deck changes, too, such as the addition of a Latin-themed bar, an expanded casino, a larger shopping area, and a new coffee bar—features currently available aboard RCI's newer vessels. Although the refit was a success, it cost a pretty penny. Don't expect Royal Caribbean to bestow it on *Enchantment*'s sisters anytime soon.

Generally, when these ships are sailing full, things can feel crowded. Getting on and off at ports can also be a hassle with so many people to move.

CABINS   To put it politely, **cabins** are "compact." Yes, they're larger than the staterooms on the line's older *Majesty of the Seas,* but smaller than those on the Oasis-, Freedom-, and Voyager-class ships and on many competitors' vessels. Still, there's an impressive amount of storage space. Bathrooms are likewise on the small side, with shower stalls that are a tight squeeze for anyone thicker than a supermodel. Overall, it's safe to say these accommodations have seen better days—though on the bright side, carpeting and bedding are in good shape.

For something grander, check out the 1,140-square-foot **Royal Suites,** which have a baby grand piano and huge marble bathroom with double sinks, a big whirlpool bathtub, and a glass-enclosed shower for two. For something in between, check the roomy, 190-square-foot **category-D1 cabins,** with private verandas, small sitting areas with pullout couches, and tons of storage space. All told, about a quarter of each ship's cabins have private verandas, and about a third can accommodate third and fourth passengers.

Each vessel has between 14 and 17 staterooms equipped for wheelchair users.

PUBLIC AREAS & ACTIVITIES   Throughout each vessel, warm woods and brass, gurgling fountains, green foliage, glass, crystal, and buttery leathers highlight the public areas, where the ambience ranges from classic to glitzy to old-fashioned. The bright, wide open, and easy-to-navigate **Promenade** and **Mariner decks** are home to most public rooms, their corridors converging at a seven-story atrium where glass elevators take passengers from Deck 4 all the way up to the glass-walled **Viking Crown Lounge** on Deck 11. Full musical revues are staged in glittery two-story **showrooms,** where columns obstruct views from some balcony seats. The ship's **casinos** are Vegas flashy, with hundreds of gambling stations so densely packed that it's sometimes difficult to move and always difficult to hear. Better nightlife is found at the **Schooner** piano bar (a great place for after-dark unwinding) and the **Champagne Terrace** at the foot of the atrium, where you can sip a glass of fine wine or bubbly while swaying to the two- or three-person band playing there.

In contrast to its showcase spaces, each ship also contains many hideaway refuges, including an array of cocktail bars, a **card room** and a **library,** though not a very well-stocked one. A couple of thousand original artworks aboard each ship (the good, the bad, and the weird) add a human touch.

For kids, there's a decent **playroom** stocked with toys, books, and games, and nearby is a roomy teen center and a small video-game arcade.

Recent refits have improved lighting in the ship's atrium, and have added high-energy acrobatic performances in these soaring, multi-story areas.

The **spas** on these ships offer a wide selection of treatments as well as the standard steam rooms and saunas. Adjacent **Solariums** have a pool, lounge chairs, floor-to-ceiling windows, and a retractable glass ceiling for inclement weather. Designed after Roman, Egyptian, or Moorish models, these bright, spacious areas are a peaceful place to lounge (except maybe during lunch and pre-dinner hours, when the snack bar in the corner takes away from their serenity). **Gyms** are surprisingly small and cramped considering the ships' size.

Each ship has a higher than expected amount of open deck space. The outdoor **pool** on the Sun Deck has the usual blaring rah-rah music during the day, along with silly contests of the belly-flop variety. A rock-climbing wall, jogging track, shuffleboard, and Ping-Pong table round out the on-deck options

DINING   The large **dining rooms** aboard these vessels span two decks connected with a grand staircase and flanked with 20-foot walls of glass. The rooms are of their era, with lots of stainless steel, mirrors, dramatic chandeliers, and, altogether, the feeling of a '90s banquet hall. At lunchtime on a recent *Rhapsody* cruise, the whole operation seemed disorganized—there was a long wait for tables and waiters seemed hassled to keep up. There's also a large indoor/outdoor **buffet restaurant** serving breakfast, lunch, and dinner. Again, on a recent *Rhapsody* sailing, the Windjammer buffet was a chaotic sea of humanity during lunchtime; it was hard to find a seat and crew seemed to struggle keeping things tidy and bins filled. A small snack counter where pizza, sandwiches, and various salads are served can be a welcome respite from the frenetic Windjammer buffet at lunchtime.

Majesty of the Seas

The Verdict

She's no spring chicken, but she sure is a bargain, sailing inexpensive 3- and 4-night cruises to the Caribbean and the Bahamas from Florida.

Specifications

Avg. Starting Per Diem $77

Size (in tons)	74,077	Crew	912
Passengers (Double Occ.)	2,350	Passenger/Crew Ratio	2.5 to 1
Passenger/Space Ratio	31.5	Year Launched	1992
Total Cabins/Veranda Cabins	1,177/62	Last Major Refurbishment	2016

Frommer's Ratings (Scale of 1–5)   ★★★

Cabin Comfort & Amenities	3	Dining Options	3
Ship Cleanliness & Maintenance	4	Gym, Spa & Sports Facilities	3
Public Comfort/Space	3	Children's Facilities	4
Decor	3	Enjoyment Factor	3.5

THE SHIPS IN GENERAL

Along with their predecessors *Sovereign of the Seas* and *Monarch of the Seas* (both of which now sail for Spain's Pullmantur Cruises), *Majesty of the Seas* was once among the largest cruise ships in the world. Today, she's literally less than half the size of her largest fleetmates. A decade and a half of hard use has imparted her fair share of bumps and bruises, and even though recent makeovers have hammered out some of the dents and updated the ship's overall look, passengers should expect a well-worn look rather than a sophisticated one. A mid-2016 refit added some fun new features, but if you want to sail aboard this classic ship, do it now: Rumor has it *Majesty* is scheduled to transfer out of the Royal Caribbean fleet sometime in 2018.

CABINS   Standard **staterooms** are very snug at only 120 square feet, bathrooms are similarly cramped, and closet space is limited. More than 100 cabins have upper and lower berths to accommodate four, albeit very tightly. Overall, decor is spartan and uninspired, with pastel fabrics and blond woods, and like other ships of this generation, relatively few rooms have balconies. Additionally, the soundproofing isn't the greatest; in some cabins you can hear every word your neighbors say.

Four cabins can accommodate wheelchair users.

PUBLIC AREAS & ACTIVITIES   A dramatic five-story **atrium** is the focal point of the ship, separating the public areas (which are mostly clustered in the stern) from the cabins forward, an arrangement that minimizes bleed-through noise and also gives the impression that *Majesty* is smaller than she is. Shops, the ship's **salon,** the **Internet center,** the **library,** several information desks, and a **champagne bar** are all clustered around the atrium at various levels. Elsewhere, you'll find a giant **casino,** a **cinema,** the popular **Schooner Bar,** and (as on all pre-*Voyager* RCI ships) the **Viking Crown Lounge,** perched on the topmost deck some 150 feet above sea level and with nifty panoramic views. It's a great place for a pre-dinner drink and after-dinner dancing. Down on Decks 5 and 7, the two-story main **show lounge** is roomy and well planned, with lots of cocktail tables for two and a huge stage.

As part of her makeover in recent years, *Majesty* has been fitted with a **Boleros Latin Lounge,** a dueling-pianos act, and drinks from Brazil, Cuba, and Central America. The ships' **children's centers** were also expanded and three teens-only hangouts added: the **Living Room** coffee bar, a disco called **Fuel,** and a private outdoor Sun Deck with a dance floor. A 2016 refit added even more features, including a massive poolside movie screen mounted just beneath the Viking Crown Lounge, and the line's new Voom high-speed Internet.

The deck layout and two good-size swimming **pools** seem plenty spacious when they're empty, but the number of passengers who typically sail these short itineraries almost guarantees that they'll fill up with wall-to-wall passengers. That said, there are many patches of more isolated deck space, from the quiet slices on the tiered aft decks to two levels of far-forward deck space.

The **Sports Deck,** up high in the stern, has Ping-Pong tables and a basketball court. The half-moon-shaped **gym** on Deck 10 is fairly spacious, with a wall of windows facing aft. Treadmills, stationary bikes, step machines, and free weights line the perimeter of the room, facing the sea, and the inner part of the room serves as the aerobics space. A smallish spa is adjacent.

Majesty also sports Royal Caribbean's signature rock-climbing wall.

DINING   The ship has a pair of one-story **dining rooms,** plus a large indoor/outdoor **buffet restaurant** with multiple self-service islands featuring regional dishes from Asia, Latin America, the Mediterranean, the U.S., and elsewhere, plus a cooked-to-order pasta station, an omelette-making station at breakfast, a carving station, a deli, and a soup-and-salad bar. You can also nosh at a dedicated **pizzeria** or grab a specialty coffee or a Ben & Jerry's ice cream from the **Latté-tudes coffee shop.** And as is now standard on Royal Caribbean, the ship features a '50s-style **Johnny Rockets** diner serving burgers and shakes (with a $6.95 cover charge).

Empress of the Seas

The Verdict

This ship offers a healthy dose of mid-1990s cruising nostalgia, but is a good match for the budget-conscious and those turned off by the line's larger ships.

Specifications   Avg. Starting Per Diem $71

Size (in tons)	48,563	Crew	668
Passengers (Double Occ.)	1,602	Passenger/Crew Ratio	2.3 to 1
Passenger/Space Ratio	30.3	Year Launched	1990
Total Cabins/Veranda Cabins	801/69	Last Major Refurbishment	2016

Frommer's Ratings (Scale of 1–5)   ★★★ ½

Cabin Comfort & Amenities	3	Dining Options	3.5
Ship Cleanliness & Maintenance	4.5	Gym, Spa & Sports Facilities	4
Public Comfort/Space	4	Children's Facilities	3.5
Decor	4	Enjoyment Factor	3.5

THE SHIP IN GENERAL

Empress of the Seas is back in the Royal Caribbean fleet after a nearly decade-long absence (when she was in the service of Pullmantur). Originally the line's *Nordic Empress* before being renamed *Empress of the Seas* in 2004, this cozy ship was one of the first to be purpose-built for three-and-four day cruises. It's no stretch to suppose that Royal Caribbean brought her back for one purpose: to eventually operate quick cruises to Cuba from Miami. That hasn't happened yet—but it's a tantalizing thought.

Like *Majesty of the Seas, Empress* is no spring chicken, and fans of the technological doodads aboard the line's Quantum- and Oasis-class ships will be disappointed. But for budgeteers, *Empress* is a fine choice for a quick jaunt to the Bahamas. With just 1,602 guests onboard, she's the smallest ship in the Royal Caribbean fleet, with a length of 692 feet.

CABINS A total of 801 **cabins** are onboard, and nothing says "I love the '90s" like the fact that just 69 of these, most of which were added during the ship's Pullmantur days, have private balconies.

On the subject of interior staterooms, the Royal Caribbean website says, "Spend your days onboard by the pool or on our sports deck. Then relax at night in the comfort of your interior stateroom." Which is a subtle way of saying these rooms are teeny-tiny. Standard interior staterooms start at just 109 square feet—only 9 square feet larger than studio accommodations aboard Norwegian Cruise Line's newest ships that are designed for one person only. Oceanview staterooms add a picture window and not much else: Entry-level rooms (Small Oceanview Stateroom) are 111 square feet, increasing to 206 square feet if you go for the top-of-the-line category. *Tip:* Some staterooms on Decks 3 and 4 have porthole windows, and some Deck 7 and 8 staterooms have views obstructed by the ship's lifeboats.

Suites come in three flavors (Junior, Owners, and Royal) and offer substantially more space, plus private balconies, separate living and sleeping areas, sitting areas, and mini-bars.

PUBLIC AREAS & ACTIVITIES Getting around the ship is a snap, thanks to her small size and convenient forward and aft staircases and elevator banks. Most of the ship's public areas start on Deck 5, with our favorite lounge—the **Schooner Bar.** Royal Caribbean has given this watering hole an entirely new look, with two sections of seating bordered by nautical window treatments and a polished wooden floor that weaves attractively through the room as the main passenger thoroughfare.

The **atrium,** which rises up six decks, has been given brand-new LED lighting and is topped by a glass skylight and bookended by two glass elevators. The ship's early '90s roots shine through with the sheer number of mirrored surfaces, but overall this space looks pleasantly modern, and serves as the social hub of the ship.

Evening production shows are held in the two-story **Royal Theatre,** while **Boleros,** situated at the stern on Deck 6, offers up a decently sized dance floor and Latin-infused live music. It functions as a sort of secondary show lounge, and features contemporary decor that wouldn't look out of place aboard the line's new *Anthem of the Seas.*

The ship also has a completely restyled **casino** that's pleasantly small (and easy to avoid if you're not interested in gambling), shops featuring all the usual logo-brand and duty-free items, an arcade, a small Internet cafe, a nice library, and the iconic **Viking Crown Lounge,** which assumes its perch up on Deck 10 and offers some pretty spectacular views.

Also on Deck 10 you'll find a single swimming **pool** and three hot tubs located amidships that are small but adequate for a ship of this size. Don't expect much from the onboard **spa:** Tucked into a corner on Deck 10, it offers the usual massage treatments and salon services but not much more (you won't find any sprawling hydrotherapy pools or thermal suites here). Royal Caribbean's trademark rock-climbing wall is located all the way aft on this deck, and one deck up on Deck 11 is a small **fitness center** that has weights, treadmills, elliptical machines, and some great views from the floor-to-ceiling windows. The ship also features a wraparound **Promenade Deck** that doubles as a jogging track during certain hours.

DINING   You won't find hundreds of different dining options aboard *Empress.* But **Windjammer Café,** which wraps around the entire forward portion of Deck 10, has superb views, not to mention buffet breakfast, lunch, and dinner. The **Main Dining Room** is a two-story affair with more stellar views from its 180 degrees of panoramic windows. Breakfast, lunch, and dinner are served here, and Sunday brunch is offered (paradoxically) every day of the week, complete with a complimentary mimosa or Bloody Mary. **Chops Grille,** Royal Caribbean's signature steakhouse, is located on Deck 5 and comes with a per-person surcharge of $39 per person.

THE CRUISE LINES: LUXURY SHIPS

On luxury ships, elbow room is abundant and service is very personal. The onboard atmosphere is much like a private club, with guests trading tales over delicious meals that often rival what's served in respected shore-side restaurants. And a full dinner can be served in your cabin, course-by-course if you like—how cool is that?

Instead of glitzy entertainment, you'll likely find informative lectures and more sophisticated activities, like wine tastings or culinary classes. When it is offered, entertainment tends to be of a more personalized variety, favoring a handful of entertainers rather than Broadway-style production numbers. The ports are often the off-beat ones, mixed with the classics.

On the flip side, these types of sailings are sometimes not the best choice for families with children, unless those kids are able to keep themselves entertained without a lot of outside stimuli. With a few exceptions, you won't find kids' clubs or a daily schedule of children-focused activities the way you would on the mainstream ships.

CRYSTAL CRUISES

www.crystalcruises.com. © **866/446-6625.**

Pros

- **Service:** Thanks to one of the highest staff-to-guest ratio in the biz, Crystal has some of the finest service of any cruise line, attentive without being intrusive, and polished without feeling stuffy.
- **Best Japanese Food at Sea:** The onboard sushi bars were developed by Food Network's Iron Chef Nobu Matsuhisa, of the famed Nobu restaurant.
- **Nearly All-Inclusive:** Drinks, tips, and even airfare are included.
- **Fitness Choices:** There are many on these ships, from well-supplied gyms, to loaner Nordic walking poles, and more.

Cons

- **Cabins:** These may be luxury ships, but onboard digs in the lower categories are significantly smaller than what you'll find on the other swank lines.

- **Big Ships:** More of a quantifier than a con, these are some of the largest luxury ships out there, and as such lack the level of intimacy found on smaller luxury vessels.

Overview

These ships aren't huge, but they're big enough to offer much more onboard excitement than their high-end peers. Service is excellent and the line's Asian cuisine is tops. Unlike Seabourn's small ships, which tend to be more calm and staid, Crystal's sociable vibe and large passenger list tend to keep things mingled, chatty, and more active. Crystal was bought in 2015 by Genting Hong Kong (owner of Star Cruises) and the new owners are in the middle of implementing the largest expansion in the company's history, introducing new luxury air charter services, hybrid expedition-luxury mega-yachts, and the company's first-ever European river cruises—all between now and 2018.

EXPERIENCE

Stylish and upbeat, Crystal provides top-shelf service and cuisine on ships large enough to have lots of outdoor deck space, generous fitness facilities, tons of activities, multiple restaurants, and more than half a dozen bars and entertainment venues. For those with money to burn, you can now fly to your destination on one of the company's Bombardier Business Jets, or—eventually—the line's very own Boeing 787 Dreamliner. With Crystal, nothing is too luxe.

ROUTES

Crystal is constantly expanding its footprint around the globe; that's particularly true for its around-the-world cruise. That being said, Europe remains a dominant region for its ships during the summer months, with winters spent in South America and the Caribbean. In the summer of 2016, Crystal made the somewhat-controversial decision to transit the (until recently) ice-choked Northwest Passage. Despite the high cost—some suites went for well over one hundred thousand dollars—the voyage sold out in record time.

PASSENGERS

Crystal's ships are generally populated with empty nesters and retirees, though during holidays and school breaks you may also see families with children, often with a nanny in tow. Guests are well-educated and well-off, and don't mind showing off their wealth. That means people *do* dress up for meals, and tend to look quite put-together during the day. However, they're also bright and congenial—so if you can walk the walk and talk the talk, you're in the club.

DINING

Service by the team of ultraprofessional, gracious, waiters is excellent. In the main dining room—and to a somewhat lesser degree in the alternative restaurants—table settings are lavish and include heavy leaded crystal and fine flatware. The line makes use of unusual ingredients and cutting edge cooking techniques, as well as offering traditional menus for the steak-and-potato set.

And the specialty restaurants are some of the best at sea. **Silk Road** serves both cooked Japanese food and sushi and sashimi, and it's helmed by Food Network's Iron Chef Nobu Matsuhisu. When there, ask about specials that the chef picked up at the fish market in port, as well as Japanese home-cooking dishes that you can order off menu. (We've seen guests from Tokyo order comfort food and scored by leaping in with a "We'll have whatever they're having.")

The Italian restaurant, **Prego,** is led by Beverly Hill's chef Piero Selvaggio. Highlights here include the mushroom soup and the lobster poached in olive oil, as well as the veal scaloppini and, for dessert, the affogato and mocha budino.

On some sea days, Crystal displays dramatic buffets on the Lido Deck, usually with a theme, such as Asian fare (which the line excels at) or seafood.

ACTIVITIES

On sunny days, most guests are by the pool or in the gym or spa, except for when there are lectures by notables or dance or golf lessons. On rainy days, the casino becomes more crowded, and you'll find both classic films and current flicks in the movie theater, where hot popcorn is served.

CHILDREN'S PROGRAMS

Crystal's ships have a small, basic playroom, and (except for on holidays and busy summer weeks) the line does not staff the space. There is also a teen space, and in-cabin babysitting can be arranged in advance for a fee.

ENTERTAINMENT

In addition to live music around the ship, the line has a partnership with **Magic Castle** to offer superb magic shows on board. Crystal also puts on small-scale, if tasteful, stage shows and has a tiny jewel-box-like nightclub with Bisazza mosaics and Philippe Starck bar stools. Most Crystal voyages feature Crystal's **Visions Enrichment Program,** which curates a host of special guest speakers and lecturers for each voyage, while the Crystal Cruises **Creative Learning** series features experts in disciplines like filmmaking, art, wellness and computer classes to share their skills with guests on select voyages.

SERVICE

The onboard service, from the wait staff to the cabin stewards and even the pool butlers, is often said to be the best at sea, and I don't think that's hyperbole. Crew members go beyond their responsibilities to make guests feel tended to, stepping in to tie a bow tie on a formal night, bring a surprise breakfast to celebrate a birthday, or solve a problem. On every sailing, there are also Gentleman Hosts to dinner companions and a dance partner.

FLEET

A two-ship line for decades, Crystal now has three ships, with more on the way. *Crystal Symphony,* which carries 922 passengers and had a $15-million-dollar redesign in 2012 is the classic favorite, and *Crystal Serenity,* which carries 1,070 passengers and went through a $17-million-dollar redesign in 2013, is the line's largest vessel. In 2015, Crystal introduced *Crystal Esprit,* a nimble, 62-guest luxury expedition ship that even comes with its own two-person submersible craft (submarine) on board.

Crystal Serenity

The Verdict

The largest ship in the Crystal fleet, *Crystal Serenity* is a modern take on the luxury cruise, offering an elegant cruise experience with a huge array of onboard amenities.

Specifications		Avg. Starting Per Diem $490	
Size (in tons)	68,870	Crew	655
Passengers (Double Occ.)	1,070	Passenger/Crew Ratio	1.65 to 1
Passenger/Space Ratio	64.4	Year Launched	2003
Total Cabins/Veranda Cabins	535/465	Last Major Refurbishment	2013

Frommer's Ratings (Scale of 1–5) ★★★★★

Cabin Comfort & Amenities	5	Dining Options	5
Ship Cleanliness & Maintenance	5	Gym, Spa & Sports Facilities	4
Public Comfort/Space	5	Children's Facilities	3
Decor	5	Enjoyment Factor	5

THE SHIP IN GENERAL

Built in 2003 but substantially refitted numerous times since then, the 1,070-guest *Crystal Serenity* is 38% bigger than fleetmate *Crystal Symphony,* but carries just 15% more guests. Everything about the ship screams luxury, from her lovely public rooms and suites to her wide-open decks (created by insetting the lifeboats into her hull). There's no crowding anywhere. After over a decade in service, she continues to sparkle like new.

CABINS **Standard staterooms** aboard *Crystal Serenity* are larger, on average, than those aboard *Crystal Symphony,* with bigger bathrooms and deeper balconies. But at an average of 226 square feet, they're still a bit snug for a luxury line. Nearly all feature private balconies, and those that don't have oceanview windows. A series of refits between 2011 and 2013 added entirely new decor to all staterooms and suites, giving them a crisp, chic look, with black or white tufted leather headboards, boldly patterned carpeting, excellent lighting, and an overall contemporary look. Bathrooms are attractive but on the small side for a luxury line.

Of 535 cabins on board, a full 100 are designated as **suites,** the largest of which—the **Crystal Penthouses**—comes with a guest bathroom, a master bathroom with heated marble flooring and a Duravit spa floatation tub with an oceanview, two walk-in closets, and a private workout area.

Eight staterooms are designated as wheelchair-accessible, and only a handful of rooms feature third-and-fourth-berth capacity.

PUBLIC AREAS & ACTIVITIES All of the amenities of a big ship are on board, but public spaces are laid out in such flow-friendly fashion that it feels like you're on a much smaller ship. For the best views, we always gravitate toward the **Sunset Bar,** situated forward of the serene **Palm Court,** overlooking the bow. The **Avenue Saloon** is pretty darn nice, too, as are the **Connoisseur Club** and the **Stardust Club,** where nightly entertainment is on offer. Bigger productions are featured in the elegant **Galaxy Lounge Showroom.** The small **Pulse Nightclub** is popular with those who want to dance the night away.

The ship has two **pools,** one of which is covered with a retractable dome for rainy weather. Active diversions available include table tennis, a putting green, and a well-equipped **fitness center.** Trainers can set up guests with two onboard specialty fitness programs: Nordic walking (poles to help those with balance issues get an aerobic workout) and "walkvests" (water-filled vests that exercisers can wear to make their workouts more intense). On the relaxation side, the **Crystal Spa** is a real stunner.

Other notable public areas include a dedicated cinema known as the **Hollywood Theatre,** a library, a massive computer center known as the **Computer University @Sea,** and even a separate lounge for games of bridge.

DINING The **Crystal Dining Room** serves as the ship's formal dining room, with two seatings at assigned tables each evening. Decor is effortlessly swank, a rich mixture of crimson and black chairs, dark oak columns, and a circular ceiling with inset murals anchored by a central chandelier. Cuisine is unusually creative, sometimes in the molecular gastronomy category (think foams, smoky containers, and other culinary magic tricks). Traditionalists can get more straightforward meals, always made with superfresh ingredients. These are some of the best meals we've had on any ship.

Crystal Serenity features two very impressive alternative dining venues: **Prego,** which specializes in Northern Italian fare, and **Silk Road and the Sushi Bar,** overseen by celebrity chef Nobu Matsuhisa. Both eateries are reservation-only, and your first visit to both is complimentary (additional visits are $30 per person). We suggest making online reservations well in advance.

Casual fare is offered at the **Lido Café,** but even this buffet is pretty spectacular, with made-to-order omelets and pastas, plus a rotating selection of dishes from around the globe (the theme switches daily to keep things interesting). Also located on the Lido Deck is **Tastes,** which serves up breakfast and small plates for lunch and dinner under the retractable dome of the Neptune Pool. Reservations are required for dinner. Still hungry? There's fast food poolside at the **Trident Grill,** snacks at **The Bistro** and an absolutely massive room service menu (24 hours a day).

Crystal Symphony

The Verdict

Few ships over two decades old have aged as well as *Crystal Symphony,* which still provides a graceful, sophisticated cruise experience with all the accouterments of a much bigger ship.

Specifications   Avg. Starting Per Diem $414

Size (in tons)	51,044	Crew	545
Passengers (Double Occ.)	922	Passenger/Crew Ratio	1.7 to 1
Passenger/Space Ratio	55.4	Year Launched	1995
Total Cabins/Veranda Cabins	461/279	Last Major Refurbishment	2012

Cabin Comfort & Amenities	4	Dining Options	5
Ship Cleanliness & Maintenance	5	Gym, Spa & Sports Facilities	5
Public Comfort/Space	4.5	Children's Facilities	3.5
Decor	4	Enjoyment Factor	5

7

Crystal Cruises

LUXURY SHIPS

THE SHIP IN GENERAL

You'd never know *Crystal Symphony* entered service back in 1995. Crystal has kept this gem sparkling with numerous refits over the intervening decades. With just 922 guests on board, she's also one of the most spacious ships we've ever been on—you'll never have problems finding a seat in your favorite bar, even when she's sailing full. Her staterooms aren't quite as big as her luxury counterparts, but she makes up for it with an array of inviting public rooms, lounges, and dining options that the little guys just can't match.

CABINS Although **standard cabins** are about 30% smaller than those found aboard competing luxury lines like Regent and Silversea, there's nothing else to complain about with these 202-square foot entry-level staterooms. Done up in elegant shades of rose and cream and with blond woods, **deluxe staterooms** now boast smart-looking leather sofas in the seating area, replacing the former armchairs. Move up one category to the **veranda stateroom** and you get your own private balcony. Deck 10 is **suite** country. **Penthouse with veranda suites** include a large living area and a bathroom with a full Jacuzzi tub, as well as round-the-clock butler service. The biggest suites in this category feature living rooms with walnut accents, Swarovski crystal chandeliers, and floor-to-ceiling windows, among other niceties.

There are five wheelchair-accessible cabins on board, and all staterooms and suites feature ocean views. It's worth noting that Category E staterooms on Decks 7 and 8 have views obstructed by the ship's lifeboats.

PUBLIC AREAS & ACTIVITIES Spanning Decks 5 and 6, the two-story **Crystal Plaza Atrium** is the place to make a grand entrance, thanks to a sweeping staircase, dazzling waterfall, and a ring of boutiques. The handsome **Crystal Cove** is a good spot to relax amid walnut wood and brass-on-blue barstools. Elaborate productions take the stage at the **Galaxy Lounge Showroom,** but in keeping with Crystal's luxury vibe, the place feels more like a classy supper club than a cavernous theater. The **Starlite Lounge** on Deck 6 is the place to be for cocktails, live music, and dancing. Those looking for the best view in the house will want to make their way to Deck 11's **Palm Court** overlooking the bow. Other fun diversions include a decently sized **casino,** a **cinema,** the posh **Avenue Saloon,** and the **Computer University @Sea.**

The **Seahorse Pool,** located on Lido Deck 11, is nearly 40 feet long; adjacent to it is a Jacuzzi and plenty of seating. The pool deck is rarely crowded, and loungers are placed a good distance apart from one another. Up on Deck 12, the Steiner-run **Crystal Spa** offers salon and spa treatments along the port side of the ship, with a spacious **fitness center** situated on the starboard side. Out on deck, walkers and joggers will love the wraparound teak **Promenade**

Deck that encircles the ship on Deck 7. A putting green, golf driving nets, and a tennis court are on Deck 12, while a small selection of outdoor fitness equipment is located all the way aft, overlooking the ship's wake.

DINING   Dining is an event aboard *Crystal Serenity.* Cuisine and service are of a very high quality that only seems to improve each year. The ship's main dining room, down on Deck 5, is as elegant as ever, with vibrant multi-colored carpeting and stylish, lantern-style shaded light fixtures that hang attractively over tables. There are plenty of tables for two (by the windows, no less), and spacing is so generous you'd have to really try to bump chairs with your neighboring tables (and you'd likely fail). The ship also features two reservations-only specialty restaurants that are available to guests once per voyage (subsequent visits require a $30-per-person charge). **Prego** focuses on Italian cuisine while **Silk Road and the Sushi Bar** serve up Asian cuisine from acclaimed chef Nobu Matsuhisa. Wine lovers will want to camp out in **The Vintage Room,** a boardroom-style venue that promotes wine education (and enjoyment) with private dinners hosted by the ship's head sommelier. Reservations (in advance of your sailing date) are necessary.

Crystal excels in the casual buffet department: The indoor/outdoor **Lido Café** offers one of the widest selections of food we've seen aboard a ship. The **Bistro Café,** meanwhile, serves up European-style coffees and lite-bites, while the **Trident Bar & Grill** is the place for poolside burgers and wraps.

Crystal Esprit

The Verdict

A scaled-down version of *Crystal Serenity* and *Symphony,* this small yachtlike ship goes where her big sisters can't.

Specifications		Avg. Starting Per Diem $749	
Size (in tons)	3,264	Crew	91
Passengers (Double Occ.)	62	Passenger/Crew Ratio	1 to 1
Passenger/Space Ratio	58.4	Year Launched	1991
Total Cabins/Veranda Cabins	31/0	Last Major Refurbishment	2015

Frommer's Ratings (Scale of 1–5)		★★★★★	
Cabin Comfort & Amenities	5	Dining Options	4
Ship Cleanliness & Maintenance	5	Gym, Spa & Sports Facilities	4
Public Comfort/Space	5	Children's Facilities	N/A
Decor	5	Enjoyment Factor	5

THE SHIP IN GENERAL

Esprit entered service for Crystal in 2015 after a massive refurbishment that added the same elegant look and luxurious amenities found on the line's larger ships. With just 62 guests on board, *Esprit* is half yacht, half expedition ship. Excursions tend to be more adventurous than on other Crystal cruises: Inflatable Zodiac rafts tender guests ashore in some of the world's most remote places, and a state-of-the-art deep-sea submersible (a cruising-world first) can carry two guests at a time on undersea explorations up to a thousand feet deep. Hiking and cycling are common, and guests that elect to stay on board can often swim, snorkel, kayak, or paddleboard off the ship's stern, thanks to a retractable marina platform. One big drawback: Those with mobility issues will find that *Crystal Esprit* isn't a good fit. In addition to the more active nature of shore excursions, the ship lacks a passenger elevator.

Crystal Esprit winters in the Seychelles and the Middle East, and typically spends her summers in the warm waters of the Mediterranean on voyages that sail between Venice, Italy and Dubrovnik, Croatia.

CABINS   There are two basic cabin categories aboard *Esprit:* **Owner's Suites** and **Yacht Suites.** Of these, Yacht Suites are what most guests will find themselves staying in. Encompassing Categories S1–4, these rooms are all 280 square feet apiece, except for Category S4, which are smaller at 223 square feet. All of the luxe amenities Crystal is known for are present: the flatscreen high-definition 42-inch TV inset into the wall, the bedside iPad that functions as an alarm clock and digital guide to the ship, ETRO bath amenities, and butler service throughout. You even get tiny bottles of complimentary sunscreen and insect repellent in case you forgot your own.

There's only one Owner's Suite on board *Crystal Esprit,* and it sells out fast. An attractive stone threshold separates the living and sleeping areas, while ceilings feature crown molding and walls with high-end wood grain and millwork throughout. The master bathroom—the biggest on board—has a separate shower and toilet area, an oversized soaker tub, a TV inset into the mirror, and a Toto Washlet toilet with a heated seat and other features.

PUBLIC AREAS & ACTIVITIES   *Esprit*'s public areas aren't as numerous or elaborate as those on her larger fleetmates, but they are every bit as serene. During the day and night, most guests will gravitate to **The Cove,** an elegant forward-facing lounge done in shades of white and grey and accented with vibrant teal and navy pillows on oh-so-comfortable chairs. An aft-facing **bar** serves up cocktails in a covered space with Scandinavian-style lounges and couches. When weather and itinerary allow, films are shown on deck.

With so much to do ashore, most time aboard the yacht is spent relaxing. Still, Sunset Deck 5 is home to a forward-facing **swimming pool** and, further aft, a small but functional **sauna** and **fitness center.** A better bet for keeping fit, though, is to take one of the complimentary kayaks, water skis, or jet skis out for a spin off the retractable marina platform at the stern.

DINING   A huge emphasis is placed on high-quality cuisine here. There aren't a lot of dining venues, but you're unlikely to leave the table disappointed. The **Yacht Club Restaurant,** done up in shades of navy blue and cool grey with eye-catching wall sconces and recessed ceiling lighting, has an open-design kitchen—a rarity aboard cruise ships, and a fun opportunity to watch chefs work their magic. Menus are four or five courses, and you can mix and match among the two (options change daily). Breakfast and lunch are served on the indoor/outdoor **Patio,** and encompass both buffet and cooked-to-order dishes. Casual snacks are available at the **Pantry;** room service is also available.

CUNARD LINE

www.cunard.com. ✆ **800/728-6273.**

Pros

o **Enrichment Is Truly Impressive:** The lecturers include big names, with politicians, noteworthy academics, and celebrities, especially on crossings.

o **Proper High Tea:** The afternoon tea is a highlight, with warm scones served with clotted cream and jam as well as finger sandwiches and pastries, delivered by white-gloved waiters. (Oh, and there's an orchestra too.)

o **Gorgeous Libraries:** The ships' wood-paneled libraries are the best at sea.

o **Classic Grandeur:** From the original *Queen Mary* to the *QE2* and now *Queen Mary 2,* Cunard ships are synonymous with glamour and the transatlantic crossing.

o **Kennels at Sea:** *Queen Mary 2* boasts the only kennel for dogs and cats at sea, used only on transatlantic crossings.

Cons

o **The Class System Can Rankle:** While life is swank if you're sailing in The Grills aboard one of Cunard's ships, the regular Britannia class experience is more mainstream than luxury. But hey—it's still plenty special.

Overview

Formed in 1840 by Sir Samuel Cunard, the line provided the first regular steamship service between Europe and North America, and was one of the dominant players during the great years of steamship travel, which lasted roughly from 1905 to the mid-1960s. In 1969, long after it was clear that jet travel had replaced the liners, the company made what some considered a foolhardy move, launching *Queen Elizabeth 2* and setting her on a mixed schedule, half-crossing, half-cruising. Through sheer persistence, the ship proved the critics wrong, and thrived throughout 40 years of Cunard service, even if the company endured some rough times.

In 1998, the line was purchased by Carnival Corporation, which injected a much-needed cash-infusion into the venerable company. Plans were immediately drawn up for a successor to *Queen Elizabeth 2.* Known initially as Project Queen Mary, the ship that would become the iconic *Queen Mary 2*—the largest purpose-built ocean liner of her kind—would make her debut in early 2004. As Carnival's Micky Arison said at the time, "We bought Cunard to create *Queen Mary 2*—not the other way around."

QM2, as she is affectionately known, also pays homage to all that went before, designed with oversize grandeur and old-world formality, even Titanic-style elitism: Some restaurants and outdoor decks are set aside specifically for suite guests only, if you please. Same story for the *Queen Victoria,* which is essentially a sister ship to *Queen Elizabeth*—both are in the 90,000-ton-plus category, carrying just over 2,000 passengers. And, unlike *QM2,* they can transit the Panama Canal. In the summer of 2016, *QM2* emerged from a massive refurbishment that added new staterooms, additional dog kennels, and revitalized public spaces and dining venues.

EXPERIENCE

This is about as traditional as cruising gets these days, with a class system that determines which dining room you eat in based on your cabin category and a stricter dress code system than you find elsewhere (there are more formal nights on these cruises than on other lines). In addition, the British influence extends to the pub (which serves pints and fish and chips and has insanely popular pub quizzes on sea days); and the nursery, where proper British nannies watch babies and toddlers in the evenings.

ROUTES

The line is best known for offering the only regularly scheduled transatlantic crossings, which sail from New York (Brooklyn) to Southampton, England (an hour and a half by train from London). Select crossings also continue on to Hamburg, Germany. In addition, Cunard offers plenty of more traditional cruises, including voyages to the Caribbean, Panama Canal, Asia, Northern Europe, and the Mediterranean.

PASSENGERS

North American cruises tend to get more North Americans and European sailings tend toward more Brits and Europeans, while crossings are often an intoxicating mix of nationalities.

DINING

Cunard is the last bastion of the old steamship tradition of segregating passengers according to category of accommodations. This means that passengers are assigned to one of the three reserved-seating restaurants according to the level of cabin accommodations they've booked: Suite-and-above passengers dine in the **Queen's Grill;** passengers in the next levels dine in the **Princess Grill;** and everyone else dines in the **Britannia Restaurant**—decor-wise, the most beautiful of the three and a fitting heir to the grand restaurants of the past. Of course, it's also the largest—and the busiest—dining venue on board. Guests in the two Grills enjoy dining in much cozier surroundings, always single seating at an assigned table, while the Britannia has early and late seatings for dinner and open seating for breakfast and lunch.

If you like the idea of dining in a smaller restaurant but can't bring yourself to splurge for the top-end suites, booking a **Britannia Club** stateroom is the way to go. Guests in this category dine in a tucked-away corner of the Britannia Restaurant, with seating for just 100 or so. Thanks to the smaller size of the dining room, service here tends to be less rushed than in the pretty, but busy, Britannia Restaurant. Guests have assigned tables, but are invited to come into the dining room at any time during opening hours.

On our recent Cunard cruises, food and service were top drawer, even in good old Britannia Class, which offers the same level of food you'd get in the main dining rooms of the Celebrity ships (see p. 132). Service in The Grills kicks things up into luxury cruise territory.

Overall, the ships' cuisine sticks close to tradition, with entrees that might include pheasant with southern haggis and port-wine sauce, roasted prime rib, grilled lobster with garden pea risotto, and scallion wild-rice crepes with mushroom filling and red-pepper sauce. The Grill restaurants also allow the option of requesting whatever dish comes into your head—if they have the ingredients aboard, someone in the galley will whip it up for you (caviar is available on request). Otherwise, it's the intimacy and cachet of the Grill restaurants that set them apart more than the food does, as many of the same dishes are served in the Britannia. At all three restaurants, **special diets** can be accommodated, and **vegetarian** dishes and health-conscious **Canyon Ranch SpaClub dishes** are available as a matter of course.

SPECIALTY   During her 2016 refit, *QM2*'s Todd English restaurant was removed, replaced instead by **The Veranda,** an elegant dining spot that echoes the original *Queen Mary*'s Verandah Grill, one of that ship's most legendary spaces. This remastered space features regional French cuisine with menus that change seasonally, and is still located on Deck 8 overlooking the stern. *QV* and *QE* also have The Veranda.

CASUAL   Almost a third of *QM2*'s Deck 7 is given over to the massive **King's Court,** a large buffet restaurant that stretches out for nearly half a deck along both sides of the ship. The casual restaurant on *QV* is fittingly smaller and has a more typical location, up on Deck 11. Though its food items are not as extensive as *QM2*'s, the *QV*'s buffet venue is far more expansive than the industry's usual "lido" cafe.

SNACKS & EXTRAS   On both ships, the **Golden Lion Pub** serves English pub grub, while *w-a-a-a-ay* up on *QM2*'s Deck 12, you can get standard burgers and hot dogs at the outdoor **Boardwalk Café,** weather permitting. Real **afternoon tea** service, usually accompanied by a string quartet, is served in the **Queen's Room** (a posh space that hearkens back to the dramatic ballrooms of yesteryear, with a high arched ceiling and crystal chandeliers). The selection of more than 20 teas includes Darjeeling, jasmine, and Japanese green tea. **Room service** is available 24 hours a day.

ACTIVITIES

While many people like to spend sea days the traditional way, on deck with a big book, a wool blanket, and a steaming mug of bouillon, *Queen Mary 2* also has an unforgettable **planetarium.** There are also visiting lecturers and a **3D movie theater,** and you can take drama classes through the line's Royal Academy of Dramatic Art (RADA) partnership.

Central to the onboard experience is *Cunard Insights,* the line's **lecture program:** Super-accomplished authorities present talks on literature, political history, marine science, ocean-liner history, music and pop culture, modern art, Shakespeare on film, architectural history, cooking, computer applications, languages, and many other topics. On crossings, there are so many worthwhile lectures that you could find yourself sitting in the theater all morning long. Cunard has even managed to attract a handful of stars, with Uma

Thurman, Rod Stewart, Lenny Kravitz, Richard Dreyfuss, John Cleese, and others having sailed, and some lectured, in the last few years. Many of these Cunard Insights presenters—even the ones that aren't famous—fill the theatres on board to capacity. On one of our last crossings, a former British Airways Concorde pilot packed the theatre for three straight days.

Particularly aboard *QM2*, Cunard offers special musical guests from time to time. These have included James Taylor, the National Symphony Orchestra, the Julliard Academy of Music, and noted blues performers as part of the spectacular BlueNote Jazz at Sea crossings. Don't let anyone tell you nightlife aboard Cunard ships is dull: We've personally sat in the Chart Room well past two in the morning on our Julliard crossing, listening to performers who went overtime and played to the still-packed room.

QM2 passengers who prefer book learning can take advantage of the largest and by far the most impressive **library** at sea: a huge, beautifully designed space that actually looks like a library, unlike the typical rooms-with-a-few-bookshelves on most megaships. The library on *QV* is smaller, but still carries an impressive 6,000 books and is staffed by two librarians. Next door on *QM2*, a **bookshop** sells volumes on passenger-ship history, as well as Cunard memorabilia. Other shops aboard the ships sell everything from high-end Hermès to low-end souvenirs and jewelry, some of it sold in a rather undignified way from long tables set up in the public corridors. Continuing the marine history topic, Cunard's ships offer an onboard museum detailing Cunard's 170-year-history. It's called **Maritime Quest** on the *QM2* and it is a history trail with a timeline set up in various places throughout the ship that highlights important moments in the story of Cunard through art and oversized archival photos; on *QV* and *QE*, it's called **Cunardia,** and it's more like a mini-museum **exhibiting Cunard artifacts.**

CHILDREN'S PROGRAMS

A Cunard cruise is more than high tea and stiff upper lips. Finger paints and cartoons are just as much a part of the ship's activities as ballroom dancing and quoits. Though you might not expect it from a grand liner that (in the popular imagination) is filled with seniors, *QM2* especially has great digs for kids (the *QV* has a decent kids' program, though not quite as impressive as the *QM2*'s). Called the **Zone** on both ships, it's open to kids ages 1 and up—an extraordinarily young minimum age shared only by Disney's ships. (Most ships with kids' programming welcome kids ages 3 and up, a few ages 2 and up.) The ages 1-to-6 set occupies half of a cheery and roomy area with lots of toys, arts and crafts, a play gym and ball pit, and big-screen TVs (and the staff do change diapers). On the *QM2*, there's also a separate **nursery** with 10 crib/toddler-bed combos for napping tots. Bring a stroller if your kids are young: The *QM2* is really long, so getting from one end of a deck to the other is a hike.

Both ships also have an outdoor play area just outside the playroom, along with a wading pool and a regular pool. The other half of the play area is reserved for kids ages 7 to 17, with the ages 7-to-12 crowd usually occupying a play area with beanbag chairs, lots of board games, TVs, and a number of Xbox video-game systems. **Activities for teens**—including ship tours, movies and production shows in the theaters, and pizza parties—are usually held elsewhere.

The kids' program is staffed by certified British nannies, plus a handful of other qualified activity counselors. The best part? Aside from 2 hours at lunchtime and an hour or two in the afternoon, the playrooms provide complimentary supervised activities and care from 9am to midnight, so you have ample time to enjoy adult company and know that your offspring are being well cared for (on other lines, you must generally pay an hourly fee after 10pm).

Though the ships' kids' program is topnotch, there are rarely more than 250 kids aboard any given sailing and usually fewer (compared to the 800–1,200 kids and teens typically aboard similar-size ships). This is a plus: Fewer kids means more attention and space for the ones who are there. Keep in mind, though, if a sailing is especially full, the counselors reserve the right to limit participation and will ask parents to choose either the morning or the afternoon session; everyone can be accommodated during evenings.

ENTERTAINMENT

Entertainment runs the gamut from plays featuring graduates of Britain's Royal Academy of Dramatic Art (RADA) to pretty run-of-the-mill song-and-dance revues. The former perform generally from April to November as part of a partnership between Cunard and the school, with RADA graduates and students also giving a variety of readings and workshops, including acting classes. Besides **theater,** a wide variety of **music** is heard throughout the ships' many lounges, from string quartets and harpists to jazz groups and high-toned dance music in the gorgeous **Queen's Ballroom** (with gentlemen hosts on hand to partner with single ladies). Both ships have a disco and a casino, which are more Monte Carlo than Vegas, with refined art and furnishings rather than the usual clangor of an arcade. Aboard the *QV,* there's an unusual show lounge arrangement where the best box seats can be reserved in advance for special performances and are first-come, first-seated for other shows.

Whereas most ships have one theater, *QM2*'s **lecture program** is so busy that there are two. As the secondary theater, **Illuminations** is smaller than the **Royal Court Theatre,** but is probably the most used room on the ship. It serves triple duty as a lecture hall, a movie theater, and also the world's only oceangoing planetarium that shows 3-D films, some of them created in conjunction with noted institutions such as the American Museum of Natural History and the Smithsonian's National Air and Space Museum.

SERVICE

The service tends toward the formal, especially in some key areas—the white-glove afternoon tea, the nanny service, and in the top-of-the-line Grills Suites. That being said, service throughout is friendly and punctual, delivered by a staff of British and International crew members.

Queen Mary 2

The Verdict

This ship is literally in a class by herself: a modern reinterpretation of the golden age luxury liner, built to sail hard seas. A massive refit in 2016 introduced new lounges and features that have left the flagship of the Cunard fleet looking better than ever.

Specifications   Avg. Starting Per Diem $189

Size (in tons)	151,400	Crew	1,253
Passengers (Double Occ.)	2,592	Passenger/Crew Ratio	2.1 to 1
Passenger/Space Ratio	58.4	Year Launched	2004
Total Cabins/Veranda Cabins	1,296/783	Last Major Refurbishment	2016

Frommer's Ratings (Scale of 1–5)   ★★★★★

Cabin Comfort & Amenities	4	Dining Options	4.5
Ship Cleanliness & Maintenance	5	Gym, Spa & Sports Facilities	4.5
Public Comfort/Space	5	Children's Facilities	5
Decor	4.5	Enjoyment Factor	5

THE SHIP IN GENERAL

Before her launch, some industry types referred to the *Queen Mary 2* as "Micky's White Elephant"—Micky being Micky Arison, chairman of Carnival Corporation. The nickname referred to the fact that *QM2*'s design and construction sucked up about $1 billion and five years of labor, a record expenditure to match her record-breaking size.

But that was before her launch, before the Queen of England did the honors at the naming ceremony, and before the fireworks and traffic jams that attended her first arrival into every port, and in some cases still continue to this day. In short, *QM2*—the longest passenger ship at sea—is remarkable: classic yet contemporary, refined yet fun, huge yet homey, and grand, grand, grand.

Inside, *QM2* is laid out in such a way that, even after a weeklong crossing, you might still find new places to explore on board. And it's very unlikely you'll feel hemmed in or claustrophobic. Our favorite rooms? The Queen's Room ballroom on formal night; the handsome, forward-facing Commodore Club; and the forward observation area on Deck 11, just below the bridge—probably the best spot aboard when sailing out of New York harbor. Artwork throughout recalls the golden age of ocean liners, but the most evocative feature might be a sound: Way up on *QM2*'s funnel, on the starboard side, is one of the original Tyfon steam whistles from the first *Queen Mary*—the same whistle that sounded when that vessel made her first crossing in 1936.

To be honest, *QM2* is really two ships in one. The top categories, the Grill classes, are very luxurious and come with their own dining rooms, lounge, and private deck space. Guests in these categories also enjoy all of the rest of the ship along with everyone else booked in non-Grill-class accommodations. For the purposes of this guide, we're rating those non-Grill categories (the largest part of the ship). It's safe to assume that ratings for the accommodations and dining for the Grill classes would be higher.

CABINS   All of *QM2*'s cabins, from the smallest inside ones to the largest outside, are decorated in a sleek, contemporary style, with light-blond woods, simple lines, and a clean, uncluttered look. They range decently sized **inside cabins** to **outside cabins with portholes** to the truly over-the-top **Grand Duplex Suites.** Each of the latter has views of the stern through two-story walls of glass. **Junior Suites** (aka Princess Grill suites) are almost twice as big as a standard and have huge bathrooms, walk-in closets, and oversize balconies.

The vast majority of cabins are outside ones with balconies, but to ensure they stay dry in even the roughest seas, many of them are recessed into the hull with steel bulkheads that block ocean views when you're seated. All Queens Grill and Princess Grill suites feature Frette linens, dedicated concierge service, a bottle of champagne or sparkling wine on embarkation, and access to the Queens Grill Lounge and a large private deck overlooking the stern (which is actually also open to Princess Grill guests as well, despite the signage). Queens Grill Suites also get stocked bars, daily canapés, and personalized stationery.

Britannia Club cabins bridge the gap between standard Britannia class staterooms (the vast majority of insides, oceanviews, and balcony staterooms are categorized this way) and Grill suites. These all-balcony rooms have been given a brand-new look, and 30 new Britannia Club balcony staterooms were added to Deck 13 during *QM2*'s 2016 dry dock.

There are 30 wheelchair-accessible cabins in various cabin grades, and 15 newly added oceanview staterooms are designed specifically for solo travelers.

PUBLIC AREAS & ACTIVITIES   Because *QM2* was designed for comfortable sailing in rough seas, most of the public areas are clustered unusually low, down on Decks 2 and 3. At midships, the relatively restrained **Grand Lobby atrium** opens onto two central promenades, decorated with huge Art Deco wall panels. Some are stunning and recall decorated glass from the opulent liner *Normandie,* while others are chintzy (they look like they're plastic) and miss the mark. Deck 2's promenade leads down to the elegant **Empire Casino** and the **Golden Lion** pub. Up one deck, the very attractive **Veuve Clicquot Champagne Bar** (serving a variety of champagnes, as well as caviar and foie gras) is decorated with slightly abstracted images of mid-20th-century movie stars. It leads into one of the ship's loveliest areas: the **Chart Room,** a high-ceilinged space with green-glass deco maps. Across, on the ship's port side, **Sir Samuel's Wine Bar** serves coffee, sandwiches, and cakes in the morning and afternoon, wine and lite bites come evening.

Forward, the **Royal Court Theatre** is a two-deck grand showroom and the principal theatrical venue on board, seconded by the striking Illuminations planetarium farther forward (see "Entertainment," above). In the stern on Deck 3, the **Queen's Room** ballroom, perfectly captures the essence of Cunard style, running the full width of the ship and boasting a high arched ceiling, the largest ballroom dance floor at sea, crystal chandeliers, and a truly royal quality. The **G32 nightclub,** almost hidden behind silver doors at the head of the Queen's Room, is decorated in industrial style to match its name—G32 was the number by which *QM2*'s hull was known at the shipyard.

REFITTING A queen

In 2016, the ship underwent its most extensive refit ever. New staterooms were designed for solo travelers, carved out of the space formerly occupied by the Photo Gallery and part of the Casino. The King's Court Buffet on Deck 7—always marred by bad passenger flow—was gutted and rebuilt from the ground up, with a better layout and more contemporary decor. The two glass elevators that once graced the Atrium were removed during this refit, and no one seems to miss them: They've opened up the Atrium in ways that just weren't possible before.

Also on Deck 7, the Wintergarden—a pretty but underused space—has been completely redone. Renamed the Carinthia Lounge, it features a dedicated patisserie and an afternoon tea service, with the option of a special Veuve Cliquot Champagne Afternoon Tea experience. In the evenings, premium wines and small bites are offered here. We hope those Canyon Ranch Spa demos don't intrude on this space like they did in the former Wintergarden.

Also getting the axe is the Todd English restaurant, which clears out to make way for **The Veranda,** a French-inspired eatery featured on board both QE and QV.

In addition to solo staterooms, Cunard has also increased the number of Britannia Club staterooms on board, perhaps not the greatest news, as that means more crowds. To be fair, the line has also refreshed all accommodations with new color palettes, linens and other "soft furnishings." The line also added 10 new kennels, bringing the total number on board to 22. Both dogs and cats can be booked on transatlantic crossings, and are taken care of by a dedicated Kennel Master. A replica fire hydrant was installed on the pet's special Deck 12 area, to make them feel, er, "more at home."

Other notable spaces include the **Winter Garden,** designed to feel like an outdoor garden, and the **Commodore Club** bar/observation lounge, with its white leather chairs, dramatic bow views, and attached **Churchill's cigar room.** There's also a remarkable library and bookshop (see "Activities," above).

The **Canyon Ranch Spa** is a two-story complex occupying some 20,000 square feet. At the center of its treatment rooms is a coed 15×30-foot aquatherapy pool whose relaxation gizmos include airbed recliner lounges, neck fountains, a deluge waterfall, an air tub, and body-massage jet benches. There's a hot tub adjacent, and nearby is a thermal suite composed of aromatic steam rooms and an herbal sauna. A **salon** occupies the top level of the complex, affording tremendous views from its lofty perch. The **gym,** one deck down, is drab and chopped up, but is adequately equipped with free weights and the latest climbers, steppers, runners, and rowers. Why not jog the wide outdoor **Promenade Deck** (Deck 7) instead? Three times around equals 1 mile.

To work on your swing, there's a pair of golf simulators adjacent to the covered pool solarium. You'll find a **splash pool** and hot tubs way up on Deck 13, and, a **wading pool, family pool,** and **play fountain** outside of the children's playrooms. Rounding out the sports options are Ping-Pong, an outdoor golf driving net, basketball, quoits, a paddle-tennis court, and, of course, shuffleboard—this is a transatlantic liner, after all.

DINING   The **Britannia Restaurant** is a large dramatic space intended to recall the old *Queen Mary*'s magnificent first-class restaurant with a vaulted, Tiffany-style glass ceiling, a curved balcony, candlelit tables, soaring pillars, and the largest art tapestry at sea, depicting a liner against the New York skyline. The new **Britannia Club** area has literally been carved out of a corner of the restaurant, providing an exclusive, old-world dining experience, just as the suite guests have in the Grill restaurants. All guests can dine in the **Veranda Restaurant** all the way aft on Deck 8. Formerly the space occupied by the Todd English specialty restaurant, the Veranda was added in 2016 and offers French regional specialties in a completely redesigned space.

The **King's Court** on Deck 7 is the ship's casual buffet option, and it's broken up into separate (complimentary) specialty restaurants each evening. It was substantially refitted in 2016 to address flow problems resulting from its disjointed layout.

See "Dining," p. 236, for more details on the ship's dining experience.

Queen Elizabeth • Queen Victoria

The Verdict

The *Queen Victoria* (QV) and *Queen Elizabeth* (QE) are more than smaller versions of the *Queen Mary 2*. These classy ships have their own style, personality, and decor while maintaining much of the line's heritage.

Specifications

Avg. Starting Per Diem $150

Size (in tons)	90,400/90,000	Crew	900
Passengers (Double Occ.)	2,092/2,014	Passenger/Crew Ratio	2.2 to 1
Passenger/Space Ratio	45	Year Launched	2010/2007
Total Cabins/Veranda Cabins	1,007/591	Last Major Refurbishment	2014/2015

Frommer's Ratings (Scale of 1–5)   ★★★★ ½

Cabin Comfort & Amenities	4	Dining Options	4
Ship Cleanliness & Maintenance	5	Gym, Spa & Sports Facilities	4.5
Public Comfort/Space	5	Children's Facilities	3
Decor	5	Enjoyment Factor	4.5

THE SHIPS IN GENERAL

Both *Queen Victoria* and *Queen Elizabeth* have the line's classic black-and-red hull on the outside and grand public spaces inside. At 90,049 gross tons, *QV* was the second-largest Cunard ship ever—until the newer and slightly bigger *QE* came along, that is. Since they were built to cater to both sides of the Atlantic, there's lots of British flavor on board—from the pub to the lovely Chart Room (though the official currency on board is still the U.S. dollar).

Sleek, smooth-running modern ships that haven't lost sight of their line's history, *QV* and *QE* have many of Cunard's signature elements along with some fresh additions. Queens Grill and Princess Grill diners have an exclusive centralized lounge for their use only (the *QM2* has two separate lounges for each of the Grills, but on the *QV/QE* they're combined), plus outside dining and sunning areas reserved for Grill-class guests only. The onboard spas are not as huge and grandiose as the *QM2*'s, and consequently they feel more casual and relaxing. There are no over-the-top stunners such as *QM2*'s planetarium, but the lack of huge spaces makes both ships feel relatively intimate despite their size.

CABINS   As might be expected on a ship that has a definite class hierarchy, there's quite a range of quality in accommodations. That being said, the non-Grill-class cabins are much nicer than they are on *QM2*. **Inside rooms** range from 152 to 207 square feet (try and get a bigger one if budget and availability allow), and all come with two beds (twin or combinable into a queen) and a shower. **Outside rooms** range from 180 to 197 square feet for those without balconies; rooms with balconies are all 249 square feet. A half-bottle of sparkling wine is given to everyone upon embarkation.

As for **suites** and **penthouses,** these are divided into 11 different categories, with the four categories of **Princess Suites** all of which have balconies their balconies. Other amenities include upgraded linens, bathrobes and toiletries, plus a pillow menu, concierge service, shoeshine service, a separate bath and shower, a larger sitting area, and a *full* bottle of sparkling wine upon embarkation. Higher up on the spectrum are the seven categories of **Queen's Grill Suites** and **Penthouses.** With these you get complimentary canapés, butler service, and sugar-iced strawberries to go along with the champagne.

Solo travelers, rejoice: There are now **single-occupancy cabins** available aboard both ships. *Queen Elizabeth* offers both inside and oceanview staterooms for solo travelers on Deck 2, while *Queen Victoria* has nine staterooms for solo travelers—eight oceanview rooms and one interior room.

There are 20 wheelchair-accessible cabins total in various categories.

PUBLIC AREAS & ACTIVITIES   There's a lot happening on Deck 2, where you'll find the first level of the extremely attractive **Britannia Restaurant** (where most guests are assigned their dining tables), as well as a series of bars all along one side of the ship (the **Chart Room, Café Carinthia, Midships Lounge, Champagne Bar,** and the **Golden Lion Pub**). Each of the bars has its own personality, ranging from the nautical Chart Room to the gentleman's club feel of the Golden Lion. There's also the **Queen's Room** ballroom with its gorgeous, 1,000-square-foot inlaid wood floor for dancing to a live orchestra.

The upper set of public decks, running from Decks 9 to 12, includes the forward-facing **Cunard Royal Spa and Fitness Centre.** Midships on Deck 10 is the indoor/outdoor space for kids, with separate spots for teens and younger kids. At the forward end of Deck 10 is the lovely **Commodore Club** lounge, probably the best place for a relaxing drink in the evening or quiet time during the day, and the 270-degree views at **Hemispheres,** which turns into a disco at night. Adjacent is the cigar bar—named after Churchill, of course.

Up above on Decks 11 and 12 are the exclusive areas for Grill-class guests: sunning areas with plush loungers, Tuscan-themed courtyards, and a **Grill Lounge.** A sign in the stairwell and restricted elevator access deny entry to non-Grill guests. They can head instead to **pools** located midships and at the aft end of Deck 9; two whirlpools are adjacent to each. Though the main pool area isn't huge, at one end is the attractive **Winter Garden,** with its rattan furniture, ceiling fans, central fountain, movable glass wall, and sliding roof.

The **spa** and **fitness center,** at the forward end of Deck 9, are impressive—a whopping 40-page guide is used to describe the extensive services available (facials, oxygen treatments, "aromasoul" massages and scrubs, nail and hair services, a Pilates institute, and a whole lot more). The gym sports 15 treadmills, dozens of other pieces of workout equipment, and plenty of free weights. Additionally, guests can stay fit by walking and jogging on several different decks, play paddle tennis or quoits, and practice their golf swing.

DINING All guests are assigned a table in one of three restaurants: the gorgeous, two-level **Britannia Restaurant** (which actually looks better than the Grill-class restaurants) or, for Grill guests, either the **Queens** or **Princess Grill,** depending on cabin category. There are two seatings for dinner in the Britannia Restaurant; it's single seating in the Grill restaurants. One outstanding feature of the Britannia Restaurant is the space between the tables—there's plenty of room for spreading out. The Grill restaurants curve along the window side, allowing for stellar views.

As for other dining venues, the most casual is the **Lido Café,** a buffet that stays open 24 hours a day. But the one you should really consider trying is the outstanding **Veranda Restaurant** (extra fees; see p. 237 for more info).

OCEANIA CRUISES

www.oceaniacruises.com.com. ℂ **800/531-5658.**

Pros

- o **Excellent Dining:** Whether you're dining in the main dining room or the two specialty restaurants, food is a focus on Oceania.
- o **Small Ships:** The relatively small size of the ships makes for an intimate, warm experience without masses of people.
- o **Longer Itineraries Than the Industry Norm:** The line offers longer sailings, giving plenty of time to experience the destination, whether that's Alaska or Japan.

Cons

- o **Cabin Size:** Cabins, particularly on the line's older ships, are small.
- o **Low Ceilings:** In some areas, the ship's low ceilings make for a somewhat cramped feeling; in the case of the main dining room, it gets quite noisy.
- o **Few Activities:** By design, Oceania generally leaves passengers to their own devices. This is a con only if you need constant stimulation.

Overview

Oceania Cruises entered the cruise industry in 2003 when it launched *Regatta,* formerly the *R Two* from Renaissance Cruise Lines (which went belly-up after 9/11) and then *Insignia* (formerly the *R One*). The launch created what was essentially a new industry category that the line called "upper premium" and it's been very successful, with Oceania adding a third former Renaissance ship to the fleet in 2005 (*Nautica,* formerly the *R Five*) and two new builds, *Marina* and *Riviera,* in February 2011 and May 2012, respectively. Oceania and luxury line Regent Seven Seas Cruises make up Prestige Cruise Holdings, a cruise division of the Apollo Management investment firm, which also owns a big portion of Norwegian Cruise Line.

EXPERIENCE

Oceania truly offers a deluxe or, said another way, upscale, experience. There's little glitz on board, but its hallmarks—dining, service, and itineraries—are impeccable. The no-charge specialty restaurants are far better than the norm.

ROUTES

Because this line offers a 180-day world cruise, it does feel like you can get just about anywhere on an Oceania ship. There are Caribbean, Panama Canal, and Mexico sailings, as well as Alaska, South America, and Canada/New Zealand. Of course, there are plenty of European itineraries, both in the Baltic and the Mediterranean. And you can go to Asia, Alaska, and the South Pacific on these ships, as well. Historically, itineraries have been port-intensive, with few sea days, so a busy shipboard agenda is not a priority.

PASSENGERS

Couples in their 50s and 60s make up the bulk of the passengers, but Oceania's ships are comfortable for both younger and older cruisers. The line is appropriate for those looking for a somewhat informal cruise, but one with topnotch dining and excellent service.

DINING

Food is a focus at Oceania, which offers menus overseen by celebrated chef Jacques Pépin, and multiple gourmet eateries on every ship. Even Oceania's smallest vessels offer an Italian eatery and steakhouse in addition to a main restaurant, and the food at all three is superb.

While you'll pay extra for drinks on Oceania, none of its restaurants come with an extra charge, in contrast to ships operated by Princess, Holland America, and Royal Caribbean. Another nice feature of Oceania's longer sailings is that entrees and featured items are not repeated, allowing the galley staff to show off their skills. Pépin, the line's Executive Culinary Director, works with Oceania's chefs to develop exciting and exotic dishes as well as more traditional ones. For snackers, Oceania's ships offer afternoon tea service, ice cream and sundae bars, and 24-hour complimentary room service. Diners with special needs are catered to with Canyon Ranch Spa Cuisine, and vegetarian and kosher meals upon request.

ACTIVITIES

Oceania does not go out of its way to provide an extensive list of things for passengers to do, in keeping with its informal style and port-intensive sailings. But there are lectures on the ports of call; dance classes and cooking lessons; and the handsome onboard libraries are well-stocked. If you like a lot of organized activities, though, this is not the line for you.

CHILDREN'S PROGRAMS

While kids may be on board, it's mostly up to their parents to entertain them. Oceania's ships have no facilities specifically for kids and really don't cater to them.

ENTERTAINMENT

Show lounges on Oceania ships are relatively small. However, there is an eight-piece orchestra for the shows put on by a small team of performers, along with cabaret acts. Depending on the cruise, there may be a string quartet, a flamenco guitarist, a concert pianist, jazz combos, local and regional folk ensembles, and the occasional headline entertainers.

SERVICE

Service is warm and friendly without being overbearing. In the dining room and bars, staff is particularly skillful at getting to know passengers' names. In the main dining room, service can be a bit rushed (there are more passengers than seats) and tables a hair too close to each other. It's a much more relaxed experience in the alternative restaurants. Cabin service is excellent, and those rooms with butler service get extra pampering.

CRUISETOURS & ADD-ON PROGRAMS

Cruisetours are a popular way to extend the cruise vacation in Alaska, and Oceania's brochure includes a 5-day pre-cruisetour package from Anchorage, a combination of rail and bus travel. All transfers and hotels as well as most meals are included in the pricing—though you can certainly arrange a pre-or-post cruise land tour on your own, often for a lot less money. Oceania also offers hotel packages in San Francisco, Vancouver, and Seattle for pre/post stays. Prices depend on number of days booked.

FLEET

One of the line's biggest strengths is the human-scale size of its first three vessels. At 30,277 tons and carrying 684 guests, these ships are really small-to-midsize by today's standards. It's an informal setting (Oceania calls it country-club casual) without crowds and lines. In 2014, the *Regatta, Insignia,* and *Nautica* underwent major multimillion-dollar refurbishments that brought new decor to public rooms, suites, and cabins; *Sirena* was refurbished in 2016. The overhaul also included the addition of a number of the popular features found on Oceania's newer ships such as an Italian-style Baristas coffee bar serving Illy espresso drinks and a transformed Terrace Café that now boasts a state-of-the-art grill.

Marina • Riviera

The Verdict

Oceania's first purpose-built cruise ships, these elegant twins are everything that made the line's existing ships so popular, delivered in a newer, larger, and more elaborate package.

Specifications — Avg. Starting Per Diem $325

Size (in tons)	66,084	Crew	800
Passengers (Double Occ.)	1,250	Passenger/Crew Ratio	1.567 to 1
Passenger/Space Ratio	46	Year Launched	2011/2012
Total Cabins/Veranda Cabins	629/591	Last Major Refurbishment	2016

Frommer's Ratings (Scale of 1–5) ★★★★★

Cabin Comfort & Amenities	4.5	Dining Options	5
Ship Cleanliness & Maintenance	5	Gym, Spa & Sports Facilities	4.5
Public Comfort/Space	5	Children's Facilities	N/A
Decor	5	Enjoyment Factor	5

THE SHIPS IN GENERAL

The first brand-new ships built for Oceania, *Marina* and *Riviera* burst on the scene in 2011 and 2012, respectively. At 68,084 tons, they're big enough to offer plenty of public rooms and open deck spaces, but still small enough to maintain Oceania's intimate, adult-oriented cruise experience. Inside, *Marina* and *Riviera* look like classic ocean liners transported to the modern era. The fit and finish throughout are impeccable, and there are just enough dramatic public areas to impart a feeling of grandeur. An excellent example: the two-story atrium flanked by staircases and anchored by a spectacular chandelier manufactured by Lalique. At every turn, passenger space is generous, particularly on the open decks, which are rarely crowded.

CABINS   Accommodations range from economical **Inside Staterooms** to the three massive **Owner's Suites** that feature furnishings from the Ralph Lauren Home Collection. These are some of the nicest suites at sea, with regal-looking colors, two walk-in closets, indoor and outdoor whirlpool spas, a grand entryway with a music room and grand piano, and keycard access to a private lounge complete with its own library.

Most guests, however, will likely find themselves in one of the ship's **Veranda Staterooms,** which feature marble bathrooms, a private balcony, and a decently sized seating area. **Concierge Level Veranda Staterooms** add amenities like early embarkation, unlimited access to the Canyon Ranch Spa Club Terrace, and priority restaurant reservations. If you don't need a balcony, **Deluxe Oceanview Staterooms** have oversized floor-to-ceiling glass windows—an unusual feature for oceanview staterooms, most of which have small, square-shaped windows. These rooms just might be one of the best values on board, with a spacious seating area, marble bathroom, and luxe amenities like a mini-bar stocked with complimentary soft drinks and bottled water, and Oceania's Prestige Tranquility Bed.

PUBLIC AREAS & ACTIVITIES The one concession to big-ship excess is the **casino,** which can get busy. The main **show lounge** is more small scale, hosting comedians, jazz musicians, and the like (no full-scale Broadway-style performances here). The bars and lounges more than hold their own, however. Our favorite **Horizons** serves as an observation lounge by day and a nightclub by night, with live music and creative cocktails.

Up on the pool deck, a spacious **swimming pool** is flanked by a pair of whirlpools. Fitness mavens will be happy to know that the ship's onboard **fitness center** is as well-equipped as those on ships twice its size, with both complimentary and pay-per-use options like yoga and Pilates. **Canyon Ranch SpaClub** is situated all the way forward on Deck 14, and has steam and sauna rooms and scented showers. The real feature to write home about is the spectacular Spa Terrace located at the front of the ship; stationed on one of its comfy loungers next to its whirlpool and pool, you can easily spend an entire afternoon here, ordering spa-themed beverages and lite bites for sustenance.

DINING With so many specialty restaurants on board, it's easy to forget about the **Grand Dining Room,** which offers up excellent cuisine overseen by legendary chef Jacques Pepin. Surrounded by windows on three walls, this chic venue is open for breakfast, lunch, and dinner. If it isn't overly crowded, that's probably because guests are taking advantage of venues such as **Jacques,** which is intended to mimic the bistros of Pépin's hometown, Lyon. Menu highlights include mussels *marinière* and freshly roasted free range chicken, duck, and lamb. Daily chef's specials are prepared from fresh ingredients purchased in local markets at ports of call.

Oceania favorites **Toscana** and **Polo Grill** are also on both ships. Toscana is sinfully overwhelming, serving half a dozen antipasti and an equal number of pasta dishes, soups, salads, and main courses such as filet mignon and swordfish steak. Polo Grill has chops, seafood, and cuts of slow-aged beef, with all the substantial trimmings. New to these vessels is **Red Ginger,** which focuses on Asian fusion. You can also opt for the tasting menu at **La Reserve.** Limited to just 24 guests, this is the only venue aboard these two ships to carry an extra surcharge, but that covers a truly luxe seven-course meal with items like stuffed brioche with duck foie gras and truffle jelly, and slow-braised short ribs with gnocchi au jus (wine pairings come with an additional charge).

If you want to keep it casual, room service is available around the clock, and the **Terrace Café** serves up buffet-style fare for breakfast, lunch, and dinner. The nearby **Waves Grill** is the place to go for burgers and other poolside eats in the afternoons. You can even get creamy homemade gelato, a made-to-order hot fudge sundae, or a thick, hand-dipped milkshake here.

Insignia • Nautica • Regatta • Sirena

The Verdict

With their smallish size, understated decor, and serene atmosphere, these ships provide a comfortable, laid-back, yet stylish way to see the world. *Sirena* was added into the fleet in the spring of 2016.

Specifications — Avg. Starting Per Diem $240

Size (in tons)	30,277	Crew	400
Passengers (Double Occ.)	684	Passenger/Crew Ratio	1.71 to 1
Passenger/Space Ratio	42.6	Year Launched	1998-2000
Total Cabins/Veranda Cabins	342/232	Last Major Refurbishment	2014-2016

Frommer's Ratings (Scale of 1–5) ★★★★ ½

Cabin Comfort & Amenities	4	Dining Options	4.5
Ship Cleanliness & Maintenance	5	Gym, Spa & Sports Facilities	4.5
Public Comfort/Space	4.5	Children's Facilities	N/A
Decor	4.5	Enjoyment Factor	4.5

THE SHIPS IN GENERAL

Imagine a stylish boutique hotel in the shape of a cruise ship and you've pretty much got the idea. Like all of the former Renaissance vessels, these four ships are comfortable and spacious, decorated mostly in warm, dark woods and rich fabrics. All are sedate, with an emphasis on intimate spaces rather than the kind of grand, splashy ones you'll find on most megaships. Only 684 passengers apiece. You'll see a lot of the globe: *Insignia* operates Oceania's extremely popular 180-day long World Cruises.

CABINS **Staterooms** aboard these ships are straightforward, no-nonsense spaces with plain, off-white walls and dark-wood trim and furniture. The highlight of each is its Tranquility Bed, an oasis of 350-thread-count Egyptian cotton sheets, down duvets and pillows, custom-designed extra-thick mattresses, and a mound of throw pillows. Spacious balconies have teak decking for a classic nautical look. Closet space is a little skimpy, but drawer space scattered around the cabin, and space under the beds, help to compensate. Rooms are midsized, by industry standards.

Suites (322–982 sq. ft., including balcony) have bathtubs and a small area with a cocktail table for intimate in-room dining. Ten Owner's Suites are located at the ship's bow and stern; they feature wraparound balconies, whirlpool bathtubs, living rooms, and guest bathrooms. **Owners Suites, Vista Suites,** and **Penthouse Suites** feature butler service. **Concierge-class staterooms** (in between regular cabins and suites) add some nice creature comforts, including a welcome bottle of champagne, complimentary shoeshine service, massaging shower heads, and luxe toiletries.

PUBLIC AREAS & ACTIVITIES Overall, these four ships present an elegant yet homey appearance, with dark-wood paneling, fluted columns, ornate faux-iron railings, gilt-framed classical paintings, frilly moldings, marble and brass accents, and deep-hued upholstery, all contributing to a kind of English-inn-at-sea look. In the bow, the spacious **Horizons** lounge has floor-to-ceiling windows and brass telescopes on three sides. It's used for dancing in the evenings and for various activities during the day. The 345-seat **show lounge** hosts cabaret and variety acts, musical recitals, magic shows, and comedy, and the smallish but comfortable **casino** allows for blackjack, poker tables, roulette, and slots. The attached **Martini Bar** has a ridiculously long martini list (some 30 recipes and an equal number of vodka choices); a jazz band performs here in the evenings. Another notable space is the comfortable **library,** decorated in traditional style with warm red upholstery, mahogany paneling, a *trompe l'oeil* garden "skylight," and a marble faux fireplace.

The attractive teak **pool deck,** dotted with canvas umbrellas, has a pair of hot tubs plus a slew of deck chairs and large daybeds for sunbathing. **The Patio,** a shaded outdoor lounge located in the aft port corner of the deck, is furnished with thickly cushioned sofas, chairs, and daybeds. Drapes and general ambience add a hint of partition from the pool goings-on, but you still feel like you're in the action. For more privacy, passengers can rent one of eight private cabanas, each with a retractable shade roof, and a plush daybed built for two. They're available either daily ($50 on port days, $100 on sea days) or for the entirety of your cruise, and they come with the services of an attendant who keeps the food, drinks, and chilled towels coming.

A small jogging track wraps around the deck immediately above the pool deck. The **Canyon Ranch** spa on Deck 9 offers a variety of treatments, including aromatherapy massages, hot-stone treatments, and various wraps and facials. Just forward of the spa there's an outdoor hydrotherapy whirlpool overlooking the bow. A decent-size oceanview **gym** and **beauty salon** are attached.

DINING The **main dining room** is an elegant single-level space surrounded on three sides by windows. It's spacious and understated, with simple wood-veneer wall panels, wall sconces, and teal carpeting. Tables seating between two and eight are available, though the smaller arrangements go fast. The ship's two specialty restaurants, the **Polo Grill** and **Toscana** (see p. 249 for full descriptions), are decorated to match their cuisine: old-Hollywood decor in Polo and Roman urns and reliefs in Toscana. On Deck 9, the **Terrace** buffet is available for breakfast, lunch, and dinner—you can have the latter out under the stars, with drink service, Spanish cuisine, and candles flickering in lovely hurricane lamps. It's a very romantic spot if you can time your meal to the sunset.

REGENT SEVEN SEAS CRUISES

www.rssc.com. ✆ **866/217-1369.**

Pros

- **A Lot Is Included in the Price:** And we're not just talking cocktails! Regent includes in its rates round-trip air (with business class on some routes), unlimited shore excursions, pre-cruise hotel stays and transfers, all beverages, and even gratuities. Stay in certain suite levels, and Wi-Fi is thrown in, too.

- **Overall Excellence:** The line serves very good food, has ultra-comfortable accommodations, creative shore excursions, and a peerless staff.
- **Tip-Top Room Service:** It's some of the best we've found on a ship, with the food served promptly, fresh, and course by course or all at once—your choice (okay, so the room-service pizza isn't so great).

Cons

- **Sedate Nightlife:** Although the line has upgraded its evening entertainment, many guests, exhausted after a full day in port, retire early, leaving only a few night owls in the disco and other lounges.

Overview

Regent's brand of luxury is unfussily elegant, its cuisine among the best in the industry.

EXPERIENCE

The Regent Seven Seas experience means outstanding food, service, and accommodations in an environment that tends to be less stuffy than Seabourn and Silversea. These are some of the most comfortable ships at sea, providing passengers with incredibly spacious outside suites and roomy public areas.

ROUTES

Regent Seven Seas offers everything from the exotic (South America, Africa, India, Asia, and the South Pacific) to the more common cruise destinations (Europe, Alaska, Canada and New England, Caribbean, and the Panama Canal).

PASSENGERS

Regent tends to attract travelers from their 50s to their 70s (sometimes even in their 30s and 40s) who have a high household income but don't like to flaunt their wealth. The typical guest is admirably well-educated, well-traveled, and inquisitive. The travelers may also be a mixed bunch. On a recent cruise, the passengers we met included an economist for an international financial institution, a retired auto-parts engineer, and an environmental lobbyist.

DINING

Regent's cuisine would garner high marks even if it were on land, with classic continental cuisine as well as more creative dishes (we're still dreaming about the avocado panna cotta we had). Service by accomplished waiters adds to the experience, as do little touches such as fine china and fresh flowers on the tables. The complimentary wines served with meals are generally quite good; there's very little reason to want to trade up (however, the wines available at extra cost are actually fairly priced). At the main Compass Rose restaurant meals are always open seating (i.e., you don't have to pre-book a time to dine); and there are a number of possible table configurations from deuces to ones that can comfortably seat 8 people.

ACTIVITIES

Days not spent exploring the ports are unstructured for most guests though there are a variety of activities thrown in for those who aren't pursuing their own relaxation. These include lectures by experts, golf instruction, card and board games, art auctions, blackjack and Ping-Pong tournaments, bingo, and big-screen movies with popcorn. Bridge instructors are on board for select sailings; check when you make a reservation. Regent ships offer free Wi-Fi for certain suite levels, and the line the offers Internet packages (an unlimited plan that is $29.99 per day, 200 minutes for $160, and pay-as-you-go for $0.99 a minute) for everyone else.

CHILDREN'S PROGRAMS

While Regent allows children on board who are one year or older, the line is geared toward the interests of mature adults. (Read: no kids club.)

ENTERTAINMENT

The small size of Regent ships limits the line's ability to provide entertainment as lavish as its big-ship competitors; however, in 2014, Regent substantially upped its game in terms of its onboard evening entertainment, introducing "Cirque Rock 'n' Roll," acrobatics with music *a la* Cirque du Soleil (but not affiliated with that company). In addition to this show, the program in the *Seven Seas Navigator*'s two-tiered showroom (the South Seven Seas Lounge) includes cabaret acts, comedians and magicians, and sometimes members of symphony orchestras and other musical groups. Other onboard productions include the soundtrack-themed "Film Flashbacks," the dance-party hit "Dancing in the Streets," and Regent's classic "Broadway," which offers samples from current Broadway productions.

SERVICE

High staff to passenger ratios means there's never any wait for service; and often the service is by real experts. The senior dining room staff generally have had experience at fine hotels as well as on ships. The room stewards and butlers are as accomplished. And we have to give special kudos to the bar staff: During our last cruise, just about all the staff members in the public lounges remembered our favorite drinks after just one meeting. The line also provides dry cleaning and full- and self-service laundry. On Regent ships, gratuities for the staff are included in the fare and are not expected.

CRUISETOURS & ADD-ON PROGRAMS

The Denali Corridor features prominently in Regent Seven Seas' land packages in Alaska. The company's brochure includes 4-night packages originating in Anchorage. The rates start at $2,299 depending on the itinerary chosen. The line also includes a free 1-night luxury hotel stay at the beginning of all Alaska cruises in Anchorage.

FLEET

Regent has four ships, the 700-passenger *Seven Seas Mariner* and *Seven Seas Voyager,* the smaller 490-passenger *Seven Seas Navigator,* and the brand-new 750-guest *Seven Seas Explorer.*

Seven Seas Explorer

The Verdict

Regent claims it's the most luxurious cruise ship ever built—and that's not far off the mark.

Specifications		Avg. Starting Per Diem $700	
Size (in tons)	54,000	Crew	542
Passengers (Double Occ.)	738	Passenger/Crew Ratio	1.3 to 1
Passenger/Space Ratio	73.1	Year Launched	2016
Total Cabins/Veranda Cabins	369/369	Last Major Refurbishment	N/A

Frommer's Ratings (Scale of 1–5) ★★★★★

Cabin Comfort & Amenities	5	Dining Options	5
Ship Cleanliness & Maintenance	5	Gym, Spa & Sports Facilities	5
Public Comfort/Space	5	Children's Facilities	N/A
Decor	5	Enjoyment Factor	5

THE SHIP IN GENERAL

This 750-guest luxury masterpiece is clearly Regent's most elaborate (and lavish) ship to-date, with the largest-ever suite at sea, a two-story spa, multiple dining options, and a look and feel that is decidedly more lavish than the line's existing fleet.

CABINS Every cabin is a **suite** aboard *Seven Seas Explorer,* and every suite features its own private balcony. Entry-level **Category H Veranda suites** are the smallest but even these are drop-dead gorgeous, with restful-on-the-eyes earth tones, elegant fixtures and more than enough room. Over half of the ship's 375 suites will measure over 470 square feet, but the real head-turner is the gi-normous **Regent Suite,** which is larger than the average North American house. It's also far more expensive to live in at roughly US$5,000 per person, per day. For that you get two bedrooms, a living room, a private garden, your own in-suite spa, biz-class airfare, roundtrip transfer from your house to the airport, a free personal guide and car to tour ashore (likely in select ports of call), guaranteed specialty restaurant reservations and more.

If you can't afford that, not to worry: There are 15 other categories of varying sizes to choose from. It's worth noting that butler service isn't included in all categories; only Explorer Suites and higher offer this amenity.

PUBLIC AREAS & ACTIVITIES The **Meridian Lounge** on Deck 5 is positioned as the prime bar to enjoy a drink before continuing on to one of the many performances in the lavish **Constellation Theatre.** Two decks in height, patrons get unobstructed views and lounge-style seating, complete with Murano glass-topped tables. The **Explorer Lounge** is also a hit, with its deep-blue color scheme, mahogany wood paneling and plush leather chairs. Nightly music is offered here on a stage framed by a golden proscenium, while the nearby **casino** offers entertainment in the form of one-armed bandits and the usual table games. The ship also carries Regent's first-ever culinary center, which has 18 individual cooking stations complete with stainless steel sinks, induction cooking surfaces, and walls of fine ingredients. Cooking classes cost $89/person, and last between 90 and 120 minutes.

Seven Seas Explorer features the largest **spa** in the fleet, operated by Canyon Ranch and offering a number of not-so-standard treatments (when was the last time you had an "Arctic Sea Ritual"?). Before and/or after treatments, guests can try out the hydrotherapy pool, heated thermal loungers, and an outdoor plunge pool. A **fitness center** is located nearby, and offers complimentary yoga and Pilates classes in addition to the usual fitness equipment.

DINING   Two brand-new dining options were introduced aboard *Seven Seas Explorer:* **Chartreuse** and **Pacific Rim.** Chartreuse is an art deco beaut with floor-to-ceiling windows and expertly prepared French Cuisine. Pacific Rim, as its name suggests, has Pan-Asian cuisine.

Returning to the ship are existing Regent favorites like the **Compass Rose** main restaurant, the always-delicious **Prime 7** steakhouse, and the **Veranda Café** for a quicker breakfast, lunch and dinner.

Seven Seas Mariner • Seven Seas Voyager

The Verdict

The all-suite, all-balcony *Seven Seas Mariner* and *Seven Seas Voyager* pamper their 700 guests with big-ship amenities.

Specifications

Avg. Starting Per Diem $623

Size (in tons)	50,000/46,000	Crew	490
Passengers (Double Occ.)	700	Passenger/Crew Ratio	1.6 to 1
Passenger/Space Ratio	71.4/65.7	Year Launched	2001/2003
Total Cabins/Veranda Cabins	354/354	Last Major Refurbishment	2016

Frommer's Ratings (Scale of 1–5)

★★★★ ½

Cabin Comfort & Amenities	5	Dining Options	4.5
Ship Cleanliness & Maintenance	5	Gym, Spa & Sports Facilities	3.5
Public Comfort/Space	5	Children's Facilities	N/A
Decor	4.5	Enjoyment Factor	4.5

THE SHIPS IN GENERAL

When she debuted in 2001, *Seven Seas Mariner* became the first all-suite, all-balcony luxury cruise ship on the high seas. In 2003, *Seven Seas Voyager* built upon the success of her younger fleetmate, introducing a single-corridor layout much like the ships of competing lines Seabourn and Silversea. Though the two vessels differ slightly, they're more similar than not, holding 700 guests apiece.

CABINS   *Seven Seas Voyager*'s accommodations used to feel more lavish than those of her sister ship (indeed, rooms on average are slightly larger), but a 2014 refit rectified that by adding a bit more zing to suites aboard *Seven*

Seas Mariner which got an all new decor of chic soft greys and earth tones. Balconies on both are decently sized, if not totally private: Dividers don't extend right to the ship's railing, so expect to say hello to your neighbors.

Beyond the "starter" suites (called **Deluxe Verandah,** and as we said all accommodations are suites with balconies), there are seven other categories: **Concierge, Penthouse, Seven Seas, Voyager, Grand,** and **Master Suites,** Butler service starts with the Penthouse level suites, and top-level suites include sniffy touches like complimentary onboard iPad and iPod use, personalized liquor bar setup, in-suite binoculars and Illy Espresso makers.

Six suites on *Seven Seas Mariner* and four on *Seven Seas Voyager* are wheelchair-accessible.

PUBLIC AREAS & ACTIVITIES   The public areas on these ship flow attractively into one another, with winding corridors that heighten the sense of discovery. And what you find are lounges, bars and other areas that are spacious and decorated with rich navy blues, brass accents, and soft earth tones.

On both ships, the **Constellation Theatre** is a multi-story affair, with superb, unobstructed sightlines from every seat in the house. The **Horizon Lounge** is a go-to spot for nightcaps, while high tea is offered here during the day, accompanied by the ship's resident pianist. A swish **Connoisseur Club** on both ships has a selection of cigars and fine cognacs.

Seven Seas Mariner has a dedicated disco, the **Stars Nightclub,** located on Deck 6, while *Seven Seas Voyager* carves a disco out of the cozy **Voyager Lounge** at night, complete with a live DJ.

Both ships have one midships **pool,** along with paddle tennis, golf tents and that ubiquitous cruise staple: shuffleboard. Both ships have a small-ish **Canyon Ranch Spa,** while a diminutive but functional **fitness center** contains everything you need to keep those dessert-pounds off.

DINING   Speaking of dessert, both ships have four restaurants apiece, starting with the main dining room, the dinner-only **Compass Rose.** We'd describe the food served as a step below what you'll get aboard rival Crystal Cruises, but still unusually good for shipboard fare. Buffet breakfast and lunch, with a la carte options available for order, are served in the casual, indoor-outdoor **La Veranda;** again these aren't as spectacular as Crystal (they could use more variety in the day-to-day selections) but still quite fine. At night, this dining space transforms into **Sette Mari at La Veranda,** featuring highly authentic, multi-course Italian meals paired with regional wines.

Better are the two dinner-only specialty restaurants: **Signatures** (French fare) and **Prime 7** (a contemporary, and very glam, steakhouse). Both are complimentary, but require advance reservations.

For lighter fare, the **Coffee Connection** serves up sandwiches, cookies and the like—not to mention caffeine-laden beverages of all kinds.

Seven Seas Navigator

The Verdict

Fresh from an extensive drydock in the spring of 2016, *Seven Seas Navigator* has never been more luxurious.

Specifications

Avg. Starting Per Diem $631

Size (in tons)	28,550	Crew	345
Passengers (Double Occ.)	490	Passenger/Crew Ratio	1.4 to 1
Passenger/Space Ratio	58.3	Year Launched	1999
Total Cabins/Veranda Cabins	245/216	Last Major Refurbishment	2016

Frommer's Ratings (Scale of 1–5)

★★★★ ½

Cabin Comfort & Amenities	5	Dining Options	4
Ship Cleanliness & Maintenance	5	Gym, Spa & Sports Facilities	4
Public Comfort/Space	4.5	Children's Facilities	N/A
Decor	5	Enjoyment Factor	4.5

THE SHIP IN GENERAL

Carrying just 490 guests, *Seven Seas Navigator* has always been one of Regent's most comfortable ships. Public rooms are numerous and smartly laid out, while outer deck areas are so spacious that you'd practically have to go out of your way to bump into your fellow guests. Staterooms are equally roomy, each facing the sea (no inside cabins here!) with nearly every cabin on board featuring its own private balcony. Throw in an extensive 2016 refit that saw sweeping aesthetic changes, and *Seven Seas Navigator* easily holds her own against her larger, newer fleetmates.

CABINS Another all **suite** ship and a full 90% of those have private balconies. All are spacious with walk-in closets, European king-sized beds (they're four inches wider than "kings" in North America), a marble bathroom with a shower *and* tub, and brand-new soft furnishings. The look of the rooms would appeal to mermaids: elegant blue headboards, sea-foam runners and carpeting, and plenty of wood and brass accents. **Penthouse Suites** and those in the categories above, feature dedicated butler service and cream-and-copper tones on the walls and drapes and carpeting. The largest of the accommodations on board are the ship's **Master Suites,** which come with a massive private balcony that's over 100 square feet in size. Each has separate living and sleeping areas and little touches like an Illy espresso machine, complementary iPod and iPad use, and an iPod docking.

Four suites are designated as wheelchair-accessible.

PUBLIC AREAS & ACTIVITIES For a ship of this size, there's a surprising number of bars, lounges and places to hang both by day and at night. After a recent renovation, the **reception lobby** now makes a stunning appearance, illuminated by a gypsum diamond cut lighting fixture. The lobby's adjacent, and entirely unexpected, eight-deck high **atrium,** comes complete with panoramic glass elevators. The ship features a small **casino;** and a number of swell lounges, including **Galileo's,** an aft-facing piano lounge. The two-story **Seven Seas Show Lounge** is where evening production shows are performed.

A large **pool** and two hot tubs can be found amidships, surrounded by relaxing lounges, and, not so coincidentally, adjacent to the **Pool Bar.** The ship's small **Canyon Ranch SpaClub** is low-key meaning there's no push from Canyon Ranch staff to purchase products you don't need. The **fitness center,** sadly, isn't large enough and tends to get crowded—particularly on sea days.

DINING   The **Compass Rose Restaurant** looks better than ever thanks to its recent refit that added new furniture, decor, and a pleasant nautical color scheme. Open for breakfast, lunch and dinner, it offers an extensive menu of options, including healthy choices curated by the Canyon Ranch SpaClub. **La Veranda** serves up breakfast and lunch buffet-style, while **The Grill** complements that at lunchtime by offering made-to-order burgers, milkshakes, sandwiches and fresh salads. The **Coffee Connection** is the place to go for all your caffeine needs, plus snacks and sandwiches. Seven Seas Navigator has two specialty restaurants: **Prime 7** (a steakhouse) and **Sette Mari at La Veranda** (Italian). Both require reservations, but are complimentary.

SEABOURN CRUISES

www.seabourn.com. ✆ **866/755-5623.**

Pros
- **Fantastic Watersports:** Thanks to a platform guests can kayak and water-ski right off the back of the ship.
- **Exclusive Beach Parties:** The line's "Caviar in the Surf" beach barbecue include plenty of champagne and, you guessed it, caviar.
- **Game-Changing Cuisine:** In late 2015, Seabourn partnered with acclaimed chef Thomas Keller to retrain its chefs and create razzle dazzle dishes unlike any being served at sea.
- **Nontouristy Ports of Call:** These small ships are able to visit smaller, less visited ports that bigger ships can't access.

Cons
- **Quiet Nights:** After dinner, most guests retire to their cabins.

Overview

Genteel and refined, these megayachts are intimate, quiet, and very comfortable, lavishing guests with personal attention and very fine cuisine. Its fleet of three (soon to be five) all entered service after 2009, making the Seabourn fleet one of the youngest in the luxury segment.

EXPERIENCE

These ships are ideal for sybarites. All rooms are suites, and all alcohol is included, so you can sip bloody marys all day long, if you like. Generally speaking, guests would rather socialize with each other than participate in organized games. Service is one of Seabourn's strong-suits, with staff that know you by name from the moment you step on board. A high guest-to-staff ratio ensures that help—or that bloody mary—is never far from reach.

ROUTES

Seabourn offers Europe and the Caribbean but also the Panama Canal, South America, Arabia, Africa, Australia and New Zealand, India and Asia. During the North American winter it offers expedition-style cruises to Antarctica. In 2017, the line returns to Alaska for the first time in over a decade.

PASSENGERS

These well-off passengers are sophisticated, well traveled, and decidedly older. Most guests will hail from the United States, Canada, or England, but a handful of European and Australian passengers are usually on board as well. While you might see the odd family with children during the holidays, Seabourn doesn't actively cater to children—and the line's loyal guests like it that way.

DINING

You could wait for months to snag a reservation at the French Laundry (the Napa Valley restaurant some consider the best on the planet)...or you could book a cabin on Seabourn. The line partnered with Per Se's chef/owner/genius Thomas Keller in late 2015, and Seabourn has been slowly rolling out his meticulously sourced, inventive French/Californian fusion fare ever since. Considering that meals at The French Laundry and Per Se (Keller's NYC restaurant) run about $600 a meal, Seabourn's partnership makes its cruise price seem (almost) like a value. Even in the highly competitive luxury cruise market, Seabourn gets deserved bragging rights for this savvy partnership.

ACTIVITIES

The enrichment classes include impressive guest lecturers and there are cooking classes, and wine tasting lessons as well as a spa and a gym. A highlight: the impressive fold-out marina on the stern of the ship for waterskiing, kayaking, and other watersports. On some sailings, the line also hosts a beach party with caviar served in the surf.

CHILDREN'S PROGRAMS

This is not a line that caters to families. There are no kids' facilities or programs, and those traveling with children are not common (and some might argue, welcome—at least as far as your fellow guests are concerned).

ENTERTAINMENT

Evening entertainment is low key: cocktails and live, quiet music, like a pianist in the Observation Bar. Guests can also dance in The Club, or catch a magic show in the Grand Salon.

SERVICE

One of Seabourn's strongest assets is its onboard service, which is polished and exacting. Mistakes are rare, and staff address guests by name throughout the voyage. In keeping with Seabourn's all-inclusive policy, all gratuities for staff members are included in the cost of the voyage.

FLEET

The 450-passenger *Seabourn Odyssey* launched in 2009, followed by sisters *Seabourn Sojourn* in 2010 and *Seabourn Quest* in 2011. Seabourn's newest ship, *Seabourn Encore,* will officially enter service in January 2017, and a sister-ship, *Seabourn Ovation,* is due out in 2018. If you're looking for the older *Seabourn Pride, Seabourn Spirit,* and *Seabourn Legend,* you're out of luck: They were sold off to Windstar Cruises and now sail as *Star Pride, Star Breeze,* and *Star Legend* (see p. 371).

Seabourn Odyssey • Seabourn Sojourn • Seabourn Quest

The Verdict

These ships are all-around winners, with magnificent interior design, spacious suites, and a high passenger-to-space ratio that means things never get crowded.

Specifications   Avg. Starting Per Diem $409

Size (in tons)	32,346	Crew	330
Passengers (Double Occ.)	450	Passenger/Crew Ratio	1.8 to 1
Passenger/Space Ratio	71	Year Launched	2009-2011
Total Cabins/Veranda Cabins	225/199	Last Major Refurbishment	2013

Frommer's Ratings (Scale of 1–5)   ★★★★★

Cabin Comfort & Amenities	5	Dining Options	5
Ship Cleanliness & Maintenance	5	Gym, Spa & Sports Facilities	4.5
Public Comfort/Space	5	Children's Facilities	N/A
Decor	5	Enjoyment Factor	4

THE SHIPS IN GENERAL

Before *Seabourn Odyssey* debuted in 2009, Seabourn hadn't had a new ship in nearly two decades—but it was worth the wait. With graceful, elegant lines from stem-to-stern, these are head-turning ships. Inside, public rooms are airy, spacious and surprisingly contemporary; designers favor brightly lit spaces that feature heavy use of glass and bold colors over "old-world elegance."

CABINS   All cabins are **suites,** all offer ocean views, and nearly all have private balconies. At the entry level are the **Ocean View Suites,** which feature an oversized picture window, generous seating area, a bed that can be arranged as a queen or two twins and a bathroom complete with separate tub and shower. **Veranda Suites** include a private balcony and are a third larger but decor is nearly identical throughout: a softly muted color palette with fashionable furniture that doesn't clutter up the room or distract by being over-the-top plush. Lighting is indirect and flattering. Suites in all categories have sizeable walk-in closets and drawers that pop open when you give them a little push.

The most over-the-top digs, the **Wintergarden suites,** have curved balconies that jut out over the side of the ship and a glass-enclosed solarium, complete with hot tub and day bed. Spa mavens will want to book the **Penthouse Spa Suites,** which offer the services of a Spa Concierge, plus private staircase access to and from the ship's spa lobby.

PUBLIC AREAS & ACTIVITIES Like a stretch version of Seabourn's earlier ships, *Seabourn Odyssey, Sojourn,* and *Quest* offer plenty of space to kick back, and a number of swellegant public rooms to do so in. **The Club** is one of the primary social gathering spots, with an attractive bar, stage, dance floor, and plenty of seating. Up top, the ship's **Observation Lounge** is the place to be for quiet sea days with a book; at night, this space turns into an posh piano bar. Evening production shows are held in the **Grand Salon,** which unfortunately suffers from poor sight lines thanks to a series of support pillars.

These ships also have a small-but-functional onboard **casino,** a **boutique,** and a breathtaking **atrium** topped with a skylight and surrounded by a spiral staircase that's one of the best examples of the architectural genre we've seen aboard any ship.

The **Spa at Seabourn** is an elaborate affair run with a thermal suite and hydrotherapy pool, a dry float, steam and sauna, and a full-service salon. The **Fitness Center** has all the usual equipment, plus a motion studio featuring a Kinesis Wall and Thai massage area. There's also a Kneipp Walk Pool overlooking the stern that is designed to sooth and relax guests with its alternating baths of cold and warm water. A **pool** and two hot tubs are located amidships, and are surrounded by comfortable lounges and tables.

DINING The **Restaurant** is downright glamorous, with unusually high ceilings and billowy white gauze curtain dividers. Open seating is the rule; some dinners require a jacket, while others are jacket optional. But all feature dazzling choices from superstar chef Thomas Keller (listed on a separate sheet of paper within the regular menu). These might include butter poached lobster with a red wine jus, or roasted king trumpet mushrooms with "lime scented" tapioca pearls. It all will tango with your taste buds in a most delightful way.

Restaurant 2, on the other hand, is open only for dinner and features nightly small-plate tasting menus. You'll have to make reservations to dine here, but there is no extra charge for the meal.

The Colonnade is the place for a quick breakfast or lunch and it is one of the most stunning indoor/outdoor dining areas we've seen. Dinner (complimentary but reservations required) is also served here, and takes its cue from Keller's **Ad Hoc** restaurant, a paean to his childhood favorites (read: fine dining presentations of comfort foods like ribs and Waldorf salads). Casual fare during the daytime is also available at **The Patio** (think: burgers), and room service is available around-the-clock.

The *Seabourn Quest* has the only floating restaurant (yet) named for the famed chef: **The Grill by Thomas Keller,** a reworking of the classic American steakhouse. Tableside preparation of traditional Caesar salads and after-meal ice cream sundaes make dining an event here as does the hip decor by interior designer Adam D. Tihany (curvilinear lines, leather banquettes, and curving wooden ceilings). The Grill will be coming to *Seabourn Odyssey* and *Seabourn Sojourn* during their next scheduled drydock periods (which is ship-speak for, "a few years from now.") There's no extra charge to eat at The Grill.

SEADREAM YACHT CLUB

www.seadream.com. © **800/707-4911.**

Pros

o **Cool Tech Stuff:** These ships were built in the mid-1980s, but they've been outfitted for the 21st century. Along with solid Wi-Fi throughout, jet skis and MP3 players are available for passenger use.

o **Late-Night Departures from Key Ports:** Instead of leaving port around cocktail hour—just when things begin to get interesting—the ships will stay late or even overnight in places such as St. Barts to allow passengers a night of carousing on terra firma.

o **Free Booze & Tips:** Unlimited wines and spirits, as well as gratuities, are included in the rates.

o **Intriguing Itineraries:** These smaller ships can get into the ports the big ships simply can't visit.

o **Raw Food Menu:** If there's a time to push the boundaries on what you like to eat, a cruise is it, and SeaDream gives you a great opportunity with its raw food menu.

Cons

o **No Verandas:** These older ships don't have any private balconies.

o **Less Stability:** While the small size of these ships is a real selling point, it can also be a detriment to those prone to seasickness: These ships bob around in even mild swells.

Overview

The focus of these cruises is on the ports, which are often less crowded than the larger ports the big ships call in. As for the onboard experience the 112-guest *SeaDream I* and *SeaDream II* have all the luxury but none of the formality of their peers.

EXPERIENCE

Most guests spend their time on shore, and the line has bikes available for those who want to explore on their own. SeaDream has also included more casual shore excursions with the crew, such as hikes, snorkeling trips, market tours (with the chef), and late-night visits to island beach bars in the Caribbean. There are a few notable features on the ships themselves: The Balinese day beds on deck feel like a serious upgrade from plastic, or even teak, lounge chairs and we love the watersports platform that drops down from the stern of the ship and features nearly every sort of aquatic toy you could want.

ROUTES

SeaDream focuses on the Mediterranean and the Caribbean primarily, mixing the standard ports with small islands and little towns (there's a good chance you won't recognize the names of all of your ports of call). If you don't mind spending a handful of days at sea, the line's transatlantic crossings in the spring and fall are a great way to get on board without breaking the bank.

PASSENGERS

Most of your fellow guests will be in their 40s and 50s, with a smattering of folks on either side of that equation. The vast majority are American, with Canadian, British, and European guests rounding out the numbers. Well-travelled and well-educated, they tend to be active, adventurous and self-entertaining (they prefer having an adult beverage with newfound friends around the pool to the "organized fun" that's the staple of so many cruises).

Some dates may not be available when you inquire because a decent portion of SeaDream's business comes from charters of the entire boat, which are usually booked by large families and other groups.

DINING

Dining is a high point of the SeaDream experience; it's roughly on a par with Windstar's cuisine, and just under Regent and Seabourn.

Open seating in the main dining rooms of each ship is *de rigueur,* meaning you can choose you tablemates each evening, or sit alone. Tables for two, four, six and eight are available. There are no formal evenings, though most male guests will, at the very least, don a collared shirt in the evenings, and a few put on sports jackets, while women opt for casual dresses to suit the warm regions SeaDream sails to. Food is prepared *a la minute* (made-to-order) rather than being pre-prepped as it is on mainstream ships. Dinners are typically five courses, and SeaDream makes a point of including locally sourced ingredients whenever possible. The line also offers a gluten-free menu, a Japanese menu, and a Raw Food menu, and will cater readily to dietary requirements provided you notify the line before sailing.

For a more casual option, the **Topside Restaurant** on Deck 5 has both a buffet and made-to-order options for lunch and dinner. Room service is available around-the-clock, and you can still get caviar on board—though it carries a small surcharge now.

ACTIVITIES

On board, there's a pool and Jacuzzi, a small gym with a sauna and steam room (and no extra charge for their use), a small casino, and a library with an extensive collection of hardbacks. That said, it's the water stern-mounted sports marina—which has glass-bottom kayaks, Wave Runners, Hobie Cats, and banana boats—that's the most fun to use on a sea day. Another SeaDream staple is the line's lavish Champagne and Caviar Splash beach barbecue, which is held on Jost Van Dyke and Virgin Gorda.

CHILDREN'S PROGRAMS

There are no dedicated children's programs, kids' rooms, or babysitting services on board, though children over the age of 1 are allowed on board (grudgingly).

ENTERTAINMENT

Evening are low key, and after dinner many couples meet for cocktails in the bars—including a piano bar and one called **Top of the Yacht**—or head up on deck, where movies are screened under the stars when the weather allows.

SERVICE

Service is never stuffy and manages to hit the mark of always being attentive. The crew-to-guest ratio is high, and it's obvious that staff have enough time to make sure you're taken care of on board.

FLEET

The line has two ships, the yacht-style *SeaDream I* and *SeaDream II*, which debuted as the original *Sea Goddess* twins back in the 1980's. Extensively refitted over the intervening years, both ships carry a maximum of 112 guests and a crew of 95, for a staff-to-crew ratio of nearly 1-to-1.

SeaDream I • SeaDream II

The Verdict

Two of the most unassuming luxury ships out there, *SeaDream I* and *SeaDream II* offers all the pampering and none of the pretensions of other luxury vessels. Whether you want to sleep under the stars or kayak off the stern-mounted-marina, these ships offer it all.

Specifications   Avg. Starting Per Diem $560

Size (in tons)	4,260	Crew	95
Passengers (Double Occ.)	112	Passenger/Crew Ratio	1.2 to 1
Passenger/Space Ratio	38.7	Year Launched	1984/1985
Total Cabins/Veranda Cabins	55/0	Last Major Refurbishment	2011

Frommer's Ratings (Scale of 1–5)   ★★★★ ½

Cabin Comfort & Amenities	5	Dining Options	3.5
Ship Cleanliness & Maintenance	4	Gym, Spa & Sports Facilities	4
Public Comfort/Space	4.5	Children's Facilities	N/A
Decor	4	Enjoyment Factor	5

THE SHIPS IN GENERAL

Originally debuting back in 1984 as *Sea Goddess I* and *II*, these two 112-guest luxury yachts were acquired from Cunard—and later Seabourn—back in 2002 when SeaDream was formed by industry vets Larry Pimentel and Atle Brynestad, the latter of which founded luxury competitor Seabourn. The line's slogan, "It's yachting, not cruising" applies perfectly to these nimble 355-foot-long ships. Deck space is generous, and public rooms are decorated with an old-world elegance. Successive refits have kept both ships looking smart, and SeaDream's dedication to onboard cuisine and friendly, personable service has never wavered.

CABINS   All of the 54 one-room **oceanview suites** are virtually identical, with the bedroom area positioned alongside the cabin's large window (or portholes in the case of Deck 2 suites) and the sitting area inside—the exact opposite of most ship cabin layouts. The standard cabins are a bit bigger than Windstar's, and about 100 square feet smaller than those of Seabourn, Silversea, and Regent. None have balconies. Soundproofing between cabins is good and engine noise minimal, as all cabins are located forward and amidships. There are 16 staterooms that are connectable.

Built in the mid-1980s, these ships have a lot more real wood incorporated into the cabins than you'll see on today's newer ships (those sport veneers and synthetics at every turn). Wood cabinetry and moldings are complemented by blue-and-white fabrics to create an appealing contemporary nautical look. A minifridge is stocked with sodas and beer (booze from any of the bars and restaurants is included in the rates, but oddly enough, if you want liquor for your minibar, you'll have to pay for it). Bathrooms are compact, but feature huge marble showers. All guests are given a set of personalized cotton pajamas with the SeaDream logo to take home.

The bigger **Owner's Suite** has a bedroom, living room, dining area, main bathroom with bathtub and separate oceanview shower, and a guest bathroom. Both ships also have a new **Admiral Suite** with a similar layout and amenities.

These ships are not recommended for passengers requiring the use of a wheelchair as the doorways aren't wide enough, many thresholds are several inches high and the tenders that shuttle passengers from ship to shore can't accommodate wheelchairs.

PUBLIC AREAS & ACTIVITIES   The SeaDream yachts retain much of *Sea Goddess*'s former sophisticated decor—stained wood floors, Oriental carpets, and striking exotic floral arrangements—but with periodic face-lifts that keep carpeting and furniture spruced up. There's a large collection of original artwork by exclusively Scandinavian artists, placed throughout the ship and commissioned or otherwise chosen by Linn Brynestad.

The **Main Salon** and its small but popular alcove bar is the place for the weekly captain's cocktail party, plus other group events. One deck above is the **Piano Bar,** the ship's small **casino,** a **gift shop,** and an attractive and book-filled **library.** By far, the favorite place to socialize is the **Top of the Yacht** bar which is partially covered and has alcove seating. On this deck, you'll also find a flotilla of queen-size sun beds; they're slightly elevated at the stern of the ship to allow for uninterrupted ocean viewing. Management allows guests to sleep on deck at night if they wish, and will outfits these beds with blankets.

The attractive **pool** area, has comfortable lounge chairs, a bar, and, not too far away, a hot tub.

On Deck 4 are the **beauty salon** and an impressively well-designed and well-equipped **spa** (spice-and-yogurt scrub, anyone?) and **gym.** The latter has equipment and room for aerobics, yoga, and tai chi classes.

DINING   Dinners are served indoors in the simple but elegant **Dining Salon.** At least once during your voyage, a festive dinner is served in the open-sided, teak-floored **Topside Restaurant,** and some special meals are served on the beach during port calls. Unlike Silversea and Seabourn, the 24-hour room-service menu is limited to salads and sandwiches, and you can't order from the restaurant menus.

SILVERSEA CRUISES

www.silversea.com. ☎ **877/276-6816** or 954/522-2299.

Pros

- **All-Around Excellence:** The cuisine, open seating for meals, exemplary service, and roomier-than-usual accommodations (even among luxury ships) make Silversea worth the outlay.
- **Very Inclusive:** All but the most top-shelf alcohol, including champagne, is included on board, as are room service and gratuities.
- **A Butler for Everyone:** Regardless of your suite category, everyone on board is treated to the services of a professionally trained butler and suite attendant.

Cons

- **Not a Great Deal of Nightlife:** Yes, the ship has a show lounge, but it's not really big enough for anything lavish. The line in recent years has been de-emphasizing production-type shows in favor of more low-key, concert performances by classically trained vocalists and other musicians.

Overview

From exquisite service and cuisine, to such niceties as free-flowing Drappier champagne and Ferragamo and Bulgari bath products in the marble cabin bathrooms, the line's fleet of classic and luxury expedition ships offer the very finest of, well, everything.

EXPERIENCE

A Silversea cruise caters to guests who are used to the good life, and nothing seems to have been overlooked. Food and service are among the best at sea, the decor is warm and inviting. Tables are set with Christofle silver and Schott Zwiesel crystal. If you want the VIP treatment 24-7, this is your line.

ROUTES

Because of the addition of the line's three (soon to be four) luxury expedition ships, Silversea offers the largest range of destinations to choose from of all of the luxury lines. This includes all seven continents, with expedition destinations including the Arctic, Antarctica, Micronesia and Melanesia, the Russian Far East, and the Galapagos. The line's classic luxury fleet covers nearly everywhere else, including Asia, Alaska, the Panama Canal, Central America, the Caribbean, South America, South Africa, the Middle East, Mediterranean, Western Europe, Northern Europe and Scandinavia, Greenland, Iceland, Canada & New England, and the Eastern Seaboard.

PASSENGERS

Overall, they're well traveled, well heeled, well dressed, well accessorized, and well into their 50s, 60s, and 70s. That being said, shorter cruises and Caribbean sailings often skew a tad younger, adding at least a handful of 30- and 40-something couples to the pot. Typically, about 50% of passengers are American and the rest are mostly from Europe, with Australians, South

Americans, and Asians. Most guests arrive in twos, though singles and small groups of friends traveling together can be part of the scene, too. Many have cruised with Silversea before.

DINING

Silversea has a partnership with venerable Relais & Chateaux, and the main dining room is as polished as you would imagine from such an association. Food is one of Silversea's greatest strengths—both in preparation and in presentation—not only in the main dining room (known simply as The Restaurant), but also in the breakfast/lunch buffets in La Terrazza. That room doubles as a low-capacity candlelit Italian restaurant with a "slow-food" philosophy.

Silversea serves very acceptable complimentary wine with dinner (and at other meals), but if you must upgrade to something really, really expensive (Opus One and Dom Perignon), you should expect to pay the going rate.

ACTIVITIES

In the past couple of years, Silversea has significantly enhanced its onboard enrichment program. Naturalists, historians, well-known authors, award-winning chefs, and wine experts host excellent sessions, often targeted to the specific cruising location. The line has also introduced a cooking school with state-of-the-art cooking theaters that allow chefs to present a variety of specialized cooking classes and demonstrations on every cruise.

CHILDREN'S PROGRAMS

These are not ships that carry a lot of children but there will be youth counselors on Silversea ships when there are a number of kids on board, offering activities appropriate to the ages of those traveling. We've seen a handful of kids on Silversea's Expedition cruises (mostly on board *Silver Explorer*), but those, too, are rare. Your fellow guests will expect your children to be quiet and well-behaved. While many will have grandkids, they picked this line for a reason—and kids weren't a part of that decision.

ENTERTAINMENT

Silverseas sails with a team of six vocalists and musicians on each ship who do a fine job on the several shows they put on every week in the main theater. There's also usually a small combo for dancing (no disco, please, for this older crowd). And many guests choose to host elaborate after-dinner drinks parties in their suites.

SERVICE

Staff have an uncanny knack for remembering your name if you've sailed before—even after a few years away from the line. Which is a long way of saying that service is exemplary; the men and women who work on these ship could take their places in the finest restaurants and hotels ashore—from where, in fact, many of them came. All gratuities are included in the fare. Ships have a self-service laundry and remarkably speedy valet service, including laundry and dry cleaning.

CRUISETOURS & ADD-ON PROGRAMS

In Alaska, Silversea offers a small number of pre- and post-cruise land packages ranging from 2 to 4 nights. The shortest, for passengers who are interested in wildlife, is a 2-night program called Flight to Bear Country that takes passengers by floatplane to Redoubt Bay. It costs from $1,529 per person, based on double occupancy. On the longer side is a 4-night trip to Denali National Park that starts at $1,899 per person, based on double occupancy. New for 2015 is a flightseeing option over the park.

FLEET

Silversea operates a fleet of luxury ships, known as the "classic" ships. Of these, the 382-passenger *Silver Shadow,* which joined the fleet in 2000, is a staunch favorite among guests, as is its identical twin, the *Silver Whisper,* which entered service in 2001. The others are the smaller and virtually identical *Silver Cloud* (1994) and *Silver Wind* (1995), along with the somewhat bigger *Silver Spirit* (2009). The line's first new build, *Silver Muse,* debuts in late spring, 2017. On the expedition front, Silversea has three luxury vessels: *Silver Explorer,* which primarily sails the Arctic, Antarctic and Atlantic routes; *Silver Discoverer,* which bases herself in the Pacific from Australia to Alaska; and *Silver Galapagos.* In late 2017, Silversea plans to refit *Silver Cloud* with a reinforced ice-class hull and transfer her to the Expedition fleet, in the process turning her into one of the most luxurious expedition vessels afloat.

Silver Spirit

The Verdict

The Silver Spirit is the largest ship in the fleet and carries the most passengers. She's also the most innovative and most filled with facilities.

Specifications   Avg. Starting Per Diem $521

Size (in tons)	36,000	Crew	376
Passengers (Double Occ.)	540	Passenger/Crew Ratio	1.4 to 1
Passenger/Space Ratio	67	Year Launched	2009
Total Cabins/Veranda Cabins	270/258	Last Major Refurbishment	N/A

Frommer's Ratings (Scale of 1–5)   ★★★★ ½

Cabin Comfort & Amenities	5	Dining Options	5
Ship Cleanliness & Maintenance	5	Gym, Spa & Sports Facilities	4.5
Public Comfort/Space	4.5	Children's Facilities	N/A
Decor	4.5	Enjoyment Factor	5

THE SHIP IN GENERAL

At 36,000 tons, the ship is 27% bigger than *Shadow* and *Whisper* and twice the tonnage of *Wind* and *Cloud.* Silversea takes advantage of this space with new dining options, a range of amenities not found on its other ships, a greater percentage of verandas, a vastly expanded spa and casino, and new lounges. As for any worries about service levels being different, with 376 crewmembers, the ratio of guest to crew is 1.4 to 1, virtually identical to the rest of the fleet. The one difference guests feel is not crowding but the awareness of other passengers on board (on other Silversea Vessels there are moments when you feel you have the ship all to yourself. Not here).

CABINS   Of the 270 **outside suites,** 258 have private verandas. All suites have butlers who provide a wide range of services, from packing and unpacking, to making spa and restaurant reservations—and, of course, providing endless amounts of Drappier champagne. Smallest suites are the **inside** ones, **Grand Suites and Owner Suites** are so big they have their own libraries! And, of course, suites can be combined for big groups.

All suites, regardless of category, can be personalized via a series of scents created by renowned Italian perfumer Laura Tonatto. Other luxury touches abound, like the marble bathrooms, the fluffy duvets, and personalized stationery. One of their best design features is the way the TVs are placed behind the mirrors; when they are not on, they are hidden from view, a classy touch. There are even iPod docking stations. If there's a weakness, it's that there are not enough electrical outlets for all of today's gadgets.

PUBLIC AREAS & ACTIVITIES   Italian architect Giacomo Mortola has used the *Spirit*'s larger space to present a 1930s Art Deco–inspired series of public rooms with a touch of old-world, Victorian elegance thrown in. Many of the rooms would be right at home on the ocean liners of the past, or in the Chrysler Building, or the many classic hotels of Europe. One of the most popular rooms is the **Bar** (which serves Italian coffees, in keeping with the line's heritage). The Bar, set next to the lobby, is a dividing line of sorts; the forward portion of each deck has suites, the aft portions have the **restaurants, lounges, spa, casino,** and the rest. The casino and boutiques are much expanded compared to earlier ships, providing ample opportunity for onboard spending.

And the **spa** is absolutely massive with an indoors/outdoor setting, a **beauty salon, gym,** whirlpool, sauna, and steam rooms (although not much in the way of luxe amenities). The changing rooms are coed, which some passengers may find uncomfortable. The **pool area** is also bigger than on other Silversea ships and has lots of wicker furniture with comfy cushions for lounging around.

DINING   Dining is a highlight of any Silversea cruise, and, with the larger tonnage of *Silver Spirit* comes an expanded range of options. The four venues, found on all Silversea ships, include the **Restaurant** with the widest range of menu options, open all three meals; **La Terrazza** for indoor or alfresco dining with breakfast and lunch buffets (a much improved setup compared to earlier ships) and authentic Italian cuisine at night; **Le Champagne** for a six-course epicurean experience in an intimate atmosphere; and the **Pool Grill** (both lunch and dinner), with a wider than normal range of options including a hot-rock dinner for the evenings. Two new restaurants fill out the menu. The **Seishin Restaurant** has a range of Asian fusion menu items, from Kobe beef and spider lobster lots of sushi choices (per-person degustation menu cost is $40); and the **Stars Supper Club** where live music, dancing, and nightclub-style entertainment complement the innovative menus. There's also 24-hour room service with menu choices taken from the Restaurant, and served course by course if so desired.

Silver Shadow • Silver Whisper

The Verdict

These handsome, well-run ships are perfect for those looking for a small-ship experience with superb dining and service.

Specifications		Avg. Starting Per Diem $499	
Size (in tons)	28,258	Crew	295
Passengers (Double Occ.)	382	Passenger/Crew Ratio	1.3 to 1
Passenger/Space Ratio	74	Year Launched	2000/2001
Total Cabins/Veranda Cabins	194/157	Last Major Refurbishment	2012

Frommer's Ratings (Scale of 1–5)		★★★★★	
Cabin Comfort & Amenities	5	Dining Options	5
Ship Cleanliness & Maintenance	4.5	Gym, Spa & Sports Facilities	4
Public Comfort/Space	5	Children's Facilities	N/A
Decor	5	Enjoyment Factor	5

THE SHIPS IN GENERAL

Silver Shadow and Silver Whisper are small enough to be intimate, but large enough to offer a classy, two-story show lounge, a dark and romantic cigar lounge, three dining venues, an impressive spa and gym, and some really great suites, in addition to the fine service and cuisine provided fleetwide.

CABINS With a chilled bottle of Drappier bubbly at your side, just settle down in the comfy sitting area and bask in the ambient luxury. Private balconies are attached to three-quarters of the plush **suites,** which are done up in an ultrapleasant color scheme focused on rich blues and soft golds, along with coppery-brown wood tones. Each one has a walk-in closet, plush bedding, lighted dressing table with hair dryer, writing desk, and wonderful marble-covered bathrooms. The separate shower stall and long bathtub, along with double sinks, make these among the best loos at sea.

PUBLIC AREAS & ACTIVITIES The impressive **two-story show lounge** has tiered seating and lots of cozy clusters of chairs; while the **Bar,** just outside the show lounge's first level, can be a social hub, with a long bar, dance floor, and plenty of seating. The **Observation Lounge,** high on Deck 10 overlooking the bow, is a swell place to watch the scenery unfold through floor-to-ceiling windows. You'll find a radar screen, astronomical maps, binoculars, and reference books, and, during the day, a self-service coffee, tea, and juice bar. At the stern, the windowed **Panorama Lounge** also affords nifty sea views, continental breakfast and high tea here, while by night it becomes an intimate nightspot, with a pianist serenading dancers. The **Connoisseurs Corner** is a dark, and plush spot for cocktails with a walk-in humidor for cigar aficionados. There's also a small **casino,** a **card room** with felt-topped tables, a **boutique,** and a **pool bar.**

The **spa, gym,** and **hair salon** occupy much of Deck 10, and are spacious for a ship of this size. There's a separate workout room with exercise machines, plus a separate aerobics room. Unfortunately, jolting grass-green Astroturf covers the entirety of Decks 9 and 10 (a teak-colored synthetic flooring would have been a better choice). There's also a golf driving cage and shuffleboard.

DINING   In the **Restaurant,** the main dining room, a live trio plays romantic oldies on some nights, and guests are invited to take a spin around the small dance floor. Breakfast, lunch, and dinner are served here in high style, while a more casual buffet-style breakfast and lunch are served in the indoor/outdoor **La Terrazza.** Service is doting even in the casual restaurant; come evening, it has a superb Italian menu that focuses on different Italian regions throughout the cruise (reservations required). A third dining spot has special wine-pairing menus in an intimate setting.

Silver Cloud • Silver Wind

The Verdict

Big enough to have a two-story show lounge and several other entertainment outlets, and cozy enough that you'll feel like you practically have the vessel to yourself, these ships are an absolute dream.

Specifications — Avg. Starting Per Diem $508

Size (in tons)	17,400/16,800	Crew	212
Passengers (Double Occ.)	296	Passenger/Crew Ratio	1.4 to 1
Passenger/Space Ratio	57	Year Launched	1994/1995
Total Cabins/Veranda Cabins	148/110	Last Major Refurbishment	2013

Frommer's Ratings (Scale of 1–5)   ★★★★

Cabin Comfort & Amenities	4	Dining Options	4.5
Ship Cleanliness & Maintenance	4	Gym, Spa & Sports Facilities	4
Public Comfort/Space	4	Children's Facilities	N/A
Decor	4	Enjoyment Factor	5

THE SHIPS IN GENERAL

Super intimate yet large enough to have multiple entertainment venues, two restaurants, and lots of outdoor deck space, sister ships *Silver Cloud* and *Silver Wind* were built in the mid-1990s, just in time to get in on must-have ship fashions such as balconies. Both have good-sized spas and gyms, and a lovely observation lounge.

CABINS   Like their fleetmates, *Silver Wind* and *Silver Cloud* are **all-suite** ships, with balconies on more than three-quarters of the staterooms. All standard suites have sitting areas, roomy walk-in closets, bathtubs, vanities, comfy mattresses, as well as new furniture, carpeting, drapes, and bathroom fixtures and finishings (recent refits gave rainfall showerheads to the *Wind* but not *Cloud*). The top of the lot, the **Grand Suites,** have two bedrooms, two living rooms, two bathrooms, and a full-size Jacuzzi tub. Color schemes revolve around creamy beige fabrics and golden brown wood. *Silver Cloud* has swirled peachy-gray marble that covers bathrooms from head to toe, and though nice, the bathrooms on these ships don't hold a flame to the larger, simply decadent loos on the line's newer fleetmates.

PUBLIC AREAS & ACTIVITIES   Public areas are spacious and open. High tea is served by day in the windowed **Panorama Lounge,** which at night hosts piano entertainment. Magic and other acts are performed in the attractive two-story **show lounge,** and, on most nights, a dance band plays oldies or a DJ spins in the intimate and dimly lit adjacent bar. There's a small **casino,** too, plus **boutiques** where you can spend your winnings, including fine jewelry shops with the requisite gold-and-diamond-studded watches.

DINING   The formal, open-seating dining room, called the **Restaurant,** is delicately decorated in pale pink and gold, and elegant candlelit tables are set with heavy crystal glasses, chunky Christofle silverware, and doily-covered silver show plates. The indoor/outdoor **La Terrazza** cafe, where buffet-style breakfast and lunch are served, is transformed into a nightly spot for more casual evening dining, featuring a scrumptious Italian menu.

POOL, FITNESS, SPA & SPORTS FACILITIES   The *Silver Cloud* oceanview **gym** occupies a roomy space by itself on Deck 9, where an observation lounge used to be (oddly, it's not attached to the ship's interior, so one must go out on deck to enter). The new **spa** has five treatment rooms, a **beauty salon,** and fitness center (similar to the layout on *Shadow* and *Whisper*). Both ships have a pool and two hot tubs.

Silver Explorer • Silver Discoverer • Silver Galapagos

The Verdict

Although these three ships are different, they're more similar than not, delivering a luxury expedition product that aims to pair the inclusive amenities of a regular Silversea cruise (think butlers, Bulgari, and champagne) with the adventure of a true expedition cruise.

Specifications   Avg. Starting Per Diem $1,068

Size (in tons)	4,077-6,072	Crew	75-110
Passengers (Double Occ.)	100-132	Passenger/Crew Ratio	1.3 to 1
Passenger/Space Ratio	40.7-46	Year Launched	1989-1990
Total Cabins/Veranda Cabins	50-66/6-24	Last Major Refurbishment	2014

Frommer's Ratings (Scale of 1–5)   ★★★★

Cabin Comfort & Amenities	4	Dining Options	4
Ship Cleanliness & Maintenance	4	Gym, Spa & Sports Facilities	3.5
Public Comfort/Space	4	Children's Facilities	N/A
Decor	4	Enjoyment Factor	5

Setting sail in the spring of 2017, *Silver Muse* is Silversea's first new ship in nearly eight years. Carrying 596 guests, she's the largest ship ever constructed for the line, although, practically speaking, she's more like *Silver Spirit* 2.0, with a few tweaks here and there, and some stylistic exterior changes, like a redesigned bow profile.

From a guest standpoint, her basic layout is near identical to the Silver Spirit. **The Bar** will still grace the entrance lobby on Deck 5, albeit in a larger format. The **Panorama Lounge** is still located all the way aft, with its dance floor and indoor/outdoor seating, and an **Observation Lounge,** similar in decor to *Silver Spirit*, with soft earth tones and blonde woods, still overlooks the ship's bow (though we are disappointed to see the latter still lacks bathroom facilities).

The real differences between *Silver Muse* and *Silver Spirit* can be found in the ship's suites and dining options. Suites are larger on average, and the number of the ever-popular Silver Suites has been increased to meet demand. All suites will feature new modern decor

(think Seabourn crossed with Viking Ocean Cruises) with amenities like USB outlets and 55" interactive flat-panel television sets.

On the dining front, Silversea has done away with the main Restaurant, carving the Deck 4 space into two distinct venues: **Indochine** (Pan-Asian cuisine) and **Atlantide** (seafood focused fare). Eight different dining options will be featured on board, from the casual, cook-it-yourself fun of **Hot Rocks** by the pool deck to the intimate **Silver Note,** the rebranding of the Supper Club found on *Silver Spirit*. Despite the new name, Restaurant No. 8 will still offer small, tapas-style dishes along with wine and cocktail offerings and live music. Also returning, and rebranded, is **Le Dame by Relais & Chateaux,** better known on Silversea's existing vessels as Le Champagne. Ditto for **Kabuki;** it's *Silver Spirit*'s Seishin Asian-fusion restaurant, renamed.

Regardless of what the brand names are, *Silver Muse* looks fully capable to carry *Silver Spirit*'s legacy—and that of Silversea—into the next decade.

THE SHIPS IN GENERAL

All three ships are hand-me-downs that Silversea has invested heavily in in order to bring up to snuff. Of the three, *Silver Explorer*—first introduced in 2008 as *Prince Albert II* and renamed in 2011—is the most elaborate, with decor, wall treatments and soft furnishings that directly recall public areas found aboard *Silver Wind* and *Silver Spirit.* Colors run toward reds mixed with a variety of blonde and walnut woods, and public spaces are more varied, with an observation lounge, piano bar, and a dedicated briefing room. *Silver Discoverer,* introduced in 2014, favors nautical blue tones and white walls in staterooms and public rooms, while *Silver Galapagos* (also introduced in 2014) underwent two sets of extensive refurbishments to brighten her decor. Each is pushing three decades in age and carries the dents and dings to go with it, but Silversea has done a good job of bringing them up to standard.

CABINS If you like balcony cabins, prepare to pony up some significant cash, because all three of these ships have relatively few of them. While all three offer all-outside accommodations, only the top-of-the-line suites feature private balconies. *Silver Galapagos* and *Silver Discoverer* lead the way here with inviting, if not exactly large, **balcony staterooms** (a perk: You can get your laundry done gratis at the higher suite levels). *Silver Explorer* only has six **suites** with true step-out balconies. Across all three ships, standard Silversea amenities remain, from butler service to Bulgari or Ferragamo toiletries (the latter is not available on *Silver Galapagos* due to Ecuadorian regulations). Sadly, walls aboard *Silver Discover* are annoyingly thin: so thin, you can hear every bit of the conversation going on in the suite next door.

PUBLIC AREAS & ACTIVITIES Across all three ships, guests will tend to congregate in **The Theatre,** a dedicated, window-lined space with its own bar and theatre-style seating that is used for lectures, presentations, and the Daily Expedition Recap and Briefing held each evening. On *Silver Explorer* and *Silver Galapagos,* this is a separate room all of its own, while *Silver Discoverer* rolls it into **The Explorer Lounge,** which also doubles as the ship's primary watering hole, done in attractive shades of navy blue and white.

Silver Explorer and *Silver Galapagos* have some pretty fantastic **libraries,** adorned with nautical memorabilia and fitted with light woods and cabinetry. A handful of computer stations can be found here as well, though both vessels are rigged with stem-to-stern Wi-Fi. *Silver Discoverer* has only a makeshift **library.**

Both *Silver Explorer* and *Silver Galapagos* have dedicated **piano bars** and the **Connoisseur's Club,** a fully glassed-in enclave serving up fine cognacs and cigars. *Silver Explorer* also features an **Observation Lounge** all the way forward on Deck 6 that is popular on scenic cruising days (or as a quiet place to nap on sea days). More books can be found here, and a small continental breakfast is placed here for the early risers.

All three ships offer a small **Spa** and **Fitness Center;** they are basic, but get the job done.

DINING Although all three ships feature the same dining options, each ship uses them a little differently.

Aboard *Silver Explorer,* almost all meals are served in **The Restaurant,** a handsome, stern-mounted room with 180 degree views. Breakfast and lunch are buffet-style with cooked-to-order options, while dinners are a multi-course affair. Occasionally, **The Grill** will be open on deck when weather permits; we're happy to say we've successfully had a cooked-to-order hamburger and a beer outdoors while cruising the ice pack in the Arctic Circle.

Silver Discoverer holds buffet breakfast and lunch in the **Discoverer Lounge** on Deck 5, while **The Grill** (located just a bit further aft) provides outdoor dining when conditions allow. While the cuisine is good, decor in the Discoverer Lounge feels chintzy, a holdover from a past, pre-Silversea life. Dinners only are held in **The Restaurant,** which is a bit of a shame: It's the loveliest public room on board, and you'll want to take all your meals here.

Silver Galapagos offers buffet breakfast and lunch in **The Restaurant,** but no one ever shows up: Thanks to the temperate climate of the Galapagos, most guests enjoy breakfast and lunch outdoors at **The Grill,** where a menu of grilled-to-order specials rotates daily. Dinners are held each evening in The

Restaurant. Ecuadorian regulations stipulate that most of the ingredients hail from Ecuador. Translation: Some of these culinary creations may not be up to Western expectations (hint: Skip the beef dishes and go for the fish instead).

All three ships feature Silversea's signature **Hot Rocks** pool grill dining, where guests cook a variety of meats and seafoods atop their very own slab of superheated volcanic rock. Room service is also offered.

VIKING OCEAN CRUISES

www.vikingcruises.com. ℂ **855/338-4546.**

Pros

- **Very Inclusive:** Everything from Wi-Fi to specialty restaurants, beer and wine with lunch and dinner, and access to the thermal suite in the spa is included in the base rate.
- **Elegant Design:** The modern Scandinavian decor, with lots of light-colored wood and references to nature, is chic and understated, a rarity at sea.
- **One of the Best Spas at Sea:** Along with individual rooms (for paid treatments) a gorgeous thermal suite is open to all passengers at no extra charge, including hot and cold plunge pools, saunas, steam rooms, and a Snow Room filled with, you guessed it, snow.
- **Exceptional Italian Restaurant:** Manfredi's, the Italian trattoria on board, is one of the best of its kind at sea—and there's no upcharge to dine there.
- **Well-Designed Bathrooms:** Cabins have large showers and heated bathroom floors.
- **Verandas for Everyone:** All cabins are outsides with private balconies.

Cons

- **Slow Wi-Fi:** The Internet access may be complimentary, but as on many ships, it can get overwhelmed when the entire vessel tries to connect.
- **Sedate:** The music you'll be given is generally classical, and if you need to be constantly entertained, this isn't the ship for you. The Viking experience is a more cerebral one than is offered on other lines.

Overview

This company, well known for being the largest river cruise operator in Europe, christened its first ocean-going ship, *Viking Star,* in May 2015. An identical sister-ship, *Viking Sea,* set sail in 2016 and two more ships are slated for 2017. In the summer of 2016, *Travel + Leisure* readers named Viking the world's best oceangoing cruise line, marking the first time in 20 years that Crystal Cruises hasn't been awarded the top honor.

EXPERIENCE

Viking has translated its river-going product to the high seas incredibly smoothly. On board, you'll find a tranquil ambiance, with guests flocking to afternoon tea and the spa's thermal suite on sea days and making dinner the main event most evenings. Ashore, a selection of excursions is offered at no additional charge, while optional tours carry a per-person cost.

ROUTES

Viking primarily focuses on the Mediterranean, Western Europe, and the Baltics, with special emphasis on Scandinavian itineraries that depart from Bergen, Norway—the homeport for *Viking Star* and *Viking Sea*. In the fall of 2016, *Viking Star* set sail on Viking's first-ever transatlantic crossing, where she operated the line's first Canada and New England, East Coast, and Caribbean itineraries.

PASSENGERS

Most passengers are older American couples, largely in their 60s and 70s with an additional number in their 50s and 80s. These cruisers tend to be well traveled, and many passengers choose the line because they have cruised on the line's river ships.

DINING

Viking offers a striking variety of cuisines on board, offering a mix of regional specialties from the areas being visited and North American favorites. Among the best dishes are the Norwegian fare, like the homemade waffles and the split-pea soup. Both are served up in **Mamsen's,** named for Chairman Torstein Hagen's beloved mother (that's her nickname); its largely her recipes you'll be enjoying when you sit down at this casual venue.

Full sit-down meals are served in **The Restaurant** for breakfast, lunch and dinner, while more casual fare is on offer in the **World Café** on Deck 7. Interestingly for a cruise ship, the World Café features an open-galley arrangement that lets guests see the behind-the-scenes food preparation. The **Pool Grill** also offers casual, pool-grill fare during the afternoon. We personally couldn't resist the Pancho Villa Burger, which still ranks as the best burger we've had on a ship outside of Carnival's Guy Fieri grill.

Each ship also has two specialty restaurants: the Italian-inspired **Manfredi's;** and the intimate **Chef's Table** that is designed to accommodate just a handful of guests at a single time, all dining on a set menu. The afternoon tea, which takes place in the **Wintergarden,** is the best at sea outside of those offered by Cunard. Guests choose from 19 varieties of tea, which are served alongside multi-tiered trays of finger sandwiches and miniature desserts.

ACTIVITIES

The focus on board is to be as all-inclusive as possible and most days the only activity with a fee attached is the wine tasting class. Other onboard activities are low key on sea days, with shuffleboard and bocce up on deck and trivia, knitting, chess, and dance classes inside. There are also cooking demonstrations in the polished **Kitchen Table** cooking school, and academic-style enrichment lectures, often (but not always) on topics related to the ports.

Less structured play time takes place in the ship's multiple **pools,** including our fave: the infinity pool on the aft deck, a first at sea. On sunny days, these spots fill up. However, on cold, grey, or rainy sea days, the most popular spot to congregate is the **spa** (for more, see p. 279).

CHILDREN'S PROGRAMS

There are no children's facilities at all on Viking Ocean Cruises, and the minimum age to sail is 16.

ENTERTAINMENT

Entertainment tries to be higher-brow. Sometimes it's a pianist, sometimes chamber music or an impromptu aria. Later at night, the most popular shows include a Rat Pack tribute show by one of the young resident vocalists. Stage shows, though, are not Viking's strong suit. Our show aboard *Viking Sea*—a tribute to, surprise surprise, ABBA—was embarrassingly amateur, and doesn't fit at all with Viking's brand of graceful elegance. But, the line is barely over a year old; it's safe to assume programming will be ironed out in time.

SERVICE

The service varies from efficient and polished to still-getting-up-to-speed, but it is always warm and friendly—just like the line's river cruises. The ship also has a complimentary self-serve laundry rooms that feature free-of-charge detergent. Viking recommends $14 USD per person, per day for gratuities.

Viking Star • Viking Sky

The Verdict

Viking hit it out of the park with these handsome vessels. They bring Viking's river cruise-style amenities and Scandinavian heritage to the oceans of the world, a contemporary interpretation of cruising's glory days.

Specifications

Avg. Starting Per Diem $425

Size (in tons)	47,800	Crew	545
Passengers (Double Occ.)	928	Passenger/Crew Ratio	1.7 to 1
Passenger/Space Ratio	51.5	Year Launched	2015/2016
Total Cabins/Veranda Cabins	465/465	Last Major Refurbishment	N/A

Frommer's Ratings (Scale of 1–5)

★★★★★

Cabin Comfort & Amenities	5	Dining Options	4.5
Ship Cleanliness & Maintenance	5	Gym, Spa & Sports Facilities	5
Public Comfort/Space	5	Children's Facilities	N/A
Decor	5	Enjoyment Factor	5

THE SHIPS IN GENERAL

Sometimes being the "new kid on the block" has its perks. Viking had the leisure to study what the other cruise lines were doing…and improve upon it substantially. The 930-guest *Viking Star* (2015 debut) and her sister *Viking Sea* (2016) brought back a number of classic features that had gradually started to disappear off many contemporary cruise ships, foremost among them: space. Too many cruise lines have been sacrificing open air decks in favor of cramming more cabins aboard each vessel. Not Viking. On these ships you'll find such delights as wraparound promenade decks, glass Magrodome-covered pools, and plenty of floor-to-ceiling windows. To this they added smartly designed common areas with few-to-no points of congestion; and snappy, chic Scandinavian decor (it echoes the design and textures found aboard the line's river cruise vessels). We also like how Viking placed the main dining room high up on the ship, with floor-to-ceiling windows that can completely open when conditions allow. That same feature was applied to the World Café, the ship's casual dining venue. There's nothing like having breakfast in Bergen, Norway in a massive, open-air restaurant at sea.

These ships do practically everything right. Elevators are quick and responsive, and signage is well-labeled. The LivNordic Spa offers the best thermal suite we've seen outside of Cunard's *Queen Mary 2,* with the major difference being that Viking provides its version completely free of charge. Furniture is soft and yielding; clearly, someone tested every piece of furniture before committing it to the ship. Books on polar exploration, Norwegian history and travel are placed throughout the ship for guests to enjoy, and Viking even produces a gorgeous print brochure that you can take home, detailing the ship's multi-million-dollar collection of artwork. In staterooms, artwork created by school children at one of Viking's sponsored schools in China grace the walls, a truly lovely touch.

On our first voyage on board *Viking Sea,* we'd been on for mere minutes when one guest exclaimed, "That's it! I'm never leaving this ship." We feel the same way.

Viking Sky and *Viking Sun* will launch in 2017, and should be more or less identical to *Viking Star* and *Viking Sea.* A fifth and sixth ship, as yet unnamed, will set sail in 2018 and 2020, respectively.

CABINS   Aboard Viking's oceangoing ships, all **staterooms** have private balconies, a lovely perk. There are essentially five categories of staterooms and suites to choose from and as you move up in category, Viking adds more amenities: The larger, more expensive staterooms and suites get to pick their excursions and dining options earlier (online, using My Viking Journey), and are able to embark the vessel earlier.

The most basic option (which aren't very basic at all) are the **Veranda Suites** which feature an embarkation time of 11am, with stateroom access at 3pm. Shore excursions can be pre-booked 60 days in advance, but Veranda Suites don't include guaranteed specialty dining reservations. That doesn't mean you can't get them; it just means that you're not *guaranteed* to. **Deluxe Verandas** are essentially the same as Veranda Suites, but rooms are available an hour earlier, at 2pm, shore excursions can be booked at 67 days out, and these rooms have the addition of an in-suite coffee maker, and a mini-bar that's replenished daily. Guests in these staterooms are also guaranteed reservations in the ship's specialty restaurants.

Jumping up a few levels, **Penthouse Suites** include the best of everything on board, with room access at 11am, shore excursion reservations at 97 days out, guaranteed restaurant reservations and complimentary pressing, dry-cleaning, laundry, and shoe-shine service.

PUBLIC AREAS & ACTIVITIES The ships are a big part of experience, with a soothing Scandinavian design that displays a thoughtfulness seldom seen in modern shipbuilding. Materials, fabrics and furniture are all top-of-the-line, and considerable thought has been put into passenger flow. Lounges are rarely crowded. Sightlines in the **main theater** are unobstructed and the outdoor **movie screen,** mounted near the midships pool, has a clever perk: Guests tune into the soundtrack with wireless Bose noise-cancelling headphones that keep that rich, movie-quality sound while allowing other guests to use the pool deck without having to hear the movie, too.

The heart of these ships is known as **The Living Room**—a casual, couch-lined space surrounding the three-story high atrium, with a grand staircase, living garden, and massive two-story LED screen that showcases itinerary-specific images of upcoming ports of call.

Tucked away on Deck 2 is one of our favorite areas: **Torshavn,** a sweet little lounge with seating clustered around a decently sized dance floor. A nightclub with live music, its bar serves up a wide array of drinks—including the largest selection of vintage Armagnacs at sea. We road-tested a 1965 one that set us back a cool $79 for four centiliters (about 1.3 fl. oz.) and now we're hooked on rare, hard-to-find Armagnac. Thanks, Viking.

Live music can also be found at the **Explorer's Lounge.** With two-story forward-facing windows and upper and lower observation areas (including an outdoor viewpoint that spans the width of the ship), this area is one of the most popular spots during the day—though you may find, that the best spots get taken early and are so comfortable some guests simply nap in them.

You'll feel like you've arrived in Cruise Heaven when you see the **pool** and **spa** offerings aboard these two ships. A midship **pool** is covered by a retractable glass magrodome roof, while an infinity pool (a first at sea) is cantilevered out over the stern. Kudos to Viking here for doing away with the ugly-as-sin standard hot tubs found on most cruise ships; the hot tubs aboard *Viking Star* and *Viking Sea* are rectangular rather than circular. Have you ever seen guests stop and admire the hot tubs on board a cruise ship? You will here.

The design sets the **spa** apart as well: Inside the dressing rooms, you use your room key to secure your things in a locker—a first at sea, but a design that needs some work since, when the ship is moving quickly, the unlocked doors swing back and forth.

The thermal suite, which is complimentary to all of the ship's passengers, regardless of whether they book a treatment, is designed around the Swedish love/ethos of alternating between hot and cold temperatures. The hot tub is adjacent to the hydrotherapy pool, and two showers—one with pressure point spouts, and the other with a wooden bucket that dumps cold water on you to cool your body down. There are also an aromatic steam room, heated ceramic lounge chairs, and the highlight of the thermal suite—a real, honest-to-gosh Snow Room. This small room has a bench and ample snow to stand in as well as icicles hanging from the ceiling.

Next door to the thermal suite is an ample **gym** with complimentary classes every morning, including Pilates, Zumba, and yoga.

DINING   The main dining room is open for breakfast, lunch, and dinner with floor-to-ceiling glass windows that can actually open to the adjacent promenade deck when conditions allow, to let fresh air in. Food here is well executed, service a bit less so, but friendly nonetheless.

The same open-window feature is featured at the buffet **World Café** (breakfast, lunch and dinner and decidedly classier than most shipboard buffets). One highlight: The chef picks up local ingredients in port on some days and serves them here. At the center of the World Café is a completely open galley space that lets you watch the chefs while they work.

At lunchtime, right outside the cafe doors, is the **Pool Grill** (see p. 276 for more). Forward in the Explorer's Lounge, **Mamsen's** serves Norwegian waffles for breakfast and smørbrød (sandwiches) and cakes at lunch. At night, the best split-pea soup we've ever had is served—but only after 10pm.

The specialty restaurants, which come with no additional charge, offer up a wide array of cuisines. The galley-style **Chef's Table** serves a set five-course tasting menu that changes every nine days. **Manfredi's** is a home run. Curiously named for the founder of luxury line Silversea (Manfredi Lefebvre d'Ovidio), everything here is perfectly executed, from the house-made pasta to the soups, salads, and grilled meats.

THE CRUISE LINES: RIVER CRUISING

Unless you've been trapped under a rock recently—or missed *Downton Abbey*—chances are good you've seen one of **Viking River Cruises** snazzy television ads. They're snappy, exciting, and surprisingly do an accurate job of showcasing what a river cruise through Europe is like.

But river cruising is neither new nor confined to Europe: Lines like **CroisiEurope** and **Uniworld** among others have been around for decades; and river cruising is now a tourism staple in many parts of the world from China and Southeast Asia to the United States, Egypt, the Amazon and, recently, India.

There are literally dozens and dozens of river cruise lines located around the world. But when most people think of river cruising, they picture sailing down the gorgeous Blue Danube. Spoiler alert: It's really more of a muddy-brown color; chalk that up to a bit of wishful thinking on the part of Mr. Johann Strauss.

What's not wishful thinking, however, is how enjoyable this type of vacation really is. The ships take you on the arteries that linked communities for centuries, meaning when you disembark you're in the heart of a small town or city (often an important one), rather than having to get in from a (sometimes) distant port to see the sights, as you would on an ocean cruise.

Much like most ocean cruises, service is faultless on river cruises. It also comes with an added bonus: Many river cruise staff actually hail from the countries you'll be sailing through, providing the unique opportunity to get the inside scoop on your ports of call from those who actually call them home.

Another HUGE plus to river cruising? Stability. If you're prone to seasickness, these are the cruises for you: Rivers tend to be far calmer than oceans, and even a slight swaying of the ship is uncommon.

River cruises are also a heckuva lot nicer than they were a generation ago. In the early days of river cruising, staterooms were small and cramped, and public spaces uninspiring. All that has changed; today's river cruise ships are modern works of art, each with its own distinctive look, feel, personality and features. Bright,

If everything about river cruising sounds all rosy and bright, it usually is. However, river cruises operate in the margins for most of the year: Some bridges have just inches of clearance between the top of your ship and the bottom of the bridge deck, and some rivers are so shallow that there may be less than a foot of water beneath the keel, or bottom, of your riverboat. So when there's too much rain—or too little—things come to a screeching halt in a hurry. This was most evident during the spring of 2013, when record flooding in Europe cancelled dozens of cruises and inundated Passau, Germany, with the worst flooding that town has ever seen. But you don't have to have record floods to have an issue: If your ship is 2 inches too tall to pass under a bridge because it's rained more than expected, things are going to get interesting.

Fortunately, that's the exception and not the rule: The vast majority of river cruises will go off without a hitch. When problems do happen, all the major river cruise lines have contingency plans they put into place. These can range from keeping the ship docked and bussing guests to important locations, to doing a "ship-swap" where guests will disembark one river cruise ship, bus to another company-owned ship and continue around the impassable stretch; or, as a worst-case scenario, continue the rest of the river cruise by land-based coaches and hotels—at the cruise line's expense.

open and spacious, they share little with their early predecessors Today, the vast majority of fleets are less than a decade old, and those that are have likely been substantially refitted thanks to the fact that the river cruise season in Europe typically shuts down between January and early March.

With more rivers, itineraries, and ships to choose from than ever before, the joke in the industry is that there are only two kinds of travelers: Those who have river cruised, and those who are going to.

COSTS

River cruises typically start at a higher price point than ocean cruises, but they also carry a greater number of inclusions. Beer, wine and soft drinks are served free of charge at lunch and dinner, and nearly all excursions ashore are provided *gratis*. Tauck even takes things one step further, providing guests with complimentary Euro coins in order to take advantage of Europe's ubiquitous pay toilets while on tour.

That being said, some lines are significantly cheaper than Tauck—we're looking at you Emerald Waterways (see p. 297) and Grand Circle (p. 300). As well, world events can have a huge impact on the cost of cruises, both on the river and on the ocean. The 2016 attacks on Belgium and France seriously depressed the costs of cruises on the Seine, and in other parts of Europe.

THE DIFFERENCE FROM LINE TO LINE

When it comes to most river cruising, everyone plays in the same sandbox. By which we mean: Due to low hanging bridges, shallow waters, and narrow locks, river cruise ships can only be so wide and so tall. So most are exactly the same size, which means each individual cruise line has to customize their onboard offerings, and ratchet up their style, in order to differentiate themselves from the competition.

And one dirty little secret about shore excursions: Most of the cruise lines share the same pool of guides, going with whichever one is free that day. So a tour on a very expensive Uniworld Cruise could easily have the same guide and commentary as one on middle-of-the road Viking, or cheapie Emerald. There are some exceptions (Tauck and Grand Circle notably create very different shore excursions), but not many.

And now, without further ado, the major river cruise lines (please note that we review American Cruise Lines on p. 335 and Un-Cruises on p. 356 as both have river boats and ocean-going vessels).

A-ROSA

www.arosacruises.com. ✆ **855/552-7672.**

After a decade of successful operations in Europe aimed primarily at German-speaking clientele, A-ROSA reached out to the North American market in 2013. The line kept their product offering essentially the same, but added English-language tours and announcements on three vessels. The cruises remain a quintessentially European experience, which works for most (but not all).

Pros

o **All Inclusive:** The line throws everything but the kitchen sink into its cruise fares.

o **Uncommon Onboard Features:** Passengers can indulge in the onboard swimming pool, enjoy a number of onboard fitness options, or spend some quality time in the larger-than-average shipboard spa.

o **Emphasis on Wellness:** Hiking, kayaking, and cycling tours ashore are offered in many ports of call.

o **Shorter Options:** A-ROSA offers a number of four-and-five-night river cruises for those who want a quick jaunt along the Danube.

Cons

o **Limited Departures:** Compared to other river cruise lines that have literally dozens of ships sailing back and forth every week, finding a sailing date on A-ROSA might be tricky thanks to the line's somewhat limited sailing schedule.

o **No Long Voyages:** If you're in the market for a 14 or 21-day long river cruise, you won't find it here. The majority of sailings are a week long.

Frommer's Ratings (Scale of 1–5) ★★★★

Cabin comfort & amenities	4	Public spaces	4
Decor	4	Dining	4
Fitness, spa & pool	4.5	Service	4
Family-friendly	4	Entertainment	4

Overview

If you think all river cruises are designed for well-coiffured senior citizens with graying hairlines, think again: A-ROSA distinguishes itself with pouty, red lips and a red rose splashed across the bow and appeals to active adults who are as interested in challenging themselves with long cycles or kayak trips as they are in soaking up sun on deck as the shore inches by. An all-inclusive experience, A-ROSA throws nearly everything into the cruise fare, from drinks to transfers and gratuities. Special offers are frequent, so it's always a good idea to check out the line's website for discounts; in the past, A-ROSA has also offered special deals for solo cruisers which eliminated the dreaded single supplement fare.

EXPERIENCE

The A-ROSA experience is aimed squarely at adult travelers who are still professionally employed, active, and curious about the world. The onboard experience caters to this, with cycling tours, a larger-than-average fitness center, enhanced wellness options, and healthy culinary choices. But that doesn't mean it's not relaxing: If you just want to lounge in a deck chair, or bathe in the onboard swimming pool, nobody will scold you.

A-ROSA is entirely all-inclusive, so you can keep your money in your wallet while on board. Enrichment options are plentiful, and guides and onboard staff display a high level of knowledge about the places you'll be seeing on your journey. Despite the fact that you're sailing on a ship operated by a European cruise line and staffed with, you guessed it, Europeans, A-ROSA's English-speaking itineraries are offered exclusively to North American guests. However, that doesn't stop the line from providing an immersive experience: Expect European and Mediterranean-influenced cuisine on board, coupled with local beers, wines and spirits.

PASSENGERS

Your fellow guests will be active and tend to skew a bit younger than guests on other cruise lines thanks to A-ROSA's attractive wellness options.

ROUTES

Constantly expanding with each passing year, A-ROSA offers voyages along the Danube, Main, Moselle, Rhine, and France's Rhône and Saône rivers. Themed voyages are also offered, like special Holiday voyages through Europe's Christmas Markets.

DINING

Open-seating dining is standard. Buffets (common in Germany) are emphasized more than on other river cruise lines, but even these are decidedly better than you might expect. Food offerings are of an unusually high quality, and healthy, Mediterranean-style fare is emphasized. If you're looking for a burger and fries, though, you won't find it on A-ROSA.

ACTIVITIES

Organized entertainment isn't nearly as elaborate as on oceangoing ships, but entertainers are brought on in most ports. Frankly, most guests prefer socializing over cocktails to organized song-and-dance routines.

CHILDREN'S PROGRAMS

A-ROSA will accept passengers under the age of 18, provided they share a stateroom with an adult (no putting the kids in their own stateroom on these voyages.) There aren't any specific provisions or programs designed specifically for children, but older teenagers travelling with their parents who have an interest in Europe or history should do all right.

Not that A-ROSA doesn't want kids on their ships; the line routinely offers some great family savings, with special promotions that allow children between the ages of 2-15 to sail for free when they're accompanied by a paying adult.

SERVICE

Expect a high level of service on A-ROSA ships from the primarily German crew. Note that while service is exemplary, it's also personable: There's no stuffiness here.

FLEET

A-ROSA boasts a fleet of ten river cruise vessels, three of which are dedicated to the English-speaking market: *A-ROSA Flora, A-ROSA Silva,* and *A-ROSA Stella.* Each is capable of carrying between 174 and 186 guests.

AMAWATERWAYS

www.amawaterways.com. © **800/626-0126.**

Founded in 2002 by industry vets Rudi Schreiner, Kristin Karst and the late Jimmy Murphy, AmaWaterways now boasts a fleet of 18 elegant, contemporary river cruise ships sailing the waters of Europe, with an additional four ships operating itineraries through Cambodia, Vietnam, Burma, and Africa's Chobe River. The line likes to say, "Welcome to the Ama Family" in their marketing, but it's more than just PR-speak: AmaWaterways is the big river cruise line that still operates like a fledgling cruise line. Schreiner and Karst still work the company's booth at trade shows, and AmaWaterways crews are some of the friendliest on the rivers. Contemporary and stylish, they're the river cruising equivalent of a cool, hip hotel gone to sea—but with the amenities and the talent to back it all up.

Pros

○ **Food & Wine:** AmaWaterways has several dining venues on each of its vessels with an emphasis on high-quality ingredients and unique recipes. The company also brings an impressive selection of wines on board and has a large portfolio of wine-themed cruises.

○ **Least Itinerary Disruptions:** AmaWaterways' president and co-owner Rudi Schreiner is one of the forefathers of modern river cruising. Schreiner's insider knowledge of inland waterways and his careful deployment of vessels means that AmaWaterways usually experiences the least (or no) disruptions on its river sailings when water levels are acting up.

o **Customer Service:** With a strong emphasis on providing top-notch customer service, AmaWaterways often makes decisions that are not necessarily in its best financial interest (think generous refunds when things go wrong) to ensure that customers go home with a positive impression.

o **Worldwide Itineraries:** AmaWaterways offers dozens of river cruise itineraries throughout Europe, along Africa's Chobe River, Myanmar's Irrawaddy, and the Mekong River in Vietnam and Cambodia.

o **Dual Balconies:** Can't decide which kind of balcony stateroom you want? AmaWaterways' newest vessels offer both French and full Step-Out balconies in many stateroom categories.

Cons

o **Playing It Safe:** Because AmaWaterways doesn't like to take risks on emerging and less predictable rivers (such as the notoriously shallow Elbe River in Germany), it generally sails on more run-of-the-mill rivers, at least in Europe.

o **Few Suites:** Those who like their staterooms spacious might find it difficult to book one on AmaWaterways: Older vessels, like *AmaLyra,* have but three on board.

o **European Electrical Outlets:** Not really a con, but more of a quantifier: Many AmaWaterways ships have only two-prong, European-style electrical outlets. That means you'll need to bring an adapter.

Frommer's Ratings (Scale of 1–5)   ★★★★ ½

Cabin comfort & amenities	4	Public spaces	4
Decor	4	Dining	5
Fitness, spa & pool	5	Service	5
Family-friendly	4	Entertainment	5

Overview

Imagine a well-staffed boutique European hotel. Now place it in a river and send it downstream: That's AmaWaterways. The line isn't the cheapest game in town—it's on a par with Uniworld (p. 314) and Tauck—but what you get for that money is a surprising level of inclusiveness, supplemented by a courteous and friendly young staff that are eager to please and a better-than-the-norm variety of culinary offerings.

EXPERIENCE

AmaWaterways includes all meals on board, at least one excursion in each port, and beer and wine with lunch and dinner. The excursions are nicely tailored for the clientele: "Active Walkers" outings are for guests who want to cover more ground; Gentle Walkers are for guests who want to linger over monuments and important sights, or for those who need more time to get from place to place; and a "Late Starter" group for those who like to sleep in. The latter is particularly rare in an industry dominated by excursions that can depart as early as eight a.m.

We'd say the line, with these well-executed excursions, is trying to find that balance between taking very good care of its passengers while also giving them the free time to explore on their own. Thus, if you want a fully inclusive river cruising experience, AmaWaterways may not be the line for you—they aren't about hand-holding the same way a company like Tauck, for instance, is.

The company does a great job catering to special groups too, which can be anything from a full-ship charter, or just a larger group traveling together, so if you're looking for a line to host a meeting, special event or reunion, this is a forte of theirs.

They also have bikes and biking excursions available to guests (AmaWaterways recently partnered up with active bike-and-hike outfit Backroads) an attractive option for more fitness-focused travelers. And the company is pushing more fervently into the family market by, for instance, having partnered with Adventures by Disney.

For those to whom it's critically important to be connected, AmaWaterways invests a lot of money into its onboard free Wi-Fi—it's still a bit spotty in between ports but it seems to be getting more reliable.

PASSENGERS

AmaWaterways' passengers are often seasoned travelers who are both affluent and well-educated. With a strong biking program, there tends to be a more active contingency on board. And though the average age range is 50 years old and up, the partnership with Disney has been such a HUGE success these specialty cruises may carry a passenger load that is one-third children. Fellow guests tend to hail primarily from the United States, with a healthy dose of Canadians and Australians intermingled (AmaWaterways is marketed in Australia under the brand name APT, and the Aussies *love* to river cruise).

ROUTES

AmaWaterways specializes in European river cruising, with 20 different itineraries offered along the Danube, Rhine, and Main; France's Seine, Moselle, Garonne, and Dordogne; and Portugal's Douro River, to name a few. Outside of Europe, the company offers voyages along Myanmar's Irrawaddy River; Vietnam and Cambodia's Mekong; and Africa's Chobe River.

DINING

AmaWaterways was among the pioneers of creating multiple dining experiences on board its river cruise vessels, including one of its venues that is now a signature, AmaWaterways' reservation-only Chef's Table dinner venue at the aft of the vessel, now available on the *AmaCerto, AmaReina, AmaSonata, AmaPrima, AmaVerde,* and *AmaBella.* These truly gourmet five-course dinners are served in an intimate restaurant at the aft of the vessel, with a view into the glass-encased kitchen where the chef and his/her team are hard at work. Dining at the Chef's Table restaurant is available to all passengers on board—they need to make sure to reserve a table as it's a smaller venue.

Weather permitting, there is also an alfresco grilling venue for casual lunches on the Sun Deck on the *AmaVista, AmaSerena, AmaSonata, Ama-Reina, AmaPrima, AmaCerto,* and *AmaVida.* This is a popular spot for serving up grilled sausages and sauerkraut, with a mug of beer to wash it down.

The *AmaVista, AmaSerena, AmaSonata, AmaReina, AmaPrima,* and *Ama-Certo* also feature charming private dining wine rooms adjacent to the main dining room for larger groups of about 10 that would like to sit together.

What kind of food should you expect from the main restaurant? There will be a decked-out breakfast and lunch buffet featuring an assortment of American standards—anything from eggs benedict and waffles for breakfast, to grilled ham and cheese sandwiches and familiar pasta dishes for lunch—alongside regional fare, with the European soups being particularly delicious. The multi-course dinner in the main restaurant is accented by impressive details such as fresh, in-house-baked bread with multiple butters and spreads and mains that sometimes have an Asian influence (it's a nice counterbalance to the European dishes, though they tend to be top-quality, too).

Lighter fare is also available in the lounge during meal times, for those who would prefer a small soup or salad and a bit of solitude.

AmaWaterways even lets you take the culinary experience ashore, with specially designed shore excursions that can include cooking school cooking classes, visits to specialty shops, or even a trip to the local *biergarten.*

ACTIVITIES

While the emphasis on AmaWaterways cruises is more often on giving passengers options for things to see and do off the ship, during the occasional longer daytime sailings, there will be informative lectures and/or demonstrations on board that highlight the theme or region of the cruise. For instance, there might be a wine lecture and tasting during a Douro River sailing, or an art history discussion on the Rhone and Saone rivers. AmaWaterways also offers a fair amount of themed sailings such as wine-themed, beer-themed or art-themed cruises, during which there will be enhanced lectures by an expert or experts and/or tastings relevant to the theme.

CHILDREN'S PROGRAMS

AmaWaterways leads the way when it comes to children's programs on the rivers of Europe. In 2016, the company partnered with Disney-affiliated travel company, Adventures by Disney, to offer distinct sailings designed exclusively for families. Some are in the summer, some in the winter during Europe's Christmas Markets season. On these partnership voyages, kids are treated to special menus, excursions, and special activities like Disney movie nights, chess lessons on a giant board, karaoke, kid-friendly cooking classes and more. Mickey and Minnie don't drop by as they do on Disney Cruise Line, but in every other way these sailings are the best choices on the rivers for families (and multi-generational families).

SERVICE

AmaWaterways places a lot of attention on hiring, training and retaining its crew members. The river cruise operator has done particularly well in recruiting charismatic and charming cruise directors—they have some of the best in the biz. The crew tend to be very hands-on and accommodating to passengers' personal requests.

When it comes to gratuities on European sailings, the line currently recommends about 12€ per person, per day, for the cruise staff; and 3€ per person, per day, for your cruise director. The onboard currency is the euro (€).

FLEET

AmaWaterways operates a total of 18 company-owned ships on the rivers of Europe, with four additional ships located on rivers outside of Europe. These ships aren't company-owned, but are operated in conjunction with local partners. The oldest European ship, *AmaDagio,* entered service in 2006, while their newest, *AmaKristina,* will set sail in 2017.

AVALON WATERWAYS

www.avalonwaterways.com. © **877/797-8791** or 907/465-3941.

Being owned by the tour operator company Globus, Avalon has solid tour operating skills backing it. You can expect well-executed excursions and VIP access to popular venues where Globus has long-held connections (don't be surprised if you skip the line at tourist hot-spots like the Eiffel Tower in Paris or at the Rijksmuseum in Amsterdam).

Avalon is also big on flexibility. In 2012, the company introduced what it calls the Avalon Choice program, the idea being to offer passengers the ability to personalize their cruise a bit more, for instance with more dining options (such as additional venues and room service), bedding options (such as choice of pillows and bed configurations), and sightseeing options (more on those below). With MyAvalon, the company's online service center, passengers can pre-register for their cruise, pre-select included excursions, choose and pre-pay for optional excursions, set bed configuration preferences (joined or separated beds), and select special celebration packages.

Avalon is definitely making a run at that middle-of-the-road segment of the river cruise market, travelers who don't want or can't afford the more luxury lines but who also like the idea of sailing on sparkling new ships with some of the latest amenities. If that sounds like you, read on.

Pros

- **Resources:** Avalon Waterways benefits from the fact that it is owned by a large travel company which translates into great value for Avalon passengers. Also, should any itinerary changes or complications arise, a global operations team is on-hand to create a quick fix.
- **Views:** Avalon's trademark floor-to-ceiling panoramic sliding glass doors in the staterooms on its 10 Suite Ship class of vessels offer sweeping views of the passing scenery, further enhanced by the fact that stateroom beds on Avalon ships face outwards towards said sweeping views.

- **The Suite Life:** With over 60 suites measuring 200 square feet or more, Avalon gives you more room to spread out than other river cruise lines.

Cons

- **Lacking Character:** While competitors have created stronger identities (Uniworld is flashy, Viking is Scandinavian-modern), Avalon ships are lacking more defining characteristics, making it hard to distinguish between the Avalon ships themselves as well as what makes Avalon different or better than others.

- **Not Great for Eaters with Issues:** Avalon states in its pre-cruise documentation that "dietary requirements cannot be guaranteed on our vacations." If you have allergies or intolerances, you're better off booking elsewhere.

- **Less Inclusive:** Unlike many competitors, Avalon charges for most drinks.

Frommer's Ratings (Scale of 1–5) ★★★★

Cabin comfort & amenities	5	Public spaces	4
Decor	4	Dining	4
Fitness, spa & pool	5	Service	5
Family-friendly	2	Entertainment	5

Overview

There's something very straightforward and no-fuss about Avalon. If you like clean, contemporary design, well-executed itineraries and solid cuisine, Avalon Waterways is probably a good choice for you. The line's undisputed hallmark lies in their Suite Ships, which prioritized personal space over passenger capacity. Avalon's ships never feel crowded as a result, and guests spend more time relaxing in their suites. Avalon also offers upscale amenities like marble bathrooms and L'Occitane bath products, minus the pretention.

Avalon's primary strength, though lies in their itineraries, which are comprehensive in Europe (with options that range from just a few days to several weeks in length) and include sails to exotic locations like the Amazon or Vietnam's Mekong River.

EXPERIENCE

Avalon once stated that their new Panorama Suites were so big, you could fit 100 cruisers into the room and still have space left over, presumably to breathe. While we don't recommend doing that, we do have to agree: On average, Avalon's staterooms and suites are larger than the competition. They're also quite nice, with beds that have been designed to face the floor-to-ceiling windows that can fully open to let the sights and sounds of Europe in.

Those compliments aside, Avalon isn't as inclusive as other river cruise lines are: Yes, Wi-Fi access is complementary throughout the day (with the corollary that it may not work) but bottled water will cost you extra, as will beer and wine with lunch. (And bringing your own wine on board will nail you with a corkage charge.) Beer and wine are provided gratis with dinners on board, while soft drinks are free of charge at lunch. All this doesn't make the Avalon experience a bad one, just less inclusive than most.

PASSENGERS

Avalon passengers span a wide age range. According to the company, 22% of passenger are 69-plus; 24% are ages 59 to 68; 21% are in the 50 to 58 range; 20% are ages 34 to 49; and 13% are between 19 and 33. They're predominantly American, with a handful of Canadians thrown into the mix. You might find the odd Aussie or Brit looking very, very lost; Avalon is primarily marketed at a North American audience.

ROUTES

Avalon's greatest strength lies in its varied itineraries around the globe. Those looking to add on a short European river cruise onto a more extensive land tour will be happy to know that the company operates European river voyages that are as short as four or five days, while travelers looking to extend their voyages can easily find itineraries lasting two or more weeks.

While Avalon's primary focus is Europe (indeed, all of the line's company-owned ships sail within the borders of the Continent), the line works closely with their partners to provide voyages to the Mekong River (Cambodia & Vietnam); the Irrawaddy River (Myanmar, formerly known as Burma); and ocean cruises around the Galapagos Islands off the coast of Ecuador.

DINING

Most river cruise ships don't include room service, and if they do, it's only for the top-of-the-line suites. Avalon, however, will serve you a tasty complimentary continental breakfast in your room, if you so choose. Otherwise, the line offers a varied breakfast in the main dining room for both early and late-risers (everything from smoothies to made-to-order eggs). Lunch offers up buffet-style food stations, with the possibility to dine in the Open Air Bistro on ships that are equipped with it. Dinners are typically four or five courses prepared with a blend of European and North American tastes in mind, and a Late Snack is served around 10:30p.m.

While Avalon's food is of a high quality, the company's relatively hardline stance on dietary requirements is unusual in an industry famous for bending over backwards to accommodate guests. The company says it will make its best effort to accommodate dietary requirements, but precedes that with the disclaimer that it makes no guarantees. If you have severe allergies, we'd recommend taking a cruise line that can offer better peace of mind.

ACTIVITIES

During sailings, Avalon embraces the cultural immersion aspect of travel with lectures by experts in various relevant fields—for instance, a World War II historian comes on board during the company's Paris-to-Normandy sailing on the Seine River to give an in-depth talk about the D-Day landings passengers will visit on the itinerary. There are also food and wine tastings to give guests the opportunity to try regional cheeses, charcuterie and wine varietals you've never heard of—especially the German ones! There is also the occasional arts, craftwork or cooking demonstration, with the latter always ending up being a highlight.

The line offers a series of complimentary shore excursions in every port of call. Passengers can see and pre-select their excursions through the MyAvalon program, an online registration option that allows passenger to pre-order their tours, whether they're included or not (the company has a minimum of one included tour at each port). Avalon offers "Essential Sightseeing" guided tours, which hit the blockbuster sites; "Leisurely Sightseeing" guided tours, for those that want to go at a gentler pace; and "Independent" exploration options for those who want to explore on their own.

Each of Avalon's European-based river cruise ships offers complimentary bicycles for guests to use while ashore. This is a great value, particularly for those who enjoy touring independently or those who are interested in keeping physically fit on their voyage. All those delicious desserts and local wines can really pack on the calories...

CHILDREN'S PROGRAMS

While Avalon doesn't cater directly to kids, the line does welcome them at certain times of the year with special voyages designed specifically for families travelling together. These are typically offered during the summer months to coincide with school breaks, but some shoulder-season voyages are also usually available. Throughout the year kids above age 8 are welcomed, provided they share a stateroom with a full-fare paying adult.

ENTERTAINMENT

Onboard entertainment is typically confined to a pianist who performs each evening in the main lounge, or local acts that are brought on board in select ports of call. Later in the evening, a DJ might take over to get the dance floor moving, and the dance floor can get pretty hopping, depending on the passengers. In general, though, the entertainment can be hit or miss.

SERVICE

There is rarely slack service on river cruises and Avalon is no exception. The Avalon crews find that delicate balance of being helpful but not overly so. Avalon recommends gratuities of 12€ per guest, per day, for the ship's crew, and 4€ per guest, per day, for the ship's program director. Gratuities can also be pre-paid at the time of booking, or settled on board by cash or credit card.

FLEET

Avalon's fleet consists of 18 river cruise ships, the vast majority of which were built after the 2011 introduction of *Avalon Panorama*. *Avalon Imagery II* and *Avalon Passion* are the line's two newest vessels, having debuted in 2016.

CROISIEUROPE

www.croisieuroperivercruises.com. ☏ **800/768-7232.**

There's nothing fancy about a CroisiEurope cruise, though some of the line's latest ships have noticeably ramped up the design and interior decor that, until recently, tended to be stuck in the mid-1990's. Staterooms are smaller on average than many competing lines and amenities are nothing to write home about, but CroisiEurope leaves the completion in the dust when it comes to diverse itineraries, and price. Few lines can touch CroisiEurope's affordability, with voyages in the under-$1,000 range. Once exclusively a European product, Croisie has turned its focus on the U.S. market in the past few years, making this the line to take if you're looking for a true cultural immersion cruise at a price that will make you think it's a typo.

Pros

o **Value:** CroisiEurope is the price leader in Europe, and voyages can often go for a fraction of the line's more well-known counterparts.

o **Original Rivers/Itineraries:** One way that CroisiEurope is trying to better compete in the dog-eat-dog river cruise industry is by charting new and unique rivers in Europe, including recently the Loire River. It also often goes further along certain popular rivers than other lines, such as further up along the Seine River.

o **Prime Docking Spaces:** When you've been around for four decades, you're awarded certain privileges. CroisiEurope is one of the few lines able to dock right in the heart of ports like Strasbourg, France, while other lines are stuck miles away in nearby Kehl, Germany.

o **European Experience:** CroisiEurope attracts a mix of Europeans and English speakers and the onboard experience has a decidedly French flavor.

Cons

o **Spartan Accommodations:** Staterooms on CroisiEurope's older ships are below industry standard, and many still have separated Pullman-style bunks that cannot be made into a queen-sized bed.

o **Frumpy Decor:** The line's older ships, which are the majority of their vessels, have a curious 1993 vibe going on. We're talking looks that went out of style around the time Jazzercise did.

o **Uneven Inclusions:** Some voyages include all beverages, like beer, wine, and premium spirits, in the cost of the cruise. Other voyages include comparatively little. Check before booking.

o **Lack of Choice:** CroisiEurope famously has traditionally offered only one entree option for dinner (though it's working to add more choices), and it has a single dining venue per boat. It also does not have the same variety of shore excursions and activities as other lines.

o **Melting Pot:** As mentioned above, while some might love the fact that they're sailing with people from France, Germany, the U.K., and Spain, others might find the announcements in multiple languages annoying and the inability to necessarily converse or connect with the other passengers limiting.

Frommer's Ratings (Scale of 1–5)   ★★★

Cabin comfort & amenities	3	Public spaces	4
Decor	3	Dining	3
Fitness, spa & pool	N/A	Service	3
Family-friendly	4	Entertainment	3

Overview

This is river cruising Euro-style, which is a different experience than river cruising built for Americans by American companies. Meals are European in taste and delivery, service is of a European standard, and entertainment has a European flair. You have to be up for the different way things are done across the pond.

CroisiEurope is run by three generations of the Schmitter family who founded the Strasbourg, France-based company in 1976. The Schmitters know river cruising and the European waterways well. And they also know they have some changes to make if they are going to continue to successfully court the U.S. market.

Since turning its focus more seriously towards the American market, CroisiEurope has been building and renovating ships that are more in line with the higher-quality interiors and amenities that Americans are coming to expect from river cruises. The company starting building a new generation of vessels that kicked off in 2014 with the launch of the 84-passenger *Lafayette on the Rhine*—this new class of CroisiEurope ships feature sleek and modern interiors with colorful accents such as Missoni-printed blankets strewn across the beds and funky chandeliers. The new generation includes the 96-passenger *Loire Princesse* that launched in 2015 and the 80-passenger *Elbe Princesse* launched in the spring of 2016. CroisiEurope is also investing in offering greater variety in its onboard meals and giving passengers more choice in general, such as with some new included excursions.

EXPERIENCE

CroisiEurope's main competitive selling points are lower prices and finding new and often unique port stops. The company is able to keep its pricing below standard U.S. market rates because all of its operations are done in-house (as opposed to contracting things such as food and beverage services, or nautical operations, out to third parties). And it's able to sail new waterways because of a recent idea to construct vessels powered by paddlewheels that allows them to have lower drafts and thus sail in shallower waters—the company has already launched its small, sleek paddle-wheelers on France's Loire River and Germany's Elbe River, and has plans to do the same on other rivers that it is still keeping hush-hush. Croisie also operates ocean-going vessels.

PASSENGERS

Perhaps because of its more accessible pricing, CroisiEurope tends to attract a younger clientele, passengers in their 40s and 50s with the average age being about 50 years old. As mentioned, it's an international mix, with about 20% coming from North America, 30% being English speakers from elsewhere (such as Brits and Australians), and 50% European passengers, mostly French and German speaking.

ROUTES

Itineraries are so varied that simply choosing where to go could be problematic. The line offers sailings along the Danube, the Rhine, Main, Moselle and Elbe, along with voyages throughout France (both barge and river cruises),

Portugal and Spain, Italy, and Vietnam and Cambodia. CroisiEurope also offers "hybrid" voyages that explore the coast of Europe along with its inland waterways; these sail to Croatia, Greece, Italy and Montenegro.

DINING

CroisiEurope vessels have one main dining room, which serves French and European cuisine. Breakfast is served buffet style, and lunch and dinner are served as sit-down, three-course meals paired with complimentary wine. In fact, all beverages including water, juice, coffee, tea, beer and wine are complimentary. The food has been notoriously so-so compared to other river cruise lines, but it was improved greatly on our last cruise (it tasted like French home cooking, which is a compliment in our eyes). The company traditionally offered one entrée at lunch and dinner, compared to the overabundance of options on other river cruise lines, but that, too, is changing on some of its ships.

ACTIVITIES

CroisiEurope offers lectures and demonstrations during its cruises. When groups that speak different languages are traveling on the same vessel lectures will be provided according to language (so a Spanish speaking group will be offered a presentation or demonstration on a given topic at one time, and an English speaking group will be offered a lecture at another time). As for shore excursions: The line offers walking excursions alongside more active options like cycling tours.

CHILDREN'S PROGRAMS

CroisiEurope allows children as young as infant and toddlers on board but does not provide cribs or any special equipment to cater to young children, so passengers are encouraged to bring their own. The company offers a discounted cruise price for kids under 10, and also has several family-friendly cruises during the summer months—there are kid friendly menus on these sailings, and active excursions such as hiking trips.

ENTERTAINMENT

Evening entertainment is offered in the form of local entertainers that board at select ports of call, or from the ship's onboard pianist. Like other river cruises, entertainment options are limited compared to ocean cruises.

SERVICE

Service aboard the ships of CroisiEurope is friendly and personable, if not polished. In hotel terms, it's closer to a family-run B&B than the Ritz-Carlton—and that's perfectly fine. Smiles are genuine, and the local crews are exceedingly helpful.

FLEET

The CroisiEurope fleet consists of 45 ships, six of which are dedicated river barges sailing the canals of France. The company's newest vessel is the *Elbe Princesse,* which uses a unique paddlewheel propulsion system to send her down the shallow Elbe on voyages from Berlin.

CRYSTAL RIVER CRUISES

www.crystalcruises.com. ✆ **888/722-0021.**

The newest player in the river market is one of ocean cruising's most established luxury lines. In late 2015, Crystal Cruises announced it would spin off an entirely new river cruise division to bring its brand of all-inclusive luxury river cruises to the waterways of Europe. Launching in the summer of 2016 with a repurposed vessel purchased from another operator and renamed *Crystal Mozart,* things will really get going for Crystal during the summer of 2017, when the line takes delivery of its first purpose-built river vessels.

These won't be any ordinary ships; Crystal plans to come out of the gate swinging. To that end, Crystal's river cruise ships—*Crystal Debussy, Crystal Bach, Crystal Ravel,* and *Crystal Mahler*—will have the largest suites on the rivers of Europe, along with ocean-liner style design and layout. They'll also boast some uncommon features, from complimentary Nordic walking sticks to GPS-enabled whisper touring guides, electrically assisted bicycles, and, apparently, jet skis and kayaks. Where you'll go jet skiing in Europe is something of a mystery, but Crystal is planning to offer it.

Pros

- **Huge WOW Factor:** Crystal isn't cutting corners or skimping on costs for their first river cruise ships. Expect the best-of-the-best at every turn, both on board and ashore.
- **Gorgeous Ships:** If Crystal's river cruise vessels turn out to be half as good as they're anticipated to be, the line will have a tremendous success on its hands.

Cons

- **Potential Growing Pains:** Crystal is entering service into a market crowded with well-established competitors. The line may experience a few hiccups here and there as it finds its footing. Then again, perhaps it will come in and be the juggernaut it seems. Time will tell.

Frommer's Ratings (Scale of 1–5)　　★★★★★

Cabin comfort & amenities	5	Public spaces	5
Decor	5	Dining	5
Fitness, spa & pool	4	Service	4.5
Family-friendly	2	Entertainment	4

Overview

Crystal Cruises brings its finely tuned luxury product from the high seas to the rivers of Europe in one of the industry's most exciting and unexpected announcements. For Crystal loyalists, sailing with Crystal River Cruises is a no-brainer—and no doubt the line hopes that will work in reverse, as legions of river cruisers try ocean cruising for the first time. The line's entry into service hadn't yet begun at press time, but we're optimistic about what Crystal has to offer river cruisers.

FLEET

The Crystal river cruise fleet debuted in 2016 with the extensively refurbished *Mozart.* A repurposed ship that originally sailed for German-operator Peter Deilmann, Crystal made substantial changes to the vessel that brought her up to the line's high standards of decor and quality. In 2017, the line will begin adding its first purpose-built ships: *Crystal Bach, Crystal Mahler, Crystal Ravel,* and *Crystal Debussey.*

EMERALD WATERWAYS

www.emeraldwaterways.com. ✆ **855/222-3214.**

One of the newest river cruise lines, Emerald Waterways began operations in Europe in 2014. An offshoot of Australia-based tour and river cruise company Scenic (see p. 306), Emerald operates a fleet of custom-built ships designed exclusively for the line, which offer many of the luxuries found on the far more expensive ships of Scenic. Targeting the price conscious consumer that still wants a high degree of quality, Emerald Waterways has grown up quickly: The line now offers voyages throughout Europe, including France and Portugal's Douro Rivers. Recently, Emerald Waterways began offering cruises throughout Southeast Asia, with sailings to Cambodia, Vietnam and Myanmar (Burma). In Australia, the line is (confusingly) marketed as Evergreen Tours.

Pros

- **Cool Contemporary Ships:** So new they still have that "new ship smell," Emerald Waterways' fleet offers some whiz-bang features, like infinity-style indoor/outdoor pool on the line's "Star Ships"—it even converts into a movie theater at night.

- **Affordable Luxury:** Snappy decor, good service, with gratuities and airport transfers included—we couldn't be happier that Emerald is keeping their fares low (because they could be charging more).

- **Great Itineraries:** The line has taken a page from parent company Scenic's playbook here, developing some truly interesting intriguing throughout Europe and Southeast Asia.

- **Fun Entertainment:** Maybe it's because there are Australians on board, but this line has more of a late-night scene than you'll find on some other river ships.

Cons

- **Quirky Stateroom Design:** Aboard *Emerald Sky* and *Emerald Star,* bathroom entrances are positioned right beside the bed instead of near the stateroom entrance. It's not an issue for couples, but friends travelling together may find this close proximity uncomfortable.

- **The Food Is Just Meh:** The cuisine is not what you'll be bragging to friends about. Still, it's plentiful and filling.

- **Awkward Menu System:** Only two menus are provided per table in the ship's dining room, which leads to some interesting games of "pass-the-menu" at larger tables.

Cabin comfort & amenities	4	Public spaces	4
Decor	4	Dining	3
Fitness, spa & pool	5	Service	4
Family-friendly	1	Entertainment	4

Overview

The Emerald Waterways experience is inclusive but unpretentious. It's a great choice for couples looking for an affordable river cruise that doesn't skimp on inclusions or little luxuries. Sure, you won't find the butlers and over-the-top technical doodads that grace Emerald's upscale sister, Scenic, but a good number of Scenic's most popular features have worked their way down to Emerald. Ships are bright, crisp and clean, and service is polished.

EXPERIENCE

This sister company to fancier Scenic brings river cruisers a value-focused proposition: Fares include free loaner bikes, pre-cruise hotel nights, transfers, wine, beer and soft drinks with meals, unlimited coffee drinks, port charges, and Internet access (you can borrow an iPad from reception if you didn't bring your own). Also included are all gratuities (which in effect means that Emerald is more inclusive than competitors such as Viking River Cruises). Best of all the lines EmeraldPLUS excursions are part of the deal, and many are designed to get away from the typical tourist experience ashore. On our sailing, that meant going in small groups to a local family home in Bratislava, Slovakia, where we learned how to make traditional baked goodies. It was one of the most entertaining and educational shore excursions we've ever had.

The line also stands out in terms of design innovation; the five nearly identical "Star Ships" boasting a modern decor (the lounge may have an ebony bar that lights up like at a club) and the standout feature of a glass-enclosed swimming pool that converts into a movie theater at night (thanks to a telescoping pool floor that comes flush with the surrounding decking at night). There's innovation in terms of cabins as well: The line's Panorama Balcony Suites have a glass wall that converts to a French balcony at the push of a button.

The ships are friendly, social and offer more nightlife than you'll find on some competing lines—which may very much be due to the fact there are likely to be fun-loving Australians and Kiwis among passengers on board.

PASSENGERS

Your fellow guests will be mostly Australian, Canadian and UK travelers, with a handful of Americans thrown into the mix to create a very international experience. The average age on Emerald Waterways tends to skew about a decade younger than the competition, so expect to see many working professionals in their 40s and 50s on board in addition to active retirees.

ROUTES

The Danube and the Rhine serve as the line's main stomping grounds, with voyages between Nuremberg and Budapest and Basel and Amsterdam being among the most popular. Emerald also operates voyages throughout France, with the new *Sensations of France* itinerary sailing for eight days between Lyon and Arles. Portugal's Douro River is also offered as an eight-day "cruise only" voyage or as a longer overland journey that includes a stay in Lisbon.

Southeast Asia is the newest destination for the company, which offers voyages along the Mekong between Cambodia and Vietnam, and the Myanmar's Irrawaddy River. The latter is a 10-day tour operating between Mandalay and Yangon, or reverse.

DINING

Breakfast and lunch are buffet-style, with hot and cold options; dinner is from a four-course menu with Continental and regional specialties, and always available items such as steak, grilled chicken and salmon. In a bit of an oddity, during the evening cocktail hour in the lounge, the chef proudly presents his featured dish of the day: a plate of, say, venison, passed around for everyone to see and smell. Preparations are okay (you won't go hungry), if not particularly memorable. Vegetarians may be disappointed by the daily veggie entrée, which gets short shrift in the creativity department.

In building new ships, Emerald had the opportunity to adopt features already popular on competitors, so as an alternative to the main restaurant you can do a light breakfast or lunch from a buffet selection on The Terrace and eat al fresco while catching forward-facing views from the ship's bow (just like on Viking's "Longships"). Room service is only available in top-suite accommodations, and even then is limited to continental breakfast. House wine and beer and soda are served at lunch and dinner, but if you order drinks during cocktail hour or other times you pay extra for them.

ACTIVITIES

Ashore, Emerald Waterways offers plenty of choice. Complimentary tours are offered in every port of call, and the line further caters to guests by offering special EmeraldACTIVE tours for those who want to stay fit and see the sights at the same time.

Each Emerald Waterways ship in Europe features a small fleet of onboard bicycles that can be checked out free of charge. You can use these to cycle through town or to head out into the countryside on the many cycle paths that border the rivers.

Other activity offerings are of the low-key variety. There are not guest lecturers on board, but we like the fact that Emerald has members of its crew do sessions where they talk from their personnel experiences—on a Lower Danube sailing, for example, the cruise director, who grew up in Romania during Communist times, talked quite candidly about what that experience was really like. The wheelhouse is always open for those interested in navigation and locks and hanging out with the officers.

CHILDREN'S PROGRAMS

None. Children under 12 years of age are not allowed to sail with the line, except on specially designated Christmas Markets river cruises—and even then, special advance permission is required.

ENTERTAINMENT

With party-loving Aussies and Kiwis on board there is a bit of a late-night disco scene. Folks hit the dance floor to a nostalgic playlist that includes the Village People and Gloria Gaynor. When the DJ plays Olivia Newton John, the crowd goes wild. After 10 pm, the crew serves snacks to keep everyone energized. Some nights there are also movies (see Activities above). Early evening a keyboardist plays tunes during cocktail hour. Not to be missed is the crew show, held one evening of the sailing. We've all seen the waiter who thinks he can sing, but on one cruise we listened to a hotel director who sang like a professional, and laughed hysterically as several members of the crew performed skits that were well rehearsed and were also well delivered. Folk troupes and other performers come on board, such as a Bavarian band on Rhine and Upper Danube itineraries, and exuberant dancers in Serbia.

SERVICE

The international crew (from various countries in Eastern Europe, Asia and elsewhere) tries hard, is very efficient and is for the most part quite friendly. Tips are included in the fare.

FLEET

The Emerald Waterways fleet consists of *Emerald Sky* (2014), *Emerald Star* (2014), *Emerald Dawn* (2015), *Emerald Sun* (2015), *Emerald Liberté* (2017), *Emerald Radiance* (2017). Two chartered vessels (*Mekong Navigator,* 2014; *Irrawaddy Explorer,* 2014) operate the line's cruises in Southeast Asia.

GRAND CIRCLE TOURS

www.gct.com. ℃ **800/221-2610.**

Once you realize that Grand Circle Tours (GCG) began life in 1958 as an off-shoot of the American Association of Retired People (AARP), you'll begin to understand more of the Grand Circle ethos. The company, which has been operating river cruises since 1997, caters almost entirely to the 55-plus set and GCT is all-American, all the time (the company won't even mail a brochure outside of the U.S.). That means travelling with American guests, eating largely American food, and taking tours that cater to "American interests and perspectives." That's either going to float your boat...or not.

Still, with its affordable pricing and attractive solo-traveler offers, GCT has amassed legions of loyal travelers (known as Inner Circle members) that come back to sail with the line again, and again, and again.

Pros

o **Affordable Pricing:** GCT's pricing, and frequent special offers, make for cruises that cost substantially less than most other lines.

o **Enrichment:** Prior to the cruise guests can expect to receive a lot of detailed information regarding destinations. Onboard guests get daily enrichment lectures from local experts in history along with various cooking demonstrations and even the occasional folk dancing troupe.

- **Solo-Traveler-Friendly:** GCL has a large supply of small cabins designed and priced for one; it also provides a roommate matching service for those sailings where solo cabins aren't available (solos bunk with another passenger of the same gender and pay the double passenger rate without a singles supplement.). Best of all: It offers reduced-rate single-supplements for those who want their own larger room.

Cons

- **Homogenous Guest Profile:** More of a quantifier than a con. Your fellow guests will be exclusively from the United States, and all over 50 years of age. If you like a diverse passenger base, this isn't it.
- **Uneven Fleet:** The GCT fleet features ships that are very different from each other, and all may not offer the same amenities. It's important to thoroughly research your itinerary and ship first before you book.
- **Small Staterooms:** Some ships in the GCT fleet, like the 1991-built *River Allegro,* feature staterooms that are a crunchy 120 square feet. Ouch!

Frommer's Ratings (Scale of 1–5) ★★★★

Cabin comfort & amenities	3	Public spaces	3
Decor	3	Dining	2
Fitness, spa & pool	2	Service	4
Family-friendly	N/A	Entertainment	5

Overview

Designed exclusively for American retirees, GCT is a basic, entry-level river cruise line that manages to provide a good number of inclusions in their fares; and unusual shore excursions (see "Activities"). Prices include beer, wine and soft drinks with lunch and dinner, and can even include economy-class flights to and from Europe. Crews are mostly European, and provide a good level of service. Mindful of the line's elderly clientele, it's not unusual to see a GCT crewmember assist passengers up the gangway and onto busses, or go out of their way to ensure that guests are comfortable and well taken care of.

EXPERIENCE

GCT features a fleet of six very diverse European river cruise ships. Comfortable but not luxurious, they feature accommodations that range in size from a snug 120 square feet to over 200 square feet. Beds are mostly Pullman-style berths that fold up to create two small sofa-style seats during the day. A few accommodations feature either French or step-out balconies, while most staterooms have simple window views. Bathrooms are plain-looking, but clean, efficient, and do what they were designed to do.

Shore excursions are where GCT really shines and have a strong educational component (see "Activities"). Because of the average age of GCT's guests, expect fewer walking tours and more bus tours.

PASSENGERS

Your fellow guests will all be from the United States, and almost all will be over 50 years of age, though GCT doesn't prohibit younger folks from booking.

ROUTES

Europe is the main area of focus for GCT, with numerous itineraries of varying lengths that ply the Danube, Elbe, Main, Moselle, and Rhine rivers. Voyages to France, including Paris, Burgundy, and Provence, are also offered. In the winter months, GCT runs special "Christmas Market" river cruises that highlight the famous outdoor markets that line the squares of Germany, Austria, and other countries from late November to mid-December.

DINING

Everyone eats in the main dining room at the same time daily. Snack options are sparse—though there may be cookies sometimes at the coffee station. Breakfast and lunch are a combination of a decent buffet spread and made-to-order entrees. Regional specialties are available and for those who get homesick you can always order a burger and fries. Dinner is a full-service, sit-down affair. The food is solidly tasty, but is more basic comfort-food than anything cutting edge. Select wine, beer, and soft drinks are complimentary during lunch and dinner, but cost extra out of the dining room. There is a coffee, cappuccino, and tea machine available 24 hours. Special requests are an area where the line seems to struggle, particularly when it comes to vegans (entrees arrive late and can be tasteless). There is no room service.

ACTIVITIES

Grand Circle places great emphasis on immersive travel as a form of enrichment. The line takes great pride in not "sugar coating" destinations by embracing cultural differences and controversial topics. Included tours go beyond the norm. On signature excursions, for instance, you visit local families in their homes or stop by a school to meet with local kids.

Personalization is another thing that sets Grand Circle apart. To enhance the onboard and destination experience, guests are divided into color-coded groups of no more than 45 persons and assigned to an onboard, English-speaking Program Director. These affable directors are chosen for their knowledge of history, geography, politics and local culture. So they act as tours guides, but they also are true hosts, there to make sure no guest gets lost in the crowd: In addition to answering questions about the destination, he or she also is the go-to person for everything from special diets to extra care for passengers with physical limitations. The relationships starts a week before departure when an e-mail is sent to each guest from their Program Director, discussing the itinerary along with important reminders and offering to answer any questions.

CHILDREN'S PROGRAMS

None. While GCT permits kids over the age of 13 to travel with adults, we don't recommend the line for kids. GCT offers no multi-generational river cruise programs.

ENTERTAINMENT

The emphasis is on enrichment lectures and demonstrations from local experts brought on board. Most guests turn in early, but there is evening musical entertainment provided by a solo keyboard singer/musician. The musical stylings are akin to Bill Murray's character from *Saturday Night Live,* "Nick The Lounge Singer."

SERVICE

Service on board is good, and designed to meet the needs of the line's older clientele in a friendly, genuine manner. We particularly appreciate the Program Director initiative on these ships (see above).

FLEET

Grand Circle owns and operates 12 river ships (though one in Russia was parked for 2016), as well as several ocean-going vessels. The fleet is older, but well maintained. Decor is best described as dated but comfortable with dark woods, colors, and heavy rich fabrics—think 1990's Marriott hotel.

Not all the ships have elevators (the ones that don't are a difficult choice for those passengers who have a hard time with stairs).

PANDAW RIVER EXPEDITIONS

www.pandaw.com. ✆ **800/729-2651.**

In 1998, Pandaw Founder Paul Strachan acquired the *Pandaw,* a steamboat built in Scotland in 1947. He renovated the vessel and operated it up and down Myanmar's Irrawaddy River for several years, and ultimately sold it. In 2001, the company built its first company-owned riverboat, which was almost an exact replica of the original *Pandaw.* Today, Pandaw River Expeditions operates a fleet of 15 such vessels, all colonial-style, three-deck ships with wraparound balconies, despite the fact that others have emerged on the Southeast Asia river cruise scene with larger vessels, indoor hallways, sprawling suites, spas, and swimming pools.

Pros

o **Experience:** Scotsman Paul Strachan, founder of Pandaw, has been operating ships up and down the Irrawaddy River for 20 years. Strachan knows the region and its rivers better than anyone else and because of that is constantly pushing the envelope with new itineraries that explore ever more exotic and uncharted inland waterways of Asia.

o **A Focus on the Destination:** Strachan himself will admit that he is no innovator. The ships the company is building today are much the same as the ships it built 20 years ago—classic, steamboat style vessels. Instead the company is focused on immersive destination experiences and creating a fun and engaging atmosphere on board.

Cons

o **No Frills:** Unlike other river cruise operators that are trying to bring a version of luxury, European-style river cruising to Southeast Asia, Pandaw is all about keeping Southeast Asian river cruising true to its original self. The company is not big on fancy public spaces or amenities such as pools on board.

Frommer's Ratings (Scale of 1–5) ★★★

Cabin comfort & amenities	3	Public spaces	3
Decor	3	Dining	3
Fitness, spa & pool	N/A	Service	4
Family-friendly	N/A	Entertainment	3

Overview

If you prefer destination knowledge over marble bathrooms, if you're more interested in authentic local experiences than in creature comforts, you'll probably fit in perfectly with the Pandaw product and with the other, laid-back passengers on board.

THE EXPERIENCE

Owner Strachan is focused on remaining true to a Southeast Asia river cruising model that fosters a more social atmosphere by drawing people out of their staterooms and into the public spaces. The wraparound balconies encourage guests to mingle and also facilitate the movement of fresh air as the vessels sail, something Strachan has said is both a comfort and safety issue, offering stability to vessels that have more shallow drafts.

While the design of the Pandaw vessels hasn't changed much in 20 years, recently the company has been pushing the envelope with new river cruise routes (see below under "Routes").

PASSENGERS

From its Scottish roots to its strong Australian and British customer base, you can expect to hear a lot of accents throughout the Pandaw experience. Whether sailing Myanmar's Irrawaddy River or the Mekong River through Vietnam and Cambodia, you're likely to be among a more adventurous bunch of more seasoned travelers than you'll find on Europe's rivers. According to Strachan, these are travelers who are "not coming for the pool or the Jacuzzi." Which is a good thing because Pandaw doesn't have those things.

ROUTES

Last year, Pandaw introduced a Mekong River sailing through Laos on the newly constructed, 20-passenger *Laos Pandaw*. Additionally, Pandaw recently introduced a new Halong Bay and Red River itinerary that inaugurated a new route along Vietnam's Red River.

Recently, Pandaw also unveiled a new itinerary that includes all six countries through which the Mekong River flows: Vietnam, Cambodia, Thailand, Laos, Myanmar, and China. Getting permission to sail across the border into China has proven the biggest challenge in achieving that goal.

Pandaw has been testing the waters beyond Southeast Asia, as well, having chartered some vessels in India recently and with the hopes of perhaps introducing its own vessels there in the near future.

DINING

Pandaw seeks to introduce its passengers to the wide variety of tastes and flavors of Southeast Asia on board its ships. Breakfast is served as a buffet and during lunch there is a soup, salad and dessert buffet but the main course is served to the table. Dinner is waiter service only. Passengers will have the opportunity to taste some of the more exotic and spicy foods Asia is known for or will be offered European alternatives. There are always vegetarian options, as well. Pandaw also prides itself on offering diners the choice of eating inside or outside (it's dining room windows also open up) so that they don't always feel cooped up in an air-conditioned spaced and removed from the fresh air and scenery. Only at night does it shut its dining room windows entirely to avoid unwanted visitors, aka insects.

ACTIVITIES

Daily excursions are in essence the whole reason for taking a Pandaw cruise, to witness the people and the traditions along the river. Pandaw offers daily excursions (at least one or two) that could be a walking trip through a village or to a unique landmark, or something a bit more adventurous such as a horse cart ride or a cycling trip—Pandaw recently brought mountain bikes on board its vessels for use on such excursions or for passengers to take out on their own. The bikes are available to book for $25 per person, and Pandaw crew will advise guests on the best routes to follow and if needed a member of the crew will accompany the guests on their cycling trip. Some excursions take place via motorboat to remote river jungles or fishing villages. In larger ports, a more comprehensive tour will be offered, such as in Phnom Penh, Cambodia or in Mandalay, Myanmar. There are also usually opportunities to visit various charity programs Pandaw is involved with in the region, as well as to head to a local market with the ship's chef.

On board, the guide will host daily briefings. In addition to these cultural discussions, there are also cooking demonstrations, fruit carving lessons (Southeast Asians are particularly adept at this art), and themed movie nights such as playing *L'Indochine* while sailing in Vietnam or the 1984 drama *The Killing Fields* in Cambodia. Otherwise, it's a good book on the sun deck or in the lounge, and/or a good drink at the bar.

CHILDREN'S PROGRAM

Pandaw welcomes children on board and has begun offering a handful of sailings designed specifically for families. On designated family departures, kids under age four travel for free if they sleep on a cot in the same cabin as their adult companions, and children ages four to 18 travel at a discounted rate. To accommodate younger passengers, Pandaw will feature more kid-friendly cuisine, will have cooking lessons on board, offer more active excursions, have bike tours at larger port calls, and will feature movie nights on board.

ENTERTAINMENT

During each expedition there will be at least one cultural performance on board. The shows might be an elaborate puppet show, as is custom in Myanmar, or a traditional folk dance performance. Otherwise, it's colorful conversations and cocktails with your fellow passengers.

SERVICE

Pandaw has been doing this for a long time. The company is intimately involved with the region, knows its people and has a solid system for training crew members. They execute extremely polite and courteous service, and it's all done with bright smiles on their faces. Many of the crew have been with Pandaw for a long time, so they know what they're doing, they know the destination and they provide comfort in their expertise.

THE FLEET

As mentioned above, the Pandaw fleet is pretty consistent in style and design. They are divided into two, relatively simple groups: Pandaw's K Class of vessels, which are the company's two-deck ships, and its P Class of vessels, which are its three-deck ships. There are 15 vessels in the Pandaw fleet, nine in its K Class and six in its P Class. The vessels sail in Myanmar, Vietnam, Cambodia, Laos and China, and Pandaw also partners on charter cruises in India, and on the Peruvian and Brazilian Amazon.

All Pandaw vessels follow the same format. For the most part, all the staterooms are the same size. They do not have private balconies but instead open up to the common wrap-around balconies not unlike those on steamboats like the American Queen in the U.S. And similarly, the shared balcony space is meant to contribute to a more social atmosphere, drawing passengers out of their cabins and into an area where they can interact with other passengers on board. There is one dining room, one bar and lounge, and an outdoor lounge and seating area. And that about does it. Simple is as simple does.

There is tons of wood everywhere, the walls, the furniture, the floors, everything is done in wood, which actually keeps the vessels looking pristine. They are no-fuss but in a way that works and doesn't feel dingy—they remind us of nice, homey local B&Bs that are simple but charming. You realize on ships like this just how few amenities we really need to have a good vacation.

PRE- & POST-CRUISE STAYS

Pandaw does offer a variety of pre- and post-cruise options. It can be a 1-night stay on board a Pandaw vessel in the Burmese capital of Yangon (with its recent explosion in tourism since opening up more to the rest of the world in 2011, Myanmar is notoriously short on hotel rooms), or a three-night extension on Thailand's River Kwai, made famous by the 1957 British World War II film, *The Bridge on the River Kwai*. There are also extensions available in Vietnam's Ho Chi Minh City, and Cambodia's Siem Reap and Phnom Penh.

SCENIC

www.scenic.com. © **855/517-1200.**

Despite arriving a smidge late to the river cruising party (2008), the Australian company Scenic is rapidly making a name for itself as a strong player at the high end of the market, with its all-inclusive pricing (meaning gratuities and alcoholic beverages, too), sleek ship interiors, and high-tech enhancements.

Scenic now sports a fleet of five-star, all-inclusive luxury river cruise ships that are among the most technologically advanced afloat. If you like your tech toys and your little luxuries, this is the river cruise for you.

Pros

o **Innovative:** Scenic has really pushed the envelope in terms of river cruise-enhancing technologies and services. They hand out custom-made GPS devices to passengers for wireless touring, loan electric-assist bikes to utilize ashore, have a very high tech in-room entertainment system, and dedicated butler services for all.

o **All-Inclusive:** Throwing in everything but the kitchen sink, there are almost no additional cost items on a Scenic cruise.

o **Adventurous Itineraries:** Scenic started life in Australia, and the Aussies love to travel. While Scenic offers short, weeklong itineraries, the line really shines with its multi-week river cruise journeys.

Cons

o **High Cost of Admission:** Everyone wants to stay at the Ritz-Carlton; few want to pay the price. Even in the costly world of river cruising, Scenic's voyages lean towards the expensive end of the scale.

Frommer's Ratings (Scale of 1–5)   ★★★★ ½

Cabin comfort & amenities	5	Public spaces	4
Decor	5	Dining	5
Fitness, spa & pool	4	Service	5
Family-friendly	3	Entertainment	4

Overview

With a fleet of 17 river cruise ships and counting, Scenic's Space Ships (so-called for their relatively high passenger-to-space ratios) offer a decidedly luxurious river cruise experience that is geared towards active individuals who are curious about the world.

Scenic offers numerous river cruise itineraries in Europe, with voyages that sail the Danube, Douro, Main, Moselle, Rhine, Rhone, and Seine rivers. Cruises along Russia's Volga River from Moscow to St. Petersburg are offered aboard the 112-guest *Scenic Tsar,* while Southeast Asia cruises sail the waters Cambodia and Vietnam along the Mekong River, and in Myanmar (Burma) along the Irrawaddy

EXPERIENCE

One of Scenic's strongest selling points is to what lengths it has gone to ensure that there are plenty of options for dining, sightseeing and engaging both on board and off the vessels.

For one, since Scenic began operating river cruises in 2008, the company has had six dining options available to passengers on it vessels (more on that in the dining section below). Scenic also has a Free Choice excursion program, which means that in addition to the blockbuster sightseeing tours it offers in each major port call, there are usually one or two additional excursions on offer that might be a bit off the beaten path or might have a unique theme, such as the Szechenyi Thermal Bath in Budapest or shopping with a chef in central Vienna's open-air food market, Naschmarkt.

And as competition heats up on the rivers, Scenic is continuing to add service options, including butler service, which covers early-morning coffee and tea, shoeshine service and help with making on-shore arrangements such as private transportation or obtaining theater tickets (the butler thing is a bit gimmicky, but it definitely makes some passengers feel special).

Then there is also the high-tech component to Scenic cruises, starting with the high-tech GPS devices that the company provides passengers in lieu of the wireless tour guide systems most other river cruise companies use. The Scenic version, which the company calls *Scenic Tailormade,* is a touch-screen device slightly larger and thicker than an average smartphone. From the device, passengers can access the traditional wireless tour guiding systems (which allows passengers to listen to their local guides via a wireless microphone and headset system), but they can also access a selection of self-guided city tours with information about various points of interest at each port call. And *Scenic Tailormade* also features a river guide, which includes a follow-along map of the river cruise and commentary about sights along the river—this last feature allows Scenic to bypass providing that commentary over the loud speaker on its ships, which can disturb passengers trying to rest, read or do other activities. Frankly, reaction to the devices can go two ways: Guests either love them or they get frustrated with them—ship staff definitely have to be prepared for the requisite handful of passengers who find the devices difficult to use.

Another technology-based feature is the entertainment system in the staterooms. In addition to the movies on demand, satellite TV and Internet access that most of river cruise lines' in-room systems have, Scenic's version also has an Internet tracker that shows how strong the Wi-Fi signal is along the river (Wi-Fi signal strength can vary quite drastically along the rivers and can range from quite good in port to non-existent during sailings—but it's getting better and more consistent each year thanks to investments and enhancements by river cruise lines like Scenic), plus fact sheets about each port call and the option for passengers to check their invoices.

Final whiz-bang feature: Scenic's ships offer a small fleet of electric-assist bicycles, which can even be used to ride from one port to another to rejoin your ship later on (always, of course, ask if you can do this first).

PASSENGERS

Scenic's bread-and-butter is the 55-plus crowd. Passengers tend to be well-traveled, well-educated, and financially well-off. They typically have already done some upscale ocean cruising prior to river cruising. This is a social bunch, predominately Australians and Brits. They like to get to know the other passengers on board as well as the local citizens in the countries they are sailing in.

ROUTES

Scenic has the major waterways of Europe covered, with sailings that operate throughout Europe, including France and Portugal. The line still operates a comprehensive 15-day *Jewels of Russia* itinerary that runs between Moscow and St. Petersburg, making Scenic one of the few operators to remain committed to the River Volga.

The new jewel in the Scenic fleet is undoubtedly the line's Southeast Asia sailings. Ranging between eight and 27 days in length, these eight voyages explore the farthest reaches of the Mekong River that runs through Cambodia and Vietnam, and Myanmar's mysterious Irrawaddy River. Particularly noteworthy is the 18-day *Mystical Myanmar* itinerary that operates roundtrip from Yangon, Myanmar.

DINING

As mentioned above, Scenic vessels all offer six dining options, so there is no shortage of variety. On each ship, there is **Crystal Dining,** the main dining room; either a **Portobellos,** an Italian-themed, or **L'Amour,** a French-themed specialty dining restaurant; **Table La Rive,** an invitation-only, six-course, wine-pairing dinner experience offered exclusively to passengers in the upper-deck Suites and second-deck Junior Suites; **River Café,** a casual cafe open from 6am to 6pm, offering a range of light meals (think mini sandwiches and small pre-prepared salads), snacks and beverages that guests can grab at their whim; **Sun Deck Barbeque,** a traditional barbeque (from burgers to seafood) served on the Sun Deck at least once per week, weather permitting; and 24/7 in-room dining.

The variety makes for a more fun and dynamic onboard dining experience, and the food churned out at each venue is first-rate. It doesn't have the uber-gourmet feel of Uniworld dining, but is rather more contemporary-chic style, with each venue putting its own little twist on things (the River Café, for instance, light and fresh tapas-style bites, whereas the Table La Rive is where the chef gets experimental with a unique nightly tasting menu, including fun dishes like a lemongrass crème brûlée appetizer). Dining on board is more casual and social, less fussy and forced. And while you'll likely see plenty of European fare woven throughout the menus, Scenic doesn't shy away from other international influences such as Asian cuisine and spices.

ACTIVITIES

Don't expect anything hokey or forced in terms of onboard activities. For one, Scenic provides its guests with tools for keeping engaged on their own while cruising, including the *Scenic Tailormade* GPS device it hands out to all its passengers, which in addition to serving as a listening device during guided shore excursions has commentary available for sights along the rivers so that passengers can relax and follow along on their headsets—kind of like an audio tour at a museum. When and where it makes sense to do so, Scenic will also bring a relevant lecturer on board or offer an interactive demonstration such as a wine or food tasting.

CHILDREN'S PROGRAMS

Children aged 12 and over are welcomed aboard all Scenic river cruises, though no special provisions are made for them. Your chances of finding fellow families traveling on board is greatest during the summer vacation months (July, August) and closer to Christmas.

ENTERTAINMENT

In addition to the nightly music in the lounge, Scenic will bring additional musical and dance groups on board during the cruise to showcase the local culture. That could be a boisterous oompah band in Germany or folk dancers in Hungary. Scenic also offers onshore entertainment in cities where that is popular or where it is available. For instance, in Vienna, passengers may take in a classical music concert in a beautiful Viennese palace. Vienna is, after all, the City of Music.

SERVICE

With its new butler service (which is included for all guests), Scenic has kicked its service standard up a notch to white-glove level. But don't expect the butler to be at your beck and call 24/7. The butlers have other duties on board the vessel, so they are there to help fulfill personal requests such as laundry service, for everything else you will still need to get assistance from the very helpful reception staff. All tips and gratuities are included in Scenic's pricing.

FLEET

The Scenic fleet consists of *Scenic Aura* (2016), *Scenic Azure* (2016), *Scenic Diamond* (2008), *Scenic Emerald* (2009), *Scenic Gem* (2014), *Scenic Jasper* (2015), *Scenic Opal* (2015), *Scenic Pearl* (2011), *Scenic Ruby* (2009), *Scenic Sapphire* (2008), *Scenic Spirit* (2016), and *Scenic Tsar* (2013).

TAUCK

www.tauck.com. ℂ **800/468-2825.**

Founded in 1925 by Arthur Tauck, Sr., Tauck has been operating land tours around the United States and the world for nearly a century. It launched its first river cruise ship on the waterways of Europe in 2006 and today boasts a fleet of nine luxurious European riverboats. Unlike other companies in these pages, Tauck doesn't directly own its ships; instead, it has worked with Switzerland-based Scylla A.G. to construct and staff its ships—but that's not a bad thing. Scylla handles all those pesky little details relating to the technical operation of its river cruise fleet, while Tauck ensures that the ship is staffed to the rafters with crews who provide some of the best service on the waterways of Europe.

Pros

o **Lofted Lower Decks:** For its newest class of vessels, Tauck created lofted lower-deck staterooms with high ceilings and a raised seating area that are a welcome departure from their smaller, darker, porthole-windowed predecessors.

- **Unique On-Shore Outings:** Tauck usually hosts at least one or two unusual outings shore-side during each cruise, so passengers might find themselves having a candlelit dinner in an ancient chateaux or being treated to a surprise musical performance in a museum.
- **Superb Service:** Taking a river cruise with Tauck is not necessarily going to be easy on the wallet, but you can expect that every single detail will be arranged to a tee.
- **Complete Inclusivity:** Unless you buy something in the gift shop, you won't spend another dime on your vacation. Tauck guides famously even provide guests with Euro coins on tours so they won't have to pay to use Europe's ubiquitous pay-per-use toilets.
- **Family-Friendly:** One of the few river cruise lines to actually *encourage* multi-generational family travel, Tauck accommodates guests of all ages through specially designed sailings known as Tauck Bridges voyages.

Cons

- **High Cost of Admission:** The Mercedes-Benz of river cruising, Tauck's inclusivity and special experiences come with a commensurate cost.
- **Older Demographic:** Even by river cruise standards, the average age on a Tauck cruise skews well north of 60. The exception to this are the family-friendly Tauck Bridges sailings that generally take place during school holidays.
- **Small Fleet:** As of 2016, Tauck's fleet consisted of nine vessels, which means the company only sails on the most traditional river routes in Europe (Danube, Rhine, Rhone and Seine), and space is limited.

Frommer's Ratings (Scale of 1–5) ★★★★★

Cabin comfort & amenities	5	Public spaces	4
Decor	4	Dining	5
Fitness, spa & pool	4	Service	5
Family-friendly	5	Entertainment	5

Overview

The Tauck model seems to be, "Yes, we're expensive, but we'll make it worth it." In other words, if you're willing to pay to play, Tauck will absolutely deliver on a luxury river cruise experience.

EXPERIENCE

Tauck is truly a full-service river cruise and land operator at the highest end of the river cruising spectrum (where it shares company with Uniworld and Scenic). Nothing is skimped on, from the food and wine to the tours and included extras. This is the river cruise experience for those who don't want to worry about a thing. A Tauck river cruise would also make for a great special occasion trip, like an anniversary or family reunion, because of the high level of service.

Tauck's secret weapon? Well, it certainly doesn't hurt that the company has 90 years of experience in guided tours. And it shows in how meticulously it executes on the daily land excursions. Tauck's operations team must search far and wide, scouring the European countryside for the awesome venues it contracts with for on-shore events, from candle-lit wine caves to ancient castles and mansions.

If you're more of a do-it-yourself traveler, there may be a bit too much hand holding in the Tauck experience for you. But if you like the idea of disconnecting and relaxing, only needing to know where to be, at what time and in what attire, safe in the knowledge that whatever awaits will not disappoint, Tauck is certainly an option to look into.

PASSENGERS

Your fellow guests are well-travelled, well-educated, and well-off. Tauck tends to draw from a primarily American passenger base, but English-speaking international guests are welcome as well.

ROUTES

Tauck sticks to Europe for its river cruises, but it's itineraries are diverse and varied. Special theme cruises are frequently offered, with options centered around music, cuisine, and Europe's famous Christmas Markets.

DINING

Tauck's riverboats have one main dining room and a more casual alternative dining venue at the aft of its vessels. Meals in the dining room are open seating, with breakfast and lunch being extremely gourmet buffets.

But Tauck is also committed to getting its passengers off the ships for one or two meals during each sailing. And when it does, the venue tends to be something more unique than a typical tourist-trap restaurant. Tauck will often find settings, such as a historic mansion or castle, in which to host these surprise seatings.

Of note, Tauck's prices include most alcoholic and non-alcoholic beverages on board, save for premium and top-shelf alcohol.

Whether on or off the ship, you can expect the quality of food to compete with the other high-end river cruise lines and is often among the several "wow" factors of the cruise. Here too, Tauck does not skimp and your taste buds will not be disappointed (your waistline, now that's a different story).

ACTIVITIES

Tauck is very much about getting its passengers off the ship to experience more of the destinations it sails to and through. Which means there often isn't much time spent on board. When there is, a relevant presentation might be given about the language, culture or cuisine of the region.

Ashore there will be at least one or two tours offered each day, and they will be well executed. Because of its long-standing tour operating business, Tauck has an extensive rolodex of local tour guides throughout Europe who are vetted by and contracted directly with Tauck, so you can expect the local guides for the daily tours to be of a really good quality (they will have excellent English skills, loads of experience and insights), as opposed to the catch-as-catch-can guides that some of the other river cruise lines rely on.

Daily excursions usually consist of either one half-day tour, two half-day tours before and after lunch, or a full-day excursion. So you can expect a mix of being on the move as well as some time to relax on board during morning or afternoon sailings. Either way, Tauck will always have something in store for its passengers—and it likely won't just be the same stereotypical landmark all river cruise lines will stop at on a given route. Tauck is very good at pushing the touring envelope and adding unique and unexpected sights and experiences to its itineraries. Our most memorable Tauck moment (of many) was when the line arranged for the In Flanders Fields museum in Ieper, Belgium, to open after-hours. Guests were invited to explore the museum on their own, without any crowds, before a multi-course dinner taken right within the museum itself, which is situated in the historic Cloth Hall that was badly damaged during World War I and meticulously rebuilt.

> **Trivia Fact**
>
> Tauck likes to surprise its guests with *lagniappes*. The word is taken from the French spoken in Louisiana and it means something given as a little bonus or extra. The company tries to incorporate at least one lagniappe into all of its tours and river cruises. So don't be surprised (or do) when some little souvenir or token of appreciation shows up randomly.

CHILDREN'S PROGRAMS

Here's where Tauck really shines. You might not expect a luxury product to cater to kids or multi-generational families, but that's exactly what Tauck offers with its specially designated Tauck Bridges itineraries. Scheduled during school holidays, these sailings offer special family-friendly adventures ashore that can include scavenger hunts in the Louvre and group bicycle rides along the Danube, all of which have a major bent on history, culture, and education. If Tauck pampers couples, it pulls out all the stops for families.

ENTERTAINMENT

Again, Tauck is all about providing that balance of on- and off-ship experiences, and that goes for entertainment as well. Like other river cruise lines, Tauck will bring local talent onto the vessels for various live performance on board (we're particular fans of the crew talent show), but also treats its guests to concerts and live shows onshore.

SERVICE

A high-end product means high-touch service. Not only does Tauck celebrate customer's special events such as birthdays and wedding anniversaries (as do most river cruise lines—in fact, sometimes it's comical how many birthday and anniversary celebrations there will be on a single sailing, regardless of the river cruise line), but the company will often throw in additional gifts, such as local souvenirs, for guests to bring home with them. The company is very tuned in to both the little and big things that make travelers feel special, and that's a level of service it takes a truly experienced company to provide. Gratuities are included in Tauck's prices. Tauck also has a Tauck Director and three Tauck Cruise Directors—as opposed to just one cruise director, which is standard on other river cruise lines—on board all its river departures to assist passengers at all times. A Tauck Director is what Tauck calls its tour directors. On its river cruise ships, this person serves as an additional point of contact and resource and will be with the groups both on and off the ship (whereas cruise directors usually stay on). They add another level of customer service and of simply helping everything to go smoothly.

FLEET

The Tauck fleet is made up of nine ships: *Emerald* (2006, substantially rebuilt 2017); *Esprit* (2015); *Grace* (2016); *Inspire* (2014); *Joy* (2016); *Sapphire* (2008, substantially rebuilt 2017); *Savor* (2014); *Swiss Jewel* (2009); *Treasures* (2011).

UNIWORLD BOUTIQUE RIVER CRUISE COLLECTION

www.uniworld.com. ✆ **800/642-0066** or 907/465-3941.

Uniworld has grabbed a hold of the highest end of the river cruise market and has firmly planted itself there. When it comes to opulent interiors, paired with fine dining and wine, Uniworld is in a class of its own.

Uniworld is also ahead of the pack when it comes to offering diverse river cruise itineraries. In addition to the popular Danube and Rhine routes, Uniworld is sailing routes that aren't even on the radar of other river cruise lines, like Italy's Po River and India's famed Ganges. The line also has a comprehensive presence in China and Southeast Asia, and is one of the few to continue to operate in both Russia and Egypt.

The line's ships are decidedly unique, with decor designed in partnership with Red Carnation Hotels. Best described as Louis XIV on acid, the decor may be polarizing, but it is undeniably Uniworld. Nothing is ordered out of a catalogue here; even the chairs in the lounge have been custom-designed.

Uniworld went all-inclusive in 2014, and each voyage now includes all beverages on board, gratuities, shore excursions, airport transfers, and even personalized butler service.

Pros

○ **High Design:** You cannot talk about Uniworld without talking about the interior design of this company's river cruise ships. We have three words for you: Over. The. Top. Think extensive marble details, lush upholstery, and tons of commissioned artwork, which have made the vessels something of a destination unto themselves.

- **Gourmand's Delight:** Uniworld's vessels are not just a feast for the eyes, they are a feast for the taste buds too. The company does not hold back when it comes to bringing impressive delicacies and wine on board.
- **Unique Itineraries:** Uniworld is the only major North American river cruise line to offer sailings that explore Italy's Po River and India's Ganges, among others.

Cons

- **Price:** Uniworld's fancy schmancy six-star, all-inclusive offering comes at a price. These river cruises are not cheap.
- **Impractical Inventory:** These decked-out riverboats are often weighed down by all the divine details inside and that means that Uniworld vessels can sometimes be at a disadvantage when river water levels are low, a situation that favors lighter boats with lower drafts. Form-over-function can be a problem on board, too: We actually had to ring the reception desk aboard *S.S. Maria Theresa* in order to ask how to open our stateroom door when the elaborate Victorian knob wouldn't turn.
- **Love-It-Or-Hate-It Decor:** You're either going to be turned on or turned off by the line's Versailles-esque decor.

Frommer's Ratings (Scale of 1–5) ★★★★★

Cabin comfort & amenities	4	Public spaces	4
Decor	5	Dining	5
Fitness, spa & pool	5	Service	5
Family-friendly	5	Entertainment	4

Overview

Its name doesn't exactly roll off the tongue, but Uniworld Boutique River Cruise Collection has been in the river cruise business far longer than most of the lines in this chapter. Founded in 1976, the company was acquired in 2004 by The Travel Corporation (owner of several major tour operators and a hotel chain), which injected a healthy amount of cash into Uniworld and allowed it to expand even further.

How much cash? The company invested more than $1 million in the purchasing and commissioning of the extensive collection of art pieces on board just one of its ships—the 159-passenger *S.S. Catherine,* which sails on the Rhone and Saone rivers in France's Burgundy and Provence regions. Other extravagant details include the intricate mosaic-tiled indoor swimming on Uniworld's newer Super Ship class of vessels, the safari-themed Leopard Lounge at the aft of several of its ships and the 10-foot blue Strauss Baccarat chandelier with sapphires, which once hung in the former Tavern on the Green in New York's Central Park and now hangs in the lobby of the *S.S. Antoinette.* Uniworld set its collective sights on becoming the first five-star boutique river cruise line—and it has largely succeeded.

Few lines have the kind of loyal passenger base that Uniworld does. They're drawn back to the line time after time by its experience, its doting staff, and ships that are as unique as the itineraries they sail. The rivergoing equivalent of Seabourn or Regent, Uniworld attracts a guest that is looking for the best of the best in every aspect, and isn't afraid to pay accordingly for it.

EXPERIENCE

Beyond its ritzy river cruise ships, Uniworld has a secret weapon similar to Avalon Waterways'—it too is owned by a major travel conglomerate, The Travel Corporation, a company that owns well-established tour brands such as Trafalgar, Insight Vacations, Brendan Vacations, and the hotel company the Red Carnation Hotel Collection (the Red Carnation team helps Uniworld design those posh interiors). What that means is that Uniworld isn't just a fleet of fancy ships. It is backed by some serious tour operating experience and decades of travel expertise.

That kind of tour operating pedigree means that Uniworld has the ability to create land programs in line with the level of expectation set by the onboard experience, whether that means finding exclusive chateaux for wine tastings in Bordeaux or taking its passengers truffle hunting in the south of France.

Back on board, you will find that, despite a certain old-world elegance that the ships evoke, Uniworld in fact has some very modern ideas about the kinds of offerings today's contemporary cruiser might want. That means top-of-the-line mattresses (from luxe Savoir® of England) and an emphasis on health and wellness. So it offers yoga and exercise classes and TRX training equipment in the fitness room. Bikes are also available to cruisers.

And passengers may find they could use that extra workout as Uniworld cuisine makes it hard to resist temptation (there are healthy options too, but who wants to eat healthy when there are mounds of pastries at breakfast, a heaping cheese station at lunch and multi-course professionally plated dinners?).

PASSENGERS

Like many river cruise lines, Uniworld's mainstay are baby boomers, but in recent years Uniworld has been attracting a wider variety of guests, including a greater number of younger passengers. Along those lines, Uniworld has been building up its wellness program, which includes higher paced "Go Active" excursions, complimentary yoga classes and TRX training, bicycles on board and Nordic walking sticks that guests can use. Uniworld also offers family-friendly departures, which helps bring down the age range.

ROUTES

Uniworld offers some of the most comprehensive river cruises around the globe. Currently, the line offers sailings in Europe, Russia, Egypt, India, China, and Vietnam and Cambodia.

DINING

When it comes to fine dining, Uniworld doesn't mess around. Passengers can expect meals that incorporate local delicacies like impressive selection of smoked salmon at the breakfast buffet, foie gras in France, hard-to-find regional cheeses throughout Europe (seriously, their cheese displays are massive) and very specialized wine pairings. This high quality, locally sourced gourmet dining experience alleviates some of the potential frustration that eating most of your meals on the ship during a river cruise can cause.

Uniworld hasn't embraced the multiple dining venue trend and appears to be more focused on simply wowing in the main restaurant.

It's also important to note that as part of Uniworld's all-inclusive pricing, unlimited beverages are available throughout the cruise including some premium spirits such as Grey Goose, Crown Royal, and Glenfiddich.

ACTIVITIES

Uniworld's discerning clientele expects lofty and engaging lectures relevant to the history, culture or current events of the region, and deeper insights into the local culinary traditions and wines of the regions through tastings and cooking demonstrations and thus that's what Uniworld strives to provide.

All excursions are included in the cost of the cruise, and Uniworld offers more than one option in most ports of call. Uniworld's Choice Is Yours program offers excursions designed for new and repeat guests alike, while "Do as the Locals Do" options focus on authentic cultural experiences.

Guests with mobility issues will find Uniworld's "Gentle Walking" tours to be an attractive option, while those seeking more active experiences ashore might want to participate in the line's "Go Active" hiking and biking excursions. Uniworld's European fleet also boasts a collection of onboard bicycles that guests can use, free of charge, for independent touring.

CHILDREN'S PROGRAMS

Uniworld does not encourage children on its regular sailings, but it doesn't prohibit them either (except for those under 4). Children under 18 must be accompanied by an adult 21 or older at all times, and there are no kid-friendly arrangements or activities for them.

All that said, for those who would like to bring the little ones on a river cruise, Uniworld has a long-standing family river cruise program on certain sailings in the summer months and during holiday season. To make these itineraries kid-friendly, Uniworld injects them with more active excursions such as biking and kayaking, more arts and crafts, opportunities to visit various amusement parks or a gladiator school (that's a thing? … apparently in Rome it is…), hands-on food activities, and anything spooky (ghost walks), creepy (such as the Medieval Crime and Justice Museum in Rothenburg. Germany) or just plain weird that "kids" will get a kick out of.

ENTERTAINMENT

Onboard entertainment is subdued, with most guests retiring to the lounge for conversation and after-dinner nightcaps. A resident pianist entertains guests nightly, and local entertainment is often brought on board in select ports of call (a fado singer in Portugal, an opera singer in Austria, you know the drill). Though the entertainment isn't all that different from the offerings on board other lines, Uniworld's ships become exceedingly cozy at night, with lounges taking on a clubby, old-world feel that helps to set the Uniworld experience apart.

SERVICE

Uniworld makes every effort to ensure that extremely well-trained staff are on-hand to meet, and hopefully exceed, customers' expectation. It could be something small like crew remembering passengers' names and preferences, to something more involved like helping passengers make special onshore arrangements and celebrate special occasions—Uniworld is tuned in to these details and appears to be aware that without them it really doesn't matter how glamorous the ships are.

Furthermore, Uniworld stepped it up a notch in 2015 by offering in-suite butler service for guests staying in the suites on four of its vessels—the *River Beatrice, S.S. Antoinette, S.S. Catherine,* and *S.S. Maria Theresa.* The service includes packing and unpacking assistance, in-room breakfast if desired, a daily fruit and cookie plate, and evening snack, a bottle of wine upon arrival, shoe shine and free laundry service. These guests are also invited to a special dinner in the Bar du Leopard.

Uniworld includes gratuities in its pricing.

FLEET

Uniworld currently has a fleet of 13 ships in Europe, with additional chartered vessels in Russia, Egypt, India, and Asia.

The company's European ships include *River Ambassador* (1996); *River Baroness* (1997); *River Beatrice* (2009); *River Countess* (1999); *River Duchess* (2003); *River Empress* (2002); *River Princess* (2001); *River Queen* (1999); *River Royale* (2006); *S.S. Antoinette* (2011); *S.S. Catherine* (2014); and *S.S. Maria Theresa* (2015).

VANTAGE DELUXE WORLD TRAVEL

www.vantagetravel.com. *℃* **888/514-1845.**

Vantage Deluxe World Travel caters to older and solo travelers—similar to Grand Circle but with some newer, shinier ships (the two companies are actually owned by members of the same family but they are completely separate entities).

Pros

o **Aggressive Prices:** Vantage is all about throwing out the 2-for-1 deals and free airfare to motivate bookings.

o **Lots of "American" Niceties:** Expect North American power outlets, English-language news programs on television, and meals that are European in nature, adapted for the American palate. Yes, you can have a hamburger if you'd like to.

Cons

o **Gimmicky:** The onslaught of 2-for-1 sales and free-airfare deals have a pushy and gimmicky feel and leave you wondering, "What's the catch?"

And once you sail with Vantage you can expect a never-ending supply of said deals.

- **Uneven Fleet:** Each of the company's five owned river cruise vessels are very different, and may not necessarily have the same amenities, or even look alike. *River Venture,* for instance, sports a bright-red hull and cream superstructure that is unlike anything else in the fleet.
- **Relatively High Gratuities:** Vantage automatically adds gratuities to your onboard account, and the recommended amounts are higher than most of the company's competitors: 17€ per guest, per day for standard staterooms, and 20€ per guest, per day, for those occupying top-of-the-line suites.

Frommer's Ratings (Scale of 1–5) ★★★★

Cabin comfort & amenities	4	Public spaces	4
Decor	4	Dining	3
Fitness, spa & pool	3	Service	4
Family-friendly	5	Entertainment	5

Overview

Founded in 1983, Vantage Deluxe World Travel started life as an organized tour company but quickly branched into both ocean and river cruising. Traditionally, the company catered solely to American guests but in 2016 began expanding to include travelers from Canada and the United Kingdom, as well as multi-generational families. Its fleet of seven river cruise ships includes five company-owned ships and two chartered ships, the latter of which operate on the Elbe and Douro rivers. The company's newest vessel, *River Voyager,* introduced a successful new jazz theme and substantially upped the quality of the company's river cruise product.

The price leader among most American-based river cruise lines operating in Europe, Vantage offers a decent river cruise at an affordable price. It's definitely nothing crazy fancy but its newer ships especially shouldn't be ruled out and present a great value for what you get—they provide many of the amenities that have become common on the rivers, such as French balconies on the majority of staterooms, and Wi-Fi and bicycles on board.

Vantage relies almost entirely on a consumer database of several million potential travelers that it markets and sells its river cruises to. The company has an aggressive customer-referral program, offering customers a discount off their next trip if a referral books, and about two-thirds of its business comes from repeat clients. So if you haven't heard of Vantage, it's probably because you're not in the system yet. But don't worry, getting in the system is no problem (and there will be plenty of enticing deals and incentives to do so).

Because of the deals and incentives, a lot of people who sail with Vantage get hooked and become Vantage loyalists. Vantage is also big with solo travelers as it sets aside a handful of cabins on each vessels as dedicated single cabins with no single supplement, and has a cabin share program whereby it will pair up solo passengers willing to room with other solos.

EXPERIENCE

Because Vantage was a tour operator first and foremost, it knows how to handle the logistic of group travel. It provides mostly inclusive river cruise packages (often bundled with appealing air deals, in fact some of its river cruise pricing is only offered as such if air is purchased together with the cruise) comprised of most meals, excursions and transfers.

While the core Vantage river cruise experience is fairly consistent, major differences in the company's river cruise fleet makes for a somewhat inconsistent onboard experience. Guests sailing aboard the line's newest ships (*River Voyager*, 2016; *River Splendor*, 2013) will find more modern decor and better fit-and-finish than some of the company's other vessels, which can vary wildly in terms of accommodations, size and amenities. Still, the overall experience is a positive one, with friendly service, good (if not adventurous) cuisine, and well-designed programs ashore.

PASSENGERS

The typical Vantage passenger used to solely consist of American retirees that had previously travelled with the line, but that's changing. Expect to see a healthy mix of American, Canadian, and UK guests, along with multi-generational families during the summer months. Vantage also gets a lot of solo travelers, as it's one of the few lines that specifically caters to that demographic.

ROUTES

Vantage currently operates European river cruises that sail the Danube, Rhine and Main rivers in Europe, along with the Rhone and Saone rivers in France. Vantage charters two ships that sail Portugal's Douro River, and the Elbe River from Berlin.

DINING

Vantage makes sure to have "safe" options on its menus, items that are familiar and perhaps not too exotic, something its customers appreciate. It does offer local specialties as well, but always alongside food that we would know or can get in the U.S. too (such as dinner salads and hamburgers, for instance).

Meals are served in the main dining room, where both breakfast and lunch are served as a buffet—the lunch buffet will always have a salad bar. The dinner menu typically includes an appetizer, soup and/or salad, choice of entrée and choice of dessert. Don't expect a ton of variety, and food is adequate but nothing overly memorable. Wine is included with dinner.

ACTIVITIES

Vantage offers a wide range of onboard and on-shore programs intended to inform cruisers (in an insightful fashion) about the destinations its ships sail through. There are often themed talks and lessons on board, which could be an art history lecture during a Seine sailing (an itinerary that includes visits to Monet's studio and the Giverny Museum of Impressionism during a port call in Giverny) or a Portuguese language lesson on a Douro river cruise. Vantage also offers local craft-making workshops (you know you have always wanted to try your hand at making your very own santon doll, the terracotta figurines that are popular in Provence). Most Vantage ships come equipped with a fleet of onboard bicycles for self-guided cycling around the many pathways of Europe.

CHILDREN'S PROGRAMS

Kids 8 to 18 can cruise for free when their traveling companions reserve a category B or higher stateroom (subject to availability), but only on "Family Cruise" sailings (which is also the only time the younger set is welcomed aboard). All of its "Family Cruise" sailings take place either during the summer or winter holidays and include kid-friendly activities such as arts and crafts and local school visits, and kids will receive a complimentary travel journal. These sailings also feature kid-friendly menus.

ENTERTAINMENT

Onboard entertainment, if any, is typically limited to a piano act in the main lounge. Special sailings sometimes feature an onboard jazz band; check the Vantage website for themed sailings.

SERVICE

Vantage has a 4:1 ratio of crew to passengers. The industry average is probably around 3.5 passengers for each crew member, with higher end lines getting closer to 3 passengers per crew member and even 2.5 passengers to crew member (on some of the Asia river cruises it can get close to 1:1). So know that a company like Vantage isn't really about coddling its customers. And when you're paying these kinds of prices, you really shouldn't expect it. You should expect a very friendly staff that is busy making sure food is being served on time, itineraries are running smoothly and cabins are being refreshed. And for some people, that's really all that matters (butlers schmutlers).

Gratuities are not included and Vantage provides passengers with a nine-to-11 euros per person per day guideline for tipping on its river cruises, which includes all of the onboard ship staff, save for the cruise director and concierge. The recommended gratuity for him/her is between three and six euros per person, per day. Five euros per person, per day is automatically applied to passengers' onboard account, but it is optional and guests can adjust the amount. All gratuities can be charged to your onboard account if you so choose. The company also recommends one to two euros per person, per day, for local guides and drivers.

FLEET

The Vantage fleet consists of five company-owned ships that include *River Voyager* (2016); *River Splendor* (2013); *River Venture* (2013); *River Discovery II* (2012); *River Navigator* (2002); as well as two chartered ships: *Douro Spirit* (2011) and *Frederic Chopin* (2002).

VIKING RIVER CRUISES

www.vikingrivercruises.com. © **855/707-4837.**

For many people Viking River Cruises *is* river cruising. It's the Big Kahuna of the industry with more than 60 ships (which account for roughly 50% of the worldwide cruise market) and it's the line you've seen in those exquisite ads on TV (most notably opposite *Downton Abbey*). Affordable, destination-focused cruising on comfortable ships is Viking's calling card.

Pros

- **Extremely Well-Oiled Operation:** You can expect a high-quality experience on any of Viking's ships.
- **Innovation:** The Viking "Longships" with their snub-noses, outdoor dining, "green" features (including solar panels), whisper-quiet engines and cabins with balconies did no less than change the course of river cruising—for the better.
- **Fun Documentation:** In a world of "print-it-yourself" e-tickets and documents, Viking's document package makes for a great surprise: Coming in a silver box, it includes a bound cruise document containing transfers, maps, flights and cruise information, along with leather luggage tags and one of the best pocket, river-specific guidebooks we've seen.
- **Diverse Itineraries:** Viking not only has plenty of European itineraries but also fascinating voyages through Russia, China, Vietnam, and Cambodia, and even along Egypt's Nile River.

Cons

- **No Pool, Spa, or Fitness Facilities:** The line will make recommendations for facilities you can visit along the way but doesn't believe in using space for that sort of stuff on board.
- **Not Kid-Friendly:** Kids under 16 are discouraged (under 12 not allowed).

Frommer's Ratings (Scale of 1–5)   ★★★★ ½

Cabin comfort & amenities	5	Public spaces	5
Decor	5	Dining	4
Fitness, spa & pool	2	Service	4
Family-friendly	2	Entertainment	4

Overview

In many ways, Viking created "Modern River Cruising." Founded in 1997 by cruise industry veteran Torstein Hagen, Viking started with cruises in Russia and has had a meteoric rise to become the king of the river cruising world with 50% of the worldwide market. In fact, Viking broke a Guinness World Record in 2013 for the number of ships launched in a single day, christening 12 new Viking Longships in a massive ceremony in Amsterdam. They beat their own record the following year by christening a whopping 18 new vessels in 24 hours over three separate cities: Amsterdam; Avignon, France; and Porto, Portugal.

The model for the river product (adopted by the ocean product as well) is value-priced, mostly inclusive cruises, with wine and beer at mealtimes, Wi-Fi, airport transfers, port charges and, most importantly, daily shore excursions included in your cruise fare.

The line's "Longships," first introduced in 2012, brought with them a whole new era of river cruising. The size of river ships is limited by the need to go under short bridges and by the width of locks, but these wonderfully contemporary ships were cleverly designed with a snub-nose rather than a traditional pointy bow. This change allowed the line to add a partially windowed, open-air outdoor dining area—what Viking calls the Aquavit Terrace. Founder Hagen, with the help of the ship architects Yran & Storbraaten (who also created interiors for ocean ships including the Disney Dream and luxury line Seabourn's Odyssey-class ships), also cleverly had the idea to move the hallways to one side so the ships could offer true two-room suites, plus cabins with real, step-out balconies as on ocean ships, without going over the river width restrictions. The de-centralized hallway also allowed for a greater number of cabin configurations and categories. "Green" advances included hybrid diesel-electric engines partially fueled by solar panels.

Spending for onboard cuisine went up. Passenger amenities were scaled up, and onboard costs scaled down. Popular shore excursion options are provided free of charge, with more off-the-beaten-path excursions offered at a modest cost. Wines are so free-flowing during lunch and dinner that you'll never see the bottom of your glass.

EXPERIENCE

The line's ships offer all the comforts of a decent hotel—the "Longships" may remind some of W Hotels with their streamlined, contemporary decor and upscale accouterments. You sleep in a cabin with a comfortable bed and can pay extra for perks such as a French balcony or a real veranda or even a two-room suite. You hang out in comfortably cushy spaces including the main lounge. All cruises come with three meals a day, with wine and beer included at lunch and dinner (you can also request complimentary mimosas at breakfast). Daily tours are included, premium tours available for an extra fee—such as a BMW Factory experience in Munich or an evening Fado concert in Lisbon.

That said, founder Hagen does things his way or the highway, and if you don't like his style, well too bad. On his ships you won't find many bathtubs (he prefers showers). You won't find pools or fitness rooms or spas on ships because Hagen believes those are underused spaces. But you will find salmon and oatmeal available every day (he's Norwegian!). And each ship carries a well-stocked library, situated on the upper level of the glass-enclosed atrium and loaded with titles on history.

A lot of people agree with Hagan's tastes. Viking is the dominant cruise line in Europe and also offers cruises in Russia, China, in Southeast Asia (the Mekong and Irrawaddy) and in Egypt. The line is gearing to introduce cruises on the Mississippi in 2018; and started offering ocean-going cruises in 2015 (see p. 275). Hotel operations for all the ships are run out of Switzerland.

Perhaps most surprising, is Viking has managed to maintain a consistent level of quality as it has grown. Itineraries are well planned and very much focused on making sure you see the key sights en route. The idea is that you explore a region without being nickel-and-dimed.

PASSENGERS

Viking gears its entire product to age 55-plus. Many on board will be *way* plus, though still active enough to do the included tours. Nearly all on board will be English-speakers and most Americans. The dress code is casual at all times (though some dress up slightly at night) and the folks on board like it that way. Expect mature, social fellow passengers who are interested in history and culture and travel.

ROUTES

Viking offers itineraries that crisscross nearly every section of Europe, with a special emphasis on Austria, France, Hungary, Germany, the Netherlands, and Portugal. The line also continues to offer some great sailings in Russia, where Viking first got its start back in 1997.

Elsewhere, China is a primary focus for the line, which operates three cruisetour itineraries ranging from 13 to 18 days there. Viking also offers cruises along the Mekong River (Vietnam and Cambodia), the Nile (Egypt), and, historically, the Ukraine's Dnieper, though it's not known when Viking will be able to operate a full season in the latter again.

DINING

Meals are served in the main dining room, and on newer ships there is alternative dining in the **Aquavit Terrace,** which is an *al fresco* extension of the main lounge. Breakfast and lunch are buffet style. Dinner is a multi-course menu that includes a choice of local specialties and continental dishes. Improved menus have added a more modern slant, so you might have potato ravioli with sabayon sauce and a sautéed black cod, tuna sashimi and carved roast veal. Always available are New York-cut steak and salmon. A light buffet is available at breakfast and lunch (the latter will be at the Aquavit Terrace on the "Longships," or on other ships in the lounge) Offered once on each sailing on the Sun Deck, don't miss the buffet of local snacks (the line calls the spread "A Taste Of…") featuring such treats as pretzels and sweet mustard leberwurst and Kölsch (beer) in Germany or grilled local sausages, vegetable skewers with feta, cevapcici (minced meat kabob), baklava and local beer in the Balkans. House wine and beer are included with dinner, and you can order complimentary mimosas if you want at breakfast. Cocktails and premium wine are extra (added to your tab). Viking also has the option of Beverage Packages that include cocktails and wine for those who prefer an all-inclusive drinks experience (priced at $210 per person for a seven-day cruise).

ACTIVITIES

The primary daily activities on a Viking River cruise are, of course, tours ashore. Viking offers a number of daily options for exploring in most cities, including a "gentle walkers" group for those with mobility issues or who want to spend more time admiring the sights and don't mind covering less ground. The line also likes to focus on options for the independent traveler, like a guided shore excursion in Vienna that teaches guests how to use the U-Bahn metro. Every port has at least one complimentary excursion options, though some additional-cost excursions are offered alongside. Note that Viking doesn't offer onboard bicycles as an option for shoreside exploration, as some lines do.

On board, there will be lectures and multi-media presentations on local history and culture. So, on Bordeaux itineraries there might be a presentation on local wine; in Holland, an included lecture could tell tales of the Dutch Masters artists; and on many sailings, the cruise director teaches words and phrases in the local language. The newer ships have a walking/jogging track and a putting green on the Sun Deck. There are no bikes on board and most of the ships do not have fitness facilities, spas or pools.

CHILDREN'S PROGRAMS

None. Viking doesn't actively cater to children, or offer any special amenities or sailings. If you're thinking of bringing kids (or even teenagers), you might do well to pick another line with dedicated family-friendly sailings.

ENTERTAINMENT

Local entertainers, singers and dance groups, come on board at select ports—such as a Hungarian folk dancing troupe on the Danube or a Fado singer in Portugal. A piano player entertains in the lounge at night, doing classical music and modern and even pop melodies, including during cocktail hour. Depending on the ship, a combo may play for dancing at night. The lounge may also double as a movie theater, the films chosen for their local connection.

SERVICE

The hardworking mixed European and Filipino crew focuses on efficiency, but the atmosphere is friendly and few passengers have any complaints. In fact, the line is so sure your needs will be attended to they offer a service guarantee—if a problem is not corrected within 24 hours you can leave the ship and get a refund. Gratuities are not included in your cruise fare, but are collected at the end of the cruise (you can pay in cash or by credit card), in one lump sum, which is then divided among the crew. Recommendations vary by itinerary, but in Europe the recommended total adds up to about $15.25 per person, per day ($2.18 for the program director and the rest for the waitstaff, bar team, room stewards and other service crew).

FLEET

Viking's fleet consists primarily of new (or close-to-brand-new) Viking Longships. While there are some noteworthy differences in things like the placement of electrical outlets, light switches, and materials used throughout, these ships are more or less identical in design and layout. Well-built and wonderfully quiet (we didn't even realize we were moving until we'd sailed halfway out of Amsterdam on our first Longship cruise), Viking has been tweaking the Scandinavian decor of these ships based on customer feedback, and the results are apparent. Each Longship holds up to 190 guests, and features accommodations ranging from value-added Riverview staterooms to each vessel's two massive Explorer Suites situated at the stern.

Viking still has a few of its older vessels clinging on for a few more seasons, but they don't have much longer to go as new Longships are added each spring. There's nothing wrong with the "older" vessels like *Viking Legend* and *Viking Prestige,* but compared to their sleek new sisters, they do look a bit dated.

THE CRUISE LINES: THE NICHE SHIPS

These are the least like what you might think a cruise would be like. Each has its own personality, from the Alaska Marine Highway System which is a bare-bones ferry service that happens to have cabins you can sleep in (on some ships), all the way to Lindblad Expeditions, which focuses on its educational program more than any other line, and Un-Cruise Adventures, whose ships feel like oversized yachts. The niches can differ greatly—and that's their charm.

ALASKA MARINE HIGHWAY SYSTEM

www.ferryalaska.com. ✆ **800/642-0066** or 907/465-3941.

In Alaska, which has fewer paved roads than virtually any other state, getting around can be a problem. In fact, some cities—like Juneau, the state capital—are not even connected to the rest of the state by roads. There are local airlines, of course, and small private planes—lots and lots of small private planes. (There are more private planes per capita in Alaska than in any other state.) But given the weather conditions for large parts of the year, airplanes are not always the most reliable way of getting from Point A to Point B.

That's why the Alaska Marine Highway System (aka the Alaska Ferry, or AMHS) is so important. The system was originally created more than 50 years ago with the aim of providing Alaska's far-flung and often inaccessible smaller communities with essential transportation links with the rest of the state and with the Lower 48. But the boats have developed a following in the tourism business, as well. Every year, thousands of visitors eschew luxury cruise ships in favor of the more basic services of the 11 vessels of the AMHS, all of which travel to the ports visited by small-ship luxury lines, along with plenty that most standard cruise ships will never see. All the AMHS ferries carry both passengers and vehicles, and passengers can embark and disembark as they please, which allows for some excellent port-hopping.

In 2005, AMHS was officially designated an "All American Road" by the U.S. Department of Transportation, and it remains the only marine route with such a designation. To qualify, a road must have qualities that are nationally significant and contain features that do not exist elsewhere—it must be "a destination unto itself." AMHS definitely fits the bill.

The AMHS's southernmost port is Bellingham, Washington. Its network stretches throughout Southeast and Southcentral Alaska and out to the Aleutian island chain to the west of Anchorage.

Pros

- **Unique Way to Travel:** The ferry system allows the opportunity for adventuresome travel that is not too taxing.
- **Lots of Flexibility:** Passengers can combine the various itineraries that the ferry system has scheduled to customize their vacation package.

Cons

- **No Doctor on Board:** None of the vessels carry a doctor, so this may not be a good way to travel if you have health concerns.
- **Space Books up Quickly:** Don't call in May and expect to get what you want in June. It ain't gonna happen! You must book months in advance.
- **Spartan Cabins:** Sleeping accommodations, when available, are basic, to say the least—no fridge, no telephone, and so on. (One traveler was overheard to say, "I've known Trappist monks with more luxurious quarters!") However, many runs—particularly in the heart of Alaska—are only a few days or hours in length, allowing guests to sleep ashore.

Overview

Ferry-riding vacations are different from cruise vacations. Don't even think about one if you're looking for a lot of creature comforts—fancy accommodations, gourmet food, spa treatments, Broadway-style shows, and the rest. You won't find any of the above on the sturdy vessels of the AMHS. In fact, not all ferry passengers get sleeping berths—5 of the 11 ferries in the fleet are considered day boats and have no bedroom accommodations at all.

BOOKING YOUR JOURNEY

Booking passage on the AMHS can be a complicated affair. First, you'll pay for a spot on the ship, which can be as little as $31 for the 1-hour trip between Skagway and Haines or as much as $547 for the 1,629-mile, 4-day voyage between Bellingham and Whittier. Then you'll pay extra if you want a cabin for the sailing, which can add hundreds of dollars more for a multi-day trip. Much like cruise ships, cabins are staggered by category, and you'll have to choose whether you want an Inside (no view) or an Outside with a picture window. You'll also have to determine whether you need a two-berth cabin or a four-berth cabin. Children between the ages of 6 and 11 are charged roughly half the adult fare throughout the system, and children 5 and under travel free.

If you're planning on bringing a vehicle, you'll have to indicate that on the booking form. For every addition you make (people, cars, cabins), the price goes up accordingly. Don't be surprised if you find yourself surpassing the cost of a reasonably priced weeklong cruise to Alaska—but then, you don't want one of those, do you? Guests booking an AMHS journey are typically looking to avoid the crowds and organized entertainment of a typical cruise.

EXPERIENCE

In general, cabins are small and spartan, coming in two-, three- and four-bunk configurations, and either inside (without windows) or outside (with windows). For a premium, you can reserve a more comfortable sitting-room unit on some vessels. Some cabins have tiny private bathrooms with showers and toilets; others have sinks only, with showers and toilets located down the hall. Cabins can be stuffy, and the windowless units can be claustrophobic as well, so try to get an outside one.

Travelers who do not book ferry passage in time to snag a cabin—or purposely eschew one to save money—spend nights curled up in chairs in lounges or in the glass-enclosed solariums found on some vessels. This being Alaska, where the frontier spirit is alive and well, some hearty travelers will bring tents and sleeping bags and "camp" in the solariums or even out on deck—a phenomenon that not only is allowed but encouraged. Only in Alaska! If you plan on setting up outside, be sure to bring duct tape to secure your tent to the deck in case you can't find a sheltered spot, as the wind blows like an endless gale over a ship in motion. No matter whether you have a cabin or not, public showers are available, although there may be lines. Lock valuables in the coin-operated lockers to keep them safe on longer, overnight runs.

PASSENGERS

More than half of the passengers on the Alaska ferry system are locals traveling between towns for everything from work to sporting events. But you'll also find a healthy mix of vacationers from the Lower 48 and beyond, everyone from young backpackers to retirees. The ferries have become especially popular with RVers, who use them to move their vehicles into and out of the state, saving thousands of miles of driving.

ROUTES

The ferries operate in three distinct areas. Year-round service is offered in the Southeast, or Inside Passage, from Bellingham to Skagway/Haines; in Southcentral, which includes Prince William Sound, the Kenai Peninsula, and Kodiak Island; and, in the summer months, the Southwest region, which includes the Aleutian chain. The Aleutian's service is not offered during the winter due to the extreme weather. One of the newest ports added to the system is Gustavus, the town recognized as the gateway to Glacier Bay National Park & Preserve. Another popular summer route connects the town of Bellingham, Washington (about 40 minutes south of Vancouver, Canada) through the Inside Passage and across the Gulf of Alaska, to Whittier, located only 60 miles south of Anchorage. See the website (www.ferryalaska.com) for more details on the many routes that the AMHS operates.

DINING

Only 2 of the 11 AMHS ferries (*Columbia* and *Tustumena*) have a full-service, sit-down dining room. The others have cafeteria-style facilities that serve hot meals and beverages. There are also vending machines on all boats, for snacks and drinks. Food is not included in the fares.

ACTIVITIES

There are no organized activities but lots of scenic viewing (either on deck or through the high-windowed solariums some boats have)—and good listening on most sailings. Some vessels have small theaters that show films of general interest and documentaries on Alaska and the outdoors. Small gift shops sell magazines, books, toiletries, and Alaska souvenirs. In addition, rangers are sometimes present on more tourist-heavy routes to provide commentary on the sights around the vessel. Still, staying a day or two in the port communities visited by the ferries is the best way experience the true Alaska.

CHILDREN'S PROGRAMS

Some ships have small video game arcades or toddler play areas.

ENTERTAINMENT

Entertainment is created by passengers on a strictly impromptu basis. It might be a backpacker strumming a guitar, or a father keeping his children occupied by performing magic tricks. Occasionally, spirited discussion groups will form in which all are welcome to participate. The subject might be the environment, politics, the effect of tourism on wildlife (a hot-button issue), or any of a thousand other topics. (It's tempting to suggest—tongue slightly in cheek—that the entertainment on many Alaska Ferry boats is better than on some cruise ships we've been on!) Occasionally, sports will be discussed—but don't look for the locals to want to talk about anything as much as dog sledding. It's almost a religion in the 49th State—their World Series, Super Bowl, and Stanley Cup rolled into one.

SERVICE

Service is not one of the things for which the AMHS is noted. The small American staff works enthusiastically, but without a great deal of distinction.

CRUISETOURS & ADD-ON PROGRAMS

None. However, those seeking a change from the more popular and frequently congested, larger Inside Passage and Gulf ports find that the ferries are an ideal way to get around the less-visited parts of Alaska. Riding on a ferry, as opposed to a cruise ship, allows you the flexibility to explore the communities for several days (as opposed to only a few hours) at your leisure. It gives you time to meet real Alaskans in large and small communities and enjoy a variety of activities such as fishing, hiking, kayaking, biking, hunting, skiing, and much, much more.

FLEET

All nine of the traditional AMHS boats are designated M/V, as in motor vessel. The two newer, catamaran-style vessels are designated FVF, for fast vehicle ferries. Below is a thumbnail description of each one:

The 382-foot-long *Kennicott,* in service since 1998, operates some of the longest runs in the system, connecting Bellingham with the towns of the Southeast before continuing on across the Gulf of Alaska as far west as Kodiak. The *Kennicott* holds up to 499 passengers and 80 vehicles, and it has 109 cabins. Five of the cabins are wheelchair-accessible.

The 418-foot-long *Columbia,* the largest of the AMHS vessels, connects Bellingham with the towns of the Southeast only (unlike the *Kennicott,* it doesn't continue across the Gulf of Alaska). It holds up to 600 passengers and 134 vehicles, and it has 103 cabins. Three cabins are suitable for wheelchair users. The vessel has a dining room for sit-down meals, a cafeteria, and a cocktail lounge.

Also sailing between Bellingham and the towns of the Southeast is the 499-passenger, 88-vehicle *Malaspina.* It has 73 cabins, a cafeteria, cocktail lounge, and a solarium. For much of the summer, it provides service from Juneau up Lynn Canal to the communities of Haines and Skagway, connecting the state capital to the road system.

The 499-passenger, 88-vehicle *Matanuska* sails between Prince Rupert, BC, and the towns of the Southeast (including Juneau, Ketchikan, Wrangell, Petersburg, Sitka, and Skagway). It has 104 cabins (one of which can accommodate a wheelchair user) as well as a cafeteria and cocktail lounge.

One of the newest and fastest vessels in the AMHS fleet is the fast ferry *Fairweather,* which operates strictly in the Southeast, mostly between Juneau and Sitka (about a 4½-hour trip; slightly longer when it stops in Angoon along the way). The 235-foot-long catamaran also makes a weekly Juneau-to-Petersburg run (a 4-hour trip). The *Fairweather* can hold 250 passengers and 35 vehicles but has no sleeping quarters. Its value to locals is immense; they now can get to the stores and government offices of Juneau twice as fast as once was possible. Its value to tourists is that it enables them to spend less time in transit. A sister high-speed vessel, the *Chenega,* similarly provides speedy service among the communities of Prince William Sound. It also has no sleeping accommodations.

Also sailing between the towns of Prince William Sound is the *Aurora,* which has room for 300 passengers and 34 vehicles but no cabins. It has a cafeteria and solarium.

The 352-foot-long *Taku,* meanwhile, is an additional option for travelers who want to get between the towns of the Southeast. It carries 370 passengers and 69 vehicles, and it has 44 cabins. The ship has a cafeteria, cocktail lounge, observation lounge, and solarium.

The *Lituya,* the smallest and slowest of the ferries, operates exclusively between Ketchikan and the nearby native village of Metlakatla. The 8-mile trip takes just 45 minutes, and the cabin-less vessel carries 149 passengers and 18 vehicles. Although built with a specific local market in mind, it offers tourists an easy way to visit the off-the-beaten-path outpost.

Another vessel that will get you to less-known towns is the 300-passenger, 34-vehicle *Le Conte* which Juneau with such small Southeast communities as Angoon, Gustavus (gateway to Glacier Bay National Park), Pelican, and Hoonah. It has a cafeteria, but no cabins.

The 174-passenger, 36-vehicle *Tustumena,* in Alaska since 1964, connects the towns of the Southwest from Homer all the way west to Dutch Harbor in the Aleutian Islands. It has 26 cabins (one of which is adapted for wheelchair use), a fine dining room, and a cocktail lounge.

ALASKAN DREAM CRUISES

www.alaskandreamcruises.com. ✆ **855/747-8100.**

Pros

o **Off-the-Beaten-Path Itineraries:** Alaskan Dream builds journeys around such little-visited Southeast Alaskan outposts as the native village of Kake and normally off-limits Hobart Bay, as well as iconic attractions as Glacier Bay National Park.

o **Local Alaskan Flavor:** Alaskan Dream is owned by a family in Sitka, Alaska, and its staff is mostly made up of resident Alaskans who are proud to show off their home state.

o **Complimentary Excursions:** At least one or two complimentary excursions are offered in each port of call.

Cons

o **Tough Embarkation & Debarkations:** Most of Alaskan Dream Cruises' itineraries begin and end in either Ketchikan or Sitka, which can be challenging to reach. A handful of voyages begin and end in Juneau.

Overview

Founded in 2011 by Dave Allan, a Southeast Alaskan resident, Alaskan Dream promises a glimpse of the "true Alaska" away from the tourist hordes, with local Alaskans as your guides. It's an admirable counterpoint to the massive ships that ply Alaska's waters, yet typically only call on the "big three" ports of Juneau, Skagway and Ketchikan. The line has five small ships, ranging in size from the 74-guest *Chichagof Dream* to the 40-guest *Alaskan Dream* (the latter is a pretty cool-looking, four-deck-high catamaran).

While the line is relatively new, the Allans are no strangers to the boat-and-ship business, having owned and run Sitka-based boat building company Allen Marine since 1967, as well as Allen Marine Tours (day cruises out of several towns). The family also owns Southeast Alaska's Windham Bay Lodge, a wilderness resort.

EXPERIENCE

Alaskan Dream focuses on small-ship cruises in Southeast Alaska with a local twist. The line has taken great pains to hire local Alaskans to staff its vessels, who bring an insider's knowledge of the region.

Other Alaskan touches include state products prominently featured on board vessels, from meals crafted from fresh Alaskan seafood and other local ingredients (and sided by Alaska-made beer and spirits) to the Alaska-made soaps and shampoos in every cabin. As is typical with most of the small-ship lines in Alaska, Alaskan Dream includes excursions in the base cost of its sailings, including adventure tours in Hobart Bay, along with transfers at the start and end of your voyage to either a hotel or airport. The cruising atmosphere on the line's ships is casual, also common for small ships in AK.

ROUTES

This line serves only Alaska, and they serve it well. Itineraries run from four to 13-days and include stops at several little-visited, "locals only" destinations in the region like Thorne Bay, Kasaan, and Metlakatla. In addition, many itineraries include a stop at scenic Hobart Bay, an unfrequented gem of a wilderness area that is within native lands and is normally off-limits to tourists. Alaskan Dream operates a private adventure camp within the Bay that has kayaks, motorized Zego boats, and ATVs for passenger use.

PASSENGERS

Alaskan Dream Cruises passengers tend to be well-traveled, well-educated people (most hold a bachelor's degree or higher) in search of an authentic Alaska experience. Often they're semi-retired or retired, and they come from all over the world, most commonly the USA, Australia, Canada, the United Kingdom, and Germany. The line also is drawing a growing number of multigenerational families, thanks to their "Become A True Alaskan" multigenerational voyages. These sailings carry a youth leader and include specially designed experiences suitable for children aged 7 years and up.

DINING

All of the line's ships have a single communal dining room where meals are served three times a day. As is often the case on vessels with fewer than 100 passengers, there is no fixed seating. In the morning, in addition to a full breakfast, an early morning Continental breakfast is put out for early risers, and you'll always find snacks available at other times, whether it be a batch of muffins or afternoon cookies. All food is sourced locally when possible, including locally caught salmon and other seafood. In addition, beer from the Alaskan Brewing Company and Alaskan Distillery spirits are prominent. Passengers with dietary restrictions and allergies will find that the line makes a great effort to be accommodating. Don't be shy about asking!

ACTIVITIES

Whether it be a kayak trip across a remote bay or a walk around a native village, most of the passenger activities take place off the ship—and they're all included in the base price of the trip. Led by naturalist guides who travel with passengers on the vessel, daily outings on a typical cruise in Alaska will include a mix of outdoorsy pursuits such as riding an ATV through a forest and visits to some of Southeast Alaska's small fishing towns. During some port calls, there's time for two excursions, though one is typical. Other usual outings: king salmon and king crab dinner at a lodge near Juneau; a small Zego sports-boat excursions at Hobart Bay; and visits to historically and culturally significant sights in the Alaskan towns of Sitka and Petersburg.

CHILDREN'S PROGRAMS

While most Alaskan Dream sailings have no formal children's program, the line features dedicated family cruises that include daily excursions aimed at kids, young adults, and families. Activities range from classes in traditional arts to geo-caching expeditions in the rain forest. When not leading a family-friendly expedition off the ship, youth leaders coordinate onboard activities.

ENTERTAINMENT

There are no shows in the traditional sense, but in the evenings, after dinner, the ships' lounges often are the site of onboard presentations and discussions led by scientific and cultural expedition leaders.

SERVICE

Alaskan Dream prides itself on hiring local Alaskans to work on its ships. Naturalists and other crewmembers facilitate all off-ship and onboard activities, as well as serve meals and perform housekeeping duties. While gratuities are not mandatory, the line suggests that passengers leave $15 per person per day to be shared among the crew.

CRUISETOURS & ADD-ON PROGRAMS

Alaskan Dream Cruises passengers can pair a cruise with a stay at Alaska's Windham Bay Lodge, owned by parent company Allen Marine. Located about 65 miles from Juneau at the end of a 6-mile bay, the lodge lies within the Chuck River Wilderness and Tongass National Forest and accommodates up to 16 people in three guest cabins and two bedrooms in the main lodge. Activities include glacier viewing, wildlife watching on Admiralty Island, kayaking along Endicott Arm, exploring Windham Bay by skiff, and a visit to the company's adventure camp at Hobart Bay.

FLEET

While the line is fairly new, its ships aren't. Alaskan Dream Cruises launched in 2011 with two vessels that had sailed before in Alaska, but had been out of commission for several years. The line has since expanded its fleet to include four small-ships that hold no more than 74 guests, with much of the fleet holding roughly half that amount. Extensively refurbished, these are comfortable, well-run ships. Just don't expect too many bells and whistles.

Admiralty Dream • Baranof Dream • Chichagof Dream

The Verdict

The *Dream* and *Baranof* are similarly designed ships, rugged explorers that hold between 49 and 59 guests apiece. *Chichagof* is the biggest and oldest in the fleet, holding up to 74 and built in 1984. All three are surprising comfortable, and features a disproportionately large amount of open deck space for ships their size, great news for nature and wildlife lovers.

Specifications   Avg. Starting Per Diem $422

Size (in tons)	95/97/1471	Crew	21/19/30
Passengers (Double Occ.)	58/49/74	Passenger/Crew Ratio	2.8/2.6/2.4 to 1
Passenger/Space Ratio	N/A	Year Launched	1979/1980
Total Cabins/Veranda Cabins	29/25/37	Last Major Refurbishment	2012/2013/2016

Cabin Comfort & Amenities	3.5	Dining Options	3.5
Ship Cleanliness & Maintenance	4	Gym, Spa & Sports Facilities	N/A
Public Comfort/Space	3.5	Children's Facilities	N/A
Decor	3.5	Enjoyment Factor	4

THE SHIPS IN GENERAL

You might remember the *Admiralty* and *Baranof* from their days with Cruise West as the *Spirit of Alaska* and *Spirit of Columbia.* Alaskan Dream Cruises has taken good care of them and their blunt appearance has a tendency to grow on you after a while. The *Chichagof* has a very different history: Built in 1984, she was given a complete overhaul at the company-owned shipyard before entering service in 2016 after nearly a decade spent out of service. With their shallow drafts, all can go into narrow channels and fjords that remain inaccessible to all but the littlest boats.

CABINS　Cabins aboard these ships can be itty bitty (even the Owner's Suite aboard the *Admiralty Dream* only measures a snug 135 square feet), but they are quite pleasant. Heavily refitted, they have new wall paneling (cherrywood accents) and lighting, plus better beds. *Note:* In some cabins, beds can't be pushed into a queen configuration, and are set in a fixed twin setup.

PUBLIC AREAS & ACTIVITIES　Guests aboard both ships will find a forward-facing **lounge** on Main Deck that serves as the social hub of the ship, at least when weather is inclement. When the weather outside is good (or the wildlife is out), the decks are the main gathering point. But let's face it: You're off of the ship most of the time anyhow, exploring Alaska's wilderness. Which is good because there's no fitness room, spa, or pool.

DINING　Meals are served in the ships' main dining room. Cuisine is designed with local ingredients and flair, and the seafood is, as you might expect, excellent. This isn't *haute cuisine,* but it's mighty tasty.

Alaskan Dream

The Verdict

You can recognize the *Alaskan Dream* a mile off, thanks to a unique catamaran design that's rarely seen in Alaskan waters. She's got some quirky features, but that just makes us like her all the more.

Specifications　　　　　　　　　Avg. Starting Per Diem $502

Size (in tons)	93	Crew	18
Passengers (Double Occ.)	38	Passenger/Crew Ratio	2.1 to 1
Passenger/Space Ratio	N/A	Year Launched	1986
Total Cabins/Veranda Cabins	19	Last Major Refurbishment	2011

Frommer's Ratings (Scale of 1–5)　　　　　　　★★★ ½

Cabin Comfort & Amenities	3.5	Dining Options	3.5
Ship Cleanliness & Maintenance	4	Gym, Spa & Sports Facilities	N.A
Public Comfort/Space	3.5	Children's Facilities	N/A
Decor	4	Enjoyment Factor	4

THE SHIP IN GENERAL

Capable of carrying just 40 guests, this 103-foot long ship can do 13 knots flat-out, making her one of the faster ships in the fleet. She plenty of windows to take in Alaska's scenery but if there's a drawback to this ship, it's that open deck space isn't as plentiful as on some of the line's other vessels.

CABINS   All staterooms and suites feature private bathroom facilities, picture window views, and beds that can convert into a queen (though beds in the Owner's Suite and Vista View Suites cannot be separated into two twins). While storage space is very decent, cabins are on the plain but pleasant side, with cherrywood furnishings. Category A and AA are *very* snug.

PUBLIC AREAS & ACTIVITIES   The **Vista View Lounge** on Main Deck has 180-degree views overlooking the ship's bow. It may be the ship's only public room, but it's an attractive one, with leather-clad chairs and attractive earth-tone colors throughout. No pool, spa, or fitness facilities.

DINING   Only one dining room is available aboard the *Alaskan Dream,* which should come to no surprise to cruisers with small-ship experience. Meals are hearty, local, and plentiful.

AMERICAN CRUISE LINES

www.americancruiselines.com. ✆ **800/460-4518.**

Pros

- **Spacious, Upscale Cabins:** At more than 200 square feet, cabins on American Cruise Lines vessels are some of the most spacious in small-ship cruising and feature large bathrooms, picture windows and even a handful of balcony staterooms.
- **Modern Amenities:** Many American Cruise Line ships boast satellite TV and complimentary Wi-Fi in every cabin, conveniences not typically found on ships of this size.

Cons

- **The Cost:** Starting at more than $4,000 per person per week for the smallest cabins, these small cruises can take a big bite out of your wallet.

Overview

Still relatively unknown to many Americans, American Cruise Lines is a niche operator of upscale small-ship voyages to Alaska, the Pacific Northwest, the Mississippi River, and to other lesser-explored areas like coastal New England, the Hudson River, and the waterways of coastal Florida.

EXPERIENCE

Founded in 1999 by Connecticut entrepreneur Charles A. Robertson, family-run American Cruise Lines offers a true slice of Americana: Sailing exclusively in the United States, its ships are U.S.–built, U.S.–flagged, and staffed by an all-American crew. Robertson's original vision of offering gracious hospitality and personalized service in an intimate, small-ship setting remains the line's mantra, and the line's vessels are relatively new, modern, and environmentally friendly, with lots of upscale amenities. Hallmarks of the line include elegant, locally sourced cuisine, nightly entertainment (something not always found on small ships), and daily lectures by historians, naturalists, and local experts.

ROUTES

American Cruise Lines vessels sail 35 different itineraries to 28 states, which include both river and ocean cruise options. The vessels operate in the U.S.'s Pacific Northwest, Alaska, New England, Mid-Atlantic, Southeast, and Mississippi River complex.

PASSENGERS

The line tends to attract experienced travelers who are mostly well educated, professional, and over 50 years old. In the mix are some singles and a smattering of younger passengers who share a common interest in history and cruising (and the money to afford American Cruise Lines' high rates).

DINING

American Cruise Lines' vessels have a single main restaurant. Each evening, before dinner, passengers enjoy complimentary cocktails and hors d'oeuvres in a lounge, then it's off to the dining room, where meals are open seating, served by waiters and ordered off menus (no buffets here for any meal).

Generally the line offers a choice of a couple of appetizers, two or three entrees, and a few dessert selections, all expertly prepared. At both lunch and dinner, wine is always on the table, included at no extra charge, and beer is also available at no charge.

There is no midnight buffet, but you can go to the main lounge any time and find snacks, coffee and soft drinks.

ACTIVITIES

During days in port, most activities take place off the ship. American Cruise Lines includes shore excursions in its pricing, and most passengers take advantage of them. Some are quite elaborate, such as the jet boat tour of Stikine River near Wrangell, Alaska. You'll talk about that one for a long time. In Glacier Bay, where American Cruise Lines has a highly sought-after permit to cruise, an official park ranger and native interpreter come on board to point out the sights and discuss folklore and history.

Onboard activities are few but on *American Spirit,* there's a small putting green. At the cruise director's discretion, additional activities such as wine tastings or a hot chocolate bar are arranged for passengers.

CHILDREN'S PROGRAMS

While kids are welcome there are no programs for them, so be prepared to create your own fun.

ENTERTAINMENT

American Cruise Lines is unusual among small-ship companies in that it has nightly entertainment. Offerings can range from lectures and slide presentations covering wildlife, geography, and history to a talk from the captain followed by a tour of the bridge to see how the ship navigates. More light-weight evenings might include activities such as bingo complete with silly prizes. On some nights, singers and musicians perform classic American songs, prompting passenger sing-alongs. In an American Cruise Lines tradition, at some point during the evening's program, a waiter makes his way through the audience with a tray full of ice cream sundaes.

SERVICE

Gracious hospitality, offered by an all-American crew, is a hallmark of the line and and passengers can expect warm, personal service. While American Cruise Lines says tipping is left to the discretion of its customers, passengers on weeklong cruises leave about $125 per person, on average.

FLEET

American Cruise Lines' vessels range in size from the 49-passenger *American Glory* to the 150-passenger *Queen of the Mississippi* and *American Eagle* paddle-wheelers. Nearly all are less than a decade old, giving American Cruise Lines one of the youngest fleets in small-ship cruising. The line's newest ship, under construction as this book went to press, is due out in mid-2017.

American Glory • American Spirit • American Star • Independence

The Verdict

With uncommon small-ship amenities like balconies, these vessels are real winners—if you can afford the price of admission.

Specifications		Avg. Starting Per Diem $585	
Size (in tons)	86–1,200	Crew	18–27
Passengers (Double Occ.)	49–104	Passenger/Crew Ratio	2.7 to 1
Passenger/Space Ratio	N/A	Year Launched	2002–2010
Total Cabins/Veranda Cabins	27–52	Last Major Refurbishment	N/A

Frommer's Ratings (Scale of 1–5)   ★★★ ½

Cabin Comfort & Amenities	5	Dining Options	3
Ship Cleanliness & Maintenance	4	Gym, Spa & Sports Facilities	3
Public Comfort/Space	3.5	Children's Facilities	N/A
Decor	3.5	Enjoyment Factor	4

THE SHIPS IN GENERAL

Launched between 2002 and 2010, these four vessels are far newer than many competing ships of the same size. Other superlatives: They offer larger cabins (some with private balconies), more space per person and a wider selection of suites than their peers. The smallest of the four, *American Glory,* still manages to offer a Grand Dining Room, outdoor observation decks, and even an exercise area and putting green. Her sisters can best be thought of as "stretch" versions, with the 104-guest *Independence* coming in at the top of the scale.

CABINS If the thought of staying in a tiny, traditional small-ship cabin has put you off, these ships are the ones for you. No **staterooms** are smaller than 200 square feet, and some of the top-of-the-line **suites** push the 400 square foot mark. Each room has double beds that can be converted to a King, with bathrooms that are as spacious. Boats even have a handful of single-occupancy staterooms available, a rare and welcome touch. That being said, decor is frumpy like something you'd see at Grandma's house, with matchy-matchy curtains, window sashes, and bed skirts paired with banquet-style furniture in the dining room. The line's newer ships are rectifying this somewhat, but don't expect cutting-edge style.

PUBLIC AREAS & ACTIVITIES For ships of this size, the amount of public rooms on board is refreshing, including several lounges for socializing, snacking and reading (one features a library). The ships' **Observation Decks** offers plenty of deck chairs, exercise equipment and a putting green but no pools or hot tubs. Sorry, no spas, either.

DINING Meals are served in the aft-facing Dining Saloon, which is large enough to seat the all guests in a single sitting. Meals tend to be comforting rather than elaborate, with an emphasis on local ingredients and specialties.

America • American Pride • Queen of the Mississippi • Queen of the West

The Verdict

Paddle-wheelers recalling the grand old days of riverboat travel, these four ships boast more amenities and features than Mark Twain could have ever dreamt of.

Specifications   Avg. Starting Per Diem $540

Size (in tons)	2,100–2,700	Crew	40-50
Passengers (Double Occ.)	120-185	Passenger/Crew Ratio	3.75 to 1
Passenger/Space Ratio	N/A	Year Launched	1995-2016
Total Cabins/Veranda Cabins	60-90	Last Major Refurbishment	2016

Frommer's Ratings (Scale of 1–5)   ★★★★

Cabin Comfort & Amenities	5	Dining Options	4
Ship Cleanliness & Maintenance	4	Gym, Spa & Sports Facilities	2.5
Public Comfort/Space	4	Children's Facilities	N/A
Decor	3.5	Enjoyment Factor	5

THE SHIPS IN GENERAL

Built between 1995 and 2016, these four ships are mostly identical despite sailing on two entirely different rivers. *American Pride* and *Queen of the West* call Washington & Oregon State's Columbia and Snake Rivers home, while *America* and *Queen of the Mississippi* can be found on the Mississippi River. Of these, the 1995-built *Queen of the West* is the most different, having been built for the now-defunct American West Steamboat Company. All offer a modern take on small-ship river cruising, wrapped up in historic packaging.

CABINS For ships of this size, cabins are positively massive. In each room, you'll find twin beds that convert (in most cases) to a king; a writing and vanity desk; a closet, and private bathroom with shower. Staterooms for singles are offered on all four ships, in both oceanview and private balcony varieties.

PUBLIC AREAS & ACTIVITIES *Queen of the West* has four passenger decks, the other three all feature five. The ship's main dining room is located on Main Deck, while one deck above it is an American Cruise Line trademark: the **Paddlewheel Lounge.** A sweet *Huckleberry Finn*–era space in looks, it has views aft over the ship's rotating, vibrant-red paddlewheel. Each ship boasts a **library** and a number of comfy **lounges.** All ships except *Queen of the West* feature a small putting green, while *American Pride* benefits from a wrap-around promenade deck on her 5th Deck that her sisters lack. Outdoor **exercise equipment** is also present on most ships. No pools or hot tubs on board.

DINING Meals are not gourmet but are usually quite tasty, reflecting the regions the ships sail through. So in the south, get ready to chow down on gumbos and mud pies; in the Pacific Northwest there are lots of succulent salmon dishes. All meals are served in the **main dining room.**

BLOUNT SMALL SHIP ADVENTURES

www.blountsmallshipadventures.com.℡ **866/730-5265.**

Pros

- **Unusual Itineraries:** These two ships reach ports that others can't get into.
- **Kick-back atmosphere:** A Blount cruise is one of the closest things you'll get to chartering your own boat. The word of the day is "informality."

Cons

- **BYOB:** The ships do not have full bars, but you can bring your own alcohol on board.
- **Small Cabins:** Cabins are small by today's standards.

Overview

These two ships were designed, originally, to go through the Erie Canal. Today, they do that, and a whole lot more.

EXPERIENCE

These friendly small ships carry less than a hundred passengers each, largely retired Americans, on domestic, Eastern Canadian, or Caribbean trips. They have shallow drafts and retractable pilot houses meaning they can sail under bridges and in waterways most ships can't get into.

ROUTES

Blount primarily cruises the Caribbean and Central America, and then a variety of American itineraries, including the Northeast, the South, the Midwest and Great Lakes, as well as up to Canada during fall foliage season.

PASSENGERS

Fellow passengers are largely Americans retirees along with a handful of Canadians and Australians.

ACTIVITIES

Onboard activities are limited, but might include photography classes, wine tastings, and lectures by naturalists. Ships sail with kayaks, snorkeling gear, and bikes. If you get a fishing license and bring your own equipment, you can fish in some ports.

CHILDREN'S PROGRAMS

Only children age 14 and older are allowed on these ships, and there are no dedicated facilities for them.

ENTERTAINMENT

There's no formal entertainment programs on these ships.

SERVICE

These ships sail itineraries that only hit U.S. ports, so (as is the nation's law) the crew is American. Service is generally quite good, but very informal. Don't expect the crew to fuss over you. Blount recommends gratuities of $12-14 per person, per day.

Grande Caribe • Grande Mariner

The Verdict

Basic but versatile, these unassuming ships can take you to some very cool places. Just don't expect much in the way of service or extra amenities.

Specifications

Avg. Starting Per Diem $284

Size (in tons)	94/97	Crew	18-27
Passengers (Double Occ.)	88/96	Passenger/Crew Ratio	2.7 to 1
Passenger/Space Ratio	N/A	Year Launched	1997/1998
Total Cabins/Veranda Cabins	44/48	Last Major Refurbishment	2010

Frommer's Ratings (Scale of 1–5)

★★★

Cabin Comfort & Amenities	3	Dining Options	3
Ship Cleanliness & Maintenance	4	Gym, Spa & Sports Facilities	N/A
Public Comfort/Space	3	Children's Facilities	N/A
Decor	3	Enjoyment Factor	4

THE SHIPS IN GENERAL

Grande Caribe and *Grande Mariner* are simple, basic ships that have nonetheless been lovingly cared for over the years. Fun features like glass-bottomed boats and onboard kayaks make them smart choices for active cruisers.

CABINS   If there's one common theme to these **staterooms,** it's that they are *small*. Most rooms feature two single berths (or an upper/lower berth), while a handful of rooms will have a double bed. That said, decor and bathrooms were updated a few years back, softening the color schemes and adding better lighting. *Warning:* Six rooms on Lower Deck have no window views.

PUBLIC AREAS & ACTIVITIES   Each ship features a **main lounge** done primarily in shades of white and slate grey, with cherrywood accents on the support columns. It ain't the height of design, but it's pleasant. There's also a large **Sun Deck** but no fitness equipment, pool or spa. But with bow ramps that lead directly onto the beach on Caribbean sailings, there's not much need for an onboard pool, is there?

DINING   Food is generous and largely American in both taste and style. Think of it as Mom's home cooking and you'll do just fine.

LINDBLAD EXPEDITIONS— NATIONAL GEOGRAPHIC

www.expeditions.com. ℰ **800/397-3348** or 212/765-7740.

Pros

- **Fab Programming:** Lindblad has innovative, flexible itineraries and outstanding lecturers/guides. The partnership with *National Geographic* has resulted in many top *National Geographic*–affiliated photographers, explorers, scientists, and researchers joining the line's voyages. Six naturalists are on board, for a 10-to-1 passenger-to-naturalist ratio.
- **Built-In Shore Excursions:** Rather than relying on outside concessionaires for their shore excursions (which is the case with most other lines, big and small), Lindblad Expeditions runs its own. Excursions are superb and included in the cost of the cruise fare.
- **Warm Crew:** The staff is friendly and accommodating.

Cons

- **Cost:** Cruise fares tend to be higher than similar adventure-focused sailings on competing lines.

Overview

In 1979, Sven-Olof Lindblad, son of adventure-travel pioneer Lars-Eric Lindblad, followed in his father's footsteps by forming Lindblad Expeditions, which specializes in providing environmentally sensitive, soft-adventure/ educational cruises to remote places in the world, with visits to a few large ports. In 2004, Lindblad Expeditions entered into an alliance with *National Geographic.* As pioneers of global exploration, the organizations work in tandem to produce innovative expedition programs and to promote conservation and sustainable tourism around the world. The venture lifts Lindblad's educational offerings out of the commonplace.

EXPERIENCE

Lindblad's expedition cruises are designed to appeal to the intellectually curious traveler. Passengers' time is spent learning about life above and below the sea (from *National Geographic* experts and high-caliber expedition leaders and naturalists trained in botany, anthropology, biology, and geology) and observing the world either from the ship or on shore excursions, which are included in the cruise package. Flexibility and spontaneity are keys to the Lindblad experience, as the route may be altered anytime to follow a pod of whales or other wildlife. Depending on weather and sea conditions, there are usually two or three excursions every day.

ROUTES

These ships sail some interesting paths, including Antarctica and the Arctic, Southeast Asia and the Pacific, South America, Caribbean, Alaska, the U.S. and Canada, and the Galapagos Islands. In 2015, Lindblad Expeditions began sailing to the protected area known as Haida Gwaii, off the coast of British Columbia, as part of its routes through Alaska and the Pacific Northwest.

PASSENGERS

Lindblad Expeditions tends to attract well-traveled and well-educated, professional, 55-year-old-plus couples who have "been there, done that" and are looking for something completely different. The passenger mix may also include some singles and a smattering of younger couples. Many passengers are likely to have been on other Lindblad Expeditions programs, and they share a common interest in history and wildlife.

DINING

Hearty buffet breakfasts and lunches and sit-down dinners include plenty of fresh fruits and vegetables. Many of the fresh ingredients are obtained from ports along the way, and meals reflect regional tastes. (Lindblad chefs will search out sustainably caught local fish as part of an overall commitment to promoting sustainable cuisine.) Although far from haute cuisine, dinners are well prepared, served at single open seatings, which lets passengers get to know one another by moving around to different tables. Lecturers and other staff members dine with passengers.

ACTIVITIES

During the day, most activity takes place off the ship, aboard expedition landing craft Zodiac boats or kayaks and/or on land excursions. While on board, passengers entertain themselves with the usual small-ship activities: wildlife watching, gazing off into the wilderness, reading, and chatting. Shore excursions are included in the cruise fare. Lindblad also has an open-bridge policy—rare in the cruise industry—that gives travelers the opportunity to spend time on the bridge to observe and interact with the captain and staff.

CHILDREN'S PROGRAMS

Family cruising is big business, and Lindblad has family activities led by specially trained staff on all sailings. Activities have a nature slant, such as exploring an Alaskan rain forest or meeting with a local ranger in Glacier Bay National Park to work toward earning a "Junior Ranger" badge. Don't expect such big-ship features as a video arcade or playroom for the little ones.

National Geographic Quest (Preview)

Lindblad's newest ship, *National Geographic Quest,* makes her debut in June 2017 in the waters of Alaska and British Columbia. Larger and more extravagant than the line's existing West Coast fleet, this new ship will hold 100 guests.

All 50 **cabins** will be outside-facing, with picture windows or private balconies.

Public areas will mirror the teal and blue of the sea outside, with a main **lounge** and a separate **dining room.** Wall-to-wall windows will line both rooms, ensuring that Alaska's scenery is never far from sight.

Like other Lindblad ships, *National Geographic Quest* will be outfitted with a fleet of inflatable Zodiac rafts, kayaks, a remote-operated underwater vehicle, bow cameras, video microscope, hydrophones, and other nifty toys for getting the most out of the Pacific Northwest.

ENTERTAINMENT

Lectures and slide presentations are scheduled throughout the cruise, and documentaries or movies may be screened in the evening in the main lounge. The line's exclusive fleet-wide Expedition Photography program features a Lindblad–National Geographic Certified Photo Instructor on every departure to help passengers take their photography skills to the next level. Several voyages are also specially designed photo expeditions that go deeper into landscape photography with *National Geographic* photographers on board. In 2011, Lindblad also began bringing a native Huna/Tlinglit interpreter on board its vessels in Glacier Bay to share local stories that date back before written history. The line's Alaska sailings are also notable for the Alaska Undersea Program, which brings on board a specialist who makes regular dives up to 80 feet below the vessel with high-intensity lighting and a video camera to capture Alaska's underwater wonders. The fascinating footage is viewed by passengers on a plasma screen in the lounge, often in real time.

SERVICE

Dining-room staff and room stewards are affable and efficient and seem to enjoy their work. As with other small ships, there's no room service. The line suggests passengers leave a gratuity of $14 to $16 per person per day.

CRUISETOURS & ADD-ON PROGRAMS

Lindblad offers add-on tours that explore overland areas of Alaska like Denali National Park. These pre-and-post voyage extensions include long stays within the park itself, and a night each in Fairbanks and Anchorage. In addition to wildlife viewing, tour-goers have the choice of hiking, canoeing, fishing, and biking. The cost of the trip, which is available pre- or post-cruise, is $5,820 per person, based on double occupancy and including all meals.

FLEET

The line has eight expedition-style ships, and they vary a greatly one to the next: The 62-passenger *National Geographic Sea Lion* and *National Geographic Sea*

Bird, for example, are basic vessels and have a minimum of public rooms and conveniences. The newly acquired *National Geographic Endeavour II,* on the other hand, features three suites, stem-to-stern Wi-Fi access, a spacious lounge, a library, and a gym and spa.

National Geographic Sea Bird • National Geographic Sea Lion

The Verdict

These 62-guest ships are among the most basic in the Lindblad fleet, but they're perfectly suited to the grand regions in which they sail.

Specifications · Avg. Starting Per Diem $734

Size (in tons)	100	Crew	29
Passengers (Double Occ.)	62	Passenger/Crew Ratio	2.1 to 1
Passenger/Space Ratio	N/A	Year Launched	1982/1981
Total Cabins/Veranda Cabins	31	Last Major Refurbishment	2015

Frommer's Ratings (Scale of 1–5) · ★★★★

Cabin Comfort & Amenities	3.5	Dining Options	3.5
Ship Cleanliness & Maintenance	4	Gym, Spa & Sports Facilities	4
Public Comfort/Space	3.5	Children's Facilities	N/A
Decor	3.5	Enjoyment Factor	4.5

THE SHIPS IN GENERAL

National Geographic Sea Bird and *National Geographic Sea Lion* make their homes in Alaska, the Pacific Northwest, Baja California, and Costa Rica and Panama. As far as expedition ships go, they're fairly utilitarian, though an extensive recent refit has left both ships with appealing new decor.

CABINS Accommodations on board are tiny but functional. An extensive 2015 refit left them looking far more cheery, though. Staterooms lock from the inside and cannot be locked from the outside, though this isn't an issue at all on these ships. Brace yourself for the stateroom bathrooms: They're Lilliputian, and the toilet is located opposite the showerhead.

PUBLIC AREAS & ACTIVITIES Each ship features a forward-facing observation lounge in the bow of the ship, home to a **bar** and small **library.** Most guests can be found gathering out on deck, even in inclement weather, as the hunt for wildlife continues. It's here that these two ships excel, with **bow viewing areas** and two decks of **outdoor promenade-style viewpoints.** A small **spa** (a treatment room, really) and a few kinds of **exercise equipment** can be found on the Sun Deck.

DINING Each ship has a main dining room where all meals are served. Thanks to the intimate size of these ships (and the open-seating policy), you'll have met all your fellow guests after a day or two. Meals are not haute cuisine, but taste like the kind of home cooking you'd get in the destination.

National Geographic Endeavour II

The Verdict

The successor to the recently retired *National Geographic Endeavour* is an improvement in every way.

Specifications

Size (in tons)	2,716	Crew	66
Passengers (Double Occ.)	96	Passenger/Crew Ratio	1.45 to 1
Passenger/Space Ratio	28.2	Year Launched	2005
Total Cabins/Veranda Cabins	52	Last Major Refurbishment	2016

Frommer's Ratings (Scale of 1–5)   ★★★★

Cabin Comfort & Amenities	4	Dining Options	4
Ship Cleanliness & Maintenance	4	Gym, Spa & Sports Facilities	3
Public Comfort/Space	5	Children's Facilities	N/A
Decor	5	Enjoyment Factor	5

THE SHIP IN GENERAL

Built in 2005 and extensively refurbished by Lindblad, *National Geographic Endeavour II* replaced the company's older *National Geographic Endeavour* in the Galapagos Islands. Carrying a maximum of 96 guests, she is easily one of the more lavish ships in the region, and the second Lindblad ship to sail to the islands along with *National Geographic Islander*.

CABINS   The ship's 96 guests stay in 42 **double occupancy staterooms** and 11 **single occupancy staterooms.** All double-occupancy staterooms feature twin beds that can be converted into a queen, and every stateroom offers outside-facing picture window views. They're simple but fine with Wi-Fi access, writing desk and chair, under-bed storage, a closet, and a bathroom stocked with botanically friendly shower products. The ship also features three **suites** with larger bathrooms and floor-to-ceiling windows.

PUBLIC AREAS & ACTIVITIES   Lindblad has given *National Geographic Endeavour II* an extensive refit adding an attractive blue-teal color scheme to the vessel, along with new furnishings. The **Lounge Deck** is even more pleasant now, redone with light, airy materials; its floor-to-ceiling windows provide a great vantage point to admire the Galapagos Islands. On Bridge Deck, a big **library** faces the stern, while the ship's **navigation bridge**—open to guests when permissible—is just a short stroll forward.

While you won't find a pool but the ship does have a small but functional **gym** and **spa** (actually just one treatment room).

DINING   The ship's main **Dining Room** takes up the better half of Main Deck. Its menu consists of ingredients culled primarily from the Galapagos Islands and the mainland of Ecuador. Breakfast and lunch are buffet-style, while dinners are plated. In all instances, seating is open and meals are casual. Snacks—including coffees, teas, soft drinks and cookies—are available all day in the library.

National Geographic Explorer

The Verdict

Ice-strengthened and rugged, this ship explores some of the farthest (and coldest) reaches of the planet, outfitted with cool toys like hydrophones, high-definition underwater cameras, and even a remote-operated vehicle (ROV).

Specifications

Avg. Starting Per Diem $961

Size (in tons)	6,471	Crew	71
Passengers (Double Occ.)	148	Passenger/Crew Ratio	2 to 1
Passenger/Space Ratio	43	Year Launched	1982
Total Cabins/Veranda Cabins	81	Last Major Refurbishment	2014

Frommer's Ratings (Scale of 1–5)   ★★★★

Cabin Comfort & Amenities	4	Dining Options	4
Ship Cleanliness & Maintenance	4	Gym, Spa & Sports Facilities	4
Public Comfort/Space	5	Children's Facilities	N/A
Decor	4	Enjoyment Factor	5

THE SHIP IN GENERAL

Introduced to the fleet in 2008, *National Geographic Explorer* was originally built for Norwegian cruise-ferry line Hurtigruten in 1982. Extensively refitted, she can carry 148 guests in 81 staterooms. Her hull is ice-strengthened and rated as Class 1A, allowing *National Geographic Explorer* to sail confidently in both the Arctic and Antarctica. Lindblad calls her, "the ultimate expedition ship," and that's not far off the mark: She carries a fleet of nimble zodiac rafts for exploration; as well as 36 two-person AIRE inflatable kayaks, a high-definition underwater bow camera, a video microscope, a camera mounted to the ship's mast that provides a far-reaching view of the terrain around the ship, and a remote-operated-vehicle (ROV) that can reach a depth of 1,000 feet. The ship also has hydrophones for listening to marine life and an open-bridge policy that encourages guests to engage with the ship's officers.

CABINS   All **staterooms** feature picture windows or private balconies. They come with either twin beds, twin beds that can convert to a queen, or fixed queen-size beds, depending on the category. Special staterooms designed for solo cruisers are also available. All have televisions with movies and *National Geographic* documentaries; reading lights; ample storage space, and surprisingly modern bathrooms that feature glass-enclosed showers and dual vanity sinks at the suite level. All bathrooms feature eco-friendly toiletries.

PUBLIC AREAS & ACTIVITIES   During the daytime, you'll often find guests on the **Bridge Deck,** visiting the Navigation Bridge (thanks to Lindblad's open-bridge policy). Further aft, a well-stocked **library** contains titles on nearly every conceivable subject, and an adjacent **observation lounge** features wall-to-wall windows and skylights. On **Veranda Deck,** an aft-facing **lounge** serves as the go-to spot for lectures, daily briefings, and post-dinner nightcaps. Our favorite nook: the forward-facing **Chart Room,** which is brimming with books and charts and boasts the same superb view that the officers on the bridge have. Wrapped in cherry woods and brass accents, there's also a nice bar here, too.

Unusually for an expedition ship, the *National Geographic Explorer* boasts a decent-sized **fitness center** with floor-to-ceiling windows, along with a small **spa** featuring two treatment rooms and a sauna. No pools or hot tubs.

DINING *National Geographic Explorer*'s main **restaurant** is uniquely positioned all the way forward on Upper Deck, providing fantastic views of the "road" ahead. Breakfast and lunch are casual, buffets, while dinners are chosen from a menu that rotates daily. Open seating is *de rigueur.* Off the main dining room is **The Bistro,** an intimate, open-seating dining venue that functions as an overflow area for the main restaurant (it has the same menu).

National Geographic Islander

The Verdict

A catamaran-style ship in the Galapagos that's big on personality, but short on open deck space.

Specifications

Avg. Starting Per Diem $744

Size (in tons)	1,065	Crew	27
Passengers (Double Occ.)	48	Passenger/Crew Ratio	1.7 to 1
Passenger/Space Ratio	N/A	Year Launched	1995
Total Cabins/Veranda Cabins	24	Last Major Refurbishment	2015

Frommer's Ratings (Scale of 1–5)

★★★ ½

Cabin Comfort & Amenities	4	Dining Options	3
Ship Cleanliness & Maintenance	4	Gym, Spa & Sports Facilities	2.5
Public Comfort/Space	3.5	Children's Facilities	N/A
Decor	4	Enjoyment Factor	4

THE SHIP IN GENERAL

Originally built to sail the Caribbean—and, oddly enough, the Scottish Highlands—Lindblad's twin-hulled *National Geographic Islander* has been sailing the Galapagos since 2004. At just 164 feet in length, she's small enough to go where the biggest ships in the Galapagos can't. The downside? Her catamaran design means there isn't a lot of outdoor deck space.

CABINS Nautical in decor, *National Geographic Islander* has 24 **staterooms** and two **suites** on board. While all staterooms are similar, you might want to splurge for the Category 4 staterooms on Upper Deck that have solarium-style glassed-in terraces that function as a sort of pseudo-balcony. The two Category 5 suites are noteworthy for being the largest on board, wrapping attractively around the front of the ship with the same view the Captain would have one deck below.

PUBLIC AREAS & ACTIVITIES The ship has a small but attractive **lounge** that can seat everyone on board at once. A **library and Internet center** flank its forward half; and the ship's **navigation bridge** functions as a sort of public room thanks to Lindblad's great open-bridge policy. The negative to the ship's lay out? Unless you're a very social being, you might find yourself wishing for a quiet corner to enjoy some time to yourself.

A small (we mean small) treatment room is set in a converted stateroom. The list of available spa treatments is short, but anyone looking for a basic massage will come away feeling relaxed. Sorry, no pool or fitness equipment.

DINING   As with all ships in the Galapagos, ingredients are mainly local due to regulations that require companies to source food products from the Galapagos Islands or the Ecuadorian mainland. Which, frankly, Lindblad would do anyway. All meals are taken in the **main dining room.**

National Geographic Orion

The Verdict

One of Lindblad's most lavish expedition ships, *National Geographic Orion* boasts the amenities of a luxury ship while sacrificing none of the educational adventure you'd expect from the line.

Specifications — Avg. Starting Per Diem $930

Size (in tons)	4,000	Crew	75
Passengers (Double Occ.)	102	Passenger/Crew Ratio	1.3 to 1
Passenger/Space Ratio	39	Year Launched	2003
Total Cabins/Veranda Cabins	53	Last Major Refurbishment	2014

Frommer's Ratings (Scale of 1–5)   ★★★★

Cabin Comfort & Amenities	4	Dining Options	4
Ship Cleanliness & Maintenance	4	Gym, Spa & Sports Facilities	3.5
Public Comfort/Space	5	Children's Facilities	N/A
Decor	4.5	Enjoyment Factor	5

THE SHIP IN GENERAL

Built in 2003, this elegant 102-guest ship was acquired by Lindblad in 2014. Bright, spacious and airy, nearly every space on the ship features sweeping views of the ocean, from the window-lined main lounge to the ship's central staircase and glass elevator, dramatically topped with a glass skylight. With fun toys for exploration like a full fleet of zodiac rafts, kayaks, an underwater camera, a remote operated vehicle (ROV), hydrophones, and snorkeling and scuba diving gear on warm-weather itineraries, this is the expedition ship that feels like a private yacht.

CABINS   Six separate categories of oceanview cabins are available. **Categories 1 through 4** feature oval-style picture windows, with French-style balconies on **Categories 5 and 6.** All are handsomely decorated (especially for an active expedition ship like this), with walnut trim and cabinetry coupled with navy blue carpeting and drapes, wall-mounted reading lights, and swanky marble-clad bathrooms with backlit makeup mirrors. It's a look that would be right at home on a more traditional cruise ship.

PUBLIC AREAS & ACTIVITIES Public areas are where *National Geographic Orion* really shines, thanks to a design that brings the outside in (with windows everywhere). The social hub of the ship is the **lounge** on Upper Deck, which faces the stern and leads to the outdoor cafe. The **lounge** houses the ship's main bar, while lectures and films are shown in **the theatre** on Observation Deck. The forward-facing **observation lounge** is also here, offering up destination-specific books and 24-hour tea and coffee machines.

Unlike most expedition ships, *National Geographic Orion* features a whirlpool hot tub, a **fitness center** and **spa** treatment room, and even a **sauna!**

DINING In addition to the main dining room, guests can dine outdoors (weather permitting) at the **outdoor cafe** on Upper Deck at tables and chairs overlooking the stern of the ship. Other meals are served in the **main dining room,** with buffet breakfast and lunch, and multi-course dinners selected from a menu that changes nightly. Seating is open.

PAUL GAUGUIN CRUISES

www.pgcruises.com. © **800/848-6172** or 425/440-6171.

Pros

- **Focused on French Polynesia:** Paul Gauguin's only ship cruises exclusively in the South Pacific, and everything on board—from the artwork to the culinary choices—reflects that.
- **Very Inclusive:** There are no extra charges for drinks or gratuities.

Cons

- **Tough to Reach:** French Polynesia is a very long flight from the United States and Canada.

The Verdict

Purpose-built for the South Pacific, the one ship line is upscale and comfortable—but never gets in the way of the scenery.

Specifications

Avg. Starting Per Diem $411

Size (in tons)	19,170	Crew	217
Passengers (Double Occ.)	332	Passenger/Crew Ratio	1.8 to 1
Passenger/Space Ratio	57.7	Year Launched	1998
Total Cabins/Veranda Cabins	166/115	Last Major Refurbishment	2012

Frommer's Ratings (Scale of 1–5)

★★★★ ½

Cabin Comfort & Amenities	4.5	Dining Options	4
Ship Cleanliness & Maintenance	5	Gym, Spa & Sports Facilities	4
Public Comfort/Space	4	Children's Facilities	3
Decor	4,5	Enjoyment Factor	5

Overview

The 1997-built *Paul Gauguin* was designed expressly to sail year-round in French Polynesia and she offers a deep focus on the culture, natural wonders, and history of the destination. Previously, the line also operated a second ship, the *Tere Moana,* but she has since been transferred out of the fleet.

EXPERIENCE

Built in 1997, the 332-guest *Paul Gauguin* offers a spectacular, all-inclusive cruise experience in the South Pacific. With a crew of 214, service levels are among the best in the industry, with many staff members having served for years with the line. Don't be surprised if your drinks arrive before you even realize you wanted one; something other lines claim to deliver but fail to actually realize. Half luxury, half soft expedition, onboard lecturers and local Polynesians provide guests with genuine insights into the destinations visited, along with locally inspired cuisines that play off the islands' French heritage. Relaxing but understated, nothing about the *Paul Gauguin* will knock your socks off—and that's precisely the idea. Here, the ship fades into the background to let the beauty of the South Pacific envelop you at every turn.

Paul Gauguin cruises are all-inclusive: Beer, wine, soft drinks, and spirits are complimentary, as are watersports activities like kayaking, windsurfing and paddleboarding. *Paul Gauguin* has a fleet of onboard Zodiac rafts for explorations ashore.

ROUTES

The *Paul Gauguin* sails the South Pacific and French Polynesia (with some visits to Fiji) year-round.

CABINS

Ranging from 200 to 500 square feet, all **cabins** aboard Paul Gauguin feature ocean views, and a full 70% of those have their own private balconies. Even at the bottom rung on the accommodations ladder, the window-only **Category E staterooms** are still plenty nice, with polished wood accents and furniture, a small sitting area, headboard-mounted reading lights, and bathrooms that, for the most part, feature a full bathtub and shower combination and L'Occitane toiletries. The color palette is Zen, with plenty of earth tones and subtle aquamarine throw pillows on the bed.

Private balconies are offered starting with **Category D staterooms,** and guests who choose **Category B Veranda** staterooms or higher are treated to butler service, an in-room bar setup, and an iPod docking station. Higher stateroom categories, including suites, increase the size of the living space and balcony accordingly. One stateroom is wheelchair-accessible, and a number can hold a third guest.

Rooms are comfortable but not over-the-top luxurious. It's appropriate for a ship and a destination where so much time is spent out on deck or on-shore, soaking in the South Pacific.

PASSENGERS

Passengers range widely in age from 40-somethings to 80-somethings, with a lot of empty nesters and retirees and some (somewhat younger) honeymooners thrown in for good mix.

PUBLIC AREAS

Paul Gauguin has everything you might expect of a larger ship, just in a scaled-down format. A small **casino** is located on Deck 5, adjacent to the comfy **piano bar** that offers up live music and cocktails every evening. All the way forward, **Le Grand Salon** is used for evening performances and daytime lectures and, like the rest of the ship, is similarly understated, with plenty of natural wood and soft colors. A small Internet corner is tucked away on the aft starboard side of Deck 5, while Deck 6 is devoted to dining, shopping and spa pursuits, including an attractive window-lined indoor Promenade that runs adjacent to the Deep Nature Spa.

Don't miss out on the **La Palette Lounge** all the way aft on Deck 8. With its indoor-outdoor seating and aft sliding floor-to-ceiling doors that can be opened, this is the place most guests head to for a nightcap or an afternoon cocktail.

DINING OPTIONS

There are three separate dining options aboard *Paul Gauguin*. Dinners are served open-seating in the lovely **L'Etoile Dining Room,** with its high ceilings and 180-degree wraparound windows. A 2012 makeover added a new, brighter color palette of golds, blues and earth tones. You'll find tables for two, four, six, and eight guests here, along with multi-course meals paired with complimentary wines.

Breakfast and lunch are taken in **Le Grille,** up on the aft portion of Deck 8. Food is buffet-style, but set selections (that don't change daily) are always available to order off of a menu. At lunch, expect standard pool grill fare, with burgers, wraps and the like. Dinner featuring Polynesian specialties is also served here, by reservation.

On Deck 6, **La Veranda** also serves up buffet breakfast and lunch, while at night it turns into a reservations-only specialty restaurant featuring dishes created by acclaimed chef Jean-Pierre Vigato. Chef Propriétaire of the Michelin-starred Restaurant Apicius in Paris, Vigato's French-inspired degustation menu includes everything from foie gras to fresh fruit.

If that doesn't tickle your fancy, there's always round-the-clock room service, with selections from L'Etoille available during operating hours.

POOL, FITNESS, SPA & SPORTS FACILITIES

The **Deep Nature Spa by Algotherm** on Deck 6 provides an assortment of treatments plus nail services, and hair styling. Spa staff members even offer an overwater massage during the day spent on Motu Mahana, Paul Gauguin's private island paradise in the South Pacific.

A small but functional **fitness center** is located on board, which is supplemented by a Polynesian-inspired sunrise Zumba class out on deck. The ship also offers complimentary watersports activities that operate when conditions permit from the stern-mounted drop-down marina. Guests can kayak, wind surf, paddleboard, and snorkel.

CHILDREN'S PROGRAMS

The ship worked with oceanographer Jean-Michel Cousteau's Ocean Futures Society to create their own Ambassadors of the Environment Youth program. The goal is to teach children and teens, between the ages of 9 and 17, about the natural habitat and culture of French Polynesia. Activities include hiking rain forests, touring Polynesian temples, and exploring the region's famously fish-filled coral reefs. Other family members are allowed to join in the excursions, and on some sailings Jean-Michel Cousteau is a special guest. Children age 1 and over are allowed on board.

ENTERTAINMENT

Evening entertainment is largely limited to dinner, drinks, and singers, storytellers, and dancers in the show lounge.

SERVICE

The service is attentive, despite the fact that the onboard atmosphere is somewhat casual.

STAR CLIPPERS

www.starclippers.com. © **800/442-0551.**

Pros

- o **Tall Ships:** Real tall-masted sailing ships—how cool is that?
- o **Unusual Itineraries:** Because of their size, these ships can get into small ports, and the line takes advantage of that well.

Cons

- o **Heavily Impacted by Weather:** Itineraries can change quickly if the weather shifts, and heavy swells are felt more on these ships than on larger ones.
- o **Europe-centric:** North American guests will find themselves the minority on these cruises, which draw heavily on European passengers—even in the Caribbean.

Overview

These sleek clipper ships have all the amenities of the sailing yacht experience, but with tall masts, white sails, and—the best seat in the house—the hammocklike bowsprit net you can climb into. Inside, a somewhat heavy-handed design evokes the Grand Age of sailing, with lots of dark wood paneling and red accents. There's also a traditional piano bar and an Edwardian-style library.

EXPERIENCE

Unlike other sailing vessels that use their sails just for show, these tall ships are *real* sailboats, and the billowing beauts that top them are actually raised to propel the ship. While there is a set plan for each sailing, arrival and departure times depend on the wind, and the plan can change as the weather shifts.

ROUTES

These ships focus on four destinations: the Caribbean, the Panama Canal, Costa Rica, and the Mediterranean. They offer many different route choices in those areas, including itineraries that specialize in part of a region, such as Spain, North Africa, or the British Virgin Islands.

PASSENGERS

Passengers range widely in age, but lean heavily toward the empty nesters and retirees. They are generally a mix of North Americans and Europeans (primarily Brits and Germans), and there can be a wide range of languages spoken on board. That's either a positive or a negative, depending on your perspective.

DINING

The ship's dress code is country club casual, and that sets the tone on board. During the day, breakfast and lunch are buffet style and, in these warm climates, most guests wear shorts. At night, you'll see lots of sundresses and polo shirts, and dinner is the main event.

ACTIVITIES

Onboard activities take full advantage of the ship. You can climb the masts, learn to tie knots, join the captain on the bridge, relax in the hammocklike bowsprit net, or just admire the scenery from one of the small pools. There's also a watersports program that guests can enjoy when the stern marina is deployed. That appendage allows guests to enter the water easily to kayak, sail, or snorkel off the side of the ship.

CHILDREN'S PROGRAMS

Children are allowed, but there are no facilities or programs catering specifically to their needs.

ENTERTAINMENT

After dinner, guests might listen to a steel-pan band on deck, or toast in the warm summer air with cocktails or at one of the bars.

SERVICE

Service is friendly and casual, which feels appropriate on these ships.

FLEET

The fleet is made up of three ships: the 170-passenger *Star Flyer* and *Star Clipper* and the larger 227-passenger *Royal Clipper.* A new ship, which the company says will be the largest square-rigged sailing ship in the world, is under construction.

Royal Clipper

The Verdict

This fully rigged, five-masted square sailing clipper turns heads wherever she goes, and her interior amenities—from marble bathrooms to an Edwardian dining room—are among the line's most stunning.

Size (in tons)	5,000	Crew	106
Passengers (Double Occ.)	227	Passenger/Crew Ratio	2.2 to 1
Passenger/Space Ratio	22	Year Launched	2000
Total Cabins/Veranda Cabins	114/14	Last Major Refurbishment	2013

Frommer's Ratings (Scale of 1–5)   ★★★★

Cabin Comfort & Amenities	4	Dining Options	4.5
Ship Cleanliness & Maintenance	5	Gym, Spa & Sports Facilities	4
Public Comfort/Space	4	Children's Facilities	N/A
Decor	4	Enjoyment Factor	5

THE SHIP IN GENERAL

At 439 feet in length, *Royal Clipper* holds the Guinness World Record for the largest square-rigged sailing ship in service, with 56,000 square feet of sails to catch the trade winds of the Caribbean and the Mediterranean. With a total of 42 sails, *Royal Clipper* uses wind power alone whenever possible to propel her to ports of call, but the ship is also equipped with traditional diesel propulsion engines in case Mother Nature refuses to cooperate.

Built in 2000, the ship recalls the grandeur of a different time. She can hold 227 guests when fully booked, along with a crew of 106. Star Clippers plays up her seagoing elegance to the hilt, pumping the Vangelis-composed theme from *Conquest of Paradise* over the ship's loudspeakers as the sails are hoisted. When conditions allow in certain ports of call, guests are invited to board the ship's tender boats for awe-inspiring exterior views of the "mother ship" as *Royal Clipper* sets sail. The miles of lines (that's ropes to you and me), old-school ventilation cowlings, brass fittings, polished woods, and ornate glass skylights and windows brings the glory days of sailing back in a way that's wonderfully different from modern mainstream cruise ships. The same holds true for the creaking, rolling, and pitching. Bottom line: This ship is a real winner for those looking for a truly unique, old-timey experience.

CABINS   *Royal Clipper*'s **cabins** have wood paneling, dark fabrics, and marble-clad bathrooms in most stateroom categories. With the exception of six **interior staterooms,** every cabin on board offers ocean views, and most are sized at a comfortable 148 square feet. Rooms are cleverly designed, with a vanity and desk area, accent lighting, twin or queen beds, and a closet. In keeping with the laid-back ambiance on board, there's no need to fill that closet with formal wear. Bathrooms are surprisingly spacious (with a full-size shower and storage hidden behind the mirror) and, with the exception of the six inside staterooms, heavy on the marble. The lip of the shower, however, stands about an inch or two off the floor, and isn't enough to keep water from sloshing out when the ship is pitching.

Select staterooms on Main and Clipper decks have the capacity for a third person, but unfortunately this spare bunk is located directly above the main bed. Even when folded, it sticks out enough so that it's easy to bump your head. If you like your cabins generously sized, a total of 14 **deluxe suites** (complete with private balconies) feature whirlpool bathtubs and minibars. The two largest suites wrap around the stern of the ship, but those prone to seasickness might want to avoid them—we noticed the most rolling near the stern on our visit.

PUBLIC AREAS & ACTIVITIES   You'd never suspect it from the outside, but the *Royal Clipper* boasts a three-story **atrium** extending from the main dining room to the main lounge, with a skylight that also functions as the floor of the midships swimming pool. That connection with the sea and water is present throughout; the **fitness center,** located below the waterline, even has porthole windows allowing guests to watch the waves while they work out. The **piano bar,** situated on the Main Deck, offers seating in an old-world setting of brass, dark polished woods, and window-lined nooks. A spiral staircase allows access to lower levels, and the outdoor **Tropical Bar,** which serves as the social hub of the ship, particularly in the warmth of the Caribbean.

A small but inviting **library** is situated in a deckhouse behind the Tropical Bar. It's stocked with maps and books in a variety of languages. All the way forward on Main Deck is an **Observation Lounge** that, like the library, is located in its own deckhouse. Sadly, the room is darkened and unused most of the time, though you will find a few Internet stations here (the rest of the ship has Wi-Fi access for purchase). For a ship of this size, the **pool, fitness club,** and **spa** offerings are a pleasant surprise. *Royal Clipper* has a total of three swimming **pools** (including the aforementioned one over the piano bar), along with a nicely sized fitness center and spa, both situated below the waterline.

DINING   Meals are taken in the eye-catching main **dining room,** which proffers a number of table sizes spread across three separate levels of Edwardian grandeur. Breakfast and lunch are buffets, while dinners are plated and chosen from a surprisingly extensive menu. The quality is excellent, especially the soups. Portholes inset into the walls are a nice touch—don't be surprised if the sea washes over them during inclement weather.

Star Clipper • Star Flyer

The Verdict

Featuring the sails and graceful lines of a classic clipper but all the amenities of a modern cruise ship, this pair of 170-guest gems provides one of the most unique experiences in the Caribbean.

Specifications   Avg. Starting Per Diem $202

Size (in tons)	2,298	Crew	72
Passengers (Double Occ.)	170	Passenger/Crew Ratio	2.5 to 1
Passenger/Space Ratio	13.5	Year Launched	1992/1991
Total Cabins/Veranda Cabins	85/0	Last Major Refurbishment	2014

Cabin Comfort & Amenities	3	Dining Options	3.5
Ship Cleanliness & Maintenance	4	Gym, Spa & Sports Facilities	3
Public Comfort/Space	3	Children's Facilities	N/A
Decor	4	Enjoyment Factor	5

THE SHIPS IN GENERAL

At 360 feet in length, *Star Clipper* and *Star Flyer* are smaller, more intimate versions of *Royal Clipper*. They sport a sleek all-white hull topped with 16 sails and four masts towering 226 feet in the air. As you might expect, this is a ship that encourages guests to be out and about on deck, taking in the action as the sails are hoisted or dropped.

CABINS   **Staterooms** aboard both ships are small, with six inside staterooms measuring a miniscule 97 square feet. The ship's outside staterooms, which come in at between 118 and 130 square feet, are significantly less claustrophobic and in fact, are quite inviting, thanks to porthole windows, wood and brass accents, and navy blues at every turn. All rooms have closets and drawers for storage and twin beds that can convert to a double. Both ships feature a single **Owner's Suite** that can be very difficult to book at certain times of the year—so it's best not to get your hopes up.

PUBLIC AREAS & ACTIVITIES   Most guests congregate around the social hub that is the **Tropical Bar,** which is situated out on deck and covered with an awning that keeps guests reasonably dry in inclement weather. The **piano bar,** just forward, is a quiet spot well-suited to lazy afternoons. A **library** is situated in a separate deckhouse aft of the Tropical Bar. Each ship sports two swimming **pools,** with the midships one offering porthole windows that look down into the piano bar—and vice versa. While there isn't an onboard fitness center as such, fitness classes like yoga are held out on deck.

DINING   The only area where crowding becomes an issue is the main **dining room,** mostly because all guests are served at a single sitting. Though the room is snug but its charms, recalling the glory days of transatlantic travel in its looks. Meals are open seating, but only tables of six or eight are available, which can be bad news when there are only single seats left and you're part of a couple. The food quality is solid, with dishes that appeal to the predominantly European passengers (like tasty pastas, seafood, and rich desserts).

UN-CRUISE ADVENTURES

www.un-cruise.com. ℂ **888/862-8881.**

Pros

- **Intimate Experience:** With just 22 to 84 passengers, Un-Cruise Adventures' vessels are the antithesis of the usual crowded megaships.
- **Built-In Shore Excursions:** Most off-ship excursions and activities (such as kayaking and skiffing) are included in the cruise fare, as is an open bar on Un-Cruise's Luxury and Heritage Adventures vessels.

- **Night Anchorages:** A great boon to light sleepers, the routes taken allow time for the vessels to often anchor overnight, making for quiet nights and gorgeous mornings in coves and inlets.

Cons

- **The Price:** On Un-Cruise's Luxury Adventures in particular, the least expensive accommodations can start at more than $600 per person per night. At a recommended 5% to 10% of the tariff, gratuities also add mightily to the outlay. In short, you pay for all the privacy and pampering.

Overview

Looking for an off-the-beaten-path adventure? That's what it's all about at Un-Cruise Adventures, which might be best thought of as the unofficial successor to the much-loved (and sadly defunct) CruiseWest.

EXPERIENCE

Un-Cruise Adventures fills a distinct niche in waterborne travel, offering vacationers the chance to explore remote areas by luxury yacht, small expedition ship, or small coastal steamer. None of the company's eight vessels holds more than 88 passengers, and a key element of Un-Cruise trips is unraveling the tradition of rigid cruise-ship schedules. Itineraries are flexible, and getting off the ship and interacting with the spectacular landscape visited, in a meaningful way, is the focus.

In short, it's not a typical cruise, hence the line's name, Un-Cruise. The idea is that this is a vacation to the outdoors that is on a ship only because that's the easiest way to get people into remote areas. It's not about cruising but about getting out into the wilderness.

All itineraries include kayaking, looking for wildlife in motorized inflatable boats, and hiking. Still, the cruises are designed so passengers who don't want to participate in the most active adventures aren't left out, and sailings offer all the creature comforts for which cruising is known, including gourmet cuisine, fine wines, and craft beers. Un-Cruise's itineraries are broken down into two categories: High-priced Luxury Adventures where the outdoor exploring is leavened with no shortage of pampering and inclusions; and similar but less-expensive Active Adventures. How can you tell the two apart? Un-Cruise Adventures' luxury ships all have blue hulls, while the more inexpensive Active Adventure ships feature a forest-green hull.

On all of the line's cruises (regardless of category), the onboard experience is informal and friendly. You won't need a keycard to access your stateroom, as doors are left unlocked during the day (but can be locked by you from the inside). An easy onboard/ashore system made up of a metallic whiteboard and magnets eliminates that awful embarking photo and the need to "zap" your keycard in and out. Finally, informal nightly entertainment put on by the crew gives sailings a real family feeling that you won't find elsewhere.

ROUTES

The ship cruises both rivers and oceans. They have a large presence in Alaska, and also cruise in the Pacific Northwest, the Columbia and Snake rivers in

Oregon and Washington state, Central America, Galápagos, Mexico's Sea of Cortes, and Hawaii.

PASSENGERS

The company targets outdoorsy types who, in the words of one manager, "are the kind of people who shop at outdoor store REI." They typically range from 40 to 70 years old but multigenerational families are also a solid market for this brand. Un-Cruise's focus on wildlife and scenery on many itineraries can be appealing to teens and even young children, although those 13 and under aren't allowed on the line's two smallest yachts, except on select family departures. Un-Cruise often attracts people who have not cruised before and who are not particularly interested in a big-ship experience. Ages skew a bit younger on the line's Active Adventure trips, which offer a lower price point.

DINING

On Luxury Adventures, shipboard chefs delight guests with multicourse, ridiculously good meals (such as fresh halibut ceviche, outstanding fresh muffins every morning, and smoked salmon). Given the opportunity, chefs barter with nearby fishing boats for the catch of the day and raid local markets for the freshest fruits and vegetables. Passengers on Luxury Adventures also can serve themselves from the well-stocked bar, which during our recent visit had two kinds of sherry and four brands of gin alone, all of them premium; there were also a variety of Alaskan beers to savor.

On Active Adventures, the dining is simpler though still scrumptious. Passengers assemble in a single dining room for breakfast, lunch, and dinner buffets. A typical dinner might include a main course of roasted Pacific cod paired with a side dish of sautéed chayote and fire-roasted tomatoes, or a filet mignon with shallot *tart tatin* and roasted asparagus. The ships' galleys also work wonders when it comes to desserts, baking items such as citrus tart or a pavlova with kiwi and strawberry sauce from scratch daily.

ACTIVITIES

When passengers aren't eating or drinking, an expedition leader is helping them into motorized rubber rafts or kayaks to explore glaciers and icebergs and to look for wildlife such as whales, bears, and sea lions. Other activities include landings by raft for guided hikes through remote forests, paddleboarding, snorkeling, "polar bear club" swims, birding, and glacier walks. The line even offers optional (extra charge) overnight camping trips from two of its Active Adventure ships.

Typically, Un-Cruise will offer guests a series of activities with varying difficulty levels, from gentle beach walks to all-out bushwhacks. On the blue-hulled luxury fleet, emphasis is placed on "soft" adventure, though sometimes that's a misnomer. On one blue-hulled cruise through Alaska aboard *Safari Endeavour,* we found ourselves crawling under old-growth tree branches and shimmying down the forest floor. The green-hulled fleet gets into even more hardcore adventuring.

The Un-Cruise ships carry high-quality equipment to use during outings, including top-of-the-line sea kayaks; trekking poles; some backpacks and day packs; binoculars; rain pants and slickers; mud boots; paddleboards; and wet suits (some, but not enough for all guests) for water activities.

CHILDREN'S PROGRAMS

Un-Cruise ships have no formal children's programs, but the outdoorsy focus of the line's Luxury and Active Adventures make them a natural for animal-loving kids; activities such as kayaking and hiking are tailored for all ages. Children ages 12 and under receive a discount of 25% off the regular cruise fare on select "Kids in Nature" sailings. *Note:* Children ages 12 and under are not allowed on the *Safari Quest* or *Safari Explorer* unless they are chartered or designated as "Kids in Nature" sailings.

ENTERTAINMENT

Onboard entertainment takes on a variety different forms: We fondly remember a Sea of Cortes cruise where the entire ship disembarked for a late-night bonfire ashore, complete with campfire stories and sing-alongs. More usual are gatherings at the small but often lively onboard bar that serves local Alaskan craft beers (on Alaskan and Pacific Northwest sailings) on tap as well as wine and mixed drinks. Flatscreen TVs in the lounge/bar area are used to show educational videos and movies—and sometimes, even videos shot by passengers. Many find themselves entranced by feeds from the bow-mounted underwater cameras (on most ships); these stream video into all TVs on board. Educational presentations are provided by onboard naturalists on select nights, with topics such as whales, glaciers, and native cultures.

Passengers can also relax in the evening under the night sky in the top-deck hot tubs or saunas found on most Un-Cruise ships. Some may choose to schedule a massage with the onboard wellness director/licensed masseuse (an extra charge on Active Adventures).

SERVICE

All of the line's ships offer top-notch service, with the most pampering coming on Luxury Adventures, where the staff-to-passenger ratio is the highest. Naturalists and crewmembers facilitate all off-ship and onboard activities, as well as serve meals and perform housekeeping duties. The company suggests passengers leave an end-of-voyage tip for the crew of 5% to 10% of the cruise fare paid, which works out to around $200 to $400 per person for the typical cabin on an Active Adventure during the peak summer months (more for passengers on higher-priced Luxury Adventures).

CRUISETOURS & ADD-ON PROGRAMS

Un-Cruise offers land-tour add-on packages into Denali National Park and an Alaskan wilderness lodge. The line also offers pre- and post-cruise stopover packages in Ketchikan, Sitka, and Juneau that utilize well-established hotels, like Juneau's Westmark Baranof, within easy walking distance of all attractions and, of course, your ship. In all instances, an Un-Cruise Hospitality Desk can be found in the hotel lobby to answer any questions you might have.

FLEET

Expanding rapidly in recent years, Un-Cruise now operates eight vessels that carry from 22 to 88 passengers. Four of the vessels, all with "safari" in their names—the *Safari Endeavour, Safari Explorer, Safari Quest,* and *Safari Voyager*—focus on the line's most upscale offerings, called Luxury Adventures (longtime cruise fans will recognize this segment of the company as what used to be called American Safari Cruises). Three other ships, all using the moniker "wilderness"—the *Wilderness Adventurer, Wilderness Discoverer,* and *Wilderness Explorer*—operate the company's less-expensive Active Adventures. A single ship, a replica coastal steamer called *S.S. Legacy,* is dedicated to what the line calls Heritage Adventures—history and culture trips.

S.S. Legacy

The Verdict

A replica coastal steamer with plenty of charm, this ship conjures the romance of the past while offering the amenities modern cruisers expect.

Specifications — Avg. Starting Per Diem $613

Size (in tons)	1,472	Crew	34-35
Passengers (Double Occ.)	88	Passenger/Crew Ratio	2.5 to 1
Passenger/Space Ratio	16	Year Launched	1983
Total Cabins/Veranda Cabins	44/0	Last Major Refurbishment	2013

Frommer's Ratings (Scale of 1–5) ★★★★

Cabin Comfort & Amenities	3.5	Dining Options	4
Ship Cleanliness & Maintenance	5	Gym, Spa & Sports Facilities	4.5
Public Comfort/Space	4	Children's Facilities	N/A
Decor	4	Enjoyment Factor	5

THE SHIP IN GENERAL

Built in 1983, the 88-guest *S.S. Legacy* is patterned after the coastal packet steamers that plied the waters of the Pacific Northwest at the turn of the last century. The ship once sailed the waters of Alaska, but now navigates the Columbia and Snake Rivers in Oregon and Washington. Heavily refitted over the intervening decades to update decor and facilities, the 192-foot-long ship is Un-Cruise Adventures' only history-focused vessel. Expect plenty of historical re-enactments and old-timey fun while aboard.

CABINS   With the exception of the gargantuan **Owner's Suite** on the Bridge Deck aft of the wheelhouse, the **cabins** aboard *S.S. Legacy* won't wow you with their size. Still, all of them feature ocean views and amenities like flat-panel television sets and well-designed bathrooms. Storage space is better than you might expect, and luggage slips neatly under the beds, which are arranged as either two fixed twins or a single queen. Despite the fact they have two fixed twin beds, our favorite staterooms are the **Commander rooms** on

Lounge and Upper Decks, which have access to large wraparound exterior promenades. For the most part, decor matches the ship's turn-of-the-century theme, with attractive dark walnut furnishings and an old-timey banker's lamp providing soft illumination (in addition to modern overhead lighting).

PUBLIC AREAS & ACTIVITIES For a ship of this size, you might be surprised at how many public areas the *S.S. Legacy* has. The forward-facing **lounge,** which slopes attractively upward along the ship's bow and features 180-degree window views, serves coffee, tea, and snacks throughout the day, and the ship's crack bartenders will whip up just about anything you can think of at the bar. For something different, head down to our favorite spot on the ship: the **Pesky Barnacle Saloon.** Tucked all the way aft on Main Deck behind the ship's dining room, this nifty room can only be accessed by either walking straight through the dining room or ascending a ladder from the exterior promenade on Lounge Deck and opening a shell door. The rewards for finding the place: a complimentary selection of scotch, whisky, and bourbons from around the world. After a few of those, guests sometimes grab a bowler hat or a parasol from costume trunks stored at the aft end of the room. Since the crew dresses like it's 1896, you might as well join them.

There's no pool aboard the ship, but there are two hot tubs located on either side of the Sun Deck. Some outdoor **fitness equipment** is located here as well, under a covered awning at the stern. The ship has two basic massage rooms, where you can enjoy a complimentary rubdown (additional massages are available for purchase).

DINING The main dining room is decorated with old-style faux tin ceilings and wood-varnished support columns and booths. If you don't sit there, you can pick one of the many tables in the center of the room; sightlines are good throughout for looking out on the water. Though tasty, meals are far from *haute cuisine.* Instead, the emphasis is on regional ingredients (the chef often visits local markets), including wines and beers brought on board at nearly every port of call. Breakfast, lunch, and dinner are plated, and typically two to three choices are offered. If you have dietary requirements, notify Un-Cruise Adventures in advance, and they'll take good care of you.

Safari Endeavour

The Verdict

Pampering and inclusive, this ship offers the best of the line in one package.

Specifications		Avg. Starting Per Diem $499	
Size (in tons)	1,425	Crew	34-35
Passengers (Double Occ.)	84	Passenger/Crew Ratio	2.5 to 1
Passenger/Space Ratio	16.9	Year Launched	1983
Total Cabins/Veranda Cabins	42/0	Last Major Refurbishment	2012

Cabin Comfort & Amenities	4	Dining Options	4
Ship Cleanliness & Maintenance	4.5	Gym, Spa & Sports Facilities	5
Public Comfort/Space	4.5	Children's Facilities	N/A
Decor	4	Enjoyment Factor	5

THE SHIPS IN GENERAL

The largest of Un-Cruise Adventures' blue-hulled luxury ships, the 84-guest *Safari Endeavour* is 232 feet in length, big enough to give her the feel of a large vessel, but small enough to let her sneak into unexpected places. She spends her summers in Alaska, and typically winters in Mexico's Sea of Cortes. She's got all the features you'd expect from a ship of this size, like plenty of open deck space, a large hot tub, and outdoor fitness equipment. The ship also features a hydrophone for underwater listening, a bow camera, and a fleet of Zodiac rafts and standup paddleboards that can be launched from a platform at the stern. Couple that with a self-serve wine bar, a small library, and a cozy lounge, and you've got one great little ship.

CABINS   Each of *Safari Endeavour*'s 42 **cabins** comes with a flat-screen TV, an iPod docking station, and generous closet space. Most suitcases should slide conveniently under the beds, which come in either fixed twin or queen varieties depending on cabin category. While snug, cabins are attractively designed, with pleasant colors and comfortable beds. If there is a low point, it's the bathrooms, which are tiny even for a ship of this size. Four **Commodore Suites** on Cabin Deck are substantially larger, and feature French balconies and bathrooms equipped with Jacuzzi tubs.

PUBLIC AREAS & ACTIVITIES   The ship's **observation lounge** enjoys outdoor access to the ship's bow via a pair of doorways all the way forward. Coffee, tea, and snacks are served here throughout the day, and a full-service bar pours up cocktails and local specialties (try the Juneau-brewed Alaskan Amber Ale if you're sailing in Alaska). A small but well-stocked **library** can be found off the port-side entrance to the ship's dining room; the latter has a self-serve wine bar, but this doesn't tend to be used outside of meal hours. A full wraparound promenade is located on Upper Deck, and an expansive Sun Deck one floor above provides great panoramic views.

Two hot tubs are secreted all the way aft on Upper Deck, and are popular at nearly every time of day. **Fitness equipment** is available outdoors on the open Sun Deck, and every guest is treated to one complimentary massage from the onboard masseuse (additional massages can be purchased).

DINING   All meals are taken in the **dining room** located amidships on Main Deck. Seating tends to be at tables of four, six, and eight, which encourages couples to mingle among their fellow passengers. Meals are plated, and usually more than one choice is offered; if you have dietary restrictions, notify Un-Cruise prior to sailing and you'll be happily accommodates. To truly appreciate the culinary staff, take part in the offered galley tour; it's a postage stamp of a space that produces some great meals.

Safari Explorer • Safari Quest

The Verdict

If owning your own yacht isn't in the cards, these two provide the next best thing.

Specifications

Avg. Starting Per Diem $457

Size (in tons)	695/345	Crew	15/11
Passengers (Double Occ.)	36/22	Passenger/Crew Ratio	2 to 1
Passenger/Space Ratio	19.3/15.7	Year Launched	1998/1992
Total Cabins/Veranda Cabins	18/2;11/4	Last Major Refurbishment	2008/2013

Frommer's Ratings (Scale of 1–5)

★★★★ ½

Cabin Comfort & Amenities	4.5	Dining Options	4
Ship Cleanliness & Maintenance	4	Gym, Spa & Sports Facilities	5
Public Comfort/Space	4	Children's Facilities	N/A
Decor	4	Enjoyment Factor	5

THE SHIPS IN GENERAL

The smallest ships in Un-Cruise Adventures' fleet are the 36-guest *Safari Explorer* and the 22-guest *Safari Quest.* Although very different on the outside, they share many of the same amenities—including some of the most spacious staterooms in the line—and an atmosphere so relaxed you'll feel like you own the place. *Safari Explorer* sails the waters of Alaska in the summer, then winters in Hawaii, offering weeklong voyages between Moloka'i and Hawai'i. *Safari Quest* also spends summers in Alaska, but in the shoulder season can be found cruising the picturesque waters of British Columbia and Washington state.

While both ships offer a remarkably similar cruise experience, there are some minute differences. *Safari Explorer* has an onboard wine bar and library, for instance, while *Safari Quest* does not. But unlike *Explorer, Quest* does have an underwater bow camera.

CABINS   Accommodations on both ships are among the line's most lavish, with comfy Tempur-Pedic memory-foam mattresses, flat-panel television screens, iPod docking stations, and large windows. Additionally, rooms have more space, on average, than many on the line's other ships. Each also has one stateroom designed exclusively for solo travelers and priced accordingly.

PUBLIC AREAS & ACTIVITIES   The **main lounge,** which can accommodate nearly every guest at once, is located next to the main dining room on both ships. *Explorer*'s lounge is supplemented by the adjacent **Wine Library**—a winning combination to be sure. Both ships feature an outdoor bow viewing area and a spacious **Sun Deck,** and both benefit from having an outdoor promenade deck for strolling and admiring the scenery. *Safari Explorer* offers guests one complimentary massage each (a perk not available on *Safari Quest*). Yoga is only offered aboard *Safari Explorer,* too, though both ships have one hot tub apiece.

Un-Cruise Adventures

DINING Meals are served in the unpretentious main dining room. A handful of choices are offered for breakfast, lunch, and dinner, and are served plated. The food is usually delicious, even aboard the small *Safari Quest,* where meals develop a family-style atmosphere as the cruise progresses.

Safari Voyager

The Verdict

A substantial $4-million refit in early 2016 has finally brought this ship, which sails year-round through Costa Rica and Panama, up to Un-Cruise standards.

Specifications

Size (in tons)	1,195	Crew	31
Passengers (Double Occ.)	62	Passenger/Crew Ratio	2 to 1
Passenger/Space Ratio	19	Year Launched	1982
Total Cabins/Veranda Cabins	32/0	Last Major Refurbishment	2016

Avg. Starting Per Diem $402

Frommer's Ratings (Scale of 1–5)

★★★ ½

Cabin Comfort & Amenities	3	Dining Options	4
Ship Cleanliness & Maintenance	5	Gym, Spa & Sports Facilities	3.5
Public Comfort/Space	4	Children's Facilities	N/A
Decor	3.5	Enjoyment Factor	5

THE SHIPS IN GENERAL

Safari Voyager is getting a little long in the tooth. Despite Un-Cruise Adventures' best efforts, she entered service for the line back in late 2013 with no shortage of technical problems. The line responded, pulling her out of service and stripping her down to the keel plating. Finally, after a series of refits in 2015 and 2016, she's been upgraded to a standard befitting Un-Cruise—and she sports some new features, to boot.

CABINS Accommodations aboard *Safari Voyager* have been rebuilt from the ground up. Most of the refitting was technical in nature, involving new plumbing, air conditioning, and electrical outlets—all of which help improve the visitor experience immensely. Not much has changed decor-wise; the interior design still relies on cherrywood furniture and plain walls decorated with photos of places around the world.

Cabins feature either queen or fixed twin beds, depending on the category. This makes it very important to consider your bed preferences before you book. All staterooms have a private bathroom, window views, an iPod docking station, and a TV and DVD player combination. Two staterooms (**207 and 208**) are set aside for solo travelers. New to the ship is a brand-new **Owner's Suite,** which takes the spot formerly occupied by the underused library. Positioned all the way forward overlooking the bow of the ship, the suite has king or twin beds, a sitting area with a wet bar and a mini-fridge, a media center, and a bathroom with a jetted whirlpool tub and a separate shower. However, the location of the bow viewing deck just outside means that guests milling about often obstruct the scenery.

PUBLIC AREAS & ACTIVITIES The social hub of the ship is the pretty, wood-paneled **main lounge,** located all the way aft on Bridge Deck, where it offers 180-degree views and a full-service bar. Daily briefings, cocktail hours, and lectures all take place here. The lounge provides easy access to the wraparound promenade just outside. Up on the Sun Deck, a variety of outdoor **fitness equipment** is available, along with a single hot tub.

DINING The 2016 refit added an expanded galley with brand-new equipment, allowing onboard chefs to prepare more elaborate meals than in the past. Breakfast and lunch are sit-down affairs with one or two options available, while dinners typically offer three choices (meat, fish, vegetarian). The food tends to be of high quality but uncomplicated in its preparation. Like all Un-Cruise ships, staff members are excellent at catering to dietary requests and restrictions. All meals are served in the sole onboard **restaurant.**

Wilderness Adventurer • Wilderness Discoverer • Wilderness Explorer

The Verdict

Un-Cruise Adventures' active, green-hulled ships are more basic (some would say spartan) than their blue-hulled luxury counterparts, but what they lack in amenities they make up for in prices—which are about a quarter lower than the others.

Specifications

Specifications		Avg. Starting Per Diem $327	
Size (in tons)	639-910	Crew	25-26
Passengers (Double Occ.)	60-76	Passenger/Crew Ratio	2.2 to 1
Passenger/Space Ratio	10-12	Year Launched	1976-1992
Total Cabins/Veranda Cabins	30-38	Last Major Refurbishment	2011-2012

Frommer's Ratings (Scale of 1–5) ★★★

Cabin Comfort & Amenities	3	Dining Options	4
Ship Cleanliness & Maintenance	5	Gym, Spa & Sports Facilities	3
Public Comfort/Space	3.5	Children's Facilities	N/A
Decor	3	Enjoyment Factor	4.5

THE SHIPS IN GENERAL

Adventures ashore are unusually active, with an emphasis placed on in-depth hiking experiences, kayaking adventures, and paddleboarding sessions. Thanks to their lower price point, these ships also attract a somewhat younger audience of adventurous thirty-to-sixtysomethings who love to get out and be at one with nature, and who are less concerned about how they get there. Which is a good thing, because the *Wilderness Adventurer* (60 guests), *Wilderness Discoverer* (76 guests) and *Wilderness Explorer* (74 guests) have minimal amenities, and cabins and public areas look somewhat clinical.

CABINS Expect the size and stylistic charm of a college dorm. Your cabin is merely a place to sleep, get dressed, and maybe dry out your clothes from an afternoon spent bushwhacking. Still, the rooms aren't uncomfortable, with quality queen or twin beds in most staterooms, flat-panel TV and DVD player combos, iPod docking stations, and windows in all cabin categories. All three ships have staterooms set aside for solo travelers.

PUBLIC AREAS & ACTIVITIES   Each ship boasts a forward-facing **main lounge;** aboard *Adventurer* and *Discoverer,* it's located underneath the bow of the ship, so picture windows are only on the port and starboard sides of the vessel. On *Explorer,* however, the lounge is situated behind the open bow viewing deck, providing spectacular 180-degree views. On all ships, a full-service bar is located in each space, which is also used for lectures, briefings, and socializing. Outside you'll find **fitness equipment** and a hot tub (*Discoverer* has two). Unlike other Un-Cruise ships, there are no massage services.

DINING   Meals are served in the main **dining room,** which is of a generous size on all ships. Seating is open and unassigned, and guests are encouraged to mingle. In keeping with that philosophy, you won't find many tables for two. Meals are served buffet style and the food is a bit simpler than what's offered aboard the line's luxury ships. But it's hearty and made with locally sourced ingredients when possible.

WINDSTAR CRUISES

www.windstarcruises.com. ℭ **888/736-4926.**

Pros

- ○ **Great Ships:** Three sailing ships and three luxury yachts make up the line; all have the amenities of much-larger ships.
- ○ **Watersports Marinas:** You can paddle-boat, windsail, or waterski off the stern of the ship.
- ○ **Sail Away Party:** The sailaway party on the older ships, on which you can watch the sails unfurl to music, is a memorable highlight.

Cons

- ○ **The Masts Are for Show:** While we've seen the sails used as the sole mode of power on rare occasions, more often than not the diesel engines are propelling the ship forward.

Overview

Long known for its masted sailing ships, Windstar also operates three ships that it acquired from Seabourn; they're small but yacht-style. Mix in some major refits for all six ships, and Windstar feels like an entirely new line.

EXPERIENCE

Talk to a past Windstar guest, and they will likely tell you about the sailaway ceremony. Set to the thudding tune of Vangelis' *1492: Conquest of Paradise* score, the sails aboard *Wind Star, Wind Spirit,* and *Wind Surf* are dramatically raised during each sailaway, and then unfurled at the song's crescendo. It's all part of the Windstar experience which also encompasses the line's notable on-deck barbecue feast, evening cocktail parties, and chill atmosphere.

Those who sailed more recently, however, may have different tales to tell. In 2013, Windstar announced it had entered into an agreement to purchase the former *Seabourn Spirit, Seabourn Pride,* and *Seabourn Legend* from Seabourn Cruises (see p. 258). All three were given stupendous makeovers and, between 2014 and 2015, entered service as the *Star Breeze, Star Pride,* and *Star Legend* to pretty much universal acclaim. Staterooms, all of which are oceanview suites, and public rooms have been lovingly redone (see below).

Windstar also put its sailing fleet through an extensive refit program back in 2012 that left all three ships with crisp, new decor. Deep blue accents intermingle with dark and light wood, and new lighting, shutters, carpeting and soft furnishings have been added throughout. If you haven't stepped aboard Windstar's ships in the last five years, you'll find yourself pleasantly surprised with the changes.

ROUTES

Windstar has a wide reach, sailing through the Caribbean, to Costa Rica and the Panama Canal, to the Baltic and Northern Europe, the Mediterranean, and Tahiti, where *Wind Spirit* makes her year-round home. The line has plans to push into Asia in 2017.

PASSENGERS

On these ships, the passengers are overwhelming American, with some Canadians, Brits, and Australians. They're also overwhelming older—empty nesters and retirees primarily. Multi-generational families are slowly discovering Windstar, so expect to see a handful of kids during peak travel times. While not as formal as, say, luxury lines like Crystal, guests on Windstar ships nonetheless like to dress up a bit at dinner, albeit in a resort-casual way.

DINING

Guests can choose to dine in the **AmphorA Dining Room** or out on deck at **Candles,** Windstar's signature dining venue that also does double-duty as the ship's casual buffet eatery during breakfast and lunch. Dishes—largely continental cuisine with some international items added—are well executed in both venues. The highlight of the sailing is always the weekly barbecue on deck, which is an all-you-can-eat spread of seafood and grilled meats that really takes advantage of the weather in warm ports.

ACTIVITIES

In the daytime, most guests are content to sit with a good book up on deck, or socialize with their fellow guests in the lounge. There are some daily activities, primarily trivia or lectures, with local performers or a resident pianist to entertain guests each evening.

The addition of *Star Breeze, Star Pride,* and *Star Legend* to the fleet, however, adds another dimension to the Windstar cruise experience. Though there are still few scheduled activities, passengers on these boats can enjoy spas, gyms, and libraries; the newer ships offer more indoor public rooms, including both a show lounge and the Compass Rose, which hosts a small but favorably trafficked casino. All the way forward on the ship's uppermost deck is The Yacht Club, a gorgeous forward-facing observation lounge that offers refreshments and beverages all day long, plus plenty of cozy seating.

All six of Windstar's ships—including the new ex-Seabourn "Power Yachts" (*Star Breeze, Star Pride,* and *Star Legend*) feature the line's signature Water Sports Platform experience, which includes a variety of water toys and boats for complimentary guest usage. This area, actually a hydraulic part of the stern that folds out flush with the water, is typically deployed in calm bays, and when weather permits.

CHILDREN'S PROGRAMS

While children aged 8 and older can technically sail the line, Windstar goes out of its way to make it clear that, "children, especially infants and toddlers, are not encouraged aboard Windstar Cruises."

ENTERTAINMENT

Highlights of evenings are dinner and cocktails on deck in the wood-lined bar by the pool. There is also a small casino and live music is offered on most nights. The larger "Power Yachts" (*Star Breeze, Star Pride, Star Legend*) offer scheduled evening entertainment in multiple lounges. Still, let's be honest: For most, these are "make-your-own-fun" kinds of cruises.

SERVICE

The staff on these ships are quick to learn; don't be surprised if they remember your favorite drink by your second day on board, or if they remember you by name on your second voyage with the line. Officers are typically European, with an international crew. Windstar recommends a gratuity of $12 USD per guest, per day, which is added to your onboard account.

FLEET

Wind Spirit and *Wind Star* are the 148-passenger sailing yachts in the fleet; the 310-passenger *Wind Surf* claims to be the "world's largest sailing yacht," and indeed, it's plenty big. *Star Pride, Star Breeze,* and *Star Legend,* originally part of the Seabourn fleet, are all 212-passenger yachts without sails, but their engineering makes them faster, sleeker, and better able to reach distant ports of call that are off-limits to the slower sailing yachts.

Wind Star • Wind Spirit

The Verdict

Romantic and cozy, these 148-guest boats strike the right balance between comfort and amenities, with modern decor to complement the relaxed atmosphere.

Specifications — Avg. Starting Per Diem $275

Size (in tons)	5,350	Crew	94
Passengers (Double Occ.)	148	Passenger/Crew Ratio	1.6 to 1
Passenger/Space Ratio	36	Year Launched	1986/1988
Total Cabins/Veranda Cabins	74/0	Last Major Refurbishment	2012

Frommer's Ratings (Scale of 1–5)   ★★★★

Cabin Comfort & Amenities	4	Dining Options	3.5
Ship Cleanliness & Maintenance	4.5	Gym, Spa & Sports Facilities	2
Public Comfort/Space	4	Children's Facilities	N/A
Decor	4	Enjoyment Factor	4.5

THE SHIPS IN GENERAL

With their high-tech, computer-controlled sails, these sleek ships are like combinations of private yachts and grand turn-of-the-century sailing vessels. They were looking tired and worn-down a decade ago, but a thorough overhaul recently brought on new drapes, carpets, lighting, wall treatments, and decor. The end result feels like an entirely new Windstar.

CABINS   Nearly all **cabins** are oceanview staterooms measuring 188 square feet. There are dual porthole windows in each, along with a completely refreshed blue color scheme. Common to all staterooms is a mini-bar, fresh fruit replenished daily, and Bose SoundDocks that are compatible with Apple iPods. Don't have one? Borrow a fully loaded device free of charge from the reception desk. Bathrooms are some of our favorite afloat, with attractive teak floors and separate crescent-shaped stalls for the shower and toilet.

Each ship has a single **suite**—a 220 square foot Owner's Suite near the stern. Unsurprisingly, it tends to sell out fast.

It's worth noting that *Wind Star* and *Wind Spirit* are not a good choice for guests with mobility impairments; both boats lack passenger elevators and contain numerous high sills that require some agility in stepping over.

PUBLIC AREAS & ACTIVITIES   Public spaces aren't especially creative but they're attractive and well laid-out. The main **lounge** is the place to be for a cold drink and nightly entertainment and lectures. The room has definite sex appeal, with dark slatted window shutters, a bustling bar, an overhead skylight, and 180-degree views from the windows. A secondary bar next to the aft pool serves as the venue for "Cigars Under the Stars." Outside the main lounge, a small wood-paneled **library** contains a decent selection of books and DVDs you can rent for free. There are also computer workstations and Wi-Fi.

Each ship has a tiny swimming **pool,** along with a small hot tub that tends to get crowded quickly. Guests tend to forget that the flying bridge, one deck above, has additional loungers for soaking up rays. The main outdoor deck has a promenade that wraps attractively around the ship; bow access is available at designated times. Impressively for ships of this size, the **fitness center** is nicely stocked, with elliptical trainers, recumbent bicycles, a ballet bar, and free weights. Treatments are available in the equally small **spa.**

DINING   **AmphorA** has a definite sense of style. Ceiling tiles with a faux woodgrain texture lend a yachtlike ambiance to the room, while crystal chandeliers class up the joint. Only dinner is served here—the sunny, window-lined **Veranda** is the place to be for breakfast and lunch. You can have your meal out on deck at one of the many tables clustered around the port and starboard sides of the ship. On the specialty restaurant front, **Candles** is an outdoor, reservations-only experience. Serving up steaks and a variety of grilled meats, it is open to about 30 guests per night. Though the dinner is free, demand is high, so sign up at reception early on in the cruise.

Wind Surf

The Verdict

An enlarged version of *Wind Star* and *Wind Spirit*, the 312-passenger *Wind Surf* is a sleek, super-sexy sailing ship that offers more of everything that made its smaller siblings great, done up in a larger and more amenity-laden package.

THE SHIP IN GENERAL

Board the Wind Surf and you just might wonder where everyone went, even at full capacity. The *Wind Surf* absorbs her 312 guests surprisingly well. And she manages to exude some of the class and charm of the bygone ocean liners, both in her interior public spaces and on her wide, open decks. For a ship with cruises starting at just under $2,000 per week, that's not too shabby.

CABINS   Like her smaller fleetmates, most **staterooms** aboard *Wind Surf* come in at a very comfortable 188 square feet. Decor and furnishings are almost identical throughout and quite chic—light browns and slate greys, and hints of sea-foam green on pillows and throws. Staterooms also benefit from stylish lighting fixtures with cream-colored shades, flat-panel TVs, and Bose SoundDocks (with pre-loaded iPods available from reception for use during the voyage). Bathrooms are decidedly luxe, with granite countertops, large showerheads, teak flooring, and L'Occitane Verbena toiletries. Light filters into rooms through decently sized porthole windows for all staterooms (including suites). Alas, no staterooms or suites have private balconies.

Those looking for a little more space will want to check out the 30 **suites** on Deck 3. Essentially two standard staterooms with the adjoining wall removed, they feature two full bathrooms and living and sleeping areas that can be separated by a thick curtain. Two 500-square-foot suites on Bridge Deck are the largest on board, with separate living and sleeping areas. Some cool perks come with these suites, including laundry and pressing service, an invite to dinner with the captain, and chilled champagne on arrival.

PUBLIC AREAS & ACTIVITIES   *Wind Surf* is the roomiest of Windstar's sailing ships, with public spaces and amenities you might expect to find on a much larger vessel. The **main lounge** is an airy space with plenty of seating options around a dance floor. The adjacent **casino** isn't huge, but it stays busy on most evenings. All the way aft, the **Compass Rose Bar** is the go-to spot for after-dinner cocktails; live music is presented each evening and views overlook the ship's wake. A comfier option is the **Terrace Bar,** where the "Cigars Under the Stars" event takes place each evening.

When it comes to pool, fitness, and spa facilities, *Wind Surf* laps many ships twice its size. Its facilities are the largest and most elaborate of the Windstar fleet. Standard spa treatments are available at the onboard **spa,** which features treatment rooms made from repurposed guest cabins. Or you can elect to have treatments administered poolside. The glass-walled **fitness center** is perched high atop the ship, where an impressive array of fitness equipment includes treadmills, bicycles, dumbbells, and a water-resistance rowing machine. You can also take part in yoga or Pilates classes for a nominal fee.

Two swimming **pools** are on board: One is inset beneath the sails on the upper deck, and another is situated at the stern. Near the stern pool are two hot tubs that tend to fill up rather quickly on certain days, as do the adjacent Balinese beds. A full teak **Promenade Deck** encircles the ship, and jogging is permitted at certain hours.

DINING   Buffet breakfast and lunch are served in the Veranda on Star Deck, while guests can enjoy dinner under the stars at **Candles** (for steaks), **Le Marché** (for seafood), **Degrees** (a reservations-only venue specializing in Mediterranean fare), or **AmphorA,** the main dining room. Food quality overall ranges from good to very good, seafood and pasta dishes being among the most memorable, along with the line's famous outdoor, on-deck barbecue with suckling pig, paella, and numerous desserts.

Star Pride • Star Breeze • Star Legend

The Verdict

Windstar has breathed new life into these three popular vessels, which, despite their lack of sails, fit in perfectly with the line's chilled-out take on cruising.

Specifications		Avg. Starting Per Diem $290	
Size (in tons)	9,975	Crew	140
Passengers (Double Occ.)	212	Passenger/Crew Ratio	1.5 to 1
Passenger/Space Ratio	47	Year Launched	1988-1992
Total Cabins/Veranda Cabins	106/42	Last Major Refurbishment	2016

Frommer's Ratings (Scale of 1–5)		★★★★	
Cabin Comfort & Amenities	4	Dining Options	4.5
Ship Cleanliness & Maintenance	5	Gym, Spa & Sports Facilities	4
Public Comfort/Space	4	Children's Facilities	N/A
Decor	4	Enjoyment Factor	5

THE SHIPS IN GENERAL

Originally built for luxury line Seabourn, these three twin-propellored megayachts were snapped up by Windstar in a package deal. *Star Pride* was the first to enter service in May of 2014, followed by *Star Breeze* and *Star Legend* in 2015. Carrying 212 guests apiece, they've been significantly revamped to fit a more contemporary sensibility. While a few areas show their age, much on the ships feels brand spanking new. Public rooms are spacious, and staterooms—all of which feature ocean views and marble bathrooms with dual sinks—are larger than those on Windstar's sailing ships. The notoriously narrow upper deck spaces above the pool deck have been widened, allowing guests (finally) to stretch out on full-length loungers.

And what about Windstar's famous sail-raising ceremony upon departure? Though *Star Pride, Breeze,* and *Legend* lack sails, Windstar still plays the score to *1492: Conquest of Paradise* upon departure from each port, complete with a flag-raising ceremony that takes place on the ship's radar mast—easily seen and admired from the pool deck bar.

CABINS Windstar has refitted all of its spacious **staterooms** with indirect lighting, snazzy midnight-blue comforters tucked around crisp white Egyptian cotton sheets, and drapes edged in that same shade of blue. Amenities are top-notch: Bose iPod docking stations, waffle-weave bathrobes, and Molton Brown toiletries. Most bathrooms feature marble-clad tub-and-shower combos, though about a dozen staterooms (well-marked on the deck plan) feature a shower only. All **suites** feature a walk-in closet, though drawer space is paltry.

All staterooms have ocean views, either by way of a picture window with a seating ledge or, in the higher categories, French balconies. These don't provide an outdoor sitting area, but serve to turn the sitting area in every stateroom into an open-air balcony. If you like to sleep with your balcony door open, however, take note: These ships don't have much height above the waterline, so in stormy or choppy seas, the officers on the bridge can electronically lock your balcony door with the push of a switch.

The four **Classic Suites** are substantially larger, measuring between 400 and 530 square feet. These include full, step-out balconies, separate living and sleeping areas separated by attractive French doors, and powder rooms. The two **Classic Suites** at the bow (Suites 01 and 02) have obstructed views. On Deck 6 all the way forward are two **Owner's Suites.** The largest accommodations on board, they're basically enlarged versions of Classic Suites. Those prone to seasickness should note that, like forward-situated staterooms on any small ship, they really move around in rough seas.

Four wheelchair-accessible suites are available on each ship.

PUBLIC AREAS & ACTIVITIES The forward-facing **Yacht Club,** located all the way at the top of the ship on Deck 8, has 180-degree wraparound windows, an outdoor viewing deck, and appealing seating separated by curved display shelves. Snacks and drinks are available here all day long. Just aft on the same deck is the **Star Bar.** Quiet during the day, it gets busy at night—and it's often standing-room only when Windstar's sailaway celebration gets underway.

All three ships sport a very decent library, with seating for a handful of guests. At the entrance to the **Compass Rose Lounge** is a small **casino,** complete with table games and slot machines. The Compass Rose often gets overlooked, but live music is offered here nearly every evening, and you can relax on leather couches or cut a rug on the dance floor. One deck below is the ship's **show lounge,** where shows, lectures, and other events are held. Curved seating translates into good sightlines.

Each ship has a small swim-against-the-current **pool** and adjacent whirlpool located amidships on Pool Deck 7. On *Star Pride,* the area occupied by The Veranda serves as a secondary swimming pool (this under-used feature was removed on *Star Breeze* and *Star Legend.*) The big thing to write home about on these ships is the retractable **Watersports Platform,** a door mounted in the stern that folds down flush with the water when conditions allow. Guests are welcome to use any of the watersports equipment: kayaks, paddleboards, snorkels, and a large floating island that lets swimmers bathe off the stern or relax on the oversized float. The downside: The marina takes forever for the crew to set up, so it's typically not deployed on short calls and can only be used when the ship is at anchor.

Each ship has a **WindSpa,** which doesn't look like much on the outside, but an amazing number of services are offered, from acupuncture to Swedish massage. The **fitness center** at the end of the hall is positively massive for a ship of this size; it's got stationary bicycles, treadmills, weights, and more.

DINING Dinners are served in the porthole-lined **AmphorA** restaurant, which has been upgraded from its Seabourn days with cut-glass chandeliers, mirrored wall accents, and plenty of open seating. Breakfast and lunch buffets are in **The Veranda,** which has both indoor and shaded outdoor seating. A small menu of cooked-to-order specialties is also available; offerings change daily. At night, this space doubles as **Candles,** a complimentary (but reservations-required) specialty restaurant dishing up a wide variety of steaks and seafood. Aboard *Star Breeze* and *Star Legend,* additional seating is available in The Courtyard, just forward of The Veranda.

Index

Map List

Photo Credits

p. i: © Crystal Symphony/www.crystalcruises.com; p. ii: Courtesy of Cunard; p. iii: © EQRoy/Shutterstock.com; p. iv: © GoToVan; p. v, top: © Andrea Izzotti; p. v, bottom: © milosk50; p. vi, top left: © jo Crebbin/Shutterstock.com; p. vi, top right: © Valentina Photo/Shutterstock.com; p. vi, bottom left: © littleny/Shutterstock.com; p. vi, bottom right: © Iakov Kalinin ; p. vii, top: © Sean Pavone; p. vii, middle: © Ann Baekken; p. vii, bottom: © Fotos593/Shutterstock.com; p. viii, top: © Brian Lasenby; p. viii, middle: © Akos Horvath Photographer/Shutterstock.com; p. viii, bottom: © Sorin Colac; p. ix, top: © Andy Newman/Carnival Cruise Line; p. ix, bottom left: © Arthur T. LaBar; p. ix, bottom right: © Cruise News Weekly; p. x, top: Courtesy of Norwegian Cruise Line; p. x, middle: © Jeff; p. x, bottom: Courtesy of Celebrity Cruises/Quentin Bacon; p. xi, top: © Andy Newman/Carnival Cruise Line; p. xi, middle: Courtesy of Royal Caribbean/Roy Riley/sbw-photo; p. xi, bottom: Courtesy of Disney Cruises/Kent Phillips; p. xii, top: © Andy Newman/Carnival Cruise Line; p. xii, middle: © Andy Newman/Carnival Cruise Line; p. xii, bottom: Courtesy of Celebrity Cruises/Quentin Bacon; p. xiii, top: Courtesy of Silversea Cruises; p. xiii, bottom: © ©2011 Seabourn; p. xiv, top: Courtesy of Alaska Marine Highway/Ron Gile; p. xiv, middle: Courtesy of Crystal Cruises; p. xiv, bottom: © Ralph Grizzle; p. xv, top left: Courtesy of Oceania Cruises/Mike Louagie; p. xv, top right: © Jennifer Lamb; p. xv, bottom: Courtesy of Cunard/Bildagentur Huber/Gräfenhain; p. xvi, top: © Dirk Weyer; p. xvi, bottom left: Courtesy of Crystal Cruises; p. xvi, bottom right: Courtesy of SeaDream Yacht Club

Frommer's EasyGuide to Cruising, 1st Edition

Published by

FROMMER MEDIA LLC

ISBN 978-1-62887-228-6 (paper), 978-1-62887-229-3 (e-book)

Editorial Director: Pauline Frommer
Development Editors: Pauline Frommer and Holly Hughes
Production Editor: Heather Wilcox
Additional material by Michelle Baran, Fran Golden, and Sherri Eisenberg
Editorial assistants: Ali Arminio, Zac Thompson, and Tom Ward
Cartographer: Roberta Stockwell
Photo Editor: Meghan Lamb
Cover Design: David Riedy
Front cover photo: © Crystal Symphony/www.crystalcruises.com

For information on our other products or services, see www.frommers.com.

FrommerMedia LLC also publishes its books in a variety of electronic formats. Some content that appears
in print may not be available in electronic formats.

Manufactured in the United States of America

10 9 8 7 6 5 4 3 2 1

ABOUT THE AUTHOR

Aaron Saunders spends half his year at sea on various cruise ships around the world. He is the founder of FromTheDeckChair.com, writes regularly about cruises for seven newspapers in Canada, and is a regular contributor to cruise and travel magazines and websites around the world. He has written two nonfiction books about maritime history, *Giants of the Seas* (Seaforth, 2012) and *Stranded*, about the 1918 sinking of the *Princess Sophia* (Dundurn, 2015). When not at sea, he ironically calls landlocked Calgary, Canada, home.

ABOUT THE FROMMER TRAVEL GUIDES

For most of the past 50 years, Frommer's has been the leading series of travel guides in North America, accounting for as many as 24% of all guidebooks sold. I think I know why.

Though we hope our books are entertaining, we nevertheless deal with travel in a serious fashion. Our guidebooks have never looked on such journeys as a mere recreation, but as a far more important human function, a time of learning and introspection, an essential part of a civilized life. We stress the culture, lifestyle, history, and beliefs of the destinations we cover, and urge our readers to seek out people and new ideas as the chief rewards of travel.

We have never shied from controversy. We have, from the beginning, encouraged our authors to be intensely judgmental, critical—both pro and con—in their comments, and wholly independent. Our only clients are our readers, and we have triggered the ire of count-less prominent sorts, from a tourist newspaper we called "practically worthless" (it unsuc-cessfully sued us) to the many rip-offs we've condemned.

And because we believe that travel should be available to everyone regardless of their incomes, we have always been cost-conscious at every level of expenditure. Though we have broadened our recommendations beyond the budget category, we insist that every lodging we include be sensibly priced. We use every form of media to assist our readers, and are particularly proud of our feisty daily website, the award-winning Frommers.com.

I have high hopes for the future of Frommer's. May these guidebooks, in all the years ahead, continue to reflect the joy of travel and the freedom that travel represents. May they always pursue a cost-conscious path, so that people of all incomes can enjoy the rewards of travel. And may they create, for both the traveler and the persons among whom we travel, a community of friends, where all human beings live in harmony and peace.

Arthur Frommer

Before, During, or After your use of an EasyGuide... you'll want to consult

FROMMERS.COM

FROMMERS.COM IS KEPT UP-TO-DATE, WITH:

NEWS
The latest events (and deals) to affect your next vacation

BLOGS
Opinionated comments by our outspoken staff

FORUMS
Post your travel questions, get answers from other readers

SLIDESHOWS
On weekly-changing, practical but inspiring topics of travel

CONTESTS
Enabling you to win free trips

PODCASTS
Of our weekly, nationwide radio show

DESTINATIONS
Hundreds of cities, their hotels, restaurants and sights

TRIP IDEAS
Valuable, offbeat suggestions for your next vacation

*AND MUCH MORE!

Smart travelers consult Frommers.com